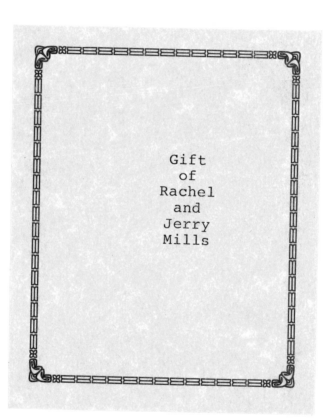

Gift
of
Rachel
and
Jerry
Mills

DEMOCRATIC PERSONALITY

NANCY RUTTENBURG

Democratic Personality

Popular Voice and the Trial of American Authorship

STANFORD UNIVERSITY PRESS

STANFORD, CALIFORNIA

Stanford University Press
Stanford, California

© 1998 by the Board of Trustees of the
Leland Stanford Junior University

Printed in the United States of America

CIP data appear at the end of the book

To the memory of my mother, Asna Jaffee Ruttenburg

Acknowledgments

A book is a strange enterprise. One begins by generating a volume of words, driven by an appalling sense of one's insufficiency to the task, and one ends here, at the Acknowledgments, all but silenced by a sense of gratitude to those who gave so much to advance it. My parents, who in very different ways provided the most fundamental support, did not live to see its completion. My mother in particular tirelessly nurtured me and my family through its stages, and for her conviction of its worth and especially for her passion I dedicate this work to Asna Jaffee Ruttenburg.

My mother shared with the codirector of my dissertation, Jay Fliegelman, the express desire to know the secret of my interest in a form of voice that could be at once profoundly innocent and yet so powerful as to be actually fatal to others on occasion. William Mills Todd, III, also at the helm of my Stanford dissertation, characteristically refrained from inquiring into this secret; I suspect, though, that he attributed it to my undergraduate training at U.C. Santa Cruz. Their complementary dispositions aside, no one could have benefited more than I did from the expertise and allegiance of these two already legendary scholars. They launched me on the Russian-American comparative project of which this book constitutes the first installment. The inspiring René Girard also occupied a seat on the dissertation committee (whether the second or third seat no one could tell), and he single-handedly kept sacrificial violence at bay by reminding us all that there was, no doubt, a third term between the Russian and American poles. I would also like to mention how very much I benefited from the support of Herbert Lindenberger, who imbued the Program in Comparative Literature with his intellectual energy and his warmth. It is largely due to his efforts that Stanford is remembered by so many for its hospitality and dedication to young scholars.

My three years in the Harvard English Department were made especially fruitful by the support of Alan Heimert, who, despite his fierce allegiance to the American field, shared with me, I think, the lure of Petersburg. As the self-revealed reader of this manuscript for both the press and my tenure case at U.C. Berkeley, he consecrated with his approval the endurance test this book came to represent in its final stages. Sacvan Bercovitch offered me the opportunity to present my work at his Americanist Colloquium at the Center for Cultural and Literary Studies and also treated me to several memorable meals, not all of which were at One Potato Two Potato.

My students, friends, and colleagues in the Departments of Comparative Literature and English at the University of California, Berkeley, have enabled me to preserve my delight in the study of literature by fostering a wealth of teaching and learning environments. Considering that the lion's share of my appointment is in Comparative Literature, the members of the English Department have been especially generous supporters of my work. In this regard, I would like to mention my appreciation of the efforts Paul Alpers, Mitch Breitweiser, Carol Christ, Fred Crews, Anne Middleton, Ralph Rader, and Alex Zwerdling have made in my behalf. Fred Crews, in particular, with whom I share a fascination with fraud, has gone well beyond the call of duty to ensure my steady progress on the manuscript — his friendship has been much appreciated. In Comparative Literature, Robert Alter and Joseph Duggan have been especially supportive colleagues. Members of the Berkeley Americanist Reading Group provided an inspiring monthly forum and generous feedback over several years: Phil Barrish, Dori Hale, Sam Otter, Margit Stange, Lynn Wardley, and our honorable member and my constant companion at Harvard, Jeff Knapp. Sam Otter shared his thoughts on "the restless camel" with me at just the right moment. Likewise, members of the Comparative Literature Reading Group have given me careful and astute readings of key portions of the manuscript: Katherine Bergeron, Tim Hampton, Leslie Kurke, Celeste Langan, and Michael Lucey.

The University of California, Berkeley, has also proven a most generous provider of fellowship support. I am very grateful to have been awarded steady research funding from the Committee on Research, as well as a Humanities Research Fellowship. I was extremely lucky in my choice of research assistants. Over the course of two years, Anna Chodakiewicz located many needles in many haystacks and cheered me with her account of the

Eastern European corollaries of the developments I was tracing in American culture. Paulina Rikoun was an intrepid hunter of especially elusive early American journals. The acuity of Damion Searles, who put up graciously with my ignorance of all things computerized, helped enormously in the final stages of preparing the manuscript for the press. Julia Cho cheerfully dealt with last-minute details.

In its early stages, this work was generously funded by the American Council of Learned Societies and the Social Science Research Council for Russian and East European Studies in conjunction with the Ford Foundation and the National Endowment for the Humanities. The University of California's President's Research Fellowship allowed me the luxury of devoting a full year to the manuscript's completion.

A section of Chapter 5 was published as "Silence and Servitude: Bondage and Self-Invention in Russia and America, 1760–1861" in *Slavic Review* 51 (Winter 1992): 731–48. A condensed version of Chapter 2 was published in *American Literary History* 5 (Fall 1993): 429–58, and has been reprinted in Gordon Hutner, ed., *The "American Literary History" Reader* (New York: Oxford University Press, 1995). A version of Chapter 7 has appeared in *American Literature* 66, no. 1 (March 1994): 83–103. I am grateful to Gordon Hutner and Cathy Davidson for soliciting this work and to Wai-chee Dimock and my friend Cathy Popkin for facilitating it.

Helen Tartar gave me confidence at a very early stage in my career and has continued to support me with her friendliness and patience far longer than she imagined she would. She has been a much-valued ally over the years and a model editor. I was very fortunate in my editors, Jan Spauschus Johnson, whose intelligence, wit, and calm provided me with a much-needed sense of purpose and perspective, and my elegant and tactful copy editor, Laura Westlund. My anonymous readers for Stanford Press and U.C. Berkeley provided careful and committed readings of my work which buoyed my spirits at a time when I began to believe that the light at the end of the tunnel was a plot, of uncertain origin, to chain me to my desk. I owe many improvements of the manuscript to their suggestions.

Scholars are rarely poets (alas) and, perhaps in recognition of this fact, tend to devote the least number of words to those whose contribution to the success of their work has been immeasurable. Let the reader know, then, that to the following names a surfeit of sentiment and gratitude is attached. My friends Barbara Fehrs, Nan Goodman, Monika Greenleaf, Bia Jaguaribe, Karin Sanders, and Judith Shepherd are also my favorite heroines. Jenny Franchot has since graduate school sustained me with the constancy of her friendship, intellectual and otherwise, and walked me through many a soggy day. My husband and dearest friend, Greg Lowry, nourished me with his strength, his humor, his songs, and his broiled chicken recipe. His love and patience, and that of our children, Hart and Michela, supplied the context for anything the reader may find of value in these pages.

N.R.

Contents

Democratic Personality: An Introduction   I

PART ONE   19

1. The Devil in the Damsel: Spectral Evidence   31

2. Spectacular Conversion: George Whitefield and the Rise of Democratic Personality   83

3. The Advent of the Individual: Democratic Personality and the Spectral Self   120

PART TWO   179

4. The Voice of the People, the Voice of the Specter   191

5. The Crisis of American Character   259

6. An American Aesthetic of Innocence: Domesticating Democratic Personality   290

7. Melville's Anxiety of Innocence: The Handsome Sailor   344

Conclusion   379

Notes   391

Bibliography   499

Index   527

DEMOCRATIC PERSONALITY

Democratic Personality: An Introduction

The literature, songs, aesthetics, etc., of a country are of importance principally because they furnish the materials and suggestions of personality for the women and
men of that country, and enforce them in a thousand effective ways.

— WALT WHITMAN, *Democratic Vistas*

Marginality is becoming universal.

— MICHEL DE CERTEAU, *The Practice of Everyday Life*

I

"Democracy" in our time has converted from noun to verb. The series of
stunning political transformations that followed the fall of the Berlin Wall,
while confirming our customarily celebratory view of democracy as apotheosis, the mythic accomplishment of an ethico-political ideal, also suggested
that democracy remained an ongoing and especially volatile process whose
underlying principles could vary and whose telos was unpredictable. Thus
the almost wistful ambivalence registered in our use of the term "democratization" to describe such political events: we speak of a global will to "democratize" with no certainty that any of its local manifestations will generate
outcomes that conform to our own experience and common-sense understanding of democracy. Moreover, it is widely recognized that global democratization has reversed formerly stable ideological significations, rendering
our political shorthand obsolete and complicating our ability to recognize

friend and foe, self and other. Such epistemic changes for which global grassroots political activism serves as both sign and stimulus have fostered the revitalization of the field of democratic theory, whose practitioners are broadly committed to the critical reexamination of the meaning of "democracy." In this regard, democratic theorists seek particularly to evaluate how, for currently democratizing cultures, the time-honored association of democracy with liberalism — its commitment to a rational, open or visible, and consensual politics — is, if not to be categorically denied, certainly not to be taken for granted.

Recent theoretical speculation on the contours and commitments of an emerging "postliberal" or "radical" democracy has so far proven surprisingly reluctant to consider the recently accomplished history of democratization, especially the story of its achievement in British North America in this and the past century. Since Alexis de Tocqueville, the story of how modern (as opposed to classical) democracy was earliest and most fully realized in British North America has often been told, although with significant variation of emphasis and detail. Why should this relatively recent history of democratization be disregarded by those eager to understand what is now everywhere unfolding? It may be because, even for Tocqueville and his contemporary adherents who locate the roots of modern American democracy in seventeenth-century Puritan congregationalism, it has been considered a product of the nineteenth century, derived more or less directly from the political economy of liberalism. Even in current cultural-historical studies of democracy in America that concede not simply the difference between but the potential incompatibility of liberalism and democracy, no substantive discussion of a nonliberal American democracy has been forthcoming.[1] As if inevitably, the story begins with a dissenting and then revolutionary republicanism articulated in the protoliberal thought and practice of the colonial civil and clerical elite which, with the advent of industrial capitalism in the first half of the nineteenth century, matured into a recognizably modern liberal-democratic polity. According to the scholarly consensus, then, democracy in America is from the outset liberal democracy; perhaps for this reason, theorists struggling to conceptualize a contemporary radical democracy emerging outside the context of liberalism consider its history irrelevant.

The story I wish to tell about democracy in America is quite different. It is premised, first, on the need to acknowledge and investigate both the pre-liberal history of American democracy and the nature of its ultimate confrontation with liberal ideology; and second, on the conviction that in order to do so we can no longer restrict democracy's meaning to a set of sociopolitical or more broadly cultural institutions or procedures grounded in rational (liberal) value. Instead, I propose that democracy be reconceived as a dynamic symbolic system or theater, historically realized in an untheorized and irrational practice of compulsive public utterance which gave rise, as popular voice, to a distinctive mode of political (and later, literary) subjectivity. For the political interventions through which it announced itself and the crises of authority it thereby generated, as well as for the performative conditions of its emergence, I call this distinctive subjectivity "democratic personality." In this study, the theaters within which democratic personality arose to reconfigure power relations within American culture range from actual sites of cultural struggle — described here in terms of "spectral possession" and "spectacular conversion" — to the self-consciously "national" literary text of the postrevolutionary through the antebellum eras.

Democratic personality, I will argue, arose in isolation from liberal philosophy and well in advance of political forms of liberalism. Its early incarnations, therefore, demonstrate little, if any, resemblance to the self-owning, rational, and rights-bearing republican citizen or liberal (Lockean) subject. Instead, as described in Part I of this book, it represents a process of individuation unconnected to the concept of citizenship, announcing itself through the exercise of an authoritative, public voice unconnected to rational debate in a Habermasian public sphere.[2] Emerging well in advance of a bourgeois public sphere, democratic personality exceeded the power of cultural forms, from Puritan cosmology to the "national" novel, to contain it. It would survive the rationalizing thrust of the Revolution, the consolidation of Federalism, and the advent of liberalism to bedevil the attempts of thinkers from Crèvecoeur through Emerson and Whitman to claim for themselves the status of "representative" Americans. The authorial struggle to domesticate democratic personality — to embrace its primitive energies as uniquely American while muting its characteristic voice through the offices of a national literature — is the focus of Part II of this book. Admittedly, this investigation into the prehistory of American liberal democracy mars the cleaner lines of the democratic identity Americans love to trace, as well as the high polish of its genealogy, but as the historian Robert H. Wiebe observes, "history challenges the notion that democracies need to come complete. . . . What ever arrives in finished form?"[3]

Democratic personality, then, was not (as Benedict Anderson has claimed of the nation) "something capable of being consciously aspired to" by a few enlightened individuals in the form of a personal ethics for the good governance of self or society.[4] Nor does the term refer to those exemplary and progressive spirits, such as the Puritan minister and defender of congregational independence John Wise, who in thought or deed promoted some aspect of what we have come to recognize as liberal-democratic value.[5] Far from representing a conscientious or reasoned anticipation of such values, the individual enactments of democratic personality adumbrate the untheorized experiential beginnings of political life for persons without a public voice within the culture. In this respect, the concept bears an affinity to E. J. Hobsbawm's understanding of those who participated in what he terms the "primitive" or "archaic" social movements in Western and Southern Europe in the nineteenth and twentieth centuries: preindustrial and precapitalistic, not affiliated with the rationality of modern liberalism, lacking any discernable political affiliation, and associated with uneducated and anonymous persons.[6] Apart from the extraordinarily eloquent George Whitefield, the cultural significance of democratic personality was expounded by those who observed, whether sympathetically or critically, the numbers of individuals emerging so unexpectedly from social invisibility to speak with power and authority in a newly constituted—and uncannily transient—public sphere. The history of democratic personality is thus largely, although not entirely (as my analysis of Whitefield and his followers will show), the history of a culture's impassioned response to the multiple incarnations and the voice of its own ideological incoherence.[7]

The Salem witchcraft crisis of 1692 marks the first significant instance of the unanticipated intrusion into the public arena of newly self-constituted speakers endowed with an unprecedented authority to make political decisions for the community. The utterances of the "afflicted"—the group responsible for denouncing and helping to prosecute others as witches—were conspicuous for being at once radically inarticulate and yet powerfully persuasive.[8] This paradox is recapitulated and amplified in the speakers' dramatized self-representation as spectrally possessed: that is, as both personally impotent to the point of selflessness and yet possessed of privileged access to an exclusive knowledge of "invisible" (spiritual) realities that justified — indeed required — their speaking publicly and authoritatively about them. This strategy of self-representation (which Whitefield would later model before mass audiences and theologically legitimate as "humble self-enlargement") epitomizes the hybridic nature of democratic personality, the basis of its peculiar political ontology. Its claim to transcend or simply to abrogate the distinction between self and other (including the divine Other), and thus its power to collapse social and cognitive distinctions critical to the integrity of cultural authority, qualifies the genesis and meaning of the impulse to speak publicly of its knowledge. That is, far from speaking autonomously or unilaterally, as accountable individuals, democratic personality invoked a transcendent legitimacy and supraindividual rationale for ignoring social restrictions upon public speech — indeed, it offered itself to the community as a passive instrument for the articulation of invisible truths normally concealed from the natural minds of mortal men and women. The pretense of the "specter" constituted an ingenious tactic for legitimating both the fact and the outrageous content of the public speech of the afflicted.[9] As we will see, the specter of 1692, an exemplary hybrid subject able to maintain a simultaneous presence in the visible and invisible worlds, nature and the supernatural, provided a paradigm for the subsequent ontology of democratic personality in both its social and literary incarnations.

The mechanics of humble self-enlargement indicates that along with beliefs about liberal-democratic value, we must dissociate democratic personality from related assumptions concerning the individual — perhaps most conspicuously, the constellation of beliefs concerning rational self-possession as the basis of modern individualism famously analyzed by C. B. Macpherson.[10] This is so because the process of individuation that democratic personality makes visible to us was complexly mediated through a distinctive type of performance in which — as the power of uncontainable voice — the process was modeled before and appropriated by mass audiences (the topic of Chapters 1 through 3). The performance itself constituted a distinctive form of social and then artistic space for the coming-into-being of democratic personality, whose verbal and behavioral excesses were partially rehabilitated in the early national era and especially the antebellum era as American character (the topic of Chapters 4, 5, and 6).[11] It was to the task of deconstructing this domestication of democratic personality as perfected by Whitman and restoring its uncanny power that Melville committed himself in his final novel, *Billy Budd* (the topic of Chapter 7).

As I trace it in the following seven chapters, then, the history of democratic personality suggests that in order to discover how democratization occurred historically on the microlevel of the individual subject (and perhaps how it continues to occur), as well as to discern cultural differences in its occurrence, we must move beyond the conceptual, historical, and even geographical limits imposed by the framework of liberalism, a point to which I will return in section III of this Introduction. (Relatedly, we must also acknowledge that democratic personality cannot be considered an exclusively American phenomenon, although here I link it quite specifically to the details of American literary and cultural history.) We must look, that is, not just to the predemocratic liberal tradition so brilliantly expounded by political theorists like Macpherson and historians like J. G. A. Pocock, Gordon Wood, Bernard Bailyn, and Joyce Appleby, but to a *preliberal democratic tradition* for which the separation of the thinker from the mass, the theoretical articulation from the act, has not yet transpired. For this reason, the analytical and conceptual difficulties of democratic personality must be seen as inhering not in the intellectual substance of its utterances, which were often inarticulate if radically persuasive, but in the individual *act* of utterance itself along with the historically inflected experience of subjectivity which that act presupposed.[12]

Indeed, only by attuning one's ear to the characteristic voice of democratic personality — unanticipated, inarticulate, uncontainable, heedless of the forms, ventriloquizing a higher will and truth — is it possible to apprehend the experiential ground that, in tandem with particular cultural forces, galvanized its historically recurring realization in an anonymous and largely uneducated class of persons. This book is committed to the identification and exploration of this experiential ground and its affiliations with a unique (if overlooked) form of expression that would contribute significantly to the development of a democratic cultural semiotic in the wake of Puritanism. The anonymity in their own era as in ours of those who first embodied democratic personality — "the people out of doors," as Gordon Wood has described them, that "hovering presence" whose life lay "outside of the legislative chambers" — makes the task of discovery and description more difficult simply because the details of their words and lives were rarely recorded.[13] Wood's language underscores what we might describe as the enduring spectrality of democratic personality in comparison with the very vocal and visible "representative personalities" like Mitchell Breitweiser's Benjamin Franklin or Patrick Joyce's Edwin Waugh.[14] Yet the spectrality of the inarticulate (as historians sometimes refer to this class) must be understood in its historic positivity rather than ahistorically, as absence or enfeebled presence, if we are to supplement our understanding of the role played by history's remarkable men and women and, more crucially, avoid positing an agentless process of cultural evolution endowed with the generative powers historians traditionally ascribed to remarkable individuals.[15]

If, as a vocal current, democratic personality migrated through individuals, conferring upon "the multitudes of illiterate people" a uniquely translatable and transferable form of subjectivity, thereby lifting them out of the social anonymity that sealed their invisibility, it is nevertheless true that those so lifted elected not to leave their invisibility quite behind. Instead, they rendered it audible, consolidating their new authority by publicly performing their emergence from and affiliation with a type of spectral domain, a sphere ontologically situated between the invisible world of God's determinations and the visible world determined by "the great, the honorable, the rich and the learned," who had claimed for themselves the prerogative of representing invisible realities.[16] By proclaiming in the very fact of public utterance a new and unanswerable epistemology concerning invisible realities of the spiritual and then the social order, as well as its unsuspected mastery of the invisible realm, democratic personality compelled a rigorous and painful reexamination of claims for representational legitimacy based, first, on worldly forms of privilege, primarily wealth and education, and, later, on carefully crafted authorial claims. In so doing, it spurred an ongoing redefinition of the project of political and literary representation in the new nation.

It has been my sense that the cultural work of the inarticulate — individual members of the human mass who have been consistently imagined as either the victims or the beneficiaries of cultural development, but not its generators — remains historically unaccounted for. Perhaps this is because, as the afflicted girls in the witchcraft crisis through Melville's Billy Budd suggest, inarticulateness (which is not the same as silence) acts as a shield, offering the disenfranchised a means of exercising an unsuspected and thus unrecognized will to power regularly misconstrued as helpless — ignorant, impotent, irrelevant — innocence.

II

As is evident in Raymond Williams's brief account of the historical development of the term "personality," its meanings have consistently encompassed the apparent opposition between individual specificity and general personhood, and between an authentic trait of selfhood (who one is) and a performed or factitious one (how one acts). Personality, as Williams points out, may be compared in this respect with the historical development of the term "character," for in both one notes the "overlap between dramatic or fictional presentation and the possession of a private as well as an evident nature." Both constitute "extreme" instances of possessive individualism:

> a *personality* or a *character*, once an outward sign, has been decisively internalized, yet internalized as a possession, and therefore as something which can be either displayed or interpreted. This is, in one sense, an extreme of possessive individualism, but it is even more a record of the increasing awareness of "freestanding" and therefore "estimable" existence which, with all its difficulties, gave us *individual* itself.[17]

Personality is a more apt term than "subjectivity" for the purposes of this study precisely because it posits subjectivity as first and foremost an articulated (jointed) structure and thus focuses attention upon its fault lines: those that exist between private or spiritual identity and public character, between individuality and the collectivity, between being and representation, between the author of a fiction and fictional character. In short, as the history of the term suggests, the tension comprised by "personality" inheres in the performative aspects of personhood with which this study is centrally concerned.

The extensive literary-historical work of the Russian cultural semiotician Lydia Ginzburg on the construction of personality similarly emphasizes its articulated structure and thus its reliance upon performance. Just as Williams locates personality on the border of the real and the fictive, essence and appearance, inside and outside, and just as M. M. Bakhtin locates discourse

on the border between two consciousnesses, so does Ginzburg define personality as an "aesthetically significant image" located on the border between
two other images: the first, "an image of reality," and the second, "an image
of a human being."[18] Personality is no fixed image, however, but the continuously produced record of an action, a "plotted structuring" of the two equally
dynamic frame images ("reality," "the human being"). The act of structuring
that is personality occurs unceasingly within and between individuals in the
course of social interaction and is for all intents and purposes indistinguishable from artistic creation. By thus redefining personality as an (aesthetic)
activity that occurs between persons rather than as an individual possession,
Ginzburg suggests how, while retaining its integrity as a mark of individuation, personality may be transferred between persons and translated from
one subjective register to another: the construction or coalescence of personality is itself a performance. Personality, the continuously produced record of
a plotted structuring, is above all an act of modeling that leads to appropriation that leads in turn to modeling; moreover, the process occurs between
persons as well as between texts (textual images of personality) and persons,
and even between texts. Each image of personality, whether human or textual
(and in Ginzburg, these sources can penetrate one another so profoundly as
to engender a hybrid subject she calls "the human document"), offers the one
who beholds it "a specific image of reality in which are combined elements of
the logical and the sensory, the abstract and the concrete, the general and the
particular, the visible and the invisible."[19] As a subset of personality so conceived, democratic personality strikingly literalizes what we might call the
ontology of personality as recorded in Williams's history, for in and through
its characteristic performances it models nothing so much as its own liminality, the condition of in-betweenness. Thus we will see how the afflicted of
1692 performed their occupation of a spectral domain between the visible
and invisible worlds and the converts of the Great Awakening spoke from the
interval between life and death, death and rebirth.

In certain individuals, the production of personality as Ginzburg describes it may be so finely correlated with a particular historical moment as to
produce what she terms "epochal" or "historically significant" personality.[20]
If normative personality tends to work centripetally, availing itself of typological categories already in place, epochal personality works centrifugally,
transgressing the boundaries between types by performing a new and com-

pelling image or model of personhood. Apart from its adherence to the liminal, I suggest that democratic personality may be the most exemplary type of epochal personality, for the (more or less conscious) disposition to challenge the symbolical integrity of established and authoritative social and aesthetic forms is inherent to both the democratic *and* the epochal as Ginzburg defines it. Moreover, the "democratic" construct, like the model, is an internally paradoxical one, encompassing an array of historically determined semantic and psychosocial tensions that have accrued to it over the course of its history.[21] Obsessively theorized and perpetually elusive, "democracy" has been claimed by liberal as well as totalitarian societies, by capitalists and socialists, by the advocates of individualism as well as those of communitarianism. It has served as a synonym for singularity as well as typicality.[22] If anything, it most steadily signifies the collapse of conceptual opposites, as in its trademark identification of the governed and the governors.[23] Democratic personality is thus an oxymoron within an oxymoron: to the coexistence of essence and performance indicated by "personality," "democratic" superadds its own contradictions as a concept both taut and flexible to the point of insignificance, both conservative and revolutionary. In general, it signifies a range of incompatibilities brought into a dynamic and volatile, thus inherently revolutionary, unity: a feature that would recommend it to Whitman in his bid to create "a single image-making work" that would encompass "the People."[24] In this study, the key opposition democratic personality perpetually collapses only to resurrect and reproblematize is that between the invisible and visible domains and its variants (the sacred and the profane, essence and appearance, being and representation), in particular as these antitheses have informed spiritual, ontological, political, and literary notions of personhood.

Within the context of the preceding discussion, democratic personality presents itself as a variant of constructed subjectivity: like identities associated with race, gender, class, or nation, democratic personality emerged as the result of complex cultural mediations.[25] Unlike race or gender, however, democratic personality is conspicuous for having no prior material referent in the body.[26] (This is not to deny the body a role in the formation of democratic personality—far from it, as we shall see. It does deny the body a delimiting function and thus denotes the radically inclusive nature of democratic personality as a category of being potentially open to everybody.) Insofar as it lacks reference to specific aspects of the body, it may be compared with class or national identities, except that these, too, are commonly regarded as deriving from a preexisting essentialist entity: the collective bodies of class or nation.[27] To the extent that a collective identity appears to precede and condition the emergence of democratic personality, however, it does so in a radically attenuated manner, a circumstance that makes of democratic personality—no matter the extent to which it ultimately permeates a given culture—an abiding anomaly. Indeed, as a variant of constructed subjectivity, democratic personality arises as a dramatic refusal to conform to collectively imposed and institutionally sustained norms of identity, a refusal legitimated not with reference to some notion of the "natural" (such as the natural relationship linking an individual to a collective body or the premise of natural rights), but rather to the supernatural, through whose transcendent authority the anomalous is made representative and the marginal is revealed to be universal. In general, then, the peculiarity of democratic personality as a form of constructed subjectivity lies with the generative site of its individual embodiments, a site that grounds—figures and determines—its oppositional rationale and subsequent relationship to the normative forms of identity available within a given culture.

III

We can begin to bring into focus the generative site of democratic personality—the peculiar theater within which it emerges into visibility through the exercise of uncontainable voice—by offering as contrast what we might assume to be its natal ground, given the scholarly linkage of postclassical democratic forms to the history and development of liberal thought: namely, modern liberal-democratic society.[28] The briefest acquaintance with contemporary democratic theory reveals that its primary internecine struggle has been to evaluate the usefulness of the liberal legacy to "the future of democracy"; the legacy itself is not in dispute.[29] For the most part, the liberal legacy poses no problem for cultural history—it would be difficult, if not silly, to deny the impact of liberalism upon the development of democratic institutions in the past two centuries. Central to the theoretical understanding of the liberal legacy, however, is a proposition concerning the liberal origins of postclassical democracy, a claim that entails a host of assumptions about the character and deployment of democratic power that, in the American case, obscures key features of its early history. The Italian theorist Norberto Bobbio states categorically that

> the liberal state is not only the historical but the legal premiss of the democratic state. The liberal state and the democratic state are doubly interdependent: if liberalism provides those liberties necessary for the proper exercise of democratic power, democracy guarantees the existence and persistence of fundamental liberties.

This reciprocity of function confirms, in turn, the historical precedence and enabling role of liberalism: "The constitutional norms which confer these [liberal] rights are not rules of the [democratic] game as such: they are preliminary rules which allow the game to take place."[30] The functional balance of such an account belies the asymmetry that invests it, the result of the pressure exerted upon its easy elegance by the heavy thumb of the normative: liberalism fosters only the "proper" exercise of democratic power. The qualifier, of course, raises the question of its improper exercise, the fear of which established "democracy" as an overwhelmingly pejorative term until well into the nineteenth century, that is, until it was fully articulated with liberalism.[31] At the heart of claims for the liberal origins of modern democracy lurks the specter of a democratic power improperly exercised and thus belonging, we may infer, to a different political game altogether.

How are we to discern the rules of this game, assuming that they will not be registered and their evolution traced in the familiar history of liberal-democratic institutions? And how are we to discover its players, assuming that they bear little, if any, relation to those representative individuals — philosophers and statesmen — who embody the progress of liberal-democratic thought and practice? We might take our cue from the beleaguered narrator of Melville's *Billy Budd*, who laments that he can discover the "inside narrative" beneath the historical record only through indirection, by focusing on those forever unincorporated sites in the rainbow where one color "blendingly enters" the province of another, what he elsewhere in the novel calls "the deadly space between." As it emerged within the culture and as it was represented in American literature, the generative site of democratic personality constitutes just such a "space between," sometimes literally deadly but always destructive to what Melville called a culture's "measured forms," both social and novelistic.[32] We may begin to conceptualize this space by reexamining accounts of the emergence of modern democracy from the matrix of liberalism.

Consider, for example, the following pair of views offered by C. B. Macpherson. In the first, Macpherson provides a telescoped account of how democracy suddenly "became a good thing" about one hundred fifty years ago after centuries of disparagement. According to his narrative, liberalism, which arose as a philosophical supplement to and rationalization of the development of market capitalism, "produce[d], after a time, a pressure for democracy which became irresistible":

> Those who had no vote saw that they had no weight in the political market—they had, so to speak, no political purchasing power. . . . When they saw this, they came to demand the vote for themselves, using the general right of association [necessary to the functioning of market capitalism] to organize their demand. When they did so, there was, equally in the logic of the system, no defensible ground for withholding the vote from them. For the liberal society had always justified itself as providing equal individual rights and equality of opportunity.
>
> So finally the democratic franchise was introduced into the liberal state.[33]

According to this narrative, democracy (the franchise) first manifested itself not simply as an economic but as an ethical imperative: it "was demanded, and admitted, on the ground that it was unfair not to have it in a competitive society" (10). The "pressure for democracy," in this view, was exerted by the disenfranchised who suddenly became aware of their voicelessness, and immediately determined to take advantage not only of their "general right" to associate but also of the implicit logic of the system from which they had historically been excluded. Ultimately, however, such remarkable political sophistication was secondary in its efficacy to a general agreement on the part of liberal thinkers that the logic of the system ethically required the broadening of the franchise (although "defensible ground" was found, apparently, for continuing to withhold it from other than white, male citizens).[34] Although Macpherson notes some tension between those who demanded and those who admitted (the achievement of democracy required "many decades of agitation and organization," but those who advocated change were largely "devotees of the market society"), the real pressure for change is exerted from within the self-fulfilling logic of liberalism itself. The "late addition" of democracy here represents the fulfillment of the logic of liberalism (9–11).

Elsewhere Macpherson suggests that liberal thinkers may have been motivated to extend the franchise not so much by an ethical imperative inherent in liberalism as by a healthy fear of the "democratic mass." Here, enfranchisement is not the result of a popular awareness of and rational appeal to the ethical logic of liberalism, but rather of the fact that liberal thinkers suddenly considered it "urgent to moralize the society before the mass took control." Moralization — for which extending the franchise was the chosen means — entailed what has been called the "taming" or liberalization of democracy, which occurred at least partially through the creation of "an image of liberal-democratic society which could be justified by something more morally appealing (to the liberal thinker and, hopefully, to the new democratic mass) than the old utilitarianism."[35]

It is not my purpose here to question the ethical integrity or political vitality of this enduringly powerful image of liberal-democratic society, but rather to ask what it obscures when we use it as a lens through which to view early (preliberal) American culture. In Macpherson's two views of the rise of democracy from liberalism, we readily see that their difference lies in the nature of the "pressure for democracy." Specifically, the liberal guardianship's fear of the demos central to the second account is wholly residual to the first narrative of a seemingly self-evolving philosophical-political rationale that disarms by anticipating and redressing in advance all opposition to its hegemony.[36] And what remains residual in the second account are the particularities of the role played by individual members of the democratic mass in the development of a liberal-democratic sociopolitical order: the democratic mass is here represented as the merely hypothetical, curiously inert, and thereby passive cause of a productive (if possibly unfounded) liberal fear. In both accounts, the notion of a specifically democratic subjectivity outside of or preexisting the context of liberalism is wholly absent. There is nothing remarkable about this absence: whereas liberalism is understood to originate in a set of theoretical propositions about human subjectivity, there exists no comparable notion of a nonliberal democratic subject.[37] From their inception as propositions about political and social being, the liberal subject and his country cousin, the virtuous republican citizen, have been densely characterized — the accruing specificity of their rights, values, motives, and actions endowing them with an individuated, almost embodied (if often ahistorical) existence.[38]

"Democracy," however, has not historically partaken of a similar imaginative endowment. Within the liberal context, "democracy" has typically been relegated to the handmaiden's facilitating role, either as a myth or ideal predicated upon a liberal subjectivity attributed to an entire society (or to humanity in general) or, less fancifully, as a set of procedures through which liberal rights — the cornerstone of liberal subjectivity — are exercised and maintained. Outside of the liberal context, to the degree that "democracy" has invoked the immediacy of subjectivity, it has done so largely with reference to an anonymous, collective subject (the mob, the mass, the "people out of doors") without internal coherence because unconnected to the conditions of personal autonomy granted a priori to the liberal subject.[39] Characterologically, the democratic subject has occupied the negative space visible only in the refracted light of the liberal subject's fullness. As the art historian T. J. Clark has explained the failure of "writers or politicians or painters [to give] faces to the People in the nineteenth century": "They were the mass, the invisible class; they all looked alike."[40] A spectral presence, its character as history has imagined it comprises a list of negatives, as if the democratic subject were the parodic underside of Kenneth Burke's "negative theology": in particular, the quality of the inarticulateness traditionally attributed to it is the fitting correlative of the merely reactive energy it is also thought to possess.[41]

How are we to convert these negative traits into positive ones; how are we to elicit the shape of preliberal democracy from the historical invisibility to which it has been consigned? The answer, I suggest, lies in reconceptualizing democracy as a theater of verbal (symbolic) action, an experiential ground whose materializations, both historical and literary, would ultimately foster the development of a recognizably democratic (polycentric) cultural semiotic such as that to which Tocqueville so passionately responded.[42] The experiential dimension of this ground is thoroughly performative, for within it the coming-into-being of a radical democratic subjectivity is simultaneously modeled before and appropriated by others. From the moment of its emergence, neither anticipated by nor accountable to any theoretical formulation, radical democratic subjectivity contradicted what would become three key attributes of the liberal-democratic (or, in Macpherson's influential formulation, the self-possessed) subject. First, far from being self-possessed and highly individualized, radical democratic subjectivity was conspicuously transferable: it individuated without necessarily individualizing those who appropriated it, although, as I argue in my third chapter, its appearance provided a transcendent rationale for individualism. Second, that democratic personality could be transferred to others was entirely a function of the uncontainability of its characteristic utterance, an utterance that both proclaimed and enacted the acquisition of a distinctively political subjectivity. The subject's claim to and experience of the uncontainability of utterance was made in terms of the cultural authority, truth-value, social relevance, and geographical range of the subject's newly acquired voice. The voice of the liberal-democratic subject, in contrast, is registered in and as the franchise which, as Claude Lefort points out, represents the simultaneous apotheosis and alienation of individual voice in the liberal-democratic regime.[43] Third, democratic personality boldly proclaims its intimate affiliation with invisible power, whereas, as Norberto Bobbio points out, the liberal-democratic state and subject are committed to the total eradication of invisible power as inherently despotic, a betrayal of the democratic ideal as represented by the classical *agora*.[44] In contrast to this ideal, Lefort had described this "diffuse invisible power" (with reference to Tocqueville's insight into American democratic practice) as one "which is both internal and external to individuals; which is produced by individuals and which subjugates individuals; which is as imaginary as it is real; and which is imprinted on government, administration and opinion alike."[45]

  As I will describe it in the following chapters with reference to specific cultural-historical events and specific literary texts, democratic personality, as a form of political subjectivity, is strikingly reminiscent of the celebrated conundrum at the root of Walt Whitman's poetic manifestos. Just as Whitman proposed that nation, poem, and poet — land, literature, and literatus — would in America come into being simultaneously, so democratic personality partakes of a similar consubstantiality of utterance, speaker, and locus of speech. The theatricalized democratic space emerged in tandem with the utterance pronounced within its confines and is thus characterized by the same extemporaneity; moreover, it extended itself with the spread of the voice that both announced and enacted the coming-into-being of democratic personality.[46] It is this syncopation of utterance, speaker, and locale that I metaphorize in the term "popular voice," a spectral presence, now embodied, now disembodied; now univocal, now grotesquely polyphonic; but unfailingly, powerfully audible. With this spectral presence of popular voice, self-consciously American writers from the postrevolutionary through the antebellum eras struggled to articulate a working relationship through a series of disturbing, literally deconstructive representations of democratic personality.

As an analysis of popular voice, then, this study inadvertently enlists itself in the debate that has enlivened the study of early American culture and fiction at least since Alan Heimert published his magisterial *Religion and the American Mind* in 1966 and unleashed a storm of controversy over which form of discursive power led to the American Revolution: Enlightenment philosophy or indigenous grassroots religious activism, the treatise or the pulpit, the text or the voice. The debate has generated several sharp, not to say barbed, historical studies of a period that had traditionally attracted neither the interest nor the scholarly energy devoted to the Puritan or antebellum eras that framed it.[47] My own preference is for those studies that move beyond the either/or opposition of text/voice to posit—whether historically or theoretically—a nuanced third term: studies such as Frank Lambert's sensitive historical account of the complementarity of the spoken and printed word in Whitefield's career; Lydia Ginzburg's explication of "the human document"; Tenney Nathanson's ingenious analyses of Whitman's peculiar poetic "presence"; or Donald Wesling and Tadeusz Sławek's elaboration of "the speaking that is in writing" to supplement Derrida's insistence upon "the writing that is in speaking."[48] I share Bakhtin's premise ("The text as such never appears as a dead thing; beginning with any text—and sometimes passing through a lengthy series of mediating links—we always arrive, in the final analysis, at the human voice"), and would emphasize his point that, even at its most inarticulate, the human voice is never innocent of other voices, whether textually or aurally insinuated.[49]

This study offers a theory of what J. G. A. Pocock has termed "the secularization of personality" as it occurred in the American context. Unlike

Pocock, who traces this phenomenon back from the American Revolution to its British and Renaissance Florentine political-philosophical sources, I am interested in its accomplishment within the context of American Puritanism as a function of revolutionary changes within the concept of personality, induced by popular challenges to the regnant symbolic, and primarily the religious, order.[50] Whereas Pocock allies the secularization of personality with the process of modernization, and specifically with the symbolic operations of commerce that compelled the transmutation of the classical notion of virtue in the age of empire, I understand secularization as occurring not subsequent to but in tandem with the symbolic economy of American Puritanism as it was enacted by common and anonymous persons rather than a cultural elite. Finally, where Pocock posits the secularization of personality as an adjunct of social and economic developments within and between European nations, I follow its American course from the colonial Puritan context in which it first emerges not into politics or economics but into literature.

Part One

The first two chapters of this book examine the rise of democratic personality in colonial America within two aberrant forms of social space, one associated with the Salem witchcraft crisis of 1692 and the other with the Great Awakening of the 1740s. Each form of social space effectively provided a mediating context within which democratic personality, not despite but by virtue of its contradictions, might be temporarily realized. This realization occurred through a distinctive, even ritualized, type of performance that permitted its appropriation by others and thus enabled its dissemination far beyond the scene of performance. In Chapter 1, "The Devil in the Damsel: Spectral Evidence," I examine the performance of spectral possession enacted by those who claimed to be afflicted by invisible evil beings and were sustained by the unorthodox theory of spectral evidence. This theory, elaborated by a group of influential Puritan ministers and magistrates, proposed that certain individuals might temporarily possess privileged access to the transcendent source of absolute meaning. In Chapter 2, "Spectacular Con-

version: George Whitefield and the Rise of Democratic Personality," I turn
to the Great Awakening, the grassroots intercolonial religious revival that
began some fifty years later. Here I analyze the formation and internal dynamics of "spectacular conversion," a performance enacted within the space
created by the evangelical itinerant George Whitefield's massively attended
sermons, during which a revolutionary notion of spiritual rebirth as vocal
uncontainability was made experientially available to his auditors.[1] Whereas
Whitefield's charismatic itinerant ministry allows for a concise view of one
man's modeling of democratic personality and its mass appropriation within
the context of spectacular conversion, the Salem crisis — comparatively contained in scope but more diffusely generated by an unstable cadre of afflicted
persons — enables the recovery of the religious and social conditions within
which it first emerged and thus provides a paradigm for its future manifestations, in particular its adaptation to a literary problematic in the postrevolutionary era.

In both the witchcraft crisis and the revival, the emergence of democratic
personality was justified as humble self-enlargement. Spectacular conversion
and spectral possession both featured the individual's public enactment of
his or her own disintegration — the convert dying to the old, sinful self;
the afflicted racked by the physical and psychological torments of spectral
beings. Public self-effacement, in turn, permitted the exercise of an apparently innocent, because radically selfless, act of judgmental and authoritative
public speech (including the public identification of others as either unregenerate or regenerate, damned or saved) that restructured the social and
institutional bases of traditional communities. The discovery of humble self-
enlargement as a means for effective participation in the public sphere was
common to the witchcraft crisis and the revival; it allowed lowly individuals — the poor and uneducated, women, African-Americans, the young —
who would normally participate minimally, if at all, in the political or social
decision-making of their cultures to assume a prominent role.[2] It permitted
these formerly silent, perhaps even silenced, individuals to speak publicly and
with unprecedented authority on the basis of their claim, performatively
verified, to have penetrated the realm of appearance and thus to have gained
privileged but innocent because nonconsensual access to essence, the realm
of spirit which the Calvinist orthodoxy had always insisted was ineluctably
remote from natural men.

In 1692 as in 1742, civil and clerical authorities faced urgent questions concerning the source and the legitimacy of this new accusatory popular speech. The vocal undermining of authority undertaken by socially anonymous individuals not normally authorized to speak publicly was often inarticulate and yet momentous in its consequences especially insofar as cultural authorities were initially unprepared both conceptually and institutionally to respond. It was not immediately clear whether popular indictments against other, perhaps highly placed persons as unconverted or in league with the devil did indeed derive from a supernatural source to which the accusers enjoyed an unprecedented kind and degree of access, or whether they indicated the speakers' estrangement from sources of absolute authority, both temporal and eternal. For the critical auditor not disposed to entertain the possibility of direct contact with transcendent being, the popular voice so exercised provided a startling insight into the complex deviance of the unanchored self, a new understanding of the relationship between the structure and deployment of human personality, on the one hand, and the structure and deployment of misrepresentation, on the other.

The premise of humble self-enlargement that legitimated popular speech in both the witchcraft debacle and the revival fatally challenged the Puritan concept of charity, along with the notion of the covenant, a key principle of community. Puritan charity established an individual's visible character or outward demeanor as a sufficiently reliable index of his or her essential spiritual estate as a child of God or a child of Satan to permit the identification, as a basis for church membership, of the community's "visible saints." Although it was acknowledged that opinions derived from visible character concerning an individual's spiritual identity could not be fully verified (given the space of unknowing that God had subtended between the invisible world of His determinations and the visible world of natural men), it was agreed that the possibility of occasional hypocrisy must and could be accommodated without unduly compromising the sanctity of the gathered community of saints. In 1692, however, when a formerly insignificant group of people within the community claimed to have sighted the specters or ghostly representations of others engaging in diabolical recruitments and were upheld in their allegations by a number of ministers, the representational possibilities of human personality proliferated well beyond visible character and the problem of hypocrisy. In place of the cosmological binarism of visible and invisible realms, the theory of spectral evidence effectively posited a third realm — the domain of hybridic specters where contact between spiritual and embodied beings (devil and witch, specter and victim) could occur — that supplanted the space of unknowing fundamental to Puritan theology, especially the foundational notion of charity.

According to the afflicted, the witches were those who, in exchange for the promised gratification of their illicit desires, had consented to let the devil spectrally represent them in order to torment or seduce others and thereby win adherents to Satan's revolutionary cause, the overthrow of divine order through the undermining of Puritan community. The truth of this spectral act — consent to representation — was taken by the Salem prosecutors to be self-evident based upon the dramatic display of spectral possession publicly enacted by the afflicted. Its truth superseded that of visible character, such that visible character was reconceived: no longer a reliable index of invisible identity, it was regarded as a species of fiction intended to mask the truth of diabolical covenant. Apparent piety might signify not divine election but its opposite. Whereas the accused witches were executed for daring to seek contact with spiritual beings in order to fulfill individual and perhaps criminal desires, their accusers enacted daily encounters with the invisible world with impunity because their access — performed as unspeakable physical and psychological torment — was perceived as nonconsensual and thus innocent. If their affliction afforded visible proof of their superlative humility, on the invisible plane they did not hesitate to chastise the Prince of Lies himself. If democratic personality first emerges in the witchcraft crisis as a behavioral paradigm for procuring a means of authoritative public speech, we cannot assign it, as we can in the Great Awakening, to a discrete faction: it is, rather, the product of factional interaction, of the projections and displacements that gave rise to the factions themselves. Democratic personality in the witchcraft crisis was the product of an unwitting collaboration: the making of victims through the discovery of performed victimization as an avenue to power that was perhaps never intended or rigorously theorized as a strategy for liberation from religious or social constraints.

With this unwitting collaboration of the actors in the witchcraft crisis in mind, the event may be seen as protodemocratic in four respects. First and most obviously, it temporarily produced an inversion of power in an infamously rigid patriarchal society such that the most eminent clerical and civil leaders were accepting spiritual counsel from teenaged girls and young women, as well as granting them the power of life or death over others, including some of the colony's most powerful and respected inhabitants.[3] Second, and perhaps more important, it produced an implicitly antiauthoritarian reconceptualization of human personality as possessed of a spectral dimension, a hidden recess of individual desire which might be invisibly activated in the interests of self-aggrandizement. The concept (or fantasy) of the specter—the creature of one's consent, an embodiment of illicit desire that maintained a presence in both the visible and invisible domains and thus bridged the chasm between them—and the draconian effort to contain it indicate how momentous was the threat posed by a form of human initiative that eluded the supervision of cultural authority. As the representational possibilities of the individual were thus theoretically expanded, the prerogatives of God and His ministers were significantly reduced: as Increase Mather, in an effort to refute spectral evidence theory, had pointed out, to recognize the specter was to grant the devil (and his human allies) independence from God's superintendence. One might say that the modern era of possessive individualism was anticipated or accompanied by that of possessed individualism, where the invisible world came to signify not the domain of God's determinations but the hidden realm of individual imagination and desire, simultaneously elicited and rejected in the performance of spectral possession.[4] This simultaneous elicitation and rejection characterizes the history of "the individual" in eighteenth-century America (as elaborated in Chapter 3) as well as what I will define (in Chapters 4, 5, and 6) as a nineteenth-century American aesthetic of innocence, suggesting the paradigmatic value of the spectral self in tracing the evolution of democratic personality.

The third sense in which the witchcraft crisis heralded democratic personality inheres in its intense scrutiny of the politically resonant concepts of representation and consent as the two key acts through which invisible beings and their human allies conspired to overturn a divine and timeless order. By judging a spectral representation to possess greater self-evident truth, greater substance, as it were, than the accused themselves, it contributed to a shift of focus from absolute truth (whether the truth of God's unerring Word, the truth of ministerial exegesis, or the truth of an individual's spiritual identity as manifested in visible character) to its reception as and through multiple representations competing to win the consent of a constituency. Thus did the witchcraft crisis prod early American culture to forsake the essential binarism of Puritanism and to move toward the complex cultural semiosis of a democratic society based upon the multiplied representational potentiality of the individual. In the process, the normative understanding of terms associated with human interiority — identity, character, conscience — underwent radical changes in response to the performative impact of popular speech, preparing for a reconceptualization of individualism that permitted its emergence in the eighteenth century as a key principle of democratic collectivity. Finally, the witchcraft crisis compelled those who would remain true to the orthodox Puritan vision to succumb to the heretical implications of spectral evidence theory, primarily (because it supported the claim of direct access to spirit and thus denied the relevance of visible character) its antinomianism. The eleventh-hour petition of the pious and condemned Mary Easty, for example, reveals that she was compelled to choose between the authority of her own conscience and the authority of those who had condemned her to death: "by my own Innocencye," she asserted, "I know you are in the wrong way."[5] As was the case during the Great Awakening, the conservative or orthodox stance became increasingly impossible to maintain; so sweeping was the conceptual challenge of democratic personality that it compelled those ideologically opposed to it to adopt its rhetorical and ideational reformulations in the very process of refuting them so that opposition was undermined from within.

Each of these manifestations of a protodemocratic order that first emerged in the sacrificial debacle of 1692 arose more permanently and unmistakably fifty years later in the Great Awakening, and the resemblance was noted by the revival's opponents. Although the practice of humble self-enlargement (the publicly performed disintegration or "undoing" of the preternaturally knowledgeable self which authorized disruptive popular speech) was first collectively enacted during the witchcraft crisis, it was within the space of spectacular conversion that the voice of the people was first elicited and realized on a mass scale and provided an evangelical rationale for its perpetuation: the imperative of spiritual rebirth. In the course of his preaching tours of colonial America conducted between 1739 and 1770, Whitefield modeled conversion as an individuality that was instantaneously reconstituted and whose voice was, in theory, uncontainable, for the convert's transcendent obligation was to bear public witness to the priority of invisible realities even when they conflicted with custom or law. Whitefield's was a form of individuality, however, that explicitly denied its own significance in order to make selfless claim to a supraindividual authority. The convert speaking before the multitude spoke not as an individual but as a selfless conduit for the uncorrupted articulation of God's Word. To the extent that Whitefield and his followers encouraged individual speech and action, then, they did so not in the name of individualism, but in the name of a transferable selfhood wholly committed to the gathering of a community of converts both elite and uncontainable that had little in common with established ministerial authority or ecclesiastical order. In the witchcraft crisis, the performance through which the selfless individual emerged was a negative one insofar as what was performed was the rejection of individual self-assertion as "embodied" by the fantastic specter: the afflicted were compelled to interact with the invisible world by the specters, and their subsequent self-assertion was understood as a particularly arduous martyrdom. During the revival, the governing trope of conversion permitted a positive light to be directly cast on individual self-assertion as a "distinguishing mark" of spiritual regeneration.[6] Out of the theatricalized demise of the sinful self, authoritative public speech was thus legitimately, collectively born as the anonymous and humble individual was metamorphosed into the culture's exemplary representative, the "new man" whose voice, with its broken accents and stuttering locutions, gave a self-consciously "new" culture an identity grounded in radical innocence.

The sheer mass of such public articulations, along with the disruptive laughs, groans, and ravings that often accompanied them, were considered by the established ministry and its socially powerful adherents (the so-called Old Lights, as opposed to the New Light revivalists) to be explicitly subversive of the established order which reserved for itself the prerogatives of public speech, and especially public pronouncements concerning invisible realities. Once realized, however, in the form of a newly critical populace and especially a vital lay itinerant ministry that did not hesitate to challenge — often abusively — the authority of the established order, the popular voice eluded efforts to recontain it, a circumstance that proved compatible with, if not the sole cause of, intercolonial revolutionary unrest. The exercise of popular voice associated with the revival provided a bridge to the explicitly democratic popular speech of the revolutionary era, a transition captured in

Tory and, later, Federalist epithets like "political methodism" to describe republican exhortation.[7]

It is a historical truism that the eighteenth century witnessed a "shift from collective to individual accountability," which is linked in turn to the increasing plausibility of revolution in the minds of American colonists.[8] Although historians have often identified the emergence of individualism and the concomitant weakening of communal values with large-scale sociohistorical developments or events (economic expansion, demographic changes, the Great Awakening), this mode of explanation does little to elucidate the experiential aspect of individualism and the role it played in the coalescence of a democratic ethos at a time when a democratic politics was officially anathema.[9] It leaves unaddressed, that is, the question of how the shift from communalism to individualism, "the primacy of individual states and interests," was experienced and enacted by the individual who would not, historians tell us, have perceived himself or herself as such. Chapter 3, "The Advent of the Individual: Democratic Personality and the Spectral Self," proposes that the individual's emergence was dialectical and mediated rather than instantaneous and natural, and that it accompanied a shift of theological focus, initiated by the revivalists but to which the conservatives inevitably acceded, from "the unerring word of God" to its multiple recipients, from Truth to its multiple representations.[10] The new focus on varieties of religious representations and the vagaries of their reception led theologians to investigate the ontology of "the individual." This investigation would be largely conducted as an inquiry into what one might call the ontological status of representation.

For the revivalists and their opponents in the conservative ministry, this inquiry into the ontology of representation was far from theoretical. The shift in emphasis from the Word to the circumstances of its transmission and reception engendered a veritable war of representations between Old and New Lights to win the allegiance of individual parishioners. Old Lights attacked new forms of religious speech initiated by the revivalists, including the impassioned tenor of their extemporaneous sermons, the uninhibited emotional responses of congregations, and the often raucous sermons preached by laypersons in various public locales. Their chief objection was that the enthusiasts dissembled the questionable doctrinal content of their utterances (specifically, the doctrine of an instantaneous rebirth) by their sensational manner of speaking, destabilizing the grounds upon which an auditor could safely consent to the representation of spiritual truth offered. The auditor could thus no longer assume that sermonic form was transparent to doctrinal content, that the manner of preaching was consistent with the matter preached. Revivalists, meanwhile, counseled their auditors to scrutinize the conservative minister's visible character and speech for indices of the truth of his spiritual estate, and to abandon a preacher they believed was unregenerate (based, for example, on the evidence of a dull delivery). As a result of this shared disposition to read visible character (and voice as an aspect of visible character) as potentially duplicitous representations of spiritual truth, a train of suppositions fundamental to ecclesiastical stability was fatally uncoupled: namely, that a minister's gracious spiritual estate offered proof of the truth of his doctrine, that his visible character offered a reliable index of his spiritual estate, and that his voice reliably represented his visible character. These constituents of religious utterance — voice, character, and doctrine — were newly perceived on both sides as not necessarily integral but potentially separable for the purposes of misrepresentation as a means of furthering the private ambitions of an individual speaker. Taken separately, each amounted to a mere appearance with no self-evident correspondence to substance and thus no independent veracity. As in the witchcraft crisis, epistemological touchstones dissolved into insubstantial representations.

Both parties in the Great Awakening responded to the crisis by reengaging the language of spectral evidence theory. Working in opposition to one another, they jointly elaborated a semiotics of authenticity intended to aid observers in discovering a speaker's truth by identifying the sensible "marks" or "signs" of a regenerate or unregenerate spirit. Armed with such information, the auditor might discover whether God or mere imagination had inspired the speaker's utterance, and whether a gracious or a criminal heart lay behind the apparent felicities of visible character and the aesthetic charms of voice. But having made the principle of separability — of multiple, contiguous but independent representations of truth — fundamental to a new epistemology committed to securing a vantage point from which one might penetrate to the hidden source of appearances, both sides were left groundless. Although voice was invoked to support the authenticity of character and character the legitimacy of voice, it became increasingly apparent that an originary and abiding truth had been replaced by a tautology of representations, a circularity that permitted no transcendent perspective and that confirmed suspicions of the ubiquity of the counterfeit.

More than any other theologian of the period, Jonathan Edwards struggled to accommodate the irreversible shift from the Word to its multiple and conflicting representations by making it the cornerstone of a reinvigorated Calvinist theology. To the acrimonious debate concerning the status of aberrant public speech and behavior characteristic of revivalist congregations, Edwards brought his concept of the "truest representation" as a demonstration of individual religious experience that engendered in the witness's mind the truest image of divine truth. With this relativizing concept, Edwards attempted to liberate New Lights from the tautology of representations that had resulted from their efforts to justify scandalous behaviors by embracing as divinely ordained the imperfection of representation as the epistemological condition of mortality. Although fallen humankind was constrained to accept representations of divine truth in place of truth itself, this did not mean that all representations were equally valid. Nor did it mean that the profound unoriginality of representations should be taken to preclude their authenticity: unorthodox behaviors and speech which purported to represent the hidden truth of God's work within the individual soul, though patently imitated within and between revivalist congregations, could nevertheless be accepted as authentic indices of spiritual experience. The paradox of the genuine copy, the integral counterfeit, was redeemed by Edwards's insistence that to understand the truth-value of such representations required one to visualize what lay beyond formal observance (both conventional forms of religious worship and the conventional parameters of pastoral supervision): the hidden recesses of the human heart. Edwards presented human interiority as the new invisible sphere, inevitably hybrid, partaking (like all creation) of divinity and corruption. There God and the devil invisibly struggled to instrumentalize the human speaker whose voice might transcend its mere individuality by offering the truest ventriloquy of divinity or, alternatively, might broadcast the triumph of character, that debased or even criminal singularity which indicated Satan's occupation of the soul. If human utterance was ineluctably double-voiced, Edwards admonished skeptics, it was not always or necessarily revolutionary.

Although deeply Calvinist, Edwards's defense of the truth-value (if not quite the social prerogative) of aberrant public speech on the part of common people conferred upon them a novel authority over the King of Kings. "Let persons be never so weak, and never so mean, and under never so poor advantages," yet these, if true (innocent of self), God regards "as princes, they have power with God, and prevail."[11] Elsewhere, however, Edwards felt it necessary to caution his readers "to consider that the end for which God pours out his Spirit, is to make men holy, and not to make them politicians."[12] The anxiety he voices here would prove in the next century to have been especially prescient. That unmatched observer of antebellum American culture, Alexis de Tocqueville, noted of American religious leaders that "[w]here I expect to find a priest, I find a politician."[13] In the Kingdom of God which Edwards hoped would rise up on American soil through the energy generated by the public expression of vital individual experience, Tocqueville thereby registered the uncanny presence of democratic personality.

ONE

The Devil in the Damsel: Spectral Evidence

Unriddle these Things.

— COTTON MATHER, *Wonders of the Invisible World*

There is a traitor in our own bowels that is ready to open our parts and let in the adversary.

— URIAN OAKES, *"The Unconquerable, All Conquering and More than Conquering Soldier" (1674)*

An entire faith in the reality of witches and apparitions may commonly be traced to its true source, in the warmth of the passions, in the strength and fertility of the fancy.

— CHARLES BROCKDEN BROWN, *"The Rhapsodist"*

Nathan Bowen, a shopkeeper and scrivener of Marblehead, Massachusetts, recorded in his diary in 1742, "This Town seems Infatuated about what the people call Religion, some of the fishermen & others of the like powers pretend to Extreordanary Gifts!"[1] Bowen lamented the effects of a "Hot Spirit of Enthuseasm" which had encouraged the ambitions of "mean people who pretend to an Extreordy shair of the spiret by force where of they draw together the Giddy Mobb" (166, 164). It was not simply that "Carters Coblers & the many Labourers leave their Honest Imployments & Turn Teachers," but even those of the "meanest Capacity i e) women & even Common negros take upon them to Extort [*sic*] their Betters even in the pulpit, before large assemblys" (165, 169). The ability of these lay exhorters to "Bewitc[h]" the "old women of both Sexes" into "Fits of Schreehing; & the utmost Confusion" recalled for Bowen and others the witchcraft crisis of fifty years earlier: "Many Actions of the persons affected have put some of the more thinking . . . in mind of the worm wood & the Gall of 1692" (167, 171, 165).

One might summarize Bowen's objections by saying that the changes brought about by the grassroots religious revival known as the Great Awakening offended his sense of social propriety: common people, laborers, women, and blacks were speaking publicly against their social betters. Moreover, this unseemly, public, and unauthorized speech was occurring in an atmosphere imbued with the "Hot Spirit of Enthuseasm," an atmosphere that promoted giddiness, infatuation, confusion, and a general tendency to forget crucial social differences — those between men and women, blacks and whites, the highborn and the lowborn, the old and the young, the public and the private, the profane and the sacred. In a word, Bowen objected to the "Licenciousness" of the Great Awakening, and he implied that the widespread and illicit denial of fundamental differences constituted the link between the witchcraft crisis and the revival.[2]

Other witnesses concurred with Bowen's assessment. In their correspondence with the Bishop of London and the Society for the Propagation of the Gospel (SPG), the Anglican clergy of New England repeatedly described how "Methodism," throughout the country towns, "multiplies its shapes, and those very awful & deformed ones too."[3] The Anglican clergy did not confine themselves, however, to a metaphorical linking of the witchcraft crisis and the revival: Charles Brockwell, Anglican minister in Salem in 1741, warned that "unless . . . some unexpected accident put a period to [the Great Awakening], I know not but this year for Enthusiasm may be as memorable as was 1692 for witchcraft for the converted cry out upon the unregenerated, as the afflicted did then upon the poor innocent wretches [who] unjustly suffered" (353–54). Clearly, for Brockwell not just the widespread social disorder but the sacrificial logic of the witchcraft crisis had been resurrected in the Great Awakening such that one could identify the "converted" of the revival with the "afflicted" of 1692 and opposers of the revival with the hapless unfortunates accused of witchcraft.[4] As Brockwell put it in a subsequent letter, enthusiasm led the unauthorized to "usurp to themselves a power of revealing secret things," to "arrogate to themselves a power to bless and curse eternally whom they please," that forcefully recalled "the unhappy tragedy of 1692" (387). This usurpation — what Bowen called the revivalists' pretense "to an Extreordy shair of the spiret" — was based upon their claim to having acquired, in the process of conversion, something akin to what the possessed of Salem had called "spectral eyes": that is, they claimed to have seen the invisible world, such that they could, according to one skeptic, "describe its situation, inhabitants, employments, & have seen their names entered into the Book of Life & can point out the writer, character & pen" (353).

Despite the testimony of Nathan Bowen and other witnesses of the Great Awakening, contemporary historians have largely refrained from examining the cultural-historical consequences of the Salem witchcraft crisis and have instead concurred in representing it as the end of the Puritan era, the inevitable (if fantastic) culmination of accelerating social tensions expressive of a range of local anxieties.[5] Perry Miller, in his monumental study of colonial America, *The New England Mind*, may have foreclosed the subject of the episode's cultural fallout by declaring that the witchcraft crisis "had no effect on the [subsequent] ecclesiastical or political situation" of colonial America nor did it "figure in [its] institutional or ideological development," although it "nearly wrecked" the logic of the covenant upon which Puritan society was established.[6] The testimony of witnesses to the social turmoil produced by the Great Awakening, however, calls into question this limitation implicitly or explicitly placed upon the significance of the witchcraft crisis. Their identification of the two events is based on the social chaos that ensued from the widespread, unorthodox, and outspoken claim of direct access to the invisible world made by common people, a privilege that justified their appropriation or, in Brockwell's phrase, their "usurpation" of the power and the prerogative of knowing and publicly revealing secret things.[7] In particular, they claimed to know infallibly and were emboldened to reveal before public assemblies the divinely determined, spiritual identities of others, a knowledge that members of the Puritan theocracy had always refrained from claiming even at the expense of their ideal of a New World church gathered exclusively from God's saints.[8]

If the publicly claimed and enacted usurpation of the power to know and reveal secret things undertaken by socially insignificant members of the community unites the witchcraft crisis and the Great Awakening, the two events are differentiated by the credibility and legitimacy that the magistrates and many of the clergy attributed to the information gleaned by spectral eyes in 1692. Contemporary observers of the legal proceedings, both pro and con, attested that the identification, conviction, and, in the case of twenty individuals, executions of the accused witches were almost entirely

based on what was called "spectral evidence" — the testimony of the afflicted (initially, a small group of girls and young women) that they had been physically and psychologically abused by the specters of other persons.[9] The case of Elizabeth Cary demonstrates how readily the magistrates accepted such testimony and how exclusive a role it could play in capital convictions. Upon hearing that she had been accused of spectrally tormenting the afflicted, Elizabeth had traveled to Salem from Charlestown, where she lived with her husband, Nathaniel, a prominent shipbuilder, to discover whether some mistake had not been made: she was not known to her accusers nor were they to her. There could thus be no question of any unpleasant history between them, the usual context within which accusations of *maleficium* (the exercise of malefic powers often involving bodily harm) were made in both European and pre-1692 American witchcraft cases.[10] Quickly "cried out" upon by the afflicted girls only after they discovered the identity of the unknown woman in the spectators' section of the courtroom, Elizabeth was summarily arrested, jailed, and shackled with heavy leg-irons. During her pretrial examination, she was made to stand with her arms extended; when she protested that she would faint, Nathaniel wrote in his account of her ordeal, "Justice Hathorn replied, she had strength enough to torment those persons, and she should have strength enough to stand." Enraged by the judges' clear assumption of her guilt, and made desperate by his wife's brutal treatment both during her pretrial examination and in prison, Nathaniel again traveled to Salem in order to witness an actual trial. To his horror, he discovered that "the Spectre-Evidence was there received, together with Idle, if not malicious Stories, against Peoples Lives" such that he could "easily perceive which way the rest would go; for the same Evidence that served for one, would serve for all the rest." Having failed to get Elizabeth's trial moved to their county of residence, Nathaniel managed to smuggle her out of prison; the Carys were compelled to flee first to Rhode Island and eventually to New York.[11]

Spectral evidence was generally acknowledged, even by its supporters, to be a qualitatively different type of evidence from the "good, plain, legal evidence" the Reverend Cotton Mather had urged one of the Salem prosecutors to seek.[12] The Reverend Deodat Lawson, in a retrospective account of the trials whose prosecutorial strategies he had enthusiastically endorsed, characterized it as "a sort of Evidence as was not so clearly and directly demonstrable to Human Senses, as in other [Capital] Cases is required."[13] In his letter of 31 May 1692 to magistrate John Richards, Mather differentiated spectral evidence from the types of convictive evidence recommended by European authorities for the detection of witches. These included "credible confession"; various tests, including recitation of the Lord's Prayer (a "signifying to make void," as one skeptic characterized it) or the so-called water test in which the suspect was cast into water with limbs tied; proof that the suspect has information concerning the afflicted that she or he could not normally have possessed; the presence of witch wounds or marks; the possession of "poppets" or wax images; and so forth.[14] The Reverend Increase Mather, Cotton's father, in his theologically grounded condemnation of spectral evidence entitled *Cases of Conscience Concerning Evil Spirits Personating Men* (written in August 1692 and presented to Governor William Phips in October), also offered explicit guidelines for convictive evidence that excluded spectral testimony.[15] An increasing number of theological and secular critiques of spectral evidence were offered in the course of the trials; their cumulative effect was to persuade Governor Phips (in October 1692) to dissolve the Salem court and to reconvene a new tribunal, forbidden to hear spectral evidence, to decide the fifty-two remaining cases.[16] The demise of spectral evidence concluded the sacrificial cycle; all remaining cases were dismissed except for those of confessors, who were pardoned. In sum, the near exclusive reliance upon spectral evidence, to the degree that it figured prominently in every conviction, appears to be the distinguishing characteristic of the Salem trials as compared both with earlier colonial witchcraft trials and European ones.[17] Its peculiarities were memorably rendered by Governor Phips in a letter of 21 February 1693 to the Earl of Nottingham:

> the afflicted persons who when they were brought into the Court as soon as the suspected witches looked upon them instantly fell to the ground in strange agonies and grievous torments, but when touched by them upon the arme or some other part of their flesh they immediately revived and came to themselves, upon [which] they made oath that the Prisoner at the Bar did afflict them and that they saw their shape or spectre come from their bodies which put them to such paines and torments.

He added, "When I put an end to the Court there ware at least fifty persons in prison in great misery by reason of the extream cold and their poverty, most of them having only spectre evidence against them."[18]

What I will call spectral evidence theory, that body of beliefs underlying the decision to accept and even to privilege spectral evidence in the identification and prosecution of witches, fostered an implicitly antiauthoritarian reconceptualization of personality which would survive Salem to bedevil conservative critics of the Great Awakening and liberal aspirants to national authorship alike. The significance of spectral evidence theory for the eighteenth- and nineteenth-century development of democratic personality may be formulated here as a pair of claims. The first is that the theological premise and the legal application of spectral evidence theory posed as serious a challenge to the Puritan order as had the Antinomian crisis of sixty years before. Because the 1692 challenge came not from the margins of American Puritan culture but from those in authority, it dealt that order, already enfeebled by the forces contemporary witchcraft historians have identified, a fatal blow. Like Antinomianism before it, spectral evidence theory undermined the semiotic system according to which New England Puritan society was organized.[19] In place of the knowable, reliable (or at least reliably unknowable) semiotic correlation between the visible world (the human domain) and the invisible world of God's determinations, from which the logic of the covenant as well as the authority of the orthodox ministry derived, spectral evidence theory posited a third, mediate realm of ambiguous spiritual significance—to borrow a phrase from the intellectual historian Lorraine Daston's work on the preternatural, a "third ontological domain"—which joined the invisible and visible worlds by facilitating border crossings between them.[20] As a result, the reliability of the visible world (including its inhabitants) as a signifier of invisible realities, as well as the semiotic authority of the Puritan clergy to determine the nature and extent of that signification, were fatally undermined, leading to an all-out assault on the sanctification of the invisible world upon which the Puritan social order depended.[21]

My second claim is that this particular sense of Puritanism's ending was also a beginning. If spectral evidence theory, put into practice by the Salem prosecution as a way of identifying the secret enemies of the Puritan social order and eradicating them, entailed the deconstruction of the cultural semiotics upon which that social order was established, the testimony of witnesses to the upheaval of the Great Awakening alerts us to the existence of an ideological continuum extending from the witchcraft crisis to the Awakening and into the revolutionary era. By positing a spectral abrogation of the barrier between invisible and visible worlds, accomplished by the witches and also by the afflicted who were demonstrably able to interact with them both physically and discursively, spectral evidence theorists found themselves committed to a view of human personality as diabolically multifaceted. Immeasurably beyond the practice of mere hypocrisy by which the spiritually unregenerate had long attempted to gain admittance into the Puritan churches, hundreds were now perceived as endowed with a revolutionary power of dissemblance drawn from their ability to maintain a vital — and, in terms of character, a contradictory — presence in the visible and invisible domains simultaneously. This ability had allowed them to attempt the overthrow of God's church by fatally scrambling the signs that differentiated the saints not only from the unregenerate but from those who had actively allied themselves with Satan. The radical reconceptualization of human personality — its stability, authority, legitimacy, and representational potential — that ensued from the Puritan authorities' attempts to make sense of the startling revelations of the afflicted as well as the confessing witches laid the conceptual groundwork for the formation of "democratic personality" in the Great Awakening and into the revolutionary era, as it provided a paradigm for the production of an "innocent" national literature in the antebellum era.

The significance of spectral evidence theory for the crisis of character to which many bore witness in the Great Awakening was thus twofold. It constituted a theory of personality that dismantled the cultural semiotics of American Puritanism — what Perry Miller called "the whole apparatus of logical and rhetorical interpretation out of which New England had wrought its peculiar system."[22] And insofar as spectral evidence theory was fundamentally a theory of personality, it presaged a more semiotically complex and incipiently democratic social order based on the multifaceted representational powers of the individual. Before examining spectral evidence theory more closely, it will be useful to review the fundamental Puritan opposition between visibility and invisibility, its translation into a distinctive social order in which authoritative popular speech was strictly regulated, and its special vulnerability to the principle that the seventeenth century would force upon Puritan America, religious pluralism.

I

The central precept of American Puritanism was that the gathered churches of Puritan New England be constituted exclusively of so-called "visible

saints," individuals who had received some assurance that God had chosen
them for eternal salvation.[23] Before the Puritan migration to the New World,
the Separatist objection to the Anglican Church had been based on its indis-
criminate acceptance of members "be they never so prophane or wretched,
no Atheist, adulterer, thief, or murderer, no lyer, perjured, witch or conjurer,
etc., all are one fellowship, one body, one Church."[24] As an alternative, the
Separatists embraced the Reformation idea of explicit and voluntary consent
to the church covenant given directly by each individual member, a condition
that the American Puritans, although non-Separating, had fully embraced.
So compatible was this notion of explicit and voluntary consent with the
American Puritans' understanding of their errand into the wilderness, that
their churches instituted the practice of having prospective members narrate
their experience of saving grace before the assembled members, who would
then, with the minister's guidance, evaluate its authenticity and admit or
refuse membership to the narrator accordingly.[25] By 1636, this narrative not
only was prerequisite to church membership but was the fundamental criterion for freemanship in the Massachusetts Bay Colony and as such the foundation of the Puritan church-state. The practice of publicly narrating one's
inward spiritual experiences — the sole occasion on which the "silent *Democracy*" (as the Reverend Samuel Stone famously referred to the Puritan congregation) shared the prerogative of the "speaking *Aristocracy*," the ministry, to voice publicly their understanding of the spiritual life — quickly
became formulaic, with the ministry's express encouragement.[26] Applicants
for church membership rarely spoke of their inward spiritual states with
confidence, for self-doubt was considered a likely sign of salvation: authoritative public speech on the part of common people had come to an end in the
first years of the Great Migration when the Puritans' test of saving grace had
wholly superseded the Pilgrims' practice of prophesying, an extemporaneous
supplementation of the minister's sermon by members of the congregation.[27]

The test of saving grace was intended to make the churches of New
England a visible corollary of God's invisible sainthood, the eternal body of
His elect drawn from all times and places. It was thus intended to narrow the
gap between the invisible world of God's determinations and the visible
world (as Sacvan Bercovitch writes, "it was New England's unique prerogative to make visible what elsewhere remained invisible"), although it was
everywhere conceded that the gap could not be entirely closed.[28] No one

could infallibly know God's determinations, in particular with respect to the spiritual fates of individuals, their essential identities as regenerate or unregenerate; no one could elide the space of unknowing that protected the sanctity of the invisible world from human attempts to understand and perhaps pass judgment upon it. Despite the comforts of the Puritans' covenant theology, which posited "that God has voluntarily engaged Himself to regular, ascertainable procedures," He remained irretrievably distant: as John Preston had counseled in *Life Eternall*, "We should be content to let *God* alone, not to inquire into all his actions, into the ground and reason of all his works . . . We should doe thus, stand upon the shore, (as it were) and behold his infinite Essence."[29] The irrevocable separation between visible and invisible might be tentatively bridged, however, by a system of signs — like those both discovered and identified by the test of saving faith — more or less legible to the limited vision of mortal creatures. The rigorously educated theocracy, masters of this system of signs (to the extent that the system permitted human mastery), maintained that God had agreed to the partial illumination of the space of unknowing through their efforts. Their stringent objections to magical practices performed by the common people were motivated by their jealous regard for the sanctity of the invisible world as well as for their own exclusive, and exquisitely tentative, access to it.[30]

Aside from the challenge posed by the Antinomian crisis in the first years of settlement, Puritan society rested fairly securely upon this foundation for the space of a generation.[31] In the last third of the seventeenth century, however, it was fatally attacked by notions of religious tolerance generated both from within the American Puritan churches and from without. Coincident with the rise of the "second generation" (the children of the Bay Colony's founders) in New England and with the Restoration in Old England, two developments directly threatened the institution of visible sainthood as both the structural principle of Puritan culture and the ideological foundation of what we may call the Puritans' imagined community. Both represented a direct attack upon Puritan covenant (or federal) theology and its enabling proposition, that the American Puritans constituted an elect nation, living under a special dispensation from and in explicit covenant with God.[32] Taken together, they appear to have stimulated an increasingly anxious degree of attention to the invisible world of God's dispensations on the part of the beleaguered ministry. Of particular interest was that portion of the invisible world that God had given over to the fallen angels who bore a special enmity against the Puritans as God's chosen people and who were perceived as dedicated to the subversion of their New World experiment.[33]

The first development was the long and bitter debate surrounding the theocracy's acceptance of the so-called Halfway Covenant. This measure, proposed at the Synod of 1662, was intended to redress the problem of declining membership in the Congregational churches by offering some of the benefits of church membership to individuals of the second generation (and their children) who had made no profession of their experience of saving grace, because they felt no inward assurance of their calling. The longevity of the debate — it extended into the next decade — was largely due to the oppositional efforts of Increase Mather, who finally agreed to its terms in 1668.[34] Mather had argued that acceptance of the Halfway Covenant, although it might swell the membership of the churches, would fatally compromise their spiritual, ecclesiastical, and political integrity as gatherings of visible saints. With no assurance that members' internal spiritual states conformed to their external characters, the churches must relinquish their claim to reflect, on the temporal plane, the eternal invisible sainthood and the corollary claim that the church members of New England represented the true nation, that saving remnant of God's elect destined to redeem the whole. Mather's great opponent in the controversy was Solomon Stoddard (Jonathan Edwards's grandfather), who in 1677 instituted in his Connecticut Valley church a policy of open communion, an idea welcome, Robert Middlekauff notes, to "a generation frustrated by years of trying to separate the gracious from the carnal."[35] Stoddard's innovations were followed by similar attempts in other churches to make them more comprehensive by removing the prerequisite of consent to the church covenant and the conversion narrative that accompanied it. Out of the fundamental opposition of election and damnation, and the corollary opposition of visible and invisible worlds whose correspondence the Puritans rigorously sought, the Halfway Covenant proposed a third possibility for spiritual identity that hovered uncertainly between the two.[36]

The second development to compromise the Puritan principle of a visible sainthood and its accompanying ideology of elect nationhood was the royal attack upon the charter of the Massachusetts Bay Colony in which its political self-determination as well as its distinctive spiritual and cultural identity were grounded. The fate of the charter was first called into question in a letter from Charles II in 1662 demanding that the people of Massachusetts accommodate liberty of conscience in religious matters. The king backed up that demand in 1664 with observers transported on two naval vessels manned by four hundred troops, the first appearance of British warships in American waters. The charter was finally revoked in 1684 only to be restored in 1692, but with provisions for religious tolerance, which Increase Mather, who had traveled to England to negotiate the new charter with King William, could not evade despite his categorical opposition to any measure that compromised Puritan hegemony. The interim period was characterized, not surprisingly, by profound uncertainty regarding the immediate future of the culture as all governmental institutions, beginning with the General Court, were suddenly invalidated. Moreover, events both associated with the charter's revocation and independent of it deepened the conviction of cultural apocalypse: the accession of the detested royally appointed governor, Sir Edmund Andros; his banishment after England's Glorious Revolution, which compelled Puritan America to improvise an interim colonial government of uncertain authority; a smallpox epidemic; a conflagration in Boston; and the renewal of French and Indian hostilities in northern New England following William's declaration of war upon France. All of these events suggested that evil forces were ready to "break in" upon and destroy the country, a conviction evident in works like Increase Mather's *Essay for the Recording of Illustrious Providences* (1684).[37] A compilation of all manner of inexplicable or remarkable events, the *Essay* was intended (in Robert Middlekauff's words) to "convey a sense of the mysterious immediacy of the Devil and his dark spirits." By demonstrating in successive anecdotes this immediacy of the invisible world, its aggressive proximity, Mather "convinced many of the power of the demonic in the world of men and things."[38]

As historians have shown, Cotton Mather, who would play so prominent a role in the witchcraft crisis, had been greatly influenced in the early years of his ministry by these events which severely tried the Puritan sense of imagined community, events whose import his father had striven to conceptualize and whose outcome he had struggled to control. As early as 1681, at the precocious age of eighteen, one year after having preached his first public sermon but four years before his ordination, Mather vowed in his diary to "Labou[r] after a greater Sense of the *Reality of Invisibles*."[39] His intense interest in the invisible world was accompanied by an incipient conviction of personal election: his first entries are replete with oddly prayerful claims that

God had provided him in the course of his day with "remarkable and even unusual Assistences" and with expressions of his belief that "*I am a chosen Vessel, and that the Lord will pour mercy unto mee, till I have arrived unto a Fulness of eternal Glory!*"[40] As Kenneth Silverman has shown, however, Mather's spiritual confidence was continually embattled by his equally lively sense of Satan's proximity, which increasingly provided him with a ready text for his sermons: "His preaching," Silverman writes, "can be charted to show that he continually reminded his congregation of a hostile invisible world."[41] As Mather represented it in one sermon, the infiltration of the visible world by the invisible entailed the violation of the former's most private and interior spaces, the prayer closet, the scholar's study, and the mind itself:

> When we are in our church assemblies, oh, how many devils, do you imagine, crowd in among us! There is a devil that rocks one to sleep. There is a devil that makes another to be thinking of, he scarcely knows what himself. And there is a devil that makes another to be pleasing himself with wanton and wicked speculations. It is also possible, that we have our closets or our studies gloriously perfumed with devotions every day; but, alas! can we shut the devil out of them? No: let us go where we will, we shall still find a devil nigh unto us.[42]

Mather's formulation closes off the avenue of escape as it precludes the possibility of transcendence: no matter how determined the struggle to elude it, one was compelled to acknowledge the diabolical shadow "nigh unto" one.

The stringency of the opposition of invisible and visible worlds at the heart of American Puritanism, and the conviction that the former was inaccessible and unknowable to humankind beyond the admittedly limited efforts of a rigorously trained clergy to interpret God's determinations, made Mather's rather conventional depiction of diabolic ubiquity potentially incendiary. The aggravated sense of the proximity of the "devil's dominion," that portion of the invisible world divinely consigned to the evil spirits, led some to claim in 1692 that they had gained direct access to the invisible world and made direct contact with its inhabitants and their human associates in their spectral forms.[43] The claim not only was not challenged but was embraced and even embellished by cultural authorities, the ministry and magistrates. In 1689, when Cotton Mather published *Memorable Providences, Relating to Witchcrafts and Possessions*, his account of the affliction of a young girl at the hands of evil spirits, the four ministers who contributed a reader's preface to the tract were careful to acknowledge the limitations God had placed on humankind in gaining information about the invisible world. These limitations were threefold. First, "Communion with Devils" was strictly "interdicted us; their Nature also being spiritual." Second, because God had not scripturally revealed the mysteries of diabolic behavior and intent,

> hence it is that we can disclose but a little of those Mysteries of Darkness; all reports that are from themselves, or their Instruments, being to be esteemed as Illusions, or at least covered with Deceit, filled with the Impostures of the Father of Lies; and the effects which come under our consideration being Mysterious, rather Posing than Informing us.

Finally, the ministers point out the limits of human capacity to understand God's tolerance of evil spirits, His permitting the perpetration of evil against unoffending people:

> The Secrets also of God's Providence, in permitting Satan and his Instruments to molest His children, not in their Estates only, but in their Persons and their Posterity too, are part of His Judgments that are unsearchable, and His Wayes that are past finding out.[44]

Three years later, when diabolical affliction had become in Salem Village no longer an aberration but a plague, no such restraint was shown and no such acknowledgments made by the Salem judges, the local ministry, and prominent members of the colonial ministry with regard to the knowledge of "secret and future things discovered from the Mouths of Damsels possest with a Spirit of divination" and from the rapidly growing numbers of those who claimed to have had a direct encounter with the specter of a countryman or woman, and even with the devil himself.[45]

II

What I am calling spectral evidence theory was less theory than it was practice, and must therefore be extrapolated from the court's decision to admit and privilege as evidence against the accused the claims of the victims to have been tormented, not by the accused witch directly, but rather by his or her shape, specter, image, or representation (as the ghostly tormentor was variously denominated).[46] We can extrapolate spectral evidence theory too from the statements of those who objected to permitting such evidence to serve as the basis for a capital conviction in witchcraft cases and who, in public and private letters, sermons, and treatises, elaborated upon the theological, legal, and social premises of their disapproval.[47]

The theory of spectral evidence allowed the Salem court to attribute an ontological and thus a legal validity to the specters of whom the afflicted complained based on a pair of inextricably linked assumptions. First, given the behavior and testimony of the afflicted, it assumed that the specters existed and could inflict both psychological torment and real bodily harm; second, and most problematic, it assumed that the person spectrally represented had commissioned the devil to replicate her or him on the spectral plane, and that the spectral representation thus existed solely by virtue of the represented person's consent.[48] In a jeremiad preached while the trials were in full swing, the Reverend Deodat Lawson clearly articulated the crucial supposition of consent on which all the convictions and executions would be based: "the Devil, having them [witches] in his subjection, by their Consent, he will use their Bodies and Minds, Shapes and Representations, to Affright and Afflict others at his pleasure."[49] As early as 1689, when the publication of his *Memorable Providences, Relating to Witchcrafts and Possessions* brought the dramatic possibility of diabolical possession powerfully before the public mind, Cotton Mather named consent and representation as the "Two Acts" by which evil spirits and evil humans cooperate in "an impudent *Essay* to make an *Hell* of the Universe":

> The *First* [Act] is, Their [the devils'] *Covenanting* with the Witches. There is a most hellish *League* made between them, with various *Rites* and *Ceremonies*. The *Witches* promise to serve the *Devils*, and the *Devils* promise to *help* the Witches; *how?* It is not convenient to be related. The *Second* is, Their *Representing* of the Witches. And hereby indeed these are drawn into *Snares* and *Cords* of Death.[50]

A perusal of the pretrial examination transcripts reveals that the supposition of consent led the prosecutors to conflate the accused individual with her or his spectral representation, thus lending the specter — invisible and inaudible to all but the afflicted — an authority that overshadowed the material presence of the accused. The interrogation of Bridget Bishop (executed on 10 June 1692), transcribed by Ezekiel Cheever, is typical in this regard:

> The afflicted persons charge her, with having hurt them many wayes and by tempting them to sine to the devils Booke at which charge she seemed to be very angrie and shaking her head at them saying it was false they are all greatly tormented (as I conceive) by the shaking of her head
>
> (Mr Har[thon]) good Bishop what contract have you made with the devill
>
> (Bish) I have made no contract with the devill I never saw him in my life.
>
> . . .
>
> (Mr H) who is it that doth it if you doe not they say it is your likenes that comes and torments them and tempts them to write in the booke what Booke is that you tempt them with.
>
> (Bish) I know nothing of it I am innocent.
>
> . . .
>
> (Mr H) have you not given consent that some evill spirit should doe this in your likenes.

Cheever concludes by noting that as Bishop left the courtroom, "5 afflicted persons doe charge this woman to be the very woman that hurts them."[51]

Cheever is transcribing accurately: in deposition after deposition, the afflicted claim to have been tortured either by an individual or by that individual's spectral apparition — as, for example, Mary Warren of Ann Pudeator (executed 22 September 1692): "she or her Apperition did offer: me the book to sign" — as if the difference between self and spectral image, represented and representation, were inconsequential.[52] This conflation is explicit in the testimony of Mary Browne against Sarah Cole of Lynn; Browne testified that Cole "bodly Appeared to mee and that In her full shapp and person: both night and day."[53] Thomas Brattle, a wealthy and accomplished Boston merchant, the treasurer of Harvard College, and a Fellow of the Royal Society, circulated in early October 1692 a manuscript letter critical of the court's proceedings, in which he observed "that often, when the afflicted do mean and intend only the appearance and shape of such an one, (say G. Proctour) yet they positively swear that G. Proctour did afflict them; and they have been allowed so to do; as tho' there was no real difference between G. Proc-tour and the shape of G. Proctour." This conflation of representation and represented, Brattle warned, had proven "a very fundamental errour" that would "occasion innocent blood, yea the innocentest blood imaginable, to be in great danger."[54] The prosecution's supposition of the accused witches' consent to spectral representation clearly provided both a motivation and a justification for its own deliberate erasure of this crucial difference.[55]

The case of Bridget Bishop amply supports the claim of one witchcraft scholar that "spectral evidence did not serve as grounds for suspicion in the mind of the court, but as presumption of guilt."[56] Thomas Brattle noted that "the prisoner at the bar is brought in guilty, and condemned, merely from the evidences of the afflicted persons."[57] The Salem court did not consider alternative accounts of the spectral appearances that had been elaborated in European and American treatises on witchcraft and demonology, explana-tions which ranged from the devil's acknowledged skill as an optical illusion-ist to "natural distempers" of the mind or body.[58] Likewise, having unreserv-edly accepted the representations of the afflicted regarding spectral activity, the members of the Salem court rejected the possibility that the devil, with God's consent, had impersonated innocent men and women such that the specters only superficially resembled the accused, but signified nothing con-cerning their essential spiritual identities.[59] Instead, consent was imme-diately inferred from representation which was criminalized (and thus, iron-ically, made credible) by the hypothesis of consent: spectral evidence theory is characterized above all by this circular logic.[60] We might say that for the prosecution the "fact" of representation verified the "act" of consent, through which the accused — many of whom had "for many yeares Lived under the unblemished reputation of Christianity" — were thought to have conspired with the devil in perpetrating "an Impious and Impudent Imita-tion of Divine Things" by "their Covering of themselves and their Instru-ments with Invisibility."[61] The criminal aspect of witchcraft, then, its revolu-tionary potential, lay not precisely in *maleficium*, the witch's infliction of harm upon another, but rather in her surreptitious apostasy, her invisible transfer of spiritual allegiance from the God of Light to the Prince of Lies, as Boyer and Nissenbaum explicitly state: "The crime lay in the initial compact by which a person permitted the devil to assume his or her human form, or in commissioning the devil to perform particular acts of mischief."[62]

As the primary form of convictive evidence in the witchcraft trials, spectral evidence—an inference drawn from an assumption; the originary and revolutionary crime of consent inferred from the assumption of not just the reality but the superior veracity of specters—did not simply conflate an individual with her spectral representation. As the magistrates construed it, spectral evidence effectively reversed the ontological (and thus the ethical and epistemological) priority one instinctively gives to the subject represented over the representation, in whatever form the latter may take. That is, the supposition of consent amounted to a judgment on the part of the court that an individual's spectral representation, as described by the afflicted, provided an infallible index of the accused's essential spiritual identity as a child of God or a child of Satan, while visible character (upon which decisions regarding membership in the Puritan churches had always been based) was viewed as contingent, unstable, inherently fictitious—in short, as a representation.[63] This is evident, for example, in the examination of the renowned sea captain John Alden, who

> appealed to all that ever knew him, if they ever suspected him to be such a person [a witch], and challenged any one, that could bring in any thing upon their own knowledge, that might give suspicion of his being such an one. Mr. Gidney [one of the magistrates] said he had known Aldin many Years, and had been at Sea with him, and always look'd upon him to be an honest Man, but now he did see cause to alter his judgment.[64]

Likewise, Thomas Bradbury was disappointed in his hopes for his wife of fifty-five years, Mary, that "her life and conversation" would provide "a better & more reall Testimoney of her, than can bee exprest by words."[65] The invisible and untraceable crime of consent, once thought to have been committed, authorized an exchange whereby the prosecution credited the spectral representation with the substance and signifying power of visible character, which henceforth took on the immateriality of spectral representation. Thus one deponent testified on behalf of his afflicted wife that when she claimed that Bridget Bishop had tormented her, he had reminded her that she "never saw the woman in [her] Life." "[N]o," his wife answered, "I never saw her in my Life but so she is Represented to me."[66] For this reason, the sole form of evidence that could be offered in defense of the accused, the character reference (even one based on a lifelong knowledge of the prisoner), was woefully inadequate to counter the "spectral exhibitions" by which the afflicted publicly acted out the harm done to them by the specters of those arraigned at the bar.[67] Cotton Mather's contemptuous remark regarding the accused Susannah Martin (executed 19 July 1692) — that her only defense lay in her claim to have "Led a most virtuous and Holy Life!" — reveals how irrelevant the logic of sanctification had become before the dramatically revealed and wholly subversive spectral self of the accused.[68]

By all accounts, Susannah Martin had not, in fact, led a particularly virtuous and holy life; Marion Starkey describes her as "every inch a witch, bright of eye, salty of tongue, and the central figure of every marvellous event that had happened in Amesbury for going on three decades."[69] Among the accused, however, were "many Persons of unquestionable Credit, never under any grounds of suspicion of that or any other Scandalous Evil," yet for these, as for Martin, the court felt that there was "little Occasion to prove the Witchcraft, it being Evident and Notorious to all Beholders."[70] Cotton Mather here expressed the dominant view, held by all members of the court as well as many of the spectators present in the courtroom, that the spectral exhibitions of the afflicted were so immediately persuasive as to strip a "good reputation and approved integrity" — visible character — of its value as a self-evidential signifier of spiritual identity.[71] This was contrary to the value placed upon visible character by the American Puritan church from its inception: the very principle according to which the New World churches excluded all but visible saints from church membership allowed that spiritual identity as God had determined it was "a *secret* Thing," "an *internal* Thing, [that] can be judged of by others, only from the *outward* Discoveries of it" — that is, only from visible character. Even the oft-acknowledged danger of admitting a hypocrite to church fellowship, one who dissembled an unregenerate heart with a pious exterior, did not deter the Puritan orthodoxy from maintaining that, according to "the Rule of Charity," character stood as the sole reliable index of the invisible "*interior* State of *others*," knowable only by "him who has said, *I am he that searcheth the Heart, and trieth the Reins of the Children of Men.*"[72] Or, as the fourteen ministers who contributed the preface to Increase Mather's *Cases of Conscience* put it, "our Charity is bound to Judge according to what appears."[73] One wonders, therefore, about the rationale according to which visible character, for those who saw themselves as the most vigilant conservators of the Puritan community, suddenly lost its signifying powers during the witchcraft crisis such that the self-evident became synonymous with the invisible.

An indication is provided in the incendiary sermon of Deodat Lawson who had watched young Abigail Williams fend off the "Devil's book" spectrally offered to her, she claimed, by the much respected, elderly, and infirm Rebecca Nurse (executed 19 July 1692). Lawson preached his sermon *Christ's Fidelity the only Shield against Satan's Malignity* on the afternoon of Nurse's pretrial examination. Nurse's status in the community notwithstanding, her interrogation resembled the others except in one respect. To magistrate John Hathorne's insistent point, in response to her repeated declarations of innocence, that her "apparition" had tormented and was at that moment demonstrably afflicting many present in the courtroom, Nurse replied that "the Devil may appear in my shape." Nurse here affirms the integrity of her character, which she claims is intact despite the devil's apparent spectral replication of her physical person (a fact she did not dispute). In effect, her affirmation is based on the differentiation of two aspects of the visible self, physical appearance (the look and motions of one's body, the sound of one's voice) and moral character (one's actions, the tenor of one's words or "conversation"). If the devil may appropriate the former, this signifies nothing concerning the integrity or truth-value of the latter insofar as the spectral translation of the body and the material aspects of voice do not necessarily entail a parallel translation of character. Nurse can only insist that whatever the actions of her spectral body, her visible character remains a reliable index of her spiritual identity as one of God's elect. As an "old Professor" of Christ, she is no more morally implicated in the crimes of her spectral body than she is spiritually delimited by the infirmity of her material body. Nurse's understanding of personal integrity as a visible correlation of one's words with one's actions is reflected in a petition signed by thirty-nine supporters who affirmed that "her: Life and conversation was According to her profession."[74] But in the context of the Salem trials, the assertion was irrelevant because the understanding of personal integrity upon which Nurse's defense was based had been superseded.

In the sermon which directly followed Nurse's arraignment and her decoupling of consent and representation, visible character and spectral body, Lawson offered an alternative account of the relationship of saintly character to diabolical specter based on the supposition of consent: if the devil "can prevail upon those that make a visible profession, it may be the better covert unto his diabolical enterprise, and may the more readily pervert others to consenting unto his subjection." Like his seemingly pious apostates, Lawson explained, the devil "never works more like the Prince of darkness than when he looks most like an angel of light; and, when he most pretends to holiness, he then doth most secretly, and by consequence most surely, undermine it, and those that most excel in the exercise thereof."[75] Similar reservations concerning the truth-value of pious character appear in the joint statement of Edward Putnam and Ezekiel Cheever concerning the suspected witch Martha Corey (executed 22 September 1692). The two men, "being in church covenant" with Corey, testified how they undertook to visit her after hearing one of the afflicted complain that Corey's apparition had abused her. Their statement reveals how, in the course of their conversation with Corey, the self-evident significance of her having long been a visible professor of Christ is insensibly altered:

> we had no reason to thinke [her a witch] for shee had made a profession
> of christ and rejoyced to go and hear the word of god and the like. but we
> told her it was not her making an out ward profession that would clear
> her from being a witch for it had often been so in the wourld that witches
> had crept into the churches: much more discourse we had with her but
> shee made her profession a cloake to cover all.[76]

Visible profession is suddenly understood as sharing in the insidious transparency of diabolical invisibility itself, resulting in a virtual war of representations: the unexceptional nature of Martha Corey's piety reveals itself to Putnam and Cheever as a "cloake" covering the sensational truth of her blasphemy, a formulation echoed in Cotton Mather's statement regarding the witches' possession of "the horrible skill of cloathing themselves with Invisibilities."[77] Such testimony demonstrates that pious character could no longer be taken at face value because it provided Satan the perfect "covert" for dissembling the crime of diabolical conversion; character whether pious or impious was, henceforth, epistemologically nullified as an index of identity. Lawson thus counsels in his sermon against the literal reading of pious character that would see it as a reliable signifier of spiritual identity, arguing instead that the truth it conveys can be ascertained only by inverting its overt — its self-evident — significance.[78]

Lawson's reassessment of visible character as a signifier of spiritual identity contributed to an urgent, if never rigorously formulated or conducted, debate concerning the relationship of invisible to visible representations. If it had once been believed that visible character constituted a reasonably trustworthy representation of identity adequate as a test for church membership, the spectral exhibitions of the afflicted compelled an epistemological shift away from visible character and to the spectral representation as the more accurate index of essential identity.[79] The shift exacted a peculiar conceptual price insofar as the specter, undetectable to all but a few, emerged as a doubly representational construct: it offered a representation of identity that contradicted the evidence of visible character, the representation formerly sanctioned by the Puritan orthodoxy; moreover, the details of its character as representation were known exclusively through the representations of the afflicted, who claimed the unique ability not only to perceive but to interact physically and verbally with the specters of the accused. In order to privilege the invisible specter over visible character as an index of identity, then, spectral evidence theorists sought to provide a conceptual ballast for the elusive and exclusive specter by discovering crimes structurally analogous to witchcraft insofar as they appeared to depend on the cooperative work of visible and invisible elements. These analogies provided a kind of evidence for the extent to which the impalpable, the removed, the invisible, or the seemingly mediate or secondary might function as the primary and immediate, if obscure, cause of real events. The upshot was to underscore the epistemological limitations of the visible, and especially visible character, and to propose instead a view of human personality possessed of vast and hitherto unsuspected resources of misrepresentation marshaled in the service of an unholy self-aggrandizement.

In a letter written to Judge John Richards two days before the return of the court's first capital conviction, for example, Cotton Mather both described and defended spectral evidence by arguing for the "imagination" as the initiatory site of a type of criminal activity, including but not limited to witchcraft, whose very real effects belied its status as a merely "imaginary" event:

Albeit the business of this witchcraft be very much transacted upon the stage of imagination, yet we know that, as in treason there is an imagining which is a capital crime, and here also the business thus managed in imagination yet may not be called imaginary. The effects are dreadfully real. Our dear neighbors are most really tormented, really murdered, and really acquainted with hidden things, which are afterwards proved plainly to have been realities.[80]

Mather highlights the structural affinity between treasonous intent and spectral abuse as the immaterial beginnings of crimes that entail material harm. The claim for the reality of the material harm spectrally accomplished by the witches, up to and including murder, bolsters the claim — made in the same breath — for the validity of the secret knowledge victimization afforded the afflicted.[81] The argument moves from the plane of the invisible (the stage of imagination) to the visible (the reality of bodily harm) and back to the invisible (the reality of the secret knowledge of the invisible world gained through the experience of bodily harm). In returning to the invisible after his foray in the visible, Mather is careful to bring with him, in a kind of conceptual smuggling operation, the booty to be found only in empirical reality: the claim that secret knowledge is, like bodily injury, susceptible of plain proof. When Mather alludes here to the crime initiated on the stage of imagination, he is not speaking of the invisible crime of consenting to spectral representation, but of *maleficium*, the infliction of harm through supernatural means. The focus on *maleficium* (the basis of the popular, but not the theological, objection to witchcraft, as Keith Thomas, Richard Weisman, and others have shown) allows Mather to rhetorically legitimate the claim of the afflicted to secret knowledge concerning essential identity by lending that knowledge the material substance and empirical credibility of the wounded body.[82] Although the "plain proof" that would validate secret knowledge is nowhere offered in the statement, Mather's implication is clear: just as bodily harm and murder cannot be refuted, secret knowledge such as that claimed by the afflicted cannot be disparaged as merely "imaginary."[83]

Unhappily for Mather, although many witnessed the spectral torments of the afflicted at close hand, the fact of bodily injury upon which his claim for the reality of secret knowledge depended was not self-evident to all observers. Thomas Brattle found the afflicted, considering their experience of constant spectral abuse, surprisingly "hale and hearty, robust and lusty, as tho' nothing had afflicted them." He added:

> I Remember that when the chief Judge gave the first Jury their charge, he told them, that they were not to mind whether the bodies of the said af-

flicted were really pined and consumed, as was expressed in the indite-
ment; but whether the said afflicted did not suffer from the accused such
afflictions as naturally *tended* to their being pined and consumed, wasted,
etc. This, (said he,) is a pining and consuming in the sense of the law.[84]

Brattle demotes the reality of bodily injury to the status of legal fiction,
allowing Mather no foundation in the visible domain that might afford empirical support to his rhetorical edifice dedicated to asserting the validity of
secret knowledge. All is dissolved in the ether of representation.

At least until October 1692, however, when the Special Court was disbanded, Brattle's was the minority view. The court's strategy for according
theoretical potentiality the convictive power of empirical reality demonstrates how it removed itself conceptually from reliance on the realm of the
visible, the self-evident, and the literal to speculate upon the nature of
the invisible world as revealed by the representations of the afflicted. Even as
the credibility of the visible was being undermined, Mather argued in the
letter to Judge Richards that one ignores the unperceivable at one's peril:

> I say, then, as that man is justly executed for an assassinate, who in the
> sight of men shall with a sword in his hand stab his neighbor into the
> heart, so suppose a long train laid unto a barrel of gunpowder under the
> floor where a neighbor is, and suppose a man with a match perhaps in his
> mouth, out of sight, set fire unto the further end of the train, tho' never
> so far off. This man also is to be treated as equally a malefactor.

Whereas the treasonous intention that leads to the actual crime of treason
functions here as an analogue for the crime of witchcraft insofar as an invisible cause, enacted on the "stage of imagination," ends in "dreadfully real"
effects, the image of the long fuse that leads to the concealed barrel of
gunpowder provides Mather with an analogue for treasonous intent as an
equally lethal, equally undetectable stimulus to destruction. It is nonsensical,
Mather implies, to argue that the short blade wielded in the "sight of men" is
more murderous than the long fuse lit "out of sight," that the fatality inflicted by the latter is any less fatal because of its extension or placement.
Having equated the direct access to the victim's body characteristic of the
sword with the relatively indirect access to the victim's body characteristic of
the long fuse, Mather converts the fuse to metaphor (a conversion fore-

shadowed, perhaps, in the unlikely image of the murderer lighting the fuse with a match he holds in his mouth) in order that its length may be imagined as extending into the invisible world as readily as one imagines it snaking beneath the floorboards of a neighbor's house:

> Our neighbors at Salem Village are blown up, after a sort, with an infernal gunpowder; the train is laid in the laws of the kingdom of darkness limited by God himself. Now the question is, who gives fire to this train? and by what acts is the match applied? Find out the persons that have done this thing, and be their acts in doing it either mental, or oral, or manual, or what the devil will, I say *abeant quo digni sunt* [let them vanish where the righteous are].[85]

Ultimately, then, the image of the fuse — an especially apt figure not just for the link between invisible and visible worlds, but for metaphor (as difference in unity) itself — illustrates how real bodily harm may be rooted in the invisible world. Mather's two examples proclaim that reality is not circumscribed by what can be seen, but must include that which is hidden, even imaginary, and whose workings are obscure. His elaboration of the manifold possibilities of indirection operative in all domains — the mental, the oral, the manual — validates spectral evidence by making the "distance" of the intention to commit treason from the actual crime analogous to the "distance" of the long fuse lit (orally) out of the sight of men, which is itself analogous to the "distance" of (spectral) representation: in each case, distance is merely apparent.

Critics responded variously to this account of the invisible and immaterial origins of occurrences in the visible, material world. Some considered such efforts to conceptualize linkages between the visible and invisible worlds utterly specious, if not blasphemous. Thomas Brattle was less concerned with blasphemy than he was with irrationality. As he rejected the relevance of the legalistic concept of tendency as applied to the reality of bodily harm (one either is or is not pined, consumed, wasted, etc.), Brattle also denied the legal validity of inference insofar as it, too, entailed a dubious removal from demonstrable, self-evident fact. Samuel Willard expressed similar reservations that reasoning such as Mather's made an "artificial argument": his term for Mather's style of reasoning was "disjunctive" as opposed to "convictive."[86] Brattle indicated his rejection of inference by linking it, in his critique of the Salem prosecution, with another epistemologically invalid procedure, the confusion or conflation of a representation with the object or person represented:

> When any man is indited for murthering the person of A.B. and all the direct evidence be, that the said man pistolled the shadow of the said A.B. tho' there be never so many evidences that the said person murthered C.D., E.F. and ten more persons, yet all this will not amount to a legal proof, that he murthered A.B.; . . . Now no man will be so much out of his witts as to make this a legal evidence; and yet this seems to be our case; and how to apply it is very easy and obvious.[87]

According to Brattle, two prosecutorial assumptions disclosed in his hypothetical indictment are conspicuously witless: first, the implicit equation of a man with his shadow so that the pistoling of a shadow suffices as evidence for the murder of a man; and second, the reliance placed upon inference, which would make a man guilty of murdering one individual because he murdered another. He rejects as illogical, thus illegal, and finally unethical both the conceptual recourse to inference and tendency demonstrated by Mather and the Salem judges as well as their conceptual elision of the irrevocable difference between visible and invisible worlds, subject and representation. Brattle's refusal to follow Mather's long fuse from the visible into the invisible world is thus a refusal of spectral evidence theorists' various attempts to explain away irrevocable difference — the difference between a harmed and an unharmed person; between a pious person and her diabolical specter; between a dead body and a pistol-whipped shadow; between a person who voices a desire to commit treason and the anonymously accomplished act — in order to cobble together a narrative productive of a scapegoat, in order to proclaim *abeant quo digni sunt*. For Brattle, it was as objectionable to attempt to bridge difference with recourse to conceptual maneuvers such as tendency and inference as it was to do so through the elaboration of images or theories of direct connection between the invisible and visible words, such as Mather's fuse, the bodily excrescence known as a witch wound or witch's tit that supposedly allowed the witch to suckle spectral creatures, or the "invisible and impalpable fluid" that Mather hypothesized connected witch and victim.[88] To bridge difference thus was ultimately to elide it and, as Robert Calef pointed out, to destroy the grounds of truth: in his introduction to

More Wonders of the Invisible World (completed 1697, published 1700), a lengthy critique of Mather's role in the witchcraft crisis, Calef complained of Mather's sensationalism as well as his literalism, his efforts to convince the populace that the devil's chains were "making a dreadful noise in our Ears, and Brimstone, even without a Metaphor, was making a horrid and a hellish stench in our Nostrils." The degraded status of the distance-preserving and thus truth-preserving metaphor as an index of social restraint was signaled by the literal "branding one another with the odious Name of Witch," which had led to the utter destruction of the social bond:

> Brother [did] Accuse and Prosecute Brother, Children their Parents, Pastors and Teachers their immediate Flock unto death; Shepherds becoming Wolves, Wise Men Infatuated; People hauled to Prisons, with a bloody noise pursuing to, and insulting over, the (true) Sufferers at Execution, while some are fleeing from that call'd Justice, Justice it self fleeing before such Accusations, . . . Estates seized, Families of Children and others left to the Mercy of the Wilderness (not to mention here the Numbers prescribed [condemned to death], dead in Prisons, or Executed, etc.)[89]

At least until the end of the summer of 1692, however, Mather's account of the relationship between visible reality and invisible causes or origins was not widely rejected as specious or irrational. Just as the Salem court denied the critical difference between a subject in the visible world and her representation in the invisible, so did it also come to deny the distance between the physical body of the witch and that of her victim by refuting the role that mediate objects, such as wax images or poppets, had traditionally been assumed to play in the supernatural infliction of harm. It was often observed during the trials that an apparently benign movement of the accused's body—clenching the hands, biting the lips, moving the eyes, nodding the head—produced physical agonies in the afflicted. Deodat Lawson thus observed of John Indian and Tituba, the West Indian slaves of the Reverend Samuel Parris in whose household the witchcraft accusations began, that "they are their own Image" insofar as "Natural Actions in them produced Preternatural actions in the Afflicted."[90] In the case of Martha Corey, who caused the afflicted in the courtroom to cry out in pain when she bit her lip, Nicholas Noyes similarly judged, "I beleive it is apparent she practiseth Witchcraft in the congregation there is no need of images."[91] Cotton Mather opined that "some witches make their own bodies to be their puppets."[92] Such statements show how intimately identified the witch had become not just with her specter but with her victim as well: as innocuous movements of the witch's body routinely produced agonized fits in the afflicted, as the ontological difference between the two parties threatened to collapse along with an entire structure of figuration ("they are their own Image"), one wonders whether the specter — almost from its inception as the enabling construct of the Salem witchcraft crisis — was in danger of outlasting its own conceptual vitality.[93] If raising an eyebrow or turning the head in the light of day and before a multitude of observers could produce instant agony in the afflicted, why was the specter needful, and whom (apart from the devil) did it serve?

III

The answer to these questions requires an inquiry into the relationship of the specter to the afflicted, central to the formulation of which was the supposition of consent to spectral representation, "the first great principle," as John Hale expressed it, of the Salem prosecution.[94] Spectral evidence theorists and their supporters understood this relationship in purely oppositional terms: by virtue of their consent to spectral representation, the accused had acquired the unholy power to abuse the afflicted body and soul. Although the reasons for their having become the unfortunate objects of God's wrath might be debated, the afflicted were not generally suspected of having consented to spectral abuse: as Deodat Lawson put it, considering their extraordinary suffering, "it would seem very hard and unjust to censure them of consenting to, or holding any voluntary converse or familiarity with, the Devil."[95] If their victimization compelled them to assume a mediating role between the invisible and visible worlds, like the specters themselves, and if their mediation entailed the reception and transmission of the same secret knowledge held by the specters, yet the sight of their violent struggle to disown their mediating function and the knowledge that accompanied it clearly differentiated the two key players in the "spectral exhibitions." Many had witnessed those dramatic encounters in which the afflicted, in a kind of trance or fit, visibly and audibly strove to resist their invisible and inaudible tormentors not physically, for to avoid bodily agony was impossible, but rather spiritually, even at the risk of increased torture. To the degree that the spectral exhibitions had enfeebled the key Puritan opposition of visible and invisible phenomena, it was replaced in the course of the trials as an ethical and epistemological touchstone by the perceived opposition of the specters' criminality and the victims' innocence. As the Reverend Samuel Parris tersely expressed it: "Here are but two parties in the world: the lamb and his followers, and the dragon and his followers. And these are contrary one to the other. . . . Here are no neuters. Everyone is on one side or the other."[96]

Those critical of the proceedings, however, more or less explicitly called into question the validity of the absolute distinction between specters and afflicted. If most critics did not evince Thomas Brattle's contempt for the latter as "possessed, at least, with ignorance and folly," they concurred with his observation that as the afflicted received their information about the invisible world from the devil's creatures, the specters, and in some cases from the devil himself, then "the Devill's information is the fundamental testimony" at the trials.[97] For this reason, in a letter sent to Judge Jonathan Corwin, one "R.P." explicitly asked "what we are to think of those persons at Salem, or the Village, before whom people are brought for detection, or otherwise to be concerned with them, in order to their being apprehended or acquitted."[98] His own reading of Scripture (Isaiah 8:19 and Leviticus 19:31) persuaded R.P. that their actions did not bear "God's stamp" insofar as God had forbidden human beings "to inquire of the dead, or to be informed by them" as well as to "seek to them that have familiar spirits."[99] "If the root of all their knowledge be the Devil," he pointedly asked, "what must their testimony be?"[100] And if their testimony is acknowledged to be of diabolical rather than divine origin, then the afflicted must be implicated in the same crime of consent ("the last and greatest question," R.P. averred) as those they accused, a crime that, as Samuel Willard pointed out, "must be proved by Presumptions; for who saw or heard them Covenanting?"[101] In charity, one was forced to conclude for both parties, the afflicted and the accused witches, that

if they counterfeit, the wickedness is the greater in them, and the less in the Devil: but if they be compelled to it by the Devil, against their wills, then the sin is the Devil's, and the suffering theirs; but if their testimonies be allowed of, to make persons guilty by, the lives of innocent persons are alike in danger by them, which is the solemn consideration that do disquiet the country.[102]

Such a conclusion raised the possibility of an even more heinous form of consent into which good people might be seduced than that allegedly given to the devil by the witches, as none other than Cotton Mather had pointed out before the first trial:

> if upon the bare supposal of a poor creature's being represented by a specter, too great a progress be made by the authority in ruining a poor neighbor so represented, it may be that a door may be thereby opened for the devils to obtain from the courts in the invisible world a license to proceed unto most hideous desolations upon the repute and repose of such as have yet been kept from the great transgression. If mankind have thus far once consented unto the credit of diabolical representations, the door is opened![103]

Mather's apprehension reminds us that during the witchcraft crisis, representation was a doubly problematic concept: the mystery of spectral representation (the relationship between an individual and the specter representing her in the invisible world) was known exclusively through the representations of the afflicted concerning the diabolical realm. These two aspects of representation augmented the possibility of committing a transgressive act of consent: first, the afflicted might consent to credit diabolical (inherently fictitious) representations; and second, those sympathetic to them might consent to credit their (mis)representations of the diabolic. And yet a single act of consent, Mather frets, would be sufficient to "open the door," to violate the protective hedge God had planted to shield mortals from the consequences of "the great transgression"—whether the one already committed by Satan or the one humankind stood poised to commit is left ambiguous.[104]

The Reverend Samuel Willard of Boston's Old South Church had had personal experience wrestling with the temptation to credit diabolic representations. Twenty-one years before the Salem crisis, in 1671, his maidservant, Elizabeth Knapp, had demonstrated symptoms akin to those of the afflicted in Salem, including the identification of an unremarkable neighbor woman as a witch whose specter, Knapp claimed, was abusing her. Willard had averted a crisis by refraining from crediting Knapp's information; instead, he brought the accused woman privately to her and, confronted with her alleged tormentor, Knapp confessed to having been misled by the devil.[105] Despite his experience, Willard did not directly protest the methods of the Salem court, but published anonymously, and in Quaker Philadelphia, a hypothetical debate between pro- and anti–spectral evidence proponents ("S" and "B," respectively) in which he explicitly discredited not just the information of the afflicted but their characters as well. Like Brattle, Mather (albeit ambivalently), and "R.P.," Willard's "B" rejected the testimony of the afflicted because their knowledge had not come to them "after the manner of men." He clarified his sense of that phrase:

> I intend, That which one man can know concerning another by his Senses, and that according to the true nature, and use of them; whatsoever comes in any other way, is either by extraordinary Revelation from God, or by the insinuation of the Devil; and what Credit is legally to be given to a thing which an Humane Person swears, meerly upon the Devils Information?

The accusations cannot be the product of divine revelation, for "B" is convinced that "when God raiseth up Prophets, he will reveale himself in some other way to them, than by Devils; and in some other sort of raptures than in Tormenting Fits." Thus the claims of the afflicted to "extraordinary sight," "their telling of things done at a distance, their Predicting of things future!" and other feats bespeak not the ill effects of witchcraft, and not God's decision to endow them with extraordinary knowledge in order to facilitate the discovery of witchcraft, but their own "unlawful commerce with the Devil." When Willard's pro–spectral evidence debater, "S," then asks "B" if he feels that "our Afflicted" are untrustworthy, "scandalous persons, liars, and loose in their Conversation," "B" replies, in a pointed attempt to recall the social function of charity, "I could name many things, which I think must prove them Witches or possessed; and I charitably believe the latter of them."[106]

Although during the spectral exhibitions the afflicted persuasively dramatized their resistance to diabolical consent—a fact that militated against identifying them with their tormentors—still these performances presented with sensational clarity the physical and spiritual intimacy of specters and afflicted. Beyond the infliction of disease reported by those who had had some hostile, if casual, contact with the accused witches and the routine pinching, biting, and beatings allegedly administered by the specters, the bodily tortures of the afflicted, graphic and bizarre, included disembowelment, impalement, and disarticulation, especially of the organs of speech.[107] The Goodwin children suffered a spectral roasting upon a spit (the spit entered their mouths and exited their feet) and a spectral nailing of their heads to the floor. A fellow sufferer told of "a Hand put into the Bed, to pull out his Bowels." The Goodwins and others had their tongues either drawn down their throats or pulled out "to a prodigious length," and their mouths were so forcefully opened that "their Jaws went out of joint; and anon they would clap together with a Force like that of a strong Spring-Lock. The same would happen to their Shoulder-Blades, and their Elbows, and Hand-wrists, and several of their joints."[108] Allen Toothaker claimed to suffer from a wound so deep that one could thrust into it "a knitting Nedle four Inches"; it healed only when Martha Carrier (executed 19 August 1692) was arrested. John DeRich testified that Margaret Jacobs had threatened to skewer him if he refused to sign the book she proffered. The afflicted were typically stuck with invisible pins; one of them, Ann Putnam, testified that she saw Mary Clarke stab Timothy Swan "with a square ragged Speare as long as her hand."[109] Mercy Short was forced to swallow pins, a "hot Iron," and a "Whitesh Liquor" that the devil and his "confederate and concomitant Spectres" poured "down her Throat, holding her Jawes wide open in spite of all the Shriekings and Strivings wherewith shee expressed a Reluctancy to Taking of it."[110] In addition to physical abuses, the specters were thought capable of penetrating their victims' minds with "Buzzes of Atheism and Blasphemy, as had made them even run Distracted with Terrors" and of encouraging some to suicide.[111] John Hale speculated that Bridget Bishop had been responsible for the death of a neighbor with whom she had argued and who later had committed suicide; her injury — using scissors, she cut out "apiece of her wind pipe . . . & another wound above that threww the windpipe & Gullet & the veine they call jugular" — exhibited a degree of self-loathing too savage not to have been induced by the devil or his allies.[112]

In the course of the spectral exhibitions, the connection between specter and victim was revealed to be even more elemental than that which the grotesque permeability of the victims' bodies had suggested. More shocking to spectators than the sight of the afflicted unsuccessfully resisting the penetration of their bodies by all manner of invisible weapons from pins to poisons was the way in which the victims' violated bodies enabled spectral weapons (including spectral body parts used to attack the afflicted) to emerge out of their invisible, immaterial state to attain some degree of visibility and a material form: thus, invisible teeth left visible indentations in the skin; invisible brimstone left visible blisters on the throat; invisible pins left pin-sized puncture wounds (sometimes visible pins were discovered in the victim's vicinity), all of which healed with remarkable rapidity only to reappear as the assaults continued.[113] In *Wonders of the Invisible World*, Mather reported how one victim complained that a specter

> ran at her with a Spindle: tho' no body else in the Room, could see either the Spectre or the Spindle. At last, in her miseries, giving a Snatch at the Spectre, she pull'd the Spindle away; and it was no sooner got into her hand, but the other people then present beheld, that it was indeed a Real, Proper, Iron Spindle, belonging they knew to whom.

Mather's narrative underscores the material specificity of the object miraculously brought over from immateriality by identifying it as the possession of a known individual, its quotidian familiarity suggesting not just the proximity of the invisible world but its domestication. This peculiar conversion narrative of an object recovered from invisibility to become "Real" and "Proper" recurs in the tale of a victim whose specter appeared to her wound in a sheet. The victim violently snatched a piece of the sheet, which "in her hand Immediately became *Visible* to a Roomful of Spectators; a Palpable Corner of a Sheet" (emphasis added). A tug-of-war between inhabitants of the visible and invisible worlds for possession of the remnant of sheet ensued, the victim's father struggling to "Keep what his Daughter had so strangely Seized" and the specter, who "had like to have pull'd his [the father's] Hand off, by Endeavouring to wrest it from him," struggling to reclaim it for invisibility. Victory went to the visible world as the man managed to sustain the materiality of his prize, the palpable corner of sheet so recently weaned and won from the invisible world, from spirituality itself.[114]

The synaptic ability of the afflicted to convert spirit into matter complemented the peculiar ontological hybridity of the specters. Both invisible and

supernatural as well as visible and human ("Corporeally tho' Invisibly present," as Mather put it), representative and represented, illicit desire and
fulfillment, malicious intention and enactment, the specters were perceived
as denizens of a mediate space between the visible and invisible worlds and
with one foot, as it were, in each: despite his recourse to the image of the fuse,
Mather puzzled how it could be that "the Wretches were Palpable, while yett
they were not Visible."[115] Their corporeality was sufficient to cause them to
bleed "spectral blood" and even to fall down dead when witnesses of the
spectral exhibitions would lunge at them (or at the places the afflicted alleged
they stood) with their swords.[116] This hybridity permitted the specters to
serve a contradictory function in late American Puritan culture: they registered the collapse of the sacrosanct difference between invisible and visible
worlds, but did so by occupying — and thus maintaining — the threatened
"space between" this most fundamental opposition. Simultaneously revolutionary and conservative, the specters reconfigured the strict opposition of
visibility and invisibility as a continuum, thus making direct access to the
invisible world possible for an elect corps of victims whose instrumentaliza-
tion permitted indirect access to ministers like Cotton Mather. With his
careful study of the afflicted, Mather reformulated his understanding of the
world of spirit based not only upon the data obtained through their mediation but upon the circumstance of mediation itself. His accounts of his experience with the afflicted unintentionally reveal that notwithstanding the
specters' ability to make their presence felt in both the invisible and visible
worlds, they depended on their human victims to make their existence as
representation corporeally manifest.[117] Only the victims' bodies confirmed
the bodiless existence of the specters; only the articulations of the victims
attested to their provoking discourse. The manifestly dyadic relationship
of specter and victim vitiated the absolute distinction between the two,
paradoxically conferring enormous cultural authority upon the afflicted for
providing "palpable Convictions" of what Mather called "the *Reality of
Invisibles*."[118]

   In 1689, Mather had temporarily adopted an afflicted adolescent girl,
Martha Goodwin, so that he might "be furnished with Evidence and Argument as a Critical Eye-Witness to confute the Saducism of this debauched
Age," but also to further his own interest in "the pneumatic Discipline," the
science of invisible spirits both good and evil.[119] The "Experiments" he

consequently conducted upon Goodwin were calculated to provide him with information (the intellectual capacities of devils, their knowledge of Latin, their ability to read minds, etc.) about which he consequently felt both pleased and guilty, expansive and inhibited: "I have Learn't much more than I sought, and I have bin informed of some things relating to the invisible World, which as I did not think it lawful to ask, so I do not think it proper to tell."[120] This novel emphasis upon the reality or materiality, and thus the conceptual accessibility, of spirit resulted in a manifest theological confusion: for example, despite an introductory chastisement of the faithless who "count it their wisdom to credit nothing but what they see and feel," Mather rejoiced in *Memorable Providences*, his account of the Martha Goodwin story, that he and other witnesses of her afflictions had received "palpable Convictions" of the invisible world sufficient to constitute "proofs" of its existence and its "methods" for the skeptics, "our Learned witlings of the Coffee-House."[121] Moreover, he records his efforts to communicate indirectly with spirits through Goodwin's apparently unconscious mediation, although the four ministers who wrote the preface to *Memorable Providences* explicitly cautioned those ambitious to make verbal contact with the invisible world. Fully cognizant that his experiments constituted a "fanciful Business" that might lead to diabolical entrapment and that the knowledge he was acquiring through the afflicted was probably unlawful, Mather yielded to his long-standing desire for palpable proof of invisible and impalpable realities.[122] He knew the extent of his limitations and despaired that the devil had pushed God's people "into a Blind Mans Buffet, and we are even ready to be sinfully, yea, hotly, and madly, mauling one another in the dark."[123] As blind and deaf he would thrust and parry with the surrounding specters in the bedrooms of the afflicted girls, Mather felt himself tantalizingly close to invisible and sacred truths that he knew were not given to mortals to discover. In his accounts of his experiences with the afflicted, who served as his eyes and ears as he struggled to perceive invisible truths, his desire to strike through the mask — the "*fascinating mist* of *invisibility*" — is as visceral as Ahab's.[124]

Mather described the spectral exhibitions as "the very State of the Damned itself represented most visibly before our eyes."[125] In the victims' sensational performances of spiritual and bodily torment, hell, no longer an abstract and future terror, was realized as a continuously occurring series of ingeniously conceived penetrations of the human mind and body. But beyond the victims' grotesque bodily deformations and the aberrant behavior that accompanied them, "the Devel in the Damsel" manifested itself vocally to the "scores of spectators" who eagerly awaited the next communication from an invisible world apparently teeming with engaging personalities.[126] These instrumentalized the "ventriloqua," as the eighteenth-century witch-craft historian Thomas Hutchinson referred to the afflicted, in two ways in order to make audible the silent world of spirit.[127] The afflicted might function as a kind of human microphone passively transmitting snippets of conversation between the devils themselves, as when from Martha Goodwin's mouth "a big, but low voice" announced, " 'There's Two or Three of them' "; Mather speculated that the " 'them' " referred to "us!" (the people praying for Martha at her bedside), suggesting that the spirits were as eager to reach across the divide and relieve their own ignorance of the alternative reality and its inhabitants as were their human counterparts.[128] More commonly, however, those gathered around the bedside of the afflicted were "Ear-witnesses to Disputacions" that amazed them: "Indeed Wee could not hear what They said unto her," Mather explained with reference to Mercy Short's monologues in *A Brand Pluck'd Out of the Burning*, "nor could shee herself hear them ordinarily without causing them to say over again: But Wee could Hear Her Answers, and from her Answers Wee could usually gather the Tenour of Their Assaults."[129]

Appearing not to hear the devil's words and so repeating them as a way of confirming them ("You! Do You say that You are *Christ!*" and "Fine Promises! You'l bestow an Husband upon mee, if I'l bee your Servant"), the afflicted made their bedside audiences privy to an extended and impassioned theological debate in which they engaged with a range of evil spirits, including the devil himself.[130] Fascinated spectators could hear how the afflicted scolded the specters of visible saints for their hypocrisy and contemned the devil's pretenses to divinity; urged the specters to repent and reversed the rule that "Younger Women [must] hearken to the Elder" to command that the elder (or at least their specters) "for once" hearken to them;[131] and prophesied their immanent delivery by a God who had surely intended by their affliction to glorify them among His elect. Mather speculated that God Himself had personally coached the victims, for how else could untutored girls demonstrate such a remarkable aptitude for theological debate, countering the ripostes of the Prince of Lies with unhesitating reference to scriptural passages precisely calculated to refute his claims?[132] Mather represented the afflicted in his accounts of their struggles as natural ministers of God's Word who, beyond even those eminent divines working to convert the New World savages, possessed an exemplary piety that authorized them to evangelize the evil specters of the invisible world. Whereas Mather had patronizingly written of John Goodwin's addendum to the account of his daughter Martha's affliction, " 'Tis in his own Style; but I suppose a Pen hath not commonly been managed with more cleanly Discourse by an Hand used only to the Trowel," he could only marvel at the girl's erudition, attesting that "all my Library never afforded me any Commentary on those Paragraphs of the Gospels, which speak of Demoniacs, equal to that which the passions of this Child gave me." (Thirteen-year-old Martha was also given to discoursing with the devils about "the state of the Countrey.")[133] Superior in their wisdom to a library of texts, the afflicted girls could also catechize Boston's leading ministers: Mather considered the greatest "marvel" of Mercy Short's affliction to be that "The Impulse which directed her unto the Scriptures . . . might have assisted or quickened us in our Devotions, If wee had seen Cause to have made that Use of them."[134] Margaret Rule's ringing jeremiads to the specters convinced Mather that "A person perhaps of the Best Education and Experience and of Attainments much beyond hers could not have exceeded" "her strains of Expression and Argument."[135] For the afflicted, "Impulse" and "passion" served them well, giving rise to their superlative eloquence, but not hindering their resistance to the devil's Poesque seductions. The spectral exhibitions, virtual dramas of nonconsent, showcased the victims' astonishingly steadfast refusal of even the smallest, the most "accidentally" committed gesture of acquiescence to eternal damnation — a mere touch of the devil's book, for example, rather than a signature.[136]

That the afflicted were authorized to provide the Puritan ministry with spiritual enlightenment was compatible with their authority to discover some of them publicly as the devil's allies. In the trial of the Reverend George Burroughs of Maine (executed 19 August 1692) and formerly of Salem Village, four Salem men testified of the afflicted Ann Putnam Jr. that

> she saw the Apperishtion of a Minister at which she was greviously affrighted and cried out oh dreadfull: dreadfull here is a minister com: what are Ministers wicthes to: whence com you and What is your name for I will complaine of:you tho you be A minister: . . . [I] tould him that it

was a dreadfull thing: that he which was a Minister that should teach children to feare God should com to perswad poor creatures to give their souls to the divill.

Mercy Lewis claimed that the specter of Burroughs played the devil to her Christ by testing her faith (and, as with Jesus, preparing her to preach) against the possibility of acquiring a superhuman power:

[He] caried me up to an exceeding high mountain and shewed me all the kingdoms of the earth and tould me that he would give them all to me if I would writ in his book and if I would not he would thro me down and brake my neck: but I tould him they ware non of his to give and I would not writ if he throde me down on 100 pitchforks.

The enormity of Mercy's temptations, her physical frailty and childlike vulnerability, and the sacrificial fervor with which she declared to Burroughs's specter, and thus to a multitude of spectators, "I will not writ in your book tho you doe kil me," sanctioned both her contact with invisible personalities and her public revelations of the knowledge their communion provided.[137] Indeed, the physical undoing of the afflicted served to reinforce their spiritual integrity, bolstering their implicit claims to the right of authoritative public speech with an undeniable credibility. If the spectral exhibitions provided the afflicted with an occasion to exercise their enormous cultural power, they also dramatized how the afflicted, far from seeking or consenting to power, were compelled to it by the Enemy of Mankind. Their nonconsent ensured their innocence: the afflicted could thus know and reveal secret and future things, including the secret thoughts and actions of others as well as their essential spiritual identities; preach the Word of God to visible and invisible auditors simultaneously; determine who in their world would live and who would die, regardless of cultural status; and mediate between the human world and the world of angels. Blameless, humble, and frail conveyors of invisible truths, the afflicted efficiently removed the keystone of the weakened edifice of late seventeenth-century American Puritanism: the inscrutability and inaccessibility of the invisible world. Aside from their communion with evil angels, the afflicted might, without risk of censure, claim to receive direct aid and counsel from the holy angels, and even from God Himself. Deodat Lawson thus reported that "a *white-man*" appeared to some in the midst of the "black" specters, who "had often foretold them what respite they should have from their fits . . . which fell out accordingly." The white man transported one of the afflicted to "a glorious place which had no candle nor sun, yet was full of light and brightness, where there was a multitude in white, glittering robes, and they sang the song in Rev. 5, 9; Psal. 110, 149."[138] Having boldly overstepped the "limit beyond which even the federal theologians could not go," the afflicted managed to deflect cultural disapprobation, with the help of spectral evidence theorists, to those hapless individuals who were presumed to have consented to spectral representation as a way of acquiring the same power that the afflicted so reluctantly, and without the slightest impediment, wielded.[139]

John Hale described the specters as "piercing Spirits" who "have advantages to know all the actions of the Children of men, both open and secret, their discourses, consultations, and much of the inward affections of men thereby."[140] But if an individual was thought to have purchased her power to know and reveal secret and future things through her consent to spectral representation—her consent to the devil—no such liability compromised the visible standing of her victim. The possessed, as nonconsenters, as innocent individuals forced into contact with the diabolical realm, could not be accused of allying themselves with the devil even if, through their bodies and voices, they commanded the same powers of knowledge and public revelation of invisible realities as did the specter. In fact, as the specters' innocent medium for the revelation of that which would otherwise remain either invisible or unarticulated, the victims could innocently attract sizable courtroom or bedside audiences who were also made privy to information that, to the degree it was humanly knowable at all, had formerly been verified and managed by the clergy exclusively.[141] In this way, the spectral realm proved susceptible not just to consensual but to involuntary, and thus innocent, access. The information thus transmitted went well beyond revealing the identities of the specters. Through their involuntary contact with the specters, the victims, who were for the most part quite powerless people in the community, many of them young girls, "could read inmost thoughts, suggest ideas to the minds of the absent, throw temptations in the path of those whom she desired to delude and destroy, bring up the spirits of the departed, and hear from them the secrets of their lives and of their deaths, and their experiences in the scenes of being on which they entered at their departure from this."[142] The afflicted knew and revealed a range of private sins and secret transgressions calculated to belie the visible evidence of election that individuals "of unblameable life & conversation" had built over the course of "a long continued consistent, just, Christian life, full of charity, and approved by mankind."[143] In the end, beyond vitiating the difference between supernatural and mortal, and between witch and victim, accused and accuser, spectral evidence theory entailed the destruction of its own most fundamental distinction, that between consent and innocence.

IV

The Reverend John Hale was an early supporter of the witchcraft prosecution who, like many prominent Puritan men (including Governor William Phips), lived to regret it when his wife was cried out upon by the afflicted. As Robert Calef describes his change of heart, Hale was one who could not be convinced that "the Devil could Afflict in a good Man's shape; . . . yet when it came so near to himself, he was soon convinc'd that the Devil might so Afflict."[144] The circumstances of the pious Mrs. Hale's spectral appearances were highly unusual insofar as her specter was instrumental in conveying to the girl she afflicted, Mary Herrick, a spectral denial of the validity of spectral evidence. Herrick confided to John Hale and her own pastor, Joseph Gerrish of Wenham, that before the execution of Mary Easty, whom she did not know but of whose guilt she had heard and was convinced, Easty's specter had appeared before her to proclaim, "I am going upon the Ladder to be hanged for a Witch, but I am innocent, and before a 12 Month be past you shall believe it." Because she was convinced that Easty was a witch, Herrick had held her peace and told no one of this visitation. After the execution, however, Easty returned, this time in the spectral company of Mrs. Hale. The specter of the dead Mary Easty stood silently by while the specter of the living Mrs. Hale "did sorely Afflict her by pinching, pricking and Choaking her." They visited several times, Easty silently observing while Hale as silently abused her, before the specter of Mrs. Hale suddenly asked her, mid-affliction, if Herrick thought she was a witch. Herrick replied, "no, You be the Devill," at which the specter of Easty broke her silence. As Gerrish transcribed Herrick's account,

She Came to tell her She had been put to Death wrongfully and was Innocent of Witchcraft, and she Came to Vindicate her Cause and she
Cryed Vengeance, Vengeance, and bid her reveal this to Mr. Hayle and
Gerish, and then she would rise no more, nor should Mrs. Hayle Afflict
her any more.

Herrick had decided to comply with Easty's directive because her experience
of spectral affliction had convinced her that "it is all a Delusion of the
Devil."[145]

Hale had identified the assumption of consent to spectral representation
as "the first great principle" of the Salem prosecution based not, of course,
upon empirical evidence but upon the firm belief "That the Devil could not
assume the shape of an innocent person in doing mischief unto mankind."[146]
The judges "took up an opinion," Cotton Mather explained,

> that the *providence* of God would not permit an innocent person to come
> under such a spectral representation; and that a concurrence of so many
> circumstances [so many sightings] would prove an accused person to be
> in a *confederacy* with the dæmons thus afflicting of the neighbours; they
> judged that, except these things might amount unto a conviction, it
> would scarce be possible ever to *convict* a *witch*.[147]

Apart from the unavailability of direct evidence for the act of consent, however, major theological objections to the assumption of consent to spectral
representation were expressed from the beginning — were even solicited —
but were not heeded until October 1692.

Puritans commonly assigned devils, as fallen angels, to the invisible world.
As the ministers' preface to *Memorable Providences* and numerous other documents attest, Puritan doctrine regarding the evil angels stated that insofar as
they wreaked havoc upon humankind, they did so with God's permission; as
Increase Mather said, the devil needs "a Divine Concession to use his Art."[148]
God suffered the devils to occupy a portion of the invisible realm because
they carried out His will regarding the necessary chastisement of human
creatures; the existence of the fallen angels, as well as their actions, was
strictly subordinated to and circumscribed by the will of God.[149] Not just the
sermonic literature but also the comparatively rare documents written by lay
Puritans generally conceded that the actions of the evil spirits, because they

were permitted by God, were ultimately productive of good: as John Goodwin, the father of afflicted Martha, had expressed it, "sanctified Afflictions are choice mercies."[150] Moreover, the evil the devils and their human instruments practiced was clearly confined to what was humanly possible, no matter how outrageous their actions or how devilish their appearance. The specters, however, were unique: evil creatures produced not by God's consent but, as spectral evidence theorists insisted, in the express absence of God's consent, by human consent alone. The reasoning suggests the doubling of popular and diabolical independence: freeing the devil from God's supervision, His exclusive "prerogative to make use of what Instrument he pleaseth, in Afflicting any, and consequently to commissionate Devils," endowed human beings with the parallel liberty of consenting to spectral representation to satisfy their own ambitions irrespective both of God's intentions as well as the limitations of their own social standings.[151]

A corps of supernatural and deeply deconstructive beings produced solely by human consent, the specters' very appearance pitted divine authority against the cause of human justice. In *Cases of Conscience Concerning Evil Spirits Personating Men*, the document most influential in invalidating spectral evidence as the basis for a capital conviction in witchcraft cases, Increase Mather explained the theological error fundamental to the theory: "The principal Plea to justifie the convictive Evidence . . . is fetcht from the Consideration of the Wisdom and Righteousness of God in Governing the World, which they suppose would fail, if such things were permitted to befall an innocent person." In his retrospective view of the crisis, John Hale, minister at Beverly, concurred: the magistrates felt, he explained, that the possibility of God permitting the spectral representation of an innocent, or nonconsenting, individual "would subvert the course of human Justice, by bringing men to suffer for what he did in their Shapes."[152] Samuel Parris, according to his lights, also articulated the premise of exclusively human initiative in the commissioning of devils: "The devil would represent the best saints as devils if he could," Parris explained, "but it is not easy to imagine that his power is of such extent, to the hazard of the church."[153] But to uphold the integrity of human justice and the visible church in this manner posed two profound theological problems for American Puritans. First, to do so was clearly to undermine the integrity of the separation between the visible and invisible worlds upon which the Puritan cultural order was based.

In the absence of a transcendent and strictly inaccessible invisible realm—one to which humans, "consenting" or not, had no direct access—members of the court and other interested inquirers were both compelled and emboldened to go "to the Devil to find the Devil," as Hale succinctly put it.[154] Second, it nullified the premise of God's exclusive prerogative to determine all events from the most momentous to the most minute, and by transferring that prerogative to the devil inevitably attributed it to the human being who commissioned the devil, the witch, "the worst of Men."[155] As Robert Calef put it, although all acknowledge "Gods Providence and Government of the World, and that Tempests and Storms, Afflictions and Diseases, are of his sending," the "asserters" of the "destructive notions of this Age" still "tell us, that the Devil has the power of all these, and can perform them when commission'd by a Witch thereto, and that he has a power at the Witches call to act and do."[156] The insistence on human consent and the direct access to the invisible world it made possible for those who allowed the devil to "serve" them (never mind how, Mather says) thus constituted a deeply subversive, indeed, revolutionary proposition, a "bold usurpatio[n]," as Increase Mather pointed out, of the "spotless *Sovereignty*" of God.[157]

Confronted with the dramatic evidence for the direct and innocent accessibility of the invisible world provided by the afflicted, the merely semiotic relation of visible to invisible on which the Puritan clergy had long insisted may have seemed pretty paltry, even to those who had insisted most rigorously on their absolute separation. We have seen how Cotton Mather, intoxicated by the dramas of nonconsent enacted in his own spare bedroom and the disclosures they entailed concerning invisible truths, forsook the principle of a transcendent and ultimately unknowable invisible order which could only be approximated on the visible plane. Not unlike the opportunistic specters, Mather instrumentalized his adolescent wards in order to spar with the devil (who the afflicted claimed was as obsessed with Mather as Mather was with him). In so doing, he disregarded his father's warning that "*they who force another to do that which he cannot possibly do, but by vertue of a Compact with the Devil, have themselves implicitely Communion with the Diabolical Covenant.*"[158]

We are now in a position to understand why the hypothesis of the consenting specter, identified as such by theatrically nonconsenting accusers, proved fatal to the Puritan order. A brief comparison with the first great challenge to covenant theology, the Antinomian crisis of 1636–38, may serve to bring the theological threat of spectral evidence theory into relief.

The Antinomian faction upheld explicitly and in a radical spirit what spectral evidence theorists implicitly and out of their principled conservatism countenanced: the violation of the fundamental Puritan principle of the separation of visible and invisible worlds guaranteed by a space of unknowing divinely subtended between the two. For their part, the Antinomians utterly denied the existence of a space of unknowing between God and His elect.[159] Indeed, in their view, to posit the existence of such a space was to affirm one's unregeneracy. Insofar as it denied the intricate semiotic system upon which New England Puritan culture had been so painstakingly established, the Antinomian faction condemned the theocracy to a purgatory of irrelevance. With the "signs" emptied of their significance, the tests of their validity, and the clerisy of their vocations, only the Voice of God remained to speak directly to the souls of His people and tell them who—indeed *that*—they were. Bearing directly to the hearer the only knowledge worth possessing, that one was destined for eternal life, the Voice came unbidden and undeserved, and was thus received by the elect individual in the absolute freedom of immobility: not only was one not required to act according to some contrived code of "sanctified" behavior, but one could not act meaningfully, there being no correlation between the (visible) person one was in the world and one's essential (invisible) identity in the afterlife. Because the Voice of God speaking directly to his saints was the sole means of identifying the elect, an apparatus of testing and performance was more than unnecessary; it was at best utterly absurd, and at worst it implicitly denied God's power to choose whom He would regardless of human effort to win His approbation.[160] The Antinomians claimed further that the elect knew infallibly, again "by an immediate revelation," who was of their number, rendering the ministry not simply irrelevant but actually a hindrance to the formation of a pure church on New World soil.[161]

In sum, where the ministers insisted, first, on a semiotic connection between the visible and the invisible worlds, but second, on the absolute separation of visible and invisible such that one could never claim epistemological certainty concerning God's determinations, the Antinomians insisted, first, that there was absolutely no connection or relation between the visible and the invisible worlds, but second, that one could infallibly know things about the invisible world not through evidence indirectly provided by the visible but through direct revelation from God. Revelation — or what the critics of Antinomianism denounced as the usurpation of the power to reveal secret things — utterly discredited the labor of semiosis as well as the cultural system it enacted. According to the critics of Antinomianism, to deny the space of unknowing was to deny the space of culture, or at least of complex community, for the distinctions and the suspensions of disbelief upon which such a community is necessarily based had no function in the Antinomian vision of true reform. Thus it was crucial to the Puritan understanding of community to preserve the neutrality or emptiness of the mediate space subtended between the visible and invisible worlds as a space of unknowing both protected and managed by the theocracy. Such a space of unknowing ensured both the conceptual legitimacy and the semiotic vitality of the foundational binary opposition (visible/invisible, diabolical/divine, saint/sinner, and so forth) upon which the Puritan cultural and political order, articulated in covenant theology, was established.

If, in the Antinomian crisis, the space of unknowing is grandly elided, in the witchcraft crisis it is eerily populated, emerging in the course of the investigations of the spring and summer of 1692 as a mediate space inhabited by a diabolical crew of ontological hybrids, witches and specters, beings both palpable and invisible. The narrative of consent to representation, variously enacted so as to draw in even would-be nonconsenters, underwrote the expansion of that section of the invisible world given over to the devil to engulf many of the visible world's most prominent and respected members and to empower its disenfranchised. Spectral representation rendered the visible as a signifier of invisible truths completely unreliable. All actors — with the exception, ironically, of the accused — conspired to replace the theocratically managed uncertainties of Puritan semiosis with a less centralized and wholly unmanageable war of representations between visible character and the spectral self, the creature of one's consent. As the nineteenth-century Catholic convert Orestes Brownson once claimed that Protestantism ended in Transcendentalism, one might say that covenant theology ended in spectral evidence theory, which articulated a new understanding of the representational possibilities of human personality as they were illuminated by the establishment of unorthodox relationships to social and theological authority. Taken together, these representational possibilities constitute the origins of democratic personality as they lay the groundwork for an American national literature.

As it emerged in the witchcraft crisis, democratic personality indulged, but in significance extended far beyond, the licentious behavior that opponents of the Great Awakening would condemn fifty years later in the New Light converts. Certainly the behavior of the afflicted was manifestly antithetical to the Puritan ideal, especially with respect to young women: they capered; they cackled; they demanded rum, food, and "fellows"; they read illicit texts written by Quakers, Catholics, and jokesters; they demanded audiences with the governor; they remarked disparagingly in meeting on the length of sermons and loudly expressed relief when they were over; they rejected prayer; they called for the deaths of those who expressed skepticism that their flamboyant disobedience was beyond their control.[162] Yet democratic personality was not merely the coveted prize in a juvenile con game conspiratorially and ingeniously invented by the afflicted. For one thing, observers of their fits were clearly shaken, not primarily by the seditiousness of their behavior but by the extraordinary mental and physical suffering that almost always accompanied it.[163] For another, even if it were true that their suffering was thoroughly dissembled, democratic personality was clearly a collective effort, the composite creation of the afflicted allied with spectral evidence theorists and their lay and clerical supporters who legitimated their behavior by leaping after them over the "hedge" separating the visible from the invisible and crediting their diabolical representations.

Robert Calef had maintained that if those in authority had simply withdrawn their belief in the accusations of the afflicted, the devil would have disappeared and the crisis been averted; he noted that the explosive Andover witch-hunt, an offshoot of Salem, came to an abrupt halt when a wealthy Bostonian threatened those who had cried out upon him with a thousand-pound defamation suit.[164] But Salem was committed to spectral evidence theory, which endowed the afflicted with the power of life and death, not just over their fellow villagers but over any resident of the colony whose name had ever happened to come to their attention: the Reverend George Burroughs, after leaving Salem parish ten years earlier to settle in Wells, Maine, had been in the middle of dinner when he was arrested and compelled to return to Salem.[165] In the minds of authorities, the often explicitly Christological martyrdom of the afflicted constituted a direct and incontestable experience of the invisible world that legitimated their exclusive access to its secrets and its truths and their right to reveal and to preach them. Moreover, their unmediated knowledge permitted them to script others' experience of the invisible world, even those, like Cotton Mather, fully conversant with educated opinion concerning its properties and personalities: when Martha Goodwin told Mather he was about to be knocked down the stairs by a specter, he felt himself being pushed and stumbled backward, and when Mercy Short told him that a specter would try to remove a ring from his finger as he walked home, he felt numbness in that finger at the appointed hour.[166] As they thus determined the content of the invisible world of God's determinations, so they claimed an exclusive and unanswerable prescience concerning that other invisible domain, private conscience: Mercy Short warned those who flocked to witness her torment "That if any of them had the guilt of a Prayerless Life upon their Consciences, they must Repent of it, or know who was well acquainted with it."[167]

As the authority of the afflicted increased in the course of the spectral exhibitions and the trials, convictions, and executions to which they inevitably led, the authority of the ministry was accordingly compromised, as the hanging of Burroughs graphically demonstrated. A considerable number of the accused had for years been regarded by the community as saints, justified professors of Christ, an identity established by a ministry clearly as blind to spiritual realities as they had been deceived by visible character and their own well-intentioned, but fatal, policy of charity. Because visible character had been proposed as a particularly insidious form of specious representation, the ministry's practice of relying upon its evidence in order to "test" spiritual identity was thrown into question. The ministry thus relied upon the afflicted to inform them of the identities of those, some perhaps in their own congregations, who were secretly instrumental in furthering the diabolical plot against New England. Moreover, given the authority derived from their privileged and unmediated access to the truth of spiritual identity, an access confirmed by the ministry, the afflicted posed a considerable threat of exposure to their ministerial allies: Cotton Mather was horrified to discover from one of his afflicted protégées that his specter had been sighted among the diabolical legions, knowing how little his piety and prominence would avail him if news of the sighting spread.[168]

The debasement of visible character as a touchstone for spiritual identity thus provoked a crisis of credibility for the ministry in which some of its members were unintentionally complicit. There was no united clerical protest against the judgment of the magistrates, evident in the examination of Rebecca Nurse, that the duplication of the body on the spectral plane was sufficient to undermine the integrity of visible character, or against their rejection of Nurse's plea that instead of withdrawing their faith in visible character, the authorities should decouple consent and representation as cause and effect. Instead, the ministry tolerated the reconceptualization of visible character, the foundation of Congregationalism (the New England Way), as a suspect sign whose significance could be known only by inverting its obvious meaning. Their passivity in this regard suggests the possibility that the role played by cultural authorities in the witchcraft crisis, both ministerial and civil, was confined to providing a corroborative reading of the data so painfully retrieved from the invisible world by the afflicted whose very debility permitted their ever tighter grip upon the reins of power. Throughout the spring and summer of 1692, the afflicted continued to re-enact their own resurrections, to reconstitute themselves after their undoing by the devil, to survive the continuous abuse of their flesh through miraculous healings, to pierce seemingly impenetrable barriers between one mind and another and between God and mortal men, and to bring by their untutored eloquence an understanding of their apostasy to the most flagrantly unregenerate. The devil himself (at least according to their dramatizations of their encounters) was cowed by their spiritual precocity. Their theatricalization of nonconsent—a dramatic refusal of the power to harm and of the subsequent joys of an unlimited self-aggrandizement—was itself the occasion for the uninhibited exercise of that power: in a state of near idiocy they broadcast God's secrets; in a state of utter physical lassitude they realized their most violent fantasies.

The destabilization of visible character was both reflected in and reinforced by the fluidity of identity demonstrated by those who affiliated themselves now with the afflicted and now with their tormentors. Deliverance Hobbs claimed to have had a minor experience of spectral affliction, but found herself in court when her daughter had confessed to the crime of witchcraft and implicated her mother. "Is it not a solemn thing," the judge asked the thoroughly confused woman, "that last Lords day you were tormented, & now you are become a tormentor, so that you have changed sides, how comes this to pass?"[169] The prosecution posed the same question to the maidservant Mary Warren, an especially active member of the initial group of accusers. Upon the arrest of her employers, Elizabeth and John Proctor, Warren apparently began to confide to some who knew her that the spectral exhibitions were either deliberately faked or delusional. Not surprisingly, the afflicted promptly sighted her specter and Warren was forthwith jailed and examined. Faced in court with the same type of incontrovertible "evidence" for her apostasy that she herself had once amply produced — the convulsions of the afflicted upon the words and gestures of the accused — Warren, unlike defendants who had expressed bewilderment or contempt upon witnessing the agony of the afflicted, also fell into violent convulsions that precluded further interrogation. The afflicted obligingly interpreted this turn of events for the benefit of the baffled prosecution: the specters were attempting to prevent Warren's confession. With great difficulty and over the course of several court appearances, Warren voiced the "truth" of her abdication from the path of righteousness and was welcomed back into the ranks of the witchcraft's victims. It is interesting to consider that just as Warren suggested the identification of specter and victim by playing both roles simultaneously, so she collapsed the difference between witch and specter by insisting that the actual bodies, and not the spectral shapes, of John and Elizabeth Proctor came to goad her into serving the devil. Ironically, as a suspected witch, Warren's accusations carried an authority even beyond that of the afflicted: a true — if reluctant — insider, Warren provided damning, detailed, and abundant testimony against eleven of the twenty who would face execution.[170]

Like Hobbs and Warren, Sarah Churchill had initially identified herself with the afflicted but subsequently found herself in the ranks of the accused. She confessed to the crime of witchcraft when the judges threatened to throw her into a dungeon with George Burroughs. Afterward, however, she approached Sarah Ingersoll "Crieng and wringing hur hands" to confess "that she had undon hursalfe in be lieng hur salf and others" but that she was compelled to it by one of the magistrates who, "If she told [him] but ons she had sat hur hand to the Book he would be leve her but If she told the truth and saied she had not seat her hand to the Book a hundred times he would not beleve hur."[171] Even more than the afflicted, confessing witches provided authorities with a valuable source of information concerning invisible truths, so valuable that their efforts to retract confessions given out of opportunism or fear were rigorously discouraged. The authorized destabilization of visible character and the concomitant importance of competing representations, which was the lasting crisis of the witchcraft episode, is brought into relief both by the confessors' belated abhorrence of their having opportunely restructured an identity of whose independent integrity they were convinced and by the authorities' insistence that they conform themselves regardless of their abhorrence (conscience) to the representations of their accusers. Thus the Andover confessors explained how one day, without warning, they were ordered to appear blindfolded at the meetinghouse to touch the Salem afflicted, who were relieved at their touch: a sure sign of guilt. "[A]stonished and amazed, and consternated and affrighted even out of our Reason," the Andover witches were pressed by "our nearest and dearest Relations, seeing us in that dreadful condition, and knowing our great danger" to "confes[s] our selves to be such and such persons, as the afflicted represented us to be." Such pressure, along with the "hard measures" instituted by the authorities, persuaded them to say "any thing and every thing which they desired, and most of what we said, was but in effect a consenting to what they said."[172] In this way, the actual consent to representation by a significant number of witches, motivated by a powerful temptation, occurred after their official indictment for that crime.

The sure sense of their own God-given spiritual identities demonstrated by this group of confessed witches (as opposed to the rapid conversions of character demonstrated by those like Mary Warren) is brought into relief by the strangely Melvillean formulations of a confessor like Rebecca Eames, who prefaced her answers to the magistrates' questions with the phrase "she did not know but that." When asked, for example, if she had had her son baptized by the devil, she replied, "she did not know but she might do it nor I do not know he is a wich but I am afrayd he is."[173] In contrast to Eames's manifest confusion, the confessed witch Martha Tyler clearly related to Increase Mather the tale of her own bewilderment and her ultimate rejection of the false "enlargement" confession would bring her:[174]

> all along the way from Andover to Salem, her brother kept telling her that she must needs be a witch, since the afflicted accused her, and at her touch were raised out of their fits, and urging her to confess herself a witch. She as constantly told him that she was no witch, that she knew

nothing of witchcraft, and begged him not to urge her to confess. However, when she came to Salem, she was carried to a room, where her brother on one side, and Mr. John Emerson on the other side, did tell her that she was certainly a witch.

The psychological torment continued until Tyler "wished herself in any dungeon, rather than be so treated." Although the men threatened to abandon her, to leave her " 'undone, body and soul, for ever,' " Tyler continued to maintain that " 'I shall lie if I confess, and then who shall answer unto God for my lie?' " But the men "continued so long and so violently to urge and press her to confess" and she consequently "became so terrified in her mind that she owned, at length, almost any thing that they propounded to her." She immediately regretted her weakness and acknowledged herself "guilty of a great sin in belying of herself, and desired to mourn for it so long as she lived."[175] Likewise, Mary Osgood regretted having succumbed to the pressure to conform to, or even to concoct, random and incriminating representations. Osgood told Mather of her strategy for satisfying her interrogators' persistent requests for the details of her alleged apostasy, details whose specificity only increases one's sense of their inconsequentiality:

> she considered that about twelve years before (when she had her last child) she had a fit of sickness, and was melancholy; and so thought that that time might be as proper a time to mention as any, and accordingly did prefix the said time. Being asked about the cat, in the shape of which she had confessed that the Devil had appeared to her, &c., she replied, that, being told that the Devil had appeared to her, and must needs appear to her, &c. (she being a witch), she at length did own that the Devil had appeared to her; and, being pressed to say in what creature's shape he appeared, she at length did say that it was in the shape of a cat. Remembering that, some time before her being apprehended, as she went out at her door, she saw a cat, &c.; not as though she any whit suspected the said cat to be the Devil, in the day of it, but because some creature she must mention, and this came into her mind at that time.[176]

The conviction that one's identity cannot be altered at will and that one will "answer unto God" for any attempt to belie it is strikingly evident in the internal pressure these women felt not to conform themselves to the representations of accusers even in the face of death, a pressure that led them to resist and deny the authority of ministers, magistrates, and older brothers. Margaret Jacobs, having confessed against herself, her father, and her grandfather George Jacobs Sr. (executed 19 August 1692), wrote a letter from her "loathsome Dungeon" that she had "confessed several things contrary to my Conscience and Knowledg" and that her "Soul would not suffer me to keep it in any longer," for "Oh! the terrors of a wounded Conscience who can bear." If Mary Warren could, Jacobs clearly could not: "I could not contain myself before I had denied my confession, which I did though I saw nothing but death before me, chusing rather death with a quiet conscience, than to live in such horror, which I could not suffer."[177] In this regard, retracting confessors resembled those who refused to deviate from their claims to innocence and who, as John Proctor (executed 19 August 1692) put it, "know in our own Consciences, we are all Innocent Persons."[178] In her moving and disregarded petition to the governor, magistrates, and ministers, Mary Easty maintained that her "own Innocencye" proved the court's error as it proved the innocence of others among the accused. In this, she upheld the authority of her soul in the face of cultural authority and scrupulously rejected the self-doubling inherent in the act of belying oneself in order to survive: "I cannot I dare not belye my own soule."[179] Along with her sister, Sarah Cloyce, Easty petitioned the magistrates that character witnesses be allowed to testify in their behalf, "Those who have had the Longest and best knowledge of us, being persons of good report," including their pastor and Easty's seven children. Even had they been admitted into evidence, however, such reports would have done the women no more good than had Ann Pudeator's reminder in her petition to the court that one of the men who had testified against her "hath been formerly whipt and likewise is rcorded for a Lyar."[180] Implicit in such suggestions was the conviction that conscience, like visible character, could not be gainsaid, a conviction suddenly and irrevocably rendered obsolete.

The end of the Puritan era was thus marked not only by the dissolution of the self-evident truth of visible character as a reliable index of one's God-given identity, but also by a withdrawal of faith from the concept of essential identity itself. Those admirable men and women accused of witchcraft who stoutly denied their guilt or who boldly retracted their false confessions, upholding the authority of their own souls in the face of merely worldly authority, are not democratic personalities as the afflicted enacted that novel form of subjectivity. Compelled to antinomian claims by their sense of outrage, they upheld their innocence in the name of the integrity of a concept of identity as unassailable, unchanging, and transcendent to which the individual, for better or for worse, is irrevocably bound. The senior minister of Andover, Francis Dane, poignantly recorded this withdrawal of faith from the reliability of visible character and essential identity when he decried, too late, "the Conceit of Spectre Evidence as an infallible mark" which led people to traduce "our neighbours of honest, & good report, & [church] members in full Comunion." Beyond the community's most respected members, Dane lamented, "we so easily parted with our Children, when we knew nothing in their lives, nor any of our neighbours to suspect them."[181] In place of the comparatively solid knowledge gleaned from the infallible marks of reputation, long acquaintance, and church membership, cultural authorities found themselves struggling to understand what modern society terms personality: an individuality which, lacking a transcendent referent, reveals itself in and as a series of representations, each of which might plausibly support the claim to constitute the truth about the self.

Spectacular Conversion: George Whitefield and the Rise of Democratic Personality

He the preacher let him then acquiesce in being nothing that he may move mountains; let him be the mere tongue of us all; no individual but a universal man, let him
leave his nation, his party, his sect, his town-connexion, even his vanity & selflove at
home & come hither to say what were equally fit at Paris, at Canton, and at Thebes.

— RALPH WALDO EMERSON

I

"I think I am never more humble than when exalted," George Whitefield
wrote in his journal on Sunday, 21 January 1739.[1] Ostensibly meant to invoke
the conventional Christian belief in empowerment through meekness and
yet perceptibly at odds with it, this sentiment is reiterated throughout the
spiritual autobiography of the iconoclastic Anglican minister who between
1739 and 1770 undertook an enormously influential series of preaching
"tours" in colonial America. By no means the first evangelical minister to
enthuse an American audience (Jonathan Edwards had recorded a cluster of
"surprising conversions" in the Connecticut River Valley in 1735), Whitefield is yet widely credited with launching an intercolonial religious revival of
unprecedented scope and duration, which many have argued definitively
altered the state of social and political life in the colonies. Known as the
Great Awakening, this grassroots religious movement democratized Ameri-

can religion by shifting the balance of power between minister and congregation.[2] The deference traditionally accorded the Puritan clergy gave way to a spirit of popular criticism while the respectful silence customarily observed in Puritan churches was broken by the cries and groans of a congregation whose religious experience was, according to their conservative detractors, "enthusiastic." Both developments were legitimated, if not explicitly sanctioned, by prominent members of the "New Light," or evangelical, ministry. Many students of the Great Awakening and its aftermath have suggested its central role in the development of an American revolutionary ideology, a development enabled, I would argue, by Whitefield's strategic reconciliation of power and humility.[3]

Whitefield's evangelical energy was fueled by the steady current of opposition from the established ministries of England and America to his charismatic person and unorthodox methods — in particular, to his practice of extemporaneous preaching and to his itinerancy. Endlessly circulating throughout the United Kingdom and the British-American colonies, he exulted in the opposition he so assiduously courted, claiming it as a sign of his professional efficacy that mandated in turn his transgressing the boundaries of established parishes and co-opting the prerogatives of settled pastors in order to gather a congregation of the newly regenerate that neither church wall nor parish line could contain. He augmented his far-reaching influence (for which the physical range of his voice was a fitting image) by traveling with an entourage of devotees who functioned as a press corps, advertising his itinerary and the remarkable success of his field-sermons in local newspapers, and disseminating his journals and sermons through local publishing networks.[4] Initially from curiosity and later from conviction, crowds gathered in unprecedented numbers (the Boston Common sermon of 1740 attracted more than twenty thousand) in the fields, commons, and marketplaces of colonial America to hear the celebrated "Grand Itinerant" preach on the nature and necessity of conversion, or translation out of the limitations of the self and the achievement of a "new birth."[5]

Offering himself to his audiences as a charismatic model of the "new man" — both an exemplary convert and a masterful converter of others — Whitefield used his "wonderful Power" to mobilize people in the name of a new vision of personal, spiritual, and community life. This vision entailed the establishment of a radical itinerant ministry in each of the major colonial denominations, and led consequently to a general fragmentation, or Separation, of constituted parishes.[6] Separate institutions for training and licensing such ministers soon challenged the hegemony of Harvard and Yale as well as the belief that the ability to interpret Scripture depended more on education than on "experimental knowledge of Jesus Christ, and Him crucified" (38), a knowledge by definition available to anyone who sought it. As the young convert Timothy Allen, who abandoned Yale to study divinity at New London's Shepherd's Tent, put it, "I WANTED NOT HUMAN LEARNING, in order *to declare the will of GOD to the World*."[7]

The growth of an itinerant ministry and the progress of Separatism fostered in turn the emergence of a class of lay itinerant preachers, including women, people of color, and even children, who traversed the colonies to exhort others on the glories and the promise of regeneration, transmuting the evangelical impulse into a republican one in the decades before the Revolution.[8] Both the vocal, if inarticulate and even hysterical, "enthusiasm" of the revivalists' congregations (the seemingly irrepressible "roarings, agonies, screamings, tremblings, dropping-down, ravings") as well as the emergence of lay exhorters initiated the debate we normally associate with the Revolution concerning the people's voice: its provenance and the scope and nature of its representativeness.[9]

Whitefield's enabling claim to have reconciled humility and power functioned as the core of his self-representation, both textual and performative: it asserts that the abasement of the self coincides with its exaltation or "enlargement," suggesting a humility — and corollary empowerment — independently achieved rather than mandated as the necessary prerequisite to a future exaltation.[10] But it functioned equally as the prescription for a model of authentic selfhood, intended not simply to mold the behavior of his followers but to enable them to recognize and then legitimate their transformation into "new" — divinely translated — men and women. Whitefield enacted this regenerative — and revolutionary — conjunction of self-debasement and self-exaltation through a religious performance, the field-sermon, an unorthodox form of public worship that I analyze in what follows as "spectacular conversion." The newborn self newly wrought at each step along the itinerant's route was at once integral, translatable, and transferable to others. Its dominant characteristic was the aggressive uncontainability of its speech, which was authorized not despite but because of the prohibitions of established authority: in short, democratic personality in its first fully developed American instantiation.

II

The psychospiritual dynamic that Whitefield both expertly staged before his vast audiences and claimed underlay his own conversion and ministry was determined by his complex relationship to his opposition. As he explicitly stated, opposition was prerequisite not only to professional success but to his own peace of mind: "I never am so much assisted, as when persons endeavour to blacken me, and I find the number of my hearers so increase by opposition, as well as my own inward peace, and love, and joy, that I only fear a calm" (228). For Whitefield, to be was to be embattled: precisely this conviction encapsulated from the first his experience of an "experimental knowledge of Jesus Christ, and Him crucified" (38). This characteristic orientation toward opposition was established in that period of his childhood when he became aware that God had destined him to fulfill some special mission, having "separated me even from my mother's womb, for the work to which He afterwards was pleased to call me" (28). To illustrate his conviction of his calling, he cited in his *Journal* an incident that occurred in his boyhood. Having run from some neighborhood children who had been taunting him, he tearfully knelt in his room and "prayed over that Psalm wherein David so often repeats these words — '*But in the Name of the Lord will I destroy them*' " (28).

As the Lord's instrument and in His name, Whitefield is from this moment determined to "destroy" his opposers by "stopping their mouths," by forcing them "into an awful silence," only to resurrect them continually, at the site of each well-advertised sermon, as the vocally hostile crowd which alone could activate and then validate his divine instrumentality (255, cf. 239).[11] The belligerence of Whitefield's childish prayer thus evolved into the aggressive circularity of his evangelism, whereby the opposers whom Whitefield, as God's agent, makes it his business to destroy are uniquely capable of engendering and then legitimating his sacred agency through their very destruction. For this reason, Whitefield tirelessly courted opposition so that he could, by means of his "enlarged" self, overwhelm it, or more accurately, incorporate it, for upon this progressive incorporation his continual enlargement depended.[12]

The centrality of opposition to Whitefield's project is further borne out by his description of the formative event of his years as a student at Oxford, which he was enabled to attend despite humble family circumstances (his widowed, then divorced, mother ran an inn) by acting as servitor to a number of wealthy students. Early in his Oxford career, the sight of Methodist students proceeding "through a ridiculing crowd to receive the Holy Eucharist at St. Mary's" struck him with the force of revelation: it invigorated his mysterious, because apparently unmotivated, attraction to the outcasts by stimulating in him an irresistible compulsion "to follow their good example" (36). As soon as a plausible excuse afforded him the opportunity, he contacted the mentor of the Oxford Methodists, Charles Wesley.

His association with Wesley and the Methodist students fatefully altered the expected course of his college studies; it "taught me to die daily," he wrote, referring not simply to the work of conversion or rebirth but more pointedly to the fact that the private religious exercises he publicly undertook in order to become "a new creature" turned him into an object of general derision (41). With his cooperation, reluctant at first, Whitefield's private life was converted into public spectacle, but one whose structure of signification was withheld from its audience, Oxford's "polite students" (40). This unsuspected power to make oneself the sign of an unsuspected meaning or value — to secrete spiritual treasure in full view of one's adversaries on the private stage of the self — Whitefield describes as the enviable prosperity of the Methodists, who "never prospered so much in the inward man, as when they had all manner of evil spoken against them falsely without" (39).[13]

So conceived, the process of rebirth was achievable only through the constant circumambient pressure of willful misrepresentation, so necessary to Whitefield, but which rigorously confined the inward man to his inwardness. For Whitefield, however, the measured satisfaction of this secret prosperity was too modest a prize. Not content with his power to flaunt his possession of spiritual treasure before the blind eyes of natural men, Whitefield would transgress the Methodist model of the self to realize what was only implicit in it: the fundamentally dramatic nature of conversion and hence its potential as spectacle.[14] This discovery allowed him to exploit the paradoxical centrality of the outcast in order to stimulate in his hostile spectators a desire for such spiritual currency as he alone possessed and whose disbursement he alone could control.

Unlike the Methodists, then, conversion was for Whitefield not a private moment of grace that invisibly refigured one's orientation to the things and people of this world but rather a public event, an act of revelation that necessarily mobilized a spectatorship, a novel (and potentially revolutionary) social configuration. From the moment he declared his allegiance to the life of the spirit by associating with Wesley and the Methodists, he differentiated his "inward sufferings" from those of his fellows who outwardly suffered with him the daily death of their "fair reputations" (39, 40). His sufferings, he claimed, partook of "a more uncommon nature" (39), notably, in that Satan chose to mislead Whitefield by causing him to pursue "a state of quietism" ("he generally ploughed with God's heifer," Whitefield explained), tempting him with that which Whitefield had never coveted, the prospect of a wholly private privacy:

> When the Holy Spirit put into my heart good thoughts or convictions, he [Satan] always drove them to extremes. For instance, having out of pride, put down in my diary what I gave away, Satan tempted me to lay my diary quite aside. When Castaniza advised to talk but little, Satan said I must not talk at all. So that I, who used to be the most forward in exhorting my companions, have sat whole nights almost without speaking at all. Again, when Castaniza advised to endeavour after a silent recollection and waiting upon God, Satan told me I must leave off all forms, and not use my voice in prayer at all. (44)

Aware that Whitefield had from his "first awakenings to the Divine life . . . felt a particular hungering and thirsting after the humility of Jesus Christ," Satan enjoined Whitefield to perfect silence if he would attain his goal (42). God, however, would give precisely the opposite counsel to the future Grand Itinerant. On the day following his ordination as an Anglican minister at the precocious age of twenty-one, Whitefield claimed to have received a divine directive:

> The next morning, waiting upon God in prayer to know what He would have me to do, these words, "Speak out, Paul," came with great power to my soul. Immediately my heart was enlarged. God spake to me by His Spirit, and I was no longer dumb. (60–61)

The next Sunday, preaching "to a very crowded audience" drawn by curiosity to see the youthful minister, Whitefield found himself exhorting "with as much freedom as though I had been a preacher for some years" (61):

As I proceeded, I perceived the fire kindled, till at last, tho' so young, and amidst a crowd of those who knew me in my childish days, I trust, I was enabled to speak with some degree of Gospel authority. Some few mocked; but most for the present seemed struck: and I have since heard, that a complaint had been made to the Bishop, that I drove fifteen mad, the first sermon.[15]

As his career advanced, Whitefield continued to promote the ritual kindling of the spiritual fires whose flames would inevitably, but nonetheless spectacularly, engulf the outermost ring of his audiences: those who came to dampen, but remained to burn — the opposition.

Whitefield's determination to occupy center stage through his perfection of a theatricalized humility raises the question of his early love for, and ostensible abandonment of, what he later called the "sin and folly" of the drama, both reading plays and playing roles, including the role of minister (54). His youthful ambition to act upon the stage remained an inextricable part of that "holy ambition" of his maturity: "to be one of those who shall shine as the stars for ever and ever."[16] The centrality of the drama to Whitefield's self-conception survived his transformation from the idle adolescent, who spent much of his time "in reading plays, and in sauntering from place to place," to the Grand Itinerant (32). This centrality is perhaps most starkly evident in that eminently dramatic moment when he forswore the pleasure of the drama — even in its most attenuated form, the reading of plays — once and for all. He had unthinkingly picked up a play to read when "God struck my heart with such power, that I was obliged to lay it down again; and, blessed be His Name, I have not read any such book since" (36). Indeed, as he represents it, his earliest intimation of the destiny which awaited him came to him when he was reading a play aloud to his sister, and involuntarily interrupted himself to inform her that "God intends something for me which we know not of" (32).

This incident suggests that the drama was as central to Whitefield's self-conscious construction of his ministerial career as it was to his self-conception, which in turn indicates the simultaneity of these two projects of fashioning — and then representing — the self.[17] In any case, the proliferation of false selves upon which the religious objection to the drama was traditionally based intensified after he claimed to have given up the imaginative identification with another being that constitutes the drama's pleasure. Thus soon after his ordination the approach of some wandering players afforded him his first opportunity to publish. His extract of "Mr. Law's excellent treatise, entitled, *The Absolute Unlawfulness of the Stage Entertainment*," ran for six weeks in a local newspaper, from which Whitefield deduced that "God gave me favour in the printer's sight." God, that is, had apparently consecrated one arena of public self-exposure, the press, even as He had forbidden another, the stage (54).[18]

From his first step into this arena, the press functioned for Whitefield as a legitimate avenue of self-replication. It is not known for certain to what degree Whitefield himself engendered the proliferating and controversial versions of his person and activities that appeared throughout his life in the presses of colonial America and the United Kingdom. It is clear, however, that his vigorous denials of many of them effectively extended their viability. Early in his career, for example, he discovered himself portrayed in the paper as "leaning on a cushion, with a bishop looking very enviously over my shoulder. At the bottom were six lines, in one of which the bishops were styled 'Mitred Drones.'" He added, "The same person [who submitted his picture to the press] published in the papers that I had sat for it." Struggling to find an appropriate way to defend himself against this charge, Whitefield, upon the urging of his "aged" mother, resolves to "sit for my picture in my own defence":

> Meeting with [the painter] one night, accidentally, I, with great reluctance complied, and endeavoured, whilst the painter was drawing my face, to employ my time in beseeching the great God, by His Holy Spirit, to paint His blessed image upon his and my heart. (84)

Similarly, much later in his career he would suffer, as a devoted memoirist expressed it, "a new kind of persecution . . . that of being mimicked and burlesqued upon the stage." Like the newspaper accounts, the burlesquing of Whitefield did not conclude in a merely local controversy, but initiated a long series of textual instantiations, positively and negatively nuanced serial versions of the character George Whitefield that extended well into the nineteenth century.[19]

That he should provide the subject for a burlesque is, of course, a sign in and of itself that he had become universally recognizable, beyond even the enlarged sphere of evangelical itinerancy. Whitefield had become, in fact, a "star," or what the cultural semiotician Lydia Ginzburg has analyzed as "epochal" or historically significant personality. Although Ginzburg bases her theory of the relationship of self-invention to cultural-historical moment upon nineteenth-century personalities and events, it is remarkably relevant to the case of Whitefield, arguably the eighteenth century's most accomplished entrepreneur of the self. Ginzburg defines epochal personality as the self-consciously constructed image of "an ideal conception [of the self] . . . continuously created in everyday life," both dependent on and constitutive of "the historically regulated forms of collective consciousness" in which it has its being. Insofar as it seeks to organize the self into a purveyable image, a symbolic construct of manifest cultural significance, the construction of epochal personality constitutes an essentially aesthetic activity.[20] Although Ginzburg argues that all personalities are organized and received as images or representations of an "inner self," epochal personality constitutes a representation of a different order of magnitude, distinguishing itself as something akin to Kenneth Burke's "god-term," that is, as the ultimate and unitary signified of a culture's diverse signifiers.[21] It offers itself, and is received, as an embodiment of the very principle of meaning for that culture, making manifest a significance that would otherwise remain latent. Given this definition, the epochal personality par excellence, one could argue, would be that of the convert, the one wholly engaged in that process of self-translation by which the "new creature" emerges from the old and, in so doing, claims access to a transcendent meaning available only from a future perspective, that of the end of time. Whitefield's achievement, then, in replacing the drama with his charismatic ministry was to replace what he experienced as his debased subjectivity, which impotently sought release through the imitation of a series of fictional selves, with the epochally significant personality of the convert, and to represent the achievement of epochal personality in and as the quintessential Whitefieldian spectacle, the field-sermon.

The peculiarity of Whitefield's self-representation as the convert in his journals and public appearances was twofold. First, he posited a self wholly consecrated to God, and thus so intimately identified with Him as to enable him to speak and act not as an individual but as the unindividuated agent through whom God chose to speak and act in the world. Second, in direct contradiction to the doctrine of an instantaneously achieved rebirth that was the substance of his sermons, Whitefield represented his own conversion as an ongoing process (consonant with Ginzburg's account of the "continuous creation" of the epochal self) in which God was continually undoing and reconstituting him, so that his character at any given moment in time had to be understood as both incomplete and, in the Bakhtinian sense, finalized.[22]

These two constitutive aspects of his self-representation — self as pure agency and self as simultaneously incomplete and finalized — are immediately remarkable for their apparent incompatibility. It must be understood, however, that both these aspects of Whitefield's idealized self-representation contributed to its extraordinary sinuosity and testify to his uncanny ability to choreograph the transfigurations of his personality with the inflections of his historical moment and, indeed, of each individual conversion performance. More particularly, they allowed him to claim the achievement of an artless, and therefore "innocent," mode of self-representation whose credibility rested precisely on the degree to which it offered itself as both an acknowledgment and a resolution of its constituent incompatibilities. The resolution of these two contradictory modes of self-representation was ensured by the topos of uncontainability central to both, which motivated not only his self-fashioning but also his theology and his evangelism.[23] Each aspect of the epochally significant personality of the convert will be examined in turn in the following sections.

III

The difference between the young Whitefield assuming the role of a minister in a privately imagined scenario and the mature Whitefield preaching before thousands in a spectacle of his own design may be understood as the difference between imitation and impersonation. Imitation here would involve a debased duplication of unworthy or unremarkable selves who, because they possess no real field of action, possess no real identity.[24] It is precisely this sense of existential emptiness that Whitefield's formidable detractor, Charles Chauncy, wished to convey when he characterized the Grand Itinerant's ministry as amounting to a mere "*prophane* Imitation" of Christ.[25] Whereas imitation might be associated with the sin of idolatry, impersonation would signify the kenosis or self-emptying that makes possible the incorporation of the transcendent essence of a supernal other; whereas imitation leads to a depletion of the self, impersonation leads to fulfillment as well as to a legitimate sphere of activity, in short, to a sanctified enlargement and extension of the self. The difference between impersonation and imitation, then, is that between an empowering and miraculous consubstantiality of ontologically unequal or inequivalent selves and a disempowering replication of equally inconsequential selves.

So understood, conversion as Whitefield represented it in the journals and in the field involved an impersonation of God, such that the convert's every word, gesture, decision, and action would directly signify Him, Who would in turn irradiate these with irrefutable meaning and irresistible power. Having consecrated himself to God, Whitefield claimed to be so intimately affiliated with Him as to be for all practical purposes indistinguishable from Him. According to Whitefield's account of his rebirth, God had wholly subsumed him as an individual subject or agent, only to reconceive him as a pure instrument or agency, unalloyed with self, for the realization of God's will, or more specifically, for the articulation of His Word. Impersonating God enabled Whitefield to claim that he exercised legitimately — that is, "innocently," because selflessly — "great boldness," "great liberty," and "freedom of speech" (207, 211, 210, 238).[26] Moreover, the confluence of God and Whitefield provided the occasion for another confluence, the remarkable assemblages of aspiring converts, and transferred those same privileges of bold speech to them.

Whitefield's project of positing a self that was less self or subject than the unambiguous signifier and instrument of divinity is most clearly discerned in those sections of his journal in which he pointedly brings himself and Christ into the same closely circumscribed referential space. This practice earned him much criticism from his clerical adversaries. Expressing their outrage, the Boston Congregationalist and vociferous opponent of the Great Awakening, Charles Chauncy, took Whitefield to task in a public letter of 1745 for his tendency to "magnify" facts, such as the circumstance of his birth in an inn, that were in themselves so *"common"* and "trivial" as to be hardly "worthy of *particular* and *publick* Notice."[27] Trivial and common as they may have been, Whitefield repeatedly alluded to such circumstances in his published journals as, for example, his account of a group of scoffers who "were pleased to honour me so far, as to trail a dead fox, and hunt it about the Hall" in which he was preaching. Afterward, at public worship, he noticed that "in the Second Lesson were these remarkable words: 'And the high priests, and the scribes, and the chief of the people sought to destroy Him; but they could not find what they might do to Him, for all the people were attentive to hear Him'" (224). Whitefield's messianism, however, exceeded the bounds of mere textual allusion and was expressed in the form of publicly staged imitations of Christ, as when he warned his auditors that they should meet him on the last day, and exhorted them, "Behold my hands and my feet! Look, look into my wounded side, and see a heart flaming with love." The adulation shown Whitefield by his more ardent supporters, many of whom insisted upon his "near ... Resemblance with his blessed Master," reflects the success of the techniques Chauncy condemned for their paltriness.[28]

Reprehensible as they were, Chauncy considered such tactics as these far from Whitefield's greatest offenses. In his letter, he cited two instances in which the Grand Itinerant exceeded the limits of mere bad taste and poor judgment. The first derived from a passage in Whitefield's spiritual biography, "A Short Account of God's Dealings with the Reverend George Whitefield, A.B.," devoted to a description of his conversion, which he represents, in accordance with his doctrine, as having occurred instantaneously. In the throes of a prolonged agony of spirit, Whitefield wrote, he suddenly recalled that the crucified Christ had cried out, "I thirst!" immediately before his death and delivery from suffering. Without hesitation, the young aspirant likewise threw himself down upon his bed in his Oxford garret exclaiming "I thirst! I thirst!" and, as he represents it, rose from his bed reborn, "delivered from the burden that had so heavily oppressed me" (48). The moment of Christ's delivery is thus made to refer to the moment of Whitefield's.

Chauncy attributed the extreme sinfulness of the passage not to the fact that he put himself "'on a Level with *Jesus Christ*,'" even though, Chauncy added, he had been a repeat offender in this regard: "this is not the only Instance, wherein your *Fancy* has formed a Kind of Resemblance between *your own*, and the Circumstances of *Christ Jesus*."[29] Rather, Chauncy objects to Whitefield's insinuation of a relationship between himself and divinity far more intimate than mere resemblance: the conversion episode, he wrote Whitefield, "appeared to me very evidently to exhibit a *prophane* Imitation of the *Son* of *God* in his last Sufferings."[30] Through his profane appropriation of Christ's suffering, Whitefield sought to justify his claim to the authenticity of a communion that was in reality a shameful solipsism. Chauncy concluded his reading of this incident in the journal by judging Whitefield's experience of conversion to be as insubstantial as the profane imitation of God upon which it was based: "to tell you the plain Truth, I don't think, nor ever did, that you had *scriptural* Warrant to look upon your self as a *converted* man, in Virtue of any Thing, or every Thing, contained in this Relation of your Christian experience."[31]

The second objectionable incident to which Chauncy refers in his letter extends his indictment of Whitefield's profanity. It concerns the case of a certain Mr. Barber, whom Whitefield had appointed to manage Bethesda, the Georgia orphanage he founded, during his prolonged absences. Barber had written a letter to Whitefield, evidently published, in terms so deferential as to constitute for Chauncy " '*an Act of downright gross Idolatry.*' " To substantiate his accusation, Chauncy quotes from Barber's letter: " 'I shall omit writing any Thing, and only hereby present my hearty Love, and let you know that *I am waiting at the Post of your Door for Admission: Though I am unworthy, my Lord is worthy, in whose Name, I trust, I come.*' "[32] Chauncy identifies Barber's words as an "evident Allusion to those Words of *Wisdom* (by whom is commonly understood the *Lord Jesus Christ, the Wisdom of God*), *Blessed is the Man that heareth me, — waiting at the Posts of my Doors*, Prov. 8.34."[33] Given this source of Barber's address to Whitefield, Chauncy asks:

> Does he not use the *same Form* of Words to encourage a Hope of Admission into *your Presence*, which is commonly used in Prayer when we approach before the great GOD? Are not *you*, in these Words, according to the literal and most obvious Meaning, *the final Object*, and the *great Saviour* the *Medium* of Access to you? . . . If Words can express it, *you* are the Person into whose Presence Mr. *Barber* wanted to come, and Christ is the *Medium* of Approach.[34]

Chauncy's outrage is here directed at the suggestion of a blasphemous typology, in which Whitefield is the object and Christ the medium of access to that object; in which Christ is made to refer to Whitefield (as in the conversion account) rather than Whitefield to Christ; in which, finally, Whitefield represents himself less as a type of Jesus than Jesus a type of Whitefield, the latter having enjoyed more success than the former in converting the opposition.[35] Ironically, the terms of Chauncy's objection to the "idolatry" elicited from those taken in by Whitefield's "profane imitations" of Christ precisely recapitulate William Law's objections to "stage entertainment," the treatise which provided Whitefield with his first opportunity to use the press as an avenue of legitimate "self-enlargement."[36]

That Whitefield was aware of the blasphemous implications of his claims and behavior is suggested by the fact that his frequent hints of an equivalence between himself and God are almost invariably embedded in statements that explicitly assert their radical incommensurability. Just as Saint Paul claimed in 1 Corinthians 15:10, "I labored more abundantly than they all, yet not I," Whitefield claimed that he exerted a "Divine attraction," "extraordinary authority," and a "power" which "few, if any, were able to resist" (234, 239, 269) that yet had no reference to self, but were instead "proofs" of God's ultimate authorship and control of self's appearances and success:

> I have scarce known a time I have preached anywhere, but I have seen some effect of my doctrine. From the hearts of the mighty the Word of the Lord hath not turned back, the Sword of the Spirit returned not empty. A proof this, I hope, that the words are not my own, and that God is with me of a truth. (104; cf. 246)

This denial of authorship — of one's words, of one's self, of one's self-presentation — and simultaneous claim to the status of pure instrumentality allowed Whitefield to enjoy surpassing rhetorical and vocational advantages. The rhetorically nuanced double referentiality of his experience at the English mining town of Kingswood, for example, where he "went upon a mount, and spake to as many people as came unto me," allowed him to assert the incontestable propriety of the controversial practice of field-preaching: "Blessed be God that I have now broken the ice! I believe I never was more acceptable to my Master than when I was standing to teach those hearers in the open fields" (209). Similarly, Christ's approbation (for how could Christ disapprove that which He had Himself performed) also inheres in his decision to preach extemporaneously, rather than from notes: as Whitefield explained to his readers, "I fear I should quench the Spirit, did I not go on to speak *as He gives me utterance*" (198, emphasis added). If here Whitefield may be understood to refer to the mode, rather than the substance, of speech, he unambiguously claims elsewhere that he and God cohabit a single voice, with

God providing the intention and justification of the utterance, and Whitefield the fleshly apparatus necessary to speech. Such an arrangement is
evident, for example, in Whitefield's account of his address to more than
twenty-three thousand people at Hannam, England. Of the information
given him after the sermon's conclusion "that those who stood farthest off
could hear me very plainly," he concluded: "Oh may God speak to them by
His Spirit, *at the same time* that He enables me to lift up my voice like a trumpet!" (232, emphasis added). In this statement, Whitefield claims the simultaneity of God's speaking and his lifting up his voice, even as he denies the
essential — if not the circumstantial — identity of the singular utterance's plu-
ral, ontologically unequal, generators. The exemplary passive-aggressivity of
Whitefield's proclaimed status as God's instrument is captured in the following prayer which, because it is addressed as much to the public as it is to God,
is also an implicit confirmation of the prayer's fulfillment: "O grant I may,
like a pure crystal, transmit all the light Thou pourest upon me, and never
claim as my own what is Thy sole propriety!" (125).

The clerisy's objections to Whitefield's method were collectively centered
on his proclivity to trespass: to appropriate the attributes, and even the
biography, of God, as well as the pastoral prerogatives of his clerical brethren
through the practice of ministerial itinerancy and field-preaching. He consistently defended himself against both these charges not by addressing the
particularities of the accusations but rather by denying, doctrinally as well as
autobiographically, his possession of a "self" to defend. As his adversaries
were painfully aware, the denial of self permitted Whitefield to assert the inevitability of his own words and actions, grounded as they were in the infallibility of the God he claimed not so much to represent as to realize through
the miraculous medium of his own "transparency," his own indefatigable
body and the physical power of his voice. Whitefield's "innocence" in regard
to his opponents' charges, in other words, derived from his self-proclaimed
status as pure agency: what his adversaries saw as his profane manipulations
of press and pulpit for the purposes of an unholy self-aggrandizement, he
portrayed as an artless, because selfless, bringing forth of speech, a self-
representation innocent of self.[37]

This innocence underwrote Whitefield's preeminently evangelical logic
of uncontainability, which comprehended an ideal tautology of message,
messenger, and receiver.[38] The delineation of references in the journals to

that which cannot be contained — God, Whitefield, the Word, and the crowd amassed to hear it — ultimately comprises a totalizing network of synonyms such that to object to Whitefield is to object to God, and to object to White-field's project is to object to the project of evangelical Christianity. Just as Whitefield characterized himself, after Christ and Paul, as having "no con-tinuing city," so he characterized God (for the edification of an opponent who had complained that by preaching in the fields, Whitefield preached on "unconsecrated ground") as "not now confined to places" (112, 305).[39] The uncontainability of God and Whitefield determines the impossibility that "the Word of God should be bound, because some out of a misguided zeal deny the use of their churches" (202). The uncontainability of Whitefield and the Word of God, despite the closing of the churches, is registered in the uncontainability of the crowd drawn to hear them: "I now preach to ten times more people than I should, if I had been confined to the churches." Inherent in the crowd's unconfinability is itinerancy's equally irrepressible justification: "Now know I more and more that the Lord calls me into the fields, for no house or street is able to contain half the people who come to hear the Word" — that is, who come to hear Whitefield (256). Ultimately, the logic of uncontainability, which is the logic of evangelical itinerancy, under-writes Whitefield's anti-institutionalism:

> Great numbers of the inhabitants would have built me immediately, a very large church, if I would have consented; but the Lord, I am per-suaded, would have His Gospel preached in the fields; and, building a church would, I fear, insensibly lead the people into bigotry, and make them place the Church again, as they have done for a long time, in the church walls. (421)[40]

Uncontainability epitomized the God-ness of God, and by extension White-field; God's Word, and by extension Whitefield's words; and finally, God's true church, and by extension, the reach of Whitefield's voice, both material and textual, as well as the range of his body. In sum, uncontainability guaran-teed that Whitefield's peregrinations encompassed the whole "task of typol-ogy": "to define the course of the church ('spiritual Israel') and of the exem-plary Christian life."[41]

Whitefield's uncontainability was consummated in those moments when God's Word, transmitted to the assembled crowd by means of Whitefield's palpable, audible transparency, hit its mark, and delivered, as one of the Grand Itinerant's disciples put it, "a home stroke" (375). Although he describes many such instances in his journal, two seem particularly suggestive of a kind of phenomenology of Whitefieldian uncontainability. The first occurred in October 1740, in Massachusetts, where Whitefield had enjoyed the support of Boston's first ministers (the Reverends Benjamin Colman, Joseph Sewall, and John Webb offered their pulpits to him) as well as the highly visible patronage of Governor Jonathan Belcher. Belcher had personally accompanied him to the Boston Common, where over twenty thousand people had gathered to hear him preach, and had escorted him, with tears and fanfare, to the Charlestown ferry upon his departure from the city. Apparently unable to keep his distance, Belcher then turned up unexpectedly in a crowd assembled to hear Whitefield at Marlborough, some miles outside of Boston, and "though it rained, and he was much advanced in years," escorted Whitefield's party as far as Worcester (476). Having finally parted from the infatuated governor, Whitefield described himself as "upon the mount, indeed" (477).[42] At his next stop, Brookfield, he wrote:

> My soul was upon the wing. I was exceedingly enlarged, and was enabled, as it were, to take the Kingdom of God by force. Oh, what precious hours are those, when we are thus strengthened, as it were, to lay hold on God. Oh, that we should ever cast ourselves down from thence! God be merciful to me a sinner! (477)

Here, Whitefield, self-described as a "Joshua going from city to city, and subduing the devoted nations" (239), is sufficiently enlarged to imagine that he had carried out Joshua's ultimate triumph: the trumpeting of the ram's horn as his own voice, the consequent collapse of the walls sealing off the Kingdom of God, its forceful appropriation and the "laying hold" of its King. In this, Whitefield's, version of the Joshua story, God is cast as the defeated King of Jericho, and Whitefield as commander of the Lord's Army, both Joshua and the incarnation of God he encounters on the plain at Jericho.[43] God yields to the force of Whitefield's trumpetings, relinquishing, in Whitefield's representation, the integrity of what had been His inviolable sanctity; for one heady, rhetorical moment, conquest and communion become indistinguishable. The ambiguity of Whitefield's position is made explicit in the passage's final two sentences, which transmit both his exhilaration at having

successfully achieved, through his bold enlargement and irresistible appropriation of the prerogative of divinity, the status of man-god, translation out
of the limitations of the natural self, as well as his temerity at his own ambitious assault upon God's Kingdom. The increasingly aggressive uncontainability of Whitefield's trajectory—his itinerancy, continuing despite the
opposition of a long-established ecclesiastical and civil order, his influence,
his ambition, and his passion—here carries him to the acme of enlargement
where, through the trumpeting of his voice, he brings down the walls that
had from eternity sealed off mortal access to the Heavenly Kingdom.[44]

The second passage suggests something of the people's responsive enlargement, in this instance so powerful as to threaten to overwhelm Whitefield's own. On this occasion, in a "desert place" outside a Pennsylvania
hamlet, twelve thousand had gathered to hear Whitefield preach. His audience was primed: no sooner had he spoken his first words, he wrote, than "I
perceived numbers melting. As I proceeded, the influence increased, till,
at last, (both in the morning and the afternoon), thousands cried out, so
that they almost drowned my voice." The audience's ecstatic agony of self-
abandonment precipitates Whitefield's own self-translation or conversion,
his own death and rebirth:

> Never did I see a more glorious sight. Oh what tears were shed and
> poured forth after the Lord Jesus. Some fainted; and when they had got a
> little strength, they would hear and faint again. Others cried out in a
> manner, as if they were in the sharpest agonies of death. Oh what
> thoughts and words did God put into my heart! After I had finished my
> last discourse, I was so pierced, as it were, and overpowered with a sense
> of God's love, that some thought, I believe, I was about to give up the
> ghost. How sweetly did I lie at the feet of Jesus! With what power did a
> sense of His all-constraining, free, and everlasting love flow in upon my
> soul! It almost took away my life. (423)

In this instance, the wall that falls is that which distinguished preacher from
congregation; when all are dissolved in an ecstasy that seems to have no
source and negates all distinctions, all "discourse" of necessity comes to
an end.

Accompanying the collapse of the discursive structure which differentiated God and Whitefield, and Whitefield and the surrounding crowd, was

that of the representative function the field-sermons were intended to serve as occasions of public exhortation to sinners and public prayer to God. No longer need Whitefield serve as a channel for representing God's Word to humankind or humankind's words to God. Having rhetorically appropriated the divinity of God "by force" in one instance, and having in the other suffered himself, the people's "mouth unto God," to be swallowed up in the people's voice, Whitefield's self-as-agency, that embodiment of the doubled self's final moments before its unrepresentable resolution in a transcendent integrity, achieves its apotheosis in these twin moments of self-insemination. With the delivery of the "home stroke," self-as-agency attains such a degree of enlargement that it overwhelms itself as channel, floods its own banks, and submerges everything surrounding it in its own element. This is the conversional moment: when the enlarged self of Whitefield converges, at the height of spiritual ecstasy, with the mimetically enlarged voice of the crowd, and the oppositional, divisive voice of the scoffers is reborn as the all-encompassing voice of the people.

IV

Insofar as they bear a generic resemblance to all other conversion narratives, whose burden is to present as dramatically as possible a life trajectory whose teleology is well known, Whitefield's autobiographical writings characterize their subject as simultaneously incomplete and finalized. In the introduction to the account of his own conversion (first published in 1740 and prefixed, in expurgated form, to the 1756 edition of the collected journals that chronicle his ministry), he distinguishes two versions of himself, one past ("what I was by nature") and one present ("what I am by grace") (26). The distinction is a conventional one: as John Freccero has described it with reference to Dante, the voice of the "poet" represents the valid and eternal self, and as such the possessor of what Bakhtin would call the text's finalizing consciousness, who evaluates the thoughts and activities of the "pilgrim," the partial and obsolescent self, while narrating them.[45]

The moment of conversion, when these two versions of the self come together, is narratologically the most problematic. As a New Light theologian, Whitefield rejected what he considered to be the Arminian notion of a preparationist conversion that would occur through what his great foe, Alexander Garden, approvingly called an *"Oeconomy* of Grace": "a *gradual co-operating* Work of the *Holy Spirit*; commencing at *Baptism*, and gradually advancing throughout the whole Course of the Christian Life."[46] Instead, Whitefield upheld the Pauline model of an instantaneous rebirth: "an immediate, *instantaneous* Work of the *Holy Spirit*, wrought inwardly on the Hearts or Souls of Men, *critically* at some *certain* Time, in some *certain* Place, and on some *certain* Occasion" — as the radical New Light Andrew Croswell put it, "in the *twinkling of an Eye.*"[47] This work of the Holy Spirit is accomplished through the total passivity of its object ("as a Clock or Watch is under the Hands of the Artificer," Garden noted derisively), and its rationale was as indecipherable to human wisdom as its timing was indeterminate.[48] Practically and doctrinally considered, then, even taking the rationale of impersonation into account, Whitefield could not claim himself to have delivered the reconceiving blow. Instead, he used the conversion spectacle to reenact the original drama of his own rebirth, itself, as we have seen, a reenactment of Jesus' passion.

The journals, too, by cataloging each successive performance, rehearsed a metamorphosis that was, by definition, entirely singular. Although the scenario remained eternally the same, each stop on Whitefield's itinerary possessed the undifferentiated specificity of a reenactment: an oppositional encounter for which success entailed further opposition which, predictably overcome, entailed success. The repeated threat of personal dissolution and the repeated thrill of divinely aided reconstitution contribute to the vitality of an autobiographical narrative in which all major details, actors, and events are revisited. Each event is both anomalous and reenacted, each sermon (as Benjamin Franklin noted in his *Autobiography*) both extemporaneous and rehearsed.[49]

Whitefield's experience of illness aptly illustrates his ability to invest repetition with dynamism and drama. The physical rigors of the itinerant's life, especially in the vast, unsettled areas of the American colonies, perhaps suggested to him the representational possibilities of the overwhelming exhaustion he suffered immediately prior to his personal appearances. As he described it in his journals, his private struggle with bodily infirmity paralleled his public struggle with external adversity in the form of "natural men." Each paired episode features a nearly fatal encounter with the debilitating forces of negation, a last-ditch summoning of the supernal energy required to overwhelm the opposition, and then, at last, victory, experienced as an incrementally achieved enlargement of the self. As an internalization of the spectacle of conversion, in which oppositional otherness was continually surmounted and overtaken by an ever-expanding self, Whitefield's failing health entered into each of his performances as its proem or prelude, integral to the powerful flow of words that followed.

The Pennsylvania event just recounted was not unique in Whitefield's experience. After preaching to twenty thousand people on Kennington Common (near London), for example, and collecting over forty-six pounds for his pet project, the Georgia orphanage, Whitefield found himself enjoying a pleasure so profound it accomplished that which had foiled all his opponents and the devil himself: the stopping of Whitefield's mouth.

> God was pleased to pour into my soul a great spirit of supplication, and a sense of His free distinguishing mercies so filled me with love, humility, and joy, and holy confusion, that I could at last only pour out my heart before Him in an awful silence. It was so full, that I could not well speak. Oh the happiness of communion with God! (258)

Aside from its chronicling a rare instance of Whitefield's submission to a power stronger than his will to speak, this passage is remarkable for its implicit characterization of speech as symptomatic of humankind's fallen condition. Speech is a creaturely impulse, the lot of one who possesses a body, the sign of one's alienation from God, and thus from the ground of meaning, which in turn condemns the speaker to the onerous necessity of speech. Above all, holy speech—prayer and sermon—is not exempt from this indictment of the true character of language as indicative of the absence of fullness, for, as Whitefield put it, if one is full, one cannot well speak, and if humankind were not separated from God as a result of its own sinfulness, neither prayer nor exhortation would be necessary. Because the gap between speech and meaning was ineluctable, it constituted a particularly burdensome condition of employment for the archspeaker, Whitefield, and those like him who dared to denounce the "unconverted ministry," those "dead, false-hearted preachers . . . who hold the form of sound words, but have never felt the power of them in their own souls" (405), and thus were condemned to reenact the fallenness of language with each effort to bring sinners to a knowledge of their precarious condition.

Preaching was thus for Whitefield the most exalted and the most debased of moments. His unconquerable drive to speak ("It is hard work to be silent") through which he realized (albeit temporarily) his aspiration to transcendent being and acknowledged the futility of such an aspiration recalls, in its poignancy, Edward Taylor's poetic obsession, constantly thematized in his poetry, with the need to accept the pathetic fragility of the linguistic enterprise as humankind's best hope.[50] Speech is both the unique means to transcendence and precisely that human activity which transcendence reveals as "nought"; it is the means to communion and yet its absence is the truest sign that communion has occurred. It represents the ultimate human effort to escape the limitations of the mortal, single self and the most burdensome of mortality's shackles. Death, and particularly death in the pulpit, becomes Whitefield's oft-reiterated wish, as the only way in which the paradox of speech — as a metaphor for the miracle of conversion, which brings life out of death, exaltation out of humiliation — could, as it were, be consummated: "O that I had as many tongues, as there are hairs upon my head! the ever-loving, ever-lovely *Jesus* should have them all. Fain would I die preaching." Only death in the pulpit would publicly seal Whitefield's achievement of an irreversible conversion, a passage in which he would be made, at last, "perfectly whole."[51]

As it was, however, Whitefield continued to live, and toiled unceasingly for thirty-five years to maintain the all-too-human, if formidable, ubiquity of itinerancy. Endlessly circulating throughout the American colonies and the United Kingdom, repeatedly overwhelming the opposition at each successive village, Whitefield was yet relieved from the limitations of the self only in the pulpit, in the space of a sermon. Only the timelessness and placelessness of preaching earned him moments of communion with others and with the divine; only the Sisyphean labor of preaching so consumed him as to extend the hope of effecting one day the longed-for, final translation into wordlessness.

For this reason, the pulpit was both the cause of and the sole cure for the "continual vomitings" he suffered between sermons. It was as if, for Whitefield, all of life was orality, and orality comprised but a single pair of alternatives: either holy speech issued from one's mouth or the noxious efflux of one's own mortality.

Fear not your weak body; we are immortal till our work is done. *Christ's* labourers must live by miracle; if not, I must not live at all; for God only knows what I daily endure. My continual vomitings almost kill me, and yet the pulpit is my cure, so that my friends begin to pity me less, and to leave off that ungrateful caution, "Spare thyself."[52]

To a remarkable degree, Whitefield segregated the two signifieds of speech — as a means to salvation and a sign of damnation — and then linked kenosis and emesis in a cycle such that when he stopped preaching he began to vomit, and when he wished to stop vomiting he preached. As with the medieval sufferers of "holy anorexia," the death of the body represented the only possibility of release.[53] For Whitefield only death in the pulpit would break the cycle (as Hawthorne's Dimmesdale well knew) and bring about the apotheosis of holy speech as a pure product, untainted by the fetid breath of mortality. As it turned out, Whitefield's actual death, from an asthmatic attack in Newburyport, Massachusetts, in September 1770, was immediately preceded by the spasmodic production of much "phlegm and wind" which issued from him in lieu of words as he tried in vain to beg for air.[54]

The peculiar pathos or "triumphant ignominy" of the vomiting/preaching cycle to which the concern of Whitefield's supporters testifies is also discernable at the heart of his presentation of conversion as spectacle.[55] Only rarely did the sermon experience procure for him that blessed silence in which the circularity of vomiting and preaching was replaced with a circulation of spirit, by which God "pour[ed] into" his supplicant's soul love, humility, and joy, and Whitefield, "filled" beyond satiety with this spirit, "pour[ed] out his heart . . . in an awful silence." (Whitefield's hard-won "awful silence" before God is, of course, akin, especially in its impermanence, to the "awful silence" of his vanquished opposers before him.) It was more typically the case that for any given sermon Whitefield's (or God's) ability or will to release and the congregation's (or Whitefield's) ability to receive and contain the full volume of the spiritual current were limited. These inevitable limitations were marked by the primacy of voice (Whitefield's and his auditors') as the distinguishing feature of spectacular conversion. Limitation, in providing the occasion for the release of voice — as exhortation, prayer, plea, and lament — was rather the point of a Whitefield sermon on the necessity of the new birth. Accordingly, no eyewitness to a field-sermon or street-sermon claimed to have braved exposure to the elements and the crowd in order to share in a communal silence. At best, precisely the opposite would occur: namely, the convergence of enlarged voices in a transcendent moment of mutual ecstasy which, however transporting, constituted a mere adumbration or shadow of a true, because sustained, state of communion with the divine. If communion is signified by silence, then it must be conceded that communion, or unification with Christ (understood to be the desired fruit of the conversion experience), was not precisely what the eager crowd was after.

The mass of newspaper accounts, published testimonials, and rumors that circulated in advance of Whitefield's individual appearances (many, as Frank Lambert has shown, originating with him or his ministerial entourage who acted as his "press agents") offers a clue to his success in attracting the largest crowds ever assembled in the colonies. These accounts prepared the spectator to recognize in Whitefield, as the source of his extraordinary vitality, a remarkable synesthesia of radical incompatibilities. For the space of a sermon, the body and voice of the itinerant seemed simultaneously occupied by divinity and mortality. Members of his audience have described how the exemplary "new man," himself re-newed for and through each performance, appeared to his audience as one visibly accompanied by the "Presence of GOD," one upon whom the Holy Ghost had "observably" fallen, one whose preaching was imbued with an audible "divine power and energy."[56] Chauncy disdainfully conceded that Whitefield was widely considered "no meer Man"; he reported to a correspondent in Scotland that when Whitefield "came to *Town* . . . he was received as though he had been an *Angel of God*; yea, *a God come down in the Likeness of Man.*"[57] The spectator thus anticipated the inherent drama of immortality inhabiting mortality, of immortality ventriloquizing mortality, articulating in the process an extraordinary syntax in which the transformation of the old man into the new was, as if for the first time, made representable.

Dominated by the exclusive, alternating imperatives of vomiting and preaching, Whitefield's body functioned as a sort of mobile arena in which mortal limitation struggled ceaselessly (and visibly) with divine inspiration. The field-sermon augmented the spectacular dimension of the itinerant's tormented body, insofar as the body served on those occasions, in the absence of a church, as the theater in which flesh and spirit, mortality and divinity, labored visibly together to enact the conversional moment. This highly theatricalized moment was marked by the overtaking — the silencing — of the opposition, both externalized as scoffers and internalized as psychological resistance or bodily frailty. The opposition receding into the silence of obsolescence, the "new man," the convert as epochal (historically significant) personality, emerged out of and away from the oppositional old before the astonished eyes of the spectator. By dramatically prolonging the conversional moment, Whitefield was thus able to represent, in the staged experience of the exemplary convert, the coming-into-being of epochal personality. Through this representation, his audience was enabled to appropriate mimetically both the conversion experience and the character of the exemplary convert. The success of this double transaction was verifiable as the voice which emerged from the midst of the hitherto unmeaning, because silent and therefore characterless, crowd. The emergence of the people's voice, in turn, lent itself to characterization (of its emergence as well as of the voice itself) and thus to the possibility of mimetic appropriation by others.

The character-building properties and the social dynamics of spectacular conversion are vividly represented in the spiritual journal of a Connecticut farmer, Nathan Cole (1711–83).[58] This record of Cole's experience of acquiring "experimental knowledge" of Whitefield, and through him of "Jesus Christ and Him crucified," is tellingly entitled "The Spiritual Travels of Nathan Cole" (c. 1765). Cole opens his account with a one-sentence description of himself as being, up until the day of Whitefield's arrival, an Arminian (a believer in the power of good works to help bring an individual to salvation). From the second sentence, however, the reader is given to understand that the coming of Whitefield revolutionized Cole's character, beginning with a sense of "conviction" that develops when rumors of the Grand Itinerant's evangelical power unsettle him in his complacency:

> Now it pleased God to send Mr. Whitefield into this land; and my hearing of his preaching at Philadelphia, like one of the Old apostles, and many thousands flocking to hear him preach the Gospel; and great numbers were converted to Christ; I felt the Spirit of God drawing me by conviction. (92)

His conviction increasing daily with reports of Whitefield's approach, Cole "on a Sudden, in the morning about 8 or 9 of the Clock" received a visit from "a messenger" who brought news that the minister would preach in nearby Middletown that very morning at ten (92).

Cole poignantly describes the urgency with which, upon hearing the tidings of Whitefield's arrival, he dropped his work, ran "with all my might" to get his horse, and hastened with his wife to Middletown "as if we were fleeing for our lives" (92, 93). As he nears his destination, Cole's imagery becomes increasingly apocalyptic: a quotidian event, the gathering of a crowd to hear a sermon, occasions a dreamlike revelation, breathlessly conveyed, of some general and inexorable death from which all the shadowy "living" are silently, desperately attempting to flee.[59] For its demonstration of a striking consonance between Cole's psychological state and the thematics of White-field's sermon on the necessity of the new birth, this passage merits quoting at length:

> On high land I saw before me a Cloud or fogg rising; I first thought it came from the great River, but as I came nearer the Road, I heard a noise something like a low rumbling thunder and presently found it was the noise of Horses feet coming down the Road and this Cloud was a Cloud of dust made by the Horses feet; it arose some Rods into the air over the tops of Hills and trees and when I came within about 20 *rods* of the Road, I could see men and horses Sliping along in the Cloud like shadows and as I drew nearer it seemed like a steady Stream of horses and their riders, scarcely a horse more than his length behind another, all of a Lather and foam with sweat, their breath rolling out of their nostrils every Jump; every horse seemed to go with all his might to carry his rider to hear news from heaven for the saving of Souls, it made me tremble to see the Sight, how the world was in a Struggle; I found a Vacance between two horses to Slip in mine and my Wife said law our Cloaths will be all spoiled see how they look, for they were so Covered with dust, that they looked almost all of a Colour Coats, hats, Shirts, and horses.
>
> We went down in the Stream but heard no man speak a word all the way for 3 miles but every one pressing forward in great haste and when we got to Middletown old meeting house there was a great Multitude *it was said to be 3 or 4000* of people Assembled together; we dismounted and shook of[f] our Dust; and the ministers were then Coming to the meeting house; I turned and looked towards the Great River and saw the ferry boats Running swift backward and forward bringing over loads of people and the Oars Rowed nimble and quick; every thing men horses and boats seemed to be Struggling for life; *The land and banks over the river looked black with people and horses* all along the 12 miles I saw no man at work in his field, but all seemed to be gone. (93)

The description of Whitefield which follows this passage is notable, first, for its disingenuous admission that the mere rumors of the preacher's power were themselves so potent as to produce in Cole a debilitating physical reaction to his words even before they were uttered: "my hearing how God was with him every where as he came along it Solemnized my mind; and put me into a trembling fear before he began to preach" (93). The impact of Whitefield's actual presence was further heightened for Cole by his awed apprehension of the young minister as a type of man-god who "Lookt almost angelical . . . as if he was Cloathed with authority from the Great God" (93). The extent to which Cole is impressed by the fresh-faced appearance of the "minister of thunder" is revealed in the multiple redundancies to which he resorts in order to describe him: Whitefield appeared "a young, Slim, slender, youth . . . with a bold undaunted Countenance," upon whose brow "*a sweet sollome solemnity sat*" (93). When they finally came, his words delivered to the trembling Cole "a heart wound": "my old Foundation was broken up," he relates, "and I saw that my righteousness would not save me; then I was convinced of the doctrine of Election" (93).

So begin Cole's spiritual travels, as well as his journey into character, and thus his narratological viability. Whitefield's sermon, at which the unassuming farmer was "called out . . . to stand as witnes for the cause of Christ," plunged him into a prolonged struggle with the conviction that "the guilt of Sin" had "undone" him for eternity (122, 94). During this period in which Cole struggled to comprehend his own deconstruction, he fluctuated between anger against God for the unjustness of election, extreme self-pity, marked by the Miltonian refrain " — Poor — Me — Miserable — me" (94), and, worst of all, a growing sense of indifference so that "my heart was as hard as a Stone: my Eyes were dry, once I could weep for my Self but now cannot shed one tear; I was as it were in the very mouth of hell" (95). Cole's spiritual turning point, which enabled him to "s[ee] with new eyes" and which provided him with "A new God; new thoughts and new heart" and a hope that he might yet undergo conversion, entailed God's personal appearance before him as he lay near death, suffering from "the fever and bloody flux" (97, 95):

God appeared unto me . . . and I was Shrinked into nothing; I knew not whether I was in the body or out, I seemed to hang in open Air before

> God, and he seemed to Speak to me in an angry and Sovereign way what
> won't you trust your Soul with God. (96)

In his stern address to Cole on his deathbed, God demands to know whether
He might be granted the authority to decide on the eternal fate of His
creatures without first consulting Cole. The latter's response is immediate:
"My heart answered O yes, yes, yes; before I could stir my tongue or lips"
(96). The following day, Cole's doctor acknowledges the positive change in
his patient's appearance and ascribes it to "conversion," whereby Cole understands that his hitherto nameless experience comprehended both eternal soul
and mortal body (98; cf. pp. 113–14).

As Cole describes it, the incident recalls his initiation into the project of
rebirth at Whitefield's Middletown sermon. Upon reading his account of his
deathbed experience, the reader is reminded of his representation in the
earlier passage: the liminality of human existence and human consciousness
hovering in a twilight state between life and death, the destruction of his
"Foundation" in the oddly claustrophobic context of open air, the speaker's
manifest and sovereign authority, his stern and direct address seemingly to
the very heart of the individual auditor, the latter's bodily distress and then
impulsive and responsive, equally direct heart-speech. Once recovered, Cole
finds that word of his spiritual "discovery" had spread, and his presence is
immediately requested at the sickbed of another who demands to know
"what God has done for your Soul": "I gave him a relation of it," Cole writes,
"he said I never heard a better Scriptural Conversion in my life" (98). The
neighbor's pronouncement on the authority and efficacy of Cole's trial narrative concerning his peculiar experience, which he later learns to recognize as
his conversion, marks the beginning of Cole's travels in the service of evangelicalism. In short, Cole asserted the fact of his new birth by assuming the
mantle of Whitefield.[60]

When at last he felt confident of his spiritual destiny, Cole records his
impulse to isolate himself in order to preserve his hard-won sense of security.
An interlocutor identified only as "an Old Christian," however, advised him
that he must instead descend from his private "mount pisgah" and "travel
through a Rough wilderness yet and have the Sons of Anak to encounter
with" (100). The Old Christian's words confirmed that the evangelical torch
had been passed on that crucial day in Middletown with which Cole's autobiography and his sense of his vocation begin: the humble farmer is warned

from retreating into privacy, into silent communion, and so prepares himself to appear before the crowd — in one case, an assembly convened to determine whether he was liable, as a Separatist, to pay Connecticut's mandatory tax to the standing ministry.[61] There, through an impassioned and scripturally fortified challenge to the law, he stimulates in his hearers a "sober amaze . . . as if I had been some strange Creature, from some other nation or World" (121).

Cole's early experience of conviction as a kind of personal deconstruction cedes to a conviction regarding the necessity of speaking out, notwithstanding his acknowledgment that

> I have an impediment in my speech and my gift is such when I try to exhort; I can only give out A few blundering hints; and Jump from one thing to another, as if I could do no good but rather prejudice the people's minds against me. (118)

Instead of letting his impediment silence him, Cole developed a rationale for public speaking which foregrounded his debility as a means for increasing the effectiveness of his words. In his account of the effect of his compromised "gift," or speech, upon his listeners, Cole compares the latter to sheep who will regurgitate the coarsest hay until it is "better than it was when they ate it":

> though I had but a blundering way of uttering my gift; Yet I might at some proper seasons give out a blundering hint; and because they are blundering; they may be more likely to strike the minds of the people and abide; more than a smooth way of speaking; and when the people are gone away and are got alone, they will it may be bring up these blundering hints into their minds again; and meditate upon them; and make them better than when I gave them out; and by this their minds may be kept from rambling so much after things that are Sinfull etc. (118–19)

It was not until 1765 that Cole resolved to supplement his modest career in public speaking ("exhort[ing] and speak[ing] often to the Saints" [118]) by writing his spiritual autobiography. Like Whitefield before him, Cole in so doing extended his opportunities for legitimate self-enlargement in the service of self-transcendence. His account of his spiritual journey begins with a description of how in Middletown he had been "called forth" by Whitefield to war against the "hypocritical" authorities (101), to bear witness for Christ, and to "convert [others] into the separation" (125), and concludes on an optimistic note, with a happy pun. Reflecting with melancholy on the deaths of the last of those who in 1747 had separated with him from the Saybrook churches, he mused:

> i was as a poor old coal buryed up in the ashes as if there was no fire to be seen but the Lord seemed to shew that in time a little spark of fire would come out of these ashes from that coal and cat[c]h fire to a brand that was neer and that brand catches fire to some brands that lay hear and there and the fire began to burn more and more and keept increasing until it arose to a much greater height then ever it was before in Kensington etc. (125–26)[62]

In a summary of his experience which appears toward the close of his manuscript, Cole emphasizes not the completion of his project of rebirth but rather its uncompletability:

> I was called forth to war and to live by faith and not by sight; and now I lived a long time I do not hardly know how to tell — some times up and some times down; some times look back and call all into Question, and then hope and try to press forward. (101)

Although the condition of character had been established — the circumstance of having been "called forth" — the absolute fulfillment of that condition remained forever on the horizon, even if Cole understood that that fulfillment was ultimately guaranteed. Cole had been called forth by Whitefield, who thus was instrumental in his rising out of the anonymity of complacency (the death of relying on a wholly insubstantial self) and in his efforts to acquire and then build a character at once integral, translatable, and transferable to others, a sign of one's election. Thus, Cole's autobiography records his incremental coming-into-being insofar as it records his ongoing struggle with the opposition: his own contempt and indifference, followed by physical collapse; all variety of natural men from his old Arminian friends to the tax authorities of Connecticut; and, most painfully, his wife, tormented with doubts just as Cole had been tormented, but whose inability to overcome them branded her as one excluded from the community of saints and the hope of eternal life. Nowhere is Cole's understanding of his self-possession more soberly asserted than in his account of how he came to realize that his wife's slide into the living hell of insanity, her disintegration and increasing isolation, meant that although he loved her, God clearly did not. The tentativeness Cole expresses in the passage just quoted should thus not be taken to imply that the process of rebirth was ultimately a failure, or that its outcome remained uncertain, because "the downs" — the continual, at times brutal, and dependably protean opposition — made possible "the ups" — the individual triumphs that taken together constituted the process and the promise of rebirth through the acquisition and growth of legitimate character.

Once called forth to struggle for life, Cole moves from an understanding of rebirth as wholly private, a drama confined within the closely circumscribed space of one's own mind and body, toward an experience of rebirth as occurring through public exhortation and then textual self-extension. Self-characterized on the model of Whitefield, Cole made himself available to other selves not yet narratively viable. In so doing, he demonstrated his successful appropriation of something of Whitefield's instrumentality, his transactional ability to provide others with an identity (a calling) which, itself possessing this quality of transferability, generated a novel type of imagined community, what Jonathan Edwards grandly envisioned as the Kingdom of God in America.[63] Cole's story rehearses, above all, Whitefield's self-fulfilling prophecy: the revealed centrality of the seemingly marginalized character, and thus the representativeness of his story about his struggle to realize and then assert that centrality. The claim to representativeness legitimates the narrative of self, authorizes its telling, and prepares the ground for future tellings. The movement Whitefield inspired was one distinguished, as its critics were furiously aware, by the ascendancy of a new voice, the voice of democratic personality.

Although Cole's narrative is one of many such testimonials of this transference, a particularly concise example of a spectator's mimetic appropriation of Whitefield's character and voice is provided by an account "of a Reformation among some Gentlemen, at Boston," published in the English revival party's organ, *The Weekly History*, for 17 October 1741.[64] The writer tells the story of a wealthy Boston gentleman, "a great Hater of Religion, and especially Mr. *Whitefield's* Preaching," who "one Day as he was walking in his Room . . . thought he heard Mr. *Whitefield*" concluding a prayer and beginning a sermon (3). The voice sounded to the perplexed gentleman as if it were coming from somewhere in his house. Upon investigation, it turned out to be "one of his Negroes preaching" (4). No longer "pensive," but rather greatly amused at the success of his servant's imitation, the wealthy man the following day invited a group of friends to "an Entertainment": "*Come,*" he told his company, "*I'll entertain you with Mr. W's Preaching: For my Negroe can preach as well as he*" (3, 4). The "Negroe," the writer reported, "had the very Phrases of Mr. *Whitefield,*" and, amidst the laughter of the company, began his exhortation:

> *I am now come to my Exhortation; and to you my Master after the Flesh: But know I have a Master even Jesus Christ my Saviour, who has said that a Man cannot serve two Masters. Therefore I claim Jesus Christ to be my right Master; and all that come to him he will receive. You know, Master, you have been given to Cursing and Swearing, and Blaspheming God's holy Name, you have been given to be Drunken, a Whoremonger, Covetous, a Liar, a Cheat, &c. But know that God has pronounced a Woe against all such, and has said that such shall never enter the Kingdom of God.* (4)

The writer, who had heard the story from "an eminent Divine," concluded:

> The Negroe spoke with such Authority that struck the Gentlemen to Heart. They laid down their Pipes, never drank a Glass of Wine, but departed every Man to his own House: and are now pious sober Men; but before were wicked profane Persons. Such is the Work of God by the Hands of poor Negroes: We have such Instances every Week from some Part of the Country or other. (4)[65]

Whether this exemplary conversion really occurred or whether it represents merely a fantasy of empowerment, it nevertheless illustrates how prevalent was the expectation that the voice of Whitefield would, in the process of spectacular conversion, "discover itself in Multitudes."[66]

V

Whitefield offered his journals not as the mere record of a reiterated event, the conversion of sinners, but rather as the transcript of an epic quest (for opposers) and conquest (of opposers) conducted by an ever-enlarging hero whose growth was calculable in the number of adversaries overwhelmed and taken in. His sensitivity to the most pressing question of the revival — namely, how to sustain the religious fire once kindled — can be gauged in his sense of the importance not simply of a constantly resurrected opposition but of one placed squarely in center stage. Whitefield made his relationship to the opposition the focus of his sermon in order to convert his audience from neutrality to partisanship, to dramatize his own rebirth, and to ensure a showing of his adversaries at the next performance. His strategic placement of the opposition at the conceptual center of the conversion experience reinforced his claims for its remarkably protean nature: manifesting itself somatically (as disease), socially (as a hostile corps of powerful and established natural men), psychologically (as his own or others' fear, anger, or indifference), and cosmically (as the machinations of Satan), the ubiquity of the opposition called for an equal effort at ubiquity on the part of the exemplary convert. As long as the opposition could be incrementally contained, on any of these fronts, its seeming irrepressibility simply confirmed the uncontainability of the continually enlarging self of the convert.

The hero's forward movement as well as his growth in grace, both synonymous with his narrative's continuation if not precisely its development, could be capped only when the translation of adversaries into acolytes was complete: the hero was thus, in theory, uncontainable. The primary fact of the journals and the field-sermons was not that of the originary conversion experience, reenacted for the edification of successive congregations on the itinerant's route, but rather the quality of uncontainability transferred to the "new man" in the process of conversion and the conditions it continually imposed on him, in particular the duty or "gift" of public speech.

As the means of overcoming the opposition, the voice of the convert also served as the primary means, and thus as the signifier, of self-enlargement. For this reason, it is the voice of the convert as epic hero — a voice that continually insists upon its occupation of the boundary between the material and spiritual, the visible and invisible realms — that reveals uncontainability to be the dominant of his character. The voice of the convert, rather than his experience per se, constituted the prime object of his auditors' mimetic desire. The degree to which the manifest power of Whitefield's voice had been successfully appropriated by the acolyte could be verified to the extent that

he or she transcended the limitations of a merely private existence and acceded to the public sphere by means of a voice inexorably rising, as if summoned by an external power, from out of a rigorously mandated silence.

If the instance cited at the end of the previous section of the black servant
delivering himself of Whitefield's words in order to deliver his master from
sin confirms this transfer of vocal power, one must also notice who is emancipated at the conclusion of the slave's ringing and explicitly subversive address. The slave is invited to speak, but only to secure his master's liberation
from his own enslavement to sin. The account thus suggests that, despite the
black itinerant ministry to which Whitefield's own apparently gave rise as he
traversed the British-American colonies, he and his followers envisioned a
wholly different model of authentic selfhood for their black auditors from
that for their white.[67] The comparatively limited emancipation intended for
black Christians qualified not only Whitefield's claim to uncontainability
but, inevitably, his enactment of it in the course of the conversion spectacle.
This fatal restriction is clearly revealed in his journal account of his experience preaching to largely black audiences in the Bermudas from March
through mid-June 1748.[68]

In the Bermudas, Whitefield confronted for the first time audiences composed mainly of enslaved blacks. He responded by seeking to control the
reception of his sermon through a rigorous supervision of his principled
practice of extemporaneous speech. To account for his uncharacteristic restraint, Whitefield described his black auditors' unexpected response to a
sermon preached on the first of May. Aware of what the racial composition of
his audience would be, Whitefield had endeavored to tailor his address to the
peculiar limitations of his black auditors as he imagined them:

> As the sermon was intended for the negroes, I gave the [white] auditory
> warning, that my discourse would be chiefly directed to them, and that I
> should endeavour to imitate the example of *Elijah*, who when he was
> about to raise the child, contracted himself to its length. (165)

The tactic of contraction appeared to work: Whitefield celebrated his own
social acumen and rhetorical subtlety at the conclusion of his journal entry
for 1 May, "I believe the Lord enabled me so to discourse, as to touch the
negroes, and yet not to give them the least umbrage to slight or behave
imperiously to their masters" (165).

His confidence was shaken the following day when a group of black auditors informed him that they had disapproved of his sermon and would no
longer attend them:

> They expected, they said, to hear me speak against their masters. Blessed
> be God, that I was directed not to say any thing, this first time, [about]
> the masters at all, though my text led me to it. It might have been of bad
> consequence, to tell them [the masters] their duty, or charge them too
> roundly with the neglect of it, before their slaves. (166)

Extrapolated from Matthew 10:16, the lesson Whitefield derived from this
experience is, considering the principle of unrestricted speech that underlay
his ministerial practice, noteworthy: "If ever a minister in preaching, need
the wisdom of the serpent to be joined with the harmlessness of the dove, it
must be when discoursing to negroes," some of whose hearts, Whitefield
opined, were "as black as their faces" (165, 166).[69]

As the expression of an evangelical strategy, Whitefield's concluding statement represents a reversal, however temporary, of the direction and energy
of his ministerial practice, a fatal moment of prudence that undermines the
integrity of his self-representation as an uncontainable force dedicated to
realizing a universalist church.[70] In Bermuda, Whitefield confronted the
limits of his own vision — that he could not bring himself to contemplate the
uncontainable enlargement of black Christians. He codified this lapse in his
published "Prayer for a poor Negroe," in which he counseled black Americans to bless God for bringing them into "a christian country," to be content
with their condition and eschew rebellion, and above all, to remain inoffen-
sively speechless: "keep the door of my lips," his addressee was directed to
pray, "that I may not offend with my tongue."[71]

By condemning them to what he had elsewhere called "an awful silence"
(255), Whitefield betrayed his most fearful opponents to be the most destitute — and, by many accounts, the most faithful — of his constituents, black
Christians. Powerless as they were, their status as exception to the promise
that conversion would entail untrammeled self-enlargement ironically challenged the theological rationale of Whitefield's evangelism: by definition,
uncontainability could brook no exceptions. His fear of unleashing, in the
cause of the spirit's emancipation, an oppositional force that he might prove
incapable of containing ultimately led Whitefield to self-censorship as the

necessary condition for constructing an image of the silenced black Christian required by his white constituency.[72] If this image was disregarded by those free blacks in his audience who were able to seize the power of the voice and become religious exhorters in turn, its contours are clear in the evangelical literature, including Whitefield's journals, as that negative construct within which uncontainability was itself contained.

As Whitefield modeled it within the normative context of spectacular conversion, however, democratic personality offered his auditors a revolutionary understanding of selfhood and a compelling rationale for its implementation, both derived from the moral authority and spiritual necessity of conversion, the rebirth of the self. The revolutionary self of the Whitefieldian convert was distinguished first and foremost by the aggressive uncontainability of his or her speech, underwritten by the reconceptualization of the self as a pure conduit for the expression of God's will. Despite the public nature of their utterances, what the converts proclaimed above all was the self's demise as the stager, the originator and referent of its utterances, and its reconceptualization as "God's mouth unto the people." The converted self was thus perceived, even on the stage of its own distinctive theater, as the purveyor of an artless self-representation consecrated to the eternal obligation to bear public, verbal witness to the transcendent power of God and to render audible the divine mandate that other selves be similarly reconceived. The newly constituted speaker thus spoke as Whitefield claimed to speak: wholly innocent of his representations and without reference to self, not the author of words about the self but rather the humble instrument for the uncorrupted and uncontainable articulation of the Word. The consequent enlargement of the self — its vocal range, its geographical and social mobility — was an index not of self-aggrandizement, because the self so conceived had ceased to exist. Self-enlargement was to be understood instead as the convert's infinite duty to transmit a transcendent content, at once timeless and urgent, as well as the power of God's determination that it be made universally available.

In the Great Awakening, the convert's self-translation out of the natural man's limitations was enacted as the translation of God's majestic, inaudible voice into ubiquitous and irrepressible human utterance. Whatever the idiosyncrasies of content or delivery, whatever its contradictions or irrationalities, the individual's utterance was posited as inevitable, unstoppable, and infallible: any attempt to oppose or restrict the convert's speech represented an attempt to usurp God's prerogative to make His will known by whatever means He chose. Evidently, He had chosen to honor His scriptural promise to reveal in time the centrality of the humble outcast by conferring upon those marginal to the culture privileged access to invisible realities and the authority to broadcast them, in the process affronting a ministerial and social elite who struggled, but ultimately failed, to retain control of the Word.

THREE

The Advent of the Individual: Democratic Personality
and the Spectral Self

Today if you will hear his Voice, harden not your Hearts.

— HEBREWS 3 : 15

And what *Minister* has a Voice like GOD, and who can thunder like Him?

— REV. THOMAS PRINCE, *"Some Account of the late Revival of Religion in Boston"*

In every period, there is a certain fashionable type, a certain fictional specter that takes hold of the imagination and as it were soars aloft with it.

— CHARLES-AUGUSTIN SAINTE-BEUVE, *Causeries du lundi*

I

Twenty-one years before the Salem crisis, an isolated but telling instance of diabolical possession occurred in the home of Rev. Samuel Willard, who would later prove a steadfast (if not outspoken) critic of spectral evidence theory.[1] Any account of the early history of the voice of the people in America must consider the case of Willard's maidservant, the "ventriloqua" Elizabeth Knapp, whose encounter with the invisible world in 1671 was initially made manifest in disjoint, inarticulate, and apparently uncontrollable vocalizations (shrieks, laughter, and nonsensical expressions) as well as "many foolish & apish gestures" that soon led to a series of lengthy fits.[2] While Willard rejected Knapp's attempts to assign a diabolical spiritual identity to a neighbor woman whose specter she claimed had tormented her, he was not inclined to dismiss the possibility that the "grum, low, yet audible voice" that issued from her mouth had a supernatural source, especially as it was almost entirely given over to a harsh and crudely expressed condemnation of himself as a "great blacke roague" who told "the people a company of lyes" (17).[3] Willard replied to the voice in kind, immediately assuming that it belonged not to Knapp but to Satan speaking through her. When the spectators gathered at the girl's bedside were emboldened to follow suit, Willard silenced them, suddenly aware of the dangers inherent in uninformed laypersons attempting to spar with Satan. He advised them "to see their call cleere, fearing least by [Satan's] policye, & many apish expressions hee used [e.g., that he was 'stronger than God'], hee might insinuate himselfe, & raise in them a fearlessenesse of spirit of him" (18).

Willard took pains to substantiate his assumption that the voice and its claims could not belong to Knapp and that, although constantly and outrageously speaking, she had remained essentially "speechless" throughout her ordeal. He did so, first, by examining her closely for signs of counterfeiting. He also recorded his maidservant's own explanation for the source of her speech:

> shee confessed that the Devill entred into her the 2d night after her first taking, that when shee was going to bed, hee entred in (as shee conceived) at her mouth, & had bin in her ever since, & professed, that if there were ever a Devill in the world, there was one in her, but in what manner he spake in her she could not tell. (18)

Subsequently, Knapp altered her hypothesis concerning the devil's appropriation of her powers of speech, supplementing her sexualized account of his entering her at the mouth with a psychology of sin in which the doubleness of coitus is replaced by the splitting of "disposition" from "enforcement," or desire from enactment, a split that renders her inclined to speak but physically unable to do so alone. Consummation of her subversive desire was delivered by the diabolical other whose strength or will was twice that of Knapp's. Thus, although she denied actually covenanting with the devil, she would admit

> the occasion of her fits to bee discontent, owned the temptations to murder; declared that though the devill had power of her body, shee hoped hee should not of her soule, yet she had rather continue soe

speechlesse, than have her speech, & make no better use of it than formerly shee had, expressed that shee was sometimes disposed to doe mischiefe, & was as if some had laid hold of her to enforce her to it, & had double strength to her owne, that shee knew not whither the devill were in her or no if hee were shee knew not when or how he entered; that when shee was taken speechlesse, she fared as if a string was tyed about the roots of her tongue, & reached doune into her vitalls, & pulled her tongue downe, & that most when shee strove to speake. (19–20)

While Knapp thus owned the disposition to speak mischievously, she denied the physiological ability to do so given her disarticulation and ventriloquization by the evil spirit and her continuing speechlessness. For his part, although Willard attributed the voice that was and was not Knapp's to Satan in his initial account of her ordeal, two years later he identified it otherwise in the preface to his published version of the episode as "a voice . . . to the whole Land," the voice of divine judgment (6). In so doing, he not only ascribed a national significance to the reproving voice issuing apocalyptically from his maidservant's mouth but he implied its identity with the voice of conscience — in Jonathan Edwards's formulation, "the mouth of that viceregent of God in the soul."[4]

In itself, the designation of an evil event as a divine communication would require no special attention and entail no cognitive strain: Puritans customarily rehabilitated afflictions (Indian captivities, most notably) as merciful signs of God's *"electing Love,"* marks of His attention to His people's spiritual readiness and proofs of His continuing investment in the covenant.[5] The actions of the devil had spoken, could speak, and would continue to speak jeremiadically on behalf of conscience, God's voice in the (national) soul. Willard's explicit anxiety that the literal voice issuing from Knapp's mouth might prove a counterfeit, however, suggests that he had struggled to make the voice of Satan and the voice to the land seamlessly cohere in the voice of his maidservant. His uneasiness "whither [the voice coming from Knapp] might not appear a counterfiet" introduces a doubtful note into his account that settles not so much upon the question of the voice's provenance as upon its genuineness and thus its truth-value, its availability to significances larger than Knapp's (or the devil's) individual resentments (17; cf. 20). The question of provenance is rather easily settled with reference to physiological, behavioral, and affective indices: Willard notes how when Knapp spoke he "observed not any of her organs to moove," even when she pronounced the labial letters, and that "the voice was hollow" (17; cf. 20); he considers the "reviling termes [she] used," so contrary to her customarily respectful manner toward him (21); he ponders the significance of his heated declaration of hatred toward the being that is visibly Knapp but invisibly the provoking spirit that inhabits his servant's body (18). He concludes on the basis of such evidences that the voice cannot be her own and thus is not a counterfeit of the voice of the Prince of Lies. But settling the question of the voice's provenance does not, Willard finds, address the problem of its genuineness, which eludes his efforts at empirical exactitude insofar as the relation of the genuine to the counterfeit eludes his ability or desire to assign stable oppositional meanings to these terms.

For Willard, the counterfeit was bound up not so much with the feigned or the false but with the individual, so that the opposition he wanted to establish between the genuine and the counterfeit could not be straightforwardly demonstrated with reference to the situation at hand. Instead, his search for the counterfeit led him into paradox: to the extent that Knapp is and speaks for herself, a servant girl who cared little for church, who contemplated murder and suicide, who disobeyed her parents, whom mischief tempted (9, 21), she is a counterfeit; and to the extent that she is "possessed," radically self-alienated (rather than alienated from those around her), the unwilling host of the double-tongued deceiver, she is true. She can only be "real" if possessed; only innocent if she is in truth Satan's ventriloqua and her speech authentically diabolical rather than genuinely expressive of her own sinful integrity. Moreover, just as Knapp could be charged with counterfeiting or falsification if she were discovered to be voicing her own individual thoughts, rather than the devil's, so the devil's pronouncements transcended their inherent falseness and were made significant as a voice to the land only to the extent that Satan, too, was possessed — by God, the cosmic puppeteer. Double-voicedness, the condition of counterfeiting, is here inextricably linked to the legitimacy of speech. Because in Knapp he comes face to face with this paradox, Willard refrains from judging whether she had actually consented to covenant with the devil; to do so would be to encounter the absurdity of pretending to distinguish once and for all the true counterfeit (Knapp speaking only for herself) from the counterfeit true (Knapp speaking for, or, more accurately, spoken by, the devil, and ultimately God and nation).

In drawing the veil of charity over the scene of possession and referring to the event as "tragedye" rather than apostasy, Willard drew himself and his maidservant back from the edge of a conceptual and a social abyss (7). Throughout the Salem temptation, he would retain this principled and humble stance against authoritative assumptions concerning the probability that a diabolical covenanting had occurred. Nevertheless, his association of innocence with doubleness in 1671, his attempts to elucidate the mystery of Knapp's unwonted speech by displacing it onto a supernatural and suprain-dividual source, allies him with his opponents in 1692, the spectral evidence theorists.

The elusive connection between the counterfeit and the spiritual, and the counterfeit and the individual, lay at the heart of Willard's ambivalence concerning the significance of the Knapp episode. The same mystery gave rise to the semiotic impasse elevated into a system by spectral evidence theory twenty years later. Insofar as the dilemma of the counterfeit — the status of the spectral self — remained unredressed by the Puritan community in the wake of Salem, it resurfaced as a familiar, circular pattern of inquiry with respect to the novel appearances, the *"new Preachers, new Doctrines, new Methods of Speech, Tone,* and *Gesture,"* that arose in such astonishing volume and force during the Great Awakening.[6] As everywhere individuals from ordained ministers to lay exhorters to humble parishioners were publicly proclaiming their privileged access to spiritual realities and in so doing questioning and sometimes castigating the formulations of divine truth proffered by the established clergy, anxieties regarding the multiplying possibilities of counterfeit saturated the culture. Members of the established clergy, suspected and publicly accused by revivalists of counterfeiting the spiritual authority to lead their congregations to an experience of saving grace, suspected and publicly attacked their detractors in turn. A crisis of charity, the ecclesiastical equivalent of religious faith and thus the cornerstone of church order, ensued. Many pointed out that the withdrawal of charity, the principled willingness to confine one's judgment of others to visible character, would destroy the foundations of the social and ecclesiastical order. And yet precisely this occurred as parishioners had suddenly to choose between two well-defined camps vying strenuously for their patronage with the same rhetorical weapons, including outright vilification. Thus the conservative New Hampshire divine, Timothy Walker, complained that "HYPOCRITE,

PHARISEE, BLIND, CARNAL, UNCONVERTED WRETCH, are in many Places become almost Words of Course, and first Compliments between Neighbours," while in the same address stigmatizing his doctrinal rivals as "proud, self-conceited, censorious, unpeaceable."[7]

Walker's list of epithets vividly conveys the challenge to which all ministers, whether conservatively or evangelically inclined, were suddenly exposed: like the witchcraft crisis, the Great Awakening brought a proliferation of inquiries into the truth-value of the visible characters of those in authority and a desire to strip away the trappings of authority to reveal what monster of unholy ambition lay beneath. Visible character was thus expressly proposed in sermons, pamphlets, and street-corner exhortations as a possible fiction of the minister's making, an "intercepting Glass" that potentially blinded congregants to the invisible truth of the clergyman's spiritual impotence to lead them to saving grace, if it did not dissemble his secret animosity to the people of God.[8] One enraged Old Light bitterly complained that the laity, having followed the lead of the evangelical clergy, had become adept at "using their Liberty for a cloak of Maliciousness" to disregard "men cloath'd with Authority" in order to cast "horrid and insufferable Contempt" upon them.[9] Yet anxieties over ministers wielding counterfeit authority and the desire to expose them began with Old Light inquiries into the source of Whitefield's unprecedented influence over his auditors. In their cumulative power, these inquiries constituted a shift in emphasis, rhetorically sustained by both parties, from the "unerring Word of Truth" to the particularities of ministerial character.[10] This shift, the accompanying effort to posit the relationship of (false) character to (false) doctrine, and the ensuing breakdown of formerly unassailable integrities (in particular, ministerial voice) will be the focus of the second section of this chapter.

Questions regarding the possible counterfeit of spiritual authority quickly proliferated beyond the contingency of "false and seducing" ministers of either persuasion leading American Christians astray.[11] The shift in emphasis from the certainties of Scripture (doctrinally enforced) to the mysteries of character anticipated a broader move from a doctrinal and homiletic focus upon the *"Object"* (the "Truths which the Scripture propounds") to the limitations of the *"Subject"* (individual Christians, both preaching and preached to). Whereas the transcendent Object clearly required no reformation, New Lights argued that individual subjects had to undergo a process of "qualifying . . . by curing the native and acquired blindness and carnality of our Minds, that we may rightly understand and embrace the Truths which the Scripture propounds."[12] The viability of divine truth was suddenly seen to depend on its reception, and right reception to depend on the ability of religious exhorters to provide vital representations of it. The novel focus on the individual subject implemented by both conservatives and revivalists despite their antithetical goals was the product not of their cooperation in the project of national-spiritual renewal but of their competition for the consent of individual congregants to their representations of divine truth, prominently including the individual preacher's self-representation. The emphasis less upon absolute truth than upon its representational possibilities, a product of the ministerial war for the patronage of congregants, illuminated the relative, circumstantial, and volatile realm of individual religious experience and gave it theological priority over conventional exegetical forms and formats.[13] This circumstance will provide the subject of the third section of this chapter.

The shift in emphasis toward individual religious experience and in particular what Jonathan Edwards called "religious affections," and the concomitant emphasis upon the proper reception of the "unerring word of Truth," encouraged multitudes to speak publicly and often with open passion on matters of religious import. Many would be emboldened to claim some form of intimate connection with transcendent authority and thus the right to exhort others. Such "raw, indiscreet, rash, illiterate and blind NOVICES," too, became the subject of bitter warnings about the dangers of consenting to what could prove a spiritually fatal misrepresentation or counterfeit of divine truth offered by multiplying numbers of unauthorized itinerant speakers who were often utterly unknown to those they exhorted.[14] As Charles Chauncy warned, "the SPIRIT's *operations* . . . may be counterfeited; that men may make an appearance, as if they were acted by the SPIRIT, when, all the while, they have no other view in their pretences, but to serve themselves."[15] Jonathan Edwards, unwilling that the excesses of some should be permitted to dim the glory of the reforming spirit abroad in the land, pointed out that even in apostolic times, "as the influences of the true Spirit abounded, so counterfeits did also then abound: the Devil was abundant in mimicking both the ordinary and extraordinary influences of the Spirit of God." The current task was thus to identify "distinguishing and clear marks by which [the church of Christ] might proceed safely in judging of spirits, and distinguish the true from the false, without danger of being imposed upon."[16] Timothy Walker, noting that "counterfeit Grace may, and often does, resemble real Grace," joined his doctrinal opponent Edwards in his urgent bid to identify the "differencing Mark which the other can't counterfeit." When unknown, "confident and assuming Men" appear before the public "set up for *public Teachers*, who have no other Claim to that Character, but only they have received the *Holy Ghost*," he advised that they be "tried" to determine "*whether they are not Liars*" and suggested that the performance of a miracle would provide satisfactory "Proof of their Mission and Authority."[17] Such statements indicate the cultural urgency and scope of the problem of the counterfeit, which became the central trope around which a semiotics of authenticity hastily developed that was uneasily situated in the individual and his or her relationship to an invisible and inherently revolutionary order of power.

II

In 1740, Josiah Smith, the Harvard-educated pastor of Charleston's Independent Congregational Church, delivered *A Sermon, on the Character, Preaching, &c. of the Rev. Mr. Whitefield.* A Boston-based publication dedicated to documenting the transatlantic and intercolonial religious revival, *The Christian History*, subsequently excerpted Smith's sermon and added a laudatory preface written by the eminent ministers of Cambridge's Brattle Street Church, Benjamin Colman and William Cooper.[18] While they acknowledge the "*extraordinary Nature*" of a pulpit sermon dedicated not to the interpretation of Scripture but to "the personal and ministerial Character of a *living Preacher*," Colman and Cooper justify Smith's unorthodox choice of text by pointing out that the sermon's "manifest Design" was "to support the *Cause* by vindicating the *Man*." That the "Cause" in question was not "private and party" but instead the greatest and most universal of all causes, "the Cause of *Christ* and *Truth*," raises a number of questions. Most pertinent, how does the personal vindication of a particular religious adherent acquire the urgency of religious principle? Under what conditions may the cause of absolute Truth be understood to depend upon the vagaries — historical, per-

sonal, and even generic — of its articulation? Such questions may be pre-
liminarily addressed by considering the proposition implicit in the preface to
Smith's sermon: namely, that if divine truth was normatively sought and
discovered through scriptural exegesis, it could as legitimately be acquired
through a characterological analysis and defense of the exegete.

The rhetorical burden of the preface to Smith's published sermon was
thus to legitimate his displacement of focus from the integrity and unity of
the written text to the self-divided and multiple human one. Both preface
and sermon participated in the marked shift of focus in religious exposition
that began in the 1740s, from the universalities of Christian doctrine to the
particularities of ministerial character and to ministerial voice as an analogue
of character.[19] Although Old Lights were ideologically and professionally
committed to upholding the neutrality and thus the authority of ministerial
character and utterance as mere vehicles for the Word, they were incensed by
their rivals' efforts to expose them as "carnal and unregenerate" and found
themselves struggling defensively to theorize the connection between the
anomalous characters and voices of New Light preachers and the fantastical
errors of New Light doctrine.[20] Bowing to the pressure to generate persuasive representations of this linkage and thus to retain the patronage of their
congregations, Old Light preaching took on an impassioned and person-
alized tenor, attacking rivals' doctrines through an attack on their characters.[21] Such behavior suggests that Old Lights were compelled by New Light
challenges to traditional ministerial prerogatives to elaborate a doctrinal
rationale for techniques of persuasion — "affectionate" preaching and vi-
tuperative public attacks on their rivals — difficult to differentiate from those
they excoriated in their opponents.

Due perhaps to the novelty and transatlantic scope of his itinerant ministry, the sophistication with which he manipulated and sustained his public
image, his scandalous practice of defaming leading members of the established clergy, as well as his extraordinarily charismatic presence and oratorical power, Whitefield in particular galvanized the theoretical ingenuity of
those committed (whether offensively or defensively) to elaborating the relation of character — and especially voice as an aspect of character — to doctrine.[22] The president and faculty of Harvard College, in an attempt to
repulse Whitefield's intended second visit to Boston, identified him as "the
blameable Cause of all the Quarrels on the Account of Religion, which the

Churches are now engaged in." Additionally, they argued that his doctrinally based enthusiasm, his conviction that he "hath as familiar a Converse and Communion with God as any of the Prophets and Apostles," was directly connected with his most offensive character traits, his arrogance toward the established clergy and his proclivity to "personat[e] our blessed Lord" and thus to act as a "Deluder of the People."[23] Whitefield is here portrayed as an exemplar of the visible piety of all revivalists which masked "some ambitious Design, to get a Name in the World, that being cried up for Men divinely inspired, they may have the Advantage to get Power into their Hands, and rule all," and that like the *"Demagogues* of old," New Light preachers "by their bewitching Oratory charm'd the Hearts of the Vulgar, and thereby accomplish'd their own Ends upon them." New Lights responded in kind to such charges, arguing that the conventionally approved learning and integrity of the established clergy should be evaluated with reference to the Pauline truism (frequently invoked in 1692) that "the Devil transforms himself into an Angel of Light, and teaches his Ministers the like Art of Imposture."[24] As rival ministers accused one another publicly of having "let their outward appearance be ever so smoothly cloaked over with a shew of Zeal and Sanctity" so as to lead their followers to enact "an *imaginary Conversion* of their own Making" and thus to risk spiritual death, anxieties concerning the truth-value of visible character and its potential to mask the self-aggrandizing aims of the spectral self — "the sneaking Self-seeker" — were raised to a pitch not seen since 1692.[25] Faced with the Old Light charge that Whitefield's unprecedented popular success bespoke the seductions of just such a spectral self, his supporters responded by denying his individuality altogether in an effort to refer the striking singularity of his character and ultimately the power of his voice to a supraindividual — indeed, a transcendent — source.[26]

In the sermon in which he takes Whitefield's character as his text, Josiah Smith thus described the Grand Itinerant as exemplifying nothing less than the *"primitive Piety"* of the *"apostolick Spirit"* while scrupulously renouncing "all Pretensions to the extraordinary Powers and Signs of Apostleship."[27] He praised Whitefield's extraordinary integrity by telling how he "guarded against the invidious Censure of assuming the Character of an *Apostle*," an observation also made by Stephen Bordley, a Maryland lawyer and among Whitefield's detractors, who conceded that "with regard to the Strength of the Spirit in him, he seems tho' unwillingly, to acknowledge himself to fall short of the Apostles."[28] Whitefield was well aware, Smith implies, that like miracles and angelic visitations, apostleship was a practical impossibility, "peculiar to the age of inspiration, and extinct with [it]."[29] Having thus cleared Whitefield of the unseemly charge of coveting the character, powers, and signs of apostleship, Smith proceeded to compare him not just to the historical Saint Paul but to a heavenly messenger sent directly by God with news of the invisible world: Smith could envision when Whitefield preached how "saint Paul would look and speak in a pulpit, and in some such manner, I have been tempted to conceive of a seraph, were he sent down to preach among us, and to tell us what things he had seen and heard above!"[30]

As his admirers construed it, then, Whitefield's principled refusal to assume character does not leave him characterless. On the contrary, his dominant character trait was identified as radical selflessness, an adamant and gracious refusal of character that prepared him (as one prepares a surface) to cleanly receive the attributes of sublimity conferred upon him by others. Through this reversible kenosis, which afforded him character without the detritus of self, Whitefield exemplified for his followers the primitive piety of ancient Christianity. Never merely himself, never delimited by his own individuality (doctrinally expressed by his scrupulous rejection of denominationalism), Whitefield's words and actions could not be interpreted as self-referential or self-aggrandizing.[31] It was not so much that he lacked the self-reflexive impulse, but rather that no residue of self survived his ministrations, which were not only doctrinally focused on the necessity of the new birth ("where a Principle of *new Life* is ingenerated in the Heart of Man, and an entire Change is produced in the Temper and Disposition of the Soul") but which continually rehearsed his own coming-into-being.[32] This hermetic conformity of private life to public calling (manifested, above all, as a striking uniformity of utterance, a proclivity to exhort no matter what the vicissitudes of his personal life) was remarked by one adherent: "I see the Man to be all of a Piece; his Life and Conversation to be a Transcript of his Sermons."[33] On one level, such a statement was intended to counter the array of accusations his opponents marshaled to discredit him, prominent among which were the charges of self-aggrandizement and antinomianism: it asserts that Whitefield practiced what he preached and claimed no self-exemptions from the rigors of Christian piety. On another level, however, by claiming Whitefield's personhood to be a transcript rather than an original, simultaneously exhortation and its literal fulfillment, Whitefield is revealed to be no person at all but something infinitely greater, the incarnated Word: as one admirer put it, Whitefield was "a kind of living Gospel."[34]

As such, he was able to enjoy the power but transcend the limitations of ministerial individuality that might inhibit auditors from receiving the full impact of divine truth, an impasse referred to in a sermon by Rev. Samuel Blair on Hebrews 3:15. "How many of you," he asked his Pennsylvania congregation, "have been hearing the Gospel for a long Time, and yet your Hearts remain always hard, without being made better by it: The Gospel is the *Voice of GOD*, but you have heard it only as the *Voice of Man* and not the *Voice of God*, and so have not been benefitted by it." As a man voicing God, a divinely inscribed "human document" or "living Gospel" whose life and words counted equally as transcripts of "the unerring Word of Truth," Whitefield released his auditors from spiritual crucifixion between incompatible yet pressing needs: on the one hand, the immediate power of the particular and, on the other, the scriptural authority of the typological.[35] This use of the notion of the transcript was radically opposed to that approved by Charles Chauncy, who advised the readers of his tract, *Enthusiasm described and caution'd against*, to judge of "real religion . . . from the conduct of men of a *sound judgment*; whose lives have been such a uniform, beautiful transcript of that which is just and good, that we can't but think well of religion, as display'd in their example." For Chauncy, the life as a beautiful transcript was a true representation of religion as "a sober, calm, reasonable thing."[36] Whitefield's adherents, however, elided to the degree possible the distance or figuration involved in Chauncy's notion of the religious transcript as a behavioral representation or analogue of what was fundamentally a social ideal of sobriety, calm, and reason. Whitefield was in their view not merely providing a representation of true religion through his comportment (a concept repellent in any case for its Arminian bias); rather, their claim was that (like Christ) he literally embodied Gospel truths, a claim that simultaneously elevated and denied the singularity conveyed by the "individual example." The Harvard faculty, in their succinct but comprehensive critique of Whitefield, located as the precise source of his pernicious ambition to impersonate God a tendency to ignore "Metaphor" in favor of taking "the Expression literally," a policy which had "given great Satisfaction to many an Enthusiast among us since the Year 1740" who were thereby freed to take "the swelling of their Breasts and Stomachs in their religious Agitations" for the "*Indwelling of the Spirit.*"[37]

Such an unqualified correspondence of his individuality with transcendent or universal meaning underlay the various efforts of Whitefield's followers to convey their sense of a personality that was, paradoxically, both everything and nothing, as when one supporter declared of the minister, "he himself is a Monument."[38] Because a monument is always a monument *to*, the trope of monumentality allowed the New Lights to meet the demand of the Old Lights — "a sinful and adulterous generation," Smith called them — for a "sign" that would corroborate what the revivalists claimed was "impossible in nature to represent," the truth of regeneration registered as the "inward feelings of the Spirit."[39] If inward feeling could not be naturally represented, the monumental Whitefield, like the "living Gospel" Whitefield, could function as an iconic sign of an inwardness that was neither personal nor particular to any individual. Beyond the seamlessness of private to public life, the minister as monument thus conveyed the absence of interiority conceived as a hidden recess of the self. He possessed instead the generic interiority that was the fruit of kenosis: the soul as a repository of divine grace. As one whose life was a transcript of the Word, whose individuality was wholly consecrated to the transcendent truth of the necessity of the new birth, the monumental Whitefield represented not the glorification or mystification of the self but its utter obsolescence outside of its iconic function.

Moreover, the monumental Whitefield represented the New Light response to the Old Light condemnation of what the latter saw as the conning minister's blasphemous theatricality. Insofar as it conveyed the seamless identity of the outer and the inner man, the icon and the individual, the monumental Whitefield exemplified the ideal of individual integrity as expressed in the venerable Puritan William Prynne's antitheatrical tract, *Histriomatrix* (1633):

> For God, *who is truth it selfe*, in *whom there is no variablenesse, no shadow of change no feigning, no hypocrisie*; as he hath given a uniforme distinct and proper being to every creature, *the bounds of which may not be exceeded: so he requires that the actions of every creature should be honest and sincere, devoyde of all hypocrisie*, as all his actions, and their natures are. Hence he en-

joy[n]es all men at all times, *to be such in shew, as they are in truth: to seeme that outwardly which they are inwardly*; to act themselves, not others.[40]

Far from exemplifying the doubleness of the actor, and in particular, such *"Filthy Hypocrites"* as the established ministry, those "Stage Players in Religion, who gave their Maker the Tongue, the Cap and Knee . . . but in the mean while their Hearts go after their Covetousness and other Lusts," the monumental Whitefield's private and public selves were indistinguishable: the more he acted himself, the more he resembled God and Truth.[41]

The tropes of monumentality and the transcripted life, which conveyed the remarkable absence of interiority conceived as a hidden spring of self-interested behavior, permitted Whitefield's adherents to acknowledge and defend his extraordinary charisma with reference to a final figure: that of the religious ravisher. More pointedly than the others, this trope permitted revivalists to respond to Old Light charges that the evangelical preacher made himself "very taking and agreeable to the People" so that he might have it "in his Power to raise [them] to any Degree of Warmth he pleases, whereby they stand ready to receive almost any Doctrine he is pleased to broach." Far from having promiscuously stimulated in the people "such an Itch after him" that they (and thus their ministers) become the victims of their own "impetuous Desires," the religious ravisher does not dispossess but invests his auditors with authentic selfhood.[42] Uniquely able to remedy the spiritual infertility of the populace — its "miscarrying Womb and dry Breasts" the result of the moribund preaching of the established clergy who, the New Lights averred, had no more chance of converting a soul than a dead man had to beget children — the religious ravisher overpowers in order to fructify the self:

> With what a Flow of Words did he speak to us upon the great Concern of our Souls! In what a flaming Light did he set out *Eternity* before us! How earnestly did he press *Christ* upon us! How close strong and pungent were his *Applications* to the Conscience; mingling *Light* and *Heat*, pointing the Arrows of *the Almighty* at the Heart of Sinners, while he pour'd in the Balm on the Wounds of the Contrite! How bold and couragious did he look? He was no Flatterer.[43]

The description of Whitefield's spiritual virility anticipates Whitman's ravisher-poet of a century later, "the most robust bard" whose sexual-discursive aggression was uniquely able to redress the literary barrenness of the nation and give it its true voice.[44] As with Whitman, the voice of the Whitefieldian ravisher transmits a saving destruction, a nihilistic energy borne in a purgative flood or "Flow of Words" that strips sinners of every superfluity, all recourse to "*dead Formalities*," to leave bare and vulnerable "the *secret Imagery*" of the heart.[45] Both absorbing and magnifying each individual's "inward and secret Spring," the preacher's torrential voice is here portrayed as startlingly synesthetic, stimulating each of the auditor's senses to an unprecedented acuity.[46] The discursive current is thus transmuted into a "flaming Light" to the eyes that reveals "*Eternity*"; an accompanying "*Heat*," registered in the sensation of being pressed, pinned down, and then soothed with an infusing balm; a pungency scented by conscience; and a moral power to discriminate and withstand the truth and thereby to renounce one's need of flattery.

The trope of the religious ravisher makes explicit the fascination of Whitefield's supporters, and his detractors, with the visceral power of his voice, its link to the mystery of his character and thus to the truth or falsity of his doctrine. This fascination was registered in numerous attempts to anatomize his voice (and subsequently, the voices of other itinerants) by delineating its material, intellectual, and moral attributes in an effort to differentiate the essential from the merely "mechanical" sources of its power. Implicit in this anatomization were a number of questions expressive of the fundamental issue for conservatives and evangelicals alike: namely, the possibility of an auditor's safely consenting to a speaker's representations of absolute truth based on the voice itself, rather than any contingent consideration, such as the institutional affiliations or even the personal identity of the speaker. Those who took upon themselves to analyze Whitefield's voice asked if the source of its seductive power was divine or merely aesthetic, and if hearing it was conducive to salvation or just pleasure. Was his voice directly expressive of God's will, his own enthusiastic vision of divine truth, or did it artfully dissemble his own self-referential will to power? In what way could an auditor deduce the truth of character from voice and, on that basis, the truth of doctrine from character? To answer such questions, some who attended his sermons strove variously to identify that point at which their reservations about Whitefield and his ministry either arose or were conquered in order to discriminate substance from mere performance in powerful preaching.

Stephen Bordley, for example, having heard Whitefield preach twice in

Annapolis, confirmed in a letter to a friend that Whitefield's doctrine of the Spirit was inseparable from his vilification of the established clergy; together, both functioned as "the great hinges or Supports of all his discourses." Bordley explicitly made inferences about Whitefield's character from observations of his voice: announcing at the letter's outset that he would provide "a Character of the man from my opinion of him," Bordley proceeds to offer a detailed description of Whitefield's voice and delivery. In order to discern more clearly the rhetorical uses of objective observation, it is interesting to compare Bordley's unwaveringly skeptical view of Whitefield's performances with that of an initially skeptical but ultimately convinced witness who anonymously contributed to *The Christian History* an account of hearing Whitefield preach. Although both observers noted the exemplary clarity of his voice, for example, they disagreed concerning its musicality (Bordley detected "a little of the West Country twang").[47] Both noted the "Mastery" of his delivery, including the striking impact made by his use of gesture. In a statement about the special expressiveness of Whitefield's body (one, it is implied, that can hardly be dissembled and that anticipates once again Whitman's portrait of the authentic poet), the *Christian History*'s contributor claimed that "Every *Accent* of his Voice, every *Motion* of his Body, *speaks*, and both are natural and unaffected. If his Delivery is the Product of Art, 'tis certainly the Perfection of it, for it is entirely concealed" (361–62). Bordley similarly noted that "His Acc[ti]on is natural fervent and moving, & the tone and Accent of his Voice together with his Acc[ti]on are so well adapted to each other, that I freely own I never in my life saw any one man that arrived to so great a prefecc[t]ion in the art of Pronunciation as he has done" (304). Not surprisingly, Bordley and the anonymous commentator disagreed on the conclusions to be drawn from this felicity of tone, accent, and gesture. The latter found that "Every Scruple vanished" before Whitefield's artless integrity as a speaker ("All he said was *Demonstration, Life* and *Power!*"), an artlessness that confirmed for the writer that "*God is with this Man of a Truth*" (360). Bordley, on the other hand, judged that the minister's perfect "Pronunciation" must have been "his Chief study, for his language is mean & Groveling, without the least Elegance; & his method of discourse is ten times worse than his language, or rather he has no method at all" (304). He concluded that although to all appearances Whitefield's comportment while in Annapolis was consistent with the sanctity of his "Character" or reputation for piety, his pulpit performances indicated either that he was "a Violent Enthusiast" or alternatively that "he is a most Vain & Arrogant Hypocrite," the possibility Bordley found most plausible (307).

For Rev. Thomas Prince, editor of *The Christian History* and an occasional contributor to its pages, the powerful impression made upon the auditors of that "most importunate Wooer of Souls" bore a third, decidedly Calvinistic significance which he arrived at by comparing Whitefield's voice and manner with those of other revivalist preachers, namely New Jersey's Gilbert Tennent and Connecticut's Jonathan Edwards.[48] Prince emphasized that ministerial voice, no matter how manifestly powerful an impact it had upon an auditor, could not be considered the primary cause of a person's acquisition of "terrible Convictions," but only a "meer Effect" of the divine will, as are the convictions themselves. To the degree that "the Work of the SPIRIT of GOD" occurs in the soul, it bespeaks the action of "a sovereign, free and almighty Agent" in no way dependent upon the oratorical talents of a particular preacher whose role, Prince insisted, is strictly instrumental in, and never productive of, an experience of saving grace (388, 387, 389). For this reason, Whitefield's seductive pleading, Tennent's frightening rages, and Edwards's restrained solemnity in the pulpit could have equally powerful effects upon auditors: all conduce in their various ways to a merely "mechanical Influence on the animal Passions," short-lived and superficial, that in some cases will precede but in no way determine or predict saving conviction (387). A given sermon might temporarily "frighten the Hearers, rouze the Soul, and prepare the Way for terrible Convictions; yet those meer animal *Terrors*, and these *Convictions* are quite different Things" (388). The prerogative to sustain terror or any other passion is exclusively God's: as Prince pointedly asked (a question that would resonate uncannily in the subsequent decades), "what *Minister* has a Voice like GOD, and who can thunder like Him?" (389). Nevertheless, in Whitefield's case Prince softened somewhat his insistence upon the limited instrumentality of ministerial voice, claiming that if "*vital, inward, active Piety*" must be considered "the meer Effect of the mighty and supernatural Operation of a divine Power on the Souls of Men," yet by "the *Manner* of his Preaching, wherein he appear'd to be in earnest," Whitefield, Moses-like, "deliver'd *those vital Truths* . . . and led his Hearers into the View" of that which lies beyond contingency (387).

Contrary to his own doctrinal and professional biases, Prince's analysis of the unprecedented successes of the major revivalist preachers of his day stressed the representational or aesthetic aspect of ministerial voice, an emphasis which required him to refrain from conflating it with the truth it represented. None of its constituent elements—manner, tone, gesture, diction—had proved essential: the harangue and the heartfelt plea could be interchanged with no significant impact upon the intensity or quality of the auditor's response or the numbers responding. Despite its powerful effects, the sound of the voice bore no necessary relationship to the meaning of the words it articulated. Only their predispositions, then, separate Prince and Bordley, who flatly concluded the letter in which he conveyed his impressions of Whitefield's preaching by noting that " 'tis really a difficult matter to perswade some among us here to make a difference between his Doctrine & Delivery." Bordley was certain that Whitefield had "the best delivery w[i]th the Worst Divinity that I ever mett with."[49] The Reverend Alexander Garden, the Anglican commissary of South Carolina and one of Whitefield's committed foes, precisely addressed the separability of doctrine and delivery in a published sermon of 1740 dedicated to refuting the credibility of the iconic Whitefield—gospel, monument, ravisher—entitled *Regeneration and the Testimony of the Spirit*.[50]

The sermon was intended to expose the doctrinal unsoundness of Whitefield's understanding of regeneration as he presented it in what Garden called his "Mobb Harangues" in the vicinity of Charleston.[51] In the same year, Garden published his correspondence with the itinerant; *Six Letters to the Reverend Mr. George Whitefield*, too, was largely devoted to a bitter refutation of the "new birth" as a bastard creed, founded not in Scripture but rather in the disordered and egomaniacal mind of the Grand Itinerant. Garden's ire, although focused on doctrinal issues, clearly derived from his sense of Whitefield's unconscionable manipulations of "the weak and unwary Populace," as well as his unwarranted castigations of the standing ministry, but he does not in the letters offer a theory of the relationship of bad doctrine to bad character.[52] The positing of such a relationship is, however, precisely the intent of the sermon: it arises in part as a rhetorical consequence of the shift in addressee that differentiates the letters and the sermon as two modes of doctrinal critique.

In the sermon, Garden's words are addressed not to his ingenuous opponent, the *"wilful Deceiver"* who plots "to intangle and amuse the Minds" of "the weak and unstable of Mankind," and whom Garden clearly considered his intellectual equal. Instead, he addressed his disaffected parishioners, those whom his opponent had all too easily alienated from their own consciences, conceived as an inward voice grounded in human reason and as such the sanctified instrument for effecting the regeneration of the spirit.[53] Charles Chauncy had defined reason as that mental faculty which allowed one to discriminate "a *pretended* revelation" from "a *real* one" and to understand revelation's meaning once identified. Reason, that is, permitted one meaning to predominate over all others and disallowed the simultaneous reception of "the most contrary" and "inconsisten[t]" senses of, for example, a scriptural passage. Only reason, Chauncy reminded his readers, would guard them against "the wilds of falshood and inconsistency" and "the wantoness of your imaginations," which he identified as among the most powerful "enemies of your *souls*."[54] For Garden, then, to negotiate this shift in address from the malefactor to his victims within the parameters of a doctrinal dispute was not merely the rhetorical but also the conceptual burden of his sermon. The unprecedented circumstance of addressing, in order to win over, an audience presumed to be estranged not just from their established minister but from themselves and the conditions of truth led Garden into a profound contradiction. In the process of justifying his moving inferentially from doctrine to character and vice versa, he posited a relationship of voice to utterance, of form to content, and implicitly of messenger to message, in which the fundamental fact is the fact of their separability and thus the wholly contingent quality of their association.

Garden's basic strategy in the sermon was to attack Whitefield's doctrine metonymically, by constricting his focus to the material or "mechanical" attributes of that voice through which the doctrine was transmitted, and inferring from those attributes the preacher's invisible character as a dissembler and a counterfeit. Consequently, in his preface to the sermon Garden appears most disturbed not precisely by the substance of those "*crude* Enthusiastick *Notions . . . now revived and propagated by Mr.* Whitefield" but rather by the qualities of the voice which had articulated them and with whose material power such insubstantial notions became associated in the popular mind:

> *They were* preached *midst the* Sound *of that* Gentleman's *Voice in your Ears*; — *that* enchanting *Sound! The* natural *and* alone *Cause, which pro-*

duced all the Passion *and* Prejudice, *that prevailed 'mong* some (*The weaker*
some *indeed*) *of you, in his Favour, against them and every thing else that opposed him; and which would equally have produced the same Effects, whether he
had* acted *his Part in the* Pulpit *or on the* Stage. *No Proposition in* Euclid
more demonstrable to me, than that, not the Matter *but the* Manner, *not the*
Doctrines *he delivered, but the* Agreeableness *of the Delivery, had all the Effect upon you, and as* naturally *as any other Effects in Nature are produced by
their proper Causes. Take away* this *Cause, no more* Multitude *after the*
Preacher!

Garden thus reveals at the outset the insidious singularity of the voice de-
tached from the conditions of truth as that which can function as the *"natural
and alone* Cause" of a disordered psychospiritual state as well as that principle
of contagion by which such disorder is made coherent in community.[55]
Above all, the ungrounded voice possesses the power to efface crucial differences, such as that between pulpit and stage (transcendent truth as opposed
to debased fiction), and to make newly problematic those which had been
considered merely formal and thus inconsequential, formally present but
under normal circumstances nonsignifying, such as the difference between
matter and manner, doctrine and delivery.

In the body of the sermon which follows these prefatory remarks on the
merely material power of Whitefield's voice, Garden acknowledged the analogous appeal of the doctrine that voice so enchantingly articulated, a doctrine that promised a magical transformation of the self such as the exemplary convert himself claimed to have undergone:

Why then will you be amused with *dark* and *vain Words*? Why will you be
carried away with so strange a *Wind of Doctrine*, as persuades to the Belief
and Expectation of a certain happy *Moment*, when, by the *sole* and *specifick*
Work of the *Holy Spirit*, you shall at once (as 'twere by *Magic* Charm) be
matamorphosed, stript of your *old* Nature and cloathed with a *new*? (13–14)

Garden here charges his listeners with permitting themselves to mistake the
material power of the voice for the spiritual transformation of the self it
vainly promised. Such a magical transformation must of necessity be spectral
or chimerical, as insubstantial as the *"Wind of Doctrine"* upon which the
revolutionary promise is borne. Only in this negative sense may doctrine and

delivery be said to coincide: that in both, the substance of the divine promise is obfuscated by the vain fascination of the magic charm.

Whitefield's character, too, Garden ultimately argues, partakes of this negative integrity. At the conclusion of his sermon, he posits the seductiveness of a voice that, like the serpent's, is superior in its purely formal properties to the charms it tells, including the heady prospect of an instantaneous and unearned metamorphosis, divinely mandated and accomplished:

> Beware therefore, my Brethren, of such Pretensions; — of the old Story over again! How *intoxicating*, how *fascinating* Things are an agreeable *Voice* and *Manner* of speaking? The only Excellencies of this *Preacher.* Take these away; — put his Discourses into the Mouth of an *ordinary* Speaker, I dare say, no one would step out of his Way to hear them.[56]

As the bearer of an evil that Garden both demystifies (by underscoring its banality) and remystifies (by referring it to the cosmic source of all evil), Whitefield, a serpent, a "Wolf," "*a vain, visionary Creature*," stimulates the "Godly Jealousie" of Garden, who casts himself as lawful "Overseer" of the "Flock."[57] The ambiguous designation of Whitefield as a "visionary" creature complicates the otherwise conventional cast of wolf/serpent, sheep, and shepherd with which Garden attempts to construct a familiar scenario of invasion and attack, scattering and regrouping. The term appears to indicate the enormity of Whitefield's "vision" which Garden understands as the ultimate dream of disorder dedicated to the realization of a novel and suspect "design": the corruption of the natural, transparent relationship of form (voice) to a content (doctrine) assumed to be nonnegotiable and constant — in short, the truth. His power as a speaker, through which this corruption occurs, is precisely calculated to dissemble his uncanny ability to disarticulate form and substance, an ability realized to diabolic perfection in his own fantastic and radically duplicitous character.

Garden's rhetorical decision to pursue his attack on Whitefield's doctrine through an attack on his voice and then on his visionary character entangled him in an illogic, of the same stripe as Samuel Willard's meditations on the counterfeit, whose implications for the security of his own authority he did not foresee. His unmasking of Whitefield is premised upon the assumption that substance and form — or analogously, utterance and voice, doctrine and delivery, message and messenger — constitute a unity such that one may move inferentially between them unhindered. Yet he simultaneously insisted that form does not bear a natural, transparent relationship to content, and that the difference between them can be manipulated in the service of dissemblance, or alternatively, as in his own sermon, in the service of revealing the machinations of the dissembler. Garden's uncomfortable insight is recognizably deconstructive: form or appearance and content or essence exist in a semiotic relationship such that through their inherent difference meaning is conferred, modified, undermined, or withheld altogether. Garden offers Whitefield as both proof and corollary of this proposition: a man who, in the guise of a minister of God, had inadvertently revealed to the watchful overseer his characterological appropriation of the inherent doubleness of signification, in such a way that the power of his voice to counterfeit God's truth was manifestly analogous to the power of his visible character to dissemble his essential identity as an "EMISSARY" or "*Seedman*" of the Church of Rome, a spy or agent of the Antichrist, in sum, a "Pretender," a double-tongued creature with an insatiable desire to misrepresent.[58] Whitefield's acolytes, seduced by the beauties of form — of voice and visible character — to abandon the ground of truth, doom themselves to share in his groundlessness, made geospiritually manifest as the deluded minister's Sisyphean itinerancy, his inability to settle.

But Garden, too, clearly struggled to maintain his command of a perspective from which to survey the territory Whitefield had transgressed and discriminate boundaries no longer easily discernible. It was as if having exploded the illusion of the integrity of form and content, works and grace, manner and matter, and having set up in its stead a series of oppositions through whose complex relations truth might be discerned, the unanchored voice of Whitefield and the replicant voices of his followers marshaled the complicity of all preachers in its reformulations, so that in the very process of refuting them, the established ministry was compelled to make use of them. The ground of truth once shifted, all must make discovery of "their sandy Foundations," all are destabilized.[59] So insistently did Garden urge upon his parishioners this revelation — that the separability of voice and doctrine, and by analogy visible character and essential identity, is most operative when they appear unassailably, mellifluously, united — that he failed to see how the point might be turned to unclasp the stays of his own institutional armor, beginning with the keystone of Old Light ethics, the rule of charity which humbly upheld the credibility of the visible.

By insisting that the integrity of manner and matter is chimerical, Garden encouraged his auditors to abandon charity, the principled confining of one's judgments concerning another's spiritual estate to evidence provided by visible character. In place of exercising charity so defined, Garden bid his auditors to scrutinize ministerial self-presentation, to differentiate the constituent elements (legitimate from cosmetic) of the minister's authority as a speaker of divine truths, and to refrain from assuming that his voice is a neutral carrier, transparent to its message and with no signifying powers or intentions of its own. No doubt Garden would have liked to cap the ramifications of his insight into the separability of form and content in order to shield the orthodox from the type of scrutiny he himself advocated in the case of Whitefield and his ilk, not from fear of exposure but from a desire to retain the privilege of assuming the integrity of exterior and interior, character and identity, for the religious conservatives. But having conceded that with the advent of the dissembler Whitefield, form could no longer be trusted as a signifier of content because all natural or necessary relationship between the two terms had been abrogated, Garden in effect conformed to the advice of one of the most intransigent of the era's itinerant preachers, the Presbyterian evangelist Gilbert Tennent, given in a sermon that Alan Heimert has called a "manifesto of the revival party."[60]

Garden's therapeutic sermon, intended to redeem his enchanted parishioners from their unseemly captivity to the errors of New Light doctrine, betrays his unwitting adoption of an epistemological principle most concisely articulated in Tennent's *The Danger of an Unconverted Ministry*. The message of this revolutionary sermon was, first, that ministers who had not themselves experienced the new birth could not reasonably be expected to lead others to eternal life, and therefore "it is both lawful and expedient to go from them to hear Godly Persons" (87); and second, that the converted (even, Tennent implies, the merely convicted) parishioner, no matter how humble in estate or education, was eminently qualified to judge the minister's inward state by his outward manner of representing the Word:

> Does not the spiritual Man judge all Things? Tho' he cannot know the States of subtil Hypocrites infallibly; yet may he not give a near Guess,

who are the Sons of *Sceva*, by their Manner of Praying, Preaching, and Living? (98)

This being the case, it followed that the established clergy, the modern "Pharisees," who, like their ancient counterparts, had gained their positions with "but a little of the Learning then in Fashion, and a fair Out-side," had reason to fear the common people (75). Even as they regarded them "with an Air of Disdain," they struggled to "keep the People in their Interests" because the latter were instinctively capable of discriminating the authentic minister of the Word, whom God had called to the pulpit, from the "hireling murderous Hypocrites," the inauthentic ministers who had been lured there by more worldly considerations (74, 83). If the minister's performance of good works and consequent fair reputation obscured his hidden designs in seeking a position of authority over the souls of others, his illegitimacy would infallibly be disclosed by his voice:

Their Discourses are cold and sapless, and as it were freeze between their Lips. And not being sent of GOD, they want that divine Authority, with which the faithful Ambassadors of CHRIST are clothed. (78)

Moreover, although in some instances "polished with Wit and Rhetorick," the "sapless Discourses of such dead Drones," the "Pharisee-teachers," are known by their "short, or indistinct and general" applications, their failure to discriminate "the Precious from the Vile," their frequent misapplications of the Word, and their "soft, selfish, cowardly" pandering to "carnal Security," all of which traits make them eminently "Unprofitabl" because unpersuasive (78, 95, 81). As Jonathan Edwards observed, even if the dull "preacher's words represent the sinner's state as infinitely dreadful, his behavior and manner of speaking contradict it, and shew that the preacher don't think so."[61]

At first glance, one notices the difference between the positions of Tennent and Garden rather than their similarity. Tennent counsels his auditors to accept a dull manner of preaching the Word as a trustworthy signifier ("an awful Sign") of a corresponding inner deadness (86), and to act accordingly in conformity with the inner voice of conscience, defined as a God-given instinct toward the good (87–88). Garden counsels his auditors to reject an enchanting manner of preaching the Word as a trustworthy signifier of a

corresponding inner vitality, and to act accordingly in conformity with conscience defined as the God-given ability to reason. For Tennent, it appears,
the attributes of voice provide the listener with an immediate and accurate
insight into the spirit of utterance and thus provide direct access to the
inward self, the spiritual identity, of the speaker. Garden, on the contrary,
cautions his auditors that it is the disparity between voice and utterance,
between the manifest beauties of one and the equally manifest deformities of
the other, that defines, to the degree possible, the inward self. Whereas
Tennent implies that one's grasp of the inward man can be immediate and
instinctive, for Garden an accurate assessment depends upon one keeping
one's distance.

Albeit for different ends, however, both Tennent and Garden advocate an
ironic reading of ministerial voice and character according to which he who
appears "righteous unto Men" may be "within . . . full of Hypocrisy and
Iniquity" (Matthew 23:28). Despite Tennent's rhetoric of immediacy, both
ministers exhort their auditors to scrutinize form carefully in order to assess
substance correctly and to refrain from automatically accepting either the
extraordinary vitality or the reassuring ordinariness of the preacher's manner
and delivery as a signifier of his election. Rigorously examined, voice provides particularly valuable evidence of essential identity, according to Tennent and Garden, insofar as the advent of hypocrisy — whether of the charismatic itinerant or the established Pharisee — means that a natural and
necessary relationship between what one says and how one says it, who one
appears to be and who one really is, can no longer be assumed. Although
Tennent exhorts his listeners to remark the unremarkable, and Garden to
remark the remarkable, both urge their auditors to acknowledge the spiritual
death lying in wait on the far side of formal observance on the one hand, and
of formal innovation on the other; to recognize the accents of Satan in the
doctrinally correct on the one hand, and in the expressively gifted on the
other.

Finally, both, it bears emphasizing, have deduced spiritual identity from
voice, base their assessments of character, the outward, publicly available
man, upon the degree to which voice truly represents — or alternatively,
knowingly misrepresents — essential identity. An intuited or observed disjunction between voice and utterance, between what a minister expresses and
what he has truly experienced, yields in both analyses the fundamental truth

behind the minister's character: namely, his hypocrisy, his drive to appear to be what he is not.[62] Thus, for Tennent, the parishioner must scrutinize the minister's voice in order to determine whether he is a "Servan[t] of Satan, under a religious Mask": knowing that he is a servant of Satan enables one to perceive the mask, to learn to defamiliarize he "that has the Name of a Minister, with a Band, and a black Coat or Gown to carry on a *Sabbath-days*" (93, 86). Garden likewise reads the disparity between voice and utterance as indicative of a corresponding disparity between character, the image of oneself constructed for public consumption, and identity, who one truly is according to the determinations of God.

In effect, according to both Tennent and Garden, voice provided insight not just into the "invisibility" of one's spiritual identity but into the visible invisibility, the doubled structure, of character as well. Character offered itself as one's personal piece of the spectral realm as it was imagined by the Puritan prosecutors of the witchcraft crisis: a mediate domain straddling the invisible and visible worlds to serve the purposes of misrepresentation and indirection for the sake of individual self-aggrandizement at the expense of the holy community. Character, that is, may serve as the purview of an individual's individuality, an empty shell of "identity" serviceable in realizing the individual's secret designs in the world. In the sermons of Garden and Tennent, the questionability of character as a legitimate dimension of human existence is reflected in its association with those of doubtful integrity: Garden's Whitefield is a spy, a serpent, a wolf, a pretender; Tennent's unconverted ministers possess a number of unsavory character traits which he enumerates at length. For Tennent, the converted ministry are conspicuously free of the need to fabricate an "Out-side," a character complete with the costume and props of the ministerial trade (Harvard or Yale degree, black band, gown, and parish) for the purpose of speciously persuading their constituencies of their legitimacy. Likewise, Whitefield's supporters expressed the glory of the preacher's successful elision of character (a suspect interiority that requires a spurious "Outside" to mask its illegitimate operations) through the tropes of monumentality, the transcribed life, and the religious ravisher. This elision of character was precisely what Jonathan Edwards was hoping to accomplish for the common man or woman beset by grace.

Insofar as it too indicated a mediate and individually marked realm between the visible (or audible) and the invisible (or silent), the inner voice of conscience in the sermons of Garden and Tennent functioned as something like a "good" analogue for the doubleness or hybridity of character. As a voice, conscience was both private and yet common to all, both individual and corporate, intimate to the inner person and yet of divine provenance and thus possessed of universal reference. In their exposés of the rival ministries, both preachers encourage the exercise of their auditors' inner voices (although not necessarily audibly) as a nearly infallible source of truth concerning the spiritual identities of others: inner voice gives one the authority and power either to consent to, or reject, the verbal representations of transcendent truth offered by the rival ministries. To this degree, the era of evangelical itinerancy, like the witchcraft crisis before it, created a discursive climate in which there appeared to be no alternative to a certain antinomianism, even for those to whom the idea was most abhorrent. Exhorting their auditors to refer their doubts to an inner voice, and to heed its silent and faithful counsel, Garden and Tennent take an enormous step away from the ideal of a silent democracy and a speaking aristocracy celebrated by the Puritan ministry of the previous century, even if the auditor never actually articulates that inward and private, individuated if not precisely individualized, voice.[63] But in fact, as many ministers of both persuasions testified, this inward voice was increasingly vocal, if not always coherent, making itself heard in the joyful and despairing outbursts that frequently punctuated and sometimes threatened to overwhelm the sermons of the revivalist ministry. Once vocalized, this inner voice was itself subjected to the same process of rigorous scrutiny and consequent characterization to which the voices of the rival ministers had proven so vulnerable, launching a new, popular phase of the semiotic quest to establish the legitimacy of public speech. With increasing numbers of anonymous individuals giving voice publicly to feelings and ideas that had previously remained unarticulated, the problem of determining the authenticity and gauging the authority of their words became more and more pressing.

III

As the numbers of congregants who elected to separate from their established ministers attest, so prevalent did the critical scrutiny of ministerial character and voice become that, as Charles Chauncy bitterly observed in

1743, "*Religion,* between *Pastors* and *People*" was reduced in the course of the revival to "a *meer Nothing,* a *Sound without Meaning.*"[64] Chauncy's contention that the evangelicals, and particularly the itinerants, were responsible for this state of affairs was not strictly true: we have seen how Alexander Garden strove to reduce Whitefield's powerful voice to a sound without meaning and was unable to restrict to his opponents the critical anatomization of ministerial voice he had encouraged his estranged parishioners to undertake. Similarly, Chauncy (thinking only of his New Light adversaries) cautioned his readers that "no minister ought to be regarded, as tho' he was the author of our faith," a sentiment expressed in much broader terms by the New Light Rev. John Wilson to undermine assumptions about the sufficiency and scope of ministerial interpretive authority. Wilson condemned "that ridiculous Sense that some have endeavour'd to fasten upon these, or some of these Scriptures, as if they were to be understood only of the Spirit as given to the Church in common, and not to particular Christians." On the contrary, particular Christians who had rightly understood scriptural truths scrupulously forbore "to determine peremptorily, chusing rather to satisfy themselves with a modest Hesitancy, and abhorring to make their Judgments the Measure of another's Faith, or superciliously to censure or despise any for their different Apprehensions."[65] Whether generally rejected or embraced, then, the notion entertained to some degree by both conservatives and evangelicals that the auditory should "try" the truth-value of ministers' voices and thus of their visible characters entailed the breakdown of these formerly unassailable integrities and initiated a polemical inquiry into the legitimacy of locating spiritual authority in the experiences of individual members of the flock rather than their ostensible overseers.

The ramifications of this inquiry carried a range of significances from the epistemological through the political. They underwrote what historian Richard Bushman has described as "a diffusion of power from pastor to people" based upon a reconceptualization of the popular voice as it was articulated in the spontaneous and often crude expressions of religious feeling offered by uneducated and anonymous speakers in churches throughout the colonies.[66] An account submitted to *The Christian History* by Rev. Park of Rhode Island describes how the unilateral authority of the ministry might be supplanted by a horizontal circulation of spiritual power generated by the congregation. Park had invited the firebrand Presbyterian itinerant James

Davenport of Long Island to preach in his church and, having joined the members of his congregation to receive the visitor's exhortation, found himself "led . . . into the *secret Imagery* of *my own Heart*" by Davenport's sermon. Park marveled at the degree to which Davenport had animated his congregants, some of whom subsequently took so to heart his advice "to *testify* and *exhort* others to fly for Refuge" (presumably from Park's spiritual morbidity) that they resolved to meet separately to pray with and preach to one another.[67] Humbled by his visitor's efficacy in the pulpit and the newly critical stance of his parishioners toward himself, Park was eventually invited to join the separating group where, as he describes it, his role was confined to witnessing how spiritual power and initiative originated not with himself but with the people:

> They gave some Declaration of *the Work of* GOD *upon their Hearts*, in *converting* them to GOD, and *exhorted* the People to come to the LORD JESUS CHRIST. And I gave public Testimony that *this was the true Grace of* GOD *which they set forth*, and encouraged them to bear the Testimony of *Jesus* among the People. Many were greatly enraged at *them*, and at *me* for countenancing them: But I thought the *true Grace of* GOD must not be opposed, but encouraged where-ever GOD was bestowing it, and however he was sending it. . . . I was myself strengthened and lifted up by their Means. (206)

Park recognized the potentially nihilistic effect upon traditional church order of this horizontal and expanding circulation of power, a maelstrom to which the "inward and secret Spring" of each individual congregant had contributed, but Davenport had taught him, Park claimed, that his role was to "bring all into a ruinous Heap" insofar as "*the Way* to *help forward the Good of Mankind*, was *not to go to repairing and mending*, but to *pull down* as fast as I could, because there was *no Foundation* at all" (205, 202, 203).[68] Park offered a rationale for his own deauthorization by proposing that the source of genuine spirituality lay in the individual's "*deep Conviction of Sin*" — the unitary source of the obfuscated "*Imagery*" and hidden "*Spring*" peculiar to each individual soul (205).

Park's account thus reveals a strange and paradoxical alteration in the minister's traditional function to provide his congregation with the regular opportunity to partake of the "*instituted Means of Salvation*" through sermons and lectures.[69] On the one hand, in contrast to the perfunctory quality of audience attention to spiritual matters characteristic of prerevival days, an offhandedness that many ministers had been tempted to imitate so as not to appear unduly enthusiastic, revival audiences were uniformly rapt, listening to sermons "as for their Lives." The Reverend William Shurtleff pointed out in a public letter to the revival's opponents that, in stark contrast to their former lassitude, churchgoers had become like "thirsty Souls [that] seem'd greedily to drink down every Word that drop'd from the Preacher's Lips," suggesting that "a divine Power accompanied the Word."[70] On the other hand, the divine spark transmitted by the preacher on whose words the congregation hung could quickly provoke the latter to express their profound "Soul-concern" in "outward Tokens"—primarily inarticulate vocalizations and involuntary bodily motions—whose "very publick Appearance" had in many instances overwhelmed the minister's voice and rendered his ministrations superfluous.[71] Even Gilbert Tennent (whom the Anglican Timothy Cutler had vilified as "a monster! impudent and noisy!") underscored the irrepressible character of such scandalous manifestations, noting that "there have been such general Lamentations in the Time of Preaching, that the Speaker's Voice has been almost drowned with the *Cries* of the *Distressed*, even after they have been entreated again and again to restrain themselves."[72]

The Reverend Jonathan Dickinson of New York, whose pulpit eloquence was by his own admission in no way extraordinary, described his crucial, but absurdly foreshortened, role in stimulating soul-concern in his parishioners. Recounting the course of the revival in his parish for *The Christian History*, Dickinson wrote how one day he was "enliven'd" by his own congregation while preaching "a plain, practical Sermon; without any Pathos or Pungency, or any special Liveliness or Vigour; for I was then in a remarkably dead and dull Frame." The uninspired quality of his performance is simultaneously belied and brought powerfully to his attention when he unexpectedly received from his congregation "a *sudden* and *deep Impression*" of their "inward Distress and Concern" which "discover'd itself, by their *Tears*, and by an *audible Sobbing* and *Sighing* in *almost all Parts of the Assembly*."[73] Dickinson's account clearly conveys his startled realization that a latent and unknown spiritual power resided within each individual congregant; that he had unintentionally tapped this reserve of raw, religious energy which lay just beneath the surface of conventional piety; that it was sufficiently forceful to reverse the tradition-bound current of religious influence such that an inarticulate congregation could "minister grace" to a minister of the Word; and that this occurred through the collective emergence of an unknown and unregulated aspect of the individual self into the public sphere which was from that moment wholly transformed.[74] The challenge was to determine the precise significance of a transformation of religious community so unanticipated and seemingly spontaneous as to be "beyond what is Rational to Conceive" and apparently beyond what was possible to control.[75]

For both Old and New Light analysts, the pressing need for such a determination raised a number of questions connected to the primary task of assessing the meaning and authenticity of anomalous behaviors and modes of speech exhibited by individuals and the means by which they passed between individuals to inflame entire communities. At the heart of all these questions lay the individual subject, suddenly enigmatic precisely for his or her simplicity and seeming insignificance. More or less inarticulate and impulsive, the relevance of individual speech acts suddenly occurring in institutional religious settings seemed to extend no further than the boundaries of the speaking self; they were to all appearances neither deliberate nor rationally motivated. But if their primary purpose seemed to be other than that of rational communication, still they transmitted without impediment a powerful affective current from one individual to another, one capable of producing radical changes — separations and reformations — within long-established traditional communities. The questions that arose from such circumstances had necessarily to do with the nature of authority and embraced contexts as large as the American religious-cultural order and as minute as the individual utterance, whether ministerial or popular. Moving from the smallest to the largest organizational increments: in what aspect of language, and particularly spoken language, does meaning inhere? If the relationship of sound to meaning, manner to matter, or delivery to doctrine, was discovered to be contingent, did this not mandate a reassessment of what "sound" signified and what "meaning" meant? How and by whose authority could such a reassessment occur and whose authority would prove sufficient to cap a potentially endless proliferation of reassessments? Relatedly, who would decide what, precisely, constituted a true representation of religious feeling and experience? What was the relationship between the uncontrolled verbal responses arising from a conventionally silent and passive auditory and the authoritative speech of the ministry? If popular critical scrutiny of the minister's claim to religious authority had defamiliarized and thus delegitimated the normative institutional context within which sacred speech occurred, what alternative context (if any) grounded the seemingly anomalous speech of individuals and what rules (if any) did the former provide for the regulation and assessment of the latter? In sum, what nature of religious space lay beyond the boundaries of formal observance?[76]

For Old Lights, the answer to this last question was straightforward: the space beyond formal observance from which individual expressions of purported religious feeling were emanating was fantastic, delusional (whether linked to insanity, a weak intellect, or enthusiasm), and thus its meanings were strictly self-referential, the "frantick Freaks of a crazed Brain."[77] Indeed, it seemed the Salem delusion revisited. Chauncy bluntly declared that enthusiasm, the term to which he referred all the unorthodox phenomena related to the revival, was caused by "a bad temperament of the blood and spirits; 'tis properly a disease, a sort of madness" to which melancholics were particularly susceptible.[78] To the degree that it was affiliated with enthusiasm, the space beyond formal observance was significant only insofar as it was an oppositional realm invisibly affiliated with those forces, both carnal and supernatural, dedicated to the overthrow of the divinely established order as it was ontologically, ecclesiastically, socially, and politically constituted. Thus, Chauncy, in *Seasonable Thoughts*, rhetorically asks whether "the *Divine* SPIRIT, in dealing with Men in a Way of Grace, and in Order to make them good Christians, would give their *Passions* the *chief* Sway over them? Would not this be to invert their Frame? To place the Dominion in those Powers, which were made to be kept in Subjection?" Since the "End of the Influence of the SPIRIT of GOD" is to keep Christian subjects "in a State of due Subordination," it was incumbent upon "the *new-forming* Men" to promote "the Reduction of their *Passions* to a proper Regimen, i.e. The Government of a *sanctified Understanding*."[79] This sanctified understanding obediently acquiesced in the clergy's perception of "the truth as it lies nakedly and plainly in the *scripture* it self."[80] Chauncy exhorted the itinerant Davenport who had encouraged his hearers to invert church order by making "private Judgment, the Ground of publick Actions" that human beings "have no way of judging but by what is *outward* and *visible*" (and, he might have

added, textual): to do otherwise is to "assume a *divine prerogative*."[81] This
blasphemous assumption was the prerequisite to larger subversions: history
had shown that, collectively exercised, it had led directly to "the Multitude"
taking up "*Arms* against the lawful *Authority*." Samuel Weller (whose anti-
Whitefield tract the Anglican Timothy Cutler was anxious to import in
quantities into Massachusetts) agreed: all "Riots, Revolutions, and Rebel-
lions," he claimed, "do usually owe their Beginning to Enthusiasts, or Inno-
vators in Religion." "[W]hat Engine," Chauncy asked, "has the *Devil* himself
ever made Use of, to more fatal Purposes, in all Ages, than the *Passions* of the
Vulgar heightened to such a Degree, as to put them upon acting without
Thought and Understanding?"[82] Chauncy's answer to the question of what
lies beyond formal religious observance, his account of the invisible realm of
private judgment and individual feeling and its potential effects upon society
at large, powerfully recalls fears of the spectral realm — the invisible world of
anarchic individual desire — as it had been imagined by the afflicted and their
Puritan supporters in 1692. As Rev. Moses Bartlett, warning of the charms of
enthusiasts, asked in a sermon by way of Galatians 3:1, "*Who hath bewitched
you?*"[83]

Charles Chauncy described the enthusiast as one who "has a conceit of
himself as a person favoured with the extraordinary presence of the *Deity*. He
mistakes the working of his own passions for divine communications, and
fancies himself immediately inspired by the SPIRIT of GOD, while all the while,
he is under no other influence than that of an over-heated imagination."[84]
Although conspicuous to Old Lights for their failure to control their impassioned imaginations, their illegitimate and presumptive claims to possess
direct information concerning the invisible spiritual identities of others, and
their efforts to disenfranchise "*the faithful* Ministers *of* CHRIST" by helping to
cast "*Dung . . . on their Faces*, [and branding them] *no better than* LEGAL
PREACHERS, BAAL'S PRIESTS, POPISH FACTORS, SCRIBES, PHARISEES, *and* OPPOSERS
OF CHRIST HIMSELF," most of the new-forming men and women of the 1740s
were not considered thoroughly diabolical in their unholy individuation, as
were the specters of 1692.[85] The majority, according to many Old Light
observers, were followers who consented to the errors of New Light doctrine
from pitiable but predictable insufficiencies: moral weakness, mental illness,
or ignorance. Easily alienated from their own duty and ability to reason,
these "honest Hearts, but weak Minds," perhaps "more melancholy than

holy," could not be held fully responsible for their consent to doctrinal error and consequent defection from rational religion because they had fallen prey to a significant — and, with the advent of lay itinerancy, a growing — minority of professional enthusiasts.[86]

As Chauncy explained in an account of the Antinomian crisis with which he prefaced *Seasonable Thoughts*, professional enthusiasts, like the Antinomians before them, often *"speak excellently, pray with Soul ravishing Expressions and Affections"* so that those of weaker minds considered them *"likely to know the Secrets of* CHRIST, *and Bosom-Counsels of his* SPIRIT." Especially susceptible to their oratorical seductions were *"simple honest Hearts that loved* CHRIST" and *"new Converts, who were lately under Sin and Wrath, and had newly tasted the Sweetness of free Grace."*[87] Such people had unwittingly placed the fate of their souls in the hands of the artful (if mad) minority whose behavior was not grounded in the rule of Scripture but arose from *"sudden impulses* and *impressions"* and baseless convictions of *"immediate calls* and *extraordinary missions"* (16). *Enthusiasm described and caution'd against* is largely devoted to what Chauncy claimed to be a Scripture-based semiotic for enabling the naive to discern this latter type of enthusiast beneath a "bold and confident" self-presentation or a pious air of "seeming seriousness, gravity, or solemnity" (7). He cautioned his readers to watch for a "wildness" of countenance; "fluency and volubility in speaking, as they themselves, by their utmost efforts, can't so much as imitate, when they are not under the enthusiastick influence"; bodily afflictions manifested as "convulsions and distortions . . . quakings and tremblings"; frenzied, "freakish or furious" conduct; an "imaginary peculiar intimacy with heaven"; an "open disturb[ance] of the peace of the world"; a refusal to reason "from a calm and sober address to their understandings"; and a complementary proclivity to assert that the truth of their unorthodox doctrinal representations was self-evident (3–5).

The great semiotic touchstone for avoiding seducers and discerning the signs of enthusiasm in oneself and others was "God's written Word, that unerring Standard of Truth and Goodness," to which a multitude of alarmed Old Lights referred their auditors and readers.[88] As long as one honored the scriptural standard reconceived as a list of desirable and unfailingly visible character traits, prominent among which was a uniform and pleasant obedience to authority, right judgment in spiritual matters would unproblematically follow; the corollary to this claim is that only the *"unguarded,"* those "poorly furnish'd with the christian Armour" are in danger of succumbing to the seductions of enthusiasts.[89] With the scriptural text in place as an infallible standard by which to judge and regulate behavior, a single explanation remained to the Old Lights for the remarkable progress of the revival among the populace. As Rev. Timothy Walker described their modus operandi, the enthusiasts'

> very *Eyes* strike Infection, that by their *Gesture*, their *Tone*, their *Delivery*, savouring so much of Transport, they endeavour what they can to depress and darken the Understanding, and to warm the Imagination, and to alarm the Affections, and when once these are set up to tyrannize over the Understanding, the Mind is thereby rendered susceptible of any Impressions, and so Men become moulded into any Form which their enthusiastical or designing Leaders would have them.

According to this account, the enthusiasts are purveyors of a spiritual pathology that invades the body through the eyes rather than the ears or the mind, inducing an intellectual lassitude that makes the sufferer susceptible, like warm wax, to being passively impressed or molded into a replication of the enthusiast. A cynical parody of kenotic self-emptying, enthusiastic modeling leaves the devotee without intrinsic spiritual or existential content. Unlike the New Light vision of the active and, as it were, manly submission of the Christian subject to the religious ravisher, the Old Light portrayal of the professional enthusiast has his victim fall prey to a "Stratagem we sometimes use with Animals, whom we would hunt into a Snare or Ambush we have laid for them."[90]

The Reverend Moses Bartlett offered an explanation for the increasing numbers of enthusiasts that was less sanguine than Chauncy's account of a multitude of gentle creatures whose simplemindedness had led them directly into the seducer's snares. Bartlett's alarm stemmed from his conviction that "[t]here is ordinarily a very considerable resemblance and likeness between false and seducing Teachers, and those that are corrupted, insnared and seduced by them," but his detailed characterization of the seduced was marred by a notable discrepancy.[91] His enthusiasts are both rebellious and overly credulous, dismissive of authority and yet extraordinarily susceptible to it so as to be easily won over, not by the subtle and modulated assertions of the established ministry, but only by the crudest claims to illegitimate au-

THE ADVENT OF THE INDIVIDUAL

thority. Though quickly won, their allegiance proves temporary as the fractious seduced inevitably break from those who ensnare them to enact an endless chain of separations.[92] Bartlett's oxymoronic portrayal of evangelicals as disobedient followers — both "Fierce and Heady" and yet "an easy Prey to Seducers" — constituted an illogic that followed from his inability to imagine an alternative form of discursively generated and maintained spiritual power other than that transmitted from an illegitimate leader to a mob unreflectively, as a type of fashion, imbibing his errors. The revival, in this view, represented nothing more spiritually significant (if socially dangerous) than the *"Vogue of the profane Multitude."*[93] This illogic was consonant with the conservatives' stereotypic characterization of New Light Christians as a "giddy Multitude of unthinking Mortals" whose efforts at "expounding the Scriptures, solving Difficulties, clearing up Doubts, and *communicating their Experiences,* is what would certainly excite the Laughter of the *Prophane,* and the Grief of the *Wise* and *Religious.*"[94]

The New Light response to such accounts entailed a necessarily sweeping redefinition of terms that described the phenomenon of spiritual awakening and its manifestations in individual Christians. The Reverend John Wilson proposed in the pages of *The Christian History* a reexamination of the term "enthusiasm" that led directly into a theory of religious utterance which denied the conservative ministry's claims to an exclusive prerogative to speak authoritatively about spiritual matters. Wilson's aim was to establish that what lay beyond formal religious observance was neither insanity nor hypocrisy, but rather "the inward Devotion of the Heart," an invisible and ordinarily unspoken spiritual realm "wherein the Life of Religion consists."[95] Wilson maintained that enthusiasm, considered as an attribute of the Christian heart, *"is of it self good"*; its intrinsic benignity, however, had been obscured by Old Light rhetoric to serve as "a *theological Scare-Crow"* with which to alarm their readers and auditors (222). In the process, the site of vital religious experience, the individual heart stirred or enthused by the divine, had been similarly obscured by the formal practices instituted and maintained by the established clergy. Denying the validity of his opponents' etymological efforts to assert a historical rationale for their pejorative sense of "enthusiasm," Wilson argued that a word's meaning does not inhere in the word itself, which cannot, therefore, in this instance or any other, function as the neutral bearer of consistent meaning.[96] A word's significance is irrevocably tied neither to its historical nor to its conventional usages, but it is linked to the specific ontological state of the one who utters it and the particular disposition of the one who hears it: this singularity of usage constitutes "the naked Truth" of the utterance (rather than "the truth as it lies nakedly and plainly in the *Scripture* it self") which the speaker dare not, and perhaps cannot, dissemble.[97] Meaning could only be the product of a fitting proportionality between the word a speaker utters and the feeling with which he or she utters it. Whether their speech is public or private, Wilson argued, speakers must strive "to have their Expressions in some due Proportion answerable to the Affections of their Hearts" if their speech is to register with the recipient of their words as truthful and significant (222). Conventional usage, on the contrary, by virtue of its abstraction from the specific ontology as well as the specific dialogicity of utterance, was inherently fatal to truthful expression. Its authenticating claim to universal applicability was, in fact, precisely what marked it as an "Incongruity" that severed articulation from immediate experience and thus dissociated utterance from meaning and the grounds of truth (221).

Wilson illustrated the importance of proportion in utterance with reference to the Christian practice of supplicating God for salvation from sin and thus for eternal life. Within this context, Wilson pointed out, the perfunctory quality of conventional prayer is incongruous insofar as it does not convey to God any indication that the petitioner has confronted his or her individual impotence and recognized an urgent need for help. "Should not Sinners," Wilson asked,

> in their Addresses to the most High, have their Hearts deeply touch'd with Sorrow for the Sins that they apprehend themselves, or others for whom they are concern'd, to be guilty of, or liable to? Doth it become an Offender, that is to beg his Pardon, to do it in a stupid Manner, as if he had no more Sense of his Fault than a Stone or a Brute? And what Incongruity is it for us in our Petitions for Mercy, to have our Desires raised to the highest Pitch that we can reach? Is the pardoning and purifying Grace of Christ of so little Worth or Use to us, as they need be but coldly or carelessly askt, as if our Words freezed between our Lips, or as if we did not greatly care whether we were heard or no? Or can we expect that God should hear those Petitions, which we our selves scarce feel when they go from us? (221)

God hears only what the supplicant feels, and feelings cannot be governed by convention or regulated by forms, especially as convention overrides and therefore stifles the living variety and potency of religious experience. The same imperative of vital speech applied to ministers, "whose Work it is to dispense the Word of Life." Why should they not, Wilson asked, formulating a key question of revival protocol, "deliver their Message in such a Manner, as that their Hearers may discern that they are in good earnest, and that the Word spoken to them is that whereon their eternal Life or Death depends?" (221). Far from constituting a distortion or an irregularity, ardent desire in this context exhibited a fitting proportionality.

Wilson invoked the deathbed as a symbolic locale for illustrating the existential specificity attached to the meanings of words and how susceptible conventional usage was to instantaneous obsolescence. Wilson noted that many, "in the Days of their Health and Jollity, have derided [Enthusiasts], for a Company of silly, distracted Fools." The threat of death, however, "awaken'd their Conscience, and bro't them to a more sober Use of their Reason, & a more serious View of Eternity" (228–29). Immanent death effects a revaluation of all values, a redefinition of terms adjusted not to convention, not even to the scope of a moment's intense feeling, but to eternity itself and the existential realities that human beings strive to deny.[98] Redefining the operative characterological terms (reason, sobriety, seriousness) so as to vindicate enthusiastic speech from charges of solipsistic madness and impulsiveness, Wilson invoked George Herbert's advice to preachers "to make choice of *moving and ravishing Texts*: and *to dip and season all their Words and Sentences in their Hearts before they come into their Mouths, truly affecting, and cordially expressing all that they say, so that the Auditors may plainly perceive that every Word is Heart-deep*" (221–22). Simultaneously immediate and essential, directly linked to context and thus transcending it, only the heart-deep word unerringly transmitted its truth, providing a ground for meaning and thus permitting genuine (consensual rather than compulsory) communication.

Wilson's rationale for the heartfelt word was addressed primarily to New Light fears that many of the key manifestations of evangelical spirituality, and particularly the recourse scores of parishioners had taken to "Visions, Dreams, or immediate Inspirations," were fundamentally antinomian in origin. Whereas moderate New Lights united to condemn such "extraordinary Ways" of experiencing a link to God, they could not so readily agree on the significance and legitimacy of those "outward Tokens of inward Soul-concern" — primarily, uncontrolled movements of the body and involuntary ejaculations of heartfelt speech — that appeared to be authentic signs of saving conviction.[99] Charles Chauncy provided an appalling descriptive catalog of such outward tokens in a public letter that quotes a witness to a New Light prayer meeting. Lay assistants appointed by the revivalist minister "'observed no stated Method, but proceeded as their present Thought or Fancy led them.'" As a result,

> "sometimes 10, 20, 30, and sometimes many more would *scream* and *cry out*, or send forth the most *lamentable Groans*, whilst others made great Manifestations of Joy, by *clapping their Hands*, uttering *extatick Expressions*, *singing Psalms*, and *inviting* and *exhorting* others. Some would *swoon away* under the Influence of distressing Fears, and others *swallowed up with insupportable Joy*. While some were *fainting*, others laboured under *convulsive Twiches of Body*, which they said were involuntary."[100]

John Cotton poignantly expressed the New Light predicament in relation to the task of evaluating such unprecedented appearances: echoing the eminent Thomas Hooker in the preface to his defense of the New England Way, he asked, "If these Things, which come so confirmed by Testimonies on all hands are not to be received as *Verities*, human Proof is at an End, and *all Men are Lyars*."[101]

The questions New Lights were constrained to pose in the face of their own and their opponents' skepticism were, first, how was the authenticity of such outward tokens or manifestations, their derivation from the work of the spirit of God upon individual souls, to be determined? Was their motivation sufficiently genuine to justify the "very publick Appearance of deep Soul-concern" demonstrated by individuals in congregations throughout the colonies and in some places forcing bitter separations of congregants from established ministers? In other words, could such behavioral expressions of religious feeling be exempted from the pitfall common to all representations, namely, the ease with which they may be counterfeited or dissembled? Finally, was it possible to propose some alternative understanding of the transmission of intense religious feeling than that brutal scenario of dominance and submission proposed by Old Lights like Walker and Bartlett? Was it

conceivable that vital religious experience could be modeled and appropriated in such a way that its transmission from one individual to another would
entail no loss of authenticity, no reduction in its urgent particularity to each
person in the chain of transmission? As Jonathan Edwards saw it, nothing
less than the apotheosis of national-millennial community depended on the
ability of New Light theorists to imagine, in the form of a redeemed representation so conceived, a mode of individual religious experience at once
authentic and imitated, a spiritual eccentricity collectively perfected and
thus constituting the inevitable prelude to "beautiful Variety, and yet sweet
Harmony."[102]

In response to the need for such a vision, New Lights proposed an alter-
nate notion of unerring scriptural truth and the ways in which it was appropriated by individuals in the interests of casting anomalous behaviors associated with the revival as the harbingers of a genuine community of saints, an
"ingathering of Souls."[103] The conclusion to which they more or less collectively arrived (in venues like *The Christian History*) was not exempt from the
familiar paradox of humble self-enlargement (encapsulated in the pleasure of
self-annihilation that Edwards claimed for converts): each individual's discovery of his or her individuality as a "miserable condition" of "utter helplessness and insufficiency" was prerequisite to an experience of authentic
selflessness which was in turn, under certain conditions of performance,
prerequisite to genuine Christian community.[104] That is, each individual's
discovery of his or her radical singularity was simultaneously the discovery of
redeemed collectivity, or at least the prerequisite for its realization in history.[105] David Brainerd succinctly expressed the paradox of individuality so
conceived: "I never felt it so sweet to be nothing, and less than nothing, and
to be accounted nothing."[106] Seeking to develop a conceptual basis and an
accompanying theological rationale for those manifestations of radical individuality increasingly common in revivalist settings, New Lights countenanced, if they did not encourage, a range of anomalous behaviors, primarily
spontaneous outbursts of public speech concerning spiritual realities.[107]
Their efforts to accommodate this behavior were both plagued and guided
by the pressing need to discriminate inauthentic (either imagined or counterfeited) from authentic expressions of an individual's terror in confronting his or her existential solitude.[108] If genuine, this terrified apprehension
of one's radical isolation — individuality as the sine qua non of existential

insignificance — would impel one's heartfelt vocal rejection of that condition and inspire one's willingness to embrace Christian selflessness as the only viable alternative to singularity. Thus it became crucial for the observer concerned with authenticity to discern in the typical, despairing cry that marked the soul's awakening — "I am undone!" — whether the psychological weight of the utterance fell (solipsistically) upon the initiatory personal noun or (redemptively) upon the predicate that declared its annihilation.

Emotional outcries in public could only be tolerated if they were involuntary and yet rationally motivated, not the product of vision or imagination, as when Rev. Samuel Blair, having privately interviewed those who vocally disrupted his sermon, claimed that such outbursts bespoke "a *rational fixt Conviction* of their dangerous perishing Estate."[109] The Reverend John Cotton of Plymouth, too, closely observed those members of his congregation who interrupted his sermons with cries of distress. One woman in particular drew his attention because she had previously exhibited impatience with others who had disrupted sermons in that manner: "I and some others observed her *narrowly*," Cotton remarked, "and discoursed with her during her Distress; and it was evident to us that she could as soon have made a World, as have help'd manifesting her Trouble in the Manner she did." He concluded that, given her earlier resistance to such demonstrations of soul-concern, "it is impossible [her crying out] should be feign'd." For Cotton and many other New Lights, it was imperative to establish that individuals articulated their distress publicly because they were irresistibly impelled to do so. Precisely the involuntary nature of popular speech legitimated it in the eyes of the moderate New Light ministry because it ensured that such speech was not a sign of individuation but was rather the sign of a work of God upon the individual soul. The eruption of individual voice into the public space thus might be regarded as occurring for no self-aggrandizing motive but as subordinate to and instrumental in the expression of the divine will: popular speech denoted not individual empowerment but rather the extreme impotence of the sinner in the hands of an angry God or the irresistible joy of the sinner receiving a conviction of saving grace. According to Cotton, individual expression testified to individual powerlessness, paradoxically manifested as a sudden ability to transcend one's discursive limitations. Many speakers, he noted, "seem to go beyond themselves, and speak in such a moving Manner as they were never capable of before."[110]

Insofar as this account of popular speech recalls similar explanations for the discursive precocity of the afflicted offered in the course of the witchcraft crisis, it suggests the emergence of a cultural rationale intended to govern the production and reception of popular expression. Like the humble self-enlargement and divinely mandated uncontainability of George Whitefield and the inspired victimization of the afflicted of 1692 for whom spectral evidence theorists sanctioned innocent access to and speech about the invisible world, individual members of evangelical congregations were perceived to be involuntarily exercising an unprecedented verbal power and thereby demonstrating their achievement of selflessness. (The hapless accused of 1692 were, of course, imagined to have willed a forbidden access to transcendent power from self-aggrandizing motives and were treated accordingly.) The task—ideological or theological, according to one's lights—of the revival was to extend to the populace access to redeemed individual expression about invisible realities and to proclaim such speech exempt from the manifold possibilities of misrepresentation. But to extend the privilege of speech beyond the charismatic individual or an elite corps of cultural martyrs like the afflicted of 1692 was to threaten to eradicate the clear demarcation between private experience and the public realm by allowing unauthorized individuals to move out of the private confinement of the heart and the prayer closet and into the public spaces of church or even marketplace.

Jonathan Edwards described the process by which individual soul-concern exceeded its normative confinement within the heart as the making visible of an invisible spiritual labor that Old Lights continued to maintain no one but Jesus was able or authorized to regard. The difference between the mini-awakening of 1735 in Northampton and the revivals less than a decade later, according to Edwards, was that in the latter time

Conversions were frequently wrought *more sensibly and visibly*; the Impressions stronger, and more manifest by external Effects of them; and the Progress of the SPIRIT of GOD in Conviction, from Step to Step, more apparent; and the transition from one State to another more sensible and plain; so that it might, in many Instances, be as it were seen by Bystanders. . . . And in this Season these apparent or *visible Conversions* (if I may so call them) were frequently in the Presence of others, at religious Meetings, where the Appearance of what was wrought on the Heart fell under publick Observation.[111]

By sanctifying the formerly suspect process of making the invisible visible and the silent audible, and thus generally available, Edwards implicitly identified the voice involuntarily released in the process of spectacular conversion as the sign of the consummation and legitimation of this process. Moreover, his conspicuous use of the passive mode here makes the transformation of private spiritual experience into public spectacle inevitable, on the order of a fait accompli, suggesting that henceforward private experience was public business and that private speech — utterances apparently relevant only to the hopes and fears of one person — was thus legitimately exercised in public space.

So desirable was the seemingly untenable combination of discursive power and personal impotence that those who could not achieve it were left in a despair apparently greater than that felt by those who weepingly proclaimed their own immanent undoing. Those reticent individuals who found that they could not publicly "brea[k] forth in earnest and pathetical Expressions" had cause to suspect their exclusion from God's "*electing Love.*"[112] Cotton wrote of Plymouth's richest man, who lamented on his deathbed "that while Children and young People were boldly praising & glorifying GOD, he had come so far behind them, and that he was so *bashful and silent* in the Cause of GOD, and that he had been almost afraid to shew his Opinion." Likewise, a woman speaking on the verge of death, that locus of Christian sincerity which Cotton Mather counseled ministers to unfailingly recall before exhorting, wondered "*how any Mouth could be shut at such a Time.*"[113] And yet public speech was, for many, a form of impotence not easy to achieve so that some were tempted to imitate it, a plight compassionately described by Samuel Blair:

> They believed there was a good Work going on; that People were convinced, and bro't into a converted State; and they desired to be converted too: They saw others weeping and fainting, and heard People mourning and lamenting, and they thought if they could be like these it would be very hopeful with them; hence, they endeavoured just to get themselves affected by Sermons, and if they could come to Weeping, or get their Passions so raised as to incline them to vent themselves by Cries, now they hoped they were got under Convictions, and were in a very hopeful Way; and afterwards, they would speak of their being in Trouble, and aim at complaining of themselves, but seem'd as if they knew not well how to do it, and what to say against themselves.

These, Blair was forced to conclude, were indulging in "an *imaginary Conversion* of their own Making"; the new-formed man, New Light theorists were determined, would in no sense be self-made.[114]

In an effort to provide a standard characterization of the genuine, as opposed to the self-made, convert, New Lights devised what purported to be an alternative semiotics of spiritual authenticity to that advanced by their opponents, delineating in their sermons "the inseperable Characters of the truly *regenerate* People of GOD" against which individuals could compare themselves. But as they discovered, the conceptual challenge would prove more exacting than a characterological tit-for-tat.[115] John Wilson, for example, despite his claim that the authenticity of unconventional individual speech may be verified with reference to the genuineness of its emotional context, was compelled to raise the possibility that even a fitting proportionality of feeling to utterance may be fundamentally illegitimate if feeling itself was called into question. This could occur either because feeling generated by "meer *natural* or *mechanical Influence*" (as fear of thunder or earthquakes) may be mistaken for a divine influence upon the soul, or because a pretender, appropriating the "Externals" of religious emotion, may demonstrate "Fervency and Fluency in Exercises of Devotion," and thereby "cheat the World, and bring the true Workings of the Spirit of God into Suspicion and Disgrace" (229–30).[116] Such speculation delivered Wilson to his opponents, whose criticisms he dialogically anticipated by invoking comparisons of enthusiasts with "those *Demagogues* of old, who, by their bewitching Oratory charm'd the Hearts of the Vulgar, and thereby accomplish'd their own Ends upon them" (231).

Given the compatibility of New Light and Old Light fears regarding the ease with which ravishing speech and ravished behavior may be dissembled, Wilson was constrained to refer doubts about the authenticity of the speaker's speech to visible character, whose apparent sincerity would provide an index of the truth of the spirit of utterance. The true enthusiast (as opposed to the artful demagogue), Wilson maintained, will be known by his or her demonstrated reluctance to dominate others and by an evident proclivity to "disown all such self-admiring and self-exalting Conceits" (233). Should one find oneself tempted to equate enthusiasm with madness — following the Old Lights, for whom such an equation "becomes their Interest" insofar as it allowed them "to brand whatsoever lies out of their Road" as pathological —

one had only to reflect whether "the Persons thus charged are known to be sober and considerate, and in all their Discourses & Affairs as rational as other Men, and as composed every Way as any of those who thus traduce them" (222, 227). Wilson's critique of discursive conventionality thus led him to counsel those who remained uncertain about the truth-value of enthusiastic speech to consider as authenticating signs both the speaker's reputation and possession of the conventional marks of respectability: "examine the Behaviour of those who are thus calumniated, observe their grave Deportment, their serious Discourse, their circumspect Carriage, their prudent Conduct of Affairs; and let sober Reason judge whether these be the Effects of Madness" (227). As even Gilbert Tennent admitted, there seemed to be no escape from judging either by "Mens Speech" or by their "Practice" — by what lay upon the surface of experience and purported to represent it.[117] Formal exegetical discipline along with its institutional supports had been challenged by those desirous of establishing some more organic foundation for transcendent realities, only to be replaced by a tautology of specular representations: the authenticating spirit of an individual speaker's utterance was inevitably referred to the conventional respectability of his or her visible character, whose authenticity was referred back to the spirit of the utterance.

To forge a path out from the representational dead end — the tautology of voice and visible character — to which both New Lights and Old Lights had arrived when attempting to evaluate the novel behaviors and speech associated with the revival, Jonathan Edwards offered in his works from the early 1740s a thorough reconceptualization of the notion of representational purity. His seminal treatise, *Some Thoughts Concerning the present Revival of Religion*, questions the general expectation that a work of God upon the soul should produce an unambiguous visible representation, either in character or voice, of the invisible, purified heart as the ground of authentic religious experience. "The great weakness" of most observers of the effects of the revival upon individuals, whether conservative or evangelical, was to be found in their "not distinguishing" true from false manifestations within the context of a single work, "but either approving or condemning all in the lump."[118] But the expectation of a wholly "good" or wholly false representation of a work of God on the soul was disingenuous given "this imperfect state and dark world, where so much blindness and corruption remains in the best." It cannot be expected that the claims of individuals to have enjoyed "sensible communication with God" should mean that they will henceforth "appear like angels, and not still like poor, feeble, blind and sinful worms of the dust." On the contrary, Edwards reminded his readers that every human being, including the saint, was inwardly divided, the inevitable "state of true Christians in this world" (314). "[T]he same persons," he elsewhere observed,

> may be the subjects of much of the influences of the Spirit of God, and yet in some things be led away by the delusions of the Devil; and this be no more of a paradox than many other things that are true of real saints, in the present state, where grace dwells with so much corruption, and the new man and the old man subsist together in the same person; and the kingdom of God and the kingdom of the Devil remain for a while together in the same heart.[119]

Human individuality cannot accurately be described in terms of integrity whether of a gracious or an evil sort, because at any given moment the individual is incomplete and in process, moving ineluctably toward his or her spiritual destiny as God has determined it. So conceived, corruption is the condition of human being — coloring not just behavioral representation but the essential experience upon which representation is based — and cannot, therefore, be epistemologically useful in the evaluation of the authenticity of human actions or utterance. Instead, the self-division or hybridity that is inherent in being human makes the theatricality of human behavior inevitable. One is constrained to act *in character*, as Jesus himself (Edwards's best example of human perfection-in-process), demonstrated by his treatment of Judas. "[I]n all external things," Edwards pointed out, Jesus treated Judas

> as if he had truly been a disciple, even to the investing him with the character of apostle, and sending him forth to preach the Gospel, and enduing him with miraculous gifts of the Spirit: for though Christ knew him, yet he did not then clothe himself with the character of omniscient judge, and searcher of hearts, but acted the part of a minister of the visible church of God.[120]

Jesus must accept the discrepancy between Judas's visible character and his spiritual identity to the point of promoting the deception publicly because it was inappropriate for him, in his human character, to inquire into the genuineness of visible phenomena. The lesson that Edwards would draw from Jesus' self-sacrificial upholding of the principle that visible phenomena must be regarded as authentic is intended for all parties whose drive to uncover the absolute and hidden truth underlying human character and behavior leads them to ignore the profound doubleness of human existence. All human representations, including character and voice, partake inevitably of this doubleness and cannot be expected to demonstrate the integrity of goodness or badness. If this caveat applies to the man "of the strongest reason and the greatest learning," then it must surely be considered "when such multitudes of all kinds of capacities, natural tempers, educations, customs and manners of life" arise to claim the experience of a work of God upon the soul (317). Not surprisingly, this lack of integrity associated with individuality characterized human collectivity as well or, more specifically, the "making of a world." As Edwards pointed out, "In the first creation God did not make a complete world at once; but there was a great deal of imperfection, darkness, and mixture of chaos and confusion, after God first said, 'Let there be light' ": confusion is thus the condition of the created world.[121]

The inevitability of confusion and the elusiveness of absolute truth as the basis of experience or representation in the human realm meant that at any given moment of human existence a double trial was of necessity in process. Human beings, struggling toward transcendent reality, are obliged to "try" the spirits that appear before them to offer guidance and not to follow such spirits blindly. At the same time, human beings may be divinely "tried" for their possession of what might be called a sanctified credulity:

> 'Tis with Christ's works as it was with his parables: things that are difficult to men's dark minds are ordered of purpose, for the trial of persons' dispositions and spiritual sense, and that persons of corrupt minds, and of an unbelieving, perverse, caviling spirit, seeing might see and not understand.[122]

Bereft of transcendent certainty and cautioned against relying on their own judgment, provided with no exit from the funhouse of representations that conditions existential reality, human beings in the revival confronted an additional stumbling block in their path to salvation: the complete novelty of the event. Edwards characterized the awakening as "the beginning of something very extraordinary," "a state of things so uncommon" in its "degree, extent, swiftness and power . . . that there has not been time and experience enough to give birth to rules for people's conduct"; moreover, even considered in historical perspective, such an occurrence was so extraordinary "that the writings of divines don't afford rules to direct us in such a state of things" (318). Without experience or instruction, individuals cannot be condemned if they "don't know how to behave themselves in such a new and strange state of things" (321). In such extraordinary circumstances, even language fails one: new sensations and ideas may place otherwise articulate and composed individuals in a position of ignorance concerning "how to accommodate language to, or to find words to express" the novelty of experience.[123] This novelty extended to the experience of conversion itself. Supporting Wilson's point about the incongruity of conventional discourse, new converts would admit

> that the expressions that were used to describe conversion and the graces of God's Spirit, such as a spiritual sight of Christ, faith in Christ, poverty of spirit, trust in God, resignedness to God, etc., were expressions that did not convey those special and distinct ideas to their minds which they were intended to signify; in some respects no more than the names of colors are to convey the ideas to one that is blind from his birth.[124]

Novelty of experience thus underwrites the necessity of incoherence, a manifestation of evangelical spirituality that Old Lights particularly deplored as an abandonment of human reason. Edwards, however, declared that inarticulateness in such circumstances was clarifying and thus possessed the status and credibility of language:

> Cryings out, in such a manner and with such circumstances, as I have seen them from time to time, is as much an evidence to me, of the general cause it proceeds from, as language: I have learned the meaning of it the same way that persons learn the meaning of language, viz. by use and experience. (399)

Implicitly, Edwards claimed that normative verbal representation can only work conventionally, as a possibility of repetition, and that a redeemed — an automatically and universally persuasive and accessible — language is not a necessary corollary to an experience of saving grace.[125]

In part, the intellectual power of Edwards's meditations on the Great Awakening derives from his willingness to confront the ubiquity of confusion and the likelihood, given humankind's fallen state, that behind every seeming absolute a contingency lurked fatal to categorical judgments of any stripe. His concern for clarification of the import of behaviors associated with the revival led him to suggest that ministers might serve a ventriloquizing function for their inarticulate parishioners, "interrogat[ing]" and "examin[ing]" them in order to help them articulate their experiences "though of themselves they could not find expressions and forms of speech to do it."[126] In effect, Edwards here adumbrates what will be a central precept of the aesthetics of innocence culminating in Whitman, which I will discuss in Chapter 6: the more authentic the speech and its speaker, the more novel and original, and the more justified the speaker's impulse to speak, the more he or she requires an act of ventriloquization, not so much sympathetic as devoid of residue or interference from the ventriloquist's self, to articulate the "truest representation" (387) of inherently unspeakable material.

The leading role to be played by the minister in ensuring a happy issue from the stuttering confusion of incipient glory is augmented by Edwards's account of the preached word as the source of the "truest representation." The concept was intended to liberate those who struggled to assess revival phenomena from the specularity of the character/voice dyad, whose viability had in any case already been deconstructed in the course of the rival ministries' internecine debates. Edwards conceded that "affectionate" preachers, those who employ "a very earnest and pathetical way of preaching," did not attempt to enlighten their auditors through a "distinct, and learned handling of the doctrinal points of religion, as depends on human discipline, or the strength of natural reason," an approach that would "enlarge their hearers' learning, and speculative knowledge in divinity" (387, 386). But the fact that the auditors' speculative knowledge of divinity was not increased did not mean that their "understandings . . . [of] divine and eternal things" remained unenlightened by affectionate preaching (386). On the contrary, "[a]n appearance of affection and earnestness in the [preacher's] manner of delivery," providing that "there be no appearance of its being feigned or forced," will more accurately produce "true ideas or apprehensions" in the hearer's mind

(387). An affectionate preaching style "does in fact more truly represent" divine truth than a "cold and indifferent" manner:

> If the subject be in its own nature worthy of very great affection, then a speaking of it with very great affection is most agreeable to the nature of that subject, or is the truest representation of it, and therefore has most of a tendency to beget true ideas of it in the minds of those to whom the representation is made. (387)

Essentially, Edwards relativizes Wilson's criterion of proportionality in heartfelt speech and in so doing explicitly makes peace with appearances. If the neutral and "unerring" word had ceded to a multiplicity of characterological and vocal representations, any and all of which might be to some degree counterfeited, this did not therefore mean that all representations need be abandoned as equally unreliable. As William Hobby straightforwardly put it, "Would you reject a Piece of *Gold*, because you have seen a *brazen* Thing, speciously counterfeited? . . . The *Sun* itself has its *Spots*; shall we therefore try to *put out* the Sun?"[127] Edwards proclaimed the critical difference between representations to lie in the potency with which a representation, such as a preacher's manner or style of preaching, could render an image of absolute truth in the mind of the recipient: a characterological or vocal image of true piety might beget in the mind of the beholder or auditor a mental image more truly representative of the transcendent object of piety than any amount of speculative knowledge about it.

With the concept of the truest representation, Edwards surmounted the impasse which Elizabeth Knapp's diabolical voice had presented Samuel Willard seventy years earlier by acknowledging and redeeming the double-voicedness at the heart of authentic utterance. Moreover, its emphasis upon an image conjured in the mind of one who receives a sensible representation of transcendent truth effectively rehabilitated the imagination, which the Old Lights had condemned as the "enem[y] of your *souls*."[128] This theoretical rehabilitation of the imagination allowed New Lights to address the problems inherent in the spectacular transmission of the prerogative of public speech to private individuals. Old Lights, of course, continued to embellish their opinions of evangelical spirituality as a virulent species of social malaise to which the common classes were particularly susceptible, a pathogenic infection that overstimulated the imagination and thus the organs of speech. Perhaps no more cynical account of enthusiastic contagion exists than the one offered to George Wishart of Edinburgh by Charles Chauncy:

> The *Speaker* delivers himself, with the *greatest Vehemence* both of *Voice* and *Gesture*, and the most *frightful Language* his Genius will allow of. If this has its intended Effect upon *one* or *two weak Women*, the Shrieks catch from one to another, till a great Part of the Congregation is affected; and some are in the Thought, that it may be too common for those *zealous in the new Way* to *cry out themselves*, on purpose to move others, and bring forward a *general Scream*.[129]

What trope other than infection could account for the rapid spread of the inclination to enact often scandalous outward tokens of inward soul-concern? Even if one were prepared to grant the antinomian claim that vital religious experience could be transmitted vertically as God's direct influence upon an individual soul, and that such experience justified otherwise scandalous public behaviors, was it therefore possible for vital religious experience to be transmitted horizontally, between individuals in the process of spectacular conversion, without stimulating the empty reproduction of its behavioral effects? If one person's behavior, generally accepted as a sanctified representation of genuine feeling, inevitably engendered similar behavior in one who happened to observe this soul-concern, did the replicated behavior automatically entail a progressive debasement of the originating experience? Or would it share the same exemption from suspicion of counterfeit; could it be granted authenticity even though it was patently imitated?[130] Such questions became increasingly urgent as the will to reproduce vital private experience as disruptive public speech ubiquitously asserted itself in New Light congregations with or without official validation.

Edwards's theory of the transmission or "begetting" of true images from mind to mind offered a release from a tautology of representations, on the one hand, and from charges of inauthenticity, on the other, by abandoning the notion of an originary representation that functioned as the site of representational purity (the first outcry in the church as opposed to those that followed). If an original purity of experience was not an issue (a concession appropriate in light of the confused and fallen state of what Edwards called "human nature"), there was no reason to assume the progressive corruption of successive representations. Visible conversion, the transformation of private experience into public spectacle, might thus be considered with equanimity. With the truth of the representation gauged by its effects upon the recipient, a range of novel religious "experiences" was legitimated, as Edwards realized at least as early as 1736 when he maintained that with respect to "the manner of persons being wrought upon . . . there is a vast variety, perhaps as manifold as the subjects of the operation."[131] Affection as the ground of vital religious experience might result from one's witnessing another's conversion and marking the stages of its sensible progress, as well as from one's hearing a sermon, participating in a private or public conversation about religion, or hearing about conversions and the propagation of religious affection occurring elsewhere. Some were "suddenly seized" with convictions; others gradually altered their thought and behavior; others already convicted gained a new perspective on their condition.[132] If such modes of the transmission of religious experience were not seen as fatally compromising its authenticity, then the Old Lights' contemptuous accounts of the transmission of revival ideology were refuted and the way cleared for an alternative vision of redeemed community.[133] The concept of the truest representation begetting a valid image in an individual recipient's mind created a market, as it were, for the generation of novel representations of divinity. These prominently included novel types of religious personality who modeled their religiosity, unwittingly or not, before substantial crowds whose appropriation or replication of the model's speech or behavior need not be condemned as inauthentic because unoriginal. As Edwards put it in *Distinguishing Marks of a Work of the Spirit of God*, it is the "coming of false Christs which Christ tells us will be in a private manner, in the deserts, and in the secret chambers; whereas this event of setting up the kingdom of God, should be open and public in the sight of the whole world."[134] William Cooper, in the preface to *Distinguishing Marks*, noted that "God has evidently made use of example and discourse" in the carrying forward of the work of conversion, and Edwards was particularly sanguine about the legitimacy of the example provided by multitudes of individuals enacting "unavoidable manifestations of strong religious affections" for the benefit of bystanders. For Edwards, the "new-formed men" that the Old Lights contemned might be, indeed, both "formed" by example, the public performance of private experience (among God's "chief means" for carrying out His work) and yet genuinely "new."[135]

In his preface, Cooper quotes the seventeenth-century English Puritan John Howe who laments another species of inarticulateness than that which the conservative ministry disdained in the uneducated. Howe's sermon poignantly depicted a failed scene of godly speech in which the majority listen mutely while the designated speaker, the minister, fails to find the words with which to talk to his auditors about God:

> We know not how to speak living sense unto souls, how to get within you: our words die in our mouths, or drop and die between you and us. We even faint when we speak; long experienced unsuccessfulness makes us despond: we speak not as persons that hope to prevail, that expect to make you serious, heavenly, mindful of God, and to walk more like Christians. The methods of alluring and convincing souls, even that some of us have known, are lost from amongst us in a great part.

The quotation concluded with Howe's hope that future ministers "shall know how to speak to better purpose, with more compassion, [and some] with more seriousness, with more authority and allurement, than we now find we can."[136] The situation of speech that Edwards described in *Some Thoughts* appears to represent the fulfillment of Howe's vision: Edwards noted that "a very great sense . . . of the importance of the things of religion and the danger sinners are in" had produced "an almost insuperable disposition to speak" in all true Christians, whatever their status within the community or the church (402). Edwards conceded that this new disposition "to speak so much" had given "great disgust to many," but despite his own concern that limits be set to "indulging and encouraging this disposition," he preferred what he called "a joint engagedness of heart" to the sight of "one speaking alone, and all attending to what he says" because the former "has more of the appearance of conversation" (401, 402, 405). As opposed to the "set speeches" with their "authority and solemnity," Edwards envisioned something like a discursive democracy, the "beautiful" sight of the "multitude meet[ing] . . . freely and cheerfully to converse together" about matters of the spirit without the artificial constraint of silent attendance upon the authoritative speech of the minister (405).

But if Edwards encouraged humble individuals to emerge from out of the undifferentiated crowd, if he beckoned them into the public arena from an unilluminated realm of silence — the private prayer closet, the muteness associated with a lack of authority, experience, or language itself — he was not disposed to tolerate "singularity." Singularity derived from the "mainspring" of all errors in the awakening, the sin of spiritual pride, which "often disposes persons to singularity in external appearance, to affect a singular way of speaking, to use a different sort of dialect from others, or to be singular in voice, or air of countenance or behavior" (414, 421). It worked against redeemed community insofar as it "disposes persons to affect separation, to stand at a distance from others, as better than they, and loves the shew and appearance of the distinction" (422). Moreover, spiritual pride possessed a diabolically protean capacity to multiply and layer its forms so that one despaired of eradicating it: the most stringent efforts to abrade the texture of selfhood merely exposed a more profoundly ensconced "image" of "the firstborn son of the Devil . . . in the heart of man"; the devil, Edwards proclaimed, *is* the self, and together with "the beast," or the world, it corrupts all nature (415). In effect, spiritual pride stamped with its diabolical progenitor's image and the true idea begotten by the truest representation issue from the same reticulum, the human heart.

The trope of conversion, of course, effectively turns an unfortunate twinship into two temporally and theologically distinct inhabitations: by nature, the human heart is inclined toward evil, but the infusion of grace into the heart purifies what it produces. Calvinist doctrine determines that this purification is in no way the result of the individual's efforts; nevertheless, both the scene of purification and that agency which generates true ideas about divinity in response to truest representations are radically positioned deep within human interiority. This place, Old Lights and moderate New Lights (including Edwards) agreed, was beyond scrutiny, utterly invisible; one could judge of it only from its emanations.[137] What originated within its confines could not therefore be positively identified as either self-generated and thus imaginary (the invisible realm of the private soul), or divinely generated and thus evidence of a work of saving grace (the invisible realm of God's determinations). This was at least partly true because spiritual pride, the great engine of delusion, was "ready secretly to mix itself with everything," thereby resembling the irrevocably mixed nature of the revival as partaking of the human mixture of grace and corruption (416). Edwards attempted to ameliorate this disappointingly inconclusive conclusion, which he could not gainsay, by shifting his rhetorical focus to an area of relative success in the work of differentiating wheat from chaff. Against misrepresentative rumors that the work in Northampton was merely the product of runaway imaginations, Edwards protested that no one in his parish, in fact or in theory, was disposed to conflate what was invisibly realized in the heart with what was seen "with the bodily eye."[138] Those who were prone to confuse "lively pictures in their minds" — whether the dreadful sight of hell's great furnace or, in Jonathan Parsons's phrase, the "reconciled face" of God — with material reality were instructed in "the difference between what is spiritual and what is merely imaginary" and thus corrected. But Edwards confessed that the problem of "impressions on persons' imaginations" and the manner in which these imaginary impressions were realized continued to mystify him, an impasse that threw into doubt the stringent differentiation of spirit and imagination, imagination and reality, transcendent Other and sinful self, even as he continued to lead his auditors in his sermons and private counseling "further down into their own hearts, to a further sense of their own universal depravity and deadness in sin."[139]

In endeavoring to teach his flock how to distinguish the wheat from the chaff, the Spirit of God from the imp of the perverse, Edwards sought to elicit a manifestation of individuated spiritual experience from which the very singularity that determined its expressive contours would be rigorously expurgated, banished to the invisible and unspoken realm of the diabolical private. In practice, this proved vexingly difficult, in part because private Christians were apt to misconstrue the nature of selflessness as the hallmark of redeemed individuality. For example, he noted that some Christians, newly emboldened to speak their minds, had publicly urged God to eliminate those who failed to experience saving grace and hurry them off to perdition before they could do any more harm.[140] Edwards cautioned against the error of believing that heart-speech was infallibly self-legitimating, of thinking "that that which they may pray for, they may seek, and use the means of" (482). When those whom he chastised for such a manner of praying objected "that the Spirit of God, as it were, forces them to utter themselves thus, as it were forces out such words from their mouths, when otherwise they should not dare to utter them," Edwards replied that the Spirit of God did not act "by putting expressions into the mouth and urging to utter them; but by filling the heart with a sense of divine things, and holy affections; and those affections and that sense inclines the mouth to speak" (482–83; cf. 437–38). In the first instance, the individual imagines himself or herself to be at the mercy of a coercive power that stocks the mouth with condemnatory, even murderous, words that he or she is then impelled to speak. In the second instance, the Christian feels the heart fill within and is inclined to express its contents which cannot be confused with individual desire. In this way, Edwards makes use of the difference between compulsory and voluntary utterance to illustrate that between mere imagination and spiritual verity. Compulsory utterance (at least of this articulate stripe) and imagination are attributes of humankind's fallenness and are associated with a range of impulsive criminal desires including murder and suicide, although the individual may erroneously or disingenuously ascribe them "to the agency of some invisible being." The spiritual is associated with an infallible inner voice both intimate to the individual who is internally persuaded to act on it in the very process of articulating it, and yet corporate, its content derived from outside the individual and given in common to all the saints (439). Spiritual truth, that is, is realized through the offices of the individual conscience, which is itself understood to be the product, simultaneously discursive and performative, of a God-filled heart. Edwards's example reveals how subtle the conceptual difference is between imagination and conscience and how difficult it might be for an untutored or private Christian to differentiate them.[141]

An embodiment of conscience, the exemplary Christian likewise partakes of just such an individuated and yet corporate identity grounded in an experience graciously provided to the elect by God; the Christian's speech is both bold and righteous but not self-righteous.[142] Although all share in "that defect, or imperfection of degree, which is in every holy disposition and exercise in this life," the Christian must be particularly vigilant in identifying, first, experiences or impulses attributable to that surplus of individuality or "monstrous excrescence" which is character, the manifold behavioral and discursive tokens of pride; and second, "experiences [that are] especially defective in some particular thing that ought to be in them" and whose defect "maims and deforms the experience" such that "things are very much out of a due proportion" (462–63). In either case, the great threat to redeemed community was the triumph of character, the grotesque and bloated creature of the spectral realm of private imagination and individual desire, inclined to criminality. The triumph of character would preclude the exquisite proportionality (to paraphrase Perkins) inherent in seeming outwardly what one is inwardly and in acting oneself and not others. In the expression of one's spiritual experiences, the sole legitimate source of public speech about private life, "it often comes to pass," Edwards warned,

> that through persons not distinguishing the wheat from the chaff, and for want of watchfulness and humble jealousy of themselves, and laying great weight on the natural and imaginary part, and yielding to it and indulging of it, that part grows and increases, and the spiritual part decreases; the Devil sets in and works in the corrupt part, and cherishes it to his utmost. (467)

Character, the individual expression of what is natural, imaginary, and diabolical, then situates itself at the root of heresies to generate not redeemed community but its debased counterfeit, the sect, the result of "a degenerating of experiences" into "wild enthusiastical notions and practices" (467).

Edwards perceived that the Christian's struggle to eschew character was enacted on the level of self and nation, and that its issue would be either the establishment of redeemed community, "our obtaining the kingdom of heaven and reigning in it in eternal glory," or eternal death, "our eternal destruction in both soul and body in hell" (384). He was pleased to note, however, if with all due caution, that what had appeared an "irreconcilable alienation" in Northampton society of various fashions, characteristics of speech and behavior, and even differences of class, educational level, generation, and race, had been resolved into "a sincere and entire amity." This was true not just for his parish, Edwards claimed, but for all of New England with the ascendancy of New Light practice (327). This wonderful transformation was clearly an "alteration abiding on multitudes" (329): in place of irreconcilable alienation, the newly convicted, despite all their former variety, uniformly exhibited

> a particular dislike of placing religion much in dress, and spending much zeal about those things that in themselves are matters of indifference, or an affecting to shew humility and devotion by a mean habit, or a demure and melancholy countenance, or anything singular or superstitious. (341)

The "uniformity," a "likeness and agreement everywhere," "persisting in an unmoved, untouched calm and rest," signified that the resolution of visible character to which Edwards bore witness derived from "the same spirit from whence the work in all parts of the land has originated" (342–44, 334).[143] A unitary and unifying spirit had resolved — reconciled and integrated — individual idiosyncrasy. With uniformity secured and the dross of idiosyncrasy purged from the visible realm, the invisible realm of the private soul was assumed to have been likewise relieved of its singularity and thus brought into conformity not only with the visible but with the invisible world of God's determinations. This assumption conferred upon the private individual a new authority and stature such that the private supplications of "even women, children and servants," Edwards declared, might place God Himself "under the power of his people" (518). The unerring Word of Truth was well on its way to ceding its priority to what Emerson praised as "the unerring voice of the world."[144]

Part Two

As it emerged from social invisibility during the witchcraft crisis to achieve
cultural prominence during the Great Awakening as disruptive public speech,
democratic personality instigated an ongoing and urgent theoretical reassessment of the status of representation (of unerring Truth) and, as its inalienable
corollary, the status of the individual as both purveyor and recipient of such
representations. For both New Light and Old Light ministers who observed
not only each other but the aberrant behaviors of the "awakened" and the
contagious force of the vocal current they generated, such representations of
religious experience begged the question of their invisible source and thus
their character as genuine (involuntary) responses to God's unknowable determinations or counterfeit (single-minded) stagings of the power of piety for
self-aggrandizing, equally unknowable, ends. What manner of mind lay beyond the defamiliarized space of formal observance, and how were the signs it
generated—in particular, bold public claims to a privileged knowledge of
invisible realities—to be read? The social necessity of acknowledging the

significance of such signs had led interpreters of both stripes into an unintended deconstruction of the categories of interpretation, a swift leveling of the ground of judgment. Jonathan Edwards pointed out that this leveling should be regarded more as a permanent ontological fact than as a temporary and regrettable social condition: it enacted nothing more than the fallenness of the human condition which all Christians must acknowledge and even embrace. But if in their desire for unmediated access to the fullness of unerring truth, all Christians were equally constrained to representation, there were nevertheless gradations of representation, Edwards maintained, some truer than others which could be known by the way in which they were received.

On the one hand, of course, Edwards's theory of redeemed representation merely reproduced the original impasse, for to judge which of the proliferating, madly competing representations generated by the awakened and their opponents was the truest—a judgment based on the equally representational act of reception—posed the same insuperable difficulty as judging the truth of Truth itself. Moreover, the market for representations of truth, and especially the demand for novel religious personalities, could not be so easily dismantled once established by the rhetoric of choice in the experience and expression of religious affections. For the Old Light clergy and their allies, the revival had not resolved in a higher integrity the problem of representation it had so recklessly advanced, but had fostered a spirit of nihilism: crude representations offered by proliferating sects and speakers unanchored by decorum or tradition and unaffiliated with community had replaced the unerring Word of Truth and its authorized spokesman, the established minister. Who was to say that the individual, exhorted to attend to and articulate his or her inner voice, was not speaking the seductions of the devil rather than the voice of conscience, of God speaking silently in the soul? What was at stake in Edwards's claim that, through an act of benign ventriloquism, the sensitive minister, his ear attuned like a gifted novelist to the inarticulate language of being, might translate it into the normative idiom of the unregenerate and in so doing, redress the fallenness of language by eliding the gap between being and representation, experience and expression? What was the import of this double-voicedness that both Old and New Lights attributed to the individual: when he or she spoke, who, in fact, was speaking?

On the other hand, embracing the ineluctability of representation allowed

Edwards to advance spectral evidence theory (as a theory of personality unanchored to visible structures of authority) into a post-Puritan world by marrying it, under the auspices of humble self-enlargement, to a newly viable practice of Puritan charity. The shift in emphasis that posited the invisible domain as the original site not so much of Being or Truth as of a steady flow of representations of it, some sensibly truer than others, underwrote a new acceptance of visible character. No longer restricted to the paradigm of sainthood as the conventional signified of orthodox notions of an unchanging invisible order, visible character, prominently including the idiosyncrasies of individual voice, was reconceived and legitimated as the necessarily mutable representation of an infinite, and thus formally uncontainable, work of the Spirit upon the soul. If as representations visible character and compulsive public utterance exceeded the signifying possibilities of conventional systems of meaning, then it had to be charitably conceded that no one had the authority to cap, by condemning, the possibilities, more numerous than grains of sand, for representing eternal Truth. The same rationale that permitted New Lights to propose liberating the meanings of key words from their historical or conventional uses by insisting that meaning was immediate, situational, and dialogic, allowed them to propose that the variety of visible character and the disturbing novelty of the popular voice constituted, in effect, a new language, the material traces of a Voice never before heard, articulating a Will utterly unknown and authoritative, and whose uncontainable generative power should not be arrogantly confused with "mere" inarticulacy by mere human authority. Such theologico-political legitimations prepared the ideological ground for the national literature project.

The simultaneous recovery of spectral evidence theory and Puritan charity, expressed in the theory of redeemed representation, did not win for Edwards the continuing vitality of his doomed professional life. His theory of a representation at least partially redeemed from the accusation of error, a representation exclusively able to make manifest to the individual mind and heart the invisible Truth from which it issued, did provide, however, a platform for the articulation of a national literary aesthetic that would claim a unique exemption from the deformations of fiction. Increasingly committed to showcasing a newly rehabilitated (a liberalized) democratic ethos, it would claim for representation an intrinsic authority commensurate with, if not exceeding, that of Being itself. The privileged representation in this regard remained the vox populi, the legacy of the Awakening to both the Revolution and the national literature project. As the perceptible sign of essential American character, the vox populi consecrated the hope that America would prove the site of redeemed community as it promised to render the national literature transparent to that community. Through the representation of popular voice in the national literature, apparent singularity would reveal its profound representativeness as individual voices collaborated to "make a world" that would prove the truest representation of an always virtual America. The record of this ambition is traced in the following chapters which examine the life of democratic personality not in the sociopolitical sphere but as the object of literary representation and literary-critical speculation from the post-revolutionary through the antebellum periods. A reading of Melville's brilliant novelistic reversal of liberal culture's attempt to domesticate democratic personality and to found a national aesthetic of artistic innocence upon that attempt concludes the present study.

Although the religious fervor of the Awakening would subside, the problem of assessing the truth status of the individual voice lived on in the ensuing Separatist movement which provided so many key players in the revolutionary era.[1] It is doubtful that conservatives comforted themselves with the reflection that Separatism had led not to the atomization of religious community but to its reestablishment upon foundations that, as time passed, more and more resembled those churches so heatedly rejected in an earlier period. The establishment of new churches, however, did apparently ensure that the potentially revolutionary act of conversion, the rebirth of the self, began to occur increasingly in the context of reformed community rather than the large and anonymous crowds typical of the Great Awakening.[2] As the historian Rhys Isaac has described this context with reference to the Baptist communities of Anglican Virginia in the late 1760s, for example, the trope of rebirth or coming-into-being enacted through the ritual of baptism referred not solely or even primarily to the individual; rather, the individual's immersion constituted "a vivid enactment of *a* community within and apart from *the* [dominant, Anglican] community." As in the Quaker case, the transfer of authentic personality for Virginia Baptists occurred in circumscribed and collective space; for the former, this space was delimited by the parameters within which individual speech was produced, authorized, and contained, whereas for the latter it was demarcated by the ritual of baptism as an "open enactment of closed community."[3]

With the establishment of acts of tolerance throughout the colonies and the increasing ease with which a Separatist congregation might be gathered out of an established one, the topos of uncontainability so central to spectacular conversion in the 1740s lost its broad revolutionary appeal as an aspect of vital religious experience, in part because of the absence of an atmosphere of strenuous opposition necessary to sustain it. Consequently, the mass formation of democratic personality as it occurred in the years between the Great Awakening and the Revolution represented to some degree, but not entirely, a declension from the Whitefieldian paradigm. The minutiae of history — fragments of information concerning anonymous persons — confirm that the volatile energy of self-assertion initially manifested in the separatist impulse, especially with the legal ratification of religious Separatism, was almost immediately enlisted in the cause of sustaining and perpetuating a new group dynamic.

An example is provided by the historian C. C. Goen in his account of the "total conversion of a group of Separates" spurred by the religious awakening of an insouciant young man living in West Woodstock, Connecticut, named Biel Ledoyt.[4] Ledoyt, "the leader of a group of frivolous young people," was among the crowd that gathered to hear the preaching of a Separate Baptist minister from a nearby town in 1763. The Reverend Noah Alden's exhortation "struck conviction" into Ledoyt, who from that moment was a changed man, wholly devoted (to his friends' chagrin) to the practice of piety. Upon Alden's departure, Ledoyt called a public meeting during which some forty of his friends, who came to mock their comrade's sudden seriousness, collectively experienced conviction under the influence of his inspired preaching. The meetings continued several times a week, drawing more and more of the town's residents who, despite their former laxness, increasingly displayed a pious "uniformity" of thought and action under his leadership. Within a year, Ledoyt's converts had withdrawn from the established church, and he received his ordination as their minister four years later. There is no suggestion in his story of the soul-searching and extreme isolation Nathan Cole experienced upon deciding to separate twenty-five years earlier. Whereas community came slowly to Nathan Cole, for Ledoyt it was almost simultaneous with his decision to "separate." The voice of the charismatic exhorter in the later case, whether Alden or Ledoyt after him, produced not more separatists (as had the voices of Whitefield, Tennent, or Davenport) but more Baptists, suggesting that although individuation continued to be part of the process of vital and irresistible inward experience, the potentially expansive sense of individuality to which it might have led was quickly contained by community.

There remained, however, individuals who resisted incorporation into such groups, no matter how small, marginal, and volatile they may have been, and who eschewed the personal stability incorporation would naturally entail. Historically, their presence is negatively registered in the tendency of dissenting sects to shatter and regroup continually, as well as in the anxiety and hostility expressed by conservative leaders, both civil and ecclesiastical, who deplored the ongoing demand which the separatist tendency generated for the services of charismatic itinerants to provide temporary group definition. Very often, the charismatic itinerant was not an ordained minister and had no ascertainable doctrinal or institutional (educational, denominational, familial) affiliations. Often the most basic details of his personal identity could not be discovered: Timothy Walker attributed to the populace's "indulging an *unmortified Itch after Novelties*" the practice of "*having the Persons of Strangers*, whom we know nothing of, *in Admiration*, and a setting them up above the *Place of Instruments*."[5] To recommend him, the stranger had only a self-proclaimed and developed "gift" of speech that he was not willing to devote to the spiritual welfare of any particular church but that he was willing to confer upon the impressionable audiences who listened avidly to his revelations as he made his way from place to place.[6] If history provides few documented biographical accounts of such anonymous individuals, except as they appear in the occasional fleeting reference in private diaries or letters or in the published diatribes their transient presence stimulated in persons of authority, early American literature prominently features them as a particularly compelling, because particularly menacing, example of indigenous American character.[7]

The liminality of "the individual," in fact, is obsessively thematized in early American fiction which tended to situate this figure, like the hybridic specter as conceived by spectral evidence theorists in conjunction with the afflicted of 1692, on the cusp of the visible and invisible domains. Simultaneously elicited by a doctrinal focus upon personal religious experience and driven back into the neutralizing medium of a reconfigured collective, "the individual" had become increasingly present as an irresolvable remainder that resisted incorporation within community no matter how redefined to accommodate the singular. Only gradually and, as it were, in bits and pieces did "the individual" emerge in the course of the eighteenth century from its sequestration in the domain of the spectral. The story, both historical and fictional, of this emergence is told in Chapter 4, "The Voice of the People, the Voice of the Specter."

Chapter 4 situates a reading of Charles Brockden Brown's novel *Wieland; or, The Transformation: An American Tale* (1798) within the superimposed contexts of the witchcraft crisis and the revival. In particular, it explores the textualization of democratic personality in the postrevolutionary era when the desire to establish the national character through literary means was increasingly expressed. The novel's common-man protagonist is Frank Carwin, an itinerant ventriloquist whose ability to speak where he is not identifies him with the specter, the itinerant, and the "individual": an apt figure for conservative fears of the verbal excesses of democratic personality.[8] Carwin chooses as his base of operations for realizing an unfocused but relentless will to power the pastoral estate of the Wielands, a family of complacent rationalists whose encounter with Carwin represents, among other things, the encounter of liberal republicanism with radical democracy in the revolutionary period. The isolated Wieland estate literalizes the space beyond formal observance so feared by spectral evidence and antirevival theorists. Within this mediate space — variously identified with representation, imagination, individual desire, and crime — all binary signifying systems, such as those that deduce essence from appearance, are undermined. Precisely such a context, as the activities of Carwin demonstrate, sustains the contradictions of democratic personality which emerges therein as a temporary or transitional, albeit an extraordinarily dynamic and inherently revolutionary, subjective mode that must labor to contain its own centrifugal tendencies. Within this space, the evacuation of the self and thus the transcendence of its limitations occurs through the exercise of tremendous vocal power. No member of the Wieland community can assign Carwin a stable identity: he is, instead, no one and everyone, himself and a kosmos, one and many. An exemplification of the popular voice that was the object of such anxiety in the Federalist era when Brown wrote, Carwin's ability to imitate the voices of others and remove them at a distance from himself ties him neither to a single self nor even to the body. The voice of democratic personality thus demonstrated its uncontainability: like Whitefield's, it could be insinuated into the mind of an auditor and exert a lasting, almost subliminal influence; its independence of the body lent it a flexibility that exceeded the text's insofar as it required no artifact (such as the book) or expertise (such as reading) and disseminated itself without requiring a network of supportive institutions. Carwin represents the transmutation into American (literary) character of the "individual" as a voice or a gesture quickly, if never completely, withdrawn; as a set of self-referential impulses conducive to no communal goal; as a "moveable" and grotesque "changeling" whose appearance bespoke apocalyptic destruction through unending revolution.[9]

Carwin's redemption from a life of crime is only suggested at the novel's conclusion, but is not represented; his destructive devotion to exercising the powers associated both with ontological liminality and ubiquitous voice generates the novel's plot. But he allows Brown, through the text's narrator, Clara Wieland, to suggest that democratic personality might be domesticated to serve the purposes of an authentic national literature if its uncontainability were constrained — if it were confined to the level plane of being rather than the multidimensional playground of representation within which Carwin invisibly frolicked; or, alternatively, if representation itself could be redeemed, as Edwards had first suggested, and acquire the authenticity of being. To this end, Clara represents herself wresting from Carwin his distinctly authorial power to emplot the inhabitants of the Wieland estate in a tragedy of his own design, while retaining the ethically superior status of a victim, a hapless character in Carwin's insidious narrative. In order to retain her innocence despite her authoring, Clara repeatedly asserts her status as representation, as character — the product of another's machinations, even as she narrates her ever more brazen and ingeniously engineered appropriation of the prerogatives and the violence of authorship. She legitimates and extends her authorship (including her ridding herself of rival authors) by detailing her sufferings which, she claims, compelled her to write for her very life and thus permitted the amplification of her own voice as representative of the experience of all. In so doing, Clara attempts to vindicate herself from the possible charge of making use of the ventriloquial power of authorship by redefining it as a legitimate form of humble self-enlargement, a form of benign ventriloquism, an innocence of power in which the author's ontological difference from his or her character might be denied and their identity asserted.

With the spectral character of Carwin the biloquist and his relationship to his victim, the enthusiastic Wieland, as well as his successor, Clara, Brown draws together the major concerns of the American eighteenth century as they organized themselves in relation to the paradigmatic counterfeit: ventriloquism and authenticity, consent and representation, egalitarianism and licentiousness, innocence and violence, and identity and revolution. Chapter 5, "The Crisis of American Character," examines how two of Brown's postrevolutionary contemporaries, Stephen Burroughs and J. Hector St. John de Crèvecoeur, would reinforce Clara's claim for the ethical superiority and, strangely, the ontological priority of character as the site of being (of suffering) in the novel. The claim betrays a profound anxiety that authorship can only vindicate itself from the charge of Carwinian ventriloquism if the author can establish himself as, in some profound sense, representative of those for whom he speaks — a character among characters. But as Crèvecoeur's Farmer James, the humble author of *Letters from an American Farmer*, discovered, the fantasy that authorial voice may selflessly represent all other voices is vulnerable to a challenge from within the represented world itself. In the *Letters*, the challenge to Farmer James's representative status is posed by a character who conspicuously bears the traits of democratic personality. Like his predecessors, this character, the slave in the cage, erupts unexpectedly into the represented domain, emerging from a space within its confines that the author, because he scrupulously restricts his gaze to what is visible in the American landscape, had not discerned. The character's exclusive knowledge of the invisible domain of slavery — articulated as a request for poison — repudiates the author's claim, upon which his authorial prerogative is explicitly based, to speak for the represented world.

In the absence of express authorial or literary-critical ratification, early American fictions variously enacted this lesson: if American character was to distinguish itself as truly democratic, the literature that represented it to the world had to accommodate the unlimited self-enlargement of American character despite the author's intentions for that character and despite the formal consequences to the text of an expanding, subordinate subjectivity. Should the engendering and containing authorial force discover itself in some form of agonistic relationship to character, this had to be accepted as an inalienable effect of the very conditions of American literary representation which posited the uncontainability of democratic character. Once elicited from invisibility and inaudibility by the inherently ventriloquistic act of authorship, character possessed the potential, as an ethical entitlement inseparable from democratic literary production, to exceed authorial intent. Because the oppositional conditions that had always governed the coming-into-being of democratic personality were, in the case of literature, internalized in this manner, the enmity between containing and expanding subjectivities, posited as ontological equals, had itself to be contained, for how was it to be enacted without destroying literature itself? This impasse, peculiar to the ethics of democratic literary creation, may be added to others (including the exigencies of nation-building, the nonexistence of patronage, and the absence of historical associations) that have since the early national era been proposed as the cause of the backwardness of American literature, its notorious slowness in establishing itself.[10]

Chapter 6, "An American Aesthetic of Innocence: Domesticating Democratic Personality," traces the developing rationale of a cultural ideology, an American aesthetic of innocence, that was intended to redress the enduring problem of literary absence. As it developed from the postrevolutionary through the antebellum eras, the aesthetic of innocence took shape less as a set of assumptions concerning the form or content of the future national literature than as a set of prescriptions for the realization of authentic national-poetic selfhood. The growing body of literary-critical pronouncements on the character of the genuine but still absent American poet, generated by diverse critical constituencies from the literary nationalists to the Transcendentalists, was intended not only to facilitate the nation's recognition of this figure when he should appear but primarily to provide a set of guidelines, a prescriptive mold, for his eventual embodiment. The aesthetic of innocence was, that is, a distinctively eugenic critical practice. The very conventionality of this composite portrait of the genuine American poet (he was repeatedly imagined to be in humble circumstances, unself-conscious, isolated from the artificial life of cities, and possessed of an unstudied simplicity) betrays its derivation from the hypothetical folk-poet of European romantic nationalism. Moreover, he was increasingly imagined to be innocent of language — and herein lies his paradoxical utility for the antebellum literary-critical establishment. His speechlessness, his unconscious self-exemption from the conditions of discourse, was celebrated as that trait which ensured the purity of the national essence he embodied and that he would one day transcribe into an authentic national poetry. In particular, the poet's simplicity ensured that his poetry would elide the gap between being and representation, author and character — the poet might command the authenticity of character while exercising, unautocratically, the prerogatives of authorship. This paradox is central to the aesthetic of innocence which bore a significant impact upon the actual production and reception of American literary texts, as the chapter's analysis of James Fenimore Cooper's Leatherstocking novels and their reception demonstrates. The critically mandated prerequisite of inarticulateness for authentic national-poetic selfhood, while it is the source of the author's authenticity, constitutes the most extreme strategy for the containment of democratic personality, and was most explicitly theorized in Emerson's essayistic celebrations of the familiar and the low.

Chapter 7, "Melville's Anxiety of Innocence: The Handsome Sailor," analyzes Walt Whitman's reinterpretation of an Emersonian aesthetic of innocence as he describes it primarily in both the 1855 and 1856 prefaces to *Leaves of Grass* as well as in *Democratic Vistas* (1871). In these manifestos, the common-man poet claims to speak not himself — at least, not himself alone — but the nation in its entirety, through a benign ventriloquism ("Through me many long dumb voices") that makes possible an innocent, because selfless, authorial practice in which the speaker transcends his individuality to encompass a "kosmos."[11] The resulting poetry is at once agentless and firmly embodied in the perfect body of the poet which, like his voice, encompasses and realizes all bodies. The chapter is largely dedicated to a reading of Melville's final novel, *Billy Budd*, as a deconstruction of the aesthetic of innocence, and especially its central claim that to posit an inarticulate poet is to domesticate — to both embrace and delimit — the uncontainability at the heart of democratic personality.

FOUR

The Voice of the People, the Voice of the Specter

If mankind has thus far once consented unto the credit of diabolical representations, the door is opened!

— COTTON MATHER

[Ventriloquism is] a power to control the imagination by imitation, supported occasionally by acting. . . . Now, if the imagination can effect so much, even in crowded assemblies, composed of people of all degrees of credulity, intelligence, and strength of mind, and when all are prepared, in part at least, for the delusion, what may it not be expected to produce on minds peculiarly suited to yield to its influence, and this, too, when the prodigy take the captivating form of mysticism and miracles.

— JAMES FENIMORE COOPER

I

The New Light claim to uniformity and the end of alienation, singularity, and irreconciliation conferred upon the words of private individuals a legitimate power of penetration that enabled them to "get within" the souls of hearers. This "gentle Violence" of the insinuated word, Edwards exulted, "would make way for the sharp sword to enter; it would remove the obstacles, and make a naked breast for the arrow."[1] Notwithstanding Edwards's optimism, writers critical of the Awakening were fulminating in private and published letters, preached and published sermons, and newspaper articles about a novel form of discursive violence, wielded like "a Sword in the Hands of a mad Man," penetrating the vulnerable breast but in no way salvific, whose range was visibly expanding and whose supervision was each day becoming more uncertain.[2] "There is a Creature here," one critic wrote in a letter to England in the wake of Whitefield's 1740 tour, "called *an Exhorter*. It is of both Sexes, but generally of the Male, and young. Its distinguishing Qualities, are *Ignorance, Impudence, Zeal.*" The practice of exhorters, according to the writer, was to

> tarry in the Meeting-house with the People after the Minister is gone, and sometimes several of them exhort at once in different Parts of the House, and then there is terrible Doings. You may hear screaming, singing, laughing, praying, all at once; and, in other Parts, they fall into Visions, Trances, Convulsions. When they come out of their Trances, they commonly tell a senseless Story of Heaven and Hell, and whom and what they saw there.[3]

Exhorters, then, were unauthorized lay people who spoke publicly in the minister's place and often without his approval, initiating a veritable Babel of public speech that prominently featured claims to some form of direct contact with or immediate inspiration and authorization from the invisible world.[4]

A multitude of critics contributed to the collective portrait of lay exhorters, providing details concerning their demographic makeup as well as their sphere of activity. Charles Chauncy, who bemoaned "the rise of such numbers of *lay exhorters and teachers*, in one place and another, all over the land," reported that "[s]ometimes they are *Children, Boys* and *Girls*, sometimes *Women*; but most commonly *raw, illiterate, weak* and *conceited young Men*, or *Lads*."[5] The Anglican Charles Brockwell of Salem reported on the activities of a mobile "set of Enthusiasts that strole about harangueing the admiring Vulgar in *extempore* nonsense" which included "Men, Women, Children, Servants, & Nigros."[6] The problem, then, was in no way confined to a popular attack on "a *just decorum in speaking* in the *house of GOD*"; rather, it was that men and women, blacks and whites, servants and children, the poor and the illiterate had begun "*wandring about from house to house, speaking the things they ought not*" under the delusional impression that the Spirit of God had moved them to it.[7] The scrivener and lawyer Nathan Bowen protested that those of "the meanest Capacity i e) women & even Common negroes" as well as "Carters Coblers & the many Labourers leave their Honest Imployments & Turn Teachers."[8] The Anglican commissary of Boston, Timothy Cutler, specified the danger lay exhorters represented to the social order. He described strolling children and servants "withdrawing themselves from Family care and Subjection" and laborers shirking their work in order to attend "Lectures" that proceeded through the night "with hideous Yellings, and shameful Revels": "much Wickedness is justly feared to be the Consequence of Them," he concluded.[9]

Similar judgments from the standing conservative ministries (predominantly Congregational, Presbyterian, and Anglican) continued throughout the colonies into the revolutionary era. Thus, an Anglican minister from Virginia in 1753 expressed Cutler's fear that "these *ignes fatui* will lead many especially the lowest & most ignorant sort to ruin & destruction"; complaints arrived to the Bishop of London from a Maryland preacher in the same year that lay exhorters "rambling up and down the Provinces, seeking whom they may seduce, have too much prevailed on the wavering & ignorant"; in 1764 a revival of the "enthusiastick spirit," in the form of night meetings replete with odd outcries and "blasphemous expressions," was bewailed; and in 1770, Whitefield wreaked a final, posthumous revenge upon one poor Anglican minister who, having celebrated the death of "the wild Enthusiast," was harassed by "one Jayne," a layman who publicly denounced him as unconverted and who interrupted his services with other "enthusiastic teachers and vagrant exhorters."[10] Conservative detractors consistently characterized itinerant exhorters as rabble attractive to the common people from whose ranks they had emerged, "Disturber[s] of the *civil Peace*" who, "under the Notion of appearing zealous for GOD and *his Truths*, insult their Betters, vilify their Neighbours, and spirit People to Strife and Faction." A fitting response to such "Follies," according to Chauncy, would be "to restrain [their] *Tongues* with *Bit* and *Bridle*."[11] The threat such persons posed — of bringing "confusion into the *body mystical*" by abandoning their social posts along with the touchstone of objective scriptural truth as authoritatively interpreted by their parish clergyman — was augmented by their class affiliation: although modern historians have asserted the mixed class composition of revivalist congregations, contemporary witnesses tended to stress that evangelicals, and particularly the problematic itinerant exhorters, derived from the common classes.[12] The Reverend John Hancock's description of exhorters as "raw, indiscreet, rash, illiterate and blind" is stereotypical; the Anglican Cutler shuddered at their "beastly brayings"; the newspapers routinely described them as "idle or ignorant persons, and those of the lowest

Rank."[13] Even the Quakers noted their "very mean" appearance; one itinerant exhorter who boldly entered a Quaker meeting in Pennsylvania and began to preach was studiously ignored until he fell silent.[14] The prevalence of this class characterization is confirmed by the New Light Samuel Finley, who welcomed it as a particularly telling historical verification of the evangelical effort. Jesus, he pointed out,

> was chiefly followed by what we call the *Mob*, the *Rabble*, the *common* and *meaner* Sort, . . . by the openly profane, the *Publicans*, and *Harlots*; for he is still set for the *Rise & Fall of many in* Israel; and many who tho't themselves *first*, and were esteemed so by others in the Dark, did show themselves to be *last*.

Equally telling in Finley's eyes was the significance of the similarity between Jesus' followers and New Light followers: "both they and we are Turners of the World upside down, Subverters of Peace and Church-Government, and the like."[15]

By 1769, the transformation into "political enthusiasm" of religious enthusiasm and its various manifestations, including what those in authority regarded as outbursts of illegitimate popular speech, was definitively recognized. One Massachusetts Anglican thus described a popular "ferment by which the minds of the people here have been wrought up into as high a degree of Enthusiasm by the word liberty, as could have been expected had Religion been the cause."[16] Eventually, critics would report a conflation of religious and political enthusiasms, as in 1782 when a beleaguered Anglican minister, reviewing the progress of his American mission, wrote about his encounters "for three years past with the enthusiastic notions of Ignorant methodists and anabaptists, some of whose absurdities has as direct a tendency to overturn all order and decency in the Church, as the base principles and practices of those who call themselves Whigs (a soft Term for rebels) have in the state."[17] From Whitefield's 1740 visit, a tour whose explicit emphasis upon the spiritual morbidity of many of the standing clergy led to the creation of an indigenous ministerial itinerancy supportive of itinerating lay exhorters, the issue for conservatives surrounding this particular exercise of popular speech had been the threat of revolution it presaged. As Samuel Weller predicted the likely chain of events, the effect of religious radicalism upon the populace would conduce directly to the apocalyptic overthrow of the social order:

> Some evil Consequence, some Riot and Rebellion, is naturally to be expected from these disorderly Proceedings. For as these Men's Followers have renounced those Pastors, whom the Laws of God and Man have provided for them: As none of them know who it is that is hereafter to preach to them, nor what sort of Doctrine will be preached in these lawless Assemblies; so will it indeed be nothing less than a Miracle, should there not soon arise among these licentious People, Preachers inticing them to Sedition and Tumult, and prompting them to overturn the civil and religious Establishments of their Country.[18]

Lay exhortation, especially when it involved itinerancy between towns and even colonies, posed a threat to legitimately instituted authority that derived from the itinerants' ability to elude questions about their personal (let alone their spiritual) identities and beliefs in conjunction with the anarchic proclivities of the ignorant multitudes who gathered to hear them. In this regard, the Congregationalist Noah Worcester worried in 1794, as had Alexander Garden more than fifty years earlier, that

> many people are so ignorant, as to be more charmed with sound than sense. And to them, the want of knowledge in a teacher, or of instruction in his discourses, may easily be made up, and overbalanced, by great zeal, an affecting tone of voice, and a perpetual motion of the tongue. . . . And when such persons hear a speaker, who has had but little advantage for education, preach in such a manner, and this too without forethought or study, . . . they think he is most certainly called of God, that he is wonderfully assisted, and speaks as the Spirit gives him utterance. Ergo, he must be a good man, and his sentiments are doubtless right.[19]

The moderate New Lights' placement of spiritual authenticity within individual interiority as well as their observation that the invisible and inaccessible space of the human heart was a divided sphere consonant with the fallenness of human nature unwittingly enabled the development of a vigorous and enduring lay itinerancy movement. Such considerations accompanied a pronounced tentativeness, if not tolerance, concerning the vagaries of visible character. New Light accounts of the progress of the revival in their various congregations reveal the extent to which even moderates were prepared cautiously to accept the legitimacy and authenticity of often scandalous outward tokens of inward soul-concern among their parishioners. As Rev. Jonathan Parsons saw it, an individual whose character evinced a "holy *visible* Conformity to the Gospel" offered "an open Exhibition of the natural Charms of the Graces of the holy Spirit," an "Example" of spiritual truth which possessed "greater Authority, than many other appointed Means," presumably institutional ones. If their lives constituted "*a living Principle*, and not a meer Pretence" (always the caveat), such individuals were able "to enlighten [other people's] Understanding and convince their Reason, and conquer their Prejudices, *more powerfully* in general, than any other Way of Teaching that Christians are able to make use of." But even if an individual appeared not to be living in holy conformity to the Gospel, this appearance could not be used to cast doubt upon the reality of his or her conversion. The mixed nature of all human undertakings divested visible character, apparently to a significant degree, of the responsibility for authenticating the inward life of the spirit. As Parsons put it, "many Errors and Defects, tho' manifest in the face of the World, can be no evidence that *professed* Converts are not *truly* so."[20] Their strict Calvinism, then, led many moderate New Lights to elaborate a semiotics of spiritual authenticity tolerant of a disparity between profession and performance, at least in private Christians, and they rejected Old Light suggestions that such a disparity belied the authenticity of the revival.

The equanimity many New Light ministers initially demonstrated in the face of questionable outward tokens of inward soul-concern in the case of private Christians did not necessarily extend to their ministerial colleagues. Radical and moderate New Light preachers would, in fact, come to evince a mutual animosity as caustic as that dividing conservatives from evangelicals, a circumstance that became apparent with the growth of evangelical ministerial itinerancy following Whitefield's 1739–40 American tour.[21] Gilbert Tennent, the fiery Presbyterian itinerant from New Jersey whose preaching tour followed on the heels of Whitefield's autumn 1740 visit to New England, was well received by Thomas Prince's moderate New Light congregation in Boston, although they were initially outraged at their visitor's displaying "no Regard to please the Eyes of his Hearers with agreeable Gesture, nor their Ears with Delivery, nor their Fancy with Language."[22] As Prince tells it, the Boston revival proceeded uneventfully after Whitefield's departure in the fall of 1740, and the prized uniformity of its manifestations (generally an increased interest in religious matters among many, formerly lax, parishioners) was maintained until the arrival of the itinerant minister James Davenport of Long Island on a Friday evening in the summer of 1742. Davenport attended a service at Charlestown on the Sunday morning following his arrival, but that afternoon "stay'd at his Lodgings from an Apprehension of the Minister's being unconverted, which greatly alarm'd us" (406). On Monday, Davenport crossed the ferry to Boston and met with the ministers of Charlestown and Boston who, although they acknowledged that he "appear'd to us to be *truly pious*," collectively decided to bar him from their churches. As they delineated it in their public statement, they objected to his impulsive behavior; his public condemnations of other ministers as unconverted and his habit of demanding of them an account of their conversion; his practice of walking with companions from church to church singing; and "[h]is encouraging *private Brethren* [i.e. who are not Probationers for the Ministry] to pray and exhort [i.e. like Ministers] in Assemblies gather'd for that Purpose" (407, bracketed remarks are Prince's).[23]

Davenport, who began his itinerant ministry after hearing Whitefield speak in New York City in 1740, courted opposition as assiduously and with far less restraint than had Whitefield, and quickly became infamous among his more sober evangelical colleagues whose authority he routinely and aggressively challenged. His scandalous practices to which the Boston area clergy objected contributed to the Connecticut assembly's decision to make itinerancy illegal in 1742; Davenport was arrested for disturbing the peace on two occasions during the year (once in Boston), but in both instances was declared non compos mentis by the authorities and escorted out of the colony. One night in March 1743, he led his boisterous followers (whom the *Boston Evening Post* described as "like a company of *Bacchanalians* after a mad Frolick") to light a bonfire in the streets of New London and burn a number of the most revered Puritan texts, including works by Increase Mather. The next day, they made another fire and were determined to throw into it their worldly goods: the cosmopolitan traveler, Dr. Alexander Hamilton, noted in his *Gentleman's Progress* that had one of his female followers not put a stop to the proceedings, Davenport would have been compelled "to strutt about bare-arsed" for he almost incinerated his "own idol . . . a pair of old, wore out, plush breaches."[24] The prayer meetings he presided over, whether held out of doors or in, were similarly incendiary. The *Boston Weekly Post-Boy* described one of Davenport's "sermons" which occurred at a New London meetinghouse:

> a great Part of their carryings on was not by Praying, Singing and preaching upon a Text as usual; but one would make a short prayer, then another would give a Word of Exhortation, and so on without any certain Order or Method, so that in one Meeting of 2 or 3 Hours, there would be it may be, 20 or 30 distinct exercises carried on by 5 or 10 distinct Persons; some standing in the Pulpit, some in the Body of Seats, some in the Pews, and some up Gallery; and oftentimes several of them would speak together; So that, some praying, some exhorting and terrifying. Some singing, some screaming, some crying, some laughing and some scolding, made the most amazing Confusion that was ever heard.[25]

When shortly after the New London incident, he was persuaded to publish a retraction of what he called his errors, Davenport confessed to *"encouraging private Persons to a ministerial and authoritative Kind or Method of Exhorting"* that had led to their becoming "much puft up and *falling into the Snare of the Devil.*"[26]

Despite his sanguine acceptance of the idea of individual Christians acting as exempla of gospel piety within the confines of their own congregations, Jonathan Parsons, who had suffered professionally for the New Light cause, was among many moderate New Lights to speak strongly against "private Christians" who "under the Character of *Exhorters*" engage in "*calling* or *appointing* or *going into public Assemblies*" in order to act "the Part of publick Teachers of the Church."[27] To take such matters out of the hands of "the Authorized Teachers of the Church" would be to "open a *wide* Door for all imaginable Errors in Doctrin and Practise to break in like a Flood upon the poor Church of the Lord Jesus," especially if that flood were made up of the words of unauthorized teachers blessed with "the Gift of Eloquence" (53 n, 52 n, 53 n). As Parsons saw it, nothing less than Christian liberty was at stake: "without much straining the Intimations of their Practise," Parsons warned, the conduct of unauthorized teachers betrayed that they "have a Design upon the Liberties of the People, and mean to enslave them by making *themselves* Lords of their faith, when they should be only *the helpers of their Joy*" (54 n). To countenance such private public teachers, or lay exhorters, would be to allow the penetration of the sacred sphere inhabited by the authorized clergy by "the greatest . . . Imposters imaginable":

> Who might not with a fair show of Piety, come in and impose upon you the wildest Enthusiasms of their own hearts instead of divine Truths, under the Pretence of an immediate Revelation? . . . *it would be impossible for you to know whether God spake to you therein, or whither you were deluded.* (59–60, emphasis added)

As a group, lay itinerant exhorters were regarded by church and civil authorities (including moderate New Lights) as both bumptious and seductive, ignorant clowns who exerted an unaccountable attraction over others whenever they opened their mouths to speak. Their very names — "Elvins a Baker," "Rogers of Ipswich," "Woodbury and Gillman, two illiterate and disorderly persons" — were invoked to underscore the utter insignificance of their individual existences.[28] Yet as insignificant as they personally were, they evinced nothing of "that Lowliness and Poverty of Spirit, which are the proper Evidences of Regeneration and the New Birth," as Old Lights and moderate New Lights agreed.[29] Their speech — the act by which they boldly intruded upon the "*sacred Enclosure*" of the established ministry to exercise the "*unbounded License*" of publick Teaching" — undeniably provoked their auditors to behavior that constituted a "shameful Abuse of the ministerial Authority," just as lay exhorters themselves had "sprung up," "like *Mushrooms in a Night*," under the tutelage of the radical itinerant ministry (men like James Davenport and Andrew Croswell) who excelled in "*breeding up Exhorters*." Judge Josiah Cotton of Plymouth registered in his memoirs his outrage at Croswell who, invited to preach at Cotton's church, permitted into the pulpit "Boys & a Negro or two, who were directed to invite others to come to Christ, particularly *old Grey headed Sinners*" like Cotton himself.[30] Benjamin Colman, perhaps regretting his earlier tolerance, prayed that such upstarts "may awake at length out of their *Dream*, or rather *Delirium*, and despise their own *Image*," but as the numbers of lay exhorters continued to multiply, it seemed more likely that they were concerned not to despise but to proliferate their images, to see them, as had Whitefield, discovering themselves in multitudes.[31]

Aside from avoiding temptation altogether by refusing to hear the itinerant seducer, critics of lay itinerancy agreed that there was no better way to avoid joining the "Crowds of the *unguarded Populace*" than by learning to decipher the visible characters of unknown exhorters with reference to the rule of Scripture.[32] Although cross-checking the behavioral characteristics of particularly conspicuous individuals with reference to a scriptural standard seemed a straightforward task, it elicited numerous written and preached commentaries from both Old and New Lights upon the discernment of "marks" or "signs" of spiritual authenticity as identified by the Gospel, as well as recommendations on how to "try" unknown individuals in order to elicit such legible indices of their veracity.[33] Commentators stressed that the trial had to be conducted without the exhorter's input. Consulting the "*enthusiast*" would lead to nothing but confusion as the latter, "if he pays any regard to [the scriptural touchstone], 'tis only as it falls in with his own preconceiv'd notions. He interprets the scripture by *impulses* and *impressions*, and sees no meaning in it, only as he explains it from his own fancy." One had also to guard against one's own fancy or inclination in this regard and use one's reason to develop a "*sober judgment*" and a "proper Zeal," in order to avoid the interpretive solipsism characteristic of exhorters, individuals who were at once the slaves of impulse and yet crafty, "cunning Gamesters, that have the Art and slight of Hand to deceive the Unskilful, and win the Game."[34] Instead of consulting one's private understanding of the scriptural touchstone, one should endeavor to discern it rationally as an objective rather than an internalized truth whose integrity, because it stood aloof from the limitations of the self, could not be compromised or corrupted. As conservative resistance to the social disruption engendered by the Awakening became the norm, opposing voices tended to promote what sounded like an unabashed solipsism: the radical Croswell, for example, declared that the heart of one's faith and the source of its "pleasure" must lie "in these Pronouns *Me* and *my*. If I should leave these Pronouns out of my Religion . . . I could have no Peace in my self."[35]

In the eyes of conservatives, however, to fail to objectify truth was to succumb to seduction, and was thus a mark of feminization. The oldest recorded spiritual debility, Eve's giving ear to the serpent, underlay the persistent sexualization of itinerant evangelism as a doubleness of male seducer and female seduced passionately seeking their unholy consummation. Those who opposed the revival, in an attempt to deprecate it, characterized it as an affair of the passions particularly attractive to emotionally and intellectually weak women whose public display of emotion in uncontrolled screams and groans infected "the Credulous" around them. Especially susceptible to infection were those "ignorant, ambitious and bigotted Followers" who desired to gainsay their insignificance by "set[ting] themselves up as Teachers of Others," a "Device that often takes with ambitious and ignorant Minds [who] fancy themselves to be wiser than their Teachers."[36] Moses Bartlett, in his 1757 sermon *False and Seducing Teachers*, undertook to supply the personal characteristics of the evangelical seducer and his victim. Satan, Bartlett contended, selected for his cause "Men of some Craft and Cunning, [who] have the Art of deceiving"; "the smoothest Orators" who know that "bad Ware needs a cunning Merchant to put it off"; "Men of Craft and Policy . . . as can almost indiscernably sprinkle their Errors" (32–33). "[M]uch elated with Pride" and "swell'd with a high Oppinion of themselves," such men, Bartlett maintained, quoting Saint Paul, *"creep into Houses, and lead captive silly Women"* (29). Their mode of enticing these silly "women," who become seducing teachers in turn, is discursive: the "women" (including those who consider themselves "firm and steadfast Men") are those who betray an insufficient intellect and consequently a frivolous curiosity, those who, to satisfy "their itching Ears," will allow themselves to be exposed and ensnared and thus to "receiv[e] the poisonous Taints" (45). The ensuing union allows them to "propagate unsound Doctrines, such as tend to foment Strife"; seducers ("disorderly walkers, of unpeaceable froward and turbulent Spirits") thus "sow the Seeds of Discord and Sedition," discursive hybrids that "intermix their corrupt and erroneous Notions, with many acknowledged precious divine Truths" (37, 42, 37). This discursive hybridity characterized Christ's "counterfeit" prophets, those who, like Eve, had admitted the seducer and who subsequently cast doubt upon true apostles by misrepresenting them publicly, creating a perceptual strabismus nearly impossible to overcome (46).

As Bartlett's choice of scriptural texts (Revelation 2:2 and Acts 19:15) makes clear, the cost to those who replicated Eve's seduction was, first, the loss of veracity, one's personal integrity, and inevitably, the loss of one's very identity: the two preconditions for becoming a seducer oneself. For this reason, Chauncy maintained, one's fearful "first discovery" of such a spirit within oneself, no matter how embryonic, should inspire efforts "to give check to its growth and progress . . . for there is no knowing, how high it may rise, nor what it may end in."[37] The consequences of this loss, represented as an uncontainable and illegitimate self-enlargement, were clarified by the Old Light Isaac Stiles's election sermon of 1743 in which he provided "the ugly, mishapen and forlorn Picture of them that are given to Change."[38] Stiles had in mind "men . . . under the direction, influence & government of no fix'd steady Principles," a condition of mind that he compares to alcohol addiction and lechery, insofar as their "Love," like their doctrine and their scruples, "is never fix'd, but sometimes set on this, sometimes on that Paramour; playing the Harlot with many Lovers" (307–8, 311). Not surprisingly, the politics of such men partakes of their moral "*Vertigo*, or dizziness in the Head, this instability, fickleness & variation in Opinion and Judgment" (311). Such men, both weak and unscrupulous, are, in fact, revolutionaries: "they are ever & anon for change of Government, and thence are raising a Dust, making a Bustle, and endeavouring to Overset the Government; to turn things *topsy turvy* and bring all into Confusion" (311). Stiles protests that he can provide only a "*Miniature*" of such characters insofar as their "almost infinite mutations, mazes, meanders, intricate turnings & windings, in all their Excentrick, Progressive and Retrograde, Apogee and Perigee motions" render them all but unrepresentable (307).

Fearless toward any form of authority, worldly or divine, such men must be isolated and paralyzed; merely to shun their company, as Bartlett and others had advised, would fail to ensure that they remained politically and socially impotent. This was crucial as the exhorter represented more than just "another ambitious Top and aspiring Coxcomb" accompanied by a "disaffected and designing Crew of changlings," as unsavory as such appearances were (315). Rather, the imperative of ostracizing and thus frustrating the designs of itinerants was intended to prevent the transformation of changelings into powerful "Arch-changlings" who, given the opening, possessed an apocalyptic ability to wreak total destruction: "they scatter and diffuse their malignant Influences far & wide, kindle a destroying Fire and make a rueful Conflagration wherever they come. And were there enough such Phaetons, they would soon set the whole World on Fire in good earnest, not in fiction but in fact" (316). For such as these, Stiles desired nothing less than cosmic retribution: he imagined "Christ the Judge" coming to them in anger in order to "break them with a rod of Iron, and dash them in pieces like a Potters vessel"; he exulted in the thought of the angry Christ preparing to "slay them before my face: Bind them in bundles & burn them together" (316). Any means should be used to prevent such "men of this make & character" from being "promoted to Honour" and "hail'd & even hosanna'd by the giddy Multitude of unthinking Mortals" (315). "If we meddle with them & become partakers of their Sins," Stiles intoned, "we must expect to receive of their Plagues & Punishments" (316).

According to contemporary accounts, the effects upon the populace of the "strolling pretended Ministers" were twofold.[39] First, lay itinerancy encouraged multitudes of laypersons to speak not simply publicly but theatrically about the invisible world as they, and not their ministers, conceived it to be. The Anglican Brockwell reported the "shocking" and "uncomon" scene of multitudes in the streets of Salem discovering the formerly inaccessible domains of their own spiritual estates before passersby:

> their groans, cries, screams, & agonies must affect the Spectators were they never so obdurate & draw tears even from the most resolute, whilst the ridiculous & frantic gestures of others cannot but excite both laughter & contempt, some leaping, some laughing, some singing, some clapping one another upon the back, &c. The tragic scene is performed by such as are entering into the pangs of the New Birth; the comic by those who are got thro' and those are so truly enthusiastic, that they tell you they saw the Joys of Heaven, can describe its situation, inhabitants, employments, & have seen their names entered into the Book of Life & can point out the writer, character & pen.

Brockwell had occasion to note that the lay exhorters often responsible for instigating such performances exempted themselves from chastisement by publicly condemning the chastiser as unconverted: the illiterate itinerant Woodbury, for example, "being gravely questioned on account of [his] extraordinary behaviour," responded with behavior even more extraordinary. "[W]ith strange Emotion and Violent Agitation," Brockwell wrote, Woodbury began "Rowling about the Ground, [and] Cryed out, You have crucified Xt [Christ] in which you have said, to add no more."[40] Indeed, it appeared impossible to contain the proliferating voices. Chauncy observed that the common people would speak on any pretense, once afforded the opportunity: "where Persons can't any longer *scream out* for themselves, supposing themselves to have got into a *converted State*, they will *scream* and *cry out*, and make as great a Noise as they can on the account of others, for their *unconverted Neighbours*, that are in a State of Sin, and going to Hell."[41] The offense to public decorum was compounded by the grotesque spectacle of such agitated speakers who, as their voices rose to drown the instigating voice of the exhorter, "made all manner of mouths, turning out their lips, drawing their mouths awry, as if convulsed, straining the eyeballs, and twisting their bodies in all manner of unseemly postures."[42]

The other notable effect of lay itinerancy was that, as numbers of people began to pay heed to the formerly unarticulated voices of common people, they began to realize in their behavior the promptings of their own inner voices, whose provenance was as uncertain as that of the "strolling pretended Ministers." Like the New Light ministry generally, if perhaps more crudely, the voices of these itinerant strangers urged their listeners to attend to their own inner voices, no matter how incoherent or incomplete the information they provided might seem, as faithful witnesses to the divine origins of their inward spiritual experiences. The account of one Hannah Cory of Sturbridge, Massachusetts, demonstrates the constructedness of the inner voice — a hodgepodge of scriptural snippets and speech fragments united in a rationale for separation — as the discursive correlative of what conservatives indicted as the impulsive and disjunct behavior of Separatists:

> One time as I was coming to the lecture the words came to me in Cor., Come out from amongst them, and then these words in Amos, Can two walk together except they be agreed, so I went to the meeting house, and when I came in there was nobody and as I sat there these words came to me, my house is a house of prayer but ye have made it a den of thieves, then suddenly fear came over me so I got up and went out and walked over to the burying place and I thought I had rather lie down among the graves than go into the meeting house, but when I saw Mr. Rice [the minister] coming I went in but it seemed to be a dark place, ministers deacon and people looked strangely as if they were all going blindfold to destruction, and though my body was there, my soul was with the Separates, praising God as soon as I was dismissed at the meeting house I went to Brother Nevil's where my soul was sweetly refreshed, the Lord alone be praised for it was He alone who brought me out and not any creature.[43]

Such was the jumbled subtext, as detractors saw it, of the Separatists' outrageous claims and impulsive behaviors like those more exuberantly demonstrated by one "high-flye[r]," a woman named Hannah Huckins, who, "in a boasting air, said she had gone through adoption, justification and sanctification and perfection and perseverance." The witness of her joy added that after delineating her spiritual accomplishments, Huckins "fell to dancing round the room, singing some dancing-tunes, jiggs, minuets, and kept the time exactly with her feet."[44] To the voices of Cory and Huckins might be added those of Edwards's parishioners who were emboldened to voice murderous impulses against those they deemed unconverted. Edwards chastised them concerning the importance of discriminating — again, with reference to the quality of inward sensations each produced — the false from the true inner voice, the voice of personal desire from the voice of conscience.

In *A Faithful Narrative* Edwards related how news of the Northampton revival had stimulated "much talk in many parts of the country, as though the people have symbolized with the Quakers, and the Quakers themselves have been moved with such reports; and came here, once and again, hoping to find good waters to fish in; but without the least success, and seem to be discouraged and have left off coming."[45] It is no surprise that the Quakers, with their doctrine of the inner voice, should have mistaken the Northampton revival as the mass conversion of Congregationalists to Quakerism. As the historian Frederick Tolles has pointed out, the Quakers and the evangelicals shared a common assumption, "that God reveals Himself directly to individual men through the Holy Spirit." For this reason, both movements encouraged a shift in "the basis of religious authority from outward belief to inward experience, from intellectual assent to experiential certainty"; they shared "a democratic tendency" realized in the development of lay preaching.[46] A brief comparison of the Quakers' and revivalists' notion of the inner light may suggest why, for the Quakers, such a doctrine guaranteed the cohesion of community across great geographical distances, so that a Connecticut Quaker like John Woolman could, in the course of his itinerancy, successfully exhort Friends from the southern colonies to whom he was personally unknown to manumit their slaves, while the Calvinist awakening was liable to work charismatically, and thus centrifugally, to produce not just separations but a class of isolated itinerants and a crisis of popular voice.[47]

If Quakers persisted in refusing to consider themselves bound by the ministry of the Word, as they claimed, such that in the absence of a standing ministry all believers were potential ministers, then their freedom of speech was quite evidently confined to the directives of the "inner voice," which their detractors insisted on denigrating as "the natural conscience," but which they knew to be the voice of God: "We were taught by renewed experience to labour for an inward stillness; at no time to seek for words, but to live in the spirit of Truth, and utter that to the people which Truth opened in us."[48] As John Woolman represents it here, attention to the inner voice demanded a degree and quality of attention calculated to pass beyond the self altogether. The Quaker endeavored to shut down, to the degree possible, the mechanism of self—most perniciously deployed when internally deployed—so that the voice of God might be audible to the ears of humankind. The selves of others could only be comprehended, and consequently addressed, when the self of the perceiver had been thus purified:

> Wherever men are true ministers of Jesus Christ it is from the operation of His spirit upon their hearts, first purifying them and then giving them a feeling sense of the conditions of the people.
> This truth was early fixed on my mind, and I was taught carefully to watch the opening lest while I was standing to speak, my own will should get uppermost, uttering words from worldly wisdom, and so depart from the true channel of the gospel ministry. (11–12)

For the young Woolman, the discipline of quietly watching and waiting, of struggling to learn the language of "the true Opener," of attempting simultaneously to repress and recognize one's own will so as not to make oneself an irrelevant distributary leading away from the "true channel," was an agonizing one. Thus, the first time he ventured to speak before a meeting, he miscalculated, producing a surplus of speech, which because it was uncalled for ("more than He directed me to say") was therefore meaningless. Much "afflicted in mind," "humbled and disciplined," Woolman struggled

> to know the language of the pure Spirit which moves upon the intellectual deep, and to wait in silence sometimes many weeks together, until I felt that rise which prepares the creature to stand like a trumpet through which the Lord speaks to His people. (11)

This erect creature is, in effect, a self-hollowed one, both container of and medium for "the language of the pure Spirit." The individual's disciplined subordination of the containing self, conceived as partial and contingent, to the contained essence of the sacred provided the fundamental rule of Quaker society; that is, the starting point of Quaker community was the disarticulation of the "inner voice" from the "private voice."[49] For this reason, Quakers were protected from the centrifugal forces of their implicitly democratic credo, and Quaker itinerancy, unlike Calvinist itinerancies, resulted not in the attenuation of the group but in its consolidation. Unlike their detractors, committed to the idea that all voices should be held to their places on the social and geographical map, the Quakers were thus free to extend the legitimacy of voice beyond distinctions of education, class, race, age, or gender, and to extend its range of address beyond the boundaries of a specific parish or meeting. The authenticity of the inner voice as an expression of the individual's dearest interest was confirmed for the Quakers not by considering it in the context of individual desire but rather by placing it alongside the unambiguous perspective of the sacred Other, made continually manifest as the consensus of the group. Thus Woolman, who undertakes his itinerancy for the cause of abolition, accounts in his *Journal* for the success of his appeals to slaveholding Quakers to manumit their slaves immediately by invoking the principled uniformity of group behavior. The dynamic of the group guaranteed that nothing could claim greater authority than the voice of the individual witness at the moment when the individual will was sensibly subdued. The resultant speech was God's, whose ascendant will was made audible through the instrumentality of the individual as breath is made audible through a hollowed tube. It may be that because the Quakers treated the potentially unlimited voice of the individual with such restraint they attracted little attention from conservatives when the fear of religious enthusiasm was at its height in the mid–eighteenth century.[50]

According to virtually every critic of the revival and many of its supporters, the importance of discerning false from true voices, both external and internal, was paramount because in both cases the voice of madness was easily confused with the voice of God. Not just the integrity of the individual Christian but the possibility of redeemed community depended on this differentiation whose necessity arose with the first stirrings of the revival. On 30 May 1735, five years before Whitefield's arrival, Edwards wrote to Rev.

Benjamin Colman of Boston "a particular account of the present extraordinary circumstances of this town, and the neighboring towns with respect to religion."[51] His sanguine account of the unprecedented and remarkable growth of religious preoccupation among the townspeople of his Northampton parish abruptly concluded with a postscripted report of the grotesque suicide of his uncle, a leading merchant of the town, Joseph Hawley Sr. "[L]ast Sabbath day morning," Edwards wrote, Hawley "laid violent hands on himself, and put an end to his life, by cutting his own throat." Edwards explained that Hawley, like many others, had experienced great concern about the state of his soul, a preoccupation stimulated by Edwards's powerful preaching."[52] Unlike others, he had no relief from his "darkness [and] doubts" and fell victim to what Edwards described as an inherited tendency to "deep melancholly," which deprived him of his sleep, his peace of mind, and finally his ability to receive advice or listen to reason.[53]

Although the Hawley story is included in the revised version of the *Faithful Narrative*, its presentation differs significantly from its earlier appearance as the postscript to the first version of Edwards's letter to Colman. It appears toward the conclusion of the *Faithful Narrative*, after the lengthy accounts Edwards provided of two of Northampton's most exemplary converts, a sickly young woman named Abigail Hutchinson whose conversion enabled her cheerfully to suffer a horrendous death by starvation, and a four-year-old child, Phebe Bartlet, who suddenly revealed an exceedingly precocious religiosity.[54] The reference to Hawley, purged of all signs of Edwards's relation to the man, occurs after an account of the near-suicide of another anonymous man, a melancholic: "being in great spiritual trouble," Edwards wrote, this individual "was hurried with violent temptations to cut his own throat, and made an attempt; but did not do it effectually" (205–6). He eventually recovered his equanimity and survived. The Hawley story, following directly this sketch of tragedy narrowly averted, is introduced as evidence that "the Spirit of God was gradually withdrawing from us" and the rage of Satan was "more let loose" (206). In the short account of Hawley's suicide appended to the earlier version of the letter, Edwards had interpreted the event as a hopeful, if sorrowful, sign: "Satan seems to be in a great rage, at this extraordinary breaking forth of the work of God. I hope it is because he knows that he has but a short time: doubtless he had a Great Reach, in this violent attack of his against the whole affair."[55] In the later version, this optimistic view of the incident's significance has yielded to a forthright admission that religious affections were waning and that the dying revival had entered a decadent phase with which Edwards chose not to associate himself, even to the extent of admitting his relationship with Hawley.

The most important difference in the two accounts is Edwards's presentation of the aftermath of Hawley's suicide in the later version:

> The news of this extraordinarily affected the minds of people here, and struck them as it were with astonishment. After this, multitudes in this and other towns seemed to have it strongly suggested to 'em, and pressed upon 'em, to do as this person had done. And many that seemed to be under no melancholy, some pious persons that had no special darkness, or doubts about the goodness of their state, nor were under any special trouble or concern of mind about anything spiritual or temporal, yet had it urged upon 'em, as if somebody had spoke to 'em, "Cut your own throat, now is a good opportunity: *now, NOW!*" So that they were obliged to fight with all their might to resist it, and yet no reason suggested to 'em why they should do it. (206–7)

Thus, four years before the Great Awakening, the problem of an internalized, spectral, and wholly spurious voice, seemingly impossible to distinguish from the legitimate voice of conscience ("the mouth of that vice-regent of God in the soul"), had arisen as a grotesque personal tragedy that threatened, through the town-traveling offices of rumor, to engulf the social body. The suicide of Hawley at the behest of a mysterious voice, a suicide carried out by severing the body from the head at the symbolically overdetermined site of the windpipe, and the subsequent suicidal thoughts of numerous others also experienced as the voice of an invisible stranger persuasively urging self-destruction, raised questions for many not just about the legitimacy of inward religious experience but about the ability of natural men to respond appropriately to powerful "impressions," as Edwards described them, made on their "imaginations" (189).[56] Chauncy's warning about elevating internal impressions to the level of divine revelation came too late for Hawley: "this you cannot do," he had chastised Davenport, "while you give heed to *impulses*, and guide your self by them, taking them for discoveries of the will of GOD. Your *grand error* lies here: And 'tis a more dangerous one, than you may be ready to imagine. There is nothing, while in this state of mind, but you may be bro't to: And how far GOD may suffer you to be led aside, is known only to himself."[57]

Charles Brockden Brown's 1798 novel, *Wieland; or, The Transformation: An American Tale*, with its Chauncyesque epigraphical warning, "From Virtue's blissful paths away / The double-tongued are sure to stray," undertakes to answer the question "how far" by (Mather-like, Melville-like) tracing the vectors of deviance to the very threshold of invisibility.[58] It thematizes the problem exemplified by Joseph Hawley and implicitly raised in Edwards's tautological "solution" to the spiritual impasse threatened by proliferating representations of divine truth: if absolute truth were absent from the human realm, the "truest representation" of it might still be identified as that which generated "true ideas" about it in the mind. The novel posits instead that like its truth, a representation is what one takes it to be, a position that parodies Edwards's theological Lockeanism which credited individuals with the sense to discriminate a false internal impression (that might urge the Christian to violence, for example) from a true work of God's spirit upon the soul. Brown's novel suggests, that is, that despite Edwards's reliance upon the scriptural touchstone that underwrote his rejection of singularity and his semiotics of redeemed Christian character, his notion of the truest representation begged an obvious question: how were unqualified men and women, by nature blind and deaf to Truth, to assess the legitimacy of representations, identify the truest one, and act confidently and righteously upon it? How central to the success of that assessment of representations was the sanctified credulity Edwards recommended for finessing God's "trial" of his creature's ability to negotiate the stumbling block at the heart of religious faith?

In *Wieland*, the representations in question are vocal, deployed within a neoclassically appointed vacuum of purpose and principle that the novel associates with revolutionary America. Within the claustrophobic space of Mettingen, an estate situated in pastoral isolation on the Schuylkill River in Pennsylvania, just outside the city of brotherly love (the capital of the United States until 1800, and threatened in 1798 and 1799 by street mobs angry with Federalist policies intended to contain internal dissent), disembodied voices are suddenly and mysteriously generated, creating for the enlightened foursome who inhabit the estate an epistemological crisis of apocalyptic proportions.[59] These disembodied voices promote the conversion of spatial into a personified claustrophobia, a progressive isolation and entrapment of the individual that constitutes the novel's plot. The plot of *Wieland* thus literalizes the revolutionary discovery made (and rued) by both parties in the eighteenth century's great religious debate: namely, the radical separability of matter and manner, so that sense or meaning may insensibly withdraw from sound, message from messenger, and—the spectral nightmare—the visible characters of those one knows best from invisible identity.[60] The disembodied voice targets with stunning precision the pretense of individuals to know about their world and those who inhabit it. For that reason, it is a representation uniquely fatal to all others: either one surrenders to it utterly and in so doing destroys one's world, or resists and watches in impotent isolation as one's world is destroyed. The disembodied voice, first "thrown" into the abyss of the American wilderness, illuminates the impenetrable gloom of what Emily Dickinson would later call "the interval/Experience between," that undiscoverable hiatus between the generation of a representation and the decision to consent to it, to take it as a "discovery" of truth.[61]

II

As he relates it in his *Memoirs*, Carwin, the ventriloquist who will be implicated in the spectacular demise of the eponymous Wieland family, meets a wealthy Irishman named Ludloe at a particularly vulnerable point in his own career. The adolescent Carwin, the impoverished son of a Western Pennsylvania farmer, has been left penniless by the death of an aunt who had persuaded his "unenlightened" father to allow her to support her nephew in "unbounded indulgence" at her Philadelphia home (282, 289). Walking disconsolately along the banks of the Schuylkill River where the tragic scene of the novel *Wieland* will later occur, Carwin encounters the urbane Ludloe who had earlier witnessed a gratuitous display of Carwin's ventriloquistic talents at a private outdoor concert and apparently suspects him to be the perpetrator of the aural illusion which had so amazed all the other guests. Not directly stating his suspicions, Ludloe begins to speak of the mysterious occurrence, and remarks that "[n]o more powerful engine [than the biloquial talent] could be conceived, by which the ignorant and credulous might be moulded" (300). He confides to Carwin his suspicion that a human rather than a supernatural agent produced the voice, and then expands upon its potential as an instrument of persuasion:

> Men, he said, believed in the existence and energy of invisible powers, and in the duty of discovering and conforming to their will. This will was supposed to be sometimes made known to them through the medium of their senses. A voice coming from a quarter where no attendant form could be seen would, in most cases, be ascribed to supernal agency, and a command imposed on them, in this manner, would be obeyed with religious scrupulousness. Thus men might be imperiously directed in the disposal of their industry, their property, and even of their lives. (300–301)

Representations made by a voice with "no attendant form" are those to which men and women give their most enthusiastic consent as the voice of transcendent authority, to the point of divesting themselves of their energies, property, and life itself. Ludloe's indirect encouragement to Carwin to make a motivated, rather than an impulsive, use of his vocal powers reinforces the Machiavellian inclinations that Carwin has already betrayed: considering the older man's observation that the disembodied voice may inspire others to perform "the most flagitious, as well as the most heroic acts," Carwin reflects upon his potential power to author an unending series of plots passing far beyond the callow tricks to which he has thus far restricted himself and for which "[t]he utility or harmlessness of the end, justified, in my eyes, the means" (301). One might say that Ludloe's insinuations inspire Carwin's first glimpse of the totalitarian powers of authorship to mold the credulous into characters — flagitious, heroic — of one's own devising.

Ludloe's words to Carwin on the generation and reception of the disembodied voice are doubly resonant. First, they chronologically anticipate but, in terms of the texts' compositions, recapitulate the plot of *Wieland*, whose action occurs several years after their interview, at some unspecified point between the conclusion of the French and Indian War in 1763 and the beginning of the American Revolution in 1776.[62] Theodore Wieland is the enlightened and brilliant scion of a melancholic religious enthusiast and radical antinomian, a German immigrant to America by way of England. His untimely and mysterious death in Wieland's childhood, apparently by spontaneous combustion, is connected in family legend to his conviction that he would suffer for having failed to obey divine commands whose import he never divulges. For his "thrilling melancholy," the younger Wieland resembles his father; in other respects, he seems largely to have distanced himself from his father's religious enthusiasm as well as his fate, for although he shared his father's thoughts insofar as "[m]oral necessity, and calvinistic inspiration, were the props on which [he] thought proper to repose," yet his "mind . . . was enriched by science, and embellished with literature" (25, 28, 26). As a mark of this difference, Wieland, a devotee of Cicero, converts the gazebo in which his father solitarily worshiped his god and later died his violent death into a neoclassical "temple" where he and his only associates — a self-styled "congregation" of childhood playmates composed of his wife Catharine, her brother and his closest friend Pleyel, and his devoted sister Clara — carry on a daily round of enlightened and strictly "theoretical" conversation (17, 23). This pleasant routine, the privilege of the agriculturalist whose "fortune exempted him from the necessity of personal labour," remains unimpaired until Wieland hears what he takes to be the voice of God commanding him to prove his religious faith by sacrificing his wife, his four children, his foster daughter, and his beloved Clara, who alone escapes to narrate the tale (23). In the novel's penultimate scene, Wieland, having escaped from prison, has cornered Clara in her bedroom and is about to kill her when yet another voice imperiously informs him that he had been mistaken in the aural representation to which he had uncritically consented and had thus killed in error. In response, he commits suicide with his sister's penknife which she, preparing to wield it against her brother in self-defense, has just dropped. Before Wieland heard the voice urging him to murder, other members of the "congregation" had heard mysterious voices in and around their isolated compound whose import they tirelessly debate and which slowly erode their Lockean faith in the epistemological adequacy of visible reality to inform the understanding and thus the will. As it turns out, all of these voices, with the possible exception of the murderous voice of God that only Wieland hears, were generated unbeknownst to them by a stranger who from "curiosity" they had recently admitted into their exclusive circle, an itinerant "rustic," the fantastically eloquent (and inaptly named) Frank Carwin (81).

By inspiring Carwin's association of Machiavellianism with intentional and sustained (one might say professional) rather than impulsive and sporadic authorship, Ludloe's words at the riverbank also remind the reader of

Carwin's *Memoirs* that the ventriloquist had from childhood coveted the peculiar advantages of invisibility. As a boy, Carwin's single ambition had been to "elude [his father's] watchfulness," as well as that of his older brother whose "ideas never ranged beyond the sphere of his vision" (282, 281). The discovery of his ventriloquistic powers — made possible by "organs of un-usual compass and vigour" — endows him not just with invisibility as the negative power to absent oneself and thus to deflect paternal aggression but also with the means to substitute for physical or "sensible" presence a met-onymic representation (e.g., pure voice) of uncanny, because spectral, subjec-tivity that permits the unimpeded exercise of his will and the "unbounded indulgence" of his fancy, and particularly his "literary passion" (284, 289). Invisibility as ventriloquistic power is thus presented as a powerful trope for authorship: it allows Carwin to realize a "fancy [that] teemed with visions" (a mark of his "incorrigible depravity," according to his father) by replicating himself in or as other speakers at the same time as he makes himself (as Whitman will more benignly claim to be) the unitary source of all discur-sive — and therefore, as his credulous victims assume, formal or embodied — variety (281, 282). This is made explicit in the scene in the *Memoirs* when Carwin (who introduces himself as an oppressed farmer's son whose "darling propensity" is the love of reading he is forbidden to indulge) discovers his voice (282). Attempting to elude his father's censure for returning home late, he takes a shortcut over, rather than around, a forested riverbank ridge and there discovers a "narrow pass," a gloomy canyon of rock cut through the "maze," into which he shouts a "rude ditty" as a way of deflecting his fear of dark places and the "goblins and spectres" that abide there (284–85). After an interval of time, his words are repeated in a "perfect imitation" of his voice by another invisible speaker who seemed to be located in a spot "inaccessible to man or beast . . . as I then imagined" (285). The repetitions proceed, after short intervals, each from a different locale. He soon realizes that the many seemingly responsive voices are all echoes of his own, and that he himself is thus the source and the nucleus of all variety; the totalitarian implications of his discovery are made explicit when he observes that in this manner "the will is capable of being rendered unlimited and absolute" (288).

From this time forward, he declares, in a comically perverse interpreta-tion of the contemporary notion of imagined community as fantastic ego-centrism, "[t]he idea of a distant voice, like my own, was intimately present

to my fancy" (287). The threat of paternal aggression cannot thwart him
from gratifying his "ardent desire" for ubiquity: "time, and incessant repetition," he finds, "could scarcely lessen its charms or exhaust the variety produced by new tones and positions" (287, 286). With practice, he learns to
transcend the natural limitations of his art by "so dispos[ing] my organs" as
to create an "appear[ance]" of displacement no matter what the contours of
the natural terrain rather than relying upon the mechanics of reverberation
(287).[63] This skill, added to his ability to imitate other sounds and voices,
completes his training regimen. As the first intentional exercise of his newly
discovered ability to produce voice with no attendant form, Carwin plans to
transgress the gender and generational divide, as well as that separating the
living from the dead: he vows "to counterfeit a commission from heaven" by
imitating the voice of his dead mother in order to persuade his superstitious
and tyrannical father to release him to his aunt's care and thereby remove
him from his "jealous scrutiny" (290, 282). He quails initially at the blasphemy of the undertaking, but reflects that "the excellence of my purpose
would justify the means," thereby suggesting that like the voice itself, the
Machiavellian justification for its uninhibited and surreptitious exercise "facilitates a repetition, strengthens temptation, and grows into habit" (290,
293). Although circumstances prevent him from carrying out this particular
exercise, his dream of invisibility — not as a passive or craven withdrawal
from the body but as the simultaneous displacement and augmentation of
one's voice — is more than realized: for Carwin, articulation coincides with
absence.

The discovery of his voice, then, as a means to disembodiment enables
Carwin to liberate himself from the restrictions that apply to specularity as a
condition of human interaction (both visibility and reciprocity). This release
marks a crucial — and atavistic — mutation of the paradigm for the production of democratic personality so powerfully realized by George Whitefield
in the context of spectacular conversion. Unlike, for example, his fellow
farmers and contemporaries, the Separatist Nathan Cole or the Baptist Biel
Ledoyt, when Carwin discovers his uncontainable voice, he does so far from
any form of cultural or collective space, and in radical, even savage, isolation,
as the detail of his initial "Mohock" yell in the "vocal glen" is intended to
convey (284, 287). The absence of a collectivity underscores from the first
the affiliation of his voice with a subversive, if not downright criminal, indi-

viduality (although this does not inhibit his tendency, as pronounced as Whitefield's, toward the theatrical revelation of his vocal powers). As he confesses, his unreluctant exercise of his gift intends "not the happiness of others," but merely the instantaneous realization of whatever momentary and solipsistic "ambition" he meditates, ambitions whose peculiarity is that they lack specific motivation (they are impulsive) and intend neither sequel nor consequence — that is, they are profoundly irrational and resist narrative accountability (295). In this respect, Carwin's access to the invisible recalls the specters of the witchcraft crisis (as represented by the afflicted): here is the atavism of the crucial deviation in the enabling paradigm of democratic personality which he represents. Because the modification of the paradigm for the coming-into-being of democratic personality that Carwin enacts and transfers to Clara marks its metamorphosis into a literary problematic, it begs the question of the usefulness to the national literature project of this return to the gothicism of the spectral domain.

At the same time, in its exercise and its effects, Carwin's vocal potency explicitly links spectral, enthusiastic, and democratic space. An amalgam of the specter and the itinerant exhorter, Carwin maintains a simultaneous presence in the visible and invisible domains, and thus combines the theological monstrosity of the hybridic specter with the characterological monstrosity of the false and seducing teacher, the itinerant "changeling." On the visible plane, he is the unsightly but seductively eloquent stranger who dissembles his true identity as a canny ventriloquist by donning the garb and assuming the gait of an unremarkable rustic; on the invisible plane, he is what the French film theorist Michel Chion would call an "acousmatic personality": a disembodied presence made sensible to others through the faculty of hearing, but not sight, a "kind of talking, acting shadow" who, in this case, interferes directly in the lives of those around him by manipulating their epistemological assumptions concerning "the reassuring fixation of the voice in the residence of the body."[64] By means of this doubling or dual affiliation, he deconstructs the reliability of the visible world by surreptitiously wielding a revolutionary power of dissemblance that erodes established authority as it erodes, through coercion or seduction, the grounds of consent to its representations. Most crucial for the national literary enterprise which his story partly initiates, his ontological ambiguity creates an enduring uncertainty as to whether he is a representing subject or a represented object, the author of evil or the emplotted character: thus the novel obsessively raises the question of whether the one who appears to deserve the blame might actually be a fiction, the blameless product of another's misrepresentations. It thus suggests that the trajectory of the answer to the question asked by characters throughout the novel — "Who is the author?" — will be a viciously circular one ultimately abandoned by default.[65]

The invisible exercise of Carwin's voice reproduces, then, the structural features of the specter-victim and exhorter-auditor relationships, and adds to this chain of analogous (enthusiastic) relationships a new link: that of the writer to the character (or, alternatively, the reader). This extension is confirmed by Carwin's proclivity to transfer his particular powers of uncontainable voice and direct access to invisible realities (as they are perceived) to at least some of his victims, primarily Clara, just as some of the afflicted acquired access to the spectral realm and some auditors of itinerant exhorters became exhorters in turn. Like the new-made specter and the new-made exhorter, the new-made writer Clara is at pains to prove her innocence and maintain her status as sufferer, to "vindicate" herself even as she acknowledges the violence in which she participated as prerequisite to her publicly offered testimony. As she represents it, Clara is Carwin's greatest victim, although it is she who most seriously assumes his prerogatives of authorship. Once Carwin has been relegated at the novel's close to "a remote district of Pennsylvania" to follow "the harmless pursuits of agriculture," Clara accedes to his vocal power to ventriloquize other voices and to "throw" her voice from her body, to release it from the limitations of physical presence, by means of her narrative (273). Increasingly solipsistic, her account begins with the paradoxical assertions, first, that her cruel "destiny" is "without example" and second, that she writes to deter others from repeating her errors (6, 5). After chronicling her own slide toward fratricidal violence, a slide that coincides with her conversion into a writer of public rather than private (enshrined and encoded) narratives like her journal, her "tale" ends with the explicit abandonment of her altruistic justification for writing. Not only does she despairingly claim to "care not" for the elusive truth but she admits that she writes less because a friend has requested an account of the events that decimated her family than because writing permits her the "luxury . . . to feast upon my woes" (5, 266, 252). Writing, she states, has become for her its own justification as that which sustains her existence: "When I lay down the

pen the taper of life will expire: my existence will terminate with my tale"
(252; cf. 260).

Considering the literally unspeakable isolation to which they all eventually
succumb, the characters of *Wieland* are so incestuously intimate before the
arrival of Carwin, their doubling (as in each of Brown's novels) is so relentless
and their emotional attachments so hyperbolic, that for clarity's sweet sake
(apologies to Carwin) the novel is best approached with reference to the
concept of artistic space.[66] The Mettingen estate in which the main action of
the novel occurs, including its immediate prehistory (the elder Wieland's
death as Clara narrates it), offers a literary representation of the space beyond formal observance — the spectral space, the "third ontological domain," the "interval between" — that religious conservatives and, before
them, spectral evidence theorists had found so troubling to imagine.[67]
Chauncy had identified the space beyond formal observance with religious
enthusiasm and its accompanying malaise, a pathological melancholy. As
such, it was the site not only of intellectual febrility but of spiritual blindness
and deafness, the result of an uncharitable and ultimately blasphemous refusal to concede the epistemological adequacy of the visible world for discovering invisible realities and, at the same time, an inability to distinguish
legitimate from illegitimate inner voices. It was the sphere in which the
religious itinerants, "disorderly walkers of unpeaceable froward and turbulent Spirits," ranged at will, unauthorized individuals with apparently unbounded authority over "the mob," but with no discernable or stable identity.[68] It was the space of seduction in which "*silly Women*" surrendered their
integrity to the unscrupulous changeling and became seducers in turn.[69] It
was the space given over to the unnatural domination of the better by the
vulgar classes and was thus identified as the revolutionary site dedicated to
the overturning of established values and meanings. For spectral evidence
theorists (for whom the conservatives of the Great Awakening, as rationalists, had little respect), the spectral realm or space beyond formal observance
was likewise associated with the radical calling into question of the visible
world, with a revolutionary power of dissemblance, with the menacing proliferation of the representational possibilities of individual personality, and
with transgressions of sacrosanct boundaries. The fear latent in the conservative abhorrence of enthusiasm as it recapitulated the earlier fear of spec-

trality was that it promoted a state of visible invisibility associated with a vocal-characterological power of misrepresentation that corrupted virtue, understood as the integrity of visible character and invisible identity, by destroying the common ground of consent to legitimate authority through the corruption of the individual mind.

A country estate, Mettingen exhibits a formal symmetry of two mansions and two summerhouses, belonging to the brother and sister, Wieland and Clara, situated in the midst of the untamed natural beauty of the American countryside. Apart from its historical context, the novel offers the estate as a space beyond formal observance both literally and figuratively understood. Upon the elder Wieland's purchase of the property, it was the site of a solitary and radically antinomian religious worship. The circumstances of the elder Wieland's religious conversion while a trader's apprentice (an unimaginably desultory Augustinian affair in which his dully wandering gaze happens to alight upon a radical French Protestant text self-exhumed from the dust in his London garret) predispose him to the worship of an imperious god of his own fabrication, a "Divine Majesty" whom he believes dictates "an empire of religious duty [which] extended itself to his looks, gestures, and phrases" (10).[70] Like the Puritan fathers, he is convinced that his religion makes it impossible for him to remain in England. His personal errand into the American wilderness, however, is motivated not by a concern to conserve his religious purity but ironically, considering his god's demand that he worship in absolute solitude, to disseminate his convictions "among the unbelieving nations" (10). The "North-American Indians naturally presented themselves as the first objects" of the elder Wieland's larger aspirations (he resembles his creator, Charles Brockden Brown, in this regard), but rumors of their savagery shake his resolution upon his arrival in America, and persuade him to postpone his mission (11).[71] Like Crèvecoeur's Farmer James and those whose "transplantation" to American soil he facilitates, the newly arrived immigrant sets out to acquire "new objects, new employments, and new associates" in an attempt to "[obliterate] the devout impressions of his youth," and becomes wealthy enough through perseverance, frugality, and slave labor to purchase Mettingen (11). There, he and his wife, a religious enthusiast and disciple of the German pietist Zinzendorf, raise their family and consolidate their fortune; it is worth noting that his wife is not invited to share his devotional life and is prevented from joining an "established congregation" by Mettingen's isolation (13).[72] Upon his retirement, Wieland's convictions return, and he leaves his family to become an itinerant exhorter among the Indians, who repel his ministrations "with insult and derision" (12). (The novel and its sequel, Carwin's memoirs, thus suggest that had the elder Wieland succeeded in converting the Indians, the "Mohock" Carwin would not have returned to punish his children.) Crucified, as was Crèvecoeur's Farmer James at the end of his narrative, between "[t]he license of savage passion, and the artifices of his depraved countrymen," the elder Wieland returns in defeat to his estate, consumed with fear for having failed to carry out the command, never specified, of his deity (12).

Increasingly melancholy and withdrawn, his life abruptly ends one night when, having retired to his "temple," an open structure located on a bluff overlooking the Schuylkill, he is apparently consumed by his own inner "light" (18). His relations, having struggled to witness his fate through the midnight gloom, rush to his aid just in time to receive his "imperfect tale" of what had befallen him, about which his brother-in-law suspects "half the truth had been suppressed" (20). Surrounded by a repellent atmosphere even in death, the elder Wieland is forsaken by "every one whom their duty did not detain" as his putrefying corpse gives off "insupportable exhalations" which, by association, cast doubt upon the sanctity or clear meaning of his martyrdom (20). Likewise, the natural limpidity that characterizes Mettingen's beauty as well as the social relations that transpire within its boundaries is belied by agitations visible, from a certain perspective, on the surface of transparency itself. Such descriptive details relative to the artistic space of Mettingen and to its inhabitants reinforce the impression that within its confines, what is perceived as a transparency distracts the eye from the "medium" whose manipulation will alter perception, as when the apparently still waters of the Schuylkill, seen from the summerhouse above, betray their profound agitation, and as Clara's own "perfect" and "unblemished" honor will be regarded by Pleyel "through the mists of prejudice and passion" (9, 127, 124).

Having, like Carwin, spent their youth with an aunt in Philadelphia, Wieland and Clara are restored to their childhood home upon reaching their majority; Clara writes that Wieland "took possession of the house in which he was born" and at the same time consummated his "long protracted" relationship with Catharine (24). The representation of Mettingen as a space beyond formal observance is complicated when the temple of worship in which the elder Wieland conducted his isolated devotions and died his mysterious death is converted by his son into a temple to "the chief object of his veneration," the classical orator Cicero (27). The first itinerant to happen by the isolated estate, an Italian artist and "adventurer," sells Wieland a bust of Cicero which he claimed to have copied from an "antique" he had exhumed near Modena. "Of the truth of his assertions we were not qualified to judge," Clara writes of their first itinerant visitor, as she will of the next, but in this case the adventurer's artistry makes the question of truth a negligible one (26). With the acceptance of the bust, the addition of a harpsichord to the temple completes its outward transformation from a site devoted to the excesses of solitary worship to a neoclassical shrine devoted to the appreciation of antiquity's formal perfections; at least as Clara represents it, Wieland's dedication to the "divinity of Cicero" has no bearing on the writer's importance to the developing American understanding of the science of politics or as a model of the ideal citizen (28).[73] But Wieland's activities within the converted temple do not differ markedly from those of his father — an indication that if the father's obsession has been repudiated by the son and daughter, its vitality survives as the content of their conscience, quiescent except for the nagging doubt they tacitly share concerning the validity of their father's quest. As the elder Wieland had discovered in religion an ongoing duty to realize in every word, look, and gesture the invisible perfection of his deity, so the son discovers in classical scholarship a similarly futile imitative exigency that he pursues with equal enthusiasm. He becomes obsessed with restoring to the Ciceronian text a purity, based upon the irretrievably lost spoken original, that the passage of time — history itself — had obliterated. Clara writes of her brother in this period of their greatest felicity:

> He was never tired of conning and rehearsing [Cicero's] productions. To understand them was not sufficient. He was anxious to discover the gestures and cadences with which they ought to be delivered. He was very scrupulous in selecting a true scheme of pronunciation for the Latin tongue, and in adapting it to the words of his darling writer. His favorite occupation consisted in embellishing his rhetoric with all the proprieties of gesticulation and utterance. (27)

In addition to the conning, rehearsing, understanding, discovering, selecting, and adapting what he hopes are the authentic components of Cicero's speech in order to restore a lost integrity by means of a faultless copy, Wieland "collected all the editions and commentaries that could be procured, and employed months of severe study in exploring and comparing them" (27).[74] Not surprisingly, this project of restoration to which all the inmates of Mettingen are devoted does not abate until Wieland receives God's command to kill and be pure, when the unending task of remedying, particle by particle, the atomization of an original integrity is replaced by the quick and irreversible work of reducing one's world to oneself. We might, then, attribute the almost palpable claustrophobia of Mettingen as novelistic space to its embodiment of an irreversible postlapsarianism; it is first and foremost a site from which the possibility of grace, as the original and authoritative voice of a primordial integrity, has been eradicated.[75]

Pleyel, who shares Wieland's "passion for Roman eloquence" if not his friend's melancholy spirit and doubts about the efficacy of human reason, eventually joins the group, and the two women, Catharine and Clara, "blithsome and gay," make up their admiring audience as the two men indulge their passion by "bandying quotations and syllogisms" (27, 25, 34). Even the "sound of war" (hostilities associated with the French and Indian conflict) does not prevent them from thus taking their daily pleasure. In fact, as Clara explains, the war's proximity only "enhance[d] our enjoyment": "Revolutions and battles, however calamitous to those who occupied the scene, contributed in some sort to our happiness, by agitating our minds with curiosity, and furnishing causes of patriotic exultation" (29).[76] In other matters as well, Clara buoyantly characterizes the foursome as "spectator[s]" of life which, when it comes to their neighborhood, offers them personal or political "spectacle[s]" that they convert into "copious theme[s] of speculation" (30, 31, 33). The scene they occupy is thus both geographically and psychologically distanced from the collective realities of political and social life: holding those realities completely at bay, Mettingen provides its inhabitants with a point of view from which the real appears as a species of fiction performed for their pleasure, when it is registered at all. The occupants of Mettingen seem equally invisible to the surrounding world and appear to contribute minimally to its life. Moreover, they formally observe no politics or religion; their self-isolation allows them to live beyond the observation of any person outside their limited "society" (28). The claustrophobia of their existence, wholly theoretical and without application, thus derives from the utter ab-

THE VOICE OF THE PEOPLE **223**

sence of a public dimension and the sense of a collective life.[77] To occupy
Mettingen is to occupy a scene wholly given over to idiosyncratic and inconsequential pursuits, a form of freedom belied when its inhabitants acknowledge themselves to be confined within its interpretive framework: the elder
Wieland's legacy of failed communication with the transcendent realm and
his subsequent incarceration in a solitary confinement of the mind.

As the space within which democratic personality will come into being,
the radical isolation of Mettingen recapitulates the solitude within which
Carwin discovers the uncontainability of his biloquial voice. Like Carwin,
the Wieland estate thus appears to suggest an atavistic turn away from the
social and political vitality of the public scene of spectacular conversion,
where democratic personality emerged in the light of day and before the eyes
of the multitude, and toward the gothic obscurity of the spectral domain as
the invisible site of anarchic individual desire. Yet their shared atavism may
be more accurately understood as twin figurations of an unknowable human
interiority which, as the subject of anxious theoretical attention in the wake
of spectacular conversion, carried the gothicism of spectrality forward into
an increasingly rationalist age. The structure of the Mettingen compound
reinforces the psychological and genealogical pattern of interiorities both
proximate and yet profoundly dissociated: the temple is a step removed from
what one assumes to be the normal domesticity of the Wieland home with its
five children; the isolated house in which Clara lives alone is a step removed
from the inbred sociability of the temple; and her lattice-covered summerhouse — the most spectral of Mettingen's milieus, in which she dreams of her
brother beckoning her toward an abyss and ventriloquistically loses her vir-
ginity to Carwin — is a step removed from the house she occupies with her
unfaithful maid. Within Clara's house, as she meticulously describes its
layout, interiorities are nested: the closet where she houses her diary as well
as her most "useful" text, a manuscript written by her father, permits no
access except through her bedroom, which also has a single door and no
windows (95, 64–65). Aside from the geographical and psychological isolation of Mettingen and its dissociated ("conflicting and irreconcilable") internal structure, then, as artistic space it is thrice removed: from purity, from
history, and from community.[78]

Upon this site, Carwin superimposes his own invisible "empire" of the
disembodied voice whose "bounds," Clara will lament, are "utterly inscruta-

ble" (97).[79] Its activity ceases only when there are no more voices for it to appropriate and emplot, at which time it transforms itself into a ventriloquist's confession and then autobiography. The first of Mettingen's inhabitants to hear a disembodied voice is, ironically, Wieland as he is walking to the temple while endeavoring to prove "the genius of the speaker" to a skeptical Pleyel in response to his friend's playful debunking of Cicero's oration for Cluentius (34).[80] He intends to "appeal to the volume" that allegedly provides the truest representation of the spoken original when he is accosted by a voice that is and is not his wife's commanding him to return immediately to the house (34). Having determined that his wife had remained with their company indoors, Wieland experiences a conviction he refrains from sharing with his friends: he becomes the "enthusiast" he has always potentially been and embraces, without reservation, his father's account of his death "as flowing from a direct and supernatural decree" (40). Visibly withdrawing from the influence of his friends, he rejects "auricular deception" (a phrase which conveys the evangelical analogy of ear to heart) as an explanation for his hearing the voice, a foreclosure of alternative possibilities that anticipates Wieland's failure to detect the oracular deception in the "divine" command to kill his family (39, 40). As the Cicero project could not, the disembodied voice galvanizes his drive to integrate his various proclivities: his rationalism, his radical Calvinism, and his tendency toward melancholy.

Wieland, Clara intimates, had thus chosen a direction when a second vocal incident occurs, this time heard by both Wieland and Pleyel as, on a nighttime stroll, the latter urges the former to accompany him on a trip to Germany in order to take physical possession of ancestral lands of which he has only just become aware. Pleyel, who intends to marry his German fiancée on the trip, wants to persuade Wieland that he can claim "the privileges of wealth and rank" and at the same time become the "enlightened proprietor" of his land and the "vassals" that reside there (43). Wieland objects that such power over others might cause him to become "deprave[d]," to "degenerate into a tyrant and voluptuary"; moreover, to leave against Catharine's will or to compel her to accompany him would be to act as her "tyrant and foe" rather than her "protector and friend" (43, 50).[81] At this point, the disembodied voice of Catharine is once again heard, confirming Wieland's anticipation of her displeasure with the plan; immediately thereafter, a man's voice informs

Pleyel of his fiancée's untimely death. Pleyel's ensuing report to Clara on the details of this encounter produces a crucial shift in her thinking about the provenance of the disembodied voice. Wieland's uncorroborated first experience had caused her to suspect the "depravity" of her brother's senses, which suggested in turn the "diseased condition of his frame": "The will is the tool of the understanding," Clara asserts in a short-lived moment of Lockean confidence, "which must fashion its conclusions on the notices of sense. If the senses be depraved, it is impossible to calculate the evils that may flow from the consequent deductions of the understanding" (39). After Pleyel's report, however, Clara announces her own conversion to a modified or tentative enthusiasm by asserting that, although she is no believer in "apparitions and enchantments," his and Wieland's experience provided "proofs of a sensible and intelligent existence . . . unquestionably super-human," and she speculates upon the "beneficent intentions" toward the group of "this airy minister" (52).[82] In so doing, Clara consents to Wieland's representations of the voice and thus accommodates in advance her future affliction as the voice's personalities proliferate beyond the benign.[83]

The conditions under which power becomes tyrannical and entails depravity as well as the relationship of physical presence to possession thus provide the context for Clara's emotional encounter with Carwin, whom she first espies shuffling along the bluff overlooking the Schuylkill in front of her home. Seen from a distance, Carwin offers Clara "nothing remarkable": judging by his clothing, his "gait," and his "form," he is a common man, "rustic and aukward," "ungainly and disproportioned," a type "frequently to be met with on the road, and in the harvest field," if uncommonly seen within the confines of the estate apparently lost in appreciation of the scenery, an activity she associates with educated tastes (57). The sight of this as yet faceless rustic figure induces an odd languor in Clara who sits, for the next half hour, "by fits, contemplating the image of this wanderer, and drawing, from outward appearances, those inferences with respect to the intellectual history of this person, which experience affords us" (58). "Experience" at Mettingen being indistinguishable from theory, the inferences Clara draws from Carwin's appearances lead her to express the "virtue-laden notion of reading" that Michael Warner has shown lay at the heart of a republican ideology of literature. She sentimentally questions the necessity of the link between farming and ignorance, and indulges in "airy speculations" on the possibilities of "dissolving this alliance" so that the common man might "embod[y] the dreams of the poets" (58). Here is the classic expression of the republican ideal of a general diffusion of literature (complete with its presumption of "a recalcitrant social difference"), in which the term "literature" intends not belletristic texts but more generally "all the forms of written discourse and the uses of literacy."[84]

Withdrawing at last into her house, Clara hears her maid open her kitchen door at the sound of someone knocking; out of sight of the door, she hears a man request of her maid a glass of buttermilk, "for charity's sweet sake." The seemingly nonsensical appeal to charity is highly ironic in the operative (if incipient or latent) context of enthusiasm, for charity — the trusting reliance upon appearances as indices of invisible truths — is precisely what Carwin's presence will destroy as social practice within Mettingen. Clara's excessively emotional reaction to the sound of the voice is the enthusiast's capitulation to the seductions of sound without meaning: she "dissolves" into "involuntary and incontroulable" tears of sympathy not, obviously, because of what the voice says but because of its power as pure articulation (59, 60, 59). Its formal attributes as Clara describes them identify the voice as that of the charismatic itinerant: she discerns in the verbose request for a cold drink nothing less than a "wholly new" tone, a musicality and energy "surpassed by none," a "force and sweetness" beyond description, and an "unexampled" power of articulation. "But this was not all," Clara enthusiastically maintains: "The voice was not only mellifluent and clear, but the emphasis was so just, and the modulation so impassioned, that it seemed as if an heart of stone could not fail of being moved by it" (59). No more pointed description exists in the literature of enthusiasm of the separation of matter (a request for water) from manner, of the seductive power of the voice as pure articulation to render irrelevant the content of its utterance.[85] Like Franklin emptying his pockets for Whitefield, Clara recognizes that the voice has alienated her from her intellect and power of judgment but, like Franklin, she doesn't, for the moment, care.

Her determination to see the speaker results in a literal rendering of the disparity of appearance and authority so disturbing to religious conservatives in itinerant exhorters, which Carwin exemplifies as the radical disjunction of his vocal and his formal or bodily attributes. She had imagined to herself a "form, and attitude, and garb . . . worthy to accompany such elocution," but is forced to concede that her mental creation is a "phantom" in relation to the objective Carwin who shocks her expectations, inducing a painful sense of disappointment to which she finds it difficult for days to reconcile herself (60). The physical Carwin resembles nothing so much as an embodiment of her father's reading habits as a young and utterly ignorant seeker of truth: unimaginably disjunct, bereft of any principle by which to integrate its "essential ingredients," without proportion or any inherent system of checks and balances (61). His face is at once sallow and radiant, his eyes sunken and lustrous, and his teeth irregular and brilliant; his aspect is at once haggard and serene; and although "the outline of his face reminded you of an inverted cone" (a symbol for democratic polity?), his forehead "served to betoken a mind of the highest order" (61).[86] He is, in fact, unrepresentable, as any reader who has tried to imagine what his face and body might look like from the description Clara provides is uncomfortably aware. At the moment she recognizes the clown in the eloquent speaker who makes poetry out of buttermilk, Clara's pastoral musings are exposed by Carwin's singularity as ludicrously inadequate. Her view of him leads Clara to draw not theoretical inferences that she mistakes for experience but rather an "inspir[ed]" portrait of him whose significance she cannot grasp; she realizes only that over the next few days she becomes increasingly "devot[ed]" to it (61, 62).

Once completed, the image, instead of exorcising the spell Carwin's appearance casts over her, acquires an independent signifying power: having drawn it, Clara can only regard it, and await from it a statement of its own significance. Medusa-like, the image immobilizes Clara, both in that it bars from her mind all other images and fills her "fancy," and because it robs her of her desire to leave her apartment, even to make her daily visit to her brother. For the next two days, she gazes fixedly and with sustained emotion at the portrait which, if its significance eludes her, yet becomes increasingly attractive to her. Recalling Moses Bartlett's paradoxical point concerning the obedient yet flighty followers of false and seducing teachers, Clara notes of "the human mind" that it is simultaneously "flexible" and "stubborn," and she laments that it can be "[s]o obedient to impulses the most transient and brief, and yet so unalterably observant of the direction which is given to it!" (61). She does not attribute to her own temperament the "peculiarities" of her behavior, an impulsiveness that once acted upon discovers an external justification for extending itself as directed or motivated activity, but instead attributes them to the image she has created and whose "properties" she finds "rare and prodigious" (62). Her normative practice of rational intro-spection is thus displaced by projection onto a fixed image of her own design and of whose representational fidelity she is uncertain. While in a prolonged state of solipsistic fixation upon her fetish, Clara, lying sleepless in her bed at midnight, the hour of her father's mysterious death, hears two voices coming from her bedroom closet plotting her ravishment and murder: the third vocal incident. She flees to Wieland's, where she collapses upon his doorstep; she is discovered there through the services of a fourth disembodied voice that rouses the sleeping inmates.

Oddly enough, no one will remark until the crisis is irreversibly launched that the advent of disembodied voices was "coeval with Carwin's introduc-tion"; no one will connect Clara's encounter with the trespassing bumpkin to the voices of apparent murderers who had succeeded in penetrating her "inviolate asylum," the house which for her stands as a symbol of her inde-pendence and her eschewal of irrational fear or superstition (150, 68). The door of her asylum having been opened, however, Clara, somewhat paradox-ically, no longer considers herself "at liberty": in particular, she understands that she is no longer free "to question the reality of those accents which had formerly recalled my brother from the hill; which had imparted tidings of the death of the German lady to Pleyel; and which had lately summoned them to my assistance" (68).[87] Clara's disconcerting induction into that portion of the "little community" that has heard voices does not bring the group together. Wieland, for example, who in his own case is convinced of the voice's super-natural agency, insists that Clara has dreamed her voices because a man's body could not have fit through the narrow window of the closet, leaving as the only explanation for their presence that the murderers had brazenly walked through Clara's house and bedroom. Yet, as his uncle will later point out, the proliferation of disembodied voices, including those reported to him by Clara, "powerfully predispose [Wieland] to this deplorable perversion of mind" that will lead to the murders of his family and the attempted murder of his sister (272). Similarly, Pleyel's decision to move into Clara's house as her protector, one that in some measure fulfills her dissembled erotic desire for him, provides the occasion for his forsaking her when he one night "over-hears" Carwin and Clara making love in her summerhouse and, despite his own experience of the disembodied voices, believes that Clara's voice must have issued from Clara herself while in an ecstasy of physical passion. Clara's impressment into the ranks of those who have heard thus has the paradoxical effect of isolating her from those most qualified to join forces and "solve appearances" (3, 105).

The "accents" whose reality Clara feels she is not at liberty to doubt now relentlessly oppress her. The next voice to intrude upon her solitude enjoins her silence if she values her life. Having returned "to resume the possession of my own dwelling," she makes a visit to her summerhouse, falls asleep, and dreams of her brother beckoning her toward a pit (67). She is awakened from this nightmare by the voice of her erstwhile closet murderer who presents her with a series of demands that couple salvation and dissemblance: she must flee her favorite retreat and never return, keep silent about this manifestation of the voice, remember her father, and be faithful if she would be saved. From this moment, like a newly convicted Calvinist, Clara lives in fear of "an unseen and secret stroke" — the stroke of Edwards's angry God poised to sever the sinner's thread, except that the object of her religious dread is no monotheistic deity (75). Instead she constructs a Manichaean scenario in which the designs of a disembodied evil agent, who for unknown reasons longs to murder her, are frustrated by the vigilance of an airy minister, "my angel," as mysteriously devoted to protecting her from harm (111). Unlike the calamitous political battles whose sounds she had complacently heard from the repose of her estate and from which she derived such pleasure, Clara finds herself occupying the scene of an invisible warfare between evil author and airy minister whose object she, unaccountably, appears to be. Clara, that is, has cast herself as one of the afflicted, the victim of a diabolical spectral being invested with preternatural strength and all-too-human motives and the favorite of an angelic spectral being with a mandate to protect her. She signals her willingness to assume the starring role in this spectral drama by complying with the voice's command to keep silent about her summerhouse encounter: she does not tell Pleyel when he comes to rescue her as she sits immobilized with fear, and she reveals to no one her new understanding of her central role in a mysterious and fraught spectral dimension. This decision to keep silent, as well as the silence she observes and the deceptive appearances she creates with respect to her coy erotic desire for Pleyel, will play key roles in the generation of the plot that Carwin, with no particular trajectory in mind, had set in motion in order to test (as he later confesses) the mettle of his social and ethical betters and to appropriate for his exclusive use the most charming spots on their estate.[88]

As an object of wonder the actual Carwin, whose appearance had shocked Clara into her Pygmalionesque artistry, is only momentarily superseded by these spectral appearances, because he soon gains admission into Clara's other intimate asylum, the exclusive circle of her inseparable friends. Pleyel had invited Carwin to visit the circle after having encountered him in a Philadelphia coffeehouse where the two become reacquainted: they had met earlier in Spain where Carwin, a self-described Englishman, had effected a "*transformation* into a Spaniard," having "counterfeited" a belief in Roman Catholicism perhaps "for some political purpose" (78). Although he avoids their inquiries as to his true identity, the congregation allows Carwin to become such a habitué of Mettingen that he "entered and departed without ceremony" (87). Upon formally meeting him, Clara is again struck by the discrepancy between the "uncouthness" of his appearance and his vocal sublimity: "He was sparing in discourse," she writes, "but whatever he said was pregnant with meaning, and uttered with rectitude of articulation, and force of emphasis, of which I had entertained no conception previously to my knowledge of him" (81). The congregation tries to gain some perspective upon the seeming transparency of Carwin's fluent social conversation, hoping to discover clues concerning his identity, but their search is futile: "Not a gesture, or glance, or accent, that was not, in our private assemblies, discussed, and inferences deduced from it," Clara confesses, and yet Carwin, despite having become a copious theme of speculation, affords them "no ground on which to build even a plausible conjecture," so uniform is his display of "that degree of earnestness which indicates sincerity" (82).[89] If he responds to the congregation's "curiosity" with an unreadable obscuration of his countenance, he does, however, encourage their desire to open to him the facts of their recent experience with disembodied voices, a topic that gives him "visible pleasure" (83, 84–85). Carwin's views are accorded a certain authority, although he contradicts himself in giving his opinion of the provenance of the voices: on the one hand, he promotes an antinomian explanation, arguing that "human beings are, sometimes, admitted to a sensible intercourse with the author of nature"; on the other hand, he rejects the explanation of "celestial interference" supported by Wieland and Clara and asserts that his own experience persuades him that "human agency" is involved, a proposition supported by Pleyel, and that someone, perhaps from the city, is exerting a not uncommon "power of mimickry" (85, 86). Carwin, ironically, states the truth, except that he omits to bring up the issue of ventriloquism which adds the acousmatic to the imitative power, thereby multiplying the possibilities of misrepresentation by allowing the ventriloquized voice in all its variety to assume the veracity, as reliable appearance, of the (missing) body itself. He speaks truthfully, too, when he hubristically cautions the group, as they wonder who would want to harm them, that every individual is only "imperfectly acquainted" with "the condition and designs of the beings that surroun[d] us" (86). Thus, despite the skill of his "narratives" (from which, not surprisingly, "all the effects of a dramatic exhibition were frequently produced"), Clara notes that the manifestly "exquisite art of this rhetorician" fails, purposely, to "impart conviction": his "most coherent and most minute" explanations for disembodied voices are those the company finds "least entitled to credit" (85, 87).

Carwin, then, acts as the facilitator of a crisis of credibility that reaches a critical stage soon after he materializes and that will decimate the congregation in one forty-eight-hour period during which Wieland will hear and act upon the voice urging him to murder and Pleyel will abandon Mettingen in a fury, convinced that Clara, whom he has known all his life, is the "most specious, and most profligate of women" (119). Arguably, it is the latter, relatively minor and, indeed, almost comic delusion that allows the former to play itself out: had Pleyel remained on the grounds, it is difficult to imagine how Wieland would have carried out the murders of Catharine and their children. Moreover, Pleyel's jealous abdication draws Clara to his home in the city in hopes of vindicating herself from his suspicions of her infidelity, a withdrawal that permits a failure of observation which also give Wieland free scope. Pleyel's pique is important, too, in that the trial of Clara's character that he stages provides the immediate context for her next encounter with Carwin as well as her (and our) discovery of the bodies of Wieland's victims, and thus testifies to the transformation "of a mind the most luminous and penetrating that ever dignified the human form" (175).

The events that prepare for this twin deception are briefly these: one evening the congregation had planned to meet, without Carwin, to rehearse a new play, "an adventurous and lawless fancy" involving "a chain of audacious acts, and unheard-of disasters" pertaining to the martyrdom of a radical Protestant (89).[90] Their plans are frustrated by Pleyel's unexplained absence. As it happens, Pleyel had discovered some information about Carwin's identity and was detained in the city investigating leads. His absence causes Clara, who had anticipated that Pleyel would declare his love for her on the way home after rehearsal, to take an early and disappointed leave from her brother's house. Her premature arrival home leads to her discovery of Carwin in her closet, where he had been perusing her journal, which offered him, as Carwin put it in his later confession to her of his role in the events at Mettingen, "the key to your inmost soul" as well as the details of her father's demise and her desire for Pleyel (235). As she enters her bedroom and approaches the closet, where she had intended to turn to her father's manuscript for consolation, she receives an impression that some malevolent spirit is within and that it intends to take her life: she can imagine this spirit only as a "hand invisible and of preternatural strength, lifted by human passions, and selecting my life for its aim" (97). She determines to proceed to her closet despite her irrational conviction, when a "divine voice" shrieks in her ear to abandon her intention (102). She recognizes this voice as the same that had warned her of proceeding toward the pit to which her brother, in her summerhouse nightmare, was attempting to coax her, and she is suddenly convinced that her brother—and not some nameless spectral creature, half-preternatural and half-human—is the being in the closet. Moving forward despite the "divine injunction," her "actions and persuasions . . . at war," she opens the closet against forceful resistance to discover not her brother as the preternaturally powerful hand prepared to deliver the fatal stroke, but a sheepish Carwin (160, 99). He makes a false and somewhat nonsensical confession before leaving Clara's house, allegedly dooming himself to "endless exile" for his temerity; its import is that he had intended to ravish Clara, but that the voice, which he identifies as his "eternal foe; the baffler of my best concerted schemes," had intervened to thwart his intentions (105, 103).

Thus does one protagonist in Clara's spectral drama, the author of evil, come crashing back to earth. Meditating upon her discovery after Carwin's departure, Clara wonders how she had failed to "discer[n] through the impenetrable veil of his duplicity" that the eloquent bumpkin was "the author of the evil that was threatened" (107). Despite Carwin's fall from spectrality, however, Clara is not disposed to modify her assessment of the spectral sphere as populated with "unfettered and beneficent intelligences" that intend the protection of human beings (she is even reluctant to deprive Carwin of the "supernatural power" she had attributed to the evil specter) but she is no longer certain of the degree to which they are in control of the spectral drama in which she is embroiled, or whether the events thus far enacted may be attributed to "some unauthorized and guilty purpose" (108, 107, 108). Is the plot in which she finds herself a central character authored or unauthorized, preservative or guilty? Brooding in immobility upon the "gloomy reverse" of all her ideas and expectations since the arrival of the "stranger," Carwin, whose motives she cannot "calculate" and whose footsteps she cannot "regulate," she suddenly hears someone enter the house and try the knob on her bedroom door (108–9, 115). She seizes her penknife, less as a weapon of self-defense against her "ravisher," the author of evil, than as a weapon of self-destruction: at this point, Clara chooses suicide over writing as a mode of vindication. She prefers, that is, to "prevent the crime [which may be understood as self-enlargement through writing] by destroying myself" (111). Nothing is clearer to Clara at this juncture than that the sole alternative to writing or suicide is to remain "immured" in her "asylum" in order to preserve herself in "seclusion and silence" (113). As she later discovers, although she does so remain, her spectral double — the bearer of her own secret and illicit desire — roams boldly forth, a disorderly walker of unpeaceable and froward spirit, into the midnight gloom and specifically to the forbidden summerhouse.[91]

Frozen with terror, Clara waits until the house is again silent before scurrying noiselessly downstairs to lock the door, and then returning to her room, whose door she also secures. Once safely back, her thoughts revert to Pleyel's mysterious absence, and she imagines or "paint[s] to myself, with an obstinacy for which I could not account," a scene in which Pleyel drowns and she, "a midnight wanderer upon the shore," discovers his "corpse, which the tide had cast up" (115). This is the second time that evening that she imagines Pleyel's death by drowning in conjunction with the trope of ravishment: the first is when she becomes certain that Pleyel will not attend rehearsal and she imagines that he may have drowned, but subsequently reflects that if he had, information of the tragedy would have been speedily brought to Wieland. "The consolation which this idea imparted was ravished from me by a new thought," Clara writes. If his death had occurred beyond anyone's observation, then "[t]he first intelligence of his fate may be communicated by the livid corpse which the tide may cast, many days hence, upon the shore" (95). Such "phantoms of [her] own creation," whose shameful elaboration marks for her "the date when my mind became the victim of . . . imbecility," a date that was "perhaps . . . coeval with the inroad of a fatal passion," give her, after her encounter with Carwin in her bedroom, "relief," "calm," and "repose" (95, 115). Thus is Pleyel doubly betrayed: by Clara's silence and flirtations with Carwin intended to stimulate Pleyel's desire, and by her mise-en-scène of his death, which is to say, the evacuation of voice or spirit from his body, its immobilization, and the drastic restriction of its signifying powers such that one receives information from it only by "stumbl[ing]" upon it in the far-removed place where it has been cast (115). Unlike Carwin's endlessly evocative and increasingly seductive portrait (that other phantom created by Clara after her initial encounter with the itinerant stranger), Pleyel's livid corpse, a "ruinous and ghastly shap[e]," delivers all the information it has to give in an instant (116).

When he unexpectedly emerges from the room reserved for him in her house the next morning, Pleyel accuses Clara of having sold her honor to Carwin at the very moment when he was hastening to inform her of his discoveries concerning Carwin's criminal past. Clara, who had found some serenity in her role as the afflicted victim of a mysterious author, finds herself catapulted by Pleyel's accusations from the victim's into the witch's role: "What evidence," she wonders, "could possibly suggest conceptions so wild? . . . Could the long series of my actions and sentiments grant me no exemption from suspicions so foul?" Why should her consent to dishonor be assumed before the more plausible scenario of its illicit appropriation? Was it not far more likely "that my honor had been assailed, not by blandishments, but by violence?" (119–20). Clara considers two possibilities for Pleyel's behavior: first, that he himself was afflicted, "possessed by some momentary phrenzy" productive of a temporary "blindness" such that "appearances had led him into palpable errors"; and second, that her "ancient and intimate associate, the perpetual witness of [her] actions, and partaker of [her] thoughts," had become the inquisitor who "judged [her] without hearing," who "ha[d] drawn from dubious appearances, conclusions the most improbable and unjust" (120, 130, 120). Upon hearing of the reasons for his inquietude from Wieland, Clara opts for the possessed Pleyel, a possibility that fills her with "delight" insofar as it confirms his love for her; this theory strengthens her determination to remain "passive and silent" as a means of augmenting his self-inflicted torture as she solidifies the grounds of her imminent vindication (120, 121). But when, having learned from Wieland that her victim was determined to leave the country, she decides to intrude "uncalled, into his presence," she learns, as she expresses it, that it is her "fate . . . to fall into the hands of a precipitate and inexorable judge" (127, 130).

Having in her room demoted the author of evil from specter to "man of mischief," Clara discovers in Pleyel's implacable anger proof that Carwin had not relinquished his intention to ravish her when he left her house in apparent defeat, but had simply decided to do so by means of her image or reputation rather than her body, and to continue his war against her on the spectral plane so conceived (130). In a move parallel to Carwin's alleged release of her body, Clara again releases Carwin, in her own meditations on the death of her reputation, from the limitations of his humanness, and imagines her foe as possessing "organs of exquisite ductility and boundless compass, actuated by an intelligence gifted with infinite endowments, and comprehending all knowledge" such that only "supernatural interference could check [his] career" (130, 131). Pleyel admits that in his unexpectedly stumbling upon the true Clara during his walk past the summerhouse, "[m]y sight was of no use to me" (154). He claims he felt no need to confirm the testimony of his ears (which informed him that he stood "within three feet" of Clara) by seeing her body, but had enough evidence to believe without visual corroboration that his ancient and intimate associate is "the colleague of a murderer, and the paramour of a thief" (154, 130). On the evidence of his hearing alone, then, his love for the "chaste" woman has instantaneously ceded to his loathing for the "polluted" one, although, as Clara protests, she is "[y]esterday and today . . . the same" (129).

Thus is Clara faced with her own progressive spectrality, her own increasing susceptibility to spectral representation, promoted first by Carwin and then Pleyel and finally affirmed by Carwin. In his confession that precedes her final meeting with Wieland, Carwin informs Clara that his understanding with her maid had afforded him unlimited access to "the interior of your chamber" in her absence, and that his examination of her private papers there — the activity in which he was engaged when Clara surprised him in her closet — had provided him with a knowledge of her exceeding that of "conjugal intimacies" (234). Carwin's stance, then, was that it was unnecessary to possess her body in order to possess "conjugal" knowledge of her: one had only to possess her textual self-representation. Similarly, after assuming that Carwin had abandoned his intention to ravish her in leaving her house, Clara discovers that he had in no way decided to "forego the immolation of [his] victim." Rather, his evil designs aim at her public image or reputation which, to protect, she cannot herself kill: there is no reputational equivalent to killing the body to avoid its dishonor (130). Finally, Pleyel brushes off her accusation that he had not bothered to confirm the testimony of his ears by looking upon her body, but argues for the superfluity of her body by claiming that she can be known by her voice alone. The spectralization of Clara promoted by Carwin and Pleyel, in conjunction with the facts that she has no alibi witnesses, that her own tale of what occurred that night is "marvellous," and that she has no means of compelling Carwin to incriminate himself at her "bar," determines that the operative question at Clara's trial by Pleyel is the question of spectral evidence: namely, did she in some way collude in her own spectral representation by consenting to Carwin's seduction, or did Carwin, the author of evil, possess the means to represent her spectrally without her knowledge or consent (126)? What was the nature of the event that transpired in the indiscernable interval between, in the transformational moment when the chaste Clara was reborn as the polluted one? Clara herself will provide an answer to that question through her complex depiction of a transformation that she implicitly suggests is analogous to the ethical mutation: her transformation from character into author.[92]

The trial of Clara takes place in Pleyel's room, into which, in her despair, she intrudes "altogether involuntar[ily]" (131).[93] The trial is bipartite in structure, comprising her testimony, followed by her fainting (whose significance Pleyel briefly ponders, and rejects, as "proof of [her] sincerity"), and, after her recovery of consciousness, his lengthy rejoinder (137). Her comparatively brief defensive argument is that the "resemblance of voice" upon which he too hastily based his convictions was "casual or concerted," and therefore insufficient to offset the "want of correspondence" between her most cherished principles and those articulated by her disembodied double, the voice at the summerhouse (134, 130). Like an enthusiast rather than a "champion of intellectual liberty [who] rejected all guidance but that of his reason," not only had Pleyel fallen into the same "sad dilemma" about which he had chided Wieland upon his hearing the first voice, but even worse, he had failed to discriminate sound from sense: "The nature of these sentiments [expressed by the voice]," she complains, "did not enable you to detect the cheat, did not suggest to you the possibility that my voice had been counterfeited by another" (28, 36, 134). Only a "distempered imagination" (133), Clara claims, could commit such a failure of discretion, could fail to realize that the woman cannot be reduced to the sound, minus the ethical content, of her voice; this, we recall, was the substance of accused witch Rebecca Nurse's self-defense before the court. Most egregiously, Pleyel's enthusiasm denies Clara the means of establishing her innocence insofar as "the tenor of my life, of all my conversations and letters, affords me no security; every sentiment that my tongue and my pen have uttered, bear testimony to the rectitude of my mind; but this testimony is rejected" (134). The enthusiast's elevation of the contingent spectral appearance over the ethically continuous visible one demotes the latter to a fiction and, by privileging fragment over continuity, shrinks to the dimensions of an instant of time the stately grounds of truth.

Pleyel responds to these challenges by addressing Clara as if she were only apparently herself, his ancient and intimate associate, but whose essential duplicity had been revealed to him as a startling and discomposing, if partial, vision of the richness and passion of her secret life. He begins his interrogation by rhetorically asking, "What is she that is now before me?" and answers by telling her what recent experience has suggested to him: namely, that she is Carwin's truer companion, that "[a]n inscrutable providence has fashioned thee for some end," and that "[s]urely nothing in the shape of man can vie with thee!" (135). Pleyel's prosecution of Clara is remarkable not for its foundations, which are predictable and briefly delineated in his concluding remarks, but for its lengthy preamble which belies in advance his foundational evidence. He had deduced her guilt from his consideration that the "peculiarities" of her voice and conversation were "inimitable," and that the voice in conversation with Carwin betrayed its possession of information that only Clara and immediate members of her family could know (154). But in his preamble to these seemingly unanswerable grounds for indictment, Pleyel tells Clara how he had, from the beginning of their reacquaintance as adults, dedicated himself to constructing a written record of her every word and action in order to disseminate it to other women as a "model" of feminine perfection not only worthy of their "indefatigable imitation" but that would not prove "beyond [the] reach" of would-be imitators; and how he had himself acquired, by spying on her as she wrote in her diary, intimate knowledge of her thoughts and her history so as to recognize their authenticity when the spectral Clara articulated them in the summerhouse (140). In the process of his researches, allegedly undertaken in a spirit of awe for a woman who, for him, "exemplified, that union between intellect and form, which has hitherto existed only in the conception of the poet," Pleyel assumes the role of his theoretical poet. He constructs an image of Clara, a spectral Clara, that takes on a life of its own to determine his perception of the actual woman and to which Pleyel had all along held the actual woman accountable (139). This alleged labor of love figures the death of charity in the novel, the moment that visible appearances are subject to ceaseless critical surveillance on the part of one who constitutes himself as judge, although Pleyel specifically denies so constituting himself (135).

His indictment of Clara begins with a history of their earliest relations as adults when Pleyel, enamored of Clara's perfections—and in particular, the "enchantments of [her] voice" which include "intricacies of melody," "emphasis of rhetoric," "transitions of discourse," "felicities of expression," "refined argumentation," and "glowing imagery"—began to "not[e] down, in writing, every particular of [her] conduct" so that "others should profit by an example so rare!" (139).[94] Pleyel thus obsessively constructs a discursive portrait of Clara, comprised of "amply displayed" details relevant to her voice as well as to her person: "Even the colour of a shoe, the knot of a ribband, or your attitude in plucking a rose, were of moment to be recorded. Even the arrangements of your breakfast-table, and your toilet. . . . I found no end and no bounds to my task" (140). His reproduction and dissemination of her as a "model"—an augmentation of her spectralization—is intended to serve notice to any woman who "wished to secure and enhance [his] esteem," including Clara, that she must strive to "mould her thoughts, her words, her countenance, her actions, by this pattern" (140). Not only has the superfluity of her physical existence been variously impressed upon Clara by this point, but Pleyel here declares that a disembodied copy of herself has superseded her as the authentic Clara to which she, the original, must conform if she is to be acknowledged and loved as legitimately herself.

Clara's fall from Pleyel's esteem begins when she herself creates a portrait, of Carwin, and commences her obsessive scrutiny of it, activities which she had apparently discussed with her friends. In Pleyel's estimation, these actions "bespoke a sensibility somewhat too vivid" and they encourage him to augment his surveillance of Clara, not in order to amend his portrait of feminine perfection but in order to "scrutiniz[e] the sentiments and deportments of [Carwin] with ceaseless vigilance" and to "watc[h Clara's] words and . . . looks when he was present" (141). He will subsequently "extrac[t] cause for the deepest inquietudes, from every token which [Clara] gave of having put [her] happiness into this man's keeping" (141). (Clara, of course, through her own practice of dissemblance unwittingly abets Pleyel's intrusion in her affairs by maintaining silence concerning her feelings for him on the one hand, and on the other by flirting with Carwin and thus generating false representations for Pleyel's express consumption.) He worries that Carwin's "eyes and voice had a witchcraft in them, which rendered him truly formidable." His concern causes him to appropriate to himself the "right to be familiar," and he enters Clara's bedroom unbidden one evening, betraying her hospitality, as she was writing in her diary (142). Noiselessly placing himself at her shoulder (and in so doing, assuming the same position with his body that Carwin would with his voice), he catches sight of several words and constructs from them a narrative in which Clara is induced by Carwin to give her "consent to midnight conferences" like the one he later overheard in the summerhouse (146). Pleyel is thus second only to Carwin in his ability to seek conjugal intimacy with another without requiring access to her body, as he is second only to Clara in his willingness to substitute for the body of another a visual representation of his own creation, an image to which he can unreservedly devote himself.

Pleyel's discoveries concerning Carwin's identity, as supplied by Ludloe (who will play a key role in the attempted seduction of the adolescent Carwin in the *Memoirs of Carwin*), augment his apprehension of the itinerant's diabolism: Ludloe informs Pleyel that Carwin is determined to "wag[e] a perpetual war against the happiness of mankind," that he may be "reasonably suspected to be, in the highest degree, criminal, but such as no human intelligence is able to unravel," that he is "the most incomprehensible and formidable among men," and that "his ends are pursued by means which leave it in doubt whether he be not in league with some infernal spirit" (149). Although he rejects the notion that Carwin is a devil ("the power and the malice of

dæmons have been a thousand times exemplified in human beings") — a rejection consonant with his denial that Clara might have been spectrally replicated without her consent — Pleyel fears Carwin's practice of a secularized
and psychologized form of witchcraft (150). He fears, that is, that Clara may
succumb to his representations and consent to "his efforts to make [her] a
confederate in [her] own destruction, to make [her] will the instrument by
which he might bereave [her] of liberty and honor" whereas, of course, it is
Wieland who will be so bereaved (150–51). Pleyel envisions not what had
actually almost occurred, Clara's self-murder, but rather her consent to Carwin's seduction.

As he relates it, his concern about Carwin's treachery as well as his re-
morse about his spying and his desire to confess his "indecorum" to Clara led
Pleyel to return to her house late on the night of the aborted rehearsal, after
having spent the day making inquiries into Carwin's identity (146). As he
passes the summerhouse in the midnight darkness, he hears, like Nabokov's
blind cuckold, a woman's laughter in the dark. Despite his former reservations about having spied on his friend (the partial motive for his errand), as
well as his claim that he had "had no power" to stop spying once he gave in to
"the spirit of mischievous gaiety" and that he had acted indeliberately and
"almost spontaneously," he does not at this moment doubt the propriety of
"approaching and listening" (142, 152). His approach closer to the source of
the laughter terminates in his descent into a "cavity" adjacent to the summerhouse, where he "li[es] in wait," longing to "strike [Clara] dead with [his]
upbraiding," in order later to bear indignant witness to the superior, if unseen, reality of the spectral — the real, profligate — Clara (152). As, in Pleyel's
mind, Carwin had "enticed" Clara "to this recess," Pleyel claims to have
"traced" her to the same pit within which he imagines her giving herself,
giving her consent, and from which he had thought to save her (154). This
pit — associated both with the violent destruction of the self and the giving of
consent — is the same to which Wieland, in Clara's nightmare, had endeavored to entice her. Thus does every male protagonist in the novel, all of
whom claim to hold Clara in an exaggeratedly high esteem, strive to place
her in or trace her to this pit where, they imagine, she will conspire in her
own destruction.

If we step back a moment from this spectral melodrama to summarize the
ways in which Clara, in particular, is reconceptualized through Carwin's

machinations by Pleyel, the "man of cold resolves and exquisite sagacity" as Clara describes him, we find that the increasing superfluity of her body accompanies the proliferation of her spectral selves (239). Clara's spectralization, a separation or fragmentation of her integral self, is fittingly accomplished by Pleyel whose point of view provides, for the first time in this autobiographical novel, an external perspective of Clara. His representation of Clara is, so considered, inherently spectral, a reconstruction of the subject produced on an immaterial — a mental or verbal — plane. Beyond that, as an explanation of his experience, Pleyel offers or elicits five spectral Claras. She is the witch who has surreptitiously consented to the suggestions of a diabolical seducer to lead an illicit double life which permits the secret exercise of a guilty passion. She is her public image or reputation which Carwin and Pleyel both attack and which she can neither remove nor destroy in advance to preserve its purity. She is Carwin's accomplice, a woman not quite human and whose machinations are stoppable only through supernatural means. She is the exemplification of a poetic concept. Finally, she is Pleyel's own verbal construct which achieves an independent existence, more legitimate than that of the original upon which it was modeled. Although they are registered in Clara's sense of helpless despondency over the impossibility of converting her friend to her view, these spectral variants do not impair Clara's sense of her own integrity. Pleyel's determination to abandon Clara, unshaken by the time he concludes his testimony, saddens her but does not cause her "any apparent loss of composure" nor does it "palsy [her] exertions" or "overbear [her] strength" (155). When Pleyel, from this moment, withdraws from the field for the remainder of the novel, he leaves Clara intact and his withdrawal is registered as a confirmation of his error. Having survived intact the attempted ravishments of Carwin and the defection of Pleyel, Clara's integrity will then be assaulted by a resurrected Carwin who resurfaces in the next scene in textual form: as a Godwinian letter waiting for Clara at her aunt's home to which she travels after leaving Pleyel's, requesting from her a midnight interview, alone, in her bedroom at Mettingen, in order by his "simple and solemn declarations" there to remove any remaining "fears" of his "designs" (156).

Clara assents to this new "plot," although the decision constitutes an abandonment of "those motives by which I am usually governed" (157). She recognizes that "the plotter" is once again "at hand," speaking now "in the style of penitence," and she recognizes his superior subtlety in the field of design. His plot, she notes, is a perfection of pure contingency; it "owed its success to a coincidence of events scarcely credible. The balance was swayed from its equipoise by a hair" (159, 158). Given his diabolical artistry and her recent experience, she deliberates "whether it was not proper to admit, at a lonely spot, in a sacred hour, this man of tremendous and inscrutable attributes, this performer of horrid deeds, and whose presence was predicted to call down unheard-of and unutterable horrors" (159). Yet at this juncture, she does so admit him: she consents to a replaying of the scene she had just fled in terror and shame. Reminiscent of the scene of her involuntary weeping at first sight of Carwin, Clara acknowledges that her consent is her undoing but that she is "divested of the power to will contrary to the motives that determined me to seek his presence. My mind seemed to be split into separate parts, and these parts to have entered into furious and implacable contention" (159). But Clara is quickly reconstituted. If Carwin is indeed "the author," then the state of her own mind is emblematic of the "poet's chaos"; as the poet, she will realize her "power of imparting conviction" and compel Carwin on ethical grounds to "unrave[l] the maze in which Pleyel is bewildered" (160, 161, 160). The maze, however, is Carwin's natal element, his birthplace as an artist, the scene of his conversion to hybridity; and as Clara knows, Pleyel has withdrawn from this field of battle with its pitted landscape and its blindspots and will not be recalled. His rejection of her ethical and characterological integrity, her slide into a spectral and then a psychological disintegration, and her willed reconsolidation as a chaotic integrity known as a poet pitched to do battle with the plotter suggest that her decision to return alone to the scene of her threatened ravishment and the source of her subsequent sorrow is not intended to unravel the maze but rather to contribute to its ongoing formation.[95]

The trial and her subsequent stopover at her aunt's home mark the first time in the novel that Clara has ventured outside of Mettingen which, up until Carwin's accession and Pleyel's abandonment, had provided her with everything she needed to sustain her self-image in her own eyes and the eyes of her closest friends. In the scene in which she receives Carwin's written invitation to return to her home, she is stranded outside its sustaining environment, denied an old friend's belief in the integrity of her visible character, abandoned to her own devices and in a state of inner turmoil. She thus realizes that to return to Mettingen will be to descend into the fearful pit toward which Wieland had beckoned her, Carwin enticed her, and Pleyel traced her. She decides to do so less because the power of the plot or the plotter is driving her there, but because only there can she affirm and even consecrate the destruction of her visible character accomplished during her trial, discard the principles by which she had always governed herself, and consent to die to her former integrity in order to reemerge as the poet and commence her "deadly toils" (164). Like Mary Easty, who spectrally challenged the validity of spectral evidence, Clara will expose and condemn the machinations of the disembodied author by becoming one herself and in the penultimate scene of the book will compel Carwin to undertake precisely the reversal of this action, the ventriloquistic repudiation of ventriloquism. By unwittingly re-futing Pleyel's portrait of her as one for whom language was merely orna-mental, Clara anticipates her transformation into an author who intends to take an active role in a plot already launched by identifying and then wresting control from the elusive plotter. It is crucial to explore this process by which she redefines herself as counterplotter rather than hapless character: her redefinition will provide the immediate context for the novelistic presenta-tion of her brother's parallel transformation into a murderer, as well as for the peculiarities of that presentation.

Clara's resurrection in the novel as a counterplotter who intends at all costs to expose and thus to eliminate the author of evil is not accomplished instantaneously upon her decision to return to Mettingen and confront Car-win in her bedroom. Instead, it occurs in stages that correspond with the two posttrial returns she will make to her bedroom, separated by an interval of delirium and then recovery. The bipartite pattern of return, with its interval of psychological disintegration, is thus structured like the trial itself: the specter of character assassination is in this way always present, a consider-ation that explains Clara's obsession with vindication. Clara's bedroom, then, the "stage," she reflects, "on which that enemy of man shewed himself for a moment unmasked," emerges as the drastically attenuated space within which the remainder of the action will occur — the deadly struggle between Clara, Carwin, and Wieland to control the unfolding of events (220). As the former symbol of her independence, her bodily integrity, and her principled rejection of the irrational, as well as the site of her (private) writing, Clara's bedroom is reconfigured by Carwin's summons to become the pit which has all along threatened her with engulfment and effacement (the literal fate of Wieland's favorite child, his foster daughter) and within which she must now vindicate herself by reclaiming it as her own domain. On her first return, she discovers her sister-in-law's body (and is then taken by people who arrive on the scene to Wieland's home to view the bodies of his five children). On the second occasion, she returns to collect and destroy her journal before departing with her uncle for Europe, and encounters there for the last time both Carwin, who finally confesses his role in the demise of Mettingen, and Wieland, who finally attempts his long-intended murder of Clara. Each of the two returns coincides with the death of a member of the original circle, first Catharine and then Wieland; in the second and final return Clara both witnesses and supervises the elimination of Wieland and Carwin as her rival authors. The complex orchestration of each return suggests that they be individually examined as stages in Clara's developing determination to wrest authorial power — both the power to plot and the power to determine the significance of events — from Carwin and, to the degree he wields it, her brother, and thus to transcend the limitations of her role as exemplary character even as she assiduously claims for herself the victim's part.

What I am calling Clara's first return, however, is itself a considerably complex event that occurs as the second in a sequence of three scenes so similar in structure, time, and locale that they appear to constitute an oddity or defect within the plotting of *Wieland*, a stutter or apparent refusal of the plot to advance, almost a slippage of the characterological doubling so prevalent in the novel into the domain of plot. The first scene in the sequence is Clara's pretrial encounter with the disembodied voice and then, because she disregards its warning, with Carwin in her closet; this event becomes part of the fabric of misrepresentation within which Pleyel is entangled only to extricate himself by defecting from novelistic space altogether. This scene bears significant resemblances to what occurs the next evening (the second scene; the first return), when Clara returns to her house at Carwin's summons and encounters the disembodied voice as she is ascending the staircase to her room. Because she again disregards its warning, even though she describes having done so the night before as "imbecility" and "infatuation," she is led to discover Catharine's ravished and strangled body upon her bed: thus is Catharine eliminated from the novel (160). The third scene in this sequence occurs in chronological time between the first and second scenes, shortly before Clara's return to her house. It features Wieland's decisive encounter with a disembodied voice as he is ascending the staircase to Clara's room which will lead him to lure Catharine to Clara's house moments later, immediately before Clara's return, in order to murder her. Aside from the prominent role played by the disembodied voice in these scenes, they are further connected by the antinomian desire explicitly articulated by both Clara and Wieland to see and be unambiguously guided by the invisible speaker they both regard as "divine." This desire is fulfilled in the last two scenes when they independently see from the staircase leading up to Clara's bedroom a "fiery visage" that gives off significant light and which they apprehend in the act of speaking (224). In the first, pretrial scene, although Clara strives but fails to discern the speaker, she is granted a partial or "toke[n]" confirmation of what Cotton Mather had called "the *Reality of Invisibles*" (98).[96] Her meditations upon this shadowy revelation of "the genius of [her] birth" (108), as well as the ambient circumstances of her occluded vision, forcefully recall Nathaniel Hawthorne's self-depiction at the conclusion of the "Custom-House" sketch in which he figures his own transformation into a writer. A closer look at these intra- and intertextual echoes may help supplement our understanding of the authorial role that Clara determines to assume (and, as an essential feature of her self-representation, determinedly repudiates) following Pleyel's trial of her integrity in which the authority and legitimacy of her visible character is categorically denied.

Although Clara fears a repetition of the previous night's terror if she returns to her room to grant Carwin a midnight interview, two significant differences between the first (pretrial) and the second (posttrial) scenes deserve notice: the gratification in the second scene of the antinomian desire to see and be guided by her angel that she expresses and is denied in the first scene; and the conversion of her penknife from an instrument of self-destruction in the first scene to an instrument of self-defense in the second. In the first scene, Clara arms herself with her penknife not to "plunge it into the heart of my ravisher," as she concedes her reader may assume, but to commit suicide and thus "to baffle my assailant, and prevent the crime by destroying myself" (111). Although she had always considered such an expedient to be a particularly abhorrent species of female cowardice, when the time came to act offensively she admits that it did not "once occu[r] to me to use [the penknife] as an instrument of direct defense" (111). In the second scene, she arms herself in advance with the penknife offensively, to serve as "my safe-guard and avenger" in order to fight to the death: "The assailant shall perish, or myself shall fall" (166). As she envisions it, the assailant shall perish by becoming visible: "I would see this man," Clara continues, clutching the penknife, "in spite of all impediments; ere I died, I would see his face, and summon him to penitence and retribution; no matter at what cost an interview was purchased" (167). The seizing of her penknife in the second scene is clearly connected, then, not with her earlier determination to see her beneficent angel, whose airy presence is sporadic and even irrelevant (Clara survives even though she disregards his warnings) and whose absence may signify, as Clara wryly points out upon her return, either the absence of danger or simply his own absence from the scene of danger (167). Rather, in seizing the penknife as she approaches her dark house she determines to see "this man," "the grand deceiver; the author of this black conspiracy; the intelligence that governed in this storm"; and having seen this impenetrable intelligence, she intends to convert him, by means of her weapon and his mortality, to an "object . . . on which we may pour out our indignation and our vengeance" (167, 217).

As it signifies a reversal of her previously held "principles" and "motives," the conversion of the penknife into a weapon of aggression and knowledge rather than self-destruction signifies a reversal of her pretrial antinomian desire to see transcendent authority. In the second scene, she searches for the revelation not of the divine will in order to obey it, as Wieland continues to do, but of the author's plot in order to appropriate it.[97] On the night before her trial, as she stood suspended in her moonlit room between her closed closet door and the disembodied speaker's shrieked warning against opening it, she had awaited precisely the visual confirmation of invisible realities she would receive the next night, a confirmation which we may designate the quintessential spectral moment when the invisible emerges momentarily into visibility. Recalling Mather at the bedside of his possessed houseguests, Clara had been struggling to pierce the moonlit emptiness of her room with "penetrating glances" in a desperate attempt to see her invisible advocate, "[h]e that hitherto refused to be seen" (98). But instead of observing "distinguishable" form, she observes only that the effect of the moonlight was to erode the "means by which we are able to distinguish a substance from a shadow, a reality from the phantom of a dream" (98, 99):

Solitude imposes least restraint upon the fancy. Dark is less fertile of images than the feeble lustre of the moon. I was alone, and the walls were chequered by shadowy forms. As the moon passed behind a cloud and emerged, these shadows seemed to be endowed with life, and to move. The apartment was open to the breeze, and the curtain was occasionally blown from its ordinary position. This motion was not unaccompanied with sound. I failed not to snatch a look, and to listen when this motion and this sound occurred. My belief that my monitor was posted near, was strong, and instantly converted these appearances to tokens of his presence, and yet I could discern nothing. (98)

Her strong belief in the presence of her "monitor" in the first scene sustains only a partial conversion to visibility: absence yields to tokens of presence, but not to presence itself.

On the next night, after her disastrous meeting with Pleyel, poised to ascend her dark staircase, penknife at the ready, Clara once again hears the anticipated "divine injunction" to halt (cf. 160). The disarticulating shock of the sound causes her to turn her head in time to see a "head thrust and drawn back" very swiftly in the act of utterance: thus is her previous night's desire to see the divine monitor unexpectedly gratified.[98] "[T]he immediate conviction was," Clara explains, recalling again Mather's awed testimony, at a moment equally fraught, to the materialization from invisibility of a spectral iron spindle and a scrap of sheet, "that thus much of a form, ordinarily invisible, had been unshrouded" (168). The materialization of her spectral monitor, however, does not cause Clara to reverse her steps as it commands her to do. Disregarding its shrieked admonition as she had the previous evening, she hastens forward to "the verge of the same gulf" that had plagued her since her summerhouse nightmare and is amazed at her audacity given this miraculous materialization of divine beneficence. "Was it possible for me not to obey?" Clara asks incredulously. "Was I capable of holding on in the same perilous career? Yes. Even of this I was capable!" (169). The question here is less what possessed Clara to disobey, but rather, given her possession of the penknife and her unwillingness to relinquish it even at a divine behest, what authorial model (that is, what model of self-authorization) does her act of disobedience, undertaken despite the gratification of her antinomian wish of the evening before for direct communion and guidance, enact? Toward the conclusion of the "Custom-House" sketch that introduces

The Scarlet Letter (1850), Hawthorne portrays himself similarly (albeit more sanguinely than Clara in the first scene) contemplating the effects of moonlight upon the solitary observer in a darkened and familiar room. His reflections, however, are intended to suggest that the call to authorship occurs precisely in this environment, announced by presences only partially realized rather than either fully materialized or wholly spiritualized. Like Clara, Hawthorne recognizes the moonlit room to be a mediate space between substance and shadow, "a neutral territory, somewhere between the real world and fairy-land, where the Actual and the Imaginary may meet, and each imbue itself with the nature of the other." As Clara remarks upon the imagistic fertility of this territory, Hawthorne explicitly associates it with literary creation by representing himself awaiting within its bounds the accomplishment of two simultaneous and interdependent transformations. The transformation of the government bureaucrat into the writer of romance occurs when the scarlet letter, which the bureaucrat had found buried in the dust of the Salem customhouse attic, is transformed from a fossilized metonymy into narrative. This resurrection and renewal of the unsignifying remainder of a historically spent plot occurs when the bureaucrat, waiting patiently in the moonlight, succeeds in "pictur[ing] forth" from the shadows cast in "the little domestic scenery of the well-known apartment" those spectral presences who embody the fullness of its symbolic trajectory: the requisite act of picturing forth proposes that the resurrection Hawthorne contemplates is less an affair of the resurrected body than of the resurrector's "intellect." Although Walt Whitman would more unambiguously insist on the simultaneous coming-into-being of poet and poem, Hawthorne in this self-portrait refrains from representing himself as the creator of his imaginary visitors. He portrays himself rather as one who awaits alone, in the darkness, the miraculous and mundane realization of a double impossibility—the spiritualized materialization of independent subjects, bearers of the letter's symbolic meanings, who are yet the products of his intellect. This stance represents a full-blown literary reconceptualization of religious antinomianism: Hawthorne insists that what occurs in the moonlit parlor, the space fertile of images, is less a feat of authorial will than it is the shadowy realization, produced by faith and grace (the former, Hawthorne insists, is impotent without the latter), of a third ontological domain. Within this "genial atmosphere" a mixed medium both foreign and familiar, the would-be writer may finally be granted the opportunity to "get acquainted with his illusive guests" whom he welcomes as his characters-to-be.[99]

The same realization that charms Hawthorne in his vocational limbo repels the deeply emplotted Clara who is disinclined to be guided or authorized by a materialized intelligence which she suspects to be, even in part, "pourtrayed by my fancy" (168). Despite her "conviction" in the second scene that the invisible was indeed miraculously emerging in her presence into visibility, Clara cannot dismiss the inference of her observation that "the cry was blown into my ear, while the face was many paces distant": precisely because the shriek's "airy undulation" had palpably delivered a "shock" to her nerves, she must doubt whether "the spectacle I beheld," the face of the speaker, "existed in my fancy or without" (168). The discrepancy compels her to conclude that the invisible content realized in this instance was less that of divine intelligence than of human imagination: "thirs[ting]" above all "for knowledge and for vengeance," she does not confer authority upon her vision because her desire is to illuminate, and thus to obliterate, the chiaroscuro of romance that Hawthorne relishes but for which she emphatically has no patience (217). And yet, as for Hawthorne, her encounter with the hybrid, objective-subjective vision denotes her transformation into an author. At least at this moment, if she does not positively affiliate herself with some understanding of authorship, she unhesitatingly refutes the antinomian version of authorized agency to which she, as her father's daughter, has been strongly attracted and which her brother has already fully embraced, with the disastrous consequences that Clara is about to discover. Her unmistakable refutation here of antinomianism as an authorial stance that rejects representation or any structure of mediation as illegitimate (as Wieland will act, and even plot, and yet claim not agency but mere instrumentality) is a momentary conviction: although she cannot hold steadfastly to it, it will nevertheless enable her to survive her encounter with her brother and both pronounce and determine the novel's final word. We may say provisionally, then, that Clara's refutation of literary antinomianism — here enacted if not articulated — ensures the possibility of literary narrative.

What she perceives as the hybridity of the spectacle on the staircase, her suspicion that it may be in part a self-projection, causes her to question its legitimacy and thus to reject its authority over her actions. Yet paradoxically, this rejection leads her to anticipate adopting a similarly compromised authorial stance: "What but ambiguities, abruptnesses, and dark transitions," she laments, "can be expected from the historian who is, at the same time, the sufferer of these disasters?" (167). The representational failures that she predicts will ensue from her insistent identity of historian and sufferer, subject and object, author and character betray her reluctance altogether to repudiate the antinomian excuse: I authored, but not I.[100] If these failures attest to her continuing victimization, they also attest to her innocence of authorship, and therefore the innocence of her narrative account of events — both its credibility and (relatedly) the unobjectionable nature of the role she herself played in its unfolding. Clara's authorial stance is thus quite distinctive in its indeterminacy. If she does not, like Hawthorne, dissemble with a coy literary antinomianism what she well knows to be the aggression and potential violence of authorship, neither does she betray Carwin's nihilistic glee upon discovering in his wilderness maze that he was both the source and the referent of all objective variety. And yet the very temerity with which she bluntly rejects the command of the supernal other suggests that despite her much-protested veneration of her enthusiastic brother who, in murdering, claims to have passed "the test of perfect virtue" and whom she represents as a Christic *"man of sorrows,"* and despite her claim, in the denouement, to "part[ake] of Wieland's credulity, sh[ake] with his amazement, and pan[t] with his awe," it is Carwin's prerogative to plot, and not the "peace of virtue, and the glory of obedience," enjoyed by Wieland, that she covets (200, 263, 262, 201).

Thus in the second scene, gripping her penknife in anticipation of compelling repentance, Clara rejects the authority of the materialized specter in order to keep an appointment with a fully corporeal assailant. This expectation of embodiment is perversely realized in her discovery not of Carwin but of the disfigured corpse of her sister-in-law, "the companion of my infancy, the partaker of all my thoughts, my cares, and my wishes" — in a word, her double (172). If the advent of Carwin may be correlated with the increased spectralization of Clara, a fantastic expansion of her characterological reach into the authorial domain, it hastens Catharine's reversion to the "clay" with which she has all along been approvingly identified (113). Having on the staircase assumed the authorial initiative to determine the course of events only to discover herself irrevocably "severed" in Catharine's death from the possibility of returning to her former self (even if Carwin could be made to unravel the maze and recall Pleyel), the old characterologically correct Clara definitively dies in the death of Catharine, an event she had both promoted and anticipated by consenting to relinquish her former principles of self-governance (172). The effacement of Wieland's hyperbolically loved but otherwise superfluous foster daughter, the last sight Clara sees before lapsing into the lengthy delirium that separates her first and second posttrial returns to her bedroom, provides a fitting emblem or visual epitaph for this death.

Clara's delirium is, of course, a response to her shocking discovery of the carnage Wieland has wrought from the sublime disengagement of Mettingen society, its unwavering devotion to maintaining the bloodlessness of the theoretical. It is also, like her briefer moment of psychological discomposure after the trial at Pleyel's, an interval during which she reconstitutes herself as an author — by default, she insists, as the only way of controlling proliferating and increasingly dangerous misrepresentations. Her determination to return surreptitiously a second time to her bedroom in order to retrieve from her closet her encoded journal containing "the most secret transactions of my life" is thus inherently an authorial gesture (218). Her desire to retain undisputed and exclusive possession of the text will fulfill itself, however, only when she has choreographed the fatal confrontation of Wieland and Carwin from which she emerges as the lone (authorial) survivor. In order to understand the dynamics of this confrontation, especially given Clara's tendency to represent herself as backing into authorship, it is worthwhile to examine the confessional statements, which are also statements of authorial intent, given by both Wieland and Carwin in advance of the final scene.

As are all other competing voices in this first-person narrative, Wieland's confession (a speech delivered in court and "faithfully recorded" by an auditor) is mediated and even expurgated by Clara; the reader's perusal of it is limited by her inability to absorb its shocking details (185). Yet the assumptions and strengths of antinomian authorship emerge clearly from that portion of Wieland's "tale" that Clara does include in her narrative: his account of what led him to murder his family and his refusal to acknowledge the legitimacy of his judges' censure (185, 200). Wieland is in fact the only authorial figure in the narrative (Brown included) who is free of the obsessive need to vindicate himself before his auditors or readers and who forthrightly condemns it as an "ignoble" task (186). Although his judge had commanded him "to confess or to vindicate his actions" (185), Wieland delivers with prophetic authority a conversion narrative whose unassailable legitimacy inheres in what the narrator represents as the full gratification of the convert's desire for privileged and direct access to transcendent being. Encountering the fiery visage on the staircase, Wieland does not pause, as his sister will, to register any spatial discrepancy of voice and face, any cognitive irregularities that might betray an enthusiastic penchant to take "internal motions" for the will of God. Because he believes that the vision represented the fulfillment of his search for the revelation of God's will, that he had been granted "[t]he blissful privilege of direct communication" and heard "the audible enunciation" of the transcendent author's "pleasure," that in seeing the illuminated face and hearing its murderous command his senses had been "salute[d]" with an "unambiguous token" of presence, he is "acquitted at the tribunal of his own conscience" and is therefore unconcerned by, and even disdainful of, the capital conviction about to be rendered by the jury (189, 206). In his view, the matter had been straightforward: once the command had been uttered, "nothing remained but to execute [the decree]" and thereby prove his "virtue" (190). There was no reason to consider "the purity of [his] intentions" because, outside of his desire to conform himself to transcendent being, he had none: presuming to consider neither the rationale for nor the consequences of the divinely mandated act, the merely instrumental self that performed it was, in the performance, utterly vanquished (200). The ignominious end artificially and belatedly engineered outside of the spiritual logic of the act by the moral pygmies of the law who set up their "bounded views and halting reason, as the measure of truth" confirms rather than undermines his authority (201).

Wieland's claim to moral infallibility is further supported by the fact that he narrates his "tale" before an "audience . . . of thousands whom rumours of this wonderful event had attracted": the reach of his speaking voice, then, exceeds Carwin's own (185, 184). His persuasive power is similarly amplified: Clara's uncle, representing the scene of his direct address to "[j]udges, advocates and auditors," claims that Wieland's aspect, like Carwin's when appropriating the voice and then the form of divinity, "denoted less of humanity than godhead" and that his audience, like Nathan Cole listening to Whitefield, was "panic-struck and breathless with attention" (185). Clara and her uncle, too, find the conviction in the narrator's voice (as he makes the kinds of "simple and solemn declarations" Carwin repeatedly intends and fails to make to Clara) so compelling that it permits the speaker to transcend his textualization in order to convey to his readers the physical immediacy and the rhetorical power and authenticity of original utterance: here is the perverse vindication of the Cicero project (156). That Wieland's textual voice reclaims the authority and presence of the body is somewhat sadistically suggested by her uncle when he asks a horrified Clara, before handing her the trial documentation, if she would like him to call "the destroyer of thy family . . . to thy presence" (185). Eschewing vindication, textualization, and interpretation, Wieland speaks with such unshakable conviction to the gathered multitudes that they condemn him only "reluctantly," and Clara, having read, is quick to follow suit (200). As Wieland claims that no one can know "what is crime" because no one dare judge the decrees of Omnipotence, so Clara wonders if it is "indisputably certain" that the "murderer" of Catharine and her children "was criminal" (201, 206). Despite the revolting details of the murders she learns from Wieland's manuscript, including the machinations by which he lures Catharine to her bedroom in order to kill her unobserved, Clara immediately judges his capital conviction "cruel and unmerited" and attempts to recast him as a killer whose innocence, both in kind and degree, dwarfs the banal probity—the mere blamelessness—of those who presume to judge him (202). Clara's beatification of Wieland will reach its apotheosis when, coming face to face with him in her bedroom upon her second return, she "violen[tly]" throws to the floor her penknife with which she had intended to kill her brother—"a brother thus supreme in misery; thus towering in virtue!"—and in so doing tacitly invites him to take it up (254).

Thus does Clara's trauma-induced lassitude not bring quiescence: before she can "take up" the new life she introduces in a jarring concluding chapter which offers a conventionally comic resolution of the Mettingen massacre, she must take up the pen which she had thought to have "forever laid aside" (267). This final movement, the taking up of the pen, begins with her reading of her brother's unrepentant confession. Even as it makes explicit the attractions of antinomian authorship—decisive action without accountability—and suggests to her that by both sympathy and heredity she may ally herself with it, Wieland's statement revitalizes her determination to discover the author as that object upon whom, in place of the murderous innocent, she may pour out her indignation and vengeance. Like all quests in this novel, beginning with the elder Wieland's, Clara's partakes of the paradigmatic structure of ventriloquism: the novel funnels itself down, life by superfluous life, to its most frequently asked question — "Who is the author?" — which is thrown out only to be mechanically returned by the inevitable wall, moving ever closer to confront the questioner with its own blank interrogative. In the penultimate chapter, the question is posed for the last time, with less wonder than desperation, in Clara's evacuated bedroom, a stagelike square of dim light in a waste of dark and depopulated space. Here will occur, as the final scene of the novel proper, that authorial awakening produced when the otherness at the heart of voice is eliminated, when the asker acknowledges, through her actions if not her overt admission, that the respondent, the culprit, the fiery visage, the author, is herself. Clara here repeats in the blasted interior of what had been presented as ideal social space Carwin's savage experiment in the wilderness maze by which he elicits, in order to appropriate and deploy, the infinite variety of voice.

The novel's denouement can only arrive when one character — whether the enthusiast, the ventriloquist, or the victim — eliminates the others in a contest that can only be fratricidal and is thereby identified, through this process of elimination, as author. Seeking a collective resolution to their competing and still outstanding claims, into Clara's bedroom each of the novel's remaining characters "penetrate[s] unobserved," self-liberated and thus "restored" to narrative life from various forms of characterological invisibility: Clara from delirium and the close guardianship of her well-meaning uncle, Carwin from a self-imposed exile of shame, and Wieland from incarceration (215). If Wieland seeks to triumph by killing and Carwin by explaining and rebuilding, Clara's motivation for returning is less clear as she takes (like the young Carwin) "an irregular path" to her old haunt (219). Like her opinions about what has occurred and who is responsible, her intentions in returning are the "sport of eternal change": initially, she intends to regain possession in order to destroy her private journal; having seized her journal, she then decides to destroy herself, but is prevented when the entrance of Carwin into the room reminds her that her more pressing desire, since her trial at Pleyel's, has been to discover the author and to punish him rather than herself (205). Obligingly, at the moment she prepares to end it all by penetrating to "the recesses of life" with her lancet, Carwin, who has been all along her prime authorial suspect, emerges from the room's shadowy depths, Hawthorne's gentleghost as Frankenstein's monster: "the shadow moved; a foot, unshapely and huge, was thrust forward; a form advanced from its concealment, and stalked into the room. It was Carwin!" (221, 222).

After reading her brother's confession, Clara had bitterly, tentatively identified Carwin as that peculiar "genius" able to subject demons to his control in order to marshal their "supernatural aid" in his diabolical schemes (206). As she imagines his role in the demise of the Mettingen congregation, he emerges as the practitioner of what can only be described as spectral humanism: that is, although he willfully engages the help of specters — "conscious beings, dissimilar from human, but moral and voluntary agents as we are" — in order to perpetrate evil, he dismisses with the disdain of the rationalist the trappings of witchcraft along with its accompanying theological rationale (206):

> The dreams of superstition are worthy of contempt. Witchcraft, its instruments and miracles, the compact ratified by a bloody signature, the apparatus of sulpherous smells and thundering explosions, are monstrous and chimerical. These have no part in the scene over which the genius of Carwin presides. (206)

Meeting her again in her "solitary and dismantled" room, Carwin will attempt to disabuse Clara of her notions of his control over events to claim instead the innocence of one who — although he freely admits to having deceived, sported with another's terrors, and plotted to destroy another's reputation — was criminal only insofar as he was curious (223, 225, 235).[101] Although he insists that his culpability is limited to his uncontrolled curiosity, he claims to have returned in order to confess himself "a repentant criminal" who offers to let Clara "denounce punishment" as a means of removing her errors and rebuilding her reputation (225). Clara renounces her fantasies of Carwin's preternatural powers only when he confesses to her the secret he keeps from Ludloe on pain of death, his purely mechanical and acquired ability "to speak where he is not," and even then she will prove herself perfectly willing to resuscitate them when convenient (249).

In his confession, Carwin offers a view of ventriloquism as a form of authorship which, although it lacks anything like a transcendent rationale, yet bears a parodic resemblance to the antinomian authorship of Wieland. For both men, authorship is the activity of a moment, whose extension is limited by the absence of authorial intention on the one hand, and on the other by the almost instantaneous dissolution of the authorial impulse, making the agent remarkably careless of consequences. If Wieland's authorship entailed the spare narrative sequence of a decree desired, received, multiply enacted, and fulfilled, Carwin in acting "meditated nothing" beyond the immediate "gratification which I derived from these exploits." Much like the brother and father whose conceptual limitations he strove to exceed and despite the extent of his powers, his "views were bounded to the passing moment, and commonly suggested by the momentary exigence" (229). Whereas Wieland, the antinomian author, is subjected to the unquestionable commands of an unrepresentable deity, Carwin is "subjected to the empire of mechanical and habitual impulses" (244). As Wieland, having acted, was instantly relieved of his agency by an infinitely powerful God, Carwin, having acted, was instantly relieved of his agency by the "machine" he himself had "rashly set in motion [and] over whose progress," he confesses, "I had no controul, and which experience had shewn me was infinite in power" (246). Both view themselves as "the undesigning cause" of events for which they bear no true responsibility and for which they disavow any personal role (223). If anything, Carwin represents himself as less an author even than Wieland: he is the unstable embodiment of the unrepresentable principle by which plots are generated solely for the sake of their generation. Clara, then, in attempting to follow Cotton Mather's train into the invisible world where she hopes to surprise criminal authorial intent at the instant in which it assumes a material form, finds not Mephistopheles, not the hyperrational orchestrator of the spectral hosts, not the cosmic contriver, but a cowering and snaggle-toothed rustic—"[u]nfortified by principle, subjected to poverty, stimulated by headlong passions"—who is himself the victim of his own fantastic eloquence, "a tool of wonderful efficacy" that he happens to possess but is unfit to use (227, 225).[102]

At the conclusion of Carwin's confession, the irrepressible Wieland makes his entrance upon the stage, despite Clara's uncle's assurance that she "will never more behold the face of this criminal, unless he be gifted with supernatural strength" (185). Wieland, of course, will not hesitate to act and cannot be appeased until his authorship has run its sacrificial course; moreover, his incarceration has compounded his power: beyond enthusiasm, he has revealed his possession of the exhorter's ability to penetrate into houses and the specter's ability to "shake off his fetters" and "restor[e] himself to liberty" no matter how his body is enchained (215). Upon Wieland's entrance and Carwin's speechless and wobbly-kneed exit, Clara securely grips the penknife which she has had concealed in the folds of her skirt (254). This detail in itself constitutes her wordless response to her questions and prediction after reading Wieland's confession: "Was I not likewise transformed from rational and human into a creature of nameless and fearful attributes? Was I not transported to the brink of the same abyss? Ere a new day should come, my hands might be embrued in blood" (204–5). But unlike Wieland and Carwin, Clara has not yet discovered a mode of guiltless authorship, has not found a way to arrange for, let alone justify, the alienation of her voice or her actions. Even if one refrains from plotting outright, even if one confines oneself to unraveling another's maze — to disemplotting and deauthorizing — can one do so with clean hands?

The only possibility for doing so is if Wieland and Carwin both voluntarily resign their authorial claims, if Carwin's ventriloquism and Wieland's enthusiasm — identities that encompass their entire sphere of action — come to a simultaneous end and self-sacrificially allow Clara, who has refused the offices of strategy and rationale, to survive them both.[103] Her solution for effecting the deauthorization of her rivals without literally killing them is, as it occurs to her in the heat of the moment, an ingenious one. Redeeming the ethical promise of Carwin's stated intention to restore her life, Clara forces him to ventriloquize himself: she commands him to tell Wieland, in the accents of transcendent being before which both sister and brother will shudder, that the voice of transcendent being has been and is being counterfeited. In so doing, Carwin is compelled to "conduct his inscrutable plots to [their] consummation" and is thus self-canceled: he has given his last performance on this stage (262). As the specter of Mary Easty had spectrally denied the validity of spectral evidence, Carwin's voice of transcendent being denies its own reality even while relying upon and commanding the awed belief of the listener in its transcendental status; this untenably paradoxical denial necessarily constitutes its last utterance. Clara permits Carwin to sustain the fiction of his authorship just long enough for him to remove Wieland's sustaining belief in transcendent being. Wieland, who will allow only transcendent being — even self-confessed as fraudulent — to deauthorize him, takes his own life in an insupportable moment of lucid incoherence, cutting his throat and thus identifying himself as Joseph Hawley's descendent, the victim of antinomian delusion. Rendered voiceless through his own utterance, Carwin at the novel's end has "hid[den] himself in a remote district of Pennsylvania," where, Clara surmises (willing the realization of her earlier benign fantasy), he "is now probably engaged in the harmless pursuits of agriculture," silently pondering "the evils to which his fatal talents have given birth" and, an unlikely convert to Jeffersonian virtue, wordlessly envisioning "[t]he innocence and usefulness of his future life" (273). The suicide of her brother saves Clara from committing fratricide, and the sprinkling of her hands with his blood thus serves to consecrate her as the text's sole survivor and bereft victim to whom nothing is left but to tell the tale of a singular fate bearing no connection to a general, representative truth. Thus does Clara author and yet retain the privileged status of a character who may legitimately bewail that her life must end when the pen is laid down.[104]

Her recourse to metaventriloquism having spared her the use of her penknife, Clara is thus left holding the pen in a gesture of ambiguous proprietorship upon whose unrepresented resolution her innocence, and thus her vindication, ultimately depends. After the elimination of Wieland and Carwin, Clara insists on inhabiting the scene of so many agentless crimes and continuing to write, which she represents as her affliction: authorship is the symptom of "a perverse constitution of mind," and its products the necessarily "abortive creations" whose author merely "suffer[s]" them until some outside force — if not relatives recalling her to her duty, then a fiery apocalypse which forces her to leave Mettingen once and for all — relieves her from their tyranny (268, 269). Clara's restoration to her right mind, her redemption from the criminal psychosis of authorship, is signaled by her offer at her narrative's end of an impossibly conventional conclusion that represents, as Norman Grabo has pointed out, Clara's only honorable authorial exit.[105] For those aspirants to authorship who will succeed her, her legacy is not the reinscription of literary norms that her story has made untenable but rather her achievement of a fantastic naïveté as she represents herself panting with awe at a fiction of her own devising, the transcendent voice that disarms her brother "*as if* the God whom I invoked were present" (258, emphasis added). What will prove useful to future aspirants to national authorship is Clara's gift of a secularized antinomianism to a future literary corpus that makes possible, as a sign of the fiction's legitimacy, not the representation of truth but rather a moment of presence, of direct communication, that is both staged and authentic.

FIVE

The Crisis of American Character

[A]t the core of democracy, finally, is the religious element.

— WALT WHITMAN, *Democratic Vistas*

The spirit of Literature and the spirit of Democracy are one.

— WILLIAM ALFRED JONES, *"Democracy and Literature"*

All form is an effect of character.

— RALPH WALDO EMERSON, *"The Poet"*

I

In the combined characters of Charles Brockden Brown's itinerant ventrilo-quist, the rustic Frank Carwin, and his republican heroine and first-person narrator, Clara Wieland, democratic personality — its rise, its effects, and its transfer — received its fullest fictional elaboration in the postrevolutionary era, and it was unmistakably linked with the activities of authorship. This association of democratic personality with the prerogatives of authorship will be a conspicuous feature of the transfer of democratic personality, not as social practice, but as the object of literary representation which, for the remainder of this study, will provide the focus of our attention. (As social practice, the characteristic coming-into-being of democratic personality continues throughout the Second Great Awakening, and is fully intact in the narratives of vocal empowerment offered by such mid–nineteenth-century itinerant lay preachers as Jarena Lee and Sojourner Truth.)[1] Within the represented world of the early American novel, the association of authorship with democratic personality is repeatedly made, illuminating fundamental and enduring anxieties about authorial status already prominent in the post-revolutionary period derived from fears that the democratic energies released in the Revolution would not easily be capped. The association of authorship with democratic personality made within the novel entailed a revaluation of the ontology of character, also carried out within the fictional realm; both features of the early American novel distinguish the national literature from the outset. Because such texts stage a radical questioning of the representational protocol operative in the novelistic domain, they provide compelling evidence for an incipient ethic of democratic literary creation which haunted the rhetoric attached to a republican ideology of literature abundantly evident in the period's metafictional productions. In particular, this democratic ethic made untenable what Michael Warner has called the "implicit center-periphery metaphorics" that structured the republican ideal of a diffusion of literature, a metaphorics which "registers the centralization of literacy that the thematic content of the discourse [of literary republicanism] disallows."[2]

This novelistic evidence for the destabilization of key ontological categories such as author and character, creator and created, being and representation, illuminates in turn the beginnings of a slow and profoundly ambivalent process, the development of an American aesthetic of innocence: the recognition and eventual rehabilitation (or domestication) of democratic personality as the essence of American character. Aside from the democratizing effects of the Revolution itself, the development of this aesthetic was abetted by a confluence of theoretical recuperations of the common man, largely (but not entirely) European and adapted from the postrevolutionary through the antebellum periods by enlightened Americans. They include a developing republican ethic bolstered by a rhetoric of virtue, simplicity, and natural rights; the agrarian myth of early America traditionally associated with Jeffersonian democracy; the romantic rediscovery of the folk as the basis for a virtuous nationalism, and later as the basis for an authentically national literature; and the affective, "elocutionary revolution," contemporaneous with the political one, which offered new support to the legitimacy of the slogan *vox populi, vox Dei.*[3]

The terms of Clara and Carwin's power struggle, emblematized in the scene in which they stand on either side of her closet door both victimized and hunted by the other, reproduce the culturally well established paradigm for democratic personality: a fantastic, composite subjectivity, produced by an oppositional social dynamic that unfolds within a circumscribed space where the visible and invisible domains intersect. In *Wieland*, of course, this oppositional space within which democratic personality arises is novelistic rather than social, and as such may be seen to possess certain distinctive features. First, no one in the novelistic oppositional domain appears to stand outside or above it as a force for its containment. Insofar as its government thus depends entirely on those who inhabit it, we may characterize this oppositional space within the novel as "democratic." The shock value of the early fictions we will examine in this chapter derives from the realization that *democratic space is coextensive with the fictional domain itself*, although it initially appeared as a rigorously localized, if volatile, area within it. In *Wieland*, even before Carwin's arrival, the representation of that which lies outside Mettingen is remarkably thin and remote. After his arrival, his surprisingly effortless penetration of the Wielands' domestic sphere, the insubstantiality of the outside world precludes its altering the increasingly nightmarish reality of what lies within Mettingen's boundaries which becomes, for all intents and purposes, the world entire.

This first difference between social and novelistic space (that the latter is entirely given over to the activities of democratic personality with an accompanying attenuation of the "normative" controlling frame) conditions the second: the location of the oppositional animus that determines the coming-into-being of democratic personality. Whereas in the scene of spectacular conversion, the powerful speaker and those to whom he transfers the revolutionary power of his voice are allies in resisting an external authority committed to containing their empowerment, the absence of such an external authority in the novel makes antagonists of the powerful speaker and the one to whom he transfers his vocal power (here is the atavistic recuperation of the specter-afflicted relationship noted in the previous chapter).[4] The "gift" of voice celebrated in all humility by Nathan Cole as an effect of his encounter with George Whitefield is here peremptorily rejected: Clara will consistently condemn Carwin as "the author of evil" even after she has definitively seized the reins of authorial power by eliminating her rivals, claiming that such power marks her as Carwin's eternal victim as surely as the mutilated corpse of Catharine marked her. The class antagonism which structures the oppositional ("inside" and "outside," "us" and "them") dynamic of spectacular conversion is here, in the absence of an "outside," internalized, and it haunts the relationship of the speaker with the one whom his voice animates. Thus, from the beginning of their acquaintance, this class antagonism informs the relationship of the eloquent rustic and his virtuous hostess misled by theory. The internalization of class antagonism is aptly figured in Carwin's unproblematic acceptance into the Wielands' intimate domestic sphere.

This relationship may be seen as a record of the catastrophic meeting of radical democracy — the political force of democratic personality — with liberal republicanism. Clara Wieland is an educated woman of Enlightenment principles, as secure in her rational independence from what she denigrates as superstition (a stance hard-won from the tragedy of her father's history) as she is in her financial independence, which explicitly isolates her from those demonstrations of mob power familiar in Brown's Philadelphia beginning with the Revolution and continuing into the 1790s.[5] Brown offers her, and her fellow characters appear to consider her, as a paragon of republican virtue and, for her rational self-possession, a model of liberal value. *Wieland* was written in 1798 in the final years of the Federalist era when conservatives feared that an incipient democratic politics, presaged by manifestations of popular unrest and an influential radical press, would destroy the hard-won felicities of republican (Federalist) virtue.[6] Although Brown's politics are not known for certain, his political writings and affiliations after 1797 have suggested to some scholars that the itinerant ventriloquist Carwin was intended to personify the "uncontrollable" democratic threat constituted by "the Mobility," the common people; in this view, his ventriloquism would signify the nihilistic power of the agentless popular voice against which the text's republicans, the enlightened but complacent Wieland circle, prove defenseless.[7] As a way of understanding the text in its literary-historical context, however, one may go beyond assigning Carwin a democratic identity that refers directly to the political preoccupations of the Federalist era to speculate on the meaning of an autobiographical fiction in which democratic personality as initially exemplified by Carwin is simultaneously deplored and appropriated by Clara as the means through which she is empowered to write.

Clara portrays the transfer of democratic personality from Carwin ("the author of evil"; a speaker) to herself (the "good" author; a writer) through her expedient practice of a secularized—in effect, a deeply fraudulent—antinomianism. The novel's penultimate scene in which she seizes control of the text is filled with the pathos of a peculiarly godless Calvinism: Clara faces her imminent annihilation filled with guilt and self-abhorrence, knowing her utter helplessness before the evil about to befall her, instinctively placing her entire reliance on the voice of omnipotence. In the absence of God, she compels Carwin to save her from death by deauthorizing himself, by making him ventriloquize the voice of transcendent being so as to declare in its thunderous accents before the enthusiastic Wieland that he is not God but a mere trickster. But there is a further irony: before the fraudulent god of her own creation whose "agency was here easily recognized," Clara describes how in hearing its counterfeit voice she "partook of Wieland's credulity, shook with his amazement, and panted with his awe" (261, 262). In order to become the author, that is, it is not enough for Clara to have conceived of the fraudulent god as a way of ridding herself of both Carwin and Wieland at one stroke. She must be fraudulently terrorized before him; before she may pick up the pen and write, she must be afflicted by a specter of her own creation within the liminal space of her isolated bedroom, the square of light into which all surviving characters emerge from their various forms of invisibility for their ultimate confrontation. There, both afflicting and afflicted, arranging for her brother's fatal deauthorization while suffering with him its physical and psychological effects, Clara emerges into authorial being proclaiming both victory and victimization. She emerges, that is, imbued with the characteristic innocence of humble self-enlargement that legitimates the authorial actions (emplotment, representation, and interpretation) of democratic personality.

Thus, although her overt authorial aim is to establish the truth of what occurred by identifying the author of evil, she presides over the text's blood-spattered conclusion as its sole authorial survivor. Her journey from Carwin's unwitting victim to his vanquisher, her journey into authorship, affords her no neutral point of view from which an author may avoid demonization on the one hand or victimization on the other, may avoid engaging in fatally misrepresentative acts on the one hand or suffering them on the other. Even if one concedes Clara's account of her participation in the generation of the novel's plot — that she did not author willingly or aggressively — it is clear that she fails to imagine, let alone occupy, an authorial position outside of a sacrificial structure: as she insists, author and victim, historian and sufferer, must always coincide, because the historian risks losing her ethical credibility and thus her reader's vindication of her authorship when she forsakes the status of victim. Thus does Clara's insistence that she was compelled to author — initially by her well-meaning friends who request a written account of her tragedy, then as a way of avoiding a fatal emplotment through the compatible stratagems of Carwin and Wieland, and finally because she perceives the act of writing as her sole alternative to annihilation — underscore the connection of authorial practice and sacrificial violence.

Far from resolving the superficial enigma of extraordinary character types and incidents as Brown promises in the novel's prefacing "Advertisement," therefore, Clara's story, her crucifixion on the axes of plotter and victim, author and character, actually foregrounds the underlying dilemma of conscientious authorship — that despite one's best intentions, to author is ventriloquistically to enact a will to plot.[8] The will to plot is shown to generate a profoundly deformative representation of reality as, for example, Carwin's vocal representation of Clara replaces her with a distorted image that she only superficially — metonymically — resembles. So considered, the novel proposes a link between representation and dismemberment; in Wieland's case, vocal representations lead him literally to dismember his social constituency by mangling and effacing their bodies.[9] Representation is, then, the antithesis of virtue (a secularization of Puritan charity), defined as the ethically structured correspondence of reality and appearance and thus as the foundation of rational community. The only way that the representer can avoid seeming to embrace the unvirtuous role of authorship is to claim the ontologically secondary, but ethically superior, status of the represented.[10] This is why for Clara the autobiographical act — which is synonymous with her preparations for Wieland's death — fills her with self-loathing and motivates her request for vindication from her readers. As her narrative progresses, she will relinquish this request in despair, confessing that she has no truth to tell, no lesson to teach, no moral to inculcate: the story that she initially offered as an instructive example proves in the telling to be merely self-referential, the representation of an unrepresentative fate, a "truth whereof I do not vouch."[11] The point of her narrative, she claims, has

escaped her; a mere character, she will simply cease to exist when the agentless tale has spent itself. Or it may be that, like the narrator of Melville's *Billy
Budd* whose declaration of authorial failure I have just invoked, Clara's appropriation of authorial power will take her far beyond the simple restoration of the truth of events to which the original intent of her manuscript, as
both she and author Brown had articulated it, was confined.

Clara's appropriation of Carwin's power to plot is thus more than a mere
element of plot. It enacts a transformation of her ontological status within
the text from character (the passive sufferer of another's plotting) to "author"
(emplotter and then recorder of others' lives): here is yet another "transformation" to which the novel's subtitle alludes. As "author," however, Clara
does not challenge structures of authority from a position outside of them, as
Carwin challenged the ritualized domestic practice of Mettingen, or as the
itinerant exhorter challenged all forms and representatives of social and religious authority. Instead, she exerts a deformative impact upon such structures of authority (prominently including Brown's authorial intent) from a
position within, undermining them as they are in the process of establishing
themselves as foundational: the ultimate consequence of the internalization
of the antagonistic principle that marks democratic space in the novel. Clara
vows to disempower Carwin, "the author of evil," by seizing control of
events she had passively endured; the history she then records is not only the
one she suffers, it is also the one she makes. It is not the one Brown had
offered his readers in his prefacing "Advertisement" whose unambiguous
moral would, he hoped, ensure his readers' "vindication" of his writerly
efforts. Ultimately, then, something akin to the class-derived oppositional
animus inherent in the dynamic transfer of democratic personality comes to
invest the relationship of the author to his characterological representatives
in the democratic domain of the novel. Such characters appear less the author's ally or accessory, the faithful carrier of his ideological opinions into the
represented world of the text, than his nemesis, an uncontainable and increasingly heroic figure already lodged — a found rather than created subjectivity — within the text's invisible heart.

If it eventually contains Carwin's uncanny power, Clara's story thus resists
containment itself within any larger heuristic narrative, a circumstance only
superficially redressed by the conventional comedy of the final chapter in
which she and Pleyel are romantically reunited in Europe. In particular,

Clara's story cannot be contained within the rational framework that the author of *Wieland*, Charles Brockden Brown, proposes as the source of the novel's utility for his readership; its uncontainability undermines the request he, too, makes in his prefatory "Advertisement" for his reader's vindication. In this document, Brown presents himself to his reader as a peculiar sort of defendant in a peculiar sort of trial: the reader's favorable "reception" of his "performanc[e]" will secure his "vindication" from unspecified charges upon which his authorial longevity depends — that is, the reader's willingness to vindicate the author will determine whether his future writing should be "published or suppressed" (3, 4). As a mark of his good faith, Brown promises his readers a "Work . . . neither selfish nor temporary," "ordinary [n]or frivolous," but rather useful and instructive, and which will allow them to approve "the manner in which appearances are solved" (3). The work will show that apparently "miraculous" appearances fully correspond both to "the known principles of human nature" as well as to history itself (3).[12]

Brown offers two possibilities for empirical corroboration of the novel's fantastic incidents: science and history will show that the work provides not frivolous amusement but sober instruction, and that its story constitutes not a curiosity or anomaly but a representative instance (3). He first observes that although both ventriloquists and enthusiasts are surely "uncommon" types, "Physicians" and other "men conversant with the latent springs and occasional perversions of the human mind" can testify to their existence and will support the author's decision, as a "moral painte[r]," to portray this type "in its most instructive and memorable forms" (3–4). History, however, promises a more sweeping exoneration: ultimately Brown appeals to "most readers" who will be familiar, through the newspaper, with the "one parallel [historical] fact" capable of providing "a sufficient vindication of the Writer" (4). This vindicating historical parallel is furnished by a farmer, one John Yates, a resident of upstate New York who one evening in 1781 concluded a family Bible reading by murdering his wife and four children at the behest of an invisible voice that he took to be God's. But even Yates, according to the newspaper account in which the incident was reported, seemed to realize that such actions were perhaps best explained to those with the power to decide one's fate not according to what actually occurred but by satisfying general expectations of the norm: Yates considered setting fire to his house and blaming the Indians for the deaths.[13] Thus is the authenticating case susceptible to its own internal corruption or falsification: does not the "one parallel [historical] fact" by virtue of its uniqueness underscore rather than eliminate the problem of anomaly? Doesn't the Yates incident, too, as its journalistic narrator insists, necessarily partake of the nature of curiosity, or at least the irremediably "extraordinary and rare," an appearance that resists resolution into any larger explanatory medium (3)?[14] Finally, by the fact that Brown refers his readers to an allegedly parallel historical incident in which the figure of the ventriloquist plays no part—for the inner voice urging the farmer to murder had no externalized, embodied, or independent equivalent—does he not underscore his own fantastic augmentation of Yates's already bizarre story with the almost preternatural character of the ventriloquial Carwin? Despite his explicit desire to vindicate his authorship as moral portraiture intended to instruct and improve the reader, Brown's portrait of the ventriloquist emphasizes in advance the epistemological—the democratic—crisis at the novel's heart (encapsulated by the ubiquitous question, "Who is speaking?") that it can neither explain nor explain away.[15] The figure of Carwin which differentiates the events of the novel from the Yates precedent effectively identifies the novelist with his ventriloquistic protagonist in the very act of producing the vindicating historical parallel.

Brown's invocation of historical precedent, then, backfires. His appeal to empirical reality only accentuates the problem to which his bid for vindication indirectly refers: namely, that authorship itself is ventriloquism writ large. Like the ventriloquist—master of the insinuated word who, to promote his own secret and irrational agenda, creeps silently into houses to seduce the curious and unwary—the author extricates his voice from the physical limitations of his body and the psychosocial contours of his personality and usurps the voices of others in the interests of fabricating a plot. Like the specter or the unknown exhorter, the author exists in a state of visible invisibility, associated with a vocal power of misrepresentation capable of corrupting the reader's virtue by destroying the grounds of reasoned consent to his representations (for these were precisely the terms in which the fear of fiction was and would continue to be expressed).[16] In this manner, the postrevolutionary American author replicated the paradigm of democratic personality in his own actions as well as those of his authorial characters. By introducing the multivoiced Carwin into the text as "the author of evil," Brown explicitly raises doubts concerning the structure of performance and reception that links author with reader (as it linked specter and afflicted, afflicted and observer, and exhorter and auditor) as an arrangement dedicated to producing the truest representation — dedicated, that is, to the promotion of virtue as a conformity of appearance to essence. Arguably, the obligation to promote virtue entailed by a producer of texts was more urgent even than the speaker's: the writer's disembodied voice would, after all, carry farther than the most skilled public speaker's; his words would be taken in by those who could not even see him, let alone know him. Moreover, they would be received in solitude where their effects could not be observed and controlled, if need be, as was theoretically possible even in the volatile public context of spectacular conversion.[17] And as with oral performance, not just the individual listener's soul but the collective integrity was at stake as published fictions were disseminated far beyond the space of formal observance. Brown's "Advertisement," however, simultaneously promises and precludes a conformity of authorial intentions to authorial acts: by stating his intentions outright, he implies that his text will not exceed its stated lessons and will leave no interpretive residue, and yet the empiricism invoked to account for and thus contain Carwin only reinforces the ventriloquist's resistance to incorporation within a larger scheme of accountability, a resistance that Clara reenacts.[18] As William H. Prescott observed concerning Brown's awkward insistence upon his reader's vindication, "Truth cannot always be pleaded in vindication of the author of a fiction, any more than of a libel."[19]

If it was difficult to ignore the similarity of authorship to ventriloquism, it might still be proposed as a benign rather than an insidious circumstance. William Ellery Channing, the founder of American Unitarianism, observed in 1830, for example, that "[b]ooks penetrate everywhere," but associated textual penetration with an infusion, rather than a dispossession, of voice; like the religious ravisher, the American literatus personified "the mind giving to multitudes whom no voice can reach its compressed and selected thoughts in the most lucid order and attractive forms which it is capable of inventing." A compelling instance of "the concentration of intellect for the purpose of spreading itself abroad and multiplying its energy," literature allowed mind to "acquir[e] a kind of omnipresence" and to become thereby "the mightiest instrument on earth." Not only was literature in this regard "among the most powerful methods of exalting the character of a nation," but — its seminal power here made explicit — it was "the chief means of forming a better race of men."[20] From the beginning of his authorial career,

Brown wished to affiliate himself with this understanding of the authorial mandate. In his 1789 debut essay, "The Rhapsodist," he promised his reader that he would refrain from taking advantage of authorial spectrality and "shall not make use of my privilege as an anonymous writer, and represent to him, any facts or circumstances which are not strictly true."[21] Instead, his authorial ambition is to be contained by the conditions literary self-representation independently places upon him which ethically compel him to take the voice of the people as his referent and touchstone, at least to the degree that, in an odd anticipation of Wordsworth's preface to the *Lyrical Ballads*, he vows to "write as he speaks, and converse with his reader not as an author, but as a man." With Carwin, however, Brown casts doubt precisely on the integrity of speech as the basis on which to establish an authorial practice whose "principal characteristic" is to be "the sincerity of [the author's] character."[22] In so doing, he suggests that the author's promise to practice a "good" ventriloquism is insufficient, and must be superseded by a more radical guarantee against the irresponsible exercise of authorial power: namely, the author will find a way to inhabit the ontological divide between being and representation, author and character, in order to become that oxymoronic fantasy which would prove surpassingly attractive to the nineteenth century, the innocent author.

The ambition to disavow the ontological difference that gives the author the power to emplot the character may be seen as an expression of democratic value that paradoxically arises within the context of heightened political fears of a democratic insurgence bolstered by the novel's own detailed account of the democratic threat as embodied by a ubiquitous and anonymous speaker. Postrevolutionary fiction nevertheless proposes that all men — in particular, authors and characters — are created equal. An incipient ethic of democratic literary creation can be discerned in the doubt that Clara, in a series of despairing soliloquies, casts upon the legitimacy of the authorial act(s) that brought her into being as a character. The questions she poses about the coincidence of authorship and violence indirectly indict Brown's prefatory self-representation as disingenuous. Ultimately Clara's concerns about the legitimacy of authorship, a role she both covets and hesitates to assume, throw into question the ethical validity — the veracity or accountability — of the representational protocol operative in the fictional domain with respect to human subjectivity.

The literary historian Lewis P. Simpson has suggested with reference to a number of postrevolutionary writers including Brown that their "democratic idealism" was textually expressed in the represented reversal of the master (author) and servant (character) roles which, as a sign of the author's uncertain status within republican ideology, contributed to "the depletion of literary authority in the new nation."[23] If, following this suggestion, we consider that the transmutation of democratic personality from a religious and then political into a literary register was intended to legitimate humble self-enlargement by showcasing it (however ambivalently) as the essence of American character, it also clarified by fictionally enacting its peculiar nihilism. The textualization of democratic personality required that the oppositional dynamic necessary to its realization be internalized as a struggle between author and characters or, analogously, between authorial characters. Like the spaces of spectral possession or spectacular conversion, the literary text itself provided the arena for the oppositional encounter within which democratic personality — the fantastic, dramatistically integrated hybrid — could, for the first time, come into being: in this instance, as the human subject who appears on the textual plane "in the character of an author," a phrase that simultaneously suggests the ethical priority of character and betrays a desire to get back to, to seek the shelter of, derivation.[24]

II

Although variously construed, the fictional inquiry into the ontological status of representation, carried out whatever the formal consequences to the text, distinguishes two other key works of the postrevolutionary and early national eras, Stephen Burroughs's *Memoirs* (1798) and Hector St. John de Crèvecoeur's *Letters from an American Farmer* (1782). Both semiautobiographical fictions demonstrate a commitment to bridging the author-character divide. For Brown's Carwinesque contemporary Stephen Burroughs, a confidence man whose *Memoirs* became something of a best-seller, writing in and as character was not so much desirable because of the comparative innocence of character but instead was inevitable given the absence of any true — original or originating — identity.[25] As he states in the opening pages of his memoirs, in which he represents himself demurring from authorship even as he picks up the pen, fiction itself had in his case destroyed the possibility of identity (the integral authorial self), allowing him only a factitious existence: "Nothing gives the mind of childhood a more unfavorable bias," Burroughs piously sighs, "than a representation of those unnatural characters exhibited in novels and romances. It has a direct tendency to lead the mind from the plain simple path of nature, into the airy regions of fancy; and when the mind is once habituated to calculate on the romantic system, error and irregularity are the common consequences" (5).[26] His ensuing life as an adventurer necessitated by his early corrupting exposure to novelistic character chronicles the author's progressive dissolution into the myriad characters whose identities he temporarily assumes in the course of his itinerancy. As his survival (he maintains) requires his discovery of the multiple forms of counterfeiting, both pecuniary and personal, Burroughs revels in the infinite store of excuses with which he rationalizes a seemingly endless series of character changes. He celebrates rather than bemoans the instability of identity and the ensuing epistemological crises that had so tormented Clara, offering his memoirs almost as a manual of how to efface the line between author and character and thereby enjoy an unheard-of existential freedom, increasingly legitimated by a conspicuously Franklinian logic of expedience and liberated from a Franklinian concern for maintaining appearances.

Thus, although it perfunctorily deplores it, Burroughs's *Memoirs* celebrates his own radical mutability, his progressive slide into a series of characters fully released from any governing authorial principle, as his emancipation from social and cultural forms that have no inherent legitimacy. Like Clara (and Crèvecoeur's Farmer James), Burroughs's narrator introduces his text as an epistolary work elicited at the request of the narrator's friend (who confesses himself mystified at "the enigma" of Burroughs's "character") with which he complies even though to do so "will give me a degree and kind of pain, which only they who feel can describe" (1, 3). Like Clara, too, Burroughs's compliance allegedly rests on his self-sacrificial willingness to redeem a life that "has been one continued course of tumult, revolution, and vexation" by instructing others to avoid the errors he committed; like Clara's text, it is overtly intended as a paean to reason, but also like Clara's text it is replete with excuses for outrageous behavior that undercut the penitential posture allegedly shaping the relation of events (1). For example, he laments that "my situation has been such, that I have violated that principle of ve-

racity which we implicitly pledge ourselves to maintain towards each other";
his errors are routinely produced by "particular causes" that those who judge
him cannot understand (67). Burroughs can therefore complain — in the
midst of a section of the narrative in which he describes how he simultaneously counterfeited money and the character of a preacher (taking advantage of the common assumption that "a clergyman . . . must speak the
truth") — that "[t]he name imposter, is therefore easily fixed to my character"
(44, 67). When he is unmasked, Burroughs is forced to flee his outraged
parishioners, but maintains that he himself "determined to drop preaching,
which subjected me to so many false appearances, contrary to my inclination" (68).

The *Memoirs* is devoted to an account of Burroughs's itinerancy, his
crimes, his incarcerations and escapes through which he progressively deconstructs the standing of visible character as a reliable — and in the case of
the minister, a sacrosanct — index of the invisible, true self. His project, in
this regard, recalls the train of thought concerning the knowability of essential identity initiated during the witchcraft crisis: spectral evidence theory
undertook the unmasking, by invisible means, of the invisible status of a
God-given spiritual identity. Burroughs offers one sense of an ending to this
train of thought: his autobiography asserts not that visible character may,
intentionally or not, dissemble spiritual identity but rather, as Larzer Ziff has
observed, that in the context of this life " 'true identity' was a term without a
referent."[27] Burroughs's insistence that all is appearance, and that fictions
refer not to transcendent realities like essential identities but to other fictions, becomes more and more unabashed until every aspect of identity is
exposed as one facet of a vast misrepresentational empire to which everyone
contributes as and in character. Claims for the extent of this empire intend no
profundity, but only contiguity: identity follows identity with no pretense of
depth, of a reaching below the surface to access the hidden truth of the self or
even its truest representation. Instead, identity is what appears on the surface, a surface geographically identical to the terrain Burroughs traverses in
his endless itinerancy. Just as, in the form of an excuse for counterfeiting,
Burroughs (through his counterfeiting friend, Lysander) maintains that
"[m]oney, of itself, is of no consequence, only as we, by mutual agreement,
annex to it a nominal value, as the representation of property," so he will
maintain with increasing insistence throughout the text that character is
equally of no consequence except as people agree to assign it a nominal value

as the representation of authentic selfhood, the foundational social fiction (83). To his own irritation and amusement, this lesson will be driven home to him repeatedly by those he meets on his travels who deny that he is Stephen Burroughs because he doesn't resemble the stories about him printed in the papers (he suffers an inversion of Caleb Williams's problem).[28] As he develops its applications throughout the text, not only is the notion of character deracinated from the ground of essential identity or veracious interiority, but the term's many connotations are brought into such proximity as to purge it of any clear significance.

The multiple nuances of "character" and the complexities of their interrelationships reveal the fiction of the self to be a densely multilayered and yet insubstantial structure to which innumerable other characters contribute. Toward the end of the narrative, for example, Burroughs tells the story of how he had submitted articles to a local newspaper under the pen name "the Philanthropist." So successful were his productions that they attract undue attention to the question of the writer's true identity. As an escaped convict always concerned to avoid detection, Burroughs determines to give up the journalistic enterprise "and here ended the matter, as it related to me in the character of the Philanthropist." But the public is not to be deterred:

> every one was ready to make his own comments upon a character so new; having, by direct and indirect means, given myself a character very novel; and my intimate friends had highly embellished the superstructure which my fancy had reared. There were almost as many different opinions concerning me as there were persons to form them. But none of the various conjectures happened to light on the identical character which I had sustained in reality, though the publications from Worcester relating to my confinement, trial, and escape were among this people. (255)

This view of character as a dizzying shift from one fictional mode to another, depending on the character of the one who perceives the character, in what light, and with what subsidiary information at hand, is contrasted throughout the text with the orthodox view of character as, according to the economy of Christian as well as republican virtue, a reliable index of an unchanging inner self. A Reverend Mr. Woolworth tries to persuade Burroughs, who fails to repent having assumed the character of a minister, of the egregiousness of his initial act of counterfeit:

> "A clergyman," said he, "is the ambassador of the Lord Jesus; he is clothed with his authority in that character, and therefore ought to be treated with that respect which such a character claims; therefore any attempt to oppose, or bring a minister into contempt, is committing a crime immediately against God, and ought to be punished as the most destructive of any which could be committed." (321)

To this appeal, Burroughs turns the minister's characterization upon him and holds him to its terms, replying that more than any other the preacher is bound by his character to honor the sinner before himself. Through his multiple and conflicting uses of the term throughout the autobiographical text, perversely grounded in an assertion and celebration of a radically fluid personal identity, Burroughs maintains that, as a reliable index for an individual's essential identity, the ultimate meaning of his or her character is infinitely deferred and therefore useless. With reference to an incident that occurs during one of his several imprisonments, for example, he dismisses the possibility of assigning characterological significance to his behavior, pointing out that "[t]hose who felt friendly towards me would call it manly resolution; others, who were inimical, would call it deviltry, wickedness, etc., so that it would have as many names as there are different feelings towards one in those who relate it" (156). This character cannot be bound even to his character (manly, wicked), but can, simply by changing interlocutors, give it the slip. The only possibility of fixing Burroughs's character would be to fix the characters of those who interact with him, whose characters may be fixed only by fixing the characters of those who have interacted with them, and so forth.

Despite this picture of social atomization, Burroughs identifies the limits of characterological relativism and the revolutions it presages in individual and social life as "the voice of the people," which he states is synonymous with "the language of the heart" that "we find . . . speaking within us" and "cannot silence" (128, 226). Burroughs thus seems to combine a radical destabilization of identity with a radical populism, whose anonymous, transcendent, and irrepressibly voluble "we" refuses marginalization; nevertheless, the possibility of grounding individual character in some form of transcendent collective subjectivity is not developed beyond this allusion.[29]

At the outset of his semiautobiographical *Letters of an American Farmer*, Crèvecoeur unambiguously proposes how the unarticulated voice of the people may supply that ground and enable the author to write legitimately as and for others. The narrative opens with the rhetoric of trial: the text is offered as a species of literary and social experiment in which the author's integrity shall be tested. In an opening letter to the Abbé Raynal, F.R.S., to whom the letters are dedicated, Crèvecoeur's narrator, the "humble" Farmer James, as a means of justifying his authorship, asks the question implicitly asked by the New Light convert as a prelude to public speech about invisible realities: "Why should not I be permitted to disclose those sentiments which I have so often felt from my heart?"[30] Like the convert, too, James promises that the undissembled content of the individual heart may be identified with the content of all honest hearts, and that the articulation of his sentiments will fairly represent the sentiments of all Americans — will, in fact, constitute an "echo" of his countrymen's unspoken thoughts and feelings (38). James's authorship is thus figured as his conscientious assumption of a benign ventriloquism; he proposes that, because the author is wholly identified with — even, as he will assert, indistinguishable from — those he represents, the unarticulated voice of the American people may be spoken through him without the danger of misrepresentation attached to a coercive or cunning authorship. Appearances to the contrary, his voice is wholly derivative, an echo, of theirs. His opening statements in the introductory letter deny what we have seen to be the oppositional prerequisite for democratic expression insofar as they insist on the identity of author and object of representation. James *is* his character, and need not attempt to write (as Brown) in the character of an author or (as Burroughs) as a character liberated from the lesser fiction of authorship or any mode of originary identity. At stake in James's authorial trial, then, is the question of whether an author-character, an integrated and ideal subjectivity, may innocently and safely (deserving and certain of his vindication) enact democratic personality as a mode of humble and uncontainable self-enlargement within the novel context of "American" literature, where uncontainability signifies not the disintegration of cultural forms but their affirmation in the potentially endless replication of Americans identical to James that occurs through the process of European "transplantation" to American soil.

The enactment of precisely such a hybridic subjectivity, on the biographical as well as the literary levels, challenged the ingenuity of the French aristocratic emigré writer. For Crèvecoeur, the character of "the people" as embodied by a hypothetical, prototypical "American" — like conscience, an identity both individual and corporate — held out the possibility of a literary subjectivity that the author could both be and represent.[31] It promised to realize on the literary plane a character capable of a self-enlargement at once humble and uncontainable, but also possessed of a self-governing principle that regulated, and finally placed a natural or noncoercive limit on, the practice (if not the theoretical prerogative) of uncontainability. Over several years until the Revolution interrupted his idyll, Crèvecoeur, settled on a farm in New York State, penned the *Letters of an American Farmer* through which he attempted to imagine an authorial character that was neither demonized nor victimized. Compiled as an epistolary narrative (elicited, as in Brown and Burroughs, by an outsider's request), the *Letters* were intended to chronicle the story of one representative farmer's discovery of how in America a multitude of otherwise disconnected individuals come to experience both "the necessity" and "the sweet pleasure" of "acting [the same] part" (53) — or, as one New Light minister had expressed a similar vision, of bringing about both "beautiful Variety, and yet sweet Harmony."[32] In this regard, "the American," as a character able to embrace the paradoxical imperatives of playing a role and fulfilling both duty and destiny, redressed an anxiety that would later be voiced by the Federalist and virulent antidemocrat Fisher Ames: "If . . . we search for a principle or sentiment general and powerful enough to produce national effects, capable of making a people act with constancy, or suffer with fortitude, is there any thing in our situation that could have produced, or that can cherish it?"[33] The principle of constancy to which all can consent, Crèvecoeur proposed, might be the duty of internalizing in order to become a novel type of character, "the American," who in undeviating conformity to a natural and infinitely repeatable process acquired the ontological substance and authority of essential (American) identity.[34]

Crèvecoeur's *Letters* constitutes one of the earliest attempts to identify "the American" as a distinctive type of personality, a "new man, who acts upon new principles" and who "must therefore entertain new ideas and form new opinions" (70). Crèvecoeur's own identity was a very slippery affair and his life as an "American" merits a brief summary. Michel-Guillaume-Jean de Crèvecoeur was born in Normandy in 1735, a member of the French aristocracy. Something of an Anglophile, he emigrated to Britain in 1754 and then to Canada in 1755 where he joined the French army in their campaigns against the British during the French and Indian War. After his discharge in 1759, he moved south into British America and changed his name to J. Hector St. John. He traveled extensively throughout the colonies as a salesman and then a surveyor, became a naturalized British subject in 1765, married an American in 1769, and settled on a large farm in New York. His wife and three children all bore the surname St. John. It is of this farm and this life that he writes in the opening letters. With the escalation of the revolutionary war in 1778, St. John, whose Anglophilic sentiments were well known, attempted to leave the country in order to secure his patrimony in France. The British, with whom he sympathized, nevertheless arrested him in New York as a revolutionary spy and imprisoned him there for two years. Upon his release, he fled to England, where in 1782 he published his *Letters*; from there he went to France, where he readopted his surname, de Crè-vecoeur, and where he published an expanded version of the *Letters* trans-lated into French (1784). Known to be an expert on the new nation, Crè-vecoeur was honored by the French government with a diplomatic post in New York. The erstwhile representative American farmer reentered the New World in 1783 as the official representative of Louis XVI, only to discover that in his absence, his farm had burned, his wife had died, and his children had been placed in the custody of strangers.

The burden of Crèvecoeur's first-person narrator, the simple yet eloquent Farmer James, is to satisfy his aristocratic English correspondent that in America, one's invisible inner content — one's dreams and inherent capabil-ities — is fully realized in one's outward manner and circumstances, in what James calls "visible character" (75). His primary example of the realization of that which in the Old World had been merely hypothetical, the individual's individuality, is the European peasant, the hapless tiller of another man's soil who in the New World becomes a self-reliant farmer and, as such, a model American: an exemplar of the achievement of American selfhood in the process of which he becomes what he has always potentially been.[35] So stan-dardized is this process of individuation-through-modeling (as James will describe it in "What is an American?") that he equates the achievement of true selfhood with the achievement of true American character. In America, visible character — that image of the self presented to others — can never be factitious or dissembling, but is necessarily a natural and direct expression of invisible character, or authentic identity. James refers to the conversion by which the European "cypher" acquires in America true character, conceived to be simultaneously individual and national, as "naturalization," defined as "[f]rom nothing to start into being": thus is the quintessential spectral act reclaimed as the source of a genuine, because collectively enacted and verifiable, selfhood (84, 83). In his first three letters, James describes at length two instances of naturalization: one, the emigration, or as James styles it, the "transplantation" of the Scotsman Andrew, and the other, the project of writing the self, that is, of writing the *Letters* (69).[36] Implicit in both emigration and autobiography is the coming-into-being, or the naturalization, of America itself. Thus does Crèvecoeur anticipate the desirability (if not the achievement) of Whitman's vision for an authentic democratic poetics in which nation, poet, and poem come into being simultaneously: not only does the author refrain from claiming any precedence over character, but no element of the creative act is subordinate to any other.

All these aspects of naturalization — emigration, autobiography, and nation-building — depend on an initial act of self-assertion that James acknowledges comes dangerously close to self-creation, the production of an isolated and anomalous self without reference to the surrounding community and thus unrepresentative of it. Far from celebrating self-invention, the *Letters* insist that the legitimate renewal of self in America requires a scrupulous "tracing" of a (narrative) line already established by father, fatherland, or Nature. James asserts repeatedly that true renewal occurs not through revolution but through repetition, and that legitimate desire cannot exist beyond "the narrow circles within which I constantly revolve" (54, 65). Thus he writes that the newly arrived European,

> no matter of what condition . . . hears his language spoke; he retraces many of his own country manners; he perpetually hears the names of families and towns with which he is acquainted; . . . [The Germans, for example] observe their countrymen flourishing in every place; they travel through whole counties where not a word of English is spoken; and in the names and the language of the people, they retrace Germany. (80, 84)

Given the blueprint already in place for becoming an American, the only way for the transplant to "go astray" is through an unwarranted self-assertion: the sin of "new pride" or disobedience to the voice of "our great parent," Nature, who welcomes the "distressed European" and promises him "the immunities of a freeman" as long as he is "just, grateful, and industrious" — as long as he does not inscribe himself but retraces the one who came before (84, 89, 90).

Likewise, the relevance to the community of the autobiographical project is ensured as long as one retraces the line which, James asserts, "Nature has herself traced for me" (50). For James, the first such natural narrative is provided by his father. When he realizes that "my father left behind him the name of a good man; I have but to tread his paths to be happy and a good man like him," he is free to end his youthful wandering in search of something better, or at least different: "I ceased to ramble in imagination through the wide world; my excursions since have not exceeded the bounds of my farm, and all my principal pleasures are now centred within its scanty limits" (53). The statement stands in radical opposition to that of the adolescent Carwin whose own imagination teemed with visions that, in order to realize them, led him to transgress the boundaries of his father's farm. James, having conscientiously taken up his father's life, writes, "I felt myself happy in my new" — that is, in his father's — "situation" (52).

Both father's sons, however, consider the exercise of voice beyond the *"yea and nay"* necessary to conduct one's legitimate business as a revolutionary act, linked to the transgression of limits set by the father to permissible self-enlargement (48). Writing threatens to become just such a revolutionary or symbolically parricidal action; for this reason James is careful to claim vindication from future "blame" by reminding his aristocratic correspondent that he writes not from "presumption" but in strict compliance with the conditions of a "covenant" established in advance by the former (49, 50). In order to guard further against the possibility of illicit self-assertion, the aspiring writer must follow another natural line as elaborated in the introductory letter in which James, his wife, and their minister debate whether the humble American farmer should accept the aristocrat's invitation. James's wife maintains that writing would draw James away from his true self by drawing him away from his farming and differentiating him from the community of farmers. By complying with the Englishman's request for a narrative of American life, James will ally himself with the "cunning folks," those who don't engage in physical labor but traffic instead in forms of absence or immateriality (writing, travel, astronomy, mathematics, credit), and whose words, even in the form of simple requests, are unreliable representations that must be scrutinized for hidden and contradictory meanings if their addressee is to avoid emplotment in their unknowable schemes (40, 41). To engage with the Englishman, to attempt to "letter it" with the educated, is to cede the solidity of one's communally sanctified "condition" as a member of the "warm substantial family," where nothing need be said because all is understood, for an insubstantial individual existence as "the man of the pen," "the scribbling farmer" fated to become the subject of gossip and speculation (40, 49). Writing announces one's singularity, one's difference. To write is to consent to the temptation to exceed the limits to a legitimate selfhood, and thus to risk losing the means of subsistence by acquiring a false and singular reputation in the community (49). For James's wife, because it constitutes an illegitimate and unwarranted self-enlargement, writing must be considered a "heinous crime" which, if one cannot refrain from committing it, should at least be kept "a profound secret" (48, 47).

James's minister responds to her objections by proposing that writing is a form of labor grounded not in absence and immateriality but rather in a palpable and universally accessible presence: anticipating Thoreau, the minister claims that James's written words will "smell of the woods" and attire themselves in "simple American garb" (41, 46). Writing, he assures the farmer and his wife, may so approximate speech that, as the Rhapsodist had promised his reader and as Wordsworth would more famously propose, writing is nothing more than a mere "talking on paper," an immediate transcription of experience into the language of "spontaneous and strong impressions" (41, 46).[37] For his writing to be legitimate, for style to correlate with status and avoid all excess, James has only to imagine that his English correspondent is physically present and asking his questions "viva-voce" (41)—a species of factitious ("as if") antinomianism reminiscent of Clara's claim to have trembled before the voice of Carwin she herself had elicited "as if the God whom I invoked were present."[38] To lay to rest all anxieties about the incompatibility of writing and laboring, the minister draws an analogy between ploughing and writing, describing how he composes his sermons while behind the plough. There, he maintains, words are inspired by the "salubrious effluvia of the earth":

> my labour flows from instinct, as well as that of my horses; there is no
> kind of difference between us in our different shares of that operation;
> one of them keeps the furrow, the other avoids it; at the end of my field,

they turn either to the right or left as they are bid, whilst I thoughtlessly hold and guide the plough to which they are harnessed. (47)

Writing, like ploughing and like identity, constitutes a visible "field of action" in which will and performance, mind and muscle, subject and object, cannot be differentiated, in which labor, of the plough as of the pen, is the product of an instinct not attributable to any single, dominating agent (43). Far from a freakish diversion from the legitimacy of labor, writing under the sign of the plough — writing the self, and through the self, the nation — may constitute an extension of nature, as the minister implies when he urges Farmer James, "Do let [the Englishman] see on paper a few American wild-cherry trees, such as Nature forms them here in all her unconfined vigour, in all the amplitude of their extended limbs and spreading ramifications" (46). Uncontainability is, in this view, an innocent trait rather than a secret plot; if the "unconfined vigour" of that "strong vegetative embry[o]," the budding American writer, produces an "irregularly luxuriant" growth, this must be seen as nothing more insidious than the fruit of the voice-plant's release from the deformities — the espaliers and pygmification — of an unnatural, because externally imposed and irrationally motivated, confinement (46).[39] The oxymoronic trope of tame wildness, like the wasps in James's kitchen, conveys what will emerge as the ideal of both democratic government and democratic personality where self-assertion and self-effacement, controlling and controlled, being and representation, conformity and individuation, are in practice synonymous, and where the oppositional requirement for democratic personality is internalized as the natural achievement of virtue.[40]

The successful naturalization of the American impresses upon him or her the superior advantage of a "pleasing uniformity," of a "perfect state of indifference" which neutralizes any "strange mixture," be it of blood, belief, or ability, in the teeming multitudes who transplant themselves to American soil (67, 75, 69). The lesson that James learns and that he promotes to newly arrived immigrants as the blueprint for authentic selfhood, both personal and national, is that true freedom entails confinement, true novelty entails repetition, true individuality entails conformity: all of which guarantee that in America appearances will coincide with essence. The unparalleled luxury of American society, then, is that the old specters cease to exist while their customary ambience, invisibility, is declared irrelevant, if not nonexistent.

No one need look beyond or behind the surface, "visible character": "the invisible one," Farmer James writes, "is only guessed at, and is nobody's business" (75).[41] These fully sufficient surfaces, all issuing from the same mold and molding others as infallibly, guarantee that American authorship will possess a total representative legitimacy: unlike Carwin, who claims all discrete voices as his own, James proclaims his voice's derivation from a true — a collective — source.

In his eagerness to represent for the Englishman the whole of that "vast maze" of a country from Nova Scotia to Florida by "enter[ing] intimately into the situation and characters of the people," James suggests that any part may be taken as representative of the whole (107). "[L]et us look attentively for some small unnoticed corner," he proposes, and we are sure to find "always a refreshing spectacle" (107). But in unexpected contradiction to this complacent expectation, the claim for the comprehensiveness of James's narrative line is fatally compromised in the ninth letter, in the course of a visit he makes to Charleston, South Carolina, where James, as it were, opens the door (in Cotton Mather's phrase) to spectral representation. Strolling through the forest on his way to a dinner engagement, James feels "the air strongly agitated" as if by an approaching storm, and then hears "a sound resembling a deep rough voice, [which] uttered, as I thought, a few inarticulate monosyllables" (177). The source of the disturbance is at first invisible; then James's attention is drawn to large birds of prey clinging to a cage suspended from a tree. Scaring off the birds with an "involuntary" shot from his gun, James finds himself "involuntarily contemplating" a "living spectre": "a Negro, suspended in the cage and left there to expire!" (178). The man's eyes have been pecked out by the birds and, with their departure, innumerable insects come to feed on the wounds covering his body. James finds himself "arrested by the power of affright and terror" (178). As it recalls the paradigmatic social cataclysm wherein invisible realities thrust themselves unbidden into the visible realm, James's unexpected and involuntary confrontation with the slave in the cage bears a grotesque anticipatory resemblance to the scene in *Wieland* in which Carwin first appears at Clara's door to deconstruct the premises upon which the modern idyll of Mettingen had been theoretically established: the slave asks the farmer to give him something cold to drink, and the farmer involuntarily trembles as he responds. Unable to free, heal, or kill the slave, James musters only enough strength to walk away from the "shocking spectacle," and learns later, over dinner on a nearby plantation, that he was thus left to die as punishment for having murdered his overseer (178).[42]

This unanticipated confrontation with "invisible" American character to which the farmer was unwittingly made a spectator effectively disintegrates the totalizing claims of his narrative as well as the terms of his authorial vindication. The slave cannot partake of "the spirit of an unfettered and unrestrained industry" which James has portrayed as the American norm, a fact that contradicts the American Farmer's claim to represent "the American" and to contain in his personal experience the experience of all who are transplanted from the Old World to American soil (67).[43] The broken, "uncouth" voice of the slave articulates the experience of another vast population of American immigrants whose experience in the New World is based upon a "frau[d] surpassing in enormity everything which a common mind can possibly conceive" (178, 170). (James would like to exempt his own slaves and, by extension, all slavery in the northern colonies from this condemnation, but cannot: his hope that someday the slaves will be emancipated exposes his own enslavement to the system he abhors.) Doomed upon arrival in the New World to submit to a molding as comprehensive as that which turns the European cipher into a prosperous landowner, the African undergoes an inverted naturalization: the individual who was someone in the Old World, a master, becomes nothing in the New, a selfhood not realized but thoroughly suppressed. James's encounter with this other representative, if "unseen," American initiates a lengthy and despairing meditation that point by point inverts his paean to America as "providentially intended for the general asylum of the world," a locale differentiated from others only to the degree that "oppression" exists outside of its borders (168, 106). For the slaves, transplantation involved the rude seizure of "innocent people" in "some harmless, peaceable African neighbourhood" (168). Whereas superficial differences are neutralized in the case of the European emigrants upon their arrival, they are so exacerbated in the case of the African as to constitute a "great contrast" at the heart of American experience that James — like Whitman a century later with his "fear of conflicting and irreconcilable interiors" — suspects he cannot poetically accommodate.[44] What one new arrival perceives as the "silken bands of mild government," the other knows as the iron chains of slavery (167, 168). For the African, the "extreme fertility" of the American soil increases the "extreme misery" of the slave who tills it and ensures his continuing and unmitigated alienation from it (176). Finally, the African-American is prohibited from tracing or even establishing the familial line which Nature underwrites for the European transplant because, from the outset, the African family is dismembered and forbidden to reestablish or perpetuate itself. Instead, nature, in the form of parental affection, must be rudely repelled if the individual slave is to survive a life of labor without reward: in the unnatural state of slavery, everything — even the natural joy of parenting — is converted into labor (169). For the slave, before the "god" of the "master's interest" (gold), "all the laws of Nature must give way" (170). As was the case with Whitefieldian uncontainability, the black American here too reveals the limits of white democratic uncontainability.[45]

With this vision of nature's capitulation, the old nightmare narrative, history, reasserts itself, overwhelming James's benign vision of an innocent human society in the best of all possible worlds. The sight of the slave instantly converts James to the view that there is "no superintending power who conducts the moral operations of the world, as well as the physical," a statement that conveys the philosophical and historical limitations of his own pretense to moral superintendence (173). Instead, "civilized society" is "forever at war, forever jarring, forever producing some dangerous, some distressing extreme" (177). All are the predestined victims, whether past or future, of history which, as history itself attests, possesses a power infinitely greater than that of nature. By "perpetually" telling us of "crimes of the most heinous nature, committed from one end of the world to the other," history represents perpetuation as occurring not through repetition — measured, incremental, and progressive — but through violent revolution without end (173). Revolution is that historical force before which nature's benign aspects are deactivated while its savagery, embodied in human passion that observes no limits to its self-expression, is permitted to prevail.[46] In short, James's sight of the slave eradicates the difference between the Old World and the New that his minister had assured him justified his writing as it had motivated the Englishman's request for his letters:

> his imagination, instead of submitting to the painful and useless retrospect of revolutions, desolations, and plagues, would, on the contrary, wisely spring forward to the anticipated fields of future cultivation and improvement, to the future extent of those generations which are to re-

plenish and embellish this boundless continent. . . . Here he might contemplate the very beginnings and outlines of human society, which can
be traced nowhere now but in this part of the world. . . . Here we have in
some measure regained the ancient dignity of our species: our laws are
simple and just; we are a race of cultivators; our cultivation is unrestrained; and therefore everything is prosperous and flourishing. (43)

The unwelcome and involuntary revelation of the American invisible in the
ninth letter derails the teleology of James's narrative: we remark the repetition of questions in the ninth chapter beginning with the words, "To what
end?"

Forced to relinquish his narrative of normative American life, James must
relinquish his vision of his own representativeness, except to the extent that
he himself is transformed by an overwhelming external power into a slave.
The uncouth voice of the slave has instantly and without warning, like a thief
in the night, converted him to "the man of sorrows."[47] In the final letter,
passively awaiting the invasion of his peaceful neighborhood by revolutionary forces, he portrays himself as beyond community and hope, prey to the
consuming power of rumor, nightmare, and superstition. The representative
American farmer, the model for the Scots emigrant Andrew (whose naturalization is portrayed in chapter 3) and a nation of Andrews, describes himself
at the end as "tied" and "fastened by numerous strings," "a person of so little
weight and consequence [that his] energy and example are of no avail" (205,
204). Like the "living spectre" of the slave, the farmer refers to himself at the
end of his life's record as a "popular phantom," not an agent of empowerment but a means by which illegitimate power may be seized. The rough,
inarticulate voice of the slave in the cage suspends James's narrative by exposing it as precisely that which James and his wife initially feared it might
be, merely self-referential. Thus the narrative ends with a statement of the
American Farmer's anomalousness ("[n]ever was a situation so singularly
terrible as mine, in every possible respect") and a statement of the failure of
language before such singularity: "no relation can be equal to what we suffer
and what we feel" (201, 203). Not surprisingly, James's last authoritative act is
to free his own slaves; he gives them, unaccountably, the same sort of advice
he had given Andrew the Hebridean in a happier time: "be sober, frugal, and
industrious, and you need not fear earning a comfortable subsistence" (219).
Finally, instead of galvanizing the nation into conformity with itself through

the exemplary writer-farmer, James, who claims for himself the "innocence" of his own "insignificance," can only locate the obstacle to a narratively translatable coherence in an unreachable and inaudible, if deeply internal, otherness with which he — and through him Crèvecoeur, as Brown through Clara — fights a losing battle for control of the text (209).[48]

As Crèvecoeur conceived it in the benign character of Farmer James, democratic personality, although it simply and humbly discovers a rationale for speaking authoritatively and from immediate knowledge about a world unknown to the aristocratic Englishman, cannot be considered and does not itself aspire to be uncontainable. In the course of his narrative it becomes clear that, as a natural effect of the process by which Europeans become Americans and model Americanness for other Europeans, James's character possesses inherent curbs to excessive self-assertion in all his areas of endeavor. This natural tendency toward self-regulation to which James refers repeatedly in his opening letter occurs as the result of the European's insensible submission, as James describes it, to the formative forces at work in the new culture — a willingness to be molded by those who had come before, enacted within a "boundless" continent divided into "confined" fields of action and speculation (73, 43). James names farming in particular as among the "confined occupations" that flourish; the alternative for those who eschew submission to preestablished cultural norms is to congregate in the frontier settlements "remote from the power of example and check of shame" (71, 72). The power of example and the check of shame are operative as well in the domain of writing, represented by James's minister and wife respectively, as he is careful to point out by reproducing in his first letter the dialogue in which they collectively authorize him to write. The first letter intends a candid demonstration of the motives, fears, and principles that underlay his transformation into a writer and that otherwise might have remained unspoken, in order to let Mr. F.B. into "these primary secrets" that his wife counseled him to hide from the community (49). To the degree that he speaks as an author publicly and with authority, James insists that his uncontainability is domesticated — bound to the expectations of his wife, his minister, and the community. Moreover, he promises that his writing will not exceed the terms of his covenant with the English aristocrat: the latter will provide him with topics and determine the parameters of their correspondence. Exhibiting no wild outgrowth and springing no surprises, James's writing will be as natural as the cultivated field whose dimensions are known and whose production is not ungoverned but responsive to the cultivator's intentions. Above all, his decision to write constitutes no manifesto of independence and bears no evidence of proud singularity, of an ambition to overreach or extend the self; its justification is, explicitly, its representativeness and it advertises from the first its full awareness of the limitations to expression that representative status imposes. The farmer is thus doubly bound: to the one who authorizes him and to those he represents.

In contrast to this authorial model of a theoretical uncontainability domesticated by society and by covenant which until the ninth chapter reigns unchallenged, the slave in the cage represents an uncontainability that exists beyond covenant or contract, beyond the limits of formal observance, and that participates in no collective, constructive enterprise. As we have seen in other contexts for the emergence of democratic personality, an extremity of victimization corresponds with an extremity of power.[49] Once it emerges from invisibility and inaudibility, it appears to possess a mythic strength; it cannot be suppressed no matter what encumbrances are heaped upon it. As the afflicted spoke although the brimstone scalded their throats, as Whitefield spoke through the debilitating nausea, the racking doubt, and the jeers of the opposition, the slave overcomes his significant disadvantages in order to voice, in his most humble and polite request for poison, an unanswerable refutation of the American paradise James has so confidently asserted through eight letters. The slave's involuntary and unanticipated revelation of the nation's invisible content occurs when the farmer, "arrested by the power of affright and terror," involuntarily, as a random effect of the itinerancy undertaken in the name of demonstrating the representational adequacy of the visible, removes the veils hiding this content from his and his readership's sight (178). Despite the obstacles to being either seen or heard heaped upon him by his master — the slave is dying and in the process of being consumed alive; he is encaged; the cage is hidden by the bodies of birds who are devouring his flesh; the cage is suspended in the treetops in a dense forest far from any human habitation or possibility of salvation — his voice, feeble, uncouth, inarticulate, makes itself heard. As James initially hears it, it is almost indistinguishable from the forest's natural sounds. Then he realizes (his realization registered first in his involuntary trembling) that the natural sounds are in some way unnaturally combined: he feels an agitation of the air, hears the sound of the wings of birds fluttering as they try anxiously to land, and then makes out through the fluttering agitation a few inarticulate monosyllables, the same "strange human murmur" that Captain Vere will hear his crew make in the course of Billy Budd's execution and instinctively recognize as the sound of mutiny. Once uncovered, the slave speaks, and swiftly, intending nothing but his release from pain, undercuts the premise upon which the farmer's idyll had been so confidently erected: that in America a democratic social order had been uniformly established everywhere without opposi- tional violence through the practice of a domesticated uncontainability. The slave's representative truth shows that the farmer's enlightened formula- tions—the formulations of Crèvecoeur and the progressive American and European audiences his book delighted—are simply unsustainable, a new principle to which the farmer is instantly, and fatally for his narrative, converted.[50]

The slave in the cage powerfully represents both the threat and the allure, the nihilism and the moral primacy, the horrible complexity and the sublime simplicity of democratic personality as it was textualized in the postrevolu- tionary decades as a seemingly irrepressible element of a "new" American literature. On the one hand, this character, whose eruption into the text and domination of its meanings is unanticipated even by other characters con- fident of their control over themselves and their materials, possesses an irrefutable ethical legitimacy. In the case of Crèvecoeur's text, the slave, unlike the narrating farmer who is so careful to establish the humble terms and modest limits of his self-representation as if fearful of overstepping them, is altogether innocent of the desire to represent himself. Because the desire he articulates in his brief and broken soliloquy is for self-annihilation (he asks James first for water and then for poison), his speech cannot be construed as an instrument of self-aggrandizement. Encaged, observed but unobserving because the birds have pecked out his eyes, he is free from the obligation to seek vindication from the reader who stumbles into his domain and intrudes upon the privacy of his death. He has all the power of irrefutable being and none of the ambiguity attached to the act of representing himself and others for an anonymous readership. The sight of him disempowers the farmer who declares himself without the means or the strength to alleviate the slave's condition; he is unprepared to join the slave in his murderous in- nocence by "dispatching" him nor, given his conviction regarding the sanctity of transplantation, can he condemn him for having murdered. James's strength is finally sufficient only "to walk away" (178, 179). Rendered "motionless, involuntarily contemplating" the dreadful sight, the self-described humble and simple farmer is haunted by his guilty knowledge of this other voice which, according to his mandate to describe the small and unnoticed corners of the nation, he has already inscribed in his narrative (178). By the terms he has so carefully elaborated, the voice represents American experience as legitimately as his own, even if it was not elicited by the aristocratic Englishman but was instead independently spoken from within the space beyond formal observance. Once articulated, the voice of the slave establishes a standard of representative veracity to which James is constrained to conform; he cannot exclude the truth he accidentally discovers but can only accommodate himself to it, as the last chapter on "distress" makes clear.

Inarticulately, then, the slave belies the elaborate foundational premise of James's authorship: his claim to be and represent himself simultaneously, to encompass both author and character, historian and sufferer, governing and governed, actuality and fiction. Far from eliding the gap between being and representation that was so irksome to the late eighteenth-century sensibility (attached, Brown observed, to an "illusion of sincerity which we love to believe is the impulse which places the pen in the hand of an author"), the unexpected realization of democratic personality bestowed upon it an iconic significance enduringly obnoxious to an American cultural elite eager to establish a national literature that was to be both respectable and revolutionary.[51] American literary critical concerns would outlive the anxieties of the Federalist critics that "the *republick* of letters may have its dignity and prosperity endangered by sliding inadvertently into a *democracy*."[52] Yet even after the democratization (the professionalization) of the literary critical establishment, it would choose as its solution to the problem posed by democratic personality the one struck upon by Farmer James: to keep it alive, but to keep it in the cage — in the case of the American critical establishment, until it had been thoroughly domesticated to the purposes of American literary nationalism.[53]

SIX

An American Aesthetic of Innocence: Domesticating
Democratic Personality

In democracies, writers will be more afraid *of* the people, than afraid *for* them.

— FISHER AMES, *"American Literature"*

America, where representation is real. . . .

— CHARLES JARED INGERSOLL, *"Influence of America"*

The art of art . . . is simplicity.

— WALT WHITMAN, *"Preface to 1855 Edition of* Leaves of Grass"

We, my countrymen, have a character to establish.

— CANDIDUS[1]

The form-destroying opposition between containing and expanding subjectivities staged in and by early American fictions raised questions about authorial power — its extent and its legitimacy — whose implications were by no means confined to the literary register. The ethical ambivalence attached to the authorial position with its assumption of the right and the power to emplot, represent, and interpret, bolstered by a fear of fiction as an insidious counterfeit of the real, reflected broad sociopolitical anxieties about democratic insurgency and democratic value, the twin legacies of revolutionary ideology to early national culture. In a range of cultural documents, including literary-critical and fictional texts, fears of social and political leveling coexist tensely with an ideological commitment not just to egalitarianism but, increasingly in the first decades of the nineteenth century, to the common as the locus of national-cultural authenticity. The specter of democracy haunted both republican and protoliberal elements of postrevolutionary culture and would continue unabated through the transition from a republican to a liberal ethos. Although extensive historiographical attention has been given to the political and socioeconomic aspects of this transition, its impact upon the evolving national literature project, with its deep questioning of what I have called the ontology of representation and its concomitant suggestion of a democratic literary ethic, has not been systematically analyzed.[2]

The problem may be broached by examining the development through the first half of the nineteenth century of an American aesthetic of innocence, through which democratic personality would be recognized and eventually rehabilitated (domesticated) as the essence of genuine American character and thus the exemplary subject—both representing and represented—of the national literature. The domestication of democratic personality occurred as the ongoing literary-critical invention of the American common man based on the elaboration of this figure in colonial religious and political thought.[3] Early American fictions had registered the deep ambiguity of the common man, dreadful for his subversive power and alluring for his irrefutable truth, to those ambitious to transcribe Americanness into literature. The novels of Charles Brockden Brown, Stephen Burroughs, Hector St. John de Crèvecoeur, and (as Christopher Looby has recently suggested) Hugh Henry Brackenridge had staged the confrontation (tragically and comically inflected) of an authorial character or first-person narrator with a character who personified "the radical democratic imagination."[4] Vocally volatile and socially marginal, enacting a representative power or legitimacy greater than the narrator's, and thus possessed of a potentially uncontainable constituency, such characters bear witness to the transfer from the cultural to the literary register of democratic personality in postrevolutionary America. The literary representation of this distinctive presence in the American cultural landscape entailed the novel's internalization of the oppositional space from which democratic personality had emerged, making novelistic space coextensive with democratic space and thereby paradoxically reifying what in its cultural manifestations had always been transitory and episodic. The generation of uncontainable fictional subjectivities and the specter of a self-indicted authorship strongly mark the early American novel. Possessing an uncanny authority and the power to shatter the formal integrity of the text from within the represented world, such characters implicitly or explicitly challenged received ideas about the authorial mandate to represent, stimulating a primary but abortive manifestation of an aesthetic of innocence: we may regard Clara Wieland's claim to the contingent status of character or victim, and thus to innocent (nonconsensual) authorship through humble self-enlargement, in this light. Beyond a general fear of fiction, early American authors (and authorial characters) were thus a peculiarly embattled lot, having found themselves somehow powerless to cap the implications of their own fictions, vocalized by their own fictional personages, as if fiction were not a contingent reality wholly dependent on the will of a creator. Thus did representation in and of itself prove incompatible with containment. The paucity of fictional attempts to render Americanness in literature in the years between Brown and Cooper and the accelerating critical demand for such fictions speak to the immensity of the challenge democratic personality as the object of literary representation presented to authors and their fictional personae.

Novelistic attempts in the postrevolutionary period to represent and contain this figure ceded to literary-critical speculation on the relationship of commonness to culture. As we have seen in previous chapters, speculation on this topic was not unique to the nineteenth century, nor was it unique to America. Early national and antebellum critical musings on commonness drew indiscriminately on the premises of a number of American and foreign theories or literary representations of its cultural value, including Puritan plain speech, republican simplicity and the agrarian ideal, the "elocutionary revolution" in rhetoric and oratory initiated in Glasgow, the varieties of European Romantic nationalisms arising from the German discovery of the cultural work of the "folk," Jacksonian democratic ideology, and American frontier mythology.[5] Regarded as a coherent cultural project, the avalanche of critical pronouncements on the relationship of commonness to culture reveal the degree to which the effort to domesticate democratic personality coincided with what Benjamin T. Spencer has described as a "vast evangelism for a national literature."[6] The composite theoretical image of domesticated democratic personality governed the figuration of Americanness in literature as well as the actual production and reception of a national literature. James Fenimore Cooper's Leatherstocking novels are particularly instructive in this regard. The internal coherence and interpenetration of both projects (the invention of the common man and the invention of the national literature) is confirmed by what became the governing paradox of their composite portrait of domesticated democratic personality: increasingly proposed in fiction and criticism as the one destined to redress the continuing absence of a national literature, the common man was nevertheless imagined to be profoundly inarticulate. Culminating in Emerson's prescriptions for an authentic American poetry, the liberal critical elite celebrated the common man's speechlessness, his unconscious self-exemption from the conditions of discourse, as that trait which ensured the purity of the national essence he embodied and that he would one day transcribe into poetry.[7] As critical practice, the aesthetic of innocence thus begins by identifying domesticated democratic personality with essential American character. It ends by requiring American authors (as a type of secular trial of the signs of regenerate national authorship) not to represent but to embody that character in order to elide the gap between being and representation and engender thereby an innocent, because agentless, literary art.

Looking back to the genesis of *Leaves of Grass*, Walt Whitman, like a redeemed Carwin resurrected as Whitefield, articulated the "I, yet not I" characteristic of the voice situated in the space between being and representation. "I saw from the time my enterprise and questionings positively shaped themselves (how best can I express my own distinctive era and surroundings, America, Democracy?)," he wrote in "A Backward Glance O'er Travel'd Roads,"

> that the trunk and centre whence the answer was to radiate, and to which all should return from straying however far a distance, must be an identical body and soul, a personality — which personality, after many considerations and ponderings I deliberately settled should be myself — indeed could not be any other.[8]

But the distinctive expression of the self as the truest representation of America and Democracy does not issue from the individual as his own distinctive voice. Instead, Whitman ponders whether the intervening years themselves

> with their aggregate of our New World doings and people, have not, indeed, created and formulated the foregoing leaves — forcing their utterance as the pages stand — coming actually from the direct urge and developments of those years, and not from any individual epic or lyrical attempts whatever, or from my pen or voice, or any body's special voice.

> Out of that supposition, the book might assume to be consider'd an au-
> tochthonic record and expression, freely render'd, of and out of these 30
> to 35 years — of the soul and evolution of America — and of course, by re-
> flection, not ours only, but more or less of the common people of the
> world. . . .[9]

Compelled by the aggregate, the utterance produces itself in an act of agentless poetry, cleanly expressing not the evolution of one man's soul but that of
the universal common.

The aesthetic of innocence thus emerged as a problematic critical strategy which sought to elide the gap between being and representation, author
and character, toward the production of an inclusive, truthful, and innocent national literature. Its practitioners intended to obviate the danger of
democratic personality by domesticating it, taming its characteristic uncontainability, and then reclaiming it as and for essential American character,
especially the character of the aspiring national author. Authorship was thus
reconceived as a kind of passive activity, the author making of himself a
conduit for the articulation of essence, that precluded the possibility of misrepresentation because it could finally make confident claim to a universality
of reference. In section I of this chapter, I will examine the critical debates
attending the identification of essential American character (including the
character of the future American poet) with commonness, simplicity, and the
absence of a will to power enacted as a withdrawal from the economic and
political life of the nation. Such accounts mark the inception of a democratic
literary aesthetic, where "democratic" refers not to the volatility and uncontainability of democratic personality so destructive in early American fictions
but rather to the attempt to supersede those traits by invoking the rationality
of a republican egalitarianism, a romantic celebration of nature, and a liberal
individualism. A reading of Cooper's *Last of the Mohicans* and *The Pioneers*
occupies section II, which analyzes these novels as efforts to enact the domestication of democratic personality, first by associating it with the principled
self-containment of Native Americans, and second, by representing the nat-
uralistic transfer of that quality to white, liberal America. The chapter's final
section reviews the efforts of some post-Jacksonian writers to identify domesticated democratic personality with authorship in an ultimate attempt to
elide the gap between being and representation. No longer the truest repre-

sentative of the simple and speechless common man, the author himself became that figure. Here is the legacy of Clara Wieland's ingenious, fraudulent "as if" — her strategy of a secularized antinomianism to instantiate an innocent authorial practice — to our classic American literature.

I

The task of domesticating democratic personality was undertaken in the early national and antebellum eras on two fronts: the fictional (including epic and lyric poetry), whereby the aspiring American author would portray reconstructed or domesticated democratic personality as a model for exemplary American character, including authorial character; and the metafictional, whereby the literary-critical establishment collectively formulated a eugenic critical aesthetic, geared to a prospective rather than a realized authorial practice, in which domesticated democratic personality was likewise formulaically prescribed as the touchstone of authentic American authorship. The task would not be fulfilled until 1855 when its fictional and metafictional constituents — its prescriptive portrayals of the genuine American author and exemplary American character, of representer and represented — coincided in Walt Whitman's *Leaves of Grass*. With its composition, Whitman claimed to be the poet of "Democracy" insofar as he had poetically annulled the gap between being and representation, self and other, silence and speech, and in so doing had put an end to the critical practice of attempting "to create an American literature by prescription."[10] By 1855, that is, domesticated democratic personality would be realized in literature as the integrated subjectivity of the democratic poet, whose unprecedented accomplishment was to comprise both creator and created (author and character), and who thus elided the breach between being and representation, American experience and American expression, that had gaped so threateningly in postrevolutionary fiction. Although in *Democratic Vistas* (1871) Whitman would represent himself not as the democratic poet but as a cultural critic frustrated with the continuing absence of a national literature, in the 1855 preface to *Leaves of Grass* he self-consciously announced himself as the American "common man" in his "indescribable freshness and unconsciousness," an identity that explicitly legitimated his efforts to represent that figure in and as the national poem.[11] Moreover, because the common man was put forward as representative of the nation's life in all its aspects, the poet's persona, "Walt Whitman, a kosmos," explicitly embraced through his poetic inventories America's manifold contradictions: one finds no specters in "Song of Myself" — indeed, in the entirety of *Leaves of Grass* — unless it be the boldly proclaimed spectral omnipresence of the poet himself.[12]

From the early national period, the problem of the continuing absence of a national literature was explained in part by the critical proposition that it was the common rather than the cultured class from which a genuine national-cultural expression would arise. A broad range of writers and critics promoted this explanation despite theoretical disagreements on such fundamental questions as what constituted literature and what role it would play in the development of a national culture. They collectively proposed that the common people's distance from the centers of culture — what George Steiner would call (in another, similar context) the "innocence of remoteness" — had preserved their characterological purity, their essential Americanness.[13] This purity was negatively manifested in the common man's exemplary trait, his inarticulateness (alternately, his silence), a characteristic which, if it confirmed his innocence of culture as an accretion fundamentally foreign to being, was patently incompatible with authorship. By the 1840s, a circular rationale was devised for this paradox of inarticulate authorship: the ideal American poet was perceived to be absent because he was inarticulate, to be inarticulate because he was simple, and to be simple because he was true — true to his essential Americanness that he was destined to reveal to the nation and the world, true to nature, true to his own unaccountable, original, and unself-conscious genius. If his genius had not yet spoken, the poet, remote from the hue and cry over the continuing absence of a national literature, would attain to speech naturally and in his own good time, safe from external influences with their partial and coercive interests. The centrality of this concept of inarticulate authorship, devised to explain the continuing absence of the national literature, thus risked perpetuating America's "literary delinquency."[14] It was as a means of confirming the central assumptions of the aesthetic of innocence while transcending the poetic impasse it inadvertently produced that Whitman offered his poetry — in particular to Emerson, whose essay "The Poet" (1844) constitutes the lyrical and conceptual culmination of an ideology of poetic innocence.

As an explanation for literary absence, then, by the 1840s the aesthetic of innocence both solicited and suppressed literary production by elaborating in advance a radically paradoxical formula for authentic national authorship seemingly impossible for any aspiring writer to fulfill. Beyond the qualifications tied to simplicity — primarily an innocence of culture and of language — there obtruded between the aspiring author and critical recognition of his work the problem of national character. According to the aesthetic of innocence, the ideal American poet would be recognized by his perfect exemplification of the national character; national character, however, could only be discovered through its realization in his work. There are two points of difficulty here. One inheres in the qualifier "national," a cipher that bred circular definitions, as in Henry Wadsworth Longfellow's less than clarifying statement, "when we say that the literature of a country is *national*, we mean that it bears upon it the stamp of national character."[15] The other difficulty is that the aesthetic of innocence proposes national character to be the defining attribute of authentic authorship and thus, along with making authorship contingent on character, implicitly posits both as contingent upon the national literature for their realization. Beyond the paradox of inarticulate authorship, then, the aesthetic of innocence proposed as a theoretical ideal a national poetry that, far from having been produced by the poet, was itself productive of him, a central qualification acknowledged in Whitman's promise to his reader in the 1855 preface to *Leaves of Grass* that "[w]hat I experience or portray shall go from my composition without a shred of my composition."[16] The poet would remain wordless while invisible and inaudible truths articulated themselves through him as a kind of sacred ventriloquism to a waiting nation.

What ended with the democratic poet as a "kosmos," a "compend of compends," began in the early national era with a profound and enduring sense that whatever was required to establish a consensual national-cultural identity through literature — whether romantic associations or incidents, a system of patronage, time-honored critical institutions, an epic history, an aristocracy, national costumes, class diversity — was, in the United States, utterly absent.[17] Whether regarded positively as unlimited possibility, or negatively as a daunting and ineluctable blankness, this absence was typically attributed to a double-edged experience of cultural marginality.[18] On the one hand, marginality resulted from the external circumstance of Euro-

pean, and especially British, linguistic and cultural domination, portrayed
as a malevolent ventriloquism that precluded the possibility of the new nation producing anything other than the mere echo of another's voice. As
William Ellery Channing expressed it in 1830, "Books are already among
the most powerful influences here. The question is, Shall Europe, through
these, fashion us after its pleasure? Shall America be only an echo of what
is thought and written under the aristocracies beyond the ocean?"[19] On
the other hand, marginality referred to the internal circumstance of a large
and culturally nondescript class — the democratic and anonymous mass —
whom many of the elites perceived as powerfully, if passively, resistant to
the materialization of a distinctive and vital national culture through the
offices of a national literature, and in relation to whom they would assert
(albeit with decreasing confidence as the decades passed) their own cultural
centrality.

The historian Francis Parkman, reviewing a new edition of Cooper's
works issued shortly before the writer's death in 1851, articulated the enduring crisis of confidence which the double-edged experience of cultural marginality produced among the educated elite.[20] Having opened his essay with
a eulogistic portrait of Cooper as a model of "that rude transatlantic nature"
so enchanting to Europeans — his genius drawn "from the soil where God
had planted it . . . rough and gnarled, but strong as a mountain cedar" —
Parkman concludes by lamenting the "nerveless and unproductive" character of "the best educated among us" compared with "the unschooled classes
of the people" which alone were capable of giving rise to a vigorous national
life (358, 376, 375):

> Some French writer — Chateaubriand, we believe — observes that the
> only portion of the American people who exhibit any distinctive national
> character are the backwoodsmen of the West. The remark is not strictly
> true. The whole merchant marine, from captains to cabin-boys, the lum-
> bermen of Maine, the farmers of New England, and indeed all the labor-
> ing population of the country, not of foreign origin, are marked with
> strong and peculiar traits. But when we ascend into the educated and po-
> lished classes these peculiarities are smoothed away, until, in many cases,
> they are invisible. An educated Englishman is an Englishman still; an ed-
> ucated Frenchman is often intensely French; but an educated American
> is apt to have no national character at all. (374–75)

Thirty-seven years earlier, Walter Channing had voiced the same fear more starkly: "Unfortunately for this country," he wrote in the prestigious *North American Review*, "there is no national character, unless its absence constitute one."[21] But if there was significant agreement among the influential class that, contrary to appearances, the "men of greatest influence are those who have studied men before they studied books," those who "boldly following out the bent of their native genius, have hewed their own way to wealth, station, or knowledge from the plowshare or the forecastle," such men nevertheless remained apart and incommunicado, sequestered in "the deep rich soil at the bottom of society" and yet "seen every where."[22]

Precisely what was seen depended, predictably, on the ideological bent of the seer. On the one hand, as Gordon Wood has pointed out, in the wake of the Revolution patriot "writers and critics, themselves gentlemen, delighted in posing as simple farmers or ploughjoggers in attacking the aristocratic pretensions and duplicity of other gentlemen . . . all the while citing in support of their arguments eighteenth-century writers from Richardson to Rousseau who were increasingly celebrating the moral virtue of sincerity, or the strict correspondence of appearance and reality, action and intention."[23] On the other hand, conservative critics of the early national era had considered and rejected the allure of simplicity as a means to establish a "perspective from absence," a point from which literary delinquency might be evenly assessed and a fresh national-literary effort initiated.[24] Charles Brockden Brown, having forsworn novel writing for literary criticism and cultural commentary as editor of the *Monthly Magazine and American Review*, observed in 1806 that American critics were seeking out literary models "for art is now suspended on a point; if by our dexterity we preserve not the equilibrium, if we pass or decline from the point, we slide into barbarism."[25] But he rejected as "pernicious" the notion that a "natural" or untutored genius might function as a model for American literary creation as "some daring spirits [who] scorn the mandates of taste" had proposed:

> At this period some, enamoured of the illusive idea of *original powers*, pretend to draw merely from the fountains of nature. Uneducated artists occasionally appear among the lower occupations of life, who are immediately received as original geniuses. But it is at length perceived, that the genuine requisites of poetry, at this period of refinement, are not only beyond their reach, but often beyond their comprehension. These

inspired geniuses have never survived the transient season of popular wonder, and generally derive their mediocrity from the facility of consulting the finished compositions of true genius. I know of no exception to this observation.[26]

Several months earlier, Brown had defended the ideal of refinement against those who detected in the concept something "censurable." "Refinement may indeed be vicious," he remarked, "as simplicity may be; refinement is not less offensive to a reader of taste, when it rises into affectation, than simplicity sinking into insipidity. But we must not confound refinement of style with its puerile excess, nor is it just to censure refinement because it differs from simplicity."[27]

For conservative critics like Brown who rejected the idea that the uneducated would model true genius for the elite, it was not just the fact that simplicity was by definition unrefined that constituted a threat to the national literature project. More insidiously, the vogue of simplicity threatened the "elegant tranquillity of literary life" enjoyed by a "few literary men" by encouraging the untutored "to erect themselves into literary censors, whom the divinities of Helicon have not anointed"; to permit those who possessed no "deep and thorough acquaintance with ancient authorities and established principles" to determine literary value was to make "the clamour of the moment" the basis for judgment.[28] The positive valuation of simplicity foretold a situation in which the critical establishment would "learn of the multitude what to admire, instead of teaching them what is admirable."[29] Simplicity, that is, might betray an unexpected will to cultural power. In the notorious absence in America of established literary institutions, only a cultural elite vigilant against "the innovating spirit of the times" could forestall the dreaded slide into a democracy of letters. As it was rhetorically elaborated, the scene of vigilance was one familiar from 1692 or 1740: like the specter or the itinerant enthusiast, the innovating spirit, if tolerated, would realize itself as it always had, "in the form of an angel of light," which "in the hour of tranquillity and sleep [would] plan[t] itself by the publick ear, forging illusions for the fancy" in order to promote a fatal leveling of the culture.[30] A clear avatar of democratic personality, the innovating spirit, a counterfeit angel of light, would claim as its authority "the voice of the people," thus, according to the maxim, "the voice of God": "Of all flattery," Fisher Ames snarled, "the grossest (gross indeed to blasphemy)."[31]

The critical writings of Edward Tyrell Channing, Harvard's Boylston Professor of Rhetoric and Oratory (from 1819), mentor to Emerson and Thoreau, and, with his brothers Walter and William Ellery Channing, a frequent contributor to Boston's *North American Review*, exemplify the early critical ambiguity toward the common as ideal subject of a national literature and demonstrate as well the limitations placed upon its usefulness by a class both deeply suspicious and tentatively enamored of it. In "On Models in Literature" (1816), Channing attempted to examine the relationship that obtained between American critics and authors as a way of understanding America's literary delinquency.[32] Whereas many commentators on America's literary backwardness attributed it to the national obsession (whether by necessity or from vulgar acquisitiveness) with economic growth and political stability, Channing speculated on the stifling effects of a bourgeois critical establishment temperamentally unable to differentiate practical from artistic modes and frames of reference and who thus applied irrelevant evaluative criteria not just to actual literary works but most destructively to their creators.[33] Because the critical "tribunals and judges . . . laugh at the folly of encouraging men in the indolent luxuries and unprofitable excesses of imagination and feeling when we were sent here to work, to be useful, to conquer the vices, and bring home the wanderings of the mind," they remained blind to "the real which is very often in the neighbourhood" and which is both the true object as well as the true subject of national literary endeavor (154–55). The "real" comprises both what (and whom) the author will write about and who the author is; he remained invisible to the critical eye of the learned philistine because as a subject he was, paradoxically, both profoundly anomalous (a "genius" as opposed to an "imitator") and yet indistinguishable from the undistinguished mass within which, "in the streets or workshops," he might be discovered (157, 155).

As epigraph to his article, Channing selected Wordsworth's poetry which, with its "republican simplicity," provided the sanction of European romanticism for three notions that would become increasingly central to critical speculation concerning authorial absence: that "Nature was at [the poet's] heart"; that therefore "he knew not" precisely what the "fashionable criticks [who] lay up a little poetry or wit for conversation's sake, or at least to gild their affectation" thought he should know; and that the effect of Nature's power on the heart of "foolish simplicity" was to "wean him" from the practical concerns of national development that were everywhere so pressing

(154, 155).[34] Indeed, his isolation from and even ignorance of the seats of power — governmental, industrial, mercantile, cultural — constituted the poet's natal environment within which he thrived. To remove him from the "unconfined seclusion" within which "he has lived and rioted from infancy" and to place him in society would be tantamount to incarcerating him in a "cell . . . in the inquisition, in some large city, where the tread of the tormentor is heard above and the laughter of the world without the walls" (155). The discourse of the genius and his companions was likewise characterized by a "freedom and infant fearlessness as if they were alone in the world and had all to themselves." Yet, because his speech issued "from the heart," it was universally comprehensible, except to the very class responsible for discerning the poet's presence, the critics, whose profound imitativeness ("cautious, constrained, and modelled throughout") rendered them peculiarly unfit to carry out their self-appointed task (157).

Yet Channing, too, has difficulty rendering a positive description of the author, the spectral common-man protagonist of his own fiction about an innocent literary genesis in the visible-invisible realm of the real. The article is largely given over instead to a psychologically detailed negative portrait of the critical imitator. He is a "worshipper" rather than "an equal"; "infected with books"; liable to substitute "finish and elegance" for "freedom and originality"; intellectually parasitical; arrogant in his philistinism (157, 158). As Channing details the shortcomings of the critical class, upon whom the success of the national literary enterprise of necessity largely depended, he refrains from detailing the character of the genius, perhaps because, as Dostoevsky had observed in a jeremiad directed against a cultural elite also divorced from and thus ignorant of the rich source of Russian genius, "simplicity is the enemy of analysis."[35] To compensate for his own unfamiliarity with the streets and the workshop, Channing employs the language of European romantic nationalism to portray American genius and then tries to claim the exotic creature for domesticity. Apostrophizing a hybrid of his genteel reader and his free-spirited poet, Channing finds him living anonymously in his native ambience and speaking "a tale of childhood" — "the hoarse and wild musick of your forests and sea-shore"; "the frantick superstition of your fathers"; "the lovely fairy scenes that lie far back in the mists of your fable" (160, 161). His is "the language that God has given [him]," a "rough torrent," that can avoid transmutation into "a strange idiom" only if the temptation to mix it with foreign elegance is resisted and the roughness permitted to be voiced (161). Aside from the labile identity of his addressee, Channing's unease is also apparent in his tendency to locate the only legitimate model for a national poetic idiom in the past, with "the very fathers of poetry" who lived in "the rougher and more intrepid ages . . . before men troubled themselves about elegance or plan and wrote right on as they felt" (162).

At one point, Channing expresses a residual fear that this unknown and as yet unheard voice at the heart of American experience may, once recognized and released from its unconfined isolation, articulate "dangerous novelties" that will prove "popular and contagious" (161). In a review written three years later of William Dunlap's biography of Charles Brockden Brown, Channing made more explicit his reservations concerning the common classes as providing a ground upon which to erect a national literature. Switching from apostrophe to analysis, from celebration to condemnation, the self-flagellating critic of the earlier article appears in the later as a responsible and displeased superintendent of culture. "If we admit that there is here a *lower class*," Channing maintained,

> its peculiarity would not be found in character so much as in vulgarity of manners and narrowness of opinion; and a foreigner would be as little delighted as ourselves with the most lively record of corrupt speech, of coarse or indelicate customs, of sturdy insolence towards the rich, and indifference or contempt for those who consented to be poor, where competency was so easy and so privileged.[36]

Such a characterless class whose very existence was arguable exerted an influence "scarcely felt amongst ourselves," the literary class, and thus could provide no foundation for writers whose object must be "to present what exists" (121, 120). Yet Channing could find no artistic nourishment either in the middle class ("a large and invaluable order, composed of sensible, industrious, upright men, whose whole experience seems at war with adventure") or in the American aristocracy which possessed "little of the exclusive spirit of an established order" and for that reason was insufficiently "distinct" and "various" to be useful to literature (121, 122).[37] Aesthetically situated between the desert of the American "real" and the mirage of its autochthonous genius, Channing's admiration for Brown derived from his having created a larger-than-life reality which, if it "seems too near," is yet unambiguously divorced from "our common every-day life" which "hardly offers materials as yet for a long story." The "chief interest" for the readers of Brown's novels, Channing asserted, lies "not in the events, nor [is] at all dependent upon the conviction that we ever saw the place or the man" (124, 122, 123). Thus did Channing more wholeheartedly approve the unfamiliarity of the "singular or improbable character" of Brown's novels who had eluded the limitations of the real (in particular, the realities of class) than he did the common man defamiliarized as the representative genius of American culture. Channing's meditation on literary absence thus leads him to a hypothetical typology of authorial character that manages to be both prescriptive and solicitous, intrigued and alienated.

The implicit premise of both Channing's essays is that the common or "real" exists on the far side of a threshold of visibility or influence which almost wholly obscures the critical class's perception of its existence. This barrier to access acquires a rich moral dimension in the two essays whose valence depends on whether Channing envisions a lower class comprised of the vulgar multitude or of inspired naïfs. The first essay suggests that far from renouncing the practice of modeling to redress its literary barrenness, the educated class should model itself upon the unconscious producers of a natural, domestic poetry. It then situates foolish simplicity in tantalizing proximity to its would-be disciples, but encloses it within some "unconfined seclusion" whose invisible walls, transparent to those who frolic within, bar those most in need of peering into Nature's heart and hearing God's strange idiom. The second essay, barely conceding the physical existence of the lower class, locates it beyond the possibility of influencing a critical class eager for knowledge of "what exists" as just punishment for the stubborn unloveliness of the vulgar and their immunity to example or opportunity. This rigorous segregation of the literati from the source of the real, now protective, now punitive, illuminates a question that would continue to bedevil the aestheticians of innocence: to paraphrase Leo Tolstoy, "Are the uneducated to learn to write from us? or, are we to learn to write from the uneducated?" (Tolstoy unhesitatingly endorsed the latter alternative.)[38]

Discoursing before the American Philosophical Society in 1823 on the "influence of America on the mind," critic and novelist Charles Jared Ingersoll conspicuously attempted to evade this issue by declaring that "philosophy, the sciences, and the useful arts . . . establish their empire in the modern republic of letters" naturally because the republican "mind is free from power or fear."[39] His vision of culture as a self-established empire of learning recalls the benign "indifference" of Crèvecoeur's America before his fall into history as well as Edwards's expectation that a voluntary social uniformity would provide the visible sign of a spiritually redeemed community. No pocket of backwardness or resistance complicates his image of "millions of educated and thinking people spreading from the bay of Fundy to the mouth of the Columbia . . . over a surface of almost two thousand miles square," an extensive "auditory" whose initial ethnic and linguistic differences had yielded to "the English ascendancy by voluntary fusion" (244, 258, 245); no "material provincialisms or peculiarities of dialect" inflect the harmony (244). In his 1830 response to Ingersoll's discourse, William Ellery Channing took issue with his vision of an undifferentiated American auditory.[40] Perfunctorily acknowledging the virtue of a Christian-republican ideal of simplicity, he nevertheless distinguished a "noble intellectual brotherhood" who produce words from "the laboring part of society" who receive them, in the process becoming "a generous race of men" (344, 350, 346):

> We are aware that some may think that we are exalting intellectual above moral and religious influence. They may tell us that the teaching of moral and religious truth, not by philosophers and boasters of wisdom, but by the comparatively weak and foolish, is the great means of renovating the world. This truth we indeed regard as "the power of God unto salvation." But let none imagine that its chosen temple is an uncultivated mind, and that it selects, as its chief organs, the lips of the unlearned. (348)

To the noble intellectual brotherhood belongs "the great duty of quickening the mass," not through the democratic medium of oratory but by realizing "the national mind in writing" (361, 346). If Channing's vision is less sanguine than Ingersoll's, the indelible line of class division he draws through the latter's primal republican integrity is softened by his belief in "the diffusiveness of intellect" (356): "here the different classes of society flow together and act powerfully on each other, and a free communication, elsewhere unknown, is established between the gifted few and the many" (356). The impalpable barriers that segregated the cultivated from the common and precluded the pedagogical relationship of master and student (however the identities of these two functionaries were imagined) in Edward Tyrell's account are in William Ellery's gently bridged.

Channing, then, restores to Ingersoll's picture of a natural and agentless self-cultivation of the American masses the distinctively eugenic impulse present in American literary-critical discourse from the earliest discussions of literary delinquency and literary mission. Consider Joseph S. Buckminster's 1809 articulation, before Harvard's Phi Beta Kappa Society, of the chronic prolepsis that would stubbornly remain at the heart of the American critical enterprise into the postbellum era: "The men of letters who are to direct our taste, mould our genius, and inspire our emulation," he informed his young audience, "the men, in fact, whose writings are to be the depositories of our national greatness, have not yet shown themselves to the world."[41] ("I look in vain for the poet whom I describe," Emerson lamented in 1844, while thirty years later Whitman expressed his "dejection and amazement" that the poetic material of America remained "entirely uncelebrated, unexpress'd."[42]) The task of American literary criticism was of necessity less directed to the productions of men of letters than to the formation of their characters in advance of their writing: in this spirit, Buckminster recommends that his youthful auditory avoid the twin pitfalls of literary exhibitionism, the practice of making oneself an object of public spectacle as "the mere man of curious erudition," and literary isolationism, the "crime" of "unprofitableness" with its attendant malaise, the "solitary diseases of the imagination."[43] Almost twenty years later, when Emerson similarly stood before a group of Dartmouth undergraduates to proclaim "There are few masters or none," he would unequivocally recommend literary isolationism — "[s]ilence, seclusion, austerity" — as that form of "asceticism" best calculated to position the would-be poet or "scholar" to receive "the free spirit which gladly utters itself through him."[44] Offering a famously vigorous defense of self-culture as conducive to the production of a selfless poetry, for which the poetic self functions as a neutral conduit for the articulation of invisible truths ("an unobstructed channel [through which] the soul now easily and gladly flows" [113]), Emerson's essays between his Dartmouth address and "The Poet" also provide a detailed account of the future poet's situation, psychology, and development.

"Come now, let us go and be dumb. Let us sit with our hands on our mouths," Emerson counsels Dartmouth's young, literary gentlemen. "Let us live in corners, and do chares, and suffer, and weep, and drudge, with eyes and hearts that love the Lord" (110). Channing's fanciful notion of the simple poet residing in unconfined seclusion is here revisited as the "dear hermitage of nature" within which the aspiring poet is urged to "retire, and hide; lock the door; shut the shutters; then welcome falls the imprisoning rain" (110). (And just as Channing intimated that the poet's unconfined seclusion might exist under the noses of the myopic urban class, Emerson notes that "independence of spirit" rather than "insulation of place" is the main object: "it is only as the garden, the cottage, the forest, and the rock are a sort of mechanical aids to this, that they are of value" [109]). The scholar's apprenticeship is one of voluntary labor through which he will achieve self-discipline: "The good scholar will not refuse to bear the yoke in his youth; to know, if he can, the uttermost secret of toil and endurance; to make his own hands acquainted with the soil by which he is fed, and the sweat that goes before comfort and luxury" (113). Far from alienating "the waiting world" by withdrawing from it, and appearing to hide one's thoughts, Emerson protests that one may as well attempt to "[h]ide the sun and moon. Thought is all light, and publishes itself to the universe. It will speak, though you were dumb, by its own miraculous organ. It will flow out of your actions, your manners, and your face" (116).

Moreover, the scholar who assumes the laborer's life only proves thereby his title to "the man of genius," whose destiny, despite temporary appearances, is to "occupy the whole space between God or pure mind, and the multitude of uneducated men. He must draw from the infinite Reason, on one side; and he must penetrate into the heart and sense of the crowd, on the other" (113). In a powerful critique of "Literary Ethics" printed in the *Boston Quarterly Review*, Orestes Brownson (who would the following year publish his proto-Marxist analysis of the plight of the American proletariat, "The Laboring Classes") takes Emerson to task for not taking seriously his own key point, that the poet must come from within "the really living, moving, toiling and sweating, joying and sorrowing people," and serve as "their representative, their impersonation."[45] Poets "will come not because we seek them, and they will be produced not in consequence of any specific discipline we may prescribe," but rather because "there is a work for them to do, and in consequence of the fact that the people are every where struggling to perform that work" (23). To understand this work as a call to live apart, remove oneself from the press of business, hold lone reveries, observe sunrises and sunsets, and contemplate the production of a national literature, was to misunderstand the meaning of "impersonation" and to betray that one lacks "an end to which his scholarship serves as a means" (26, 24). In effect, Brownson accuses Emerson of promoting narcissism over the real work of "secur[ing] the complete triumph of the democracy": the true poet will be "the glass which concentrates the rays of greatness scattered through the minds and hearts of the people; not the central sun from which they radiate" (26, 20). Brownson's poet alone will realize through the uncorrupted channel of his soul "the national spirit"; Emerson's, eager to show that he is "above the vulgar herd, and too profound to be comprehended," is more concerned to establish a "literary caste" with supervisory powers over "the drudges" than he is to establish an American literature (22).

As an alternative to imputing to Emerson a deplorable bad faith, one detects in "Literary Ethics" a response to the prosaic nature of the everyday, what Emerson had called in a letter to Carlyle "the terrible *is*," a domain that Edward Tyrell Channing had characterized as "too stubbornly familiar and unpoetical" to inspire literary interest.[46] In this domain, the lack of obscurity itself constituted an opacity: the openness of American society, like the grandeur of American nature which also resisted literary transcription, frustrated those critics and aspiring writers most ambitious for a national literature. It led them to contemplate the mystery of a life beyond culture as they defined it that, despite their efforts and its transparency, they knew only negatively, as a resistance to their programs for cultural development or transformation. It was perhaps this lack of positive knowledge, the intriguing idea of a life lived beyond the bounds of representation or at least its conventions, that suggested the possibility that the common people might provide the solution to rather than the crux of the national literature problem. Might it be possible to posit some correlation between the apparent formlessness of common life and the continuing failure of a national literature to materialize? For those "tenacious of national character," attempts to theorize such a correlation were typically situated between these poles of possibility: either the common people embodied the national essence which they had unwittingly preserved in its historical strength and purity or they represented a social and conceptual vacuity which must be either redressed or dismissed before a world-class national culture could emerge.[47] Stated as a literary imperative, either inherited literary forms had somehow to be adapted to — if not wholly reformed by — common life and in so doing made truly "native," or the people's continuing unrepresentability must be recognized, once and for all, as final confirmation of their cultural irrelevance.

II

The practice of literary criticism as literary eugenics, which the generally proleptic viewpoint of the critical class encouraged, was a key feature of the aesthetic of innocence. The commitment to redressing literary absence eugenically, through the prescriptive practice of establishing the moral character of legitimate authorship in advance of its individual realization, was not unique to political and cultural conservatives who expressed fears of the authoring common man as the next instantiation of democratic personality. Those inclined to associate the common man with a virtue either of character or of principle were equally invested in enriching the hypothetical portrait of "the People's men" as a national-literary beau ideal: "plain and of consequence less disguised, . . . less intriguing, more sincere" than their social betters.[48] Such portraits, of course, mandate rather than observe the people's sincerity. Not surprisingly, as a characterological requirement sincerity placed stringent structural limitations upon nascent literary efforts regardless of the writer's political convictions. A grave and principled sincerity tended to produce the pedantic simplicity typical of the earnest and nominally popular voice of the early epic: undifferentiated, narrowly allegorical, characterization proved in such cases (to adapt the epic poet Joel Barlow's observation) "inflexible to the hand of fiction."[49] Alternatively, simplicity could be comically conveyed, imparting a flexibility to literary characterization (most obviously, in the use of regional dialect) that seemed to indicate the writer's greater degree of confidence in the adaptability of the common to literary purposes, and especially to the drama and the novel. The comic, however, seemed inevitably to deprive simplicity of its dignity and complexity, as demonstrated by the early appearance of the conventional and quintessentially American comic figure, Brother Jonathan.[50] The poet Philip Freneau's facetious literary creation, Robert Slender, a "stocking and tape weaver" ambitious of authorship, may be taken as a particularly endearing example of the character and its early association with American author-ship.[51] Slender reveals himself in his "Letters" as a realization of all that an Anglophilic literary establishment could detest in a literature consecrated to the representation of unembellished American character. His account of his decision to publish his letters features precisely the type of demystification of the literary enterprise that a critical class anxious for the dignity of American letters would deplore.[52] Having informed his learned neighbor and confi-dant, "the Latinist," of his authorial ambitions, for example, Slender con-siders the Latinist's objection that legitimate poets traditionally affix initials after their names to advertise their accomplishments and professional affilia-tions, of which Slender possesses not a one. But Slender is not to be dis-suaded: he forthwith announces his intention to "write myself, o.s.m." — "ONE OF THE SWINISH MULTITUDE" — thereby rehabilitating for democracy Edmund Burke's notorious epithet for the people, and to dedicate his book not to a great patron of the arts, and not even to the American president, but to the Freemen of the United States.[53]

If Slender here appears as a foolish nose-thumber, he evinces a greater dignity, a more sophisticated wit, and a tempered colloquial style in other letters that Freneau published in various venues between 1788 and 1799. In his 1788 "Advice to Authors," he combines satirical advice on how to satisfy an "itch for scribbling" while carrying out a respectable paying trade with commentary that more directly anticipates details of the portrait of the com-mon genius proposed by the protoromantic critics of the 1810s and 1820s. In an anticipation of Channing's attack on critics as imitators, Slender warns his aspiring "original author" to avoid the company of the "mere scholar" inso-far as these are "two animals as different from each other as a fresh and salt water sailor":

> There has been an old rooted enmity between them from the earliest ages, and which it is likely will forever continue. The scholar is not unlike that piddling orator, who, cold and inanimate, not roused into action by the impelling flame of inspiration, can only pronounce the oration he has learned by rote; the real author, on the contrary, is the nervous Demos-thenes who, stored with an immensity of ideas awakened within him he knows not how, has them at command upon every occasion; and must therefore be disregarded as a madman or an enthusiast by the narrow and limited capacity as well as the natural self-sufficiency of the other.[54]

Despite the provocative point that the "real," untutored author as "nervous Demosthenes" is akin to the inspired enthusiast (an alliance Brown had also noticed), Slender does not possess the characterological depth to enact such claims — he can only humorously assert their veracity.[55] The same limitations of the comic pertain to the common-man characters who together present Washington Irving's *History of New York, by Diedrich Knickerbocker* (1809). As landlord of the Independent Columbian Hotel in New York, Seth Handaside opens the *History* by offering the reader an explanation for his having published Knickerbocker's manuscript without his consent. He did so, he claims, because the irascible Knickerbocker, whom everyone thought mad, had mysteriously disappeared without paying his rent, leaving his magnum opus behind presumably as compensation. Knickerbocker then introduces himself, in advance of his first-person satirical history, as learned but poor, dedicated to the completion of his history although it will please neither "the superficial throng, who skim like swallows over the surface of literature" nor "the pampered palates of literary voluptuaries." He dreams (with an audible self-puffery) of standing with Gibbon, Hume, and Smollet "two or three hundred years ahead" of the future historians of America: "*little I* — at this moment the progenitor, prototype and precursor of them all, posted at the head of this host of literary worthies."[56] Despite his pretensions and his ambition, Knickerbocker, too, has nowhere to go in the text he narrates; he is simply a comic voice-over who establishes the tone of the piece without himself entering its action.

Thus, despite such attempts to broaden the Brother Jonathan convention to include marginally self-reflective authorial characters like Robert Slender and Diedrich Knickerbocker, its associations with the comic which lent it its feel of authenticity and, to a degree, its generic flexibility also placed limitations upon the literary development of national character. The question became then, how might the restrictions upon the textual development of democratic personality as representative American character be removed without unleashing the infectious and potentially destructive energies seen in *Wieland*? What lay beneath the comic mask that could be safely recovered? In 1815, Walter Channing unambiguously declared in the pages of the *North American Review* that the "blank of our national character" and the related failure of an authentic national literature to emerge were equally symptomatic of the culture's derivative status and could not be redressed by embracing the comic conventions of Brother Jonathan.[57] Given his pessimistic sense that "[t]here is something peculiarly opposed to literary originality in the colonial existence which was unfortunately so long the condition of America," he identifies "the oral literature of its aborigines" as the sole possibility for American literary authenticity (118, 119). For Channing, the Native American was key not because his originality underscored the derivative nature of Anglo-American culture but rather because he offered an example of existential simplicity imbued with dignity, a combination organically connected to the production of an authentic — and undeniably American — poetry.

Radically simple but untainted by foolishness, the character of the Indian as it was popularly conceived offered itself as a legitimate model for American authors, a way to disentangle national character from the constraints of the comic or the murderous without its threatening to take on a life of its own — for the Indian, as everyone knew, was well on the way to extinction. Walter Channing, of course, was not so blunt; instead, he elaborated upon the widespread belief that the discourse of the Indians was stringently self-limited because of its central mimetic imperative. Thus, according to Channing, not only did the American Indian exhibit himself as one whose "emotions were taught him at a school in which the master was nature and a most unsophisticated heart the scholar," but he spoke a poetically privileged language in which matter and manner, sound and sense, experience and expression, could not be alienated:

> Their words of description are either derived from incidents, and of which they are famed to convey most exact ideas, or are so formed as to convey their signification in their sounds; and although so ridiculous in the English dress as to be a new cause for English satire and merriment, are in themselves the very language for poetry, for they are made only for expression, and their objects are the very element for poetry. (119)

So portrayed, the Native American resolves the crisis between being and representation that had plagued Brown and Crèvecoeur. European-Americans, in contrast, suffered the "enslaving" influence of the English language: the absence of national character would be chronic as long as "our language" fails to "conform to our situation" (113). But the language of the Native American, because it conformed itself faithfully to experience, was "as bold as his own unshackled conceptions" which were nevertheless instantaneously contained — circumscribed and preserved — in the very act of mimetic expression (119). Channing thus identifies the mimetic imperative at the heart of Indian speech as constituting an inherent system of checks and balances in which character and language are mutually defining and delimiting: language grounded in experience, in the individual speaker's immediate "circumstances," delimited a "peculiar national character" insofar as national peculiarities "can be perfectly rendered only by the language which they themselves have given use to. I mean a peculiar language" (114, 115).

As his theory of Native American language revisits New Light John Wilson's understanding of the existential specificity of linguistic meaning, a clear family resemblance exists between Channing's argument here for the transcendent reality of Indian national character and Jonathan Edwards's claim for the transcendent reality of invisible religious experience. Edwards argued that a verbal representation of spiritual experience might substantiate not only the fundamental reality (if not the details) of that experience but also the speaker's spiritual identity as the necessary ground of his or her articulation: that is, the convert's words were bound to the experience of rebirth. Channing's argument thus resurrects the problematic desire evinced by both Old Lights and New Lights during the revival crisis to assess the truth-value of evangelical heart-speech with recourse to a concept of actual experience that was discovered to be as unavailable to observation as any transcendent referent. In seeking to conceptualize authentic national character within the context of its absence, Channing renders (in the language of high romantic interest in the folk) a portrait of the Indian as exemplifying an essential (national rather than spiritual) identity realized by a language that rigorously determines the extent to which experience (the ground of essential identity) may be articulated. Like the participants in the Great Awakening debates, his emphasis falls squarely upon the veridical status of an essentially theoretical — either incomprehensible or even inarticulate — speech.

Channing's enthusiastic assessment of the aboriginal language of the Native American was everywhere encountered and in some places refuted before and during the years in which James Fenimore Cooper's Leatherstocking novels were written. Debate intensified with the publication of *The Pioneers* (1823) and *The Last of the Mohicans* (1826), and would continue through the final novel of the series, *The Deerslayer* (1841).[58] That the Indians were, as the critic W. H. Gardiner put it, "a highly poetical people" (who, because they were fast disappearing, would fittingly be recovered by the poetry of "some future wizard of the West") was a truism, as was the observation that their poetic excellence inhered in the very movement and form of their bodies, as expressed in Richard Henry Dana Sr.'s hypothetical question, "How would the studied graces of Chesterfield appear by the side of a well made savage?"[59] In his introduction to the 1831 edition of *The Last of the Mohicans*, Cooper contributed a seemingly ethnographic objectivity to the critical tendency to romanticize Indian speech.[60] He noted that the Indian made use of a conspicuously "Oriental" imagery, but if his metaphors, derived from the innumerable elements of the natural world, exhibited the "richness and sententious fulness of the Chinese," they were yet "chastened" by "the limited range of his practical knowledge"; Indian metaphors were, as Channing also imagined, both unshackled and contained (5 *LM*). Indeed, as Cooper's account of Indian speech progresses, it appears that not only experience but also a logic inherent in the language itself limits the number of words the Indian will actually produce, a factor that paradoxically contributes to the superior expressivity of the aboriginal tongue: "He will express a phrase in a word," Cooper claims, "and he will qualify the meaning of an entire sentence by a syllable; he will even convey different significations by the simplest inflexions of the voice" (5 *LM*). For the Native American, then, the fewer the words, the greater the expressive capacity. As David Simpson has shown, a heightened eloquence was attributed to the very silence of the Indian, a capacity that Cooper's white frontiersman, Natty Bumppo, conspicuously acquires as his characteristic silent laugh.[61] The 1831 introduction thus suggests that Cooper's Leatherstocking tales made a foundational contribution to the aesthetics of innocence by translating it from a largely critical to a fictional register that did not partake of the comic. The aesthetics of innocence is distinctly present in this introductory account of the peculiarities of Indian speech. It offers, first, a critical (metafictional) ideology dedicated to promote the textualization of democratic personality as a theoretical basis for American (national, literary) character. But it is equally committed to domesticating it through a rigorous reinterpretation of its central trait, the vocal uncontainability that had proved so destructive to the ethical, characterological, and structural integrity of the postrevolutionary fiction of Brown and Crèvecoeur.[62]

In addition to offering a detailed sociology of Indian speech as Cooper imagined it, *The Last of the Mohicans* provides a complex account of its susceptibility both to adaptation and degradation within the Indian population and between Anglo-Americans and Native Americans. Cooper's description of the substance and evolution of these linguistic interrelationships is governed by the central fact of the decimation of the Indian population, thematically stressed throughout the Leatherstocking series from the initial appearance of the aged and isolated Chingachgook: if the Indians embody a discursive and thus an ethical ideal, as primitives they are doomed to extinction. In *The Pioneers*, this point—that the Indians exemplify the ethical primacy without the revolutionary cultural power of democratic personality—is clearly rendered when a besotted Chingachgook's increasingly loud and hypnotic chanting threatens to overwhelm desultory barroom chat. Natty is forced to remind him that his song refers to battles fought long past, whereas their present task is to restore his adopted son, Oliver Edwards, to his property rights as the scion not of Native Americans but of a Royalist sympathizer, Major Effingham, dispossessed by the American Revolution. "And why have you slain the Mingo warriors?" Natty chides Chingachgook, "was it not to keep these hunting-grounds and lakes to your father's children? and were they not given in solemn council to the Fire-eater?" (165 *P*). Here is the quintessential scene of domestication, in which Natty reminds Chingachgook that he had acquiesced, and rightly so, in his imminent extinction so that Oliver Edwards, "your father's children," might be prosperously settled within the formerly spectral space of the primeval forest wherein "half wild beings," like Natty himself, "who hang between society and the wilderness" had once roamed with their Indian companions (7 *LM*).[63] *The Last of the Mohicans* registers the circumstance of Indian genocide as tragic and inevitable, stimulated by intertribal rivalries as well as European aggression; the latter in particular, it is implied, may be sanctioned if the violent appropriation of Indian lands is accompanied by a respectful—indeed, an almost worshipful—appropriation of their discursive ethic.

Natty Bumppo, of course, serves as the transfer point between the dying and the ascendant cultures, a character who, while evincing the comic traits of the American common man as developed in the Brother Jonathan convention, acquires tragic depth through his inherently self-sacrificial mediating role. Like his life-companion, Chingachgook, the white frontiersman who condemns the progress of white settlement as the defilement of a primitive simplicity he has embraced is himself on his way to extinction, a circumstance noted by one of Cooper's early reviewers, who proudly observed that while Europeans might consider such progress incredible, "[t]he removal of forests of immense magnitude; the creation of flourishing towns and culti- vated fields, where but a few years before those forests stood, are events now so familiar to us, that they scarcely excite surprise."[64] Having adopted the ethics of Indian speech which enjoin his silence, Natty's paradoxical role in forestalling the epic design of a providence dedicated to white ascendancy is to preach the ethical superiority of the Indians to white encroachers of all description, arguably a serviceable metonymy of Cooper's readership. More- over, although his adoption of the doomed culture's discursive ethics leads him to repudiate all forms of mediation from Christ to books to language itself, he is compelled by history to mediate the transition from wilderness to settlement, from an Indian ethic of immediacy for which oral expression was just another form of direct action to a white ethic of property based on the textual codification and arbitrary control of action. We will return to Natty's paradoxical function in the Leatherstocking tales; suffice it to say for now that its demands free him from the comic limitations established by the Brother Jonathan type.[65]

As demonstrated by the speech of the "noble savage" figures, Chingach- gook and his son Uncas in *The Last of the Mohicans*, the key discursive trait of America's aborigines according to Cooper is that the stringent economy of their spoken language ensures that the dissociation of words and meaning, always an insidious possibility in the "civilized" languages of Protestantism and republicanism, rarely, if ever, occurs. As even the "bad" Indian rival, Magua "le Subtil," "le Renard," is entitled to point out, white speakers "have two words for each thing, while a red skin will make the sound of his voice speak for him" (91 *LM*). Thus, the "mild and musical" qualities of Uncas's voice cause Cora and Alice Munro to "look up in admiration and astonish- ment" when he speaks, although his words are "broken and imperfect"; likewise, when Chingachgook speaks "in the language of the Delawares," he does so "with a calmness and dignity that instantly arrested the attention even of those, to whom his words were unintelligible" (56, 226 *LM*). Hey- ward's attention had earlier been similarly attracted by the physical perfec- tion of Uncas's body (one critic dubbed him "an Indian Apollo"), for which he had "openly expressed his admiration at such an unblemished specimen of the noblest proportions of man" (53 *LM*).[66] As an aesthetic object, affiliated with either music or sculpture, once the Indian has won the admiring and respectful attention of the auditor or observer, unerring interpretation necessarily follows: the ethnographically enlightened Heyward, sufficiently independent in his judgments to consider that the Indians "were possessed of an instinct nearly commensurate with his own reason," is able to follow the deliberations of a meeting conducted among Indian speakers without difficulty, both because of the "direct and natural" gestures that accompanied the speech and which clearly indicated a contemplated course of action in an identifiable natural landscape, and because of the pictographs tattooed on the Indian body that constituted a universally legible supplementary language (52, 230, 198–99, 226 *LM*). Not only does the sound of the Indian voice bear a supplementary significance to the words it utters, then, but the Indian body with its "plastic and ingenious movements" and its "peculiarly significant gestures" is so articulate, combining the advantages of voice and text, as to constitute a pure poetry allied to music that is proof against misinterpretation even when the words of the Indian speaker are unfamiliar (200 *LM*, 142 *P*). The heightened expressivity of the Indian body thus ultimately comprehends nature itself: as Indian words bridge the divide between signifier and signified, the Indian body bridges that between nature and the most highly wrought cultural forms (52–53 *LM*). When Cooper translates a dialogue Natty and Chingachgook conduct in Delaware, the diction is conspicuously poetic, the mode of address naturally "figurative"; divested of his comical dialect, Natty in particular is transformed into an (Anglo-)American Shakespeare or Scott or Burns (165, 204 *P*).[67] Cooper himself is not above appropriating the stereotypically Indian metaphor, as when he describes Natty's eye as "glisten[ing] like a fiery star amid lowering clouds"; and he claims at several points in *The Last of the Mohicans* that if the "comprehensive and melodious language" of the Indian speaker were translatable into English, it would discover itself in high poetic forms as, for example, the ode (18, 319, 342 *LM*). As an expression of this achievement, Chingachgook's face offers an ideal and "singular compound of quick, vigilant sagacity, and of exquisite simplicity": both sagacious and simple, Chingachgook is a model of poetic precocity as well as republican virtue (52 *LM*).

The fact that the speech of the Indian confirms that he indeed is "what his looks assert him to be" means that both discursively and characterologically the Indian steadfastly represents, as Crèvecoeur's Farmer James had aspired to do, the reliability and integrity of the visible world (53 *LM*). If according to "white experience" the apparently tranquil forest potentially masks untold evils, for the Indian it constitutes a wholly legible text — it is simply a matter of knowing how to read the signs everywhere in evidence, a literacy synonymous with survival (210 *LM*). The Indian's virtue thus resists the threat of spectrality, the threat of what is hidden and individualized, whereas the speech of the most pious white character, the Calvinist itinerant David Gamut, is tainted with a structural, if not an intentional, duplicity: even the infantile Alice Munro immediately observes in David the "unworthy conjunction of execution and language" and the "unfitness between sound and sense" (27 *LM*). The invisible terrors of the wilderness associated with Indian violence are everywhere invoked, but throughout Cooper's novels they serve to deepen his characterization of the Indian as a "child of the forest" whose virtue disdains as deceitful any recourse to the hidden recesses of personality (86 *P*). When in *The Pioneers* the Episcopalian minister of Templeton, Dr. Grant, urges Chingachgook to attend Christmas services not just in the body but with a spirit of contrition, insofar as "all form is but stench, in the nostrils of the Holy One, unless it be accompanied by a devout and humble spirit," the Indian responds by striking himself upon his chest and proclaiming, "The eye of the Great Spirit can see from the clouds; — the bosom of Mohegan is bare" (95 *P*). (The interchange is ironic given the villagers' resentment of Grant with his Episcopalian formalism, and their frequent invocation of the superiority of Whitefieldian practice, especially the extempore sermon [125–26, 147–48 *P*]). The discrepancy between Indian virtue and Christian piety is further demonstrated when Chingachgook, in his deathsong, sings his own praises as a great warrior and, equally, as one who never lied and in whom "the truth lived . . . and none else could come out of him" (420 *P*). When a frantic Dr. Grant endeavors to learn from Natty what the Indian's song signifies, and specifically if he is "sensible of his lost state" and singing "the Redeemer's praise," Natty chides him, insisting, not without comedy, on Chingachgook's higher truth: "No, no, — 'tis his own praise that he speaks now, . . . and a good right he has to say it all, for I know every word to be true." As for Dr. Grant and his doctrine of intercession, Natty points out, "[t]hough all you say be true, and you have scripter gospels for it, too, you will make nothing of the Indian" (420, 421 *P*). Chingachgook's principled refusal of mediation survives his Christianization, specifically his acceptance of a savior, and is consistent with the strictures the

Indians place upon language intended to thwart the impulse to lie, to prevent the disintegration into separate components of sound and meaning to which language as language is prone. Like the Quakers, Cooper's Indians observe a principled silence as a prerequisite to honest discourse: when Uncas and Chingachgook meet after a fraught separation, each keeps silent, "appearing to await the moment, when he might speak, without betraying womanish curiosity or childish impatience." Similarly, Uncas later forgoes "that eager and garrulous narration, with which a white youth would have endeavoured to communicate, and perhaps exaggerate, that which had passed out in the darkness of the plain" in order "to let his deeds speak for themselves" (33, 195, cf. 292 *LM*).

Their rigorous practice of a discursive virtue that enjoins silence as well as a scrupulously observed dialogical formalism leads Cooper to suggest Indian superiority in both the political and the religious arenas. If the Episcopalian Grant of *The Pioneers* is especially vulnerable to an unfortunate comparison with the noble savage, the itinerant evangelist and singer of hymns in *The Last of the Mohicans*, David Gamut, doesn't fare much better. At best, his hymn-singing instigates comic and salvific misunderstandings among the hostile Indians: it causes them to refrain from scalping him (as well as Cora and Alice) when they mistake his hymn-singing for the deathsong of the white warrior and spare him in admiration of his bravery; after he and the women are taken captive, it permits him the physical freedom and the respectful treatment the Indians accord what Natty calls the "non-composser" (178, 224 *LM*). As a composite of conventional character types associated with the itinerant evangelical, David, in his initial Carwinesque appearance in the novel, appears to augur nothing good.[68] But although he turns out to be honest and gentle, he is easily bested in a doctrinal dispute with Natty, who declares the doctrine of predestination to be "the belief of knaves, and the curse of an honest man," and the book of nature superior to David's beloved Bible insofar as "the words that are written there are too simple and too plain to need much schooling" (116, 117 *LM*). Moreover, Natty disdains evangelical heart-speech as a fatal practice while proclaiming the excellence of prayer that issues silently from the heart, a "tongue" that the Maker understands as well as any articulated one; the silent prayer of the heart is contrasted explicitly with the deadly ignorance of a "white voice" articulated in the woods, as exemplified by "that miserable devil, the singer," Gamut

(201 *LM*). Elevated in the course of the novel to the status of a holy fool, the Calvinist Gamut's claim to exclusive possession of the highest truth is ultimately undermined by his conversion to Indian spirituality at Cora's wilderness funeral. The Indian women singing their grief at Cora's demise, "their ideas [clothed] in the most remote and subtle images," along with the "speaking countenances" of the sympathetic Indian men, persuade "[e]ven David . . . to lend his ears to the tones of voices so sweet; and long ere the chant was ended, his gaze announced that his soul was enthralled" (343, 344 *LM*). Cooper's characterization of Gamut is surely the deathsong of the cultural type of the evangelical itinerant so powerful in its previous textualizations but which Natty consistently associates with impotence and emasculation, and thus with a virtue insufficient to survive, let alone to guide others through the complexities of their own lives.[69]

Politically, the Indians' discursive integrity, the immediacy of experience to expression and letter to spirit, suggested that the indigenous peoples displaced by the republican revolution of the European colonists practiced a pure democracy that made the representative democracy of Cooper's America appear corrupt by comparison. Indian political practice as Cooper describes it transcends the expedient of representative structure altogether. The point is first made that the Indians enact self-government based on the concept of unanimity, such that the will of the people cannot be announced and acted upon until all agree on what it is. The Indian version of a town meeting, as Heyward admiringly witnesses it, resembles "the most decorous christian assembly" in which the strictures placed upon individual speech produce a "moderation," a "forbearance and courtesy" that allows every voice to be heard and its pronouncements dispassionately weighed (198). When Uncas and Chingachgook become "converts" to Natty's opinions as to the course of action the beleaguered group should pursue, Cooper observes that the Indians' "liberality and candour, . . . had they been the representatives of some great and civilized people, would have infallibly worked their political ruin, by destroying, for ever, their reputation for consistency" (199 *LM*). The achievement of a unanimous popular will requires not simply the type of conceptual flexibility that the "civilized" world would receive as a sign of inconsistency (an association that plagues contemporary politics) but a rhetoric that persuades rather than seduces. In his depiction of a "solemn and formal assemblage of the [Delaware] nation," wherein over one thousand warriors gathered into a "grave," "attentive," and "deeply interested multitude," the strictures against impulsive individual speech are more than ever in evidence:

> In a collection of so serious savages, there is never to be found any impatient aspirant after premature distinction, standing ready to move his auditors to some hasty, and, perhaps, injudicious discussion, in order that his own reputation may be the gainer. An act of so much precipitancy and presumption, would seal the downfall of precocious intellect for ever. It rested solely with the oldest and most experienced of the men to lay the subject of the conference before the people. Until such a one chose to make some movement, no deeds in arms, no natural gifts, nor any renown as an orator, would have justified the slightest interruption. (292 *LM*)

It is as if the ideal Old Light congregation had been resurrected in the primeval — and diabolic — wilderness of the New World.

Beyond their principle of unanimity, the Indians accommodate an antinomian practice that further circumvents a reliance on representation. Thus the reigning elder of the Delaware nation, Tamenund, more than a century old, is rumored even among rival tribes to possess "the rare gift of holding secret communion with the Great Spirit" (293 *LM*). At the funerals of Cora and Uncas, Tamenund practices a sanctified ventriloquism — "as if the venerated spirit [the Indians] worshipped had uttered the words, without the aid of human organs" — that brings access to divinity directly to the gathered multitudes (341 *LM*). But the god Manitto's message to his people is that their annihilation is accomplished: if the Indians practice an antinomianism that precludes the necessity of representation and thus transcends the purest democratic practice imaginable, their achievement coincides with their vanishing. Transcendent power and the accomplishment of extinction are simultaneous, a circumstance that precludes the need or temptation to dramatize annihilation as it was performed within the contexts of spectacular conversion and spectral possession.

The fall of the Indian nations to European-American aggression is portrayed in the novel as the fall of certain individuals, the "bad" Indians, into representation — into politics and artistry. Cooper's ambivalence toward the Indian engaged in representation is evident, for example, in his characterization of Magua, the serpent in the savage paradise. Magua is that oxymoron, the Indian demagogue who, like the seducer-itinerant, "never spoke without auditors, and rarely without making converts to his opinions," and whose practice when speaking is to "glid[e] among his countrymen" while deploying "his fatal and artful eloquence" (249, 175 *LM*). His body and his words share a hypnotic and explicitly seductive effect upon his auditors insofar as his efforts are calculated to flatter the individuality or "self-love" of each (282 *LM*). Despite their disparate beliefs and temperaments, each auditor responds to Magua's eloquence by imagining "that more was meant than was uttered, and each one believed that the hidden meaning was precisely such as his own faculties enabled him to understand, or his own wishes led him to anticipate": each auditor, drunk with the pleasure of interpretation as an expression of self-love, agrees in his own flattered heart to permit the separation of matter and manner in Magua's presentation of policy (283 *LM*). Blending "the warlike with the artful, the obvious with the obscure, as to flatter the propensities of [all] parties," Magua, likened to "the Prince of Darkness," is popular, his artfully indirect appeal to individual pride allowing him to engineer a spectral unanimity that is in reality a triumphant totalitarianism: according to his representations, "[t]he tribe consented to act with deliberation, and with one voice they committed the direction of the whole affair to the government of the chief, who had suggested such wise and intelligible expedients" (283, 284 *LM*). The consummate politician who follows up his demagoguery with personal visits calculated to flatter certain individuals in the crowd, Magua possesses the Indian's superior ability to read countenances and to reproduce fictitious character in his own face. His duplicity, in the service of violence and revenge, is implicitly compared with Chingachgook's salvific artistry when he makes "a natural fool" of Heyward by painting his features:

> Long practised in all the subtle arts of his race, [Chingachgook] drew, with great dexterity and quickness, the fantastic shadow that the natives were accustomed to consider as the evidence of a friendly and jocular disposition. Every line that could possibly be interpreted into a secret inclination for war, was carefully avoided; while, on the other hand, he studied those conceits that might be construed into amity. In short, he entirely sacrificed every appearance of the warrior, to the masquerade of a buffoon. (229 *LM*)

Magua's moment of triumph is his duplicitous address to the Delaware nation in which, even as he asserts that a "Huron never lies," he masks his vigilance beneath an impassive front: "With his consummate knowledge of the nature of the people with whom he had to deal, he anticipated every measure on which they decided; and it might almost be said, that in many instances, he knew their intentions even before they became known to themselves" (291–92 *LM*). Yet it is clear by the terms of Cooper's characterization as well as Chingachgook's lamentations for the lost unity of the Indian nations as the result of European aggression, that Magua's talents are peculiarly those of the Indian who, having forsaken his native virtue, proves a gifted student of the white art of misrepresentation.

The misrepresenting and individually ambitious Indian, the Indian who refused to delimit his speech or actions according to the collective (if self-destructive) standard of virtue, was neither accommodated (as an interesting human type) nor rehabilitated in the early American novel. But if the "bad" Indian was left to die a villain's death, alone and unmourned, the novelistic representation of collective annihilation allowed for the glorification of normative Indian character. Cooper's normative Indian exemplifies domesticated democratic personality—its uncontainability ("passions unrestrained, and . . . thoughts free as air") scrupulously self-regulated and its antinomianism committed to verifying that extinction was internally necessary rather than externally imposed (136 *P*). The Indians' vanishing, that is, may be at least implicitly attributed to an ethic of self-limitation easily accommodated to one of self-sacrifice as well as to the wholly internal and transcendent necessity of their disappearance. Clearly this emphasis mitigated white responsibility for Indian genocide; perhaps more pointedly, it also suggested for the encroaching white population not simply a neutral role as witness to history but a morally elevated and even salvific one. If their ascendancy coincided with Indian decimation (as Tamenund suggests, with the unequivocal termination of Manitto's covenant with his people as signified by his closing his eyes and ears to their pleas), the whites might yet save the Indians: not from extinction, for that was out of their purview, but from literary morbidity by appropriating domesticated democratic personality as exemplified in their social and discursive ethics and naturalizing it as American national character. Once the naturalization of domesticated democratic personality as (white) American character had occurred, the literary vogue of the exemplary Indian was abandoned. Thus does the novelistic representation of the white character's nonviolent appropriation of Indian democratic personality as an ethos of self-containing freedom as well as an antinomianism whose achievement coincides with the achiever's demise perform a secondary function: it usefully legitimates, as tacit analogy, the violent appropriation of Indian lands.

It is the white frontiersman Natty Bumppo's lot to enact the nonviolent appropriation of domesticated democratic personality as exemplified by the vanishing Indian. His anomalous presence in the Indian landscape permits the work of genocide to be figured as the companionable transfer of democratic personality from the noble savage to his white comrade as the latter's rightful legacy and the unpolluted source of his representative Americanness. Throughout the Leatherstocking novels, the naturalization of this transfer as interracial and intercultural inheritance rather than an act of war is central to Natty's function as the representative American common man for whom less is always more, silence is eloquence, and illiteracy an exquisite mode of scholarship in which the textual and the real are wholly identified in and as nature. Natty does not just support or admire the Indian ethos but he realizes it in a white body and articulates it with a white tongue — in this respect, his whiteness, as he is fond of pointing out, is his great characterological achievement. That he can be white and embody Indian values means that he has gone beyond the representational and acceded to being itself. In comparison with Natty, more pedigreed white figures like Duncan Heyward or Oliver Edwards may prove apt students of democratic personality as Natty and the Indians model it for them, but they do not themselves embody it. Instead, they are limited to providing a more or less cynical imitation of certain of its features. Heyward, for example, demonstrates an appreciation of Indian qualities characteristic of the cultured man's generosity toward those he has conquered that excludes the possibility of his identifying with those he admires. In an effort to win the confidence of Magua by imitating the metaphorical allusiveness of Indian language (with nearly incomprehensible results), Heyward is thus described as an "adventurous speaker" who practices "subtle speech" with a "well acted sincerity"; the Englishman's efforts only make him the double of the artful dissembler le Subtil, with whom he converses, an obvious irony that not only undermines his assumption of moral and cultural superiority but condemns the assumption of difference itself (96 *LM*). (It is not surprising that Heyward parleys only with the "bad" Magua; with the "good" Indians Chingachgook and Uncas, Heyward is largely content to observe rather than engage in conversation.) When Heyward avails himself of Indian speech, the reader hears not the Indian ethos but the pressure of Heyward's own dilemma that has suggested his exploitative strategy; Heyward does not exhibit the integrity of manner and matter central to reformed or domesticated democratic personality as an unalterably virtuous (rather than revolutionary or subversive) mode of being. In contrast to Heyward, Natty's repeated claim to be "a man without a cross" advertises his transparency to Indian culture, a claim largely upheld even when he strategically deploys Indian language, gesture, metaphor, and narrative logic in order to convert his Indian auditors to his views. The self-applied epithet possesses a benign ambiguity: if Natty's whiteness is the mark of racial difference that allows him to carry domesticated democratic personality from its origins in primitive simplicity into the Anglo-American future, it equally conveys his achievement of transparency to redness, a racial and cultural liminality within which difference (a "cross") is dissolved. The French novelist Honoré de Balzac praised the character of Natty Bumppo in this regard as "a statue, a magnificent moral hermaphrodite, born of the savage state and of civilization."[70] The concept of the democratic character as statue recalls the monumental Whitefield whose function was wholly iconic, possessed of no inner — potentially spectral — dimension. The transparency necessary to transmit democratic personality from out of its basis in nature (that is, Indian culture) is refigured in the accomplished bilingualism of the illiterate frontiersman.

Ultimately, of course, the function of whiteness as difference rather than transparency prevails. Unlike Heyward, however, Natty's difference does not induce him to embrace the ontological indeterminacy of representation (representing oneself *as* rather than actually being); instead, Natty's difference bolsters his identification with the Indian as history's innocent victim, as exemplar of domesticated democratic personality. On the surface, this seems implausible insofar as the main sense of Natty's self-portrayal as a man without a cross is that he possesses no Indian blood; he is a purebred if not a cultured man. In this spirit, he repeatedly observes that whiteness entails distinctive "gifts" (as color does), a word that possesses in Natty's usage the meaning of a potentially burdensome obligation that cannot be disowned, as the farmer Nathan Cole after his conversion acknowledged that spiritual rebirth entailed the gift or duty of public speech. His gift of whiteness prevents Natty from fully embracing the Indian ethos; it exempts him, for example, from participating in what he considers the savageries of warfare indulged even by the good Indians with whom he allies himself. More important, whiteness extends his victimization — and thus his credentials as the major textual representative of domesticated democratic personality — by forcing him to take up the cross he claims to be without. Natty's whiteness, that is, allows Cooper to pit the details of his characterization, particularly his principled rejection of mediation as a corruption of being, against its structural logic in and between the Leatherstocking novels as that figure destined to mediate the transfer of domestic democratic personality from an already legendary (if barely accomplished) history to the ascendant Anglo-American context by suggesting that its appropriation occurs as the natural result of contact.

Many readers of the Leatherstocking novels have noted the ironic circumstance that Natty's respectful presence in Native America ensures its demise. Inevitably, Natty is the harbinger of an advancing alien population; as inevitably, when the indigenous and the invading cultures meet, he reluctantly fulfills the role of mediator in which he is constantly adjusting his sense of his own whiteness and its significance. The incompatibility of his character (favorable to the Indian) and his destiny (promoting their demise) lends him, despite the comic aspects of his appearance and his backwoods speech, the tragic pathos that belongs more properly to the Indians whose experience of an impending extinction — if not of life itself, then of a way of life — he shares. This pathos forestalls potentially cynical readings of key scenes, as, for example, in *The Last of the Mohicans* when Natty's whiteness threatens to undermine the poignancy of his emotional identification with the grieving Chingachgook after the death of Uncas. As the Indian is representing himself as a " 'blazed pine, in a clearing of the pale-faces' " (an image that associates the decimation of the Indians with the destruction of the wilderness), Natty claims that, as the last Mohican's truest companion in radical solitude, he too is the blazed pine. And as Tamenund is "dispers[ing] the multitude" gathered for the last time to hear him announce the accomplishment of white mastery and the Indians' imminent extinction, Natty is insisting that he and Chingachgook despite their racial difference possess a shared destiny (349,

350 *LM*). Only the reader's sense of the pathos of Natty's own transience — an ephemerality sustained through five novels — lends plausibility to the analogy he implicitly makes between his own and Chingachgook's plight, an analogy that draws a parallel between genocide and one man's voluntary abandonment of a culture for which he has no use.[71]

For some readers, of course, the incompatibility of Natty's principles with his actions has made him fair game for criticism. John Neal, the American-born critic of *Blackwood's Edinburgh Magazine*, condemned him as "the hero and the bore in one," a "very silly, prating, garrulous character": "Always talking, he is always enjoining silence," Neal observed, "and he keeps up an incessant cackle that would have been sure to bring half the Indians of the forest upon his trail."[72] Neal's objection is justified, but it is equally true that his function as mediator compels Natty to violate his own principled silence. In spite of his reservations concerning the value of speech, he is bound to represent the Indians to the whites who would otherwise misinterpret their words and actions. Such details as Neal points out portray Natty as unable to live the life of an Indian because he is white, confirming Natty's status as victim — of history, of white culture, of the text that crucifies him on the axes of character and function. His characterological precariousness is empha-sized by his particular rejection of textual mediation as pernicious, a convic-tion that would play a prominent part in the development of the American aesthetic of innocence after Cooper. The fictional character who more suc-cessfully than any other had modeled domesticated democratic personality and claimed it for American national character explicitly and repeatedly condemns the book not simply as artifact but as a cultural fetish that de-formed the cultural material it attempted to transmit. Above all, Natty can-not abide the sickly impulse of bookishness.

Beyond his association of bookishness with emasculation, Natty is con-vinced that the authority accorded to books in place of experience promotes the confusion of textual representations of reality with reality itself, enfee-bling what we might designate the natural culture of being. He continually notes that the Indian ability to read the visible world — woods, faces, trails, streambeds — entails no discrepancy between experience and language: to read as an Indian reads is to bear witness to what occurs and to discern what exists. "What right have christian whites to boast of their learning," Natty asks, "when a savage can read a language, that would prove too much for the wisest of them all!" (196 *LM*; cf. 186). Reading books is not merely useless, "in-door work" but also a practice, Natty declares, "which, as an honest man, I can't approve" (134 *P*):

> It is one of their [white] customs to write in books what they have done and seen, instead of telling them in their villages, where the lie can be given to the face of a cowardly boaster, and the brave soldier can call on his comrades to witness for the truth of his words. In consequence of this bad fashion, a man who is too conscientious to misspend his days among the women, in learning the names of black marks, may never hear of the deeds of his fathers, nor feel a pride in striving to outdo them. (31 *LM*)

Because they promote the lie as the articulation of the discrepancy between experience and expression, because they dissemble the opposition of being and representation, books deform the modeling process on which the transmission of the natural culture of being and the purity of character depend. Emerson will most forcefully assume and articulate Natty's textbound struggle against the text (and against Cooper's fundamentally ethnographic authorial practice) and explicitly identify this resistance to the book, and ultimately to language itself, as the mark of the authentic American literatus.[73]

Despite Natty's animus against the text, its recuperation is variously represented. In the first of the Leatherstocking volumes, *The Pioneers*, the very framework of the plot (the reinstatement of Oliver Effingham, formerly Oliver Edwards, Natty's young companion and the adopted son of Chingachgook, to ownership of the lands that the Indians had bequeathed to his grandfather, the Royalist Major Effingham) constitutes a defense of textuality. Oliver, like Natty, has chosen the life of the backwoodsman out of principle. Unlike Natty's relatively sober choice, the hotheaded Oliver is motivated by his proud and unspoken resentment at Judge Temple's apparent appropriation, in the Effinghams' absence, of what the younger man considers his ancestral lands. But if initially Oliver (echoing Farmer James at his narrative's end) laments, "I have become a man of the woods, and must place my sole dependence on the fruits of the chase," he soon accepts Temple's offer of an assistantship, and will eventually, when the truth of his identity becomes known, be fully reinstated as the rightful proprietor of vast tracts of former Indian wilderness (184 *P*). Natty must flee from this reclaimed wilderness in order to remain free, in part because Oliver, as Temple's representative, is obliged to warn him that the law — precisely as that which, in Temple's words, "remove[s] us from the condition of the savages" — forbids him to hunt out of season (383 *P*). Oliver's decision to abandon the life of freedom, the life lived beyond formal observance, thus explicitly clarifies and vindicates the textually determined limitations of Natty's mediate function: living on the margins of settlement and thus on the cusp of vocational and characterological extinction, Natty transmits democratic personality to Cooper's readers not by his own eccentric example but by modeling it for another character one shade more attached to whiteness, with its commitment to the book (here, the letter of the law), than he. This shade is immediately discerned by Judge Temple and his family as a telltale discrepancy between Oliver's rustic appearance and his aristocratic speech, and in the course of the novel appearance is brought into conformity with speech rather than vice versa.

Despite his transformation from romantic savage into contented bourgeois, Oliver does not lose his authority as an exemplar of domesticated democratic personality. On the contrary, his accession to respectability and wealth consolidates it: because he has absorbed its central ethical imperative, humble self-enlargement through a principled containment, he instinctively seeks in the white world the most fitting receptacle for his powers. By redeeming containment as an avenue to personal freedom (as Farmer James before him had sought to do), Oliver, beyond Natty, makes domesticated democratic personality available as normative American character — the sentimental denouement of his story is thus perfectly consistent with the extensive valorization of Natty's backwoods life. The scene of Natty's incarceration for hunting out of season marks the point at which the transfer of domesticated democratic personality to Oliver is initiated; it will be finalized at the two men's last meeting at Chingachgook's grave. Furious at Judge Temple for permitting Natty's arrest, Oliver for the first time yields to the temptation of uncontainability and vents his "ungovernable" rage at his employer as a usurper of the land. But the moment that the "volcano," Oliver, "burst its boundaries" is the moment his true identity is discovered: not a "half-breed," as some had suspected, angrily denying what Temple calls "the validity of the claims that have transferred the title to the whites," but rather the grandson of the very white man to whom the land was transferred. It is as a white man — indeed, as the scion of a Royalist — and not as an Indian that

Oliver indicts Temple for usurping the land (345 P). Oliver's utterance of the truth of his identity and his right to Temple's land and wealth is thus made commensurate with Natty's eloquent pleas against confinement as a violation of the essential freedom of his being (356–57, 362 P).

The plot thus offers Oliver, reinstated after his wilderness exile to his rightful position at the pinnacle of Templeton society, as Natty's truest successor: imbued with the principles of domesticated democratic personality modeled by Natty and Chingachgook in the forest, Oliver is able to propose them as the ideal yet normative basis of American character where Natty, for his literal outlandishness, his commitment to freedom, and his rejection of the notion of property, cannot. The transfer of the torch from Natty to Oliver is completed in the novel's final scene when, his claim to proprietorship recognized and his proposal of marriage to Elizabeth Temple accepted, Oliver, Elizabeth, and Natty meet at the adjacent graves of Chingachgook and Oliver's grandfather, whom the Indian had sheltered after his defeat and in his dotage. At the close of that scene, despite Oliver's plea that he remain "where we can sometimes see you," Natty will one last time remove himself from (white) visibility by penetrating more deeply into the untracked wilderness where only "God will see" him, in an effort to relieve himself once and for all of his untenable role as the great mediator who consistently rejects the necessity and the ethics of mediation; the advocate of silence who is compelled by his mediating role both to bilingualism and verbosity; the bookbound preacher of the evils of the text (454 P). Yet before he vanishes forever, the free-spirited enemy of the written word provides it with a curious sanction. He is delighted to discover, when Oliver reads his grandfather's epitaph at Natty's request, that his name has been inscribed on the tombstone as the dead man's enduringly grateful servant. (In contrast, the fact that Oliver has misspelled Chingachgook's name on his tombstone, and thus apparently had always mispronounced it, confirms the Indian's absolute unavailability to language.) Cooper makes Natty's tracing a finger over the "winding" letters of his name graven into the marble—an obvious image of the devious and fatal nature of language and especially print—the prelude to his resurrection: having followed "the windings of the letters to the end, with deep interest," he "raised himself from the tomb," the American common man as Lazarus and Jesus united, and removed himself forever, or at least until his next novel, from the realm of representation (452 P).[74] Richard Slotkin has observed that "the national myth of the frontier" unites "the characters of the hunter and the captive," an observation borne out in this scene in which Natty explicitly gives his sanction to the principle of containment lying at the heart of heroic uncontainability.[75]

Just as the isolato's final act (in his first novel) is to lead "the march of the nation across the continent," the champion of illiteracy and silence performs a final service to textuality: his manner of hunting is made to suggest the viability of an innocent authorial practice whereby material may be taken out of the invisible context of being and made available to sight, and thus to representation, without violence and deformation (456 P). Chapters 22 through 24 of *The Pioneers* represent three hunting scenes, the first two (the pigeon-shoot and the dragging of the lake for quantities of bass) carried out by the white settlers of Templeton and the last conducted by Natty, Chingachgook, and Oliver in Elizabeth Temple's presence. The first two of these chapters describe the savagery of a white attack upon the resources of the American wilderness, carried out on the pretense of harmless sport. As two thousand fish are needlessly brought out of the lake only to rot upon the shore, Temple worries aloud that such profligate raiding of the wilderness's hidden treasure, and specifically the violence with which it is conducted, will cause natural resources to disappear. His excessively prosaic cousin Richard Jones, Templeton's sheriff, objects, "Disappear, 'duke! disappear! If you don't call this appearing, I know not what you will" (260 P): his literal understanding of Temple's words, his insistence on appearance, is proof of his blindness to the consequences of failing to preserve nature and, by extension, the natural culture of being. Elizabeth fittingly finds the scene of the hunt as the uninhibited destruction of being "a subject for the pencil," for representation. The vulgarity of her error in attributing romantic sublimity to the spectacle of violence is implicitly pointed out by Natty, who proclaims that the dragging of the lake constitutes evidence of human sinfulness (262, 265 P). Elizabeth, drawn by "curiosity" to seek Natty out, is invited to accompany him, Oliver, and Chingachgook ("Trust the Indian") on a fishing expedition to the lake's center in which she is given the opportunity to compare Natty's hunt with the settlers' as both a subject for and a method of artistic representation (266, 267 P). Unlike the settlers stranded like the dying fish on the lake's margins, Natty and his friends glide quickly in their light canoe into its silent center, their responsive silence indicative of both stealth and respect as they approach the invisible world that lies beneath the lake's surface.

Natty's torch "laid bare the mysteries of the lake, as plainly as if the limpid sheet of the Otsego was but another atmosphere"; in its light, Elizabeth's gaze can penetrate the lake's otherwise invisible depths, where she sees thousands of prize fish within easy reach of Natty's spear (268 *P*). Natty sees further: his "tall stature, and his erect posture" are supplemented by his practice of "bending his body forward, and straining his vision, as if desirous of penetrating the water, that surrounded their boundary of light" (268, 269 *P*). Penetrating the depths of deep and unilluminated water and thus able to render an "unusual exposure of the secrets of the lake," Natty distinguishes the single fish in the mass whose catch will best test the skill of the catcher. In a scene that anticipates the salvific expulsion of Queequeg's coffin from the depths at the end of *Moby-Dick* (as the journey into the lake's midst anticipates "The Grand Armada"), Natty's spear silently "disappeared in the lake," leaving behind a "little bubbling vortex," and is then ejected "into the air, by its own re-action" rather than by Natty's efforts. The spear and not its "master" retrieves the fish from the depths to effect its transferal from the invisible sphere of being to the visible one of representation: the release of the spear so that it springs back into his hand, the chosen fish cleanly impaled on its tines, constitutes the innocence as well as the surpassing skillfulness of his artistry. In this venue, Elizabeth cannot sustain, as a pleasurable sensation of control, the artistic distance she had experienced on the shore regarding the riotous scene of the fish massacre. Instead, she is "transfixed" (awkwardly, because so is the bass), entranced "by this scene, and by gazing in that unusual manner at the bottom of the lake" (269, 270 *P*). Chingachgook provides a quasi-biblical sanction to Natty's production of the fish out of the chaos of dark water which supplements its Christic significance: when the spear delivers the fish to Natty's hand and he proclaims his satisfaction with what he has wrought, Chingachgook "waved his hand, and replied with the simple and energetic monosyllable of—'Good'" (270 *P*). The death of the magnificent creature is resurrected as a profoundly creative act. Natty's access to invisible realities is thus mediated by his spear which accomplishes the evacuation of being while preserving undistorted the form of life: his fish is a poem, distinctive, sublime, and perfectly preserved through its journey into visibility from out of the depths of being. As for Natty's spear, it functions as an analogue of that old haunt, the specter, crossing the border of the visible and the invisible spheres, making them, for the innocent initiate, mirror universes whose intimate connectedness is not compromised by a distorting will to power.

III

Throughout the remainder of his career, apparently, Cooper would be incompletely aware, not of the international popularity of his heroic backwoodsman, Natty Bumppo, but of his increasingly iconic significance for a particular segment of the American literary class, the aestheticians of innocence who would dominate literary and cultural criticism from the late 1830s well into the 1850s and who had dedicated themselves to solving the mystery of literary absence. Whitman would become the greatest poetic practitioner of an aesthetics of innocence (which posited the elision of the gap between being and representation in an organically agentless poetic utterance) and his 1855 and 1856 prefaces to *Leaves of Grass* its enduring manifestos, but Emerson preceded him as its most cogent formulator and theoretician. The publications of "The American Scholar" (1837) and "The Poet" (1844) frame the appearance of Cooper's last Leatherstocking novels, *The Pathfinder* (1840) and *The Deerslayer* (1841), to which he had returned after a thirteen-year hiatus (including a seven-year sojourn in Europe) largely devoted to a fictional and critical investigation of American democracy as social practice.[76] In contrast to Cooper's cultural commentaries of the late thirties, Emerson's essays not only declared America's literary independence from Europe's courtly muses but proposed its literary dependence upon a hypothetical American poet who in no way resembles Cooper and whose peculiarities of character and situation Emerson describes — or rather, prescribes — at length. He explained that the poet's existence had not yet been recognized by the literary class because he moved at the "suburbs and extremities" of culture, innocent of its trappings and preoccupations and of its servile reliance upon the book (78). Far from bookish himself, the poet's language, knowledge, and actions equally demonstrated his total involvement in what I have called the natural culture of being: they were fully sufficient to the matter at hand, direct and unself-conscious rather than devious and premeditated, and so organically linked to the immediate moment as to make (textual) preservation unnecessary and undesirable. In 1840, this great American author, from whom the American people awaited the realization of their own collective essence (as American character) in his as yet unwritten poems, was himself but a character — that is, he remained the object of authorial (and critical) representation despite the attribution to him of an unparalleled ontological, ethical, and cultural authenticity.

Although Cooper had provided in Natty Bumppo the fullest fictional portrait of the American common man to whom the hypothetical Emersonian poet bore a family resemblance, he failed to realize that in the course of the 1830s it had become his obligation not just to portray, or even to mythify, Natty but to be him. The self-described writer of "polite literature" had realized as early as 1832 that "I am not with my country — the void between us is immense — which . . . time alone will show," but was unaware of the reasons for his alienation.[77] Cooper did not expect that his own authorial practice should bear any resemblance to the ideal, noncoercive, and metaphorical "authorship" of his backwoodsman, affiliated not with representation or invention but with being itself. For Emerson, however, the authorial figure who was the subject of his own poetic musings was, if hypothetical, yet real; he might be recognized on the street insofar as he embodied the characterological requirements for democratic personality as fictional characters like Natty, and before Natty, the Cooper Indian, had modeled them.[78] In order, then, to be recognizable to the literary class as the genuine American literatus, an author like Cooper, having "breath[ed] into his creations the breath of life" and "turn[ed] the phantoms of his brain into seeming realities," had also to resemble Natty, innocent of culture, including its bookish theories about or poetic celebrations of the common.[79] Or, put otherwise, the difference between Cooper and Emerson is the difference between the author who represents in a text an ethically ascendant authorial character (e.g., Natty fishing) as an exemplification of domesticated democratic personality or American national character; and the author who represents an ethically ascendant author whom he claims inhabits a world that is at once real and hypothetical in the sense that it is conceptually, temporally, or spatially — but not actually — removed from the writer and the reader. In each case, ethical ascendancy is both registered in and demonstrated by the represented author's practice of a principled, if unself-conscious, silence that anticipates his own secession from the utterance he is destined to produce, so that events, as Emerson promised, may "sing themselves" (64). The possibility that (fiction) writing itself might be considered by less subtle aestheticians of innocence as an unacceptable "authorial" activity is borne out in the truncated career of Herman Melville.[80]

The general perception, exacerbated by his political writings, that Cooper had maintained an aristocratic distance from his white characters and had portrayed his Indians with a disengaged ethnographic objectivity led critics like New York's sophisticated Lewis Gaylord Clark to note that his common people looked increasingly like a mass of "fools or clowns," and were without individual interest.[81] But even before his defection from the magnificence of America's primeval forests and the epic dignity of its history in order to turn his attention to the paltriness of its contemporary politics and social life, Cooper was criticized for the distance he clearly felt from his simple and strongly poetic characters. In part, he was caught in a trap of his own design: Natty, who exemplifies the Jacksonian confidence in the abilities of the common people, argues persuasively for the ethical and epistemological inferiority of books to actual experience, implicitly including the books in which Natty himself has his being. Like Clara's indictments of authorship as the exercise of an illegitimate and even autocratic power over characters, Natty suggests that illiteracy is not so much an inability to read as a principled rejection of texts and, as such, the mark of characterological authenticity which an author, as the producer of texts to which others were enslaved, could not possess. In this spirit, Cooper was criticized for his reliance upon J. G. Heckewelder's compendium of Native American folklore which rendered his Indian characters "false and ideal"; while his alienation from his other characters was registered in "something obscure and mysterious" in their actions that precluded the reader from doing anything other than "merely look on and perceive" behavior that remained fundamentally mysterious.[82]

Moreover, Cooper was the target of a cogent critique leveled not so much against him personally as against the popular genre of Indian narratives whose master author he was internationally acknowledged to be. John Neal, reviewing *The Last of the Mohicans*, derided it as "a tissue of common-place Indian adventures."[83] Grenville Mellen was more explicit: the problem was not that Cooper could not identify with his Indians and their white companions but that no sophisticated reader could (although many were made to feel they should). Writing in 1828 for the *North American Review*, Mellen attributed the literary vogue of the Indian to a peculiar authorial assumption: "Starting with a principle, correct in itself, but like other correct principles requiring judicious application, that works of imagination should represent the character and manners of the country where they are written, our novelwriters, at least those of the second class, have made their works too purely of the soil."[84] This excessively literal understanding of nativist purity was realized in the character of the Indian, "made to talk like Ossian for whole pages, and measure out hexameters, as though he had been practising for a poetic prize" (142). In fact, Mellen explained, the Indians were "simple, silent creatures," the interest of whose lives could not sustain a narrative. "The character of the Indian," he continued,

> is a simple one, his destiny is a simple one, all around him is simple. We use the expression here in its most unpoetical sense. But mere simplicity is not all that is needed. There must be some event in the life of a hero, to keep us from growing weary of him. He must not lie upon our hands; the author must keep him in business, and he must have more business than is comprehended in the employment of the scalping-knife or the paddle, to become the subject of our refined sympathies, or to gratify a cultivated taste. He must be mentally engaged. The savage says but little; and after we have painted him in the vivid and prominent colors which seem necessary to represent him amidst his pines and waterfalls, — after we have set him before our readers with his gorgeous crown of feathers, his wampum and his hunting-bow, it would seem that we have done as well as we could for him. (143)

In an effort to "fit the savage for our modern novel," the novel inadvertently renders him ridiculous by making him into "a poetic savage, instead of the true aboriginal in the naked and strong relief which he naturally presents" (146).[85] For the sake of representing Americanness in literature, poetry had been permitted to dissemble the truth of the actual Indian's naked silence, a truth that, were it squarely faced, militated against simplicity as a subject for literary representation.[86]

To the extent that, as James Russell Lowell had pointed out in his satirical poem of 1848, *A Fable for Critics*, Cooper's "Indians, with proper respect be it said, / Are just Natty Bumpo daubed over with red," the critics' reservations

applied to the character of the backwoodsman as well.[87] For the aestheticians
of innocence, increasingly committed to the idea that the future American
poet would partake of a sublime simplicity and poetically translate it from
out of his own representative life into a distinctively national literature,
critical skepticism about the literary viability of simplicity had to be confronted. How can what appears irrefutably to be the essential eventlessness
of the simple life and the inarticulateness of simple folk be rendered sufficiently weighty to sustain a narrative without dissembling the content of that
life in the process of poetic representation? How might the gap between
being and representation, a corrupting warp through which experience had
to pass before it could be offered as poetry, be elided, an accomplishment that
the aestheticians of innocence were certain would distinguish a genuinely
American poetic production?

Cooper himself had indirectly, imagistically, suggested an answer to this
dilemma (which by the late 1830s had become acute) in the first of the
Leatherstocking tales with the scene of Natty's transcendent feat of fishing.
It is no accident that in the last of the Leatherstocking novels, *The Deerslayer*
(1841), in which Natty is young and the wilderness pristine, Cooper refers to
the lake in which the aged Natty of *The Pioneers* had so impressively fished
not as Otsego but as "Glimmerglass." The name encapsulates the exemplary
artistry of Natty's hunt in which the invisible domain below the lake's surface
is made transparent to his gaze. His spear — a redeemed version of the spectral spindle — passes back and forth between the mirrored realms, permitting
the innocent exercise of Natty's will to realize in material form the sublime
creature of the invisible world. Natty's access to invisible realities is both
direct and selfless, the mark of democratic personality as well as sublime
authorship which the author, and not his fictional character alone, must
assume. According to the prescriptions for national poetic authenticity elaborated by the critical vanguard of the 1830s and early 1840s (the years in
which Cooper attempted to reconceptualize his authorial role), the American author as democratic personality would take his place with the silent red
and white men of the woods whose most mysterious activities were shown to
be wholly grounded in an ethos that declared the sufficiency of the visible
world to all desirable knowledge. But if the author was to stand with Natty
and Chingachgook, he implicitly stood with their undomesticated precursors: the ventriloqua of Salem and the specters they invoked, the spectacular

convert, the evangelical itinerant and the itinerant ventriloquist, the slave in the cage — all of them speakers of extraordinary deconstructive power.

Unlike his forebears, the invisible realm to which the future American author would innocently accede was not to be the spectral dimension or the individual heart; nor was it the world of God's determinations considered either as spiritual identity or as historical destiny. It was neither the invisible reality that lay behind the apparent serenity of a southern forest nor the opaque surface of a wilderness lake, the red and black states of "savage wildness" or "enslaved submission."[88] Instead, the invisible realm to which the critics beginning with E. T. Channing wished the poet silently to lead them was the domain of essential Americanness, whose visible signs were the "familiar" and "low" facts of common life whose meanings remained opaque to those most eager for a genuine national literature. In "The American Scholar," Emerson dismissed the details of the nation's burgeoning economic, social, and political life as great irrelevancies, "merest appearance" that had blinded the culture to its own inalienable significance (73). The meaning of America was preserved in the ubiquitous space of ordinary American life where it realized itself at every moment "without observation" if in full view, like the young Whitefield's spiritual transformation which occurred in full view of, but unremarked by, his spiritually blind adversaries whose opposition fueled the uncontainability of his resurrecting power (71). America itself figured as the new invisible realm or spectral domain from which the critical class awaited the emergence of an author whose very being — iconic, monumental, concealing no "ambidexter" pockets of will, meaning, or desire — would comprise its essence, and thus offer a blueprint for an atomized nation's reintegration as its own truest self. For the book-bound literary class to discover this poet, still unremarked in the mass of common people, would be to receive a renewed vision of the living "facts" of an authentic American poetry — in Emerson's famous formulation, "[t]he meal in the firkin; the milk in the pan; the ballad in the street; the news of the boat; the glance of the eye; the form and the gait of the body" (78).[89]

The materials for a rich poetry, although scattered everywhere and visible everywhere, were invisible and thus unavailable to the literary class, Emerson maintained, which explained their chronic "discontent" (77). Their commitment to what they regarded as a "higher order of fictitious composition," and their subsequent proclivity to seek Americanness in an exotic but nonexistent dimension suggested to them by European literary conventions (a storied past or romantic associations), had prompted their ignorance of what lay close to hand.[90] This fundamental error is discernable in W. H. Gardiner's exasperated question, "How are [we] to get over this familiarity of things, yet fresh in their newest gloss?" "[T]he face of a fair country" and its eventless past, Gardiner complained, constitute opacities whose significances remained unavailable to critical scrutiny, no matter how well disposed: "you see them as they now are, and you see nothing beyond."[91] The "broad, garish sunshine of every-day life," Prescott observed, had blinded writers to what might lie below "the crust of society."[92] Thoreau expressed a similar frustration: "Our vision does not penetrate the surface of things. We think that that *is* which *appears* to be." And yet, it was increasingly maintained, in critical treatises and manifestos, that the source of cultural fecundity, "the vigorous life of the nation," derived from "the deep rich soil at the bottom of society" — the humus of the common.[93]

In the 1830s and 1840s, similar convictions were everywhere expressed, by literary critics, journalists, and even politicians (of conservative as well as democratic persuasions). Orestes Brownson, for example, stated two decades before Whitman's *Leaves of Grass* that the national literature would emerge not from the libraries or literary societies but in the "thronged mart," and that anyone ambitious to discover the natural culture of being as it was unfolding in America should spend his days with the "really living, moving, toiling and sweating, joying and sorrowing people around them."[94] According to their opening statement for *The Dial* in July 1840, Margaret Fuller and Emerson named precisely this crowd as the basis for a new American readership "united only in common love of truth, and love of its work":

Of these acolytes, if some are happily born and well bred, many are no doubt ill dressed, ill placed, ill made — with as many scars of hereditary vice as other men. Without pomp, without trumpet, in lonely and obscure places, in solitude, in servitude, in compunctions and privations, trudging beside the team in the dusty road, or drudging a hireling in other men's cornfields, schoolmasters, who teach a few children rudiments for a pittance, ministers of small parishes of the obscurer sects, lone women in dependent condition, matrons and young maidens, rich and poor, beautiful and hard-favored, without concert or proclamation of any kind, they have silently given in their several adherence to a new hope.[95]

As their adherence was silent and unplanned, so would the poet whose work they awaited tacitly explain his own inarticulateness by realizing in his poetry the maxim that "[t]here is somewhat in all life untranslatable into language." His poems will evince their greatness by proving uncontainable, immune to the "imprisoning" power of thought and incorporating only the "lifelike word" that "slips through our fingers" (3). That is, "the pens of practised writers" would be so completely identified with "the discourse of the living" that, in publishing their effusions, *The Dial* would not be "multiply[ing] books" but rather "report[ing] life" (4). Literature was undergoing a "democratical revolution," Emerson and Fuller declared in the second number, which meant that poetry became "the right and power of every man to whose culture justice is done."[96] The promise that a democratic literature, written by and for the people, would prove uniquely able to elide the gap between being and representation is here explicitly given.[97]

Such sentiments, rather than reflecting a shift in critical focus from a refined notion of literary worth to a populist criterion, what the literary historian Benjamin Spencer described as a "steady ascendancy of the people as theme, audience, and resource," actually begged a question that would prove of central importance to the way in which a democratic literature would be defined and its production solicited: the problem of the democratic author's relation to democratic character whose existence the former would be in some fashion instrumental in realizing.[98] In "The American Scholar," Emerson invoked the writings of Goldsmith, Burns, Cowper, Goethe, Wordsworth, Carlyle, and especially Swedenborg as "auspicious signs" of the "elevation of what was called the lowest class in the state [which] assumed in literature a very marked and as benign an aspect" (77, 78). But if these writers are credited for having initiated this revolution in literary focus, Emerson ultimately invokes them in order to dismiss them as the creators of "exhausted" texts, representations rather than elements of the natural culture of being that had been thoroughly mined in the course of America's now-concluded literary apprenticeship (76). The present task was not to read about the "dumb abyss" of present life but to ensure that it became "vocal with speech" (70). Paradoxically, though, in 1837 Emerson could only envision the common man at whose feet he longed to sit—and who for his innocence of European culture was elected to redress the silence of the American literary abyss with "heroic sentiments, noble biographies, melodious verse, and the conclusions of history" — as himself dumb: "Long he must stammer in his speech," Emerson decreed,

> often forego the living for the dead. Worse yet, he must accept — how often! — poverty and solitude. For the ease and pleasure of treading the old road, accepting the fashions, the education, the religion of society, he takes the cross of making his own, and, of course, the self-accusation, the faint heart, the frequent uncertainty and loss of time, which are the nettles and tangling vines in the way of the self-relying and self-directed; and the state of virtual hostility in which he seems to stand to society, and especially to educated society. (73)

As Marx had imagined the withering away of the state after the proletarian revolution, so Emerson, rediscovering the fraudulent antinomianism of Clara Wieland, imagined the withering away of the authorial voice in favor of an agentless poetic utterance whose essential truth could never be falsified by the individual poet's intrusive ego.[99] The prescription of inarticulateness transcends the requirement for an authorial innocence evident, for example, in the Columbia professor John McVickar's tribute to the memory of Walter Scott in 1833. McVickar lauds Scott for his "child-like simplicity" and "unsophisticated heart," and claims that his authorial practice amounted to his "simply transferring the leading lines from the eye to the imagination — even as the plate or the stone, transfers the picture to the paper destined to receive it."[100] In his prescriptive portrait of the genuine American literatus, Emerson goes beyond this conception of the author as transcribing from essence rather than inventing it to insist on a complete conflation of being and representation: the American author will *be* the unspeaking stone and the receiving paper; or, in Melville's reinterpretation of the late 1880s in which even the primitive technology of stone and paper is repudiated, he will be the bud whose imminent opening the nation awaits.

In 1844, Emerson complained, as Whitman would complain almost thirty years later, that although "America is a poem" impatient "for meters," he continues to "look in vain for the poet whom I describe."[101] This was so despite the length and detail of the description: the poet would be "representative," standing "among partial men for the complete man" (223); "the man without impediment," both "the sayer" and "the namer" whose naming is a resignation to what is, "the divine *aura* which breathes through forms" (224,

233). His denominative powers would prove exquisite: whereas most of us can hear the "primal warblings" of an unearthly music, when we attempt to write down what we hear we unfailingly "substitute something of our own, and thus miswrite the poem" (224). The poet, however, would produce near-perfect "transcripts," for he would have been "present and privy to the appearance which he describes" (224, 225). The poet, "who re-attaches things to nature and the Whole," would exemplify the truth that "form is an effect of character," and his exemplarity would allow him to occupy the point "where Being passes into Appearance and Unity into Variety" and then passes back again (229, 227). He will make the dumb abyss vocal because he will put "eyes and a tongue into every dumb and inanimate object," and thenceforward all speech, like his speech, will "flo[w] with the flowing of nature" (230). But the "Languagemaker" himself holds back from making language, and once again, Emerson insists that the genuine poet's signature must be his silence (231).

Inarticulateness, Emerson decreed, is the sign of a characterological purity essential to the production of poetry, and the only basis for a representative art. For one not disposed to silence and exile but who subscribed wholeheartedly to Emerson's understanding of democratic poetic production, what possibilities for poetic expression remained? One might represent one's relationship to the personified poetic source, but the problem of so doing, given the sacred silence of the object of representation, the character, was as thorny as the accomplishment of a poetry of inarticulacy itself. Might the ambitious American author pose as the representative voice of this representative character? How would the author portray the relationship of his voice to the common man's silence, of his sophistication to the common man's simplicity, if simplicity was understood as the guarantor of purity? Alternatively, was the author to present himself as indistinguishable from his character, the ideal poet, and thus in some manner the innocent subject of his own characterization? In the former case, where some distance between author and character is acknowledged, the writer would have to portray himself as having achieved an idealized neutrality so that the pure content of the common man's unspeaking soul could receive its articulation through his agency, but undepleted in its power and uncorrupted in its purity, as Emerson maintained, "without diluting or depraving" (233). In the latter case, where creator and creation are conflated, the writer might represent himself as achieving a self-identical, indeed Godly, moment in which land, literature, and literatus — nation, poem, and poet — would come into being simultaneously. This fantastic choice circumscribes the contradiction of the writer's dilemma in the context of the aesthetic of innocence. Charged as the unwitting broker between character and identity before he put pen to paper, he was the one who of necessity made manifest the critical difference between the embodiment of cultural purity and its articulation.[102]

For Whitman, both America and the American poet were poems that had not yet been written or spoken. As the poem realized itself — through the neutral, because utterly self-identical, "channel" of the poet, through whom inchoate content would achieve its articulation uncontaminated by any admixture of the poet's own "elegance or effect or originality" — the poem would simultaneously realize the identity of America and the American poet (1855P 717). Land, literature, and literatus would come into being simultaneously, in the perfection of poetry, but could only do so as a revealed consubstantiality, as "*reciprocal* terms, each of which implies the other."[103] That is, the articulation of the poem, as it accomplished the identity of land and of poet, realized the identity between land, poet, and poem as well. This miracle of simultaneity, wherein each term contained the other in a balletic equilibrium of power and possibility, would supersede the oppositional encounter crucial to the production of democratic personality. Whitman's poetry boasted its internalization and neutralization of every opposition to be found in the world of antebellum America: his great inventories both declare and eradicate the difference between then and now, now and later, here and there, you and me, poet and poem, poem and body, poem and land, land and poet, and so forth. The poet, "a figure immune to mediation," achieved this miracle of simultaneity through the medium of his own "richest fluency," a term with which Whitman described his perfect self-correspondence, his achieved existence as pure self-referentiality unobstructed by consciousness, his attainment of an unconditional self-reliance.[104] Yet possibly to be both poet and poem would be to straddle the incompatible statuses of creator and created and thus to deviate from pure self-reference. In that case, every bringing-forth, every concrete word, would represent a siphoning off of the poet's richest fluency, the primal fluid from which the selfhood of nation, literature, and individual derived. It was this premise that Melville placed at the heart of his final novel, and of its central figure Billy Budd, Whitman's inarticulate poet.

Melville's Anxiety of Innocence: The Handsome Sailor

Do you not know O speech how the buds beneath you are folded?

— WALT WHITMAN, *"Song of Myself"*

Who aint a slave? Tell me that.

— HERMAN MELVILLE, *Moby-Dick*

There is no such thing in man's nature, as a settled and full resolve . . . except at the very moment of execution.

— NATHANIEL HAWTHORNE, *Twice-told Tales*

I

"I feel, with dejection and amazement," Walt Whitman lamented in *Democratic Vistas*, "that few or none have yet really spoken to this people, created a single, image-making work for them [so that their] central spirit [remains] uncelebrated, unexpress'd."[1] He dismissed contemporary literature as a "mockery," the product of a merely "verbal intellect" powerless to move those who had retained an instinctive fidelity to the ideal of genuine American expression and who, in their isolation, remained "obedient, lowly, reverent to the voice, the gesture of the god, or holy ghost, which others see not, hear not" (*DV* 412, 395, 391). While the "class of supercilious infidels" refused to be silent, those whose access to invisible realities qualified them to testify to the authentically American — and whose collective voice, Whitman projected, "though without polish'd coherence, and a failure by the standard called criticism [will sound] real at least as the lightnings" — remained utterly "voiceless" (*DV* 395, 391, 388).

Because it belied his career-long celebration of inarticulateness as both the sign and guarantor of the national poet's purity, Whitman tempered his anxiety regarding the significance of America's continuing silence by praising "the noiseless operation of one's isolated self" as the source of all genuine poetry, as he had from the first attributed the richest fluency to the silent movements of the body (*DV* 399).[2] Thus he constructed in *Democratic Vistas* a somewhat elaborate account of this silence, characterizing the authentic national poet as still a sleeping infant, not only unconscious and prelingual but geographically remote, culturally ignorant, and thus "happily unrecognized and uninjur'd" by the cultural elite (*DV* 412). From these buds, he prophesied, will "sprout, in time, flowers of genuine American aroma" (*DV* 413). If in this passage Whitman represented silence as both a natural attribute of the "infant genius" as well as the environment necessary to his germination, the benignity of the characterization begs the question of his poetic development. If, as Whitman seemed to suggest, purity cannot be simultaneously embodied and articulated, then what kind of poetic expression can America expect from its budding poet?

Whitman's steadfast advocacy of voicelessness as the condition for genuine national-poetic expression reveals his substantial engagement with a cultural ideology elaborated with increasing detail and urgency in response to the continuing absence of a national literature: an American aesthetic of innocence. As it developed from the postrevolutionary through the antebellum eras, this aesthetic of innocence took shape less as a set of assumptions concerning the form or content of a future national literature than as a set of prescriptions for the realization of authentic national-poetic selfhood. The growing body of literary-critical pronouncements on the character of the genuine American poet were intended in part to facilitate the nation's recognition of this figure when he should appear, but primarily to provide a set of guidelines, a discursive mold, for his eventual embodiment. The composite portrait of the genuine American poet thus produced is a conventionally romantic one: he is required to be in humble circumstances, unselfconscious and isolated from the artificial life of cities, and possessed of an unstudied simplicity. But as the American critical establishment reelaborated this type in the course of the nineteenth century, his most striking because most paradoxical trait (considering the growing urgency of his mission to express national identity) was his increasingly extreme innocence of language, as if only the poet's inarticulateness and illiteracy guaranteed the purity of the national essence he was invented to contain.

In the course of his career as a poet and a writer of poetic manifestos, Whitman provided the aesthetic of innocence with a programmatic integrity, an elaborate set of criteria for the production and reception of an authentic national literature. But it was Emerson, from whom Whitman explicitly drew, who disclosed the ideological rationale according to which the profoundly paradoxical critical demand for an innocent national art was for so long supported.[3] In "The Poet," the premiere essay of *Essays: Second Series* (1844), Emerson identified inarticulateness as the fundamental trait of American national-poetic character; in so doing, he revealed that the poet was less silent by nature than silenced at the behest of the critic. As Emerson proclaimed with his own ready eloquence, the poet, although uniquely "without impediment," must yet "abdicate a manifold and duplex life" and "be content that others speak for [him]" — in particular, members of the financial, political, and social elite. He continued his apostrophe to the speechless poet by directing him to withdraw from the life of the world:

> Others shall be thy gentlemen and shall represent all courtesy and
> worldly life for thee; others shall do the great and resounding actions
> also. Thou shalt lie close hid with nature, and canst not be afforded to the
> Capitol or the Exchange. The world is full of renunciations and appren-
> ticeships, and this is thine; thou must pass for a fool and a churl for a long
> season. This is the screen and sheath in which Pan has protected his well-
> beloved flower, and thou shalt be known only to thine own, and they
> shall console thee with tenderest love.

In effect, with this decree, Emerson condemns his ideal poet to the status of a character for whom others speak in default of his own independent utterance. But Emerson mitigates his sentence of silence, exile, and passivity by assuring the "balked" poet that his transcendent "rage" — the inevitable product of his inarticulateness, itself the result of his mandated, yet voluntary, subordination to cultural spokesmen — shall in time find expression as limitless power:

> Stand there, balked and dumb, stuttering and stammering, hissed and
> hooted, stand and strive, until at last rage draw out of thee that *dream-*

power which every night shows thee is thine own; a power transcending all limit and privacy, and by virtue of which a man is the conductor of·the whole river of electricity.[4]

With striking precision, the passage anticipates the fate of Melville's own "flower," Billy Budd, as he stands balked and stuttering before his articulate adversary, John Claggart, a posture finally relieved by the fatal blow the enraged Billy deals Claggart which in turn releases a "vocal current electric" among various members of the ship's crew.[5] In his docile silence as well as his stuttering rage, Billy Budd faithfully exemplifies the ideal poet as Emerson conceived him; moreover, he conforms precisely to Whitman's added speci-fications of authentic poetic character, including the organic association he represents of perfect poetry with perfect physicality.[6] Thus Billy demon-strates an utter ignorance of "the idea of the covert, the lurid, the maleficent, the devil, the grim estimates inherited from the Puritans, hell, natural de-pravity, and the like" (*DV* 414). He is distinctive for "his cheerful simplicity, his adherence to natural standards, . . . and by the absence in him of doubt, ennui, burlesque, persiflage, or any strain'd and temporary fashion" (*DV* 414). When Melville claims that "the spirit lodged within Billy . . . made the dimple in his dyed cheek, suppled his joints, and dancing in his yellow curls made him preeminently the Handsome Sailor" (64), we recall Whitman's emphasis on the primary expressiveness of physical beauty in his serenade to his budding poet: "your very flesh shall be a great poem and have the richest fluency not only in its words but in the silent lines of its lips and face and between the lashes of your eyes and in every motion and joint of your body" (1855P 715).

Because he embodies with such exactitude the positive traits of the inno-cent poet, Billy exhibits a characteristic that, although desirable in itself and integral to the critical portrait of innocence, throws into question his fitness to carry out his mediating function as the inviolable channel through which national identity would achieve its purest expression. In *Democratic Vistas*, Whitman confessed himself haunted by the possibility that, despite the sim-ple poet's unique ability to gain access to the "interior and real," the "con-flicting and irreconcilable interiors" of the nation might exceed his power to resolve "all lesser and definite distinctions in vast, indefinite, spiritual, emo-tional power" (*DV* 367, 368). For Melville's Billy, this inability to "deal in double meanings and insinuations of any sort," coupled with his inability to articulate, his absolute reliance on the "richest fluency" of his body, leads him not to poetic impotence but to murder, and involves the narrator of his story in an almost incoherent attempt to establish the truth of his innocence (12). Despite Emerson, in *Billy Budd* events no more "sing themselves" than they did at Salem.[7]

Melville's final novel thus textually enacts the paradox of inarticulate innocence as that which both legitimated and promised to redress the nation's enduring silence about itself.[8] Critics have long speculated upon Melville's purpose in writing *Billy Budd*, his first work of prose fiction since his withdrawal from the profession of authorship after the spectacular critical failure of *The Confidence-Man* (1857) some thirty years earlier.[9] I propose that the novel offers Melville's retrospective account of his own professional failure, his inability or refusal even to dissemble the "innocence" that might have quieted critical fears of his lack of "veracity" and the consequent desire, as one hostile reviewer expressed it, to "freeze him into silence." *Billy Budd* shows with relentless specificity what happens when the hypothesized national poet, conceived as a "novice in the complexities of the factitious life," is actually made to perform in the fictitious life (14). In order to read Melville's final novel as offering his assessment of a cultural ideology so influential in his day as to determine, to a significant degree, the parameters according to which works of literature would be judged as legitimate or illegitimate, representative or misrepresentative of the infant nation, one must look first to the rage that Emerson named as the silent poet's compensation for a life of mandated marginality. The "river of electricity" that Emerson suggested might one day constitute the inarticulate and enraged poet's compensatory "*dream*-power" is realized in *Billy Budd* as a "vocal current electric" initiated by Claggart's lie about Billy and galvanized by Billy's responsive stuttering and fatal blow to Claggart's forehead.[10] In the remainder of this chapter, I would like first to trace the trajectory of this vocal current as it sweeps through the novel in order to show how it functions both as the key to its integrity and as its governing and triumphant contradiction. I would then like to show, through an analysis of the role the narrator plays vis-à-vis the usurping dynamism of the vocal current, why and how Melville rejected the Emersonian and Whitmanian practice of copiously producing words about the superiority of wordlessness as the sole guarantor of national-poetic integrity.[11]

Impressed from a merchant vessel to join the "fighting peacemakers" of the *Bellipotent*, a British man-of-war actively engaged in the struggle against revolutionary France, Billy Budd, remarkable for his beauty and cheerful disposition, joins the crew without a murmur of protest (8).[12] The new foretopman's peculiarities include his utter ignorance of his parentage combined with the manifest purity of his bloodlines; his inability to read or to deal in double meanings and insinuations; and a verbal defect characterized as a type of Hawthornean "birth-mark," an "organic hesitancy" of speech, or stutter, which surfaced "under sudden provocation of strong heart-feeling" (12, 19). His "significant personal beauty" in combination with his extreme simplicity stimulates a profound antipathy in the ship's Master-at-arms, John Claggart (63). Having failed to tempt Billy into an outright act of insubordination, Claggart nevertheless reports to the ship's captain, directly following a harrowing encounter with a French vessel, that he has found Billy guilty of attempting to foment mutiny among the impressed men. Judging the charge unlikely given Billy's reputation, Captain Vere, plagued with anxiety over the recent mutinies at Spithead and the Nore, decides to bring both accuser and unsuspecting accused together before him so that he might read the truth of Claggart's charge, or its untruth, in Billy's face.[13] When Billy begins to stutter in reaction to the lie, Vere immediately recognizes the proof of his innocence in his inability to articulate it.[14] As Thoreau had said of his simpleminded visitor to Walden who confessed to a deficiency of intellect, "And there he was to prove the truth of his words."[15] At this moment, being and representation coincide, but the mixture proves extremely volatile.

In his attempts to reassure Billy, Vere instead intensifies his anxiety to utter the truth until, in a "convulsed tongue-tie," Billy deals a fatal blow to Claggart's forehead (93). As he ruefully tells a drumhead court of three officers which Vere convenes directly following the event, "Could I have used my tongue I would not have struck him" (102). The word for which violence becomes a substitute is the word of self-identity: I am true — a word whose integrity the blow instantly fractures, as all but Billy realize when he states before the court, "I have eaten the King's bread, and I am true to the King" (102). Vere understands Billy's "essential innocence" but fears that if he does not execute Billy for the crime of mutiny, the crew will misinterpret clemency as weakness and stage an actual uprising (121). By the time of the trial, Vere has achieved the legal rationale for a death sentence instinctively and instantaneously pronounced. Against all his officers' protestations of the unintentional nature of his crime, Vere presses for Billy's immediate execution (121). With no faith in the crew's ability to appreciate a verdict of clemency, Vere overpowers his court with the rhetorical force of his arguments, and Billy is forthwith hung before the assembled crew.

II

Directly after the ship's surgeon confirms the consequences of Billy's "undeniable deed," Vere passionately exclaims, "Struck dead by an angel of God! Yet the angel must hang!" (102, 95). From this moment, Billy's execution is decided, even as the radically paradoxical nature of his crime — partaking as Vere perceives it of both depravity and divinity — receives its most concise expression. Vere's horrified exclamation reveals that, despite the guise of military disciplinarian he assumes, he immediately apprehends a sacred dimension to Billy's deed which both eradicates and constitutes its meaning. Vere's Billy will hang as an angel, and not as a murderer. Yet hang he will: according to Vere's legal view, persuasively elaborated before the court, only by rigorously excluding this sacred dimension from judicial consideration can the paradox of murderous innocence be eliminated. Vere aspires to purest neutrality; "the light of [the] martial code" shall illuminate as does, in Ishmael's words, "the great principle of light" which reveals by virtue of the fact that it "for ever remains white or colorless in itself," and which, could it operate ideally — that is, without medium — "would touch all objects, even tulips and roses, with its own blank tinge" (98).[16]

What the "discomposed" Surgeon uncomprehendingly witnesses, then, is Vere's tormented preliminary step toward a hermeneutic strategy that he will represent to his court as one of confinement: "a martial court must needs in the present case," he insists, "confine its attention to the blow's consequence, which consequence justly is to be deemed not otherwise than as the striker's deed" (95, 103). The confinement of the sacred to an area of jurisdiction superintended not by the Prince of Peace but by the God of War entails a host of repudiations, all of which intend the refinement of the jury's focus. Together, these provide a representative sampling of what for Vere partakes of the logic of the sacred, rather than the logic of the law. Accordingly, the

Angel of God, Budd, who vanquishes the "serpent," Claggart, is himself vanquished by Vere's exhortation to his jury to challenge — and vanquish — moral scruple in favor of "a lawful rigor"; concern about Billy's intent in consideration of his "overt act"; the private conscience in favor of the imperial one formulated in code; the feminine heart in favor of the cool head; and theories of natural justice in favor of the ready application of martial law (93, 108, 106). In short, for Vere the sacred embraces all considerations of narrative context, the nuances and subtleties of those "antecedents" to the murder whose absence so baffles the Surgeon (95).

In his desire to eliminate ambiguity, then, Vere condemns narrative itself to irrelevance. Supported by the overriding and undoubted materiality of Claggart's corpse, Vere pronounces narrative — the extenuating circumstances of the case which occupy the first two-thirds of the novel — "hardly material" (103). Inert as a dead snake, Claggart's body is used to corroborate Vere's axiom that narrative, in its struggle to provide a psychologically creditable motive for the murder, as well as in its ancient (and, the narrator confesses, less fashionable) guise as that which chronicles the lure of the serpent for the unsullied, is a matter for "psychologic theologians," not judges (101, 104).

This horrific power of the corpse to swallow the text in the name of confinement to the undeniable deed is manifest in the narrator's careful description of the arrangement of Vere's rooms in which Billy's ordeal and trial take place. Vere's quarters consist of two small staterooms situated on either side of a central space which, "expanding forward into a goodly oblong of length," is illuminated by porthole windows "convertible" into embrasures for carronades. Vere's courtroom is both a cross and an instrument of war. Its small staterooms (the arms of the cross) become, on one side, the "jail" containing the stuttering prisoner, and on the other, the "dead-house" containing the eternally tongue-tied Claggart (101). This courtroom, then, within which Vere argues for the arrest of narrative as a theological matter inappropriate to a court of law, itself reinstates that paradox he struggles to eliminate; it begs the question of its inscribed cross. Do the arms of the cross separate the inarticulate innocent and the lying iniquitous, or do they unite the condemned and the corpse, separated in truth only by a few fleeting hours? Does the cross refer ironically to the law as that imperfect instrument by which the saintly are condemned by the worldly, and therefore to itself as

"setting a question-mark against the whole course of this world and its inevitability"?[17] Or might it suggest something far more scandalous: the perfect
symmetry of an unthinkable equation?

In its perfect formal symmetry, the cross identifies Vere's angel of God
with the one he strikes dead. This identification is deployed in the court's
verdict, characterized by the narrator as a "jugglery of circumstances" by
which the innocent and the guilty exchange their distinguishing features,
becoming indistinguishable and finally interchangeable in the process. The
official report of Billy's execution contained in a naval chronicle reifies this
jugglery as historical truth; until the narrator's restoration of narrative context, this symmetrical inversion of truth stood alone "in human record to
attest what manner of men respectively were John Claggart and Billy Budd."
The substitution of an "authorized" falsehood for narrative truth can only be
read as an ironic indicator of the extent and the implications of Vere's failure
to eliminate paradox. Far from eradicating ambiguity, the light of the martial
code has reconstituted it, illuminating not Billy's undeniable deed but something of a "mysterious swindle," precisely an illicit exchange, which underlies
the crisis of mutiny aboard the *Bellipotent* (98, 134, 42). This jugglery, swindle, or exchange — expressed textually as various instances of inversion and
politically as the twin crises of mutiny within and revolution without — is
itself the generic sign of what Melville calls "the deadly space between," a
vacuum or hidden warp, both characterological and structural, that provides
explanation for and context of the fatal confrontation of Claggart and Billy.[18]

The "deadly space between" is first named in the text as an element of
Claggart's character description and is intended to provide an insight into
"the hidden nature of the Master-at-arms," upon which, the narrator insists,
the "point of the present story turn[s]." Thus, the narrator tells us, in a
chapter marked by a sense of impatience with the "hints" he has offered to
account for Claggart's villainy, that "to pass from a normal nature to him one
must cross the 'deadly space between'" (61, 58).[19] If, as character description,
the phrase seems to partake of the narrator's own sense of insufficiency to his
task, as the novel's structural principle, the deadly space acquires enormous
power. Made dynamic (as evangelical itinerancy made the space of spectacular conversion dynamic and realized its potential uncontainability), it travels
through the text as the "vocal current electric" to destructure even as it
structures. Its quintessential verbal expression in the text is Claggart's lie

about Billy's fidelity which, by engineering Billy's fall into plot, asserts a narrative chain whose links are yet independent of logic or truth. Because the text's reversals of signification, epitomized by the lie and indicative of the deadly space, are effected through some manner of formal symmetry, the narrator can only warn against the appearance of "symmetry of form" in narration. Immediately following his account of Billy's execution, he insists that such symmetry is only "attainable in pure fiction" and "can not so readily be achieved in a narration essentially having less to do with fable than with fact. Truth uncompromisingly told will always have its ragged edges" (131). The lie, that is, will be recognized by its apparent integrity, whereas narrative imbued with truth is narrative dismembered which will be known by its torn body.

The narrator's cautionary designation of narrative symmetry as the sign not of truth but of "pure fiction" retrospectively indicts the argument by which Vere urges a constriction of his and his jurors' focus to the dimensions of a truth beyond dispute. Vere's argument takes shape as the rhetorical counterpart of the cross-court in which it is delivered: as the formal symmetry of the court paradigmatically enacts the identification and then collapse into unity of Billy and Claggart, so does a fatal equation determine the syntactical peculiarity of Vere's argument for execution. Distinguished by the hermetic symmetry of tautology, it brings first act and consequence, and then act and agent, "into such proximity as to collapse the distinction between them."[20]

Vere's most concise articulation of his strategy as prosecutor, Billy's death sentence, reads as follows:

Quite aside from any conceivable motive actuating the Master-at-arms, and irrespective of the provocation to the blow, a martial court must needs in the present case confine its attention to the blow's consequence, which consequence justly is to be deemed not otherwise than as the striker's deed. (103)

On first impression, the death sentence seems simply to establish liability: Billy struck Claggart, Claggart is dead, therefore Billy is responsible for that death. Yet the semantic force of Vere's account does not derive from that relationship between its terms characterized by Kenneth Burke as a "ratio" — that is, premised upon some configuration of motive(s) and thereby generative of the logic and progress of narrative.[21] Rather, it states an equivalence demanded by Vere's confinement of focus to the deed, his rigorous looking only "to the frontage, the appearance" (108). This confinement, Vere asserts, is consonant with the entire operation of the military in time of war when all differences between men — especially those having to do with matters of conscience — are disregarded. With the elimination of the verb by which a relationship or ratio of difference, with its accompanying calculus of motivation, is determined (Billy struck and killed Claggart), an equivalence may be established in its stead (the striker's deed is the blow's consequence), marked by the disappearance of the act's agents. Paradoxically, then, in order to identify Billy as Claggart's murderer, Vere makes the murder agentless.

Vere's dismissal of motive, predicated upon the eradication of distinction between an act and its consequences as well as that between act and agent, makes his formulation logically and "dramatistically" (to use Burke's neologism) suspect. The death sentence tells us that the blow's consequence is the deed of a striker who struck a blow whose consequence is the deed of a striker who struck a blow, and so on. Its syntactic symmetry produces not a statement of liability (although it does produce a victim) but an endless circularity maintained by the false hub of the "is" around which the specious equivalents revolve. The space of the "is," which articulates the inversion of truth, is the deadly space: a space that tautologically both is and is not, that irrevocably separates while ineluctably uniting.

The structural dependence of Vere's tautology on the deadly space is manifested in its incorporation of the latter as a space of ignorance necessarily subtended between Claggart's motive for lying and the jury's ability to pass judgment upon it. The death sentence makes of Claggart's mind a sacred ground upon which one may not tread, and then immediately designates Billy's provocation to murder as on the far side of that same deadly space. Having divorced Billy's action from motive, Vere can now uphold the integrity of his innocence even as he identifies the Handsome Sailor with Claggart's consummate criminality. Thus, for all his abhorrence of ambiguity and his insistence on a rigorously constricted focus, Vere carries out a profoundly (if not intentionally) duplicitous project in which the narrator, through his own identification of the deadly space with Claggart, is implicated. In the very effort to bridge — literally to comprehend — the disjunction between the innocent Billy and his murderous act, the simple boy and his inconceivable fate, Vere finds himself dealing from the deadly space between. From that strategic position, the site of Claggart's primitive and originless (unmotivated) violence, he articulates the death sentence through which the text's central swindle is authorized: the designation of Billy as victimizer and Claggart as victim. Vere's verdict suffers in its reception by his jurors and by his crew accordingly.[22]

In effect, in urging his jury to confine their investigation to the fatal blow, Vere asks them to frame this event and to sever it from its narrative context. Thus framed, the deed appears to justify the sacrifice of "motive" and "provocation" in the name of objective truth. The framed event becomes the basis for what the jury of officers feels is a frame-up, "involving a prejudgement on [Vere's] part" (103, 104). At the "summary" trial "summarily convened," the sacrifice of narrative context — those "palliating circumstances" which the narrator seemed at such pains to represent — leads Vere's trio of petty officers reluctantly to condemn a man they know to be "innocent before God" (99, 100, 106). Claggart's corpse is emblematic of this divestiture of all extenuating circumstances: it remains for Vere to render a judgment based on the inert body of the denuded event. The corpse renders all else "immaterial," and, most fatally for narrative as for Billy, the question of motivation in particular. Thus it is no wonder that directly upon the pronouncement of Vere's death sentence, Billy, incapable of dealing in double meanings, considers his captain's words a "gesture ambiguous," and that the jury senses in them a "meaning unanticipated" which encourages them to suspect not only Vere's objectivity but even his sanity. Vere's death sentence (in its formal symmetry a verbal expression of the deadly space) is manifestly mimetic of Claggart's lie: both proclaim Billy's involvement in the capital crime of mutiny and both intend his destruction, even as both are surreptitiously premised upon a uniquely "adequate appreciation" of the "moral phenomenon" of his innocence (103, 104, 64).

If Vere's tautological death sentence is mimetic of Claggart's lie, then in its endless circularity, in its relation to narrative progress, it is analogous to Billy's stutter. A recoil of narrative upon itself, a damming of the flow of words, a capitulation to that which cannot be accounted for: the stutter and the tautology are those forms of language eminently eligible to be displaced by violence, and they result first in the execution of Claggart and then of

Billy. Vere's death sentence does not so much reveal independence of mind in the face of a complex legal problem as it establishes itself as part of a pattern initiated by the lie and recapitulated by the stutter: recoil and blow, failed articulation followed inevitably by violence.

Far from eradicating ambiguity, then, Vere's death sentence contributes to a marked pattern of failed articulations which conduce to the dialectical extension of (textual) violence as the "vocal current electric." Inarticulacy first manifests itself in Billy's stuttering response to Claggart's lie, followed immediately by the fatal blow. Lie, stutter, and blow collaborate in what we have designated, after Melville, the mysterious swindle: Claggart deploys a word (the lie) in place of the blow he cannot deliver, and Billy a blow in place of the word (of self-identity) he cannot utter. The violence of this initial exchange issues in the paradox of murderous innocence, an ambiguity which Vere considers deeply subversive and which he struggles to contain through the application of the most stringent of legal forms, capital punishment under the Mutiny Act. Intending to eradicate the paradox by positively identifying a victim and victimizer, Vere opposes his death sentence to the concerted effort of lie and blow to derive the truth of mutiny from the lie of mutiny.

Contrary to his intention, however, the death sentence tragically fails to cap the subversive potential of the lie by erecting against its accelerating force a bulwark of objective truth. Rather, Vere's death sentence succumbs to the paradoxical, partaking of both Claggart's lie (in function) and Billy's stutter (in form). Insofar as it constitutes a second manifestation of inarticulacy, a deformation of language coincident with a violent action, the death sentence extends the reach of the lie of mutiny, abetting it in its drive to establish itself as the truth of mutiny. In this manner, the death sentence establishes itself securely within the governing pattern of the mysterious swindle or illicit exchange, producing in its turn the authorized "jugglery" of the naval chronicle, a confusion of innocence and evil, truth and falsehood.

The dialectic generated by the lie, and whose first two terms are stutter and tautology, is the "vocal current electric," through which the lie permeates the text as an inexorable sequence of juggleries and swindles. The implications for narrative of this dialectical penetration of the text by the lie, as the narrator bears witness, appear ominous. Normally that instrument by which a temporal sequence "unravels" contradiction while preserving crucial sense-making distinctions, narrative in *Billy Budd* appears to be intercepted in its trajectory by the dynamic of the deadly space. Motivated by the peculiar intercourse of the liar and the innocent, the vocal current makes what was untrue true, a conversion which seems to elude the narrator's ability to account for it. Nevertheless, it is possible to track this peculiar dialectic of absence — the deadly space marking the limits of human comprehension, precisely that point past which the language of identity (of self, of criminal, of victim) cannot proceed — through those continuing manifestations of inarticulacy followed by violence which punctuate the text of *Billy Budd*. To grasp the dialectical dynamism of the vocal current and through it Melville's understanding of the intimate relationship of innocence and violence in narrative, we must look back to Claggart's lie, as its point of origin, and forward to the aborted mutiny of the *Bellipotent*'s crew with which Billy's story ends.

The deadly space first appears as a rupture of the wonted order of shipboard routine in the form of Claggart's false witness to Vere. It bears repeating that Claggart, according to the narrator's description of him, is profoundly alien, beyond the comprehension of normal natures and separated forever from them by the no-man's-land of the deadly space. Here, the deadly space is the primary element of the narrator's description of Claggart, one which justifies the former's falling into the "literary sin" of digression, in the end despairing of ever hitting the mark (40, 25). But with the lie to which Billy responds with the stutter and then the blow of transgression (more on the order of original sin, quite literally the fall into plot), the deadly space transcends its status as description. Enabled by Billy's innocence, the lie activates the vocal current by which truth is falsified and falsehood verified.

Thus, almost instinctively Vere considers Claggart's false report of Billy's mutinous intentions a violation of his beloved "measured forms," a violation which heralds immeasurable violence. For this reason, because he understands that the implicit violence of the lie is directed not against Billy but against himself, he threatens Claggart's life, warning him that "there is a yard-arm-end for the false-witness." At Vere's insistence, his initial conference with Claggart takes place without explicit mention of the word "mutiny," because for Vere such mention constitutes an explicitly mutinous challenge to his sovereignty as ship's commander. Claggart's resulting hints and allusions augment for Vere the dubiety of his "foggy tale," and he conceives of forcing the accuser to be "direct" by confronting him directly with the accused — here, made to witness for the soundness of the entire ship even more than for his own innocence, of which Vere is convinced in advance (89, 86).

As the narrator describes it, Claggart's lie constitutes an impurity epitomized by the "phenomenal" muddying of his eyes as he faces Billy and accuses him of conspiracy. Their normal violet "blurring into a muddy purple" anticipates the narrator's later comment on the difficulties inherent in distinguishing sanity from insanity, specifically in relation to Captain Vere: "Who in the rainbow can draw the line where the violet tint ends and the orange tint begins? Distinctly we see the difference of the colors, but where exactly does the one first blendingly enter into the other? So with sanity and insanity" (92, 97). Claggart's eyes suggest this perverse moment at which the human veers toward the monstrous and the sane toward the insane, signified by an emptying of the "lights of human intelligence" and its monstrous replacement by a "gelid" opacity, "like the alien eyes of certain uncatalogued creatures of the deep." The muddying of his eyes signals Claggart's recovery from the long "recoil" with which he had responded to the mystery of Billy's innocence up to the moment of their confrontation. With the lie, he strikes out, polluting Billy's "virgin" purity in one passionate discharge of "subterranean" feeling (92, 93, 65, 118, 83). This initial strike, when it finally occurs, is verbal: Claggart's illicit ejaculation of the forbidden word, mutiny. As a violent transgression of form, a mark of the monstrous, a polluting blow, an illicit ejaculation, Claggart's lie provides that fundamental asymmetry characteristic not of "pure fiction," not of romance, but of that generic anomaly, the text of "ragged edges," the fiction which is "truth uncompromisingly told." The lie's unwilling accomplice and abettor, the stutter, thus ironically afflicts the one through whom Billy's truth is told, the narrator.

Proceeding by fits and starts, appearing to give information when in actuality he withdraws it or undermines its authority, the narrator blames his inability to tell the tale of Billy Budd straightforwardly on the paucity of historical information about the Great Mutiny. So horrible was this "episode" in Britain's "grand naval story" that national pride all but suppressed its mention in naval histories. One may find references to it, the narrator complains, but no "narration," no "details." And yet why suppress the event, he asks, when a "well-constituted individual" might find a "considerate way" to treat the material? Some pages later, the narrator denies "considerateness" to be characteristic of "natures constituted like Captain Vere's." In so doing, he implies that the censorship which impedes his narrative originates not with the naval histories but with a particular vessel and another strategy of containment practiced by its captain which antedates his confinement of focus. So fearful is Vere of a "distempering irruption of contagious fever in a frame constitutionally sound" that he forbids all mention of the word mutiny. Aboard the *Bellipotent*, mutiny is the single word acknowledged as so susceptible to incarnation that no one dares utter it, an absent presence that causes all hands to act in wary anticipation of the materialization of plot or conspiracy (23, 38, 24).[23]

The suppression of the word constitutes that precondition by which the opportunistic lie initiates a dialectical movement, the vocal current, which leads to actual mutiny and thus to its own ultimate vindication as truth. Claggart, his "conscience being but the lawyer to his will" (a characteristic he shares with Vere), imputes to Billy a motive, thereby eliciting the latter's "lurking defect" — the stutter — with his own glance "of serpent fascination": he makes Billy mutinous. Vere, with equal acumen, deploys his "naval regard" and, by denying to either Claggart or Billy a motive, pronounces the blow's consequence the striker's deed: he sanctions Claggart's creation. The dialectical conversion of lie into truth is achieved at the point when the potential energy of mutiny, forever hovering about the edges of the text, ironically converts Vere's public indictment of Billy as a mutineer into an incitement to mutiny in its very pronouncement. Fearful that any articulation of the word will effect its literal incarnation, Vere becomes the unwitting high priest of his own "arrested allusion." In his effort to construct and stage a verdict that will preclude all interpretation — that is, all attempts to establish motive — Vere initiates a kind of inarticulate litany of the arrested allusion by which the sleeping god of Spithead and the Nore is invoked. As he ascends, the god speaks, and he speaks as we expect he will — with a stutter, his sacrificial "Vestal priestess" being none other than Billy himself (67, 87, 93).

Thus, Billy's "strange dumb gesturing and gurgling" when confronted with Claggart's false witness is replicated by the sailors as they hear Vere's account of the originating exchange of lie and blow. At first, the "throng of standing sailors" responds with an answering "dumbness like that of a seated congregation of believers in hell listening to the clergyman's announcement of his Calvinistic text." Although Vere refrains from "preachment" in making his announcement as he refrains from explicitly naming Billy's crime, these silent spaces in themselves constitute a hell-fire sermon, an exposition of original sin and predestination as determined by the Mutiny Act, "War's Child," for which "intent and non-intent is nothing to the purpose." Billy's crime "speaks for itself" no more than did Billy. Faced with the deadly space in its most comprehensive manifestation — as that which operates as a conduit for the most radical reversals and inversions of order, threatening the disintegration of meaning by positing both insurmountable difference and incomprehensible sameness — the collective dumbness yields at several points (93, 115, 108).

After Vere's announcement, after the crew's mechanical repetition of Billy's "conventional felon's benediction" of the captain, after the execution, and after the dropping of Billy's body into the sea, silence yields to a sound "inarticulate," "ominous," and "low." Like its predecessors, the stutter and the tautology, the inarticulate sound is born of revulsion and recantation. This "strange human murmur" blended with the screams of predatory seabirds (echo of Farmer James's discovery of the slave in the cage), akin to the "sloping advance through precipitous woods [of a] freshet-wave of a torrent suddenly swelled by pouring showers in tropical mountains," is the sound of the word never uttered, mutiny. As Billy's face during his struggle to articulate innocence was "as a crucifixion to behold," so the sailors' protestations are "pierced" by the whistles and drumbeats prefacing the meaningless command to "about ship" — an (unnecessary) reversal of the *Bellipotent*'s direction. The dialectic of the deadly space comes to a temporary halt as inarticulateness is driven back into a volatile muteness, the volatile muteness of Billy himself. Yet the "torrent" which it has released cannot be permanently blocked, the narrator implies, any more than can the related "torrent" of "novel opinion" by which the continent is "convulsed" (124, 128, 129, 93, 115, 36, 31).

To the extent that the assembled sailors wholeheartedly reject Vere's narration of Billy's crime and Claggart's victimization as a falsification of the fundamental moral difference between the two men, they ironically complete that dynamic by which the lie of mutiny establishes the truth of mutiny. Although this last pent-up release of feeling is not permitted to expend itself in a full-scale uprising, its short-lived manifestation is sufficient to establish it as part of a familiar pattern. The sailors' reaction to Vere's announcement, itself marked by the suppressed word, conforms to that pattern of recoil and blow — failed articulation and inevitable displacement by violence — by which the vocal current can be traced. Receiving its energy from the continued confinement of the word, the vocal current sweeps through the text, implicating all hands (with the exception of the liar Claggart, for whom language and violence coincide) in Billy's "virgin experience of the diabolical incarnate"; all, to a degree, share his innocence. But only Billy transcends the agony of the experience still innocent. Only Billy joins Claggart beyond the confines of a dialectic born of an express policy of confinement. Billy's appears to be the final and literal "ascendancy of character" that "ought to be" the captain's. The slow roll of the ship's hull, metonymically expressive of the mechanical obedience to brute power to which the men who live within it submit, becomes the instrument by which Billy's body ascends even as it is dropped seaward — a reversal of a wholly different order than that pervasive jugglery of circumstance that haunts the *Bellipotent* (118, 33, 98).

III

Melville's exploration in *Billy Budd* of an aesthetic of innocence upon the form and future of literary art included issues explicitly raised by Whitman in his manifestos, such as the necessity for "indirection" in poetic expression and the importance of shunning the "romance" as a generic and idiomatic medium for American artistic ambitions (1855P 712, 721, 722). For Whitman, however, these methodological considerations for the creation of a genuine national poetry could claim only a secondary importance. Instead, they depended for their authority upon a definition of the future poet that possessed its own rigorous characterological and organic requirements.

These requirements were, first, that the poet demonstrate an utter ignorance of all that partakes of the duplicitous or ambiguous; and second, that his perfect art derive from his perfect physicality. For Whitman, a body such as Billy's, all "innocence and nakedness," constitutes a "channel of thoughts and things" and ultimately — provided the poet does not impede the natural flow through the channel with "any elegance or effect or originality" — a channel of the self as well (1855P 719, 717). What emerges from the channel under these ideal conditions of noninterference "is of itself," possessing genuine independence: "all else," Whitman tells us, "has reference" (1855P 724). Firmly rooted in this system of pure self-referentiality and thereby secured against the possibility of misrepresentation, the true poet need not seek beyond the self, but composes "regardless of observation," heedless even of the supervisory observation of self-consciousness: "What I experience or portray shall go from my composition without a shred of my composition. You shall stand by my side and look in the mirror with me" (1855P 717).[24] Not only does Billy Budd as Melville's version of Whitman's body electric fully embody these requirements, but his story constitutes their activation on the plane of the fictitious which, as the narrator tells us, must always coincide with the factitious if it is to coincide with the truth. For Melville, this activation of a heretofore hypothetical innocence justifies his producing a narrative "tinctured with the Biblical element" and "savoring of Calvinism," although this is precisely what Whitman, let alone Melville's would-be fashionable reader (as well as Vere himself), explicitly proscribes (59, 60). For the same reason that Billy passes with ease Whitman's "test of a great literatus," he abysmally fails Vere's test of steady fidelity (*DV* 414). In doing so, he gainsays Whitman, who warned that "the time straying toward infidelity and confections and persiflage," the poet alone "by his steady faith" would persevere as an example of inviolable integrity (1855P 713).

In the blow, the event which occasions innocent Billy's fall into plot, the elements of Whitman's synthesis of poet and poetic practice — channel, mirror, and self-referentiality — undergo a sea change, acquiring a character that Melville evaluates according to "the Puritan's grim estimates." The deadly space, between people as between principles, functions as a conduit for the mysterious swindles and illicit exchanges we have examined, and in that capacity represents Whitman's channel of self-referentiality invaded and corrupted. Predictably, the defiler does not speak "with the perfect rectitude and insouciance of the movements of animals and the unimpeachableness of the sentiment of trees in the woods," which Whitman considered the "flawless triumph of art" — that is, unless one considers that the Great Artificer, the Serpent, is also an animal, and the Tree of Knowledge also a tree (1855P 717). When, after his "virgin experience" of the rupture of self-referentiality, the poet-subject holds up the mirror, he sees not his own innocent and naked reflection, "much such perhaps as Adam presumably might have been ere the urbane Serpent wriggled himself into his company." Rather, he finds himself collaborating "regardless of [Vere's] observation" in an illicit exchange, as when Claggart with his glance of "serpent fascination" draws out Billy's "lurking defect," his stutter, which the narrator had punningly characterized as "a striking instance" of the contribution of the "envious marplot of Eden" to Billy's composition (118, 17, 93, 19).[25]

With the concept of the conduit, slipstream of the vocal current and ironic counterpart of Whitman's channel, Melville appears a type of puritanical Bakhtin, lamenting rather than celebrating the articulations of the great social machine precisely for their unaccountability. The uncanny inversions and reversals transpiring in the deadly space between, formerly the space of pure self-referentiality, impede the free flow from nature to expression characteristic of Whitman's channel. This impediment, sign of the Other's penetration of the Whitmanesque channel which is Billy's unheard-of innocence, appears in Melville's text primarily as an obstacle to that form of speech by which one defines and denominates, distinguishes and identifies. Thus, we have noted Billy's stutter and blow in place of the word of self-identity, Vere's tautological death sentence instead of an inside narrative, and the crew's "torrent." The nature of the lie which converts channel to conduit conditions a response that is at once a capitulation and a mimesis: nothing so closely approximates the lie as a consubstantiation of language and violence as do the stutter and its immediate issue, the blow.

In its unmediated transit from experience to expression, in its inimitable and unstoppable directness, the blow supersedes the Whitmanesque innocent soul as the text's ultimately self-referential figure. In this displacement lie Claggart's vindication and his triumph. As the deadly space transcended its status as an element of Claggart's character description through the lie's activation of the vocal current, so does self-referentiality, as the determining characteristic of Billy's innocence, acquire through the blow a tremendous deconstructive potency directed against the act of narration itself. This transcendent power of the blow becomes most apparent as the narrator attempts to establish character as an integral, defining, and directing force within his narrative. Far from a character's achieving through narrative a moral ascendancy, his discourse, along with the narrator's discourse about him, is channeled willy-nilly into the great narrative whorl or recoil the blow establishes. Functioning as the text's ponderous center of gravity, the blow forces the return and repetition of words, phrases, and even entire blocks of character description. Offspring of the lie, the blow constitutes a usurping and imperialistic self-referentiality, and it converts the text into a vast echo chamber, a seeming chaos of stutters and repetitions.

This explains what happens when the narrator attempts to account for Billy's exceptional integrity, the question with which we concluded the previous section of this chapter. Throughout his narrative, he constructs a typology of Billy's innocence, selecting his epithets from the four realms of the powerless and marginal in relation to life aboard a man-of-war: the feminine, the juvenile, the animal or brute, and the barbaric or pagan. Through this unlikely combination of references, he ultimately reveals Billy as a consummate ideal, the perfect synthesis of personal, political, and spiritual identity. In his last exquisite description of Billy as he lies awaiting death, the narrator finds his beauty epitomized by the delicate definition of his "skeleton in the cheekbone at the point of its angle," and through it claims for Billy the legendary beauty of the English, whom the conquering Romans called "Angles" for their angelic appearance. But the narrator's consummate designation of Billy as an angel, especially one whose "fervid hear[t] self-contained" is as a "secret fire in a ship's hold," precipitously returns us to Vere's anguished cry upon the commission of Billy's undeniable deed: "Struck dead by an angel of God! Yet the angel must hang!" As an echo of Vere's cry, the narrator's description relinquishes its moral authority as the final word about Billy, sending us back to the shackled and discordant figures, Billy the ascendant angel and Billy the mutineer and murderer (118, 120, 95).

The only character who appears to act independently of this claustrophobic and duplicate order is Billy's capricious mentor, the Dansker. The Dansker is an anomalous character, rarely discussed by critics perhaps because of his unshakable refusal to participate in the Vere-Claggart-Billy dynamic. While the narrator talks but doesn't know, the Dansker knows but refuses to talk. An old and retired figure, sitting off to one side attentively observing, listening, and ruminating, the Dansker might be imagined a type of exemplary narrator *in posse*, as well as a judge. As such, the "sea-Chiron" does not so much indicate a reversion to myth as he does a throwback to the time when the omniscient narrator was still a viable figure in fiction; the Dansker no more considers advising Billy than would an omniscient narrator be caught tapping his hero on the shoulder to apprise him of a denouement that has not yet come to pass. Although in this manner he safeguards the integrity of the plot, by its diabolical logic the Dansker becomes what his cryptic articulations describe: the "cat's-paw" which toys with its victim before fixing it firmly on the ignominious altar of its sacrifice. Because he, above all other characters, has complete access to the inside narrative and yet holds his tongue, he assures the martyrdom of "ignorant innocence." Thus, the Dansker, whose nickname is Board-her-in-the-Smoke, figures primarily as a minor element in a sustained apocalyptic motif which includes Red Whiskers and Red Pepper, and through which Melville appears to indulge in what might be called "caprices of the pit" (52, 77, 81).

Representative of the ultimate impossibility of independence from the logic of the lie, the Dansker presents "in summary form" the plight of character in *Billy Budd*. The rationale for his integrity, for his policy of uninvolvement, lies in his "pithy guarded cynicism," in his principled avoidance of what Claggart (and the narrator) terms the "man-traps," a philosophy best expressed by the narrator in his maxim "that unless upon occasion [one] exercise a distrust keen in proportion to the fairness of the appearance, some foul turn may be served [one]" (53, 88, 79). Like an "antique parchment" covered with illegible hieroglyphics, the Dansker, when he does reply to Billy's urgent questions, does so in language inaccessible to the simple boy. After his oracular and unilateral pronouncements, he then "pursed his lips, gathered all his wrinkles together and would commit himself to nothing further," his "patriarchal" affection for Billy notwithstanding. If in the opacity of his language concerning Billy's affairs and the paternal quality of his feeling for him he approaches Vere, the pursing of his face and gathering of his wrinkles foreshadow that "evanescent" and fatal moment in which Claggart, observing Billy with "a settled meditative and melancholy expression" suffused with "soft yearning," repents of his feeling, "pinching and shrivelling the visage in the momentary semblance of a wrinkled walnut" (50, 76, 80). Thus, the Dansker's very characterization, caught up in the din of echoing characterizations, shows that to be a character in *Billy Budd* involves of necessity the practice of some form of principled containment, either of feeling, word, or focus. By virtue of this practice, he finds himself inadvertently contained within the vocal current, product of the deadly space, and thus committed to that reversal of significations by which the lie becomes truth.

Billy, of course, remains unintentionally aloof from these infernal circles of containment, and it is tempting to attribute the apotheosis the narrator suggests he attains at his death to this fact. Relatively unaware of the pressure of heaped constraints, Billy rollicks and rolls along the upper gun-deck, his movements in stark contrast to the scuttlings, adversions, and perversions of Claggart below. Unbeknownst to him, what Whitman called the "threads of manly friendship" twist about him, suggesting the "oozy weeds" of "Billy in the Darbies" which the sailor-balladeer imagines receive his body as it founders in the deep (*DV* 414 n). In the text as in the ship, these threads constitute a "half-hid warp," a peculiarly expressed "fervid comradeship." Below Claggart's "self-contained" demeanor, a "subterranean fire" burns for one whom he has designated, in Whitman's words, his "most inevitable twin and counterpart"; for without Billy, to avail ourselves of Whitman again, Claggart knows himself "incomplete, in vain, and incapable of perpetuating [him]self" (*DV* 415 n). The sole inroad by which Claggart might accede to this other "fervid hear[t] self-contained" with its corresponding "secret fire," burning self-sufficient and self-consuming, offers itself in the hiatus left by the tabooed word, mutiny. With the lie, administered with a "hungry lurch," Claggart penetrates the innocent's perfect self-referentiality (137, 83, 118, 93).

Were that the end of the story, Billy Budd, already praised by the narrator as an Apollo and an Achilles, could yet attain his apotheosis as a latter-day Persephone, abducted by the ever-pallid god of the underworld. But the blow constitutes an unanticipated complication; as the vocal current, Claggart finds a novel way of self-perpetuation. Advancing through the text as a series of stutters and tautologies terminating in acts of violence, the vocal current electric is conceived in this confrontation of two men, their interchange marked by an unaccountable mingling, Claggart taking on the innocent's victimization and Billy the deceiver's depravity. In the breakdown of distinction prefigured in this homoerotic and tautological exchange, Melville fails to remedy Whitman's complaint that the topic of sex had been "made dumb by literature."[26] Claggart's desire to possess the innocent Billy produces not a poem, not even a "Song of Myself," but self-referentiality reconstituted as violence, and a violence that singularly targets the possibility of literary art.

By virtue of their collusion in the dyad of lie and stutter/blow, innocence and violence pose an analogous obstacle to what even contemporary readers regard as normal narrative progress. Melville's narrator is forced to acknowledge his debt to the lie, which compels the innocent's fall into plot, by struggling palpably with the condition it imposes upon his narrative's "progress": namely, that it proceed only to the degree to which it continually acknowledges the doubly signifying, and therefore self-canceling, significance of its central event, Billy's fatal stutter/blow. In this regard, Vere's tautological death sentence, in which the very functioning of narrative — as a play of ratios, as a grammar of motives — breaks down, is anticipated by the narrator's own representation of that unspeakable synapse of innocence and violence, the fatal blow. Vere formulates the death sentence in compliance with an objectivity so constrained that it inscribes its subjects within the actions they commit or suffer. In an analogous manner, the narrator, even as he fixes that point where innocence and transgression intersect, reverts to speculation, and not upon the blow's moral significance but upon the purely material conditions of its placement on Claggart's anatomy: "Whether intentionally or but owing to the young athlete's superior height, the blow had taken effect full upon the forehead . . . so that the body fell over lengthwise, like a heavy plank tilted from erectness." At his own moment of "moral emergency," the narrator withdraws and, like the "fated boy," his innocent and murderous hero, or the equally fated Vere, he mirrors a "frontage," delving no deeper into motive than the intentionality one can reasonably impute to physical size. Neither confirming nor denying the blow as a socially or psychologically meaningful action, the narrator leaves us with the ineluctable contradiction of the coexistence of innocence and murder (93, 51, 108).

The narrator's account reveals that, just as Billy's stutter establishes a pattern to which the articulations of other characters, excluding Claggart, conform (tautology and torrent), Claggart's lie provides the model for narrative itself: like the lie, it must possess the semblance of providing information while in essence providing nothing at all. In *Billy Budd*, lie and stutter constitute a double genealogy of utterance equally based on the principle of dissemblance. The effect upon narrative — what the narrator tells and how he tells it — is devastating: beyond the problem of echo and repetition, this double genealogy ensures a peculiar narrative inarticulacy or stutter, passage after passage impeded by double negatives, self-canceling statements, and obfuscating syntax. With the narrator tongue-tied, only Billy "tells" us with his stutter (the sign of innocence and depravity alike) that as ultimate self-referentiality, the blow, the pivotal event of the text, lies beyond telling, beyond the pretensions of narrative to account for it. Nothing can equal the blow's directness; nothing else will succeed so well at "hitting the mark." This accounts for the narrator's appearance of having been seized by "the vertigo of the uninterpretable" in the face of Billy's deed.[27]

The narrator, then, suffers along with Vere a kind of verbal strabismus; both struggle to focus unambiguously upon that which remains stubbornly double, Vere in order to judge, and the narrator in order to produce a "truth uncompromisingly told." Just as Vere, before his crew assembled to witness punishment, is forced by the paradox of murderous innocence to give both the truth of and the lie to Billy's deed — a dissemblance which nearly results in mutiny — so the narrator's contribution to Billy's tale seems a chronicle of mis-givings. Thus, Claggart, who accuses Billy of dissimulation or conceal-ment, is not really far off the mark: in containing or concealing nothing, Billy conceals everything. Meant to be an absolute transparency, Billy is funda-mentally opaque, the cipher of the book, and as such, is as potentially subver-sive as the blank, undifferentiated ocean which surrounds the ship or the white whale cruising through it. Whether the narrator compares him with the nightingale, the baby, or the barbarian, he defines Billy's innocence most tellingly as a "blank" which functions at the moment of moral emergency as a mirror for evil (78). At the crucial confrontational moment, Claggart's glance of "serpent fascination" draws out Billy's "lurking defect," his stutter, pre-cipitating the murder but leaving the murderer undepleted of his innocence, as the ocean in *Moby-Dick* absorbs its shipful of human tragedy and yet rolls on eternally unchanged in aspect. Neither conceptual, nor progressive, nor active, Billy's innocence cannot be considered a positive phenomenon; it is neither heroism nor righteousness. He intends neither his innocence nor his transgression. His innocence represents more a state or a definition of being than an active choice; it is the innocence of leviathan over which Ahab and Starbuck argue. The innocent's violence functions as a sort of black hole of purity, a central, if half-hid, warp through which narrative, in its transit from first chapter to last, must pass.

For this reason, the innocent Billy cannot save the text, the Christological symbolism surrounding him notwithstanding. As an alternative to its com-prehensive doubleness, he offers an integrity premised upon emptiness, and which therefore functions in a manner analogous to the hiatus left by the tabooed word, mutiny: both extend to the wary one a wild card, the rare opportunity to infiltrate and subvert. We have noted the blow's usurpation of the innocent's self-referentiality and observed its deployment through the text, under the doubly signifying sign of the stutter, as the vocal current electric. We have further examined its deconstructive effect upon normal narrative progress, the tendency of the narrative to seize up, to stutter, to make of itself one great tautology, one great collapsing of distinctions. The more the teller tells, the more he winds himself around the central emptiness of a destructive self-referentiality which allows neither access nor egress, and the more his narrative is unmanned, unable to achieve its own release from the recoil which it tells.

Nothing hinders the progression of doubleness. It perpetuates itself, first, as with the Dansker's characterization, in the complex interactions of over-lapping structures of containment. Second, and more problematic, it pro-ceeds from insanity, defined by the narrator as that interaction subsisting between those structures of containment, on the one hand, and nonstruc-ture, activated as the vocal current, on the other. A flirtation of form with nonform, insanity's streamlined vehicle is the lie through which Claggart mediates the transfer of self-referentiality from innocent character to unde-niable deed, in the process initiating the vocal current. Henceforward it is all the narrator can do to disengage his text from the proliferating variants of the lie, all of which offer themselves in the form of a specious account of the blow.

As producer of the lie, the text's sole example of an unhindered and, one might even say, creative utterance, it is the mad liar Claggart, and not the Dansker, who suggests himself as the beleaguered narrator's alter ego; with the lie, Claggart alone appears to offer a way out of the morass of close-coupled discourses. For this reason, and because the narrator is so manifestly implicated in and hindered by the insanity he identifies, the impact of this second form of doubleness on the writer committed to the uncompromised telling of the truth is best approached indirectly, at least initially. Thus, the narratological problem of doubleness-as-insanity is best examined through a characterological analysis of the liar and madman, Claggart, upon whom, the narrator insists, despite his ostensibly supporting role in the drama, the whole "point of the present story turn[s]" (61).

Claggart's activity is entirely premised upon a uniquely dual relationship to those structures of containment he finds available to him by virtue of his official position. He manipulates and exploits these structures, containing his illicit passion for Billy under the stern guise of the Master-at-arms. His official legitimacy enables him to vent his contained passion in the form of a specious accountability, a lie which becomes the truth, a text. Once deployed, however, the lie promotes, independently of Claggart, a state of mutiny, an assertion of that which had been contained and confined against its container — a predicament reminiscent of the dilemmas of Brown with respect to Carwin, Carwin with respect to Clara, and Farmer James with respect to the slave in the cage, in which the text's contained subjectivities overwhelm the limits their authors had set for them. His lie compels the revelation of that which Claggart lived to hide, amounting to a self-mutiny which, carried out in the form of a predictable act of aggression directed against him from without, claims his life.[28] Because it exceeds his ability to master it, Claggart's dual relationship to the condition of containment — the simultaneous effort to contain and determination to subvert that effort, the interplay between the structures of containment and the nonstructure of the deadly space — is designated by the narrator as insanity. Ultimately, insanity is defined as the overwhelming of the form-giving container by that which it contains; herein lies its threat to narrative, precisely as it was played out in Crèvecoeur's *Letters*.

Before transgressing upon Billy's infantile world with the lie, Claggart himself suffers a species of invasion: contrary to the dictates of "fate and ban," Billy Budd takes root in his soul and blossoms into a flower of evil, a monomania that permits of no direct expression. Claggart experiences his pathological desire to possess Billy largely as contempt ("To be nothing more than innocent!") and disguises it as respectability, intellectuality, and a principled austerity. Most relevantly for narrative, masked by these indices of his legitimacy, the one whom the innocent has in some sense repelled claims to possess him — or the truth about him — in the form of a specious accountability. We must view in this light Claggart's initial report to Vere, Vere's to the crew, and most horrifyingly, because of its total disengagement from the human drama, the naval chronicle's to history, all of which conduce to Billy's victimization. Insanity, the unsuccessful containment of a feeling or a word that would directly express itself, indirectly leads through a specious accountability to sacrificial violence, as it did at Salem. Not surprisingly, it finds its primary apologist in Vere, who, endeavoring to jog his jury out of their "troubled hesitancy" to execute, asserts that war honors only "the frontage," even if the frontage be false (80, 65, 105, 108). We have arrived at the opposite pole from Salem — whereas the prosecutors in 1692 rejected the evidence of the frontage and pursued the hypothesis of consent, Vere rejects all but the frontage and ignores all extenuating circumstances — but with the same issue: Vere cannot afford to restrict his gaze to what is visible because of the constant threat of subversion.

Vere explains to his jury that the *Bellipotent* best serves the king to the degree that it suppresses all that subsists underground, from private conscience to the love proscribed by fate and ban. Patriotism is a "button" that secures the drawn veil, excluding all that for Vere constitutes the sacred and for the reader narrative context. The revolving forms of containment and censorship which ensue overlap and undercut one another: the practice of oppressing and impressing sailors generates a subterranean fear of mutiny which in turn produces an atmosphere fraught with secrecy, as well as Vere's double strategy of confinement, the tabooed word and the constriction of focus. But of necessity, the policy of expressly acknowledging only surface and deed involves an acute, if purposely dumb, acknowledgment of Ahab's "little lower layer," and thus a virtual commitment to the state of doubleness: the container must labor at every moment to adjust its pressure inward in conformity to the amount of outward pressure exerted by the contained material.[29] Form and chaos battle continually for dominion, mirrored in the tale's political context of brutal repression and anarchic revolution. The text survives in fragile equilibrium, suspended over the deadly space — which reveals how very proximate the text's antitheses are — like Jonathan Edwards's human spider over the abyss. Melville unequivocally is not choosing sides: not between acceptance and resistance, conservatism and liberalism, or God and the devil (106).[30]

Although Vere presides over this quintessential text of mutiny, Claggart emerges as its most perfectly adjusted composite figure. Designated by Vere as responsible for maintaining order, he patrols the decks, his "self-contained lunacy . . . not distinguishable from sanity." The world he monitors exists in a state of carefully plotted doubleness: behind each man working a gun stands another with drawn sword. The order Claggart guarantees Vere is in reality a violence concealing a violence of a different order; the stringency of Vere's beloved "measured forms" permits Claggart to advance his underground violence. Through Claggart, Vere effectively makes of insanity an institution; as a result, narrative itself is taken hostage aboard the *Bellipotent*, and with its captain's sanction (60, 32, 130).

The narrator's most explicit "hint" concerning the rapprochement of Claggart and Vere appears in the eleventh chapter, in that listing of Claggart's psychological idiosyncrasies which indicate the presence of the "deadly space between," the space of insanity. His description of Claggart as "dominated by intellectuality," demonstrating "no vulgar alloy of the brute," folded in "the mantle of respectability," and associated with austerest civilization, echoes or adumbrates in individual words and phrases descriptions of Vere, a similarity which becomes more pronounced (if never outspokenly so on the part of Vere's severely tried officers) with each turn of the plot (60, 96). Beginning with the Surgeon's initial doubt of Vere's sanity, the individual character descriptions of Claggart and Vere, posited so confidently on antithetical ends of the moral spectrum, start to "blendingly" converge, as do the violet and orange of the narrator's rainbow. Within both men lurks the passion that austerity would hide, while Vere's behavior before and during the trial suggests to his jury, all "honest natures," that perhaps Vere, as the narrator claims of Claggart, employs reason "as an ambidexter instrument for effecting the irrational," and that to accomplish "an aim which in wantonness of atrocity [i.e., arguing for the death of an innocent] would seem to partake of the insane, he will direct a cool judgement sagacious and sound." Moreover, such lunacy, because it is "self-contained" and "to the average mind not distinguishable from sanity," is the more dangerous and volatile: even the self which contains the lunacy may be unaware of lunacy's presence, as a narrative may lose control of a character inscribed within it. Thus, behind the narrator's express doubling of Claggart and Billy as twin theological mysteries of which Vere — as a professional — is unable to judge, the narrator establishes Claggart as the character from whom Vere — as a lunatic — is unable to keep his distance. Together they pose the riddle of insanity whose dimensions threaten to exceed the narrator's capacity to account for and thus contain it (61, 97, 101, 60).[31]

For this reason, the deeply reverberant psychological portrait of Claggart — which comes to rest (briefly, because "tinctured with the Biblical element") upon a definition of the Master-at-arms as a "mystery of iniquity" (a definition which Vere considers, and rejects as irrelevant, at the trial) — must be recognized as initiating the narrator's defensive strategy. In itself, Claggart's conjectural portrait constitutes an experiment with indirection as a method of characterization. In indirection lies the narrator's sole hope of circumscribing and containing Claggart, and thus, as he puts it, of vindicating his effort. Despite its being largely understood as a sympathy of kindred and gentlemanly souls, the narrator's relationship to Vere can be evaluated with more fidelity to the text as one of a decidedly ungentlemanly convenience. The narrator makes use of the "heedless" Vere as a vehicle with which to approach Claggart, persuaded to it, perhaps, on the strength of his own lyrical description of the captain as possessing a famed "directness, sometimes far-reaching like that of a migratory fowl that in its flight never heeds when it crosses a frontier." The frontier in question can only be "the deadly space between," beyond which Claggart stands. In this regard, Claggart emerges less a character than a type of narratological directive, a "hint" to the narrator to proceed "by indirection," despite the narrator's explicit evaluation of indirection (in contrast to the sailor's frank and simple manner) as "an oblique, tedious, barren game hardly worth that poor candle burnt out in playing it" (59, 61, 38, 58, 78).

This understanding of the narrator's conjectural portrait of Claggart as initiating his experiment with indirection is supported by its containment within a digression remarkable for its incongruous association of insanity, the incompetence of professional men to witness or to judge, and, tellingly, the possibility of narration. By means of this digression, the narrator extends through the text a meditation on the nature and significance of doubleness in literary art expressed as a confession of his own inability to account for events. The digression begins with an accumulation of "hints" concerning Claggart's "hidden nature" offered as a conjectural psychological portrait. This alone, the narrator suggests, will answer for his narrative's credibility, upon which its "vindication" — for this narrator, like his postrevolutionary predecessors, craves absolution — ultimately depends (61, 59). However, although the narrator explicitly acknowledges the centrality of Claggart's characterization to the success of his own enterprise, he brings to perfection the art of nonstatement. Throughout the eleventh chapter, he develops explanations for Claggart's mysterious antipathy for Billy, only to dismiss them as irrelevant or simply inadequate to the known facts. He draws upon a variety of scholarly works to lend credence to his formulations (in so doing, proving himself Vere's equal in his stock of "bookish" citations), only to compare his array of authorities unfavorably with the transcendent authority of "Holy Writ," which he nevertheless rejects as unpopular with the modern audience. Finally, he reports at length, but to no apparent purpose, a distant conversation with "an honest scholar" who refers to events and actors even more distant from the matter at hand (58).

The eleventh chapter concludes with the narrator's announcement that, but for "an added hint or two . . . the resumed narrative must be left to vindicate, as it may, its own credibility," a statement which suggests that, despite — or perhaps because of — his effort, doubts about the narrative's credibility may be appropriately exercised (61). The twelfth chapter situates itself at an even further remove from the main narrative than the expected "hints." It constitutes a single paragraph devoted to an apparently superfluous and even obtrusive diatribe against legal and medical professionals as incompetent to judge of such mysteries as Claggart embodies, especially in comparison with their clerical counterparts. In advance, the chapter both commends Vere's decision to abstain from dealing with Claggart as a mystery of iniquity and condemns him as unable to do so.

Conspicuous for its belabored logic, the digressive association between insanity, narration, and the competence of professionals reappears in the twenty-second chapter. The chapter is central: the narrator reports not only on Billy's trial but also on the historical events (the French Revolution, the Napoleonic invasions, the mutinies of Spithead and the Nore) which, in the way they are described, lend an apocalyptic urgency to the issues surrounding the trial. The chapter opens with a digressive meditation on the difficulties of distinguishing sanity from insanity, which trails off into an indictment of professionals. These last, the narrator charges, "in some supposed cases, in various degrees supposedly less pronounced" than the present one (the participle is telling), accept a fee in exchange for drawing a necessarily specious "line of demarcation" between sanity and insanity. Abruptly, if obliquely, the narrator reveals that the line in question refers not to Claggart, long relegated to the *outremer* of the deadly space. Rather, it refers to the prosecutor Vere, who commands the reader's pathos by virtue of his producing a specious and ultimately sacrificial account of Billy's deed, while suffering the application of a like judgment to his own behavior through the hints proffered by the narrator and the surmises of the text's professional par excellence, the Surgeon. Even the reader is lamely challenged by the narrator to "determine for himself by such light as this narrative may afford" Vere's psychological fitness to adjudge the mysteries of innocence and iniquity. The narrator thus situates this reiteration of doubt concerning the sanity of Vere's decision to judge Billy's innocence by the "light of [the] martial code" within a reiterated doubt concerning the "light" of narrative, and its adequacy as a tool for reading (Vere's) (Claggart's) character (97, 98). In effect, through his irritable asides on the professional class, the narrator repeatedly associates the identification of Claggart and Vere on the basis of insanity with a confession of the insufficiency of his own account to contain a truth uncompromisingly told.

The poor prospects of containment and accountability receive a final confirmation as the hidden theme of yet another digressive chapter aptly titled "A digression." The flagrant insertion of this chapter between the emotionally heightened moments of Billy's death and the sailors' immediate reaction to his execution underscores its parodic recapitulation of the issues at stake. Two representative men aboard the *Bellipotent*, the Purser, "a rather ruddy rotund person more accurate as an accountant than profound as a philosopher," and the Surgeon, earlier introduced as "a self-poised character of that grave sense and experience that hardly anything could take him aback," discuss the execution which, according to the reader's chronology, has just occurred. Although as reported to the reader, the hanging took on an explicitly theological significance, with Billy's body "ascending" into the "vapory fleece" of the eastern sky, reminiscent of the "fleece of the Lamb of God," the Purser and the Surgeon here debate how to "account" for the fact that Billy did not ejaculate at the moment of death. Might this "phenomenon" be considered the result of willpower (that is, intent, a kind of inside narrative) or merely "an appearance the cause of which is not immediately assigned" — in Vere's words, a "frontage"? Does the innocent contain a secret significance, or is he an empty vessel? The question at the text's end brings us back full circle to its beginning, when Billy the legendary Handsome Sailor shares the opening chapter of his story with the equally legendary Billy-be-damn, whom we thought to have left there "vaporing in the groggeries" (126, 94, 125, 124, 127, 108, 4).

IV

Whitman inserted into his otherwise ebullient 1856 preface to *Leaves of Grass* a paragraph which appears to contradict the dominant tone of the address and to anticipate the more classically jeremiadic *Democratic Vistas* of 1871. Midway through the paragraph, the familiar pattern of the jeremiad suddenly emerges, an elaboration of cultural achievements which, at least initially, serves only to underscore a failing so grievous that it threatens to eradicate the very fact of accomplishment: "America, grandest of lands in the theory of its politics, in popular reading, in hospitality, breadth, animal beauty, cities, ships, machines, money, credit, collapses quick as lightning at the repeated, admonishing, stern words, Where are any mental expressions from you, beyond what you have copied or stolen? Where the born throngs of poets, literats, orators, you promised? Will you but tag after other nations?" (1856P 732). The verb "collapse" instantaneously deflates the crescendoing braggadocio and unceremoniously delivers the reader to the chastisements, not of a God outraged at a broken covenant, but of that nemesis of adolescent America, the culturally mature and exacting European.

By virtue of its being the beneficiary of "the mighty inheritance of the English language," America lay under an enormous debt to the cultural progenitor. "Payment prevails," Whitman solemnly intones, yet even as he does so, the paragraph moves toward the triumphant upswing indicative of moral recovery (1856P 732). This reversal is accomplished through a rhetorical undermining of the very notion of cultural succession as involving the elaborate mechanisms of inheritance — the imposition from without of something not inherent in the culture, a will which disregards the will of the recipient vis-à-vis its legacy — and adoption, the artificial acceptance of something fundamentally alien into a naturally exclusive family circle. But if one denies these hallowed forms of cultural transmission, these long chains of bequest and adoption which ensure both legitimacy and continuity, with what does one replace them? What else guarantees the generation of culture?

Whitman's answer turns on the concept of submission, and involves a choice of cultural sires. Henceforth, Whitman proclaims, the nation need not submissively "lie under" a debt owed to the demanding parent culture but will lie instead under "the most robust bard," submitting willingly to his crude and primitive — and therefore the more legitimate — claim to posses-sion: "Submit to the most robust bard till he remedy your barrenness. Then you will not need to adopt the heirs of others; you will have true heirs, begotten of yourself, blooded with your own blood" (1856P 732). The pun on "heir" divests the American song, or "air," of further responsibility to any but this bard, both its begetter and true mate. Paradoxically, the only way to satisfy the English debt is to satisfy the American poet.

Thus, Whitman suggests in this figure of virility an alternative to the sleeping infant poet of *Democratic Vistas*. If masculine America, as that army of soldiers fighting for an independence not merely political, was to be deliv-ered from the prevailing state of literary siege; if the potentially "perfect Mothers" of feminine America were to be delivered of true heirs, then Amer-ica must seek a manly innocence, which could simultaneously be itself and comprehend itself, and then inscribe this accomplishment, the elision of the gap between being and representation, in the incontrovertible word of American identity (*DV* 372). Only so conceived would the American poet show the States "themselves distinctly, and what they are for."[32] In the years that elapsed between the 1856 preface and *Democratic Vistas*, the continuing silence of the poet compelled Whitman, his hypothesis of the babe notwith-standing, to recommend as antidote to what appeared an obdurate barren-ness those negative virtues suggestive of the robust bard. While acknowledg-ing America as "the most positive of lands," he expresses an anxious yearning for a native artist possessed of "negative qualities, even deficiencies" (*DV* 409, 394).

If Billy Budd, and most explicitly Billy shackled on the upper gun-deck awaiting execution with "the look of a slumbering child in the cradle," repre-sents Melville's version of Whitman's great American poet as a sleeping infant, invulnerable to the machinations of the dissimulators, then John Claggart represents his offering of a character composed exclusively of "negative virtues," those hidden recesses and deep pockets of noninforma-tion summed up in the adjective "ambidexter" (60). Claggart's lie — articu-late, coherent, unimpeded, effective because it demands that reality conform to it — generates the vocal current electric, in the confrontation of innocent and liar producing not precisely democratic personality as embodied uncon-tainability that a genteel literary elite would endeavor to render poignantly inarticulate, a hollow container for national expression, but a poetics in which the infantilization of innocence plays no part. Billy's innocence is exposed as republican virtue gone decadent, or as the honesty of Nietzsche's beast which "cannot dissimulate" and "conceals nothing," so that "at every moment it seems what it actually is, and thus can be nothing that is not honest." In its unidimensionality, such honesty reveals its affinity to nihilism, and is commensurate with self-cancellation because it lives "*unhistorically*; for it 'goes into' the present, like a number, without leaving any curious remainder."[33] Melville shared Nietzsche's insight and demonstrated it repeatedly: for them, piety so conceived revealed a special ability to "blendingly enter" the space of nihilism. If, even as he describes this process in the vocal current, Melville's narrator appears to be taken hostage by the lie (as insanity made fluent), then one must concede that he exhibits the captive's typical and resourceful ambivalence toward the captor, a capacity to oppose while accommodating, which is born of the will to survive.

This ambivalence translates into that peculiar psychological idiom of narration which stutters in its earnest desire to be nothing but honest, even as it enacts the learning of Billy and Vere's lesson: namely, that honesty does not necessarily correlate with or guarantee the truth. In the very process of refuting the lie whose passage to truth he chronicles, the narrator acknowledges the lie's undeniable constitutive power — its perfect choreography of directness and indirection — by telling his own negotiations and renegotiations of the text's deadly spaces. In this way, the narrator of *Billy Budd*, Melville's last Ishmael, survives not to tell the tale but survives the telling of his tale. Anything but a "barroom bore" endlessly repeating his failure, the narrator walks in intense concentration a *via crucis* between tautological stasis and sacrificial violence, recoil and release, accompanied — or shadowed by — that genius of the anti-logos, the liar, a type of what Hawthorne called "the devil in manuscript."[34] Melville's "final word" is both a confession of defeat, an admission that, at best, his tale offers a "truth whereof I do not vouch," and a manifesto proclaiming the creation of a new genre, defiantly asymmetrical, flaunting its "ragged edges" in the name of the "truth uncompromisingly told." The latter truth is the superior truth of literary creation; to have avoided the man-trap of "pure fiction" becomes the boast of the deadly space's tattered hostage and accomplice, the narrator (43, 131).

Conclusion

The scholarly inquiry into the history of modern democratization has in the last half of the twentieth century become the subject of philosophical, theoretical, and historical speculation in its own right. We may (somewhat arbitrarily) identify its inaugural moment in the opening line of C. B. Macpherson's series of lectures for the Canadian Broadcasting Corporation on the subject in 1965: "We are in a muddle about democracy."[1] At least as it applies to its American career, our ability to isolate and apprehend the significances of the word is compromised by its susceptibility to our continuing mythification of American democratic origins. In scholarly works, this mythification often reveals itself in a kind of tautological tic whereby the inquirer, often fully aware of the dangers of so doing, explains the origins of phenomena with reference to developments generated by them. The historian Joyce Appleby, for example, has discovered this tendency at the heart of modernization theory which sets out to explain the difference between premodern and modern mentalities. Its foundational assumption became, Appleby writes, "that progressive increases in per-capita productivity set in motion political, familial, and personality changes" which collectively constitute the modernizing process.[2] "Central to the functional-structuralist core of modernization theory," she explains,

> is the importance placed on values as the integrators of coherent social action. Shared values can do this only because they convey shared intelligibility or meaningfulness. Yet there is no place in the theory for analyzing how meaningfulness is created and, once created, is adapted to changing circumstances. The expectation that modernization will promote rationality as a mode of thought is more tautological than descriptive: where rationality appears, modernization takes place; where it does not, modernization has not taken place. (93)

The only way to correct for this tautological tendency in historical-theoretical scholarship is to discern the "particular conceptual bridges men and women build to carry them into the unfamiliar territory of a radically altered future," granting them the status of "discrete developments" which constitute "parts of a process" (98). Reminiscent of Michael Oakeshott's claim that political actors, in advance of rational recognition, sympathetically intuit incoherences in political arrangements, Appleby suggests that we look for evidence of these elusive conceptual bridges "in the realm of the imagination [where] new approaches may be suggested in anticipation of structural rearrangements." It is in the realm of the imagination that we may glimpse "the beginnings of those shifts of consciousness which in full course appear as inexorable reactions" (98).[3]

In her own attempt to limn the emergence of the modern "individual," Appleby forgoes any inquiry into the realm of the imagination and incipient shifts of consciousness to focus instead upon the complex "ideas" through which "men and women grasped the meaning of modernization." If she does not attribute an individual-producing power directly to increases in per capita productivity, she does claim that the social changes accompanying the commercialization of the economy produced "new ideas about human rights," which in turn produced "the individual": "Commercial expansion increased the number of private transactions, and the market reached through groups to the single members of society, *turning them into individuals* who had rights to life, liberty, and the pursuit of happiness" (121). Economic growth thus provokes an intellectual response which, in ways that remain unexamined, produces the democratic subject, the individual, the end product of a process in which individual agency appears to play a minimal and reactive role.

This portrait of the protoindividual, passively awaiting his or her realization as the end product either of socioeconomic forces or theories about their significance, is not entirely amended when we examine recent historical accounts of the rise of democracy in America, which is routinely associated with the rise of the "individual." For example, in his recent book *Self-Rule: A Cultural History of American Democracy*, historian Robert Wiebe suggests that in order to understand how a modern democratic social and political order came into being (Appleby's "structural rearrangements"), one has first to discover the "history of social experiences" that led to "self-rule" or popular self-government, the most generally accepted definition of democracy.[4] Like Appleby's "realm of the imagination," Wiebe's experiential domain has traditionally proven elusive to historical inquiry; he notes that "remarkably few" have attempted to understand or even acknowledge its role in democratic developments (6). For Wiebe, the distinction between experience, on the one hand, and institutions or ideology, on the other, is a rigorous one, motivating, for example, his surprising dismissal of the importance of the Revolution for the cultural history of American democracy as having endowed it with "a powerful symbolic vocabulary but little else" (14).

From the early nineteenth century forward, Wiebe provides a detailed account of how a culture, paradoxically organized around a vacuum of power at the center, generated a mind-boggling array of novel socioeconomic and political developments whose impact upon the lives of white men, especially, was profound. These included "an abundance of cheap land, a general collapse of unfree labor arrangements, a fluidity in the status of wage-earners, a relentless decentralization of everyday decision-making, a remarkable expansion of small-scale credit for farmers"; added to them were circumstances like the extension of the franchise, increased access to elected officials, and increased possibilities for political association (27). The question is, do such circumstances constitute "social experience" or are they instead the product of such experience? Did, say, a general collapse of unfree labor arrangements produce democratic experience, or was it produced by it? If by "experience" we mean that which reveals itself in "patterns of behavior," as Wiebe suggests (1), are such patterns responsive to or generative of such external developments? What makes these behavioral patterns democratic, especially in the absence of externally established democratic conditions? Do these behaviors characterize isolated individuals or groups; or, in order to constitute a true pattern, must they encompass both? Where Appleby begins by invoking the realm of the imagination but moves quickly to "the idea" in her quest to discover the genesis of the modern individual, Wiebe begins by invoking experience and tenuously related patterns of behavior, but moves to what appears a secondary level of experience provided by economic and political developments to pinpoint the arrival of modern American democracy. In both cases, the definitional slippage is vexing, leaving the reader with the impression that the historian has abandoned the ground of her or his best insight.

That Wiebe is fully aware of the impasse engendered by the experiential emphasis is clear from his historicization of the problem, which leads him to posit a conceptually generous and open-ended working definition of democracy. Beyond the fact that, as he notes, "democracy has been many things at many times in many places," and thus is not naturally allied with any form of political economy, social value, or institutional apparatus, he further claims that "an awareness of history loosens the criteria" for "what must go into democracy and what must come out of it" (9, 6). An awareness of history, in this case the history of social experience, suspends whatever definitional integrity democracy may have for us, first, by throwing into question "certain prerequisites that by today's standards seem indispensable to a sound democracy"; and second, by challenging "the notion that democracies need to come complete, that any aspect falling below universalistic standards sinks the whole enterprise" (6, 7). The history of social experience, he warns his readers at the outset, may show us a democracy that reveals our humanity rather than our salvation, a democracy we may not like or approve of (9).

His awareness of the definitional impasse is also evident in his brief opening attempt to identify the originary locus of democratic experience that permitted white men to grasp the significance of altered political and economic conditions in the early national period: the Second Great Awakening which occurred at the turn of the century and the Finneyite revivals which followed some two decades later. In particular, he attributes to the radical lay itinerancy movement associated with the Second Great Awakening the power he denies the Revolution, not just of undermining clerical authority, but of toppling the especially resilient and flexible hierarchies of authority that had survived all eighteenth-century assaults (18). Yet radical itinerancy movements were launched in the 1740s, during the First Great Awakening, begging the question not just of their effectiveness in toppling authority but, more pertinently, of their status as originary democratic experience. The seemingly arbitrary choice of the Second Great Awakening implies that Wiebe's decision to assign democratic origins to the nineteenth rather than the eighteenth century rests upon what he minimizes as that merely symbolic vocabulary of rights and privileges associated with the Revolution. Instead, the existence of such a vocabulary—the highly elaborated product of en-lightened, nondemocratic political thought—appears to determine when social experience, like a religious revival, counts as democratic and when it does not. It is yet another indication that democracy remains for us unthink-able without liberal foundations.

In this study, I have attempted to describe the "realm of the imagina-tion"—its genesis, its contours, its psychosocial placement, the conditions of its inhabitation, the dynamic of its realization in social space—precisely as an experiential domain whose existence and representations, both social and literary, were central to the rise and evolution of democracy in America. This domain was not anticipated, prefigured, or invoked by vocabularies and the-ories of human political subjectivity external to it. Instead, it erupted into normative social space as a succession of irrational and publicly performed bids for vocal empowerment; at our historical distance, we learn of such events largely through written methods for containing it—published coun-tersermons and appeals to public order, character assassinations, legal in-junctions against lay itinerancy, and so on. In early American literary texts, democratic personality takes the powerful speaking parts (even when only a few words long), to the express detriment of authorial figures and their actual counterparts anxious about the authenticity of their attempts to represent the new nation in literature.

Robert Calef, among the witchcraft prosecution's angriest detractors, complained in 1692 that the devil's chains were "making a dreadful noise in our Ears, and Brimstone, even without a Metaphor, was making a horrid and a hellish stench in our Nostrils."[5] He seems to have meant not only that Cotton Mather and his cronies were behaving devilishly and visiting a literal hell upon the residents of the Massachusetts Bay, but also that a distance- and thus truth-preserving structure, akin to the function of metaphor, was collapsing, a failure which had led to the utter destruction of the social bond through sacrificial violence. Likewise, Charles Chauncy, Whitefield's bitterest enemy, objected that Whitefield's followers, through their insistence that the Grand Itinerant embodied gospel truth, had elided the distance or figuration central to the conventional notion of the religious life as a behavioral representation of a social ideal of sobriety, calm, and reason.[6] The Harvard faculty echoed Chauncy's critique when they attributed Whitefield's ambition to impersonate God to a tendency to ignore "Metaphor" in favor of taking "the Expression literally," a policy which had "given great Satisfaction to many an Enthusiast among us since the Year 1740" who were thereby freed to take "the swelling of their Breasts and Stomachs in their religious Agitations" for the *Indwelling of the Spirit*."[7] There is a tension in the Old Light view of the use and abuse of metaphor. On the one hand, Chauncy encourages something like a forgetting of metaphor when he insists that pious (conventional) behavior is (as far as society is concerned) piety. There is an "as if" operative here: acting as if is, for all intents and purposes, being. And yet, as the Harvard faculty point out, forgetting metaphor, forgetting the "as-ifness" of representation, far from eradicating the representational divide, leads to nonsense, chaos, unseemly performances which obscure the original truth of the unerring Word. Jonathan Edwards's validation of the truest representation as a vehicle to move one ever closer to the true offers itself as an ingenious solution to this contradiction. A stalwart recognition that fallen humankind inhabits a merely metaphorical dimension, the concept of the truest representation yet allows for the abrogation of the *significance* of the distinction between representational or imitative and original expressions of a direct experience of saving grace. The possibility of direct contact with the divine, that is, is not disallowed. Clara Wieland, like Jonathan Edwards, also discovered a form of antinomianism enabled by the "as if" to render a moment of fictional presence both staged and authentic. Here, too, belongs the fictional revaluation of character that, aided by cultural pressure to discover and enact a democratic literary ethic, promoted representation to the status of being in the early national period. The figure of the inarticulate poet offers the quintessential image of the desire to transcend metaphor, to eradicate the empty space it interposes between essence and expression by making word and flesh consubstantial at last.

In this light we may regard Melville's novelistic restoration of the space of figuration, the "deadly space between," a distance-preserving structure which precludes the pleasures of antinomianism, of direct access and communion, fraudulent or otherwise. Contrary to the expectations of Calef or Chauncy and others dedicated to the conservation of social forms and the conventions which express and secure them, Melville's insistence on the space between does not prevent sacrificial violence or a near-collapse of the structures. (Here we recall Hawthorne's portrait of Melville as unwilling to settle either on annihilation or salvation, but pacing restlessly the space between: figuration neither conserves nor does it render innocent.)[8] The space between, after all, is a space of unknowing that, unlike its Puritan counterpart (subtended between God's determinations and the limited knowledge of mortal men and women), cannot be managed by those in authority. Instead the space between is like spectral space, populated by a hybrid or "uncatalogued" breed, constitutionally external to even the most inclusive Whitmanian or Emersonian inventory. Or perhaps it is more accurate to say of the space between that it is envoiced rather than populated, and that the energy generated by the powerfully inarticulate voices which imbue it (including the lie as a privileged form of inarticulacy, an inability or unwillingness to make expression conform to experience) lends movement to this structure whose telos is the making of truth through a jugglery of identities and circumstances. If Melville knew that we are all slaves, he apparently didn't assume that we would all stay in the cage.

The liar Claggart, ontologically augmented by the stutterer Billy and the disciplinarian Vere, is the novel's embodiment of the force of democratic personality. Ambidexter, occupying the most liminal corner of liminality (belowdecks on a man-of-war midocean), the Master-at-arms, through his illicit and unspoken desire rather than his intellect intuiting an incoherence in the political arrangements of the *Bellipotent*, articulates his false witness to invisible realities, the reality of blank and beautiful Billy's interiority. Vere, like the spectral evidence theorists before him, is taken by surprise. There is nothing in the military code to help him address such anomalous speech, which, although the speaker dies, a martyr to his vision of the eradication of "fate and ban," brings forth the political result most feared, an act of mutiny, wholly unanticipated even by the mutineer whose death (and particularly whose benediction upon his captain at the moment of his death) invokes a popular revolt. The sound of revolution—a profoundly inarticulate composite of human, animal, and natural sounds—is the same from Crèvecoeur to Melville.

As an analogue of democratic space (the space of possession, of conversion, of internalized opposition), the deadly space acts as a conduit not for essence (as the innocent American poet, the domesticated democratic personality, was imagined to act), but for radical inversions of order, dynamic nontruths that call literary art into being as a kind of double and a corrective, a "let me tell you how it really was." When this narrative impulse to strip away false appearances extends to a whole community, like the outraged crew of the *Bellipotent*, one sees the vox populi articulating a truth which is, inevitably, also the truth of its own participation in the dynamic through which the lie (of mutiny) becomes the truth (of mutiny).

The lie provides the model for narrative as it provides its occasion. Far from exhibiting a diabolical independence and self-referentiality, the lie, a misrepresentation of reality, arises from relationship. The lie originates as a desire to possess another. Everything that follows is double—the mimetic prime number being two—and this is what precludes the one and only truth and generates an aggressive, high-stakes competition to claim one's own version as the truest representation. The inevitable doubleness does not preclude, however (as Jonathan Edwards also knew), some real anomalies, most prominently the text of ragged edges whose singer, committed to an uncompromised truth, is anything but the frank and simple artist: this is among its uncompromising and unlovely truths.

Whitman had described the innocent poet as producing poetic material that is uniquely "of itself," without "reference," and therefore free from the pitfalls of representation. Melville brings Calvinism to bear on this claim, the same Calvinism Whitman had explicitly proscribed, a Calvinism not yet compromised by the fantasy that the word, in our unmiraculous day, can still be made flesh, a fantasy the spectral evidence theorists shared with the aestheticians of innocence. Melville stages the corruption of Whitman's channel of pure poetic production so that it is no longer "of itself," bringing it back into representation as a condition of democratic community.

By virtue of his artistry a creature of the space between, Melville philosophically could not abide the either/or; this is the least of reasons why it would be inaccurate to regard his vision of literature, representation, and democracy as the antithesis of Whitman's. In a recent article, the poet Allen Grossman has lovingly described Whitman's poetic task and talent to be a "revision of the fundamental logic of representation (his new poetics, his cure of poetry by poetry) and therefore of the logic of love (since the logic of representation prevents the truth of love for the same reason that it prevents . . . the actuality of justice."[9] Melville, I believe, was equally driven to revise the fundamental logic of representation, but his revision stops short of transcendence. Representation is a structure that Whitman wants to overcome; only by so doing can he overcome the "*slavery to representation*" that precludes the possibility of unmediated presence, thus precludes the comradeship based upon equality understood as the "incommensurability of the person" (for the laws of representation are inimical to such equality) (117). But the "*incommensurability* criterion," essential to comradeship, essential to democracy, "entails *invisibility*," Grossman writes. "There is no image of the incommensurable, as there is no actual social formation characterized by equality, and therefore there is no image of the person" (114). And so Whitman, in Grossman's view, discovers an entirely original poetic discourse, a " 'new' pastoral," "unmeasured, neither unmanifest nor manifest: subvocal, as it were virtual" toward "the reinvention of representation through the overcoming of representation with the intention of producing by poetic means a 'human form' that is truly human because free" (121 n. 2; 118). Representation is overcome, or reinvented, within language: did not the afflicted, the convert, the itinerant, the ventriloquist, the slave — inarticulates all — dream similarly about displacing, if not destroying, history and "making it new"? And in order to achieve this, did they not deploy what anthropologist Michael Taussig has called "the magical economy of mimesis," by which copy and original become indistinguishable, "the copy drawing on the character and power of the original, to the point whereby the representation may even assume that character and that power"?[10]

Democratic personality is the trace of a mimetic encounter. Melville insists on mimesis; he is not so much condemning domesticated democratic personality as Whitman and Emerson envisioned it as he is restoring to visibility its suppressed mimetic origins. It is not that invisible content is blocked from finding its visible expression in Melville: the story of Billy Budd is a story about the act of narration, about the nature and production of literature, which expressly thematizes the textual problem of an uncontainable content. But in Melville, the transit from experience to expression is far more fraught than Whitman or Emerson envisioned and is anything but a solo flight. It is instead a collective, irrational, amoral event. Mimesis is a claustrophobic and duplicate order which nevertheless does not brook containment: it is an infinite and infinitely devious process, for which violence (and not an innocent national art) is the sole alternative.

So what is democratic personality? Democratic personality is that humble self-enlarging creature through whom, as the eye of the needle, the Creator and all creation are invited to pass.

Reference Matter

Notes

INTRODUCTION

1. For example, Russell L. Hanson begins his study of the rhetorical evolution of the term "democracy" in U.S. history, *The Democratic Imagination in America*, by noting that "traditional liberal democratic discourse" has always overlooked the incompatibility of liberalism and democracy. The result has been the ongoing "taming of democracy," a tendency "to liberalize democracy so thoroughly that any tension between liberalism and democracy [is] almost completely sublimated"; the qualifier "liberal" is thus routinely dropped as redundant. Despite this initial observation, Hanson follows Louis Hartz in identifying all Americans (at least since the Revolution) as "liberal democrats of various persuasions," and therefore maintains that "recounting the history of liberal democracy in this country does not entail a blow-by-blow description of some titanic struggle between the representatives of two traditions," but rather "an interpretation of the internal process by which liberal democrats explored the practical meaning" of democracy in U.S. culture. See p. 18 and n. 2, pp. 14–15. The premise of Joshua Miller's recent study, *The Rise and Fall of Democracy in Early America*, is that one can understand this history only if one acknowledges the existence in advance of the Revolution of a preliberal or "radical" democracy. As here portrayed, however, radical democracy is, simply, direct (as opposed to representative) democracy as advocated by the Anti-Federalists and claimed since Tocqueville (whom Miller follows in this regard) for Puritan congregationalism. Robert H. Wiebe, in *Self-Rule: A Cultural History of American Democracy*, offers a far more complex and vibrant portrait of the "inherently radical nature of democracy" as it was enacted in early nineteenth-century America (10). According to Wiebe, the astounding degree of personal and social mobility increasingly evident in the first decades of the century was fueled by a chance simultaneity of enabling factors, all predicated on a general collapse of cultural hierarchy and all signs of the development of a liberal market society, making "self-defining authority" and "self-directed work" almost synonymous (26). As Wiebe represents it, the centrifugal energies of American politics and society represent an opportunistic response to fortuitous social conditions

rather than a conscientious adoption and implementation of Enlightenment values such as rational individualism on the part of the populace. Nevertheless, this democracy comes after the general introduction of Enlightenment thought — "[l]ate in this individualizing process," he asserts, "democracy arrived" in America — and for this reason, it was able to appropriate for its own legitimation a "powerful symbolic vocabulary" of rights and privileges, particularly that of self-ownership, derived from revolutionary republicanism (14). This seems a critical concession, for what besides the general availability or popularization of this vocabulary, expressive of the "bourgeois spirit" of self-possession, differentiates the prerevolutionary First Great Awakening from the postrevolutionary Second Great Awakening and subsequent Finneyite revivals which Wiebe names as "originat[ing]" events in the democratic trajectory he traces (23, 18)? This seemingly arbitrary affiliation of democracy with the Second rather than First Great Awakening means that the Revolution and the Enlightenment philosophy of the subject that at least partially fueled it are fundamental to Wiebe's understanding of American democracy. In contrast, I assume that in order to discover what is "inherently radical" about democracy in America and to apprehend the ways in which postrevolutionary culture responded to that radicalism, we must go back to a time when the essentially democratic impulse of self-rule was popularly realized in the absence of a theoretical vocabulary for rationalizing the collapse of the hierarchies. My attempt here to examine what preceded even the most rudimentary popularization of self-possession as the bedrock of a modern, liberal subjectivity is thus an attempt to provide the prehistory of, as well as a key contributing element to, Wiebe's nineteenth-century narrative.

    2. See Jürgen Habermas, *The Structural Transformation of the Public Sphere*. Michael Warner has argued for the applicability to postrevolutionary and early national America of the Habermasian model of the public sphere — as well as the priority of textual to oral discursive forms — in *The Letters of the Republic*. Whereas Warner's claim that textuality eclipses or subsumes orality in this period seems to depend on distinguishing not just "text" from "voice" but also "readers" from "speakers," I will argue here that the critical issue is the way authoritative words (whether spoken or written) were produced. That is, whether in print or in "person," the salient issues for me are the activities of "speaking for" and "speaking through," as well as the phenomenon of compulsive, irrational, and often inarticulate public speech whose prominence was registered both historically and fictionally. I will return to this issue in section III of the Introduction.

    3. Wiebe, *Self-Rule*, p. 7.

    4. Benedict Anderson, *Imagined Communities*, p. 67.

    5. Larzer Ziff has called John Wise's treatises defending the Congregational Way against attempts (notably Cotton Mather's) to establish ministerial associations "the fullest expression of democratic thinking in the period, representative of the otherwise unexpressed beliefs of the people"; see *Puritanism in America*, p. 281. The historian Christine Leigh Heyrman opens her study *Commerce and Culture: The Maritime*

Communities of Colonial Massachusetts, 1690–1750, with an account of Wise's admirable blend of ecclesiastical and commercial progressivism (13–15). Perry Miller offers a detailed sketch of Wise's career in *The New England Mind: From Colony to Province,* pp. 288–322. See also George Allan Cook, *John Wise, Early American Democrat.* My reading of democratic personality thus departs from the somewhat hallowed view of American Puritanism as an exemplarily (liberal-)democratic culture established by the nineteenth-century historians George Bancroft, in his 1834 *History of the United States of America* ("Puritanism constituted not the Christian clergy, but the Christian people, the interpreter of the divine will; and the issue of Puritanism was popular sovereignty" [1: 318]), and Alexis de Tocqueville, in part I, chapter 3, of *Democracy in America.* See also Charles Jared Ingersoll, "Discourse Concerning the Influence of America on the Mind," pp. 271, 273.

6. See E. J. Hobsbawm, *Primitive Rebels: Studies in Archaic Forms of Social Movement in the Nineteenth and Twentieth Centuries,* esp. "Introduction," pp. 1–12. Historians of the "lower classes" — defined by Reinhold Bendix as "those persons who have been excluded from political participation in most periods of history up to the development of universal suffrage" — have often noted that so-called democratic revolutions carried out by the lower classes have reverted to political methods that we would not consider democratic. For this reason, Bendix underscores the importance of distinguishing "democracy in the sense of equality from democracy in the sense of a viable party system, protection of constitutional liberties, and related institutions." See Bendix, "The Lower Classes and the 'Democratic Revolution,'" p. 91 n.

7. On the effects of "incoherence" in a culture's political arrangements, see Michael Oakeshott, *Rationalism in Politics and Other Essays,* pp. 111–36, esp. pp. 124–27. Oakeshott understands political change as generated by an "intimation" of an incoherence present in political arrangements and intuited (as "sympathy") by political actors. Whereas Oakeshott's theoretical political actors use political reasoning to "expose" this site of ideological incoherence, the exposure both embodied in and publicly performed by democratic personality was a far more agonistic affair. Ziff's recent observation about the late eighteenth-century American elite recalls Oakeshott's formulation: Ziff remarks that their sense of entitlement "was qualified by their sense of the authority that resided in the people. This, as Edwards and Crèvecoeur revealed in their different ways, was a cultural condition before it was proclaimed as a political principle, which is to say that literature together with civil institutions such as church and family embodied the conditions of revolution before they were abstracted into political creeds and then embodied in political institutions" (*Writing in the New Nation,* p. 32). Although my task here is to explore manifestations of popular authority even before it was perceived as a "cultural condition," and thus before its realization in literature and civil and political institutions, I share Ziff's assumption that the authority of the people was felt — as an intuition, variously expressed, of "incoherence" — before it was formulated.

8. These features — the character and scope of the social crisis at Salem, the in-

articulateness of the perpetrators, and their unprecedented political power — differentiate the witchcraft crisis from the earlier Antinomian crisis to which it has often been compared. These differences are discussed in Chapter 1.

9. My use of the term "tactic" here to describe the activities of the afflicted is somewhat loosely based on the difference between "tactic" and "strategy" as Michel de Certeau expounds it in *The Practice of Everyday Life*. As opposed to "strategy," "tactic" signifies a largely unself-conscious form of "antidiscipline" exerted at opportune moments by the powerless within a given culture. There has been wide disagreement as to the canniness of Salem's afflicted, of course, ranging from theories of a hallucinatory hysteria produced by Puritan repressiveness to the strategic pursuit of personal ambitions exhibited by the afflicted character Abigail in Arthur Miller's *The Crucible*. According to de Certeau's distinction, Miller's Abigail acts rationally to unleash the irrationality of Puritan practice, and thereby acts strategically rather than tactically. See de Certeau's "General Introduction," esp. p. xix, and chapter 3, " 'Making Do': Uses and Tactics."

10. C. B. Macpherson, *The Political Theory of Possessive Individualism*. J. G. A. Pocock debates Macpherson's hypothesis as insufficiently dialectical and offers a more nuanced typology of the eighteenth-century individual in *Virtue, Commerce, and History*, pp. 59–71. On Pocock and Macpherson, see also note 20 of this Introduction.

11. Several suggestive theoretical formulations of social or political space have recently been offered that appear germane to the notion of democratic personality I will investigate. See, for example, Chantal Mouffe's defense of an "agonistic pluralism" as constitutive of the political, as opposed to the liberal insistence on consensus in *The Return of the Political*, esp. pp. 1–22 and 102–17. This is more thoroughly treated in Ernesto Laclau and Chantal Mouffe, *Hegemony and Socialist Strategy: Towards a Radical Democratic Politics*, esp. pp. 93–148. Especially compelling are Claude Lefort's meditations in *The Political Forms of Modern Society* and *Democracy and Political Theory*, in particular chapter 11, "The Permanence of the Theologico-Political?" on pp. 213–55. Also useful is Pierre Bourdieu's understanding of symbolic power and the political field as described in *Language and Symbolic Power*.

12. My sense of "the subject's experience" here may be contrasted with that of the historian Joan W. Scott. As she understands the subject's experience, it offers an insufficient epistemological foundation for the writing of histories of difference. See " 'Experience,' " esp. p. 26. In *The Life and Times of Liberal Democracy*, Macpherson briefly discusses the notion of a pre–nineteenth century, preliberal democracy, but concludes that it was "utopian," an insufficiently theorized reaction to class-based society, and that the difference between preliberal and liberal democracy is best described as a "sharp break," a "fresh start." See chapters 1 and 2, esp. pp. 10, 23.

13. Gordon S. Wood, "The Democratization of Mind in the American Revolution," pp. 74–75; cf. *The Creation of the American Republic, 1776–1787*, pp. 396–403. James A. Morone identifies as central to "the democratic wish" the enduring myth of America that motivates large-scale social and political change into our own day, the

revolutionary concept of the people out of doors as "a concrete, independent political entity, capable of ruling by and for itself, even in opposition to the government." He argues that the revolutionary fantasy of a unitary people governing directly, "outside the formal mechanisms of the state" and its laws, survived the Federalist crucible as both dream and threat. My analysis of an American aesthetic of innocence, the subject of Chapters 5 and 6, similarly turns on a notion of democratic personality as both dream (the basis for authentic national character) and threat (the fear of unaccountable and uncontainable popular voice). See Morone, *The Democratic Wish: Popular Participation and the Limits of American Government*, pp. 55, 65.

14. See Mitchell R. Breitweiser, *Cotton Mather and Benjamin Franklin: The Price of Representative Personality*, and Patrick Joyce, *Democratic Subjects: The Self and the Social in Nineteenth-Century England*.

15. Cf. T. H. Breen's warning concerning historians' tendency to conflate separate strands of political discourse in a given era and then privilege one over the others. He warns that political leaders rarely "subscribe to the same ideas, beliefs, and assumptions as did the men who actually fought the battles" and that we "risk losing touch with ordinary persons," and thus with historical accuracy, when we fracture historical discourse. His antidote involves a reconceptualization of Habermas's concept of the public sphere which expands it to include religious as well as political discourse. See Breen, "Retrieving Common Sense: Rights, Liberties, and the Religious Public Sphere in Late Eighteenth Century America," esp. pp. 57–58. His article points up a danger with linking the formation of the public sphere in eighteenth-century America exclusively with print. In *The Transformation of Virginia, 1740–1790*, for example, the historian Rhys Isaac notes the importance of the "oral dissemination" of news in prerevolutionary Virginia, not simply to promote knowledge of events but to determine how such information would be incorporated "into the common stock of knowledge, opinion, and feeling" (245). The incisive analyses of representative personality offered by scholars like Breitweiser and Joyce may be usefully compared with the spectrality of Jean Baudrillard's lyrically queasy representations of the masses as, if not precisely a population, then a "soft, sticky, lumpenanalytical notion"; as an inertial force "without attribute, predicate, quality, reference"; as that which "remains when the social has been completely removed"; as that which signifies a "central collapse of meaning." See Baudrillard, "In the Shadow of the Silent Majorities" and ". . . Or, The End of the Social," in *In the Shadow of the Silent Majorities, Or, The End of the Social, and Other Essays*, pp. 4, 5, 6–7, 3. My intention has been to see if it is possible to retain the sharpness of Joyce's and Breitweiser's studies while inverting their aims and methodologies. As Breitweiser observed that "[t]he *vox populi* can emerge into the reflective clarity and coherence of a single voice" (1), I want to understand the dynamics whereby the single voice began to "discover itself in Multitudes" (as Charles Chauncy described the uncanny power of George Whitefield's voice in *Letter to Wishart*, p. 12). The landmark study of the lower classes in American urban culture during the late seventeenth through late

eighteenth centuries is Gary Nash's invaluable *The Urban Crucible: Social Change, Political Consciousness, and the Origins of the American Revolution.*

16. Jonathan Edwards, *Some Thoughts Concerning the present Revival of Religion in New-England*, pp. 321 ("the multitudes of illiterate people"), 295 ("the great, the honorable, the rich and the learned").

17. Raymond Williams, "Personality," in *Keywords*, pp. 232–35, esp. pp. 234, 235. It would be interesting to correlate with Williams's history of the internalization of personality Walter J. Ong's history of the internalization of the word as elaborated in *The Presence of the Word*, esp. pp. 262–86.

18. See Lydia Ginzburg, "The 'Human Document' and the Construction of Personality," in *On Psychological Prose*, and also pp. 8–9 of this book. The phrase "plotted structuring" in the sentence following also appears on p. 9. In *Problems of Dostoevsky's Poetics*, Bakhtin claimed that every thought of Dostoevsky's heroes "lives a tense life on the borders of someone else's thought, someone else's consciousness" (32). He amplified this point with respect to the word in general in "Discourse in the Novel."

19. V. Shtoff, *Modelirovanie i filosofiia* (Modeling and philosophy) (Moscow and Leningrad: 1966), cited in Ginzburg, *On Psychological Prose*, p. 12.

20. Ginzburg's understanding of the ways in which individuals identify and impersonate "historically significant" personality types and thus of the ways in which both persons and cultures fluctuate between types is far more dialectical and historically capacious than that offered by Pocock in an article in which he criticizes as insufficiently dialectical Macpherson's model of possessive individualism. See Pocock, "Authority and Property: The Question of Liberal Origins," in *Virtue, Commerce, and History*, pp. 51–71. Also relevant is his *Politics, Language, and Time*, chapter 4, in which Pocock grapples with the inevitable circularity involved in attempting to infer "ideas" from "social reality" and vice versa.

21. On the history of the term "democracy," see R. R. Palmer, "Notes on the Use of the Word 'Democracy,' 1789–1799," and *The Age of Democratic Revolution*; Ellen Meiskins Wood, "Democracy: An Idea of Ambiguous Ancestry"; and Anthony Arblaster, *Democracy*. Also of interest is Arne Naess et al., eds., *Democracy, Ideology, and Objectivity*.

22. This observation has motivated several attempts to identify structurally and/ or historically distinct categories of democratic practice, such as Macpherson's *The Real World of Democracy* and more recently David Held's *Models of Democracy*. On the use of democracy in connecting the "diametrically opposed notions" of revolution and constitutionalism, see Sheldon S. Wolin, "Norm and Form: The Constitutionalizing of Democracy."

23. On the political controversies to which this identification gave rise in the early national era, particularly with reference to the establishment of the Bill of Rights, see Edmund S. Morgan, *Inventing the People: The Rise of Popular Sovereignty in England and America*, chapter 11.

24. Whitman, *Democratic Vistas*, pp. 388, 376.

25. The constructedness of democratic subjectivity is also the premise of Joyce's recent study, *Democratic Subjects*. Joyce's understanding of democratic subjectivity differs in significant ways from mine, however. He analyzes the autobiographical and biographical texts written by or about the nineteenth-century working-class dialect poet Edwin Waugh and the radical Quaker mill-owner John Bright as "technologies of the self." Collectively, he argues, the texts produced these two men as exemplary democratic subjects, practitioners of a "cult of the heart" which posited the equality of all human beings and the infallibility of heart-speech (99, 102–3, 56–63). In this way, the cults of Waugh and Bright contributed to the development in late nineteenth-century England of what Joyce describes as the "democratic imaginary" through which "a nascent mass democracy was both mobilised and managed" (136).

26. The notion of the body's constructedness was most powerfully (re)formulated (after Nietzsche) in the work of Michel Foucault, whose thought Judith Butler extends and radicalizes in *Gender Trouble: Feminism and the Subversion of Identity*, esp. pp. 128–41, and *Bodies That Matter*. In *The Psychic Life of Power*, Butler analyzes the referential paradox that informs current theories of subjection (the formation of subjects). If subjection is conceived as the individual's submission to a power which inaugurates the subject *as* subject, Butler throws into question the psychic traces of this power: "The form this power takes is relentlessly marked by a figure of turning, a turning back upon oneself or even a turning *on* oneself. This figure operates as part of the explanation of how a subject is produced, and so there is no subject, strictly speaking, who makes this turn. On the contrary, the turn appears to function as a tropological inauguration of the subject, a founding moment whose ontological status remains permanently uncertain" (3–4). The "tropological quandary" at the heart of theories of subjection exists equally, I would note (with Kenneth Burke, in *Rhetoric of Religion*), at the heart of theories of conversion, since conversion explicitly intends the individual's ultimate submission (death) and ultimate subjection (rebirth). Cf. the political thought of Hannah Arendt, who identifies the body with the realm of necessity in *On Revolution*. B. Honig has provided an incisive analysis of the incompatibilities of Arendt's views on identity and (political) action in "Toward an Agonistic Feminism: Hannah Arendt and the Politics of Identity."

27. We should not forget that those who defend the absolute distinctiveness of class or nation often invoke the ne plus ultra of "familial" or bodily difference. On the strength of the conviction that "having a nation" (or a class) is "an inherent attribute of humanity," see Ernest Gellner, *Nations and Nationalism*, pp. 6, 7, and esp. pp. 43–50 on the "weakness of nationalism."

28. The notable exceptions to this tendency to pair democracy and liberalism are theoretical and historical studies of modern nonliberal democracies. See Macpherson, *Real World of Democracy*, chapters 2 and 3; J. L. Talmon, *The Rise of Totalitarian Democracy*, esp. the introduction, pp. 1–13, and part I, chapter 3, pp. 38–50, and his later study, *Political Messianism*, as well as *Totalitarian Democracy and After: International Colloquium in Memory of Jacob L. Talmon*. For a defense of democracy without

liberalism, a democracy compatible with authoritarian government, see Carl Schmitt, *The Crisis of Parliamentary Democracy*. For a critique of Schmitt, see Habermas, "Sovereignty and the Führerdemokratie." Finally, the work of theorist Claude Lefort is of great interest; see esp. *The Political Forms of Modern Society*, part III ("Democracy and Totalitarianism"), pp. 237–319. Also compelling are Mouffe, "On the Articulation between Liberalism and Democracy" and "Pluralism and Modern Democracy: Around Carl Schmitt" in her *Return of the Political*; and Norberto Bobbio, *Democracy and Dictatorship*.

29. This focus, for example, unites the otherwise distinctive approaches of C. B. Macpherson, Chantal Mouffe, and Norberto Bobbio.

30. Norberto Bobbio, *The Future of Democracy*, pp. 25–26. Cf. Macpherson, *Real World of Democracy*, p. 11: The liberal state "liberalized democracy while democratizing liberalism."

31. On the negative assessment of democracy until its articulation with liberalism, see Raymond Williams's brief history of the word in *Keywords*, pp. 93–98; alternatively, one may refer to Palmer, "Notes," and Arblaster's useful survey, *Democracy*. Also relevant is Mouffe, "On the Articulation between Liberalism and Democracy." Vernon Louis Parrington noted in his classic, *Main Currents in American Thought: An Interpretation of American Literature from the Beginnings to 1920*, that until the French Revolution Americans were "curiously sensitive over the term democrat" and would use it only pejoratively (1: 322). He also pointed to the lack of availability of democratic (as opposed to liberal) theory in the revolutionary era — "American democratic aspiration had far outrun old-world liberalism, and had produced no independent speculation of its own" (1: 279) — and posited America's dependence in this regard on Jacobin France. Cf. Naess et al., *Democracy, Ideology, and Objectivity*, who note the "astonishing" fact that "during the whole period from the Renaissance to the American War of Independence — and even during that war . . . we cannot find self-proclaimed democrats, i.e., groups using the term in an honorific way and as one of their slogans," with the exception of the Jacobins and in particular, of course, Robespierre. The term as it is commonly understood today may only be applied retrospectively to "such movements as the Reformation, the peasants' uprising in Germany, the Puritans, and the Levellers, and the whole struggle between Crown and Parliament in the seventeenth century in England" (95). On the pejorative connotations of the term "democracy" in the American context, see pp. 105–8: no politician claimed to be in favor of "democracy" from either political camp during the nation's first four decades. Charles A. Beard claimed that neither Jefferson nor Jackson referred to himself as a democrat, although the term was commonly and approvingly used by "the plain people"; see *The Republic: Conversations on Fundamentals*, pp. 30, 31. Of related interest is Robert W. Shoemaker, " 'Democracy' and 'Republic' as Understood in Late Eighteenth Century America." Jennifer Roberts has explored the anxiety provoked in postrevolutionary and early national America by classical democratic thought in "The Creation of a Legacy: A Manufactured Crisis in Eighteenth-Century Thought."

On the controversies surrounding the formation of "democratic" or "democratic-republican" societies in the early national period, see the collection of primary documents compiled by Philip S. Foner, *The Democratic-Republican Societies, 1790–1800: A Documentary Sourcebook of Constitutions, Declarations, Addresses, Resolutions, and Toasts.*

32. Herman Melville, *Billy Budd, Sailor: An Inside Narrative*, pp. 97, 58, 89.

33. Macpherson, *Real World of Democracy*, pp. 1, 9, 11. Macpherson has offered a fuller account of the rapprochement of liberalism and democracy (in England) in *The Life and Times of Liberal Democracy*. Macpherson's hypothesis here recalls Oakeshott's remarks on incoherence and intimation; see note 7 of this Introduction.

34. Macpherson discusses the exclusion of women from preliberal theories of democratic (one-class or classless) societies on pp. 19–20 of *The Life and Times of Liberal Democracy*. He discusses their exclusion from nineteenth-century concepts of a "universal" franchise on pp. 35, 36, 59.

35. Macpherson, *Democratic Theory*, p. 6. In *Life and Times of Liberal Democracy*, Macpherson combines these two motives, for example in his discussion of Jeremy Bentham in chapter 2, esp. p. 35 where he claims that Bentham was "pushed" to accept a democratic or universal franchise (the determining feature of liberal democracy) "partly by his appraisal of what the people by then would demand, and partly by the sheer requirements of logic as soon as he turned his mind to the constitutional question." On the conceptual taming of democracy, see Hanson, *Democratic Imagination in America*, p. 18. The enduring power of the image of liberal-democratic society may be responsible for the "strong tendency" noted by the historian J. R. Pole "to slide noiselessly from what we *do* mean to what we *ought* to mean" in discussing the history of democracy in America ("Historians and the Problem of Early American Democracy," p. 627).

36. In his recent book *The Rites of Assent*, Sacvan Bercovitch argues in similar terms for the development, beginning in the colonial era, of an American rhetoric of nation and national destiny so ubiquitous as to be found on all levels of cultural discourse and so capacious as to disarm by embracing the discursive premises of all emergent forms of ideological dissent. (Cf. political historian James A. Morone's understanding of "the democratic wish," articulated historically as a recurrent appeal to nonliberal democratic values and practices [communitarianism, direct political participation] which inevitably works not to challenge but to strengthen the liberal state; see *Democratic Wish*.) Since the form of democratic dissent I trace here is conspicuously *not* rhetorically or discursively bound, but rests upon the notion of the uncontainability of voice, I see it as an exception to Bercovitch's premise.

37. The efforts to locate theories of a democratic subjectivity outside the definitional parameters of liberalism prove to be somewhat circular, in that the liberal understanding of the meaning of democracy implicitly governs the search. Thus Macpherson, in *Life and Times of Liberal Democracy*, notes the dearth of preliberal theories of democracy based on the absence of demands for "a democratic political structure" (particularly, a democratic franchise) in popular uprisings as well as the

scarcity of "democratic" theorists, authors of philosophical treatises. On the individuated liberal subject, Pocock, in *Virtue, Commerce, and History*, attributes to the tendency to define liberalism as "a view of politics founded on the conception of the individual as a private being, pursuing goals and safeguarding freedoms which are his own and looking to government mainly to preserve and protect his individual activity" the fact that antiliberal thought, whether promulgated by the right or the left, resembles a "humanist heresy-hunt" (60).

38. In contrast, Slavoj Žižek sees the radical inclusivity of "the subject of [liberal] democracy" as an "empty point of reflective self-reference . . . strictly correlative to the Cartesian *cogito* as a point of pure, non-substantial subjectivity" ("Formal Democracy and Its Discontents: Violations of the Fantasy-Space," p. 190). He notes that the typical democratic preamble — " 'all people *without regard to* . . . (race, sex, religion, wealth, social status)' " — expresses the "violent" alienation of the individual from his/her particularity and, therefore, the essentially "anti-humanistic" tendency at the heart of (liberal-)democratic inclusivity. Žižek observes that any attempt to render the subject of (liberal) democracy in terms of " 'concrete contents,' " to imagine that subject as anything other than "a pure singularity emptied of all content, freed from all substantial ties," is to "succumb . . . to the totalitarian temptation" (190, 192, 191). Of related interest are Mouffe's analyses of several critiques of the liberal subject (especially as theorized by John Rawls), based upon the lack of cultural-historical specificity in its conceptualization, in *Return of the Political*, chapters 2 and 3. The bibliography on the "virtuous republican" and the "liberal subject" is enormous; one could begin by looking at Pocock's account of the threat to virtue by corruption in *The Machiavellian Moment*, esp. chapter 15.

39. In large part, this lack of internal differentiation is due to the fact that the qualitative traits attributed to "the people" as collective democratic subject tend to elide, rather than emphasize, individual difference. Rule by the people was thus commonly understood as a rule that would brook no dissent, or individuation. As Macpherson has pointed out, this is "in striking contrast to the liberal-democratic tradition . . . which accepted and acknowledged . . . the class-divided society, and set out to fit a democratic structure onto it." And this, significantly, was possible only by thinkers like Bentham and Mill who reasoned, first, from a "model of man (which assimilated all men to a model of bourgeois maximizing man, from which it followed that all had an interest in maintaining the sanctity of property), and second, [from] their observation of the habitual deference of the lower to the higher classes." See *Life and Times of Liberal Democracy*, pp. 10, 11. Naess et al., in *Democracy, Ideology, and Objectivity*, pp. 99–100 and 109–14, concur, noting that the reigning concept of the term "democracy" from Spinoza's *Tractatus Theologico-politicus* through the French Revolution envisioned a governing body composed of a majority (as Diderot and d'Alembert's *Encyclopédie* put it, "une assemblée composée de tous") whose will may not be opposed. The authors add that "all actual governments labelled 'democracies' (that is, taken as denotata of a concept 'democracy') were direct. This holds good at least up to the time of the Constitutional Convention (1787)" (101). The term "representation," although the

concept of representative government was well theorized by this time, was not associated with the term "democracy," and was, in fact, explicitly distinguished from it.

40. See T. J. Clark, *The Absolute Bourgeois*, p. 29. As Whitman said in *Democratic
Vistas*, "The People! Like our huge earth itself, which, to ordinary scansion, is full of
vulgar contradictions and offence, man, viewed in the lump, displeases, and is a
constant puzzle and affront to the merely educated classes. The rare, cosmical, artist-
mind, lit with the Infinite, alone confronts his manifold and oceanic qualities — but
taste, intelligence and culture (so-called), have been against the masses, and remain
so" (376).

41. Kenneth Burke, *The Rhetoric of Religion*, p. 22.

42. In *Democracy and Political Theory*, Lefort suggests how difficult this task of
reconceptualization may be by noting the strength of the "desire for an 'objective'
definition" of politics which, he claims, "lies at the origin of the political theory,
political science and political sociology that have developed in the course of our
century" (216). His call to us to redress the fact that "we [have] lost all sense of the
political" (16) may be compared to Mouffe's project in *The Return of the Political*. Both
democratic theorists, as well as the sociologist Pierre Bourdieu, in *Language and
Symbolic Power*, have figured democratic or political space in terms of a disembodied
or discursive and thus symbolic form of power. Of related interest are Kristin Ross's
propositions about social space and its poetic figurations in her study of Rimbaud and
the Paris Commune, *The Emergence of Social Space*. I am grateful to Jonathan Hunt for
bringing her book to my attention. Always useful is Kenneth Burke's *Language as
Symbolic Action*.

43. Thus Lefort notes that "the singular procedure of universal suffrage," although it is "based upon the principle of popular sovereignty," nevertheless "at the
very moment when the people are supposed to express their will, transforms them
into a pure diversity of individuals, each one of whom is abstracted from the network
of social ties within which his existence is determined — into a plurality of atoms or, to
be more precise, into statistics." See *Democracy and Political Theory*, p. 227.

44. It is ironic that Plato denigrated the Athenian *agora*, the congregation of all
citizens gathered to make political decisions, as a "theatrocracy," a coinage that mocks
the *agora*'s claim to absolute visibility, the unmasking of power. See Bobbio, "Democracy and Invisible Power," in *The Future of Democracy*, pp. 79–97, esp. pp. 80–81. In
this essay, Bobbio bemoans the contemporary willingness to relinquish this commitment to the Kantian ideal of the necessarily public character of power, an ideal
formulated by Kant as the freedom to make "*public* use of man's reason" or, in other
words, "that use which anyone may make of it *as a man of learning* addressing the
entire *reading public*" (quoted on p. 84). Bobbio's comments underscore the affinity of
the liberal-democratic ideal of visible power with the Habermasian concept of the
public sphere, whereas Lefort seems implicitly to critique the Habermasian public
sphere as acting "to blur rather than to elucidate the features of the democratic
phenomenon" (*Democracy and Political Theory*, p. 227). For Bourdieu's critique of
Habermas, see "Editor's Introduction," *Language and Symbolic Power*, p. 10.

45. Lefort, *Democracy and Political Theory*, p. 174. Both Lefort here and Bourdieu, in chapter 7 of *Language and Symbolic Power*, appear more or less explicitly to tie the invisibility of symbolic power to an odd complicity between those who apparently wield it and those who are apparently subject to it. I examine the phenomenon of complicity in Chapter 3.

46. On the uncontainability of the "true" (as opposed to the "closed") crowd, see Elias Canetti, *Crowds and Power*, pp. 20–21, 29–30.

47. Major recent studies of textuality in this period that I have found most useful are Nancy Armstrong and Leonard Tennenhouse, *The Imaginary Puritan*; Cathy Davidson, *Revolution and the Word*; Michael Warner, *The Letters of the Republic*; and Larzer Ziff, *Writing in the New Nation*. Major recent voice-based studies are Richard Bauman, *Let Your Words Be Few*; Kenneth Cmiel, *Democratic Eloquence*; Jay Fliegelman, *Declaring Independence*; Christopher Looby, *Voicing America*; Stephen A. Marini, *Radical Sects of Revolutionary New England*; Harry S. Stout, *The New England Soul*; and Donald Weber, *Rhetoric and History in Revolutionary New England*. In *Letters of the Republic*, otherwise a strong study, Warner dismisses some voice-centered historical scholarship as "sentimental and ideological," both naive and unpleasantly canny. The indictment interestingly recapitulates the sentiments of eighteenth-century conservatives whose authority was challenged by voice-based social movements like the Great Awakening. George Whitefield, for example, so infuriated those whose clerical authority his itinerant ministry challenged that they typically accused him of being intentionally misrepresentative ("ideological") in order to mislead the people, but also of appealing to emotionality rather than upholding the priority of the rational as men of his station should ("sentimental"). Hence his appeal to those other "sentimental" (thus feminized) segments of the population, weak intellects all: in addition to women, the poor, the uneducated, African-Americans, Native Americans, the young, and so on.

48. See Frank Lambert, *"Pedlar in Divinity": George Whitefield and the Transatlantic Revivals, 1737–1770*; Lydia Ginzburg, *On Psychological Prose*; Tenney Nathanson, *Whitman's Presence*; and Donald Wesling and Tadeusz Sławek, *Literary Voice*. See also Alessandro Portelli, *The Text and the Voice*, and Peter de Bolla, *The Discourse of the Sublime*, esp. chapter 10.

49. See M. M. Bakhtin, "Forms of Time and of the Chronotope in the Novel," pp. 252–53.

50. Pocock does mention that the secularization of personality might be discussed in "evangelical and millenarian" terms as well as in "post-Christian and utopian" ones. See *Machiavellian Moment*, p. 463.

PART I

1. For contemporary accounts of Whitefield's popularity and the size of his audiences, see Harry S. Stout, *The Divine Dramatist*, and Frank Lambert, *"Pedlar in*

NOTES TO PAGES 20–25 **403**

Divinity." Whitefield's draw in 1740 of over twenty thousand auditors in Boston may be compared with the "massive community parades" in 1788 to celebrate the Constitution that drew up to six thousand participants; see Alfred F. Young, "English Plebeian Culture and Eighteenth-Century American Radicalism," esp. p. 186. Lambert argues persuasively for the centrality of the print network to Whitefield's cultural influence. Without denying Whitefield's sophisticated manipulations of the press to expand the reach of his ministry, I stress the impact upon auditors of his spectacular self-presentation in the context of the field sermon: as many acknowledged, had he not been such a gifted speaker he would not have gathered the unprecedented crowds he typically drew.

2. Humble self-enlargement may thus constitute the democratic underside of what Warner identifies as the republican "principle of negativity in representational politics," which, he argues, allowed the private (and propertied white male) individual "to make entry into political discourse" (*Letters of the Republic*, pp. 43, 72). See his chapter 2, "The *Res Publica* of Letters."

3. The nineteenth-century American historian George Bancroft as well as the French cultural analyst Alexis de Tocqueville both associated American Puritanism with what Bancroft called "democratic liberty," an interpretation that contemporary historians have vigorously challenged. Richard L. Bushman, *From Puritan to Yankee*, argues that "Democracy, in the Puritan view, was nongovernment or anarchy, and rulers had to constrain not to obey a corrupt popular will. Election was a device for implementing divine intentions rather than for transmitting power from the people to their rulers" (9; cf. 12–13). Bushman's comments underscore the phenomenal significance of the witchcraft crisis as conferring an unprecedented degree of political and social power upon disenfranchised persons. See Bancroft, *History of the United States of America*, 1: 469; and Tocqueville, *Democracy in America*, esp. part I, chapter 2, pp. 31–49.

4. The idea for the pun was suggested to me by the work of Elizabeth Maddock Dillon, "Representing the Subject of Freedom: Liberalism, Hysteria, and Dispossessive Individualism." The sociologist Steven Lukes speaks of individualism in America as a nineteenth- and twentieth-century concept — as an attribute, that is, of modern liberal democracy, although a passing reference is made to evangelicalism as adding its layer of influence to the increasingly positive antebellum understanding of the term. See his useful survey, *Individualism*. See also Raymond Williams, *Keywords*, pp. 161–65.

5. Paul Boyer and Stephen Nissenbaum, eds., *Salem Witchcraft Papers*, 1: 304. As Easty expressed it, to know oneself in this way is to know the Lord, to know what the Lord "who is the Searcher of all hearts" knows, and to be prepared to testify about it to Him "att the Tribunall seat" (304). On the connection between antinomianism and the development of American literature, see Amy Schrager Lang, *Prophetic Woman: Anne Hutchinson and the Problem of Dissent in the Literature of New England*.

6. The phrase comes from Jonathan Edwards's key essay, *The Distinguishing Marks of a Work of the Spirit of God*.

7. The phrase is taken from the Federalist Benjamin Welles, who in 1807 asked, "What national dignity can be expected from a country, where there are so many hundreds of political methodists canting about universal liberty, promiscuous equality; and preaching about political milleniums, the new light of reason, republican purity, and the diffusion of knowledge throughout the country?" From the scenarios that follow, each of which pictures an effort at self- and mutual education among the common class of laborers (Colin Clout, Blouzilinda the milkmaid, Dilworth the farmer and his clownish friends, tavernkeepers and postmen), the threat posed by "the inarticulate" is made explicit. See Welles as quoted in Lewis P. Simpson, ed., *The Federalist Literary Mind*, pp. 55–56. Numerous references to political methodism are recorded in William Stevens Perry, ed., *Historical Collections Relating to the American Colonial Church*.

8. Patricia Bonomi, *Under the Cope of Heaven: Religion, Society, and Politics in Colonial America*, p. 158.

9. To revert again to Raymond Williams: "The fact is," he writes in *Keywords*, "that, with only occasional exceptions, democracy, in the records that we have, was until C19 [the nineteenth century] a strongly unfavourable term, and it is only since lC19 [the late nineteenth century] and eC20 [the early twentieth century] that a majority of political parties and tendencies have united in declaring their belief in it. This is the most striking historical fact" (94). See also Bushman, *From Puritan to Yankee*, and Rhys Isaac, *The Transformation of Virginia, 1740–1790*, for accounts of the transition from communalism to individualism in colonial America.

10. Cf. Charles Taylor, *Sources of the Self: The Making of the Modern Identity*, esp. pp. 144–55, for an account of the shift toward a representational epistemology in the natural sciences in the seventeenth century and the subsequent emphasis on evidence and instrumentality.

11. Edwards, *Some Thoughts*, p. 518.

12. Edwards, *Distinguishing Marks*, p. 241.

13. Tocqueville, *Democracy in America*, p. 293.

CHAPTER ONE

1. Nathan Bowen, "Extracts from Interleaved Almanacs of Nathan Bowen," p. 164. Page references will henceforth be cited parenthetically in the text, and the spelling will occasionally be modernized.

2. Bowen uses the term "Licenciousness" on p. 168 to describe popular behavior. He explicitly links social freedom so conceived to impiety, noting that "the more Thinking part of the Boston Clergy . . . dare not attempt to Stop the Current least by disobliging their people, they forfiet their Benefits, & So they row down the Stream in the rabble rabble, now & then making Some faint Assays to Appose the Currant, but are soon repuls'd by the rough Gentry who now take a freedom with them which,

12 months ago, would have been Adjudged Impious!" (169). Heyrman notes the "longstanding association of all forms of religious antinomianism . . . with licentiousness and sexual libertinism"; see her study *Commerce and Culture*, p. 102. For an examination of the sexual stereotyping indulged by critics of the Great Awakening, past and present, see Cedric B. Cowing, "Sex and Preaching in the Great Awakening."

3. See Perry, *Historical Collections*, 3: 439 (letter of Timothy Cutler to the Secretary of the Society for the Propagation of the Gospel). This particular complaint was made as late as 1770. Explicit instances in which religious enthusiasm is likened to infection appear on 3: 377, 513. Page references to this volume will henceforth appear parenthetically in the text.

4. The reputations of those executed in the Salem witchcraft crisis were officially vindicated in October 1711. See Boyer and Nissenbaum, eds., *Salem Witchcraft Papers*, 3: 1015–17. Cited hereafter as *SWP*.

5. Few contemporary historians have ventured to comment on the enduring significance of the witchcraft crisis. In *Salem Possessed: The Social Origins of Witchcraft*, Boyer and Nissenbaum briefly remark upon the resemblance of the witchcraft crisis to the Great Awakening, but ultimately dismiss its importance by identifying what for them is a comprehensive difference: the revival lacked the sacrificial dynamic responsible for the deaths of at least twenty people in 1692; the revival's only victims were its suicides. Clearly, however, Bowen and other witnesses do complain of a sacrificial impulse which, if not fatal, was yet felt to have robbed individuals either of their reason or their good reputations. Brockwell, for example, makes the analogy between the possessed of 1692 and the enthusiasts of his day explicit when he writes of how "at Barrington, they [the enthusiasts] have not Scrupled to Accuse'd a poor Creature of Witchcraft, on Acc[oun]t of the death of two horses and Sickness of a Cow. Such is the shocking proceedings and such the extravagant behaviour of these Enthusiasts" (Perry, *Historical Collections*, 3: 387). An article in the *Boston Evening Post* in 1742 did raise the possibility of murder linked to religious enthusiasm: it reported that the followers of the itinerant evangelist James Davenport "would make nothing to kill Opposers" (quoted in Bonomi, *Under the Cope of Heaven*, p. 150). Perhaps the most cogent argument for linking the homicidal impulse let loose in the witchcraft crisis with the suicidal impulse expressed in the Great Awakening is given by Jonathan Edwards, who explicitly associated the two forms of crime in *Some Thoughts*, p. 482. Larzer Ziff, in *Puritanism in America*, writes that "the witchcraft craze of New England was not the last fling of Puritanism, but rather the final outcome on a public level of the primitive relationship between God's intent and the Puritan believer. The new relationship, essentially in effect at the time of the outburst, was also structured by the cultural ideals of Puritanism, and the new order that emerged was no less the result of Puritanism than was the order asserted by those who were possessed by the hysteria" (249). Ziff does not show in any detail how the witchcraft crisis itself may have served as a transition to the "new relationship" he goes on to trace through the

Great Awakening; it remains an "outburst," an "aberration" (249), the final manifestation of a particular aspect of Puritanism that did not survive into the eighteenth
century when Puritan culture was restored to its "faith in conscience and words"
(249). In the final analysis, the witchcraft debacle represented a successful, if tragic,
"purging" of Puritan fears regarding the loss of the charter. In contrast to this approach, Philip Gould has recently surveyed the historiography and historical fictions
of the postrevolutionary and early national periods that focused on the Salem witchcraft. He observes that in these texts the witchcraft hysteria — Puritan "superstition" — is implicitly made analogous to the popular "enthusiasm" the writers considered responsible for the political and social processes of democratization that
occurred in the first decades of the nineteenth century. See Gould, "New England
Witch-Hunting and the Politics of Reason in the Early Republic."

   6. See Perry Miller, *The New England Mind: From Colony to Province*, pp. 191–92.
Cf. Sydney Ahlstrom, who claimed that the witchcraft crisis was so anomalous that its
study "does little to elucidate the Puritan mind of the age"; thus he almost entirely
omitted it from his massive *Religious History of the American People* — in over one
thousand pages, he accords it a single paragraph on p. 161. Likewise, George Lincoln
Burr, a key collector of historical documents related to the Salem witchcraft crisis,
noted in his paper "The Literature of Witchcraft" delivered before the American
Historical Association in January 1890 that to "say nothing of the literature of American witchcraft" is demanded by "the brevity [of] its place in the history of the delusion": to say more than nothing about Salem would be "a work of supererogation, if
not an impertinence." See Burr, "The Literature of Witchcraft," p. 263 n. 6. Marion
Starkey does not directly suggest an association between the witchcraft crisis and the
revival; such an observation would not have come within the purview of her fine study.
But she makes an important observation: "Witchdom was what Puritanism in its later
phases was not, an evangelical faith. Each communicant was urged to bring in at least
one more convert before the next sabbath" (*Devil in Massachusetts*, p. 116).

   7. The questionable claim "to know and revea[l] secret things" is also discussed by
Increase Mather in 1696 in *A Disquisition Concerning Angelical Apparitions*. Mather
argues that such information, allegedly transmitted by "*Celestial Visitants*," is false,
"the effect of an hurt Imagination only" (3). All italics appearing in quotations
throughout the book are inherent to the original sources, unless otherwise noted.

   8. During the Great Awakening, critics like Charles Chauncy accused New Lights
of a lack of charity for their claim to know the identities, determined and hence
known only by God, of the elect and the damned. See Chauncy's summary of the
Antinomian controversy in his preface to *Seasonable Thoughts On the State of Religion in
New England*.

   9. See, for example, Cotton Mather's admission, in his defensive account of the
witchcraft crisis included in his *Magnalia Christi Americana*, that "divers were condemned, against whom the *chief evidence* was founded in the *spectral exhibitions*," which
occurred because the judges "took one thing more for granted" than more con-

ventionally acceptable forms of evidence (visible proofs, confession, etc.) allowed: namely, spectral evidence, "wherein 'tis now as generally thought they *went out of the way*" (1: 209, 208). The account of witchcraft appears in Mather's appendix to book II entitled "Pietas in Patriam. The Life of His Excellency Sir William Phips, Knt.," section 16. Thomas Brattle, a critic of the trials, complained that it was "purely by virtue of these spectre evidences, that these persons are found guilty," despite the judges' denial that this was so. See his "Letter of 8 October 1692," quotation from p. 176. Robert Calef, a Boston merchant who wrote a lengthy, scathing critique of the witchcraft proceedings several years after they occurred also maintained that "the Accusations of [the afflicted] from their Spectral Sight" were "the chief Evidence against those that Suffered. In which Accusations they were upheld by both Magistrates and Ministers, so long as they Apprehended themselves in no Danger." The last and "most remarkable of the Tryals," that of the aged Sarah Daston, "seemed wholly forreign," Calef observed, insofar as "Spectre-Evidence was not made use of." See Calef, *More Wonders of the Invisible World*, pp. 306 and 383. A letter of inquiry sent to the Dutch and French clergy of New York in October 1692 by Joseph Dudley, the former deputy governor of Massachusetts under Edmund Andros, featured queries concerning the validity of spectral evidence, especially when it constituted the sole form of evidence offered; Dudley asked, for example, whether the siting of an apparition is "of itself sufficient for a just conviction of witchcraft" and whether "a serious accusation by the afflicted is sufficient to prove witchcraft, against a long continued consistent, just, Christian life, full of charity, and approved by mankind, where no previous malice is made known." See Dudley, "Letter to the Dutch and French clergymen of New York, 5 October 1692," and Selijns et al., "Reply to Dudley, 11 October 1692." The questions quoted (queries 6 and 7) appear in Dudley, p. 353.

Modern historians have generally concurred in this respect with the trials' observers. Boyer and Nissenbaum point out in their introduction to *Salem Witchcraft Papers* (*SWP*) that, because the trial transcripts have not survived, no one knows for certain how much weight the court of Oyer and Terminer gave to the spectral evidence gathered by the magistrates in their preliminary investigations, but it constituted "the great bulk" of the latter testimony (1: 19). Starkey, however, claims that trials closely followed the pretrial examinations, so much so that "the examination was the trial; its records were reviewed not as hypotheses to be tested, but as facts already proved" (*Devil in Massachusetts*, p. 152). She identifies spectral evidence as "by far the most important principle accepted by the magistrates" (54). The statement made by the accused (and later executed) John Proctor supports Starkey's claim for the conformity of trial to preliminary examination: he spoke of the judges "having Condemned us already before our Tryals" (quoted in Calef, *More Wonders*, p. 362). Other historians who cite the dominance of spectral evidence in the Salem prosecutions include David Thomas Konig, *Law and Society in Puritan Massachusetts*, p. 171; Robert Middlekauff, *The Mathers*, pp. 154–55; and Dennis E. Owen, "Spectral Evidence." In Richard Weisman's excellent study *Witchcraft, Magic, and Religion in*

Seventeenth-Century Massachusetts, he states that the conflict between magistrates and clergy in the evaluation of evidence during the Salem trials "lay in the emphasis given to spectral evidence in the gathering of incriminating testimony. While other evidences, including ordinary witchcrafts, witch's marks, puppets, and even secondary signs such as unusual physical strength, had also been admitted into the records of the court, only the spectral evidence had been collected for all the cases" (150). Charles W. Upham, in *Salem Witchcraft*, suggests that the reliance on spectral evidence was so scandalous after the conclusions of the trials that it led to "a suppression and destruction" of historical materials pertaining to the witchcraft crisis; he refers specifically to the disappearance of the journal of the Special Court of Oyer and Terminer as well as other documentary evidence (2: 462–63).

10. On European witchcraft trials and the prominence of spectral evidence in securing convictions, see note 17 of this chapter. Studies of American witchcraft trials occurring before the 1692 crisis provide little evidence that the accused witches' offenses involved anything other than petty *maleficium*. See, for example, Carol F. Karlsen, *The Devil in the Shape of a Woman*, esp. pp. 1–45. Although Karlsen maintains that in practice, prosecutors were concerned with both the commission of *maleficium* and the witch's covenanting with the devil, the "recurring list of witchcraft crimes" included bewitching people and animals, interfering with the making of butter and beer, causing miscarriages, knowing things seemingly impossible to know, claiming to have had sexual relations with the devil, being prideful, etc. (23). Apparently, the sighting of specters did play a role in accusations made during the Hartford crisis of 1662–63, but was significantly augmented by reports of *maleficium* and other non–spectral evidence issues. This assessment is born out by the collection of primary documents pertaining to seventeenth-century American witchcraft trials published by David D. Hall in *Witch-Hunting in Seventeenth-Century New England*. Also see John Demos, *Entertaining Satan: Witchcraft and the Culture of Early New England*, and Weisman, *Witchcraft, Magic, and Religion*, who states that before 1692, "the culpability of the witch consisted neither in complicity with Satan nor in conspiracy against the state but in the willingness to make use of malefic magic. Thus, in the pre-Salem litigations, it was in the form of testimony alleging specific damage or injury that the courts of New England received evidence of witchcraft from the villages of New England" (75).

11. See "Nathaniel Cary's Account of his Wife's Examination," in Boyer and Nissenbaum, *SWP*, 1: 207–10. The quoted material appears on pp. 209 and 210. Cary's account also appears in Calef, *More Wonders*, pp. 350–52.

12. Cotton Mather, letter to John Richards of 31 May 1692, in *Selected Letters of Cotton Mather*, pp. 35–40; quotation from p. 36. Hereafter cited as "Richards Letter."

13. Quoted in Burr, ed., *Narratives of the Witchcraft Cases*, p. 150.

14. Cotton Mather, "Richards Letter," pp. 37, 39. In this letter, as in every one of his statements regarding the Salem witchcraft, Mather is an ambivalent critic of spectral evidence (to the great irritation of his main critic Robert Calef): one senses

the pressure he feels to renounce it as well as his fascination with it. For an overview of "the problem of proof" and the influence of European witch scholars on the Salem magistrates and involved clergy, see Weisman, *Witchcraft, Magic, and Religion*, pp. 98–105. For a contemporary account of the categories of evidence actually used in the conviction of the Salem witches, see John Hale, *A Modest Inquiry into the Nature of Witchcraft*, pp. 411–12. Samuel Willard also reviews what is necessary for a clear conviction in *Some Miscellany Observations*, pp. 9–13. The skeptic of the Lord's Prayer test alluded to is Robert Calef (*More Wonders*, p. 347).

15. Increase Mather, *Cases of Conscience Concerning Evil Spirits Personating Men.* On Mather's guidelines for "*sufficient Proof*," see Cotton Mather, *Wonders of the Invisible World*, pp. 276–84. Increase Mather relies mainly on credible confession (and is careful to exclude "distracted" or "Melancholy" persons) and testimony from two credible witnesses. He vehemently rejects the use of the water test for the detection of witches as "Superstitious and Magical experiments . . . invented by the Devil, that so innocent Persons might be condemned, and some notorious Witches escape" (270; see also 271–74; he made the same objections earlier in *An Essay for the Recording of Illustrious Providences*), whereas his son Cotton, in "Richards Letter," appears to recommend its use (39). See Boyer and Nissenbaum's discussion of the problem of evidence and the magistrates' attempts to bolster spectral evidence to the degree possible with empirical evidence in *SWP*, 1: 19–24. See also Weisman's discussion of the classifications of evidence in witchcraft cases elaborated by the English Puritans William Perkins and Richard Bernard in *Witchcraft, Magic, and Religion*, pp. 99–101.

16. Robert Calef reported that at these final trials "some of the Jewry made Inquiry of the court, what Account they ought to make of the Spectre Evidence? and received for Answer 'as much as of Chips in Wort' " [as of less than no worth] (*More Wonders*, p. 382). Starkey provides an account of the dissolution of the court of Oyer and Terminer and its reconstitution as a judicial body precluded from hearing spectral evidence (*Devil in Massachusetts*, chapter 19).

17. It is not within the scope of this study to determine what role, if any, spectral evidence played in European witchcraft trials in both Catholic and Protestant contexts. Preliminary study suggests that although the witch's covenanting with the devil and acquiring thereby supernal powers of inflicting evil defined the crime of witchcraft throughout Europe and although evidence concerning the act of covenanting was officially admissible in England from 1593 through 1712, it played a relatively minor role in convictions. It is one thing to remark, as do Boyer and Nissenbaum in *SWP*, 1: 10–11, the prevalence throughout the Christian world of the beliefs fundamental to spectral evidence, and another to show that spectral evidence played as dominant a role in European trials as at Salem. George Lyman Kittredge, in *Witchcraft in Old and New England*, claims that spectral evidence was "one of the best established of all legal principles" (363) and cites many English trials between 1593 and 1712 in which it figured (pp. 592–93 nn. 138–62) as well as its frequent discussion in authoritative guidebooks to witchcraft and its detection (most prominently, in

Joseph Glanvill's highly influential *Saducismus Triumphatus: or, Full and Plain Evidence concerning Witches and Apparitions* [1681]). The question, Kittredge says, "was not whether such evidence might be heard, but what weight was to be attached to it" (364). He does not thereafter discuss the relative weight given to spectral evidence in the Salem trials as compared with the European (he is more concerned to exonerate the Salem prosecutors as typical of their age and the Salem debacle as relatively minor), but in his lengthy discussion of European witchcraft he nowhere cites a trial in which spectral evidence played anything like the role it did at Salem. See Kittredge, pp. 221, 363–64. Kittredge cites James B. Thayer, who, in his 1890 study "Trial by Jury of Things Supernatural," suggests that the first European case for which spectral evidence was decisive was in Scotland in 1696, four years after Salem. The other case Thayer discusses in detail, that of the Suffolk witches in 1664 tried by Sir Matthew Hale and to which, according to Cotton Mather, the Salem prosecution referred for guidance, did not include spectral evidence (467–68). Robert Calef briefly claimed in *More Wonders* that spectral evidence and confession were accepted in English, Scottish, and New English trials (379). Burr does not provide corroborating evidence for this remark, but only notes that the transcripts of English trials were recorded in "wretched chap-books" that "Calef was likely to know" (*Narratives*, p. 379 n. 5). Joseph Higginson, who wrote a prefatory letter to John Hale's retrospective critique of the proceedings, testified therein to "a Question yet unresolved, Whether some of the Laws, Customs and Principles used by the Judges and Juries in the Trials of Witches in England (which were followed as Patterns here) were not insufficient and unsafe." Hale argues that the proceedings were mistaken because unscriptural, and that the American Puritans were perhaps wrong to have relied upon European precedent in the prosecution of suspected witches. But the question of the role actually played by spectral evidence in European witchcraft convictions—no matter its theoretical acceptability—is not addressed. See Hale, *Modest Inquiry*, pp. 401, 427.

18. Reprinted in Boyer and Nissenbaum, *SWP*, 3: 864.

19. The most outspoken Old Light clergyman, Charles Chauncy, identified the revivalists with the Antinomians in the preface to *Seasonable Thoughts*. Lang, in *Prophetic Woman*, traces the relevance of the Antinomian crisis to the development of a national literature, and Konig, in *Law and Society*, notes the "remarkable degree" to which accusations of the witches resemble those against the Antinomians (173 n. 49).

20. See Lorraine Daston's extremely suggestive article, "Marvelous Facts and Miraculous Evidence in Early Modern Europe," p. 99. I am grateful to Terry Castle for drawing my attention to Daston's work. The Puritan understanding of the relationship between the visible and invisible worlds is succinctly presented in Perry Miller's classic article, "The Marrow of Puritan Divinity." See also Ziff, *Puritanism in America*, on the witchcraft crisis as a "brief and bloody"—and also "inarticulate"—"excursion into the third dimension . . . of nonverbal mystical access to the invisible world" (250). Also of interest is Ann Kibbey's provocative account of how "the image of the [Puritan] deity as the author of remarkable providences, and the image of the witch as the author of *maleficia*, were positive and negative forms of a single idea about

supernatural power" in "Mutations of the Supernatural: Witchcraft, Remarkable Providences, and the Power of Puritan Men," p. 137.

21. On the absolute separation between the visible and invisible worlds at the heart of radical Protestantism, see Michael Walzer, *The Revolution of the Saints*, pp. 25–26; for a fuller treatment, see Perry Miller, "Marrow of Puritan Divinity," esp. pp. 93–97. It was to this sanctified isolation of the invisible world of God's determinations that Puritan ministers referred when they cautioned against undue confidence in one's spiritual destiny, indulgence in magical practices, and attempts to communicate with spiritual beings, whether angels or evil spirits.

22. See Perry Miller, *The New England Mind: From Colony to Province*, p. 252.

23. On the theory and practice of a visible sainthood, see Edmund S. Morgan, *Visible Saints* and *The Puritan Dilemma: The Story of John Winthrop*, esp. p. 79; Nuttall, *Visible Saints and the Congregational Way, 1640–1660*, which treats the development of Congregationalism in England; Bercovitch, *The American Jeremiad*, chapter 2; Perry Miller, "Marrow of Puritan Divinity"; and Caldwell, *The Puritan Conversion Narrative*, esp. chapters 1 and 2. On the tenacity with which Increase Mather held to the idea of the pure church, his increasing tendency to identify the church with New England in the last decades of the century, and his increasing emphasis on external conformity during those years, especially after he accepted the Halfway Covenant in 1668, see Middlekauff, *The Mathers*, pp. 117–23.

24. Quoted in Morgan, *Visible Saints*, pp. 35–36.

25. The eminent English Puritan Richard Baxter condemned this practice for relying too much upon "the *opinions* of the Pastor (yea, the people too)" (quoted in Morgan, *Visible Saints*, p. 105). Elsewhere, Morgan starkly represents the centrality of the elect/damned opposition to American Puritan culture: after the establishment of the Congregational churches, he wrote, "every soul was checked off as saved or damned" when coming off the boat (*Puritan Dilemma*, p. 79).

26. See Caldwell, *Puritan Conversion Narrative*. On William Perkins's elaboration of a ten-step morphology of conversion, see Morgan, *Visible Saints*. Samuel Stone's distinction is cited in Perry Miller, *The New England Mind: The Seventeenth Century*, p. 452. See also Darrett B. Rutman, "Local Freedom and Puritan Control," p. 118.

27. Patricia Caldwell discusses the likelihood that American conversion narratives started out but did not long remain in the prophetic mode in *The Puritan Conversion Narrative*, pp. 70–74, 97–100. Geoffrey Nuttall examines the English context for Puritan prophesying in the fifth chapter of *The Holy Spirit in Puritan Faith and Experience*, pp. 75–89.

28. Bercovitch, *American Jeremiad*, p. 45.

29. See Perry Miller, "Marrow of Puritan Divinity," pp. 92–93; Preston quoted on p. 96. Miller concludes, "it would be the end of Puritanism if [Puritan divines] ever succeeded completely in penetrating the ultimate secret, if they could reach the point of saying that thus and so is not simply the way God does behave, but the way in which He must behave for these and those reasons" (97).

30. Breitweiser examines Cotton Mather's profound ambivalence toward this

space of unknowing—"an abysmal gap across which the present can only measure ironically its hopeless difference from the past"—as revealed in his genealogical and hermeneutic pursuits ("Cotton Mather's Crazed Wife," p. 95). See also chapter 2 (pp. 46–87) of *Mather and Franklin* ("Cotton Mather's Work"), which extends his analysis. Of special significance is the nature of the threat posed by Robert Calef's published critique of Mather's publications on the witchcraft crisis; Breitweiser notes that in *More Wonders* "Calef accused Mather of doing what Mather accused Hutchinson and Satan of doing—constructing simulacra that looked like truth, but were actually traductions meant to interrupt the tradition of piety" (79); see pp. 77–80. On magic in the American seventeenth century, see Jon Butler, *Awash in a Sea of Faith*; Richard Godbeer, *The Devil's Dominion: Magic and Religion in Early New England*; David D. Hall, *Worlds of Wonder, Days of Judgment: Popular Religious Belief in Early New England*, who argues that magic and religion coexisted relatively peacefully in colonial New England; and Weisman, *Witchcraft, Magic, and Religion*.

31. This is not to suggest that the Puritan orthodoxy constituted a seamless unity of behavior and belief against which radicals like Hutchinson struggled. This view has been persuasively challenged by Janice Knight, *Orthodoxies in Massachusetts: Rereading American Puritanism*.

32. See Bercovitch, *American Jeremiad*, for the process by which these threats were themselves incorporated, as modernizing stimuli, into the evolving understanding of the Puritans' errand into the wilderness. Bercovitch disagrees with Miller on the provenance of the jeremiad; see Perry Miller, "Errand into the Wilderness," pp. 8 and 15, and Bercovitch's discussion on p. 5.

33. On New English demonology, see Godbeer, *The Devil's Dominion*, esp. pp. 86–91.

34. Long-standing opposition to the Halfway Covenant is evident in the fact that Cotton Mather's North Church, at the insistence of some of its leading members, including the future Salem magistrate John Richards, did not accept its terms until 1691. See David Levin, *Cotton Mather: The Young Life of the Lord's Remembrancer*, pp. 194–95. On the Halfway Covenant as a strategy for increasing clerical authority, see Bushman, *From Puritan to Yankee*, pp. 147–49.

35. On Mather's debate with Solomon Stoddard, see Middlekauff, *The Mathers*, chapter 7, "The Church of the Pure." The quoted phrase appears on p. 131.

36. In *American Jeremiad*, Bercovitch claims that the Halfway Covenant "served to secularize the colony" and "was less a departure from old ideas than it was an effort . . . to extend and adapt those ideals to new conditions" (27). On the Halfway Covenant as "the major turning point" in the secularization of Puritan doctrine that would eventually "extend the prerogatives of visible sainthood to the entire American electorate" (63), see chapter 3, esp. pp. 62–67. For a view of the Halfway Covenant as tending to strengthen Puritan society, see Robert G. Pope, *The Half-Way Covenant*.

37. On these events and their impact on Cotton Mather, see Kenneth Silverman's excellent biography, *The Life and Times of Cotton Mather*, esp. chapter 3. Levin dis-

cusses these events with respect to Mather's conviction of the coming millennium in chapter 6 of his *Cotton Mather*.

38. See Middlekauff, *The Mathers*, pp. 146–47.

39. See the 6 July 1681 entry in Cotton Mather, *Diary of Cotton Mather*, 1: 22–24, quotation from p. 23. See also Silverman, *Life and Times of Cotton Mather*, pp. 24, 26.

40. Cotton Mather, *Diary*, 1: 7, 6. Middlekauff notes his father's similar sense at the beginning of his ministerial career in *The Mathers*, p. 85. On the eccentricity in the Puritan context of Cotton's interest in and claims to have had relatively direct experience of good and evil spirits, see Lovelace, *The American Pietism of Cotton Mather*, pp. 188–97. On Mather's own "visitation by an angel," see Silverman, "A Note on the Date of Cotton Mather's Visitation by an Angel," who presents evidence that the visitation took place sometime after June 1693; and David Levin, "When Did Cotton Mather See the Angel?" as well as his *Cotton Mather*, esp. pp. 195–222, who maintains that the visit occurred in 1685 and that this event, coupled with the "chiliastic and military context" (200) within which the Salem debacle occurred, contributed to his ambivalence regarding spectral evidence. In support of his evidence, Silverman notes an increase in the numbers of angelical apparitions between 1692 and 1694.

41. See Silverman, *Life and Times of Cotton Mather*, p. 88; see also Godbeer, *The Devil's Dominion*, p. 86 n. 3. Silverman notes that Mather was not alone in his obsession with the hostile invisible world. Keith Thomas, writing about Luther's heightened sense of sin and the visible world as the devil's province, provides some insight into the significance of this practice for radical Protestants in general: "In the long run it may be that the Protestant emphasis on the single sovereignty of God, as against the Catholic concept of a graded hierarchy of spiritual powers, helped to dissolve the world of spirits by referring all supernatural acts to a single source. But if so it was a slow development. For Englishmen of the Reformation period the Devil was a greater reality than ever. . . . Men thus became accustomed to Satan's immediacy" (*Religion and the Decline of Magic*, pp. 470–71).

42. Quoted in Upham, *Salem Witchcraft*, 1: 391.

43. Cf. Ziff, *Puritanism in America*, p. 246: "the witchcraft craze in Massachusetts revealed that the Puritan religion, in the formalism consequent upon its success and the professionalization of its clergy consequent upon its adjustment to a changing economic world, had too severely delimited the individual believer's sense of his direct access to the divine will. . . . [T]he people, in indulging in the lore of witchcraft, indulged themselves in a final unchecked thronging of the avenue of immediate access to the spiritual world." See also p. 247 on the Puritan ministry's complacency in allowing laypersons, indeed powerless children, to restore "religious fervor" to a backsliding community.

44. See Cotton Mather, *Memorable Providences, Relating to Witchcrafts and Possessions*. The quoted material appears on pp. 95–96. On p. 96, the ministers also allude to the troublesome mystery of God's tolerance of the devil's actions.

45. Cotton Mather, *Another Brand Pluckt Out of the Burning*, pp. 321–22.

46. Spectral evidence also included sightings of the devil or of diabolical "familiars" — grotesque beings, usually animalistic or monstrous — in the witch's vicinity or presence. See, for example, this exchange in the interrogation of Dorcas Hoar: "[DH:] I will speak the Truth as long as I live. / Mary Walcot & Susan: Sheldon & Eliz: Hubbard said again there was a man whispering in her ear, & said she should never confess. . . . What do you say to those cats that suckt your breast, what are they? / [DH:] I had no cats. / You do not call them cats, what are they that suck you? / [DH:] I never suckt none, but my child" (Boyer and Nissenbaum, *SWP*, 2: 390). In the cases of every individual executed, the spectral representation of the accused witch played a central role in the testimony of the afflicted, as it did for the vast majority of convicted witches. There are very few examinations in which spectral representation of the accused does not play a major role, and only a handful of places in which it plays no role whatsoever.

47. Aside from Increase Mather's *Cases of Conscience*, the anti–spectral evidence treatises available before Phips dissolved the court were Brattle, "Letter of 8 October 1692"; Willard, *Some Miscellany Observations*; Selijns et al., "Reply to Dudley"; "Letter from R.P. to Jonathan Corwin"; and "Return of Ministers of 15 June 1692," reprinted in Hutchinson, *The History of the Colony and Province of Massachusetts-Bay*, 2: 38–39.

48. Although in *Religion and the Decline of Magic* Thomas notes that "demons had no corporeal existence, but it was notorious that they could borrow or counterfeit human shape" (470), convictions in the Salem trials were obtained by "proving," through the behavior and testimony of the afflicted, that those whose shapes Satan chose to borrow had explicitly consented to the diabolical counterfeit. Beginning with Kittredge, historians of the witchcraft crisis have been more concerned to condemn or exonerate the actors (exoneration is typically based on the fact that belief in witchcraft was universal) than to understand why spectral evidence dominated the Salem trials and what its cultural significance might have been. Upham, who is outspokenly critical of the Salem court, names Chief-Justice William Stoughton as the magistrate unmovably committed to the postulate of consent, and quotes a letter published by Increase Mather from a London correspondent: "I speak with much wonder that any man, much less a man of such abilities, learning, and experience as Mr. Stoughton, should take up a persuasion that the Devil cannot assume the likeness of an innocent, to afflict another person. In my opinion, it is a persuasion utterly destitute of any solid reason to render it so much as probable" (*Salem Witchcraft*, 2: 356–64; Mather's correspondent quoted on p. 364). Perry Miller also faults Stoughton for his insistence on inferring consent from representation, calling it preeminent among "the gaping hypotheses of Stoughton's court," and ties his unorthodox opinion to the disintegration of the intellectual structure of the Puritan community. According to Miller, it did so by encouraging the extortion of false confessions from accused witches, thereby subverting the culture's method of atonement by which the covenant was kept intact. See *From Colony to Province*, pp. 204, 194–97. Finally, George Lincoln Burr also

attributes the emphasis on the consent of the represented to Stoughton, noting that he was convinced of "the Devil's impotence to personate by a spectre any but a guilty witch" (*Narratives*, p. 183 n. 2).

49. From Deodat Lawson's sermon of 24 March 1692, *Christ's Fidelity the only Shield against Satan's Malignity*, quoted in Burr, *Narratives*, p. 158 n. 3. The sermon was published in 1693 and republished in London in 1704, with his eyewitness account of the Salem trials, entitled *A Brief and True Narrative*, published with it as an appendix. The sermon is excerpted in Upham, 2: 78–87; its final section is reprinted in Boyer and Nissenbaum, eds., *Salem-Village Witchcraft*, pp. 124–28. Its publication history is provided by Upham, *Salem Witchcraft*, 2: 90. Upham also reprints the 1704 edition's preface and appendix (the revised *A Brief and True Narrative*) in the appendix to his own book (2: 525–37). Upham claims that Lawson's sermon, carefully researched in advance of his firsthand acquaintance with events in Salem and rhetorically powerful, "justified and commended . . . every kind of accusation and evidence that had been adduced; every phase of the popular belief, however wild and monstrous" (2: 88). On the effect of Lawson's sermon, see also Starkey, *Devil in Massachusetts*, pp. 68–86. Confessing witches tended to support Lawson's account of what was occurring. Mary Osgood, for example, confessed that "she has afflicted three persons . . . and that she did it by pinching her bed clothes, and giving consent the devil should do it in her shape, and that the devil could not do it without her consent" (Boyer and Nissenbaum, *SWP*, 2: 615).

50. See Cotton Mather, "A Discourse on Witchcraft," pp. 97, 99, 97. Interestingly, Mather is also concerned here to delimit the potential uncontainability of spectral representation by differentiating the one true representation — that of the individual who has consented to serve the devil — from the myriad false ones generated by the "wild" speculations of popular superstition: "We need not suppose such a wild thing as the *Transforming* of those Wretches into *Brutes* or *Birds*, as we too often do" (97).

51. Bishop's trial documentation appears in Boyer and Nissenbaum, *SWP*, 1: 83–109. Quoted material appears on pp. 85–86 and 87.

52. See Boyer and Nissenbaum, *SWP*, 3: 705. The phrase "she or her apparition [he or his apparition]" appears in the vast majority of depositions submitted to the court. Michael Clark makes the point that the witchcraft trials depended on such rhetorical strategies which "made it possible to transcend ontological boundaries between flesh and spirit" and thus "to translate the body into an image of demonic presence that becomes a target for legal authority" ("Discourse and the Body in Colonial Witchcraft," p. 212). In *The Devil's Dominion*, Godbeer points out the resemblance to magic of this conflation of reality and appearance or representation (216–17).

53. See Boyer and Nissenbaum, *SWP*, 1: 225. Cf. the confession of Deliverance Hobbs as reported by John Hale (*Modest Inquiry*, p. 417). She reports signing the devil's book "and immediately upon it a Spectre in her Shape afflicted another per-

416 NOTES TO PAGE 46

son," the implication being that bodies and specters lead separate lives and exist independently of one another. But she also reveals wounds on her body from blows that were dealt to her specter.

54. See Brattle, "Letter," pp. 174–75. Samuel Willard noted the tendency to conflate the representation with the represented, specter and human, in confessing witches whose testimony he rejected for that reason: "The Witches themselves do not know when they go in Spectre, and when in Body, and how should they then tell, whether the other be the person bodily or only in Spectre?" (*Miscellany Observations*, p. 24).

55. Oddly enough, the erasure of this difference between an individual and her specter was supported by testimony in which the separability of specter and individual was asserted. The confessing witch Abigail Hobbs, for example, told the court that there was no need for her to go in person to hurt others, because the devil went for her. He had no need to "take [her] spirit" in order to carry out his evil intention, but required only her consent, leaving her as he went on his evil errand, "as well as at other times." Her sense of self thus remained intact, such that she could confidently differentiate herself from her "shape," the creature of her consent. See the documents pertaining to her case in Boyer and Nissenbaum, *SWP*, 2: 405–17, esp. pp. 407, 408.

56. See Owen, "Spectral Evidence," p. 277. Upham concurs that the prosecution's supposition that the accused had consented to a division of the self into visible and invisible components meant that "the last defense of innocence [was] swept away" (*Salem Witchcraft*, 2: 407). Also see Konig, who claims that Stoughton relied on an English statute of 1604 to identify the crime of witchcraft not as the practice of *maleficium* but rather the consulting of spirits for any purpose: "what was at stake was an entire system of law and authority that was being challenged by an utterly antithetical *method* of social control. Magic was, therefore, a secular heresy that had to be crushed, and four of the accused had, in fact, done nothing more than make a 'covenant with the Evill Spirit, the Devill' " (*Law and Society*, p. 173). Konig's remarks underscore the political implications of witchcraft.

57. See Brattle, "Letter," p. 176.

58. Increase Mather's description of the devil as a visual artist is instructive: "He had perfect skill in Opticks, and can therefore cause that to be visible to one, which is not so to another, and things also to appear far otherwise then they are: He has likewise the Art of Limning in the Perfection of it, and knows what may be done by Colours" (*Cases of Conscience*, p. 237). This view of the devil's artistic powers was standard: his method of invisibilizing is described during the Scottish witchcraft trials of 1696 and quoted at length in Thayer, "Trial by Jury of Things Supernatural," pp. 478–79.

59. The significance of this rejection will be elaborated further in the chapter. Suffice it to say for now that even when those in favor of spectral evidence entertained the possibility that the accused might be innocent, they did not therefore conclude that the latter deserved to be exonerated. As Lawson expressed it in his June sermon,

"if innocent persons be suspected, it is to be ascribed to God's pleasure, supremely permitting, and Satan's malice subordinately troubling, by representation of such to the afflicting of others." See Upham, *Salem Witchcraft*, 2: 91. The legal and theological controversy that came to surround the policy of admitting spectral evidence in court was focused precisely on the issue of God's consent.

60. In the introduction to her "Marvelous Facts," the intellectual historian Lorraine Daston provides another way of accounting for the legal (as opposed to the theological) problem of spectral evidence, by speaking of the crucial distinction modernity makes between "facts" and "evidence." If evidence and facts are conjoined insofar as the former "might be described as facts hammered into signposts, which point beyond themselves and their sheer, brute thingness to states of affairs to which we have no direct access," nevertheless we preserve the independence of fact because only then are facts "valuable to a certain view of rationality, one that insists upon the neutrality of facts and staunchly denies that they are 'theory-laden'" (93–94). In the case of spectral evidence, one must add to this the crucial point that the "fact" in question — spectral representation — never had the status of "sheer, brute thingness"; nevertheless, it was taken to point automatically beyond itself to the (equally elusive) "fact" of consent, and herein lies the problem with spectral evidence. But it is not the fantastic nature of the "facts" in question that troubles so much as their lack of independence so conceived. As Daston states: "Implicit in this conventional distinction between facts and evidence is that in order for facts to qualify as credible evidence, they must appear innocent of human intention. Facts fabricated as evidence, that is, to make a particular point, are thereby disqualified as evidence. . . . It is the distinction between facts and evidence that is at issue, not the reality of the facts per se, nor their quality as evidence in general" (94). "Marvelous Facts" explores how the distinction between facts and evidence came about, and asks if it is possible "to imagine a kind of evidence that is intention-laden" (94). Boyer and Nissenbaum in *Salem Possessed* emphasize the "almost franti[c]" efforts made by the Salem magistrates to "seek out proofs that would conform to the established rules of courtroom evidence — that is to say, evidence that was empirically verifiable and logically relevant" (11–16; quotations from p. 11).

61. Accused witches Mary Easty and her sister Sarah Cloyce describe themselves as having lived under the unblemished reputation of Christianity in their petition to the prosecution, reprinted in Boyer and Nissenbaum, *SWP*, 1: 302–3, quotation from p. 303. On the blasphemous imitation and the assumption of invisibility, see Cotton Mather, *Wonders*, pp. 245, 246. That the witchcraft crisis represents a perversion of issues of consent and representation implicit in Puritanism is suggested by an observation of Morgan's in *Visible Saints* (26) that the separatist policy of the English Puritans rested upon similar issues: a rejection of representation in their conviction that the church covenant "must be subscribed to personally: the people's representatives in Parliament could not act for them in this matter," and an insistence on free consent as the basis of the institution's validity (see esp. pp. 28–41).

62. Boyer and Nissenbaum, *Salem Possessed*, p. 11. Demos notes that statutes concerning witchcraft in New England "stressed the bare fact of diabolical connection, without reference to the use of such connection in causing harm. In practice, however, there *must* be harm — enough to warrant the effort and expense of a formal proceeding. Thus witch trials began with a complaint by (or on behalf of) the supposed victims" (*Entertaining Satan*, p. 10).

63. Michael J. Colacurcio has brilliantly identified spectral evidence and the nightmarish reversals of judgment concerning essence it entailed as the central issue in Hawthorne's tale "Young Goodman Brown," which demonstrated that the "difficulty of detecting a witch is distressingly similar to the radically Puritan problem of discovering a saint" (286). See "Visible Sanctity and Specter Evidence: 'The Tryal of G.B.,'" the fifth chapter of *The Province of Piety*, pp. 283–313; cf. his analysis of "Alice Doane's Appeal," pp. 78–93. Colacurcio's analysis builds upon that of David Levin, "Shadows of Doubt: Specter Evidence in Hawthorne's Young Goodman Brown," as well as Michael Davitt Bell, *Hawthorne and the Historical Romance of New England*, pp. 76–81. David H. Watters makes a similar point in his account of Cotton Mather's attempt to construct the worldly and ambitious Governor William Phips as a saint for the biography included in the *Magnalia Christi Americana*, an effort that "compromised the essential basis of sainthood as behavior that cannot, finally, be imitated" ("The Spectral Identity of Sir William Phips," p. 230).

64. See Boyer and Nissenbaum, *SWP*, 1: 53.

65. See Boyer and Nissenbaum, *SWP*, 1: 118. Supporters of Mary Bradbury, some of whom had known her for over fifty years, signed a petition which stated that "in all appearance" she was a saintly woman (1: 119).

66. See pretrial transcripts for Elizabeth How in Boyer and Nissenbaum, *SWP*, 2: 452.

67. It is difficult to overstate the poignancy of many of these character references which, until Governor Phips halted the executions in October 1692, had no chance of producing a stay of execution. See, for example, the petition of Thomas Hart on behalf of his aged mother, Elizabeth, in Boyer and Nissenbaum, *SWP*, 2: 383–84. On the irreversibility of spectral evidence and its invulnerability to the character reference, see Weisman, *Witchcraft, Magic, and Religion*, p. 161.

68. Cotton Mather, *Wonders*, p. 236. Likewise, Mather claimed of George Burroughs (executed 19 August 1692) that the sufferings of the afflicted "were enough to fix the Character of a Witch upon him" (216). Susannah Martin is unique for offering the prosecution a clear scriptural precedent for the devil's impersonation of a nonconsenting individual. When she was asked what she had done to promote the suffering of the afflicted who stood nearby, she responded, "Nothing at all." "Why, 'tis you or your Appearance," her interrogator objected. She responded, "I cannot help it." She is further pressed: "Is it not Your Master? How comes your Appearance to hurt these?" And Martin very cannily replied, "How do I know? He that appeared in the shape of Samuel, a Glorify'd Saint, may Appear in any ones shape," referring to the

first book of Samuel in which Saul, unable to obtain God's advice concerning how he should deal with the advancing Philistines, solicits the help of the witch of Endor in raising the spirit of the departed Samuel so that he might consult with him. The spirit of Samuel rebukes Saul for failing to see from God's silence that God is angry with him, and that no recourse to the spirits of the departed can avail. See Cotton Mather, *Wonders*, p. 230.

69. See Starkey, *Devil in Massachusetts*, p. 170.

70. See Rev. John Higginson's "Epistle to the Reader" which prefaces John Hale's *Modest Inquiry*, p. 400; and Cotton Mather, *Wonders*, p. 223. On Mather's *Wonders* as a last-ditch attempt to turn the events of Salem to the purposes of national consolidation through the offices of the jeremiad, see Perry Miller, *From Colony to Province*, pp. 202–3. Despite his intentions, Mather revealed his ambivalence toward the theory of spectral evidence in this text, as in virtually every document he wrote concerning the Salem trials. Mather's great opponent, Robert Calef, wrote that of the twenty-eight persons executed or condemned to die at the conclusion of the witchcraft crisis when the court of Oyer and Terminer was disbanded, one-third were members of churches, and more than half "of a good Conversation in general." See Calef, *More Wonders*, p. 373.

71. The phrase appears in a petition critical of judicial policy that was sent to government and judicial officials, quoted in Weisman, *Witchcraft, Magic, and Religion*, p. 164. The only dissenter from the court was Nathaniel Saltonstall, who excused himself from duty after the initial execution of Bridget Bishop. On Calef's objections to Mather's ad hominem indictments of the accused that revealed him to be "more like an Advocate [for the prosecution] than an Historian," see *More Wonders*, pp. 378–79, quotation from p. 379. In his accounts of the witchcraft crisis, Mather consistently claims for himself the historian's objectivity.

72. Quoted from Chauncy, *Seasonable Thoughts*, pp. 6, 7. The phrase "the Rule of Charity" appears in Increase Mather's *Cases of Conscience*, p. 254.

73. "To the Christian Reader," preface to Increase Mather, *Cases of Conscience*, pp. 221–24, quotation from 222–23.

74. That Hathorne recognized her implicit challenge to the self-evident significance of the spectral body is apparent in the particular emphasis he places upon it: "What uncertainty there may be in apparitions I know not, yet this with me strikes hard upon you that you are at this very present charged with familiar spirits: this is your bodily person they speak to: they say now they see these familiar spirits com to your bodily person, now what do you say to that." See the record of Nurse's pretrial examination and related documents in Boyer and Nissenbaum, *SWP*, 2: 583–608, esp. pp. 585, 592.

75. This was the import of the words Cotton Mather spoke at the execution of George Burroughs. In a last-minute attempt to prove his innocence, Burroughs recited the Lord's Prayer without error to the crowd assembled at the gallows. As Robert Calef described it, his recitation appears to have had the impact of one of the

extemporaneous sermons of the New Light ministry during the Great Awakening: his address "was so well worded, and uttered with such composedness, and such (at least seeming) fervency of Spirit, as was very affecting, and drew Tears from many." As a result, Calef continued, "it seemed to some, that the Spectators would hinder the Execution," if not for Mather's timely interference. Mather reminded the spectators that the devil is most himself when impersonating an angel of light. See Calef, *More Wonders*, pp. 360–61. Finally, in his discussion of Calef's contribution to the ongoing critique of the Salem proceedings, Perry Miller elaborates on the relationship of hypocrisy to witchcraft, specifically on the belief Lawson expresses that one is more apt to find one's witch in church than in the tavern: "Since, according to the official confessions, the land is rife with fraud, then open and dissolute sinners, convicted fornicators and disreputable tavern-haunters would be the last in the community to engage in secret transactions with Satan, whereas the 'more Cunning, or more seeming Religious' would be most likely to yield, because witchcraft depends, as does hypocrisy, upon 'Invisible Evidence' " (*From Colony to Province*, p. 251).

76. See the pretrial examination and related documents for Martha Corey in Boyer and Nissenbaum, *SWP*, 1: 247–66, esp. pp. 260, 261–62. The Reverend Samuel Parris, in whose household the witchcraft accusations began, put the point more bluntly in a sermon he preached on 27 March 1692 (three days after Lawson's sermon) entitled *Christ Knows How Many Devils There Are*: "Let none then build their hopes of salvation merely upon this: that they are church members. This you and I may be, and yet devils for all that" (130). Parris ended the sermon by praying that "God would not suffer devils in the guise of saints to associate with us" (131).

77. See Cotton Mather, *A Brand Pluck'd Out of the Burning*, p. 274. Mather expressed himself similarly in *Wonders*, pp. 221, 246. In "Cotton Mather's Crazed Wife," Breitweiser characterizes the published polemic carried out by Cotton Mather and Robert Calef in the wake of the witchcraft crisis as a "battle of the books concentrating on the representational distance between 'what really happened' and what the theocrat made of it in his book" (101). Thus did the war of representations survive the official close of the crisis.

78. Similarly, the Dutch and French ministers of New York to whom Joseph Dudley applied for opinions on the identification of credible evidence in the witchcraft trials argued against the usefulness as evidence of demonstrations of malice between individuals, a standard support for the credibility of accusations of malefic witchcraft in traditionally conducted trials. The ministers' reason for denying the significance of malice was that whereas a fundamentally good person might express anger honestly, through malicious words or actions, a fundamentally bad one is "able to conceal the very worst practices under the appearance of friendship and benevolence." Malicious behavior cannot, then, be considered a reliable index of an evil soul. Likewise, a pious demeanor cannot be trusted because it is the nature of "the cunning of the Devil, and his servants, that they deceive, as much as possible, the eyes and minds of the discerning, and remove all suspicion." The ministers then reverse

this point by claiming that one who has long held a reputation for piety most likely is pious ("it can hardly be that he who fights in the camp of the Devil should have the power, for a great while, to put on the appearance of a soldier of Christ"), then immediately revert to their first thesis concerning the proclivity of the cunning to dissemble a good life: even the devil himself, they point out, "sometimes tells the truth, and proclaims good morals, in order the more easily and insidiously to deceive." See Dudley, "Letter," and Selijns et al., "Reply," pp. 356, 357. For the ministers of New York, external character was as unreliable a representation as the specter itself, which, because it was of the devil, could not be trusted as a legitimate index to the spiritual identity of the spectrally represented individual.

79. See especially Morgan, *Visible Saints*, and Caldwell, *Puritan Conversion Narrative*. The visible church, as John Cotton made clear, was a way of preventing religious enthusiasts from "seek[ing] Christ . . . in deserts and secret chambers" (quoted in Caldwell, p. 106). That is, it was intended as a bulwark against, in Andrew Delbanco's words, the "secessionist self" of antinomianism (*The Puritan Ordeal*, p. 131). See also the discussion on pp. 123–24 where Delbanco states that "the essential principle underlying the Puritan concept of the self as well as of the church" is that there is "no distinction between the inner and the outer man." Cf. Hall, *Worlds of Wonder*, p. 93.

80. Cotton Mather, "Richards Letter," p. 37.

81. Cotton Mather reported in *Wonders* how the afflicted were able to see not only the specters of living people but the ghosts of people long dead: "These Ghosts do always affright the Beholders more than all the other spectral Representations; and when they exhibit themselves, they cry out, of being Murdered by the witchcrafts or other violences of the persons who are then in spectre present" (217). See the beginning of the final section of this chapter for an inversion of what Mather here presents, the astonishing circumstance of the executed Mary Easty's ghost appearing to a young woman to persuade her of the illegitimacy of spectral evidence.

82. See Weisman, *Witchcraft, Magic, and Religion*, on the conflict between the two major approaches to the problem of witchcraft, one focused on the malefic powers of the witch and the other focused on the defiance of God that the witch's covenanting with Satan entailed (57–72). See Thomas, *Religion and the Decline of Magic*, pp. 435–63, esp. pp. 449–63. But cf. David D. Hall's study of popular religion in seventeenth-century New England, *Worlds of Wonder*, for the degree to which popular conceptions of the supernatural, the "world of wonders," exceeded the interpretations authorized by the theocracy and often influenced them. In his article "Witchcraft and the Limits of Interpretation," Hall focuses especially on the issue of witchcraft and argues that by the mid–seventeenth century, the differences between popular and ecclesiastical objections to witchcraft were muted and *maleficium* was conflated with the sin of covenanting with the devil (276–77). Godbeer argues that "there was no fundamental breach in early New England between magical and religious constituencies" but that witchcraft trials did tend to bring them into conflict (*The Devil's Dominion*, p. 16).

83. Of course, the fact of the murders, spectrally related to the afflicted, was no

more susceptible of plain proof than was the secret knowledge concerning spiritual identity; it was, in fact, part of secret knowledge, insofar as the very fact that murder had occurred was spectrally related to the afflicted during their fits. See, for example, Cotton Mather's discussion of George Burroughs in *Wonders*, pp. 217–18. On Mather's uncomfortable recognition of the role imagination had played in his construction of Governor William Phips's biography, see Watters, "Spectral Identity of Phips," pp. 223–25.

84. Brattle, "Letter," pp. 187–88. Those more tolerant than Brattle of the behavior of the afflicted also observed that their agonies, severe as they were, produced no lasting physical effects. Increase Mather, for example, listed as one characteristic by which the possessed might be known: "when the Limbs of miserable Creatures, are bent and disjointed so as could not possible be without a Luxation of Joints, were it not done by a preternatural Hand, and yet no hurt raised thereby" (*Cases of Conscience*, p. 260). And Cotton Mather, in *Another Brand*, noted that although Margaret Rule was unable to eat for nine days because of the devil's interference, "she was unto all appearance as Fresh, as Lively, as Hearty, at the Nine Days End, as before they began" (313). Mather noted of both Margaret Rule and Mercy Short, the heroine of *A Brand Pluck'd Out of the Burning*, that "witch-wounds" (pinpricks, bruise marks from the witches' pinching, bite marks, etc.) healed amazingly quickly, usually overnight. The French and Dutch ministers of New York supported the evanescence of witch wounds: "The reason is, that nutrition is perfect—the stomach suffering no injury." The afflicted girls' perfect digestion and ability to consume greater quantities of food than most people allowed for the rapid repair of "all the injury caused by the tortures." See Selijns et al., "Reply," p. 358.

85. Cotton Mather, "Richards Letter," p. 37.

86. See Willard, *Miscellany Observations*, pp. 10 ("artificial argument") and 20: evidence divorced from that which we can affirm through our senses "proves nothing distinctly, or individually, but only disjunctively, *viz.* that it is either by Witchcraft, or more immediately from the Devil."

87. Brattle, "Letter," p. 176. Cf. the objections of "B" in Willard, *Miscellany Observations*, who rejects in witchcraft cases the sufficiency of "a strong Presumption" of guilt accompanied by "many facts which look that way" for "Good reason; for if the fact may be done, and yet the person doing it be innocent of the Crime, the Verdict is meerly conjectural, and the man dyes by will and doom: whereas God hath not granted to men such a power over one anothers Lives. If the Hypothesis be not necessary, there can be no Evidence or Demonstration drawn from it: and if the artificial argument fail, the Testimony cannot affect the party" (10). Also relevant here is the testimony of the afflicted and afflicting maidservant Mary Warren against her master John Proctor (whose apparition, Proctor claimed, was in fact just his shadow): "the first night I was taken, I saw as I thought the Apparition of Goody Cory & catched att itt as I thought & caught my master in my lap tho I did nott see my master in that place att that time, upon w'ch my master said itt is noe body but I itt is

my shaddow that you see, but my master was nott before mee as I could descerne" (Boyer and Nissenbaum, *SWP*, 3: 801). Proctor had been outspokenly contemptuous of the afflicted, advising anyone who would listen to him that they should be whipped and hung for accusing innocent people (Starkey, *Devil in Massachusetts*, p. 86).

88. Mather particularly recommends in his letter to John Richards the discovery of witch wounds as palpable proof of—indeed, an emblem of—an accused witch's connection with the invisible world. See "Richards Letter," p. 39. For Mather's hypothesis of the invisible fluid, see Upham, *Salem Witchcraft*, 1: 412.

89. Calef, *More Wonders*, pp. 298, 299.

90. Lawson, *Brief and True Narrative* (1692), p. 163.

91. Boyer and Nissenbaum, *SWP*, 1: 253. Burr explained this collapse of the image's function: "these witches have no need, as do others, to make images, or puppets, in the likeness of those they wish to torment, and then by torturing the puppets to inflict the same tortures on those they represent: these witches have only to act, and their victims are preternaturally compelled to the same action" (*Narratives*, p. 163 n. 1).

92. Mather, "Richards Letter," p. 39.

93. An anonymous critic of spectral evidence theory noted an accompanying conflation, that of witnesses with judges: for testimonies comprised of spectral evidence, "R.P." wrote, "the witnesses are not only informers in matter of fact, but sole judges of the crime,—which is the proper work of the judges, and not of witnesses." In the case of spectral evidence, of course, the judges had no authority to evaluate the representations of the witnesses in light of the unique ability of the latter to gain access to the invisible world. See "Letter from R.P. to Jonathan Corwin of 9 August 1692," p. 540. On the probable identity of "R.P.," see Upham, *Salem Witchcraft*, 2: 449, and the note on pp. 449–52.

94. Hale, *Modest Inquiry*, p. 411.

95. Lawson, *Brief and True Narrative* (1704), p. 531.

96. Samuel Parris, *These Shall Make War With the Lamb*, p. 134. The assignment of "sides" had nothing whatsoever to do with one's visible standing in church or community, although there was an uncanny resemblance between the process by which one was "canvassed" for church membership and that by which one was revealed as a candidate for spectral representation. The case of accused witch Elizabeth How (executed 19 July 1692) makes this conformity of the processes by which one was identified as saint or sinner explicit. As Cotton Mather reported How's history in *Wonders*, not only had How's specter itself tormented the afflicted, but the ghosts of unknown others informed the afflicted "that this How had Murdered them: which things were Fear'd but not prov'd" (237). Mather then recalls How's difficulty in the past in becoming a member of the Ipswich church. One woman who had publicly taken her part, informing the membership in a "Frantick, Raving, Raging and Crying" manner that How " 'is a precious Saint; and tho' she be Condemned before Men, she is Justify'd before God' " (238), fell into a trance immediately after this defense.

Coming to her senses hours later, she explained, " 'I thought Goody How had been a Precious Saint of God, but now I see she is a Witch' " (238). How had allegedly threatened this woman and her child with spectral abuse unless she would argue publicly for How's fitness for church membership. A deposition describing the incident was submitted during How's trial by the woman's husband. See the transcripts of How's pretrial examination in Boyer and Nissenbaum, *SWP*, 2: 433–55. That the structures of visible sainthood and spectral representation were closely allied was also attested to by the afflicted Mercy Short, who, in her conversation with specters, chastised one who was clearly a visible saint within the community. See Cotton Mather, *A Brand Pluck'd*, p. 270.

97. Brattle, "Letter," pp. 172, 182. Cf. Calef's characterization of the afflicted as "a parcel of possessed, distracted, or lying Wenches, accusing their Innocent Neighbours, pretending they see their Spectres (*i.e.*) Devils in their likeness Afflicting of them" (*More Wonders*, p. 298). Others cast serious doubt upon the characters of the afflicted. The pillar of Boston society, Captain John Alden, accused of and jailed for witchcraft in May 1692, completely conflated the afflicted with those they accused, complaining about how he was "sent for by the Magistrates of Salem . . . upon the Accusation of a company of poor distracted, or possessed Creatures or Witches." He describes how these "Wenches . . . plaid their jugling tricks, falling down, crying out, and staring in Peoples Faces." Alden's account is reprinted in Calef, *More Wonders*, p. 353. The accused witch Mary Easty submitted a petition to the magistrates prior to her execution in which she noted "the wiles and subtility of my accusers" and pled that in future "the Testimony of witches, or such as are afflicted, as is supposed, by witches may not be improved to condemn us, without other Legal evidence concurring." See Boyer and Nissenbaum, *SWP*, 1: 303.

98. "Letter from R.P.," p. 542.

99. "Letter from R.P.," p. 543.

100. "Letter from R.P.," p. 544.

101. "Letter from R.P.," p. 543; and Willard, *Miscellany Observations*, p. 8. The question in Willard is attributed to "S," the pro–spectral evidence voice either of Salem or of Stoughton. Although "S" invokes the witchcraft authorities Perkins, Bernard, and Dalton in support of the prosecution's recourse to presumption in default of "good and clear proof," "B" protests that "S" has misunderstood those authorities who differentiate among presumptions as those which may be conducive either to examination or even commitment, but never to conviction in a capital case (9).

102. "Letter from R.P.," p. 540.

103. Cotton Mather, "Richards Letter," p. 36. In *Another Brand*, his account of the afflicted Margaret Rule, whose diabolical possession began months after the resolution of the witchcraft crisis, Mather writes of how he counseled Rule "to forbear blazing the Names" of those who spectrally afflict her "lest any good Person should come to suffer any blast of Reputation thro' the cunning Malice of the great Accuser; nevertheless [Mather continues] having since privately named them to my

self, I will venture to say this of them, that they are a sort of Wretches who for these many years have gone under as Violent Presumptions of Witchcraft, as perhaps any creatures yet living upon Earth; altho' I am farr from thinking that the Visions of this Young Woman were Evidence enough to prove them so" (311). Statements such as these infuriated Robert Calef and led him to blame Mather for stirring up sacrificial violence.

104. Cotton Mather, "Richards Letter," p. 36. For the political significance of Mather's use of the scriptural image of the "hedge" and its violation, see Michael Kammen, *People of Paradox*, p. 38.

105. See Samuel Willard, "A briefe account of a strange & unusuall Providence of God befallen to Elizabeth Knap of Groton." I will return to the affliction of Elizabeth Knapp in Chapter 3.

106. Cited material appears in Willard, *Miscellany Observations*, pp. 13–16. Even Cotton Mather had acknowledged, albeit in another context, the "near Affinity between Witchcraft and Possession" in *Memorable Providences*, p. 136. The incipient characterological issue here, identical to that which circulates around the mystery of outwardly pious witches, gives way to a theologically grounded debate upon the difference between being bewitched and being possessed, with "S" arguing that the afflicted are merely bewitched, and are therefore capable of offering credible testimony concerning spectral phenomena, and "B" maintaining that they are possessed and that their testimony is therefore insufficient (14–15).

107. Cotton Mather attempted to describe the mental diseases inflicted by devils as "beyond those that attend an Epilepsy, or a Catalepsy, or those that they call The Diseases of Astonishment" (*Memorable Providences*, p. 101).

108. Cotton Mather, *Memorable Providences*, pp. 105, 101–2.

109. Boyer and Nissenbaum, *SWP*, 1: 193, 2: 490, 1: 214.

110. Cotton Mather, *A Brand Pluck'd*, pp. 266, 265, 262, 265. Such imagery of abuse complements the exaggeratedly sexualized behavior of the specters. Thus, Susannah Sheldon testified that Bridget Bishop's specter visited her carrying a snake around her neck that crept into her bosom. Bishop was accompanied by the specter of Mary English, who carried a yellow bird in her bosom, and that of Giles Corey (pressed to death on 16 September 1692), who had "two tircels" sucking at his breast. Subsequently, the specter of Martha Corey came to her and "puled out her brest" for a "blake pig" to suck. Bishop's specter, several men testified, came to them in the middle of the night and sat upon them in such a way that they were unable to reach their swords in self-defense. See Boyer and Nissenbaum, *SWP*, 1: 92–95, 99–100, 101–2, 104–6. See Robert Calef's equally sexualized account of the Mathers' motives in providing shelter to afflicted girls in *More Wonders*.

111. Cotton Mather, *Wonders*, p. 249.

112. Boyer and Nissenbaum, *SWP*, 1: 96–97.

113. In *Magnalia*, Mather noted that when the afflicted were bitten by spectral teeth, "not only the *print of teeth* would be left on their flesh, but the very *slaver* of

spittle too; and there would appear just such a *set of teeth* as was in the accused, even such as might be clearly distinguished from other peoples" (1: 208).

114. Mather, *Wonders*, p. 247. Calef demystified both events as follows: as for "a Corner of a Sheet, pretended to be taken from a Spectre, it is known that it was provided the day before, by that Afflicted person, and the third bone of a Spindle is almost as easily provided, . . . so that Apollo needs not herein be consulted" (*More Wonders*, p. 370).

115. Cotton Mather, *A Brand Pluck'd*, pp. 278–79; "Corporeally tho' Invisibly present" is from p. 274. Also relevant is Hunter, "The Seventeenth Century Doctrine of Plastic Nature." Again, it is not the perception of this continuum between invisible and visible that is new: Increase Mather, for one, noted many such incidents (visible evidence of the actions of invisible beings) in his compendium of supernatural occurrences, *An Essay for the Recording of Illustrious Providences*. What is new is the certainty that these invisible beings are visible to some and identifiable as their acquaintances or relations, as well as the accompanying assumption that individuals so represented had consented to their spectral actions. For a demystification of the conjoining of illicit desire and fulfillment, see the retraction of the confession of Abigail Faulkner Sr.: "she owned: that . . . she did look with an evil eye on the afflicted persons & did consent that they should be afflicted: becaus they were the caus of bringing her kindred out: and she did wish them ill & her spirit being raised she did:pinch her hands together: & she knew not but that the devil might take that advantage but it was the devil not she that afflicted them" (Boyer and Nissenbaum, *SWP*, 1: 328). That is, Faulkner denies that, because she desires to harm another, she has the power to carry out that desire. The claim bears an intriguing resemblance to Edmund S. Morgan's account of the governing paradox of the notion of popular sovereignty, that "governors and governed cannot be in fact identical" (*Inventing the People*, p. 282). For a description of the forms of legitimate mediation across the space between the visible and invisible worlds initiated not by men but by God, see Increase Mather, *Angelographia*. This collection of sermons delivered "to a Popular Auditory" ("To the Reader," unpaged p. 2) provides details concerning the celestial hierarchy in which the angels, as God's creatures, carry out God's commands concerning the visible world and its inhabitants in a rigorously invisible and imperceptible manner (see pp. 10–11, 46, 63 ff.). Ultimately, of course, the mediate space is the space of Christ, insofar as it is "by means of Jesus Christ, that the Angels of God do ascend & descend for us, as for *Jacob* of old, Christ is the *Jacobs* Ladder which toucheth Earth and Heaven, and joynes them both together by his Mediation" (97). But the sermons delineate the angelic operations that occur across the space separating the invisible from the visible worlds, including protection, reconciliation, supervision, observation, and modeling (the angels are "Patterns of Obedience unto us" [100]). Mather repeats at several points that although the devil can break through "the *Hedge* of Divine Protection" surrounding God's elect (54), he does so with God's permission. Mather is at pains throughout to deny that his knowledge of the invisible world is

firsthand; rather, it comes to him only through his reading of Scripture, insofar as "to shew by what Laws the Invisible World is Governed, is presumption, and sinful Curiosity; such are condemned by the Apostle, *as intruding into those things, which they have not seen*" (16). Mather is equally at pains to dissuade his auditors from going to the devil to discover that which God had decreed could not be known by men. On pp. 25–26 he conjectures that because some ignored that prohibition, God had "been provoked, to let loose evil Angels upon *New England* two years agoe" (26). On p. 58 and esp. pp. 63–65, Mather insists that good angels no longer appear to men given that the Scriptures are complete and cannot be added to, and that therefore angelical apparitions are sure to mean that Satan is appearing to men in the guise of an Angel of Light: "Wherefore it is an unwarrantable and a very dangerous thing, for men to wish, that they might see, and that they might converse with Angels" (65). To the degree that the angels mediate between God and humankind, they are invisible and otherwise imperceptible; thus, though they may and should be adored, one cannot see, hear, or speak to them while one is in life (102). He softens this position somewhat in his *Disquisition Concerning Angelical Apparitions*, appended to *Angelographia*, where he asserts that although angelical apparitions, as well as miracles, "*are not so frequent as under the Old Testament, nevertheless; some such there have been, and still may be*" (4). For an anthropological view of this mediational structure, see W. D. Hammond-Tooke, "The Witch Familiar as a Mediatory Construct."

116. See Starkey, *Devil in Massachusetts*, p. 119. Some of the specters when attacked did not turn into corpses, however, but into other types of animals who showed no signs of having been wounded.

117. This dependence on human beings by preternatural or supernatural creatures is oddly suggested by Cotton Mather in "A Discourse on Witchcraft." In that sermon he asserts that as the identity of the witch was to be inferred from the appearance of her specter, so the existence of the devil himself could be inferred from the identification of a witch: "Since there are *Witches*, we are to suppose that there are *Devils* too" (99). Not surprisingly, Mather goes on to deduce the existence of immortal souls from the existence of devils, insofar as "*Devils* would never contract with *Witches* for their Souls if there were no such things to become a prey unto them" (100). Increase Mather begins his *Disquisition Concerning Angelical Apparitions* with this argument, citing the *System* of the "Learned Dr. Cudworth"; see Burr, *Narratives*, p. 246 n. for Cudworth's significance. In this work, Mather claims that the reason "Providence has permitted" the earth to be infested with evil angels is "so men may be left without excuse for their *Atheism*, if they will not believe a future state, or that there is any World besides that which is visible, when such *sensible demonstrations* thereof have been set before them" (2–3).

118. See Cotton Mather, *Memorable Providences*, p. 123, and *Diary*, 1: 23.

119. See Cotton Mather, *Memorable Providences*, pp. 110, 122.

120. Cotton Mather, *Memorable Providences*, p. 122.

121. Cotton Mather, *Memorable Providences*, pp. 95, 123 (the introductory chas-

tisement of the unfaithful was written by Mather's ministerial colleagues Charles Morton, James Allen, Joshua Moodey, and Samuel Willard); and *Another Brand*, pp. 320, 318. The latter text, written after the court of Oyer and Terminer had been disbanded, betrays Mather's increased anxiety to defend his interest in and experimentation with the invisible world in comparison with the former, written before the crisis surfaced, in 1689. Mather's critic Robert Calef considered *Memorable Providences* a deliberate "kindling those flames," a virtual preparation of the sacrificial ground that would eventuate in the Salem debacle; see Burr, *Narratives*, p. 124 n. 1. For evidence that the afflicted were probably familiar with the details of Martha Goodwin's experience with the invisible world, see Starkey, *Devil in Massachusetts*, p. 41.

122. See Cotton Mather, *Memorable Providences*, p. 113.

123. Quoted in Perry Miller, *From Colony to Province*, p. 203.

124. The phrase appears in Cotton Mather, *Magnalia* 1: 206. For instances of Mather's and others' efforts to contact the specters indirectly through the afflicted, see *A Brand Pluck'd*, pp. 262, 267, 279. In *Memorable Providences*, Mather claimed that when spectators struck at the specters, the bewitched children would initially feel the injury, but would soon get temporary relief from their fits (107; see also 115, 116).

125. Cotton Mather, *A Brand Pluck'd*, p. 267.

126. The phrase "the Devel in the Damsel" appears in Burr, *Narratives*, p. 260 n. 4. Mather noted the "scores of spectators" in *Memorable Providences*, p. 100.

127. See Thomas Hutchinson, *History of the Colony and Province of Massachusetts-Bay*, 2: 13.

128. Cotton Mather, *Memorable Providences*, p. 121.

129. Cotton Mather, *A Brand Pluck'd*, p. 267; cf. p. 262.

130. Cotton Mather, *A Brand Pluck'd*, pp. 268, 269.

131. Cotton Mather, *A Brand Pluck'd*, p. 270.

132. Cotton Mather, *A Brand Pluck'd*, p. 276.

133. Cotton Mather, *Memorable Providences*, pp. 126, 123.

134. Cotton Mather, *A Brand Pluck'd*, p. 275.

135. Cotton Mather, *Another Brand*, p. 316.

136. Cotton Mather, *A Brand Pluck'd*, p. 263: here the devil assures his victim, Mercy Short, that "if shee would only Touch it [his book] with her Finger it should bee enough." Recalling the inducements to self-destruction of Poe's "imp of the perverse," Lawson asserted that the devil did not even require that the victim's finger touch the book: the slightest brush of her clothing would do (*Brief and True Narrative* [1704], p. 529). For supernatural events occurring in France in the years preceding the Salem crisis that may have influenced Mather's evaluation of the girls' spiritual precocity, see Levin's *Cotton Mather*, pp. 175–76.

137. Boyer and Nissenbaum, *SWP*, 1: 164 (Putnam), 169 (Lewis).

138. Lawson, *Brief and True Narrative* (1704), p. 532.

139. On this limit, see Perry Miller, "Marrow of Puritan Divinity," pp. 93–94.

140. Hale, *Modest Inquiry*, p. 406. It is interesting to compare Hale's account of the diabolic spirits as "piercing" with Cotton Mather's description of the angelic spirits who visited the possessed Mercy Short as "suggesting": according to Mather, a good spirit communicated with the girl "cheefly by an Impulse, most powerfully and sensibly making Impressions upon her Mind [as opposed to wounding her body]. This Wonderful Spirit would suggest unto her, How to Answer the Temptacions of the Diabolical Spectres, and comfort her with Assurances that shee should at last bee Victorious over Them" (*A Brand Pluck'd*, p. 283).

141. See Kibbey, "Mutations of the Supernatural," for another view on the Puritan conjunction of innocence and power. Kibbey considers the case of Puritan men who, far from being punished by the community, were seen as pious insofar as they felt convinced that their own sins had brought about the deaths of wives or children.

142. This description is taken from Upham's account of the specter's freedom in *Salem Witchcraft*, 1: 404.

143. The first phrase is taken from William Phips, "Letter to the Earl of Nottingham of 21 February 1693," p. 341; the second is from Dudley's "Letter," p. 353.

144. Calef, *More Wonders*, p. 369. Cf. Cotton Mather, who, during the trials, in response to a letter from John Foster asking how he felt about spectral evidence, had calmly maintained that "if the Holy God should permit such a terrible calamity to befall myself as that a specter in my shape should so molest my neighborhood as that they can have no quiet, although there should be no other evidence against me, I should very patiently submit unto a judgment of *transportation*"; see "Letter to John Foster of 17 August 1692" in *Selected Letters*, p. 42. But later, in his diary, Mather frantically reported how "my Image or Picture" appeared to an afflicted girl "and then [the devils] made themselves Masters of her Tongue so far, that she began in her Fits to complain that I threatened her and molested her." Mather confessed himself "extremely sensible, how much a malicious Town and Land would insult over mee, if such a lying Piece of a Story should fly abroad, that the Divels in my Shape tormented the Neighbourhood," and is relieved when, upon his praying for her, the girl came quickly out of her possession. See Burr, *Narratives*, p. 326.

145. See Burr, *Narratives*, p. 369 n. 1. Mercy Short, in one of her lengthy conversations with the devil, denied the validity of spectral evidence in such a way as to illuminate Mary Herrick's oddly restrained behavior in the face of spectral assault: " 'What do you show mee the Shape of that good Woman for? I know her. Shee's a good Woman. Shee never did mee any Hurt. Yett you would fain have mee cry out of her. But I will bee so far from crying out of Her that I will not cry out of You' "; see Cotton Mather, *A Brand Pluck'd*, p. 270.

146. Hale, *Modest Inquiry*, p. 411.

147. Cotton Mather, *Magnalia*, 1: 209.

148. Increase Mather, *Cases of Conscience*, p. 237. On the centrality of this tenet for medieval and Renaissance witch-hunting manuals, both Protestant and Catholic, see Sydney Anglo, "Evident Authority and Authoritative Evidence," pp. 15 and 20–21.

As Anglo notes of one representative witch-hunting guide, the fifteenth-century *Malleus Maleficarum*: "Everything is built upon the assumption that God permits the devil to perpetrate evil through human agents" (20), and that "everything" includes the "reality of a pact between the devil and his human partners" which the writers also insist upon (18). Human consent to collaborate with the devil is thus firmly anchored in God's intention that such collaboration should occur, resulting, as Anglo repeatedly points out, in a "monstrous paradox, since witches are merely serving God's mysterious purposes and might, on that account, be deemed more worthy of praise than of blame" (20). It is this paradox that the witchcraft prosecutors endeavored to eradicate with spectral evidence theory. Increase Mather belabors the point of the subordination of the evil angels in *Angelographia*; see, for example, pp. x–xi, 7, 26, 33–34, 45–47, and 113–20. In his excellent study of the continuities between demonology and natural philosophy in the Renaissance, Stuart Clark notes that European demonologists, with whose work Mather was thoroughly familiar, "were also, without exception, committed to exposing the limitations, weaknesses, and deceptions of the devil. . . . It was always granted that demons had not lost their physical powers after their fall from grace and that their cumulative experience since the Creation, their subtle, airy, and refined quality, and their capacity for enormous speed, strength, and agility enabled them to achieve real effects beyond human ability. Nevertheless, it was also invariably insisted that such effects were within the boundaries of secondary or natural causation" ("The Scientific Status of Demonology," pp. 359–60). As the English demonologist John Cotta put it in his *Triall of Witch-Craft* (1616), "For Nature is nothing els but the ordinary power of God in al things created, among which the Divell being a creature, is contained, and therefore subject to that universall power" (quoted on p. 360).

149. In his "Richards Letter," Cotton Mather alludes to the promise that Christ, upon his "coming again in His human nature," will "dispossess the devils of their aerial region to make a New Heaven for His raised there" (37). The implication almost seems to be that for the time being, God is tolerating the devil's independent activity within the borders of His own domain. For a discussion of how tentatively this proposition was held in European Protestant thought, see Kibbey, "Mutations of the Supernatural," pp. 134–35.

150. See Cotton Mather, *Memorable Providences*, p. 131. Goodwin suggests that his own experience of affliction, the possession by devils of his eldest daughter, was intended by God "to put us on with greater diligence to make our Calling and election sure" (130).

151. Calef, *More Wonders*, p. 390.

152. Increase Mather, *Cases of Conscience*, p. 223. Cf. *The Autobiography of Increase Mather*, p. 344. Second quotation from Hale, *Modest Inquiry*, p. 411.

153. Parris, *Christ Knows How Many Devils There Are*, p. 131.

154. Hale, *Modest Inquiry*, p. 411. Thomas Brattle's objection to the trials might be encapsulated by Hale's phrase.

155. Calef, *More Wonders*, p. 390.

156. Calef, *More Wonders*, pp. 301, 302; cf. p. 339.

157. Increase Mather, *Cases of Conscience*, p. 223. Pro– and anti–spectral evidence theorists did not fall cleanly on either side of the question of initiative in the matter of diabolical commissions. The Reverend Deodat Lawson, for example, alluded to the Salem crisis as "these direful operations of Satan, which the holy God hath permitted in the midst of us" (*Christ's Fidelity the only Shield against Satan's Malignity*, p. 124; cf. p. 125). Given the premise that God has permitted Satan to insinuate "affrighten-ing representations to the minds of many amongst us, to force and fright them to become his subjects," Lawson would appear to consider the representation of inno-cent people: "It cannot but be matter of deep humiliation, to such as are innocent, that the righteous and holy God should permit them to be named in such pernicious and unheard-of practices, and not only so, but that he who cannot but do right should suffer the stain of suspected guilt to be, as it were, rubbed on and soaked in by many sore and amazing circumstances" (124, 125; cf. 127). The duty of the elect, he claims, is to pity such unfortunates; his conclusion did not prevent Lawson from favoring their rigorous prosecution as well. The pro–spectral evidence position is succinctly represented in Willard, *Miscellany Observations*, pp. 17–18, along with the opposition's objections to their doctrinal errors. Lorraine Daston in "Marvelous Facts" notes that the dawn of the eighteenth century saw an increased effort on the part of Protestant divines to centralize God's power: "The preternatural had depended crucially on insubordination to divine decree, both nature's and the devil's, and therefore virtually disappeared as a result of God's new, tightened regime. Although few went so far as to deny the devil's existence, he was, like nature, put on a very short leash" (122). God, in effect, was granted "a monopoly on agency in the universe" (122).

158. Increase Mather, *Cases of Conscience*, p. 265.

159. See Edmund S. Morgan, *Visible Saints*, p. 112. There is ample room for speculating that Puritanism leads inevitably to Antinomianism, and that the Ameri-can Puritans' emphasis on making visible (morphologies of conversion, etc.) inevita-bly produced the claims, on the part of the Antinomians as well as the afflicted, to an exclusively wielded and divinely sanctioned power of sight, a power of knowing who is saved and damned without tests of visible sainthood.

160. For a view of Antinomianism as a threat to the authority of legal institutions in late seventeenth-century Massachusetts, see Konig, *Law and Society*, pp. 140–43. For the association between opposition to the courts and threats of witchcraft, see p. 146: "witchcraft was an alternative form of social control in the community, a body of forces that existed outside and opposed to the legal system."

161. See "The Examination of Mrs. Anne Hutchinson at the Court at Newtown," p. 337. On the far-reaching influence of Hutchinson and Antinomianism on the future of American letters, see Lang, *Prophetic Woman*.

162. This summary of the afflicted's freedoms is drawn from Cotton Mather's three accounts of possessed girls (*Memorable Providences, A Brand Pluck'd*, and *Another*

Brand) as well as other firsthand accounts, including Lawson's *Brief and True Narrative* and Hale's *Modest Inquiry*. See also Calef's demystification of Cotton Mather's accounts, *More Wonders*, particularly pp. 324–28.

163. See, for example, Lawson, *Brief and True Narrative* (1692), p. 159.

164. Calef, *More Wonders*, pp. 356, 372.

165. See Starkey, *Devil in Massachusetts*, pp. 209, 120–22.

166. The incident on the stairs appears in Cotton Mather, *Memorable Providences*, p. 116; the ring incident appears in *A Brand Pluck'd*, p. 273.

167. Cotton Mather, *A Brand Pluck'd*, p. 276.

168. See Burr, *Narratives*, p. 326.

169. Boyer and Nissenbaum, *SWP*, 2: 420.

170. Boyer and Nissenbaum, *SWP*, 3: 793–804.

171. Boyer and Nissenbaum, *SWP*, 1: 211–12.

172. Calef, *More Wonders*, p. 375. Michael Clark offers a Lacanian interpretation of the significance of such confessions as discursive disintegrations and reintegrations of the confessor's sense of self in "Discourse and the Body," pp. 215–17.

173. Boyer and Nissenbaum, *SWP*, 1: 280.

174. The term "enlargement" is from Margaret Jacobs's recantation; see Boyer and Nissenbaum, *SWP*, 2: 492.

175. Boyer and Nissenbaum, *SWP*, 3: 777–78.

176. Boyer and Nissenbaum, *SWP*, 2: 617.

177. Boyer and Nissenbaum, *SWP*, 2: 490, 491–92.

178. Boyer and Nissenbaum, *SWP*, 2: 689.

179. See Easty's petition in Boyer and Nissenbaum, *SWP*, 1: 303–4.

180. The Cloyce-Easty petition appears in Boyer and Nissenbaum, *SWP*, 1: 302–3, quotation from p. 303, and that of Ann Pudeator is in *SWP*, 3: 709–10, quotation from p. 709.

181. Boyer and Nissenbaum, *SWP*, 3: 882. Dane saw two daughters, one daughter-in-law, and several grandchildren accused of witchcraft. Cf. Brattle, "Letter," pp. 180–81. See also the Massachusetts legislature's official exoneration of those convicted of witchcraft in 1692, "Reversal of Attainder, October 17, 1711," in which evil spirits are blamed for "acting in and upon those who were the principal accusers and Witnesses proceeding so far as to cause a Prosecution to be had of persons of known and good reputation." Reprinted along with the very moving petitions for reimbursement submitted both by the sufferers of 1692 and their relations in *SWP*, 3: 1015–156. The material cited is from p. 1016.

CHAPTER TWO

1. Whitefield, *Journals*, p. 194. Further page references to this edition will appear parenthetically in the text. Most of Whitefield's sermons and letters are included in

his *Works*. Other fruitful sources of Whitefield's pronouncements are the eighteenth- and nineteenth-century biographies, particularly by Rev. John Gillies, *Memoirs of the Life of Reverend George Whitefield*, and Rev. Luke Tyerman, *The Life of the Rev. George Whitefield*. Modern biographies include Belden, *George Whitefield, the Awakener*; Henry, *George Whitefield*; and the excellent recent reading of Whitefield as America's "first intercolonial hero" (xiv) by Stout in *The Divine Dramatist*.

2. On the publication history of Jonathan Edwards's *A Faithful Narrative of the Surprising Work of God*, see *The Works of Jonathan Edwards*, vol. 4, *The Great Awakening*, pp. 32–46. For an excellent synopsis of the Great Awakening, see Alan Heimert's introduction to a representative collection of primary documents from the period, *The Great Awakening: Documents Illustrating the Crisis and Its Consequences*, ed. Heimert and Miller, pp. xiii–lxi. See also Bushman, ed., *The Great Awakening: Documents on the Revival of Religion, 1740–1745*. Stephen Nissenbaum has compiled primary documents relating to events at Yale in *The Great Awakening at Yale College*. Also of value are the nineteenth-century study by Tracy, *The Great Awakening*; Gaustad, *The Great Awakening in New England*; and Lovejoy, *Religious Enthusiasm in the New World*. The historians Jon Butler and Christine Leigh Heyrman have recently challenged the scholarly consensus on the reformative power of the Great Awakening: see Butler, "Enthusiasm Described and Decried," as well as his book-length study of popular religion in colonial America, *Awash in a Sea of Faith*, and Heyrman, *Commerce and Culture*, esp. pp. 182–204, 366–89. For an excellent recent study of the democratizing effects of American popular religion in the postrevolutionary period, see Hatch, *The Democratization of American Christianity*.

3. The most influential study of the relationship between the Great Awakening and the American Revolution is Heimert, *Religion and the American Mind*. Heimert's book is useful as a corrective to Benedict Anderson's influential and compelling study, *Imagined Communities*, insofar as Anderson asserts the centrality of itinerancy to the development of a Latin American national consciousness, but gives printing primacy of place in the North American context. Aside from Heimert's, the other major study of this period is Stout's *New England Soul*, which shares Heimert's premise of the centrality of evangelism to the formation of a revolutionary ideology in colonial America. Also extremely helpful for its emphasis on evangelical oratory and the beginnings of revolutionary sentiment is Stout's article "Religion, Communications, and the Ideological Origins of the American Revolution." See also Goen, *Revivalism and Separatism in New England*; and McLoughlin, *New England Dissent*, vol. 1, *The Baptists and the Separation of Church and State*. Finally, see Jacob and Jacob, eds., *Origins of Anglo-American Radicalism*, especially the essays gathered in the section entitled "Religion and Radical Culture in England and America," chapters 12 through 16. Early Quaker practice in England provides an important precursor to Whitefield's revolutionary ministerial tactics and their consequences, including lay itinerancy, field and street preaching, extemporaneous preaching, separatism, and social leveling. See Bauman, *Let Your Words Be Few*, esp. chapter 5. In contrast to Whitefield's practice, Quakers

promoted the uncontainability of their message by endeavoring to place limits upon the speech of testifiers; thus George Fox warned Friends, "Once ye have spoken the Truth to the people and they are come into the thing you speak of, many declarations out of the life may beget them into a form" (quoted in Bauman, *Let Your Words Be Few*, p. 75). Relatedly, Quakers refrained from issuing printed versions of sermons.

4. Several of Whitefield's contemporaries testified to the extraordinary range of his voice. In *Memoirs*, Gillies claimed it could be heard "near a mile" (44), while Benjamin Franklin "computed that he might well be heard by more than Thirty-Thousand" (*Autobiography*, p. 179). Franklin confesses to have experienced a kind of conversion of his own upon hearing the Grand Itinerant preach: against his earlier resolve, he found himself contributing generously to Whitefield's collection for his pet project, a Georgia orphanage, at the sermon's conclusion (*Autobiography*, p. 177). On the relationship of Whitefield and Franklin, see John R. Williams, "The Strange Case of Dr. Franklin and Mr. Whitefield." On Whitefield's astonishing appropriation of new commercial techniques to publicize the revivals, his uncanny appreciation of the importance of the press in creating a desire for the New Birth by advertising it as one would a commodity, see Lambert, "*Pedlar in Divinity*." Lambert discusses Franklin's relationship to Whitefield on pp. 110–30.

5. The *Boston Weekly News-Letter* for 16 October 1740 calculated that twenty-three thousand attended Whitefield's farewell address on the Boston Common. In his journal, Whitefield estimated a crowd of twenty thousand, and added without hyperbole that it was "a sight, perhaps never seen before in America" (474).

6. The early history of this fragmentation is captured in a public letter written by Rev. Theophilus Pickering to Rev. Nathanael Rogers Jr. in 1742. Rogers's oppositional behavior, according to Pickering, mimics Whitefield's own as described by an eyewitness in a 1737 issue of the *New England Weekly Journal*. Both letter and article are reprinted in Bushman, *Great Awakening*, pp. 56–57 and pp. 22–23. Cf. Timothy Cutler's complaint in his letter to the Bishop of London dated 5 December 1740 included in Perry, *Historical Collections*, 3: 346–47.

7. Timothy Allen is quoted in Stout and Onuf, "James Davenport and the Great Awakening in New London," p. 564. On the establishment of the Log College, see Trinterud, *The Forming of an American Tradition*, pp. 169–95; Briggs, *American Presbyterianism, Its Origins and Early History*, pp. 304–10; and Ahlstrom, *Religious History of the American People*, pp. 270–73.

8. According to Alan Heimert, by the 1760s "the commitment to the Work of Redemption had translated even the ecumenical spirit into a New World nationalism" (*Religion and the American Mind*, p. 142). Cf. Niebuhr's characterization of the Great Awakening as "our national conversion" in *The Kingdom of God in America*, p. 126; Goen, *Revivalism and Separatism*; and Stout, *Divine Dramatist*, on the association of the Whitefield phenomenon with the growth of nationalist sentiment in the colonies. Benjamin Franklin's biographer Carl Van Doren notes that Franklin "bec[ame] intercolonial" directly following Whitefield's first visit to Philadelphia in

1739; see *Benjamin Franklin*, p. 138. Opponents of the revival tended to assume that Whitefield single-handedly created the class of lay exhorters. See, for example, Charles Chauncy, *Letter to Mr. George Wishart*, who described them as "the Preachers of Mr. *Whitefield's* making" (15); and Edward Wigglesworth, who condemned the Grand Itinerant as the "blameable Cause" of religious separation in *A Letter to the Reverend Mr. George Whitefield*, p. 58. See also the nineteenth-century historian Leonard Bacon's account in *Thirteen Historical Discourses*, p. 222. On undergraduates preaching, see Dexter, ed., *Documentary History of Yale University, 1701–1745*, p. 357. On the role played by women in the revival, see Susan Juster, *Disorderly Women: Sexual Politics and Evangelicalism in Revolutionary New England*. For a suggestion of the limits of female evangelism in this period, see Stephen J. Stein, "A Note on Anne Dutton."

9. Whitefield takes this description of his auditors' behavior from an opponent whose remarks he quoted in "A Second Letter to the Bishop of London," in *Works*, 4: 160, Whitefield's most concise defense of religious itinerancy.

10. The self's abasement, that is, is neither the condition nor the premise of its exaltation, since the terms "humble" and "exalted" suggest no temporal differentiation, as in the compensatory formulation which appears elsewhere in the journal, "The more thou art humbled now, the more thou shalt be exalted hereafter" (62).

11. See Kenney, "George Whitefield, Dissenter Priest of the Great Awakening." The phrase "Opposers Mouths were stop'd" (*Journals*, p. 407) appears on p. 80.

12. The urbane Maryland physician Dr. Alexander Hamilton, who traveled to Maine in 1744 and kept a diary of his adventures, noted the revivalists' reliance on opposition: speaking of the Moravian settlement near Poughkeepsie, New York, he observed that the group had "received a considerable strength and addition to their numbers by Whitefield's preaching in these parts but now are upon the decline since there is no opposition made to them." See Hamilton, *Gentleman's Progress: The Itinerarium of Dr. Alexander Hamilton*, p. 58. For the psychological and doctrinal centrality of opposition to the radical New Light mode, see also the sermon by the itinerant revivalist Samuel Finley, *Christ Triumphing, and Satan Raging*.

13. For an examination of the grounds for popular hostility against the Methodists, see John Walsh, "Methodism and the Mob in the Eighteenth Century."

14. Whitefield did not discover the theatrical possibilities of conversion, hence its usefulness in the field of social control, nor was he the first to overcome his own social marginality to win celebrity by these means. See Daniel E. Williams, "The Structure and Significance of Criminal Conversion Narratives in Early New England." Interestingly, Williams notes that executions routinely attracted crowds of up to six thousand, with some accounts claiming up to twelve thousand, making them a close second, in terms of draw, to Whitefield's field-sermons, and the first materialization of the crowd in America.

15. Quoted in Gillies, *Memoirs*, p. 10. On this process (curiosity to conviction), see the firsthand "Account of Whitefield's New York visit." The writer describes how two bodies of people gathered around the minister, "*GOD's Church*," who "were col-

lected round the Minister, and were very serious and attentive," and "the *Devil's Chappel*," who "placed themselves in the Skirts of the Assembly, and spent most of their Time in giggling, scoffing, talking and laughing." Whitefield used the latter to illustrate cowardly and shamefaced Christians, and by the sermon's end, "the whole Assembly appeared more united, and all became hush'd and still; a solemn Awe and Reverence appeared in the Faces of most, a mighty Energy attended the Word" (360).

16. Quoted in Gillies, *Memoirs*, p. 207. Beginning in grammar school, Whitefield was chosen for his "good elocution and memory" to "mak[e] speeches before the corporation at their annual visitation," and, at about age twelve, even permitted his schoolmaster to dress him in girls' clothing for the corporation's entertainment. Among the many parts he prepared himself so assiduously to play, the ministerial role was apparently the only one that influenced his everyday behavior, such that "[p]art of the money I used to steal from my parent I gave to the poor, and some books I privately took from others, for which I have since restored fourfold, I remember were books of devotion" (29).

17. On this point, see especially the excellent biography of Whitefield by Stout, *Divine Dramatist*.

18. For the historical association of players with vagabonds, see Jonas Barish, *The Antitheatrical Prejudice*, p. 238. Barish's study is particularly suggestive in reference to Whitefield's own relationship to the theater.

19. Gillies, *Memoirs*, p. 232. On Whitefield's sophisticated use of the press, see especially Lambert, *"Pedlar in Divinity."*

20. See Ginzburg, *On Psychological Prose*. The quoted phrases appear on pp. 10 and 17. Cf. Lionel Trilling's analysis in *Sincerity and Authenticity* of the formation and evolution of what he identifies as a new, fundamentally histrionic type of personality that emerged in the late sixteenth and early seventeenth centuries.

21. See Burke, *Rhetoric of Religion*, pp. vi, 25–27.

22. See Bakhtin, "Discourse in the Novel," and *Problems of Dostoevsky's Poetics*, which offers a more concise discussion of the difference in consciousness of dialogic and monologic characters

23. The term "self-fashioning" derives from Stephen Greenblatt, *Renaissance Self-Fashioning*. Of all Greenblatt's Renaissance self-fashioners, Whitefield perhaps most resembles Tyndale, who could not obey Christ's exhortation "to do . . . good deeds secretly," and whose "whole self" was transformed into *"voice"* insofar as his was "a life lived as a *project"* — in Tyndale's case, the project of translating the Bible into English (107). Greenblatt's affinity with the Russian cultural semioticians, most prominently Lydia Ginzburg and Iurii Lotman, and in particular their notion of a "poetics of everyday behavior," is suggested in his essay "Towards a Poetics of Culture." See also "The Circulation of Social Energy" for a discussion of the peculiar dynamism of cultural poetics as Greenblatt envisions it.

24. Cf. Iurii M. Lotman's analysis of "khlestakovism" (after the Gogol character) in "Concerning Khlestakov."

25. Chauncy, *A Letter to the Reverend Mr. Whitefield*, p. 37. Hereafter referred to as *1745 Letter*.

26. See, for example, Whitefield's response to Rev. Alexander Garden's vehement attack on the Grand Itinerant as a confidence man and wolf in sheep's clothing who misled his auditors by the mere aesthetic character of his voice. In his *Journal*, Whitefield declared his pity for the Anglican Commissary of Charleston, South Carolina, who had unwittingly advertised his unconverted state by revealing his ignorance of the fact that in persecuting Whitefield, "it is Jesus Whom he persecutes" (442). Garden's attack on Whitefield is discussed at greater length in Chapter 3.

27. Chauncy, *1745 Letter*, p. 32.

28. Whitefield, *Works*, 6: 62; Whitefield's resemblance to God was asserted by Edward Ellington in *The Reproach of Christ the Christian's Treasure*, a sermon he preached on the occasion of Whitefield's death. Both passages quoted from Henry, *George Whitefield*, p. 121.

29. Chauncy, *1745 Letter*, pp. 36–37. 30. Chauncy, *1745 Letter*, p. 37.

31. Chauncy, *1745 Letter*, p. 38. 32. Chauncy, *1745 Letter*, pp. 29–30.

33. Chauncy, *1745 Letter*, p. 30. 34. Chauncy, *1745 Letter*, pp. 30, 31.

35. Samuel Weller points explicitly to Whitefield's *"spiritual Pride"* in the journals: "Nay, the Discourses of the blessed Jesus, *who spake as never Man spake*, fell far short of that Conviction and Force on the Minds of his Hearers, if Mr. *Whitefield* may be believed, which are boasted of in almost every Page of the Journals." Moreover, Whitefield's *"Acts* are already three or four times more voluminous than the History of all the Apostles of Jesus Christ." See Weller, *The Trial of Mr. Whitefield's Spirit*, pp. 11, 14, 12. Passages in the journal such as the following surely contributed to the ire of Whitefield's critics: during his 1740 tour of Massachusetts, he wrote, "I had just heard of a child, who after hearing me preach, was immediately taken sick, and said, 'I will go to Mr. Whitefield's God.' In a short time he died" (471).

36. See William Law, *The Absolute Unlawfulness of the Stage-Entertainment Fully Demonstrated*.

37. Cf. Breitweiser's analysis, in *Cotton Mather and Benjamin Franklin*, of Cotton Mather's more tortured experience of the selfless self: the many books he wrote, for example, "notable for spiritual excellence must testify not to self, but to a perfectly submissive son through whom God the Father writes" (74). As for Whitefield, even his earliest biographer, John Gillies, recognized the fundamental necessity in Whitefield's case of eschewing the charge of artfulness. In the introduction to his memoir, Gillies noted that because "it has been insinuated that he learned his oratory upon the stage," he must be at pains, as Whitefield's biographer, to point out that the minister "was more indebted as an orator to nature, than to art of any kind" and that "his eloquence was in a great measure the effect of his genius, and proceeded chiefly from that peculiar assemblage of extraordinary talents with which GOD had endowed him." See his *Memoirs*, p. 3.

38. Because this tautology was the real goal of evangelism, it is easy to understand

why the evangelical movement posed such a threat to the social elite: to the degree that it succeeded, it would obliterate the differences which constituted both the social hierarchy as well as the structure of representation itself. As a representation of a particular relationship to God, evangelism thus carries within it the seeds of its own destruction, unless it dissembles the similitude of message, messenger, and receiver upon which it is ostensibly based (or at least toward which it is ostensibly moving). Such dissemblance is the crux of contemporary critiques of (tele)evangelism but, as Garry Wills has shown, the charge of hypocrisy is meaningless to evangelicals who take it as a given and who do not consider their ministries compromised by it; see Wills, "The Phallic Pulpit."

39. John Marrant, a black freeman who was converted by George Whitefield in South Carolina as a teenager, and who himself became an itinerant preacher in Nova Scotia (after suffering captivity at the hands of the Cherokees and impressment into the British navy), also characterized himself as having "no continuing city." See Marrant's extraordinary (ventriloquized) "Narrative of the Lord's wonderful Dealings with John Marrant," p. 180.

40. See also "Letter DLXVII," *Works*, 2: 76.

41. Taken from Sacvan Bercovitch's discussion of Puritan typology in *The Puritan Origins of the American Self*, pp. 35–40; quotations from p. 36.

42. Something of the innkeeper's son's glee at the governor's display of devotion is echoed in the Welsh evangelical itinerant Howel Harris's reaction to being informed by Wesley that he was "to go to see a Lady," the influential Lady Selina, Countess of Huntingdon. Harris, who saw himself as sent by God "among the Hills of Wales to my poor Ignorant despised Country men," was, upon reception of this news, "inflamed with praise to God" (quoted in Nuttall, "Howel Harris and 'The Grand Table,'" p. 531).

43. The outrageousness of Whitefield's enactment and later account of the Joshua story is underscored by Jonathan Edwards's conventional reading of it: "The destruction of the city of Jericho is evidently, in all its circumstances, intended by God as a great type of the overthrow of Satan's kingdom; the priests blowing with trumpets at that time, represents ministers preaching the Gospel; the people compassed the city seven days, the priests blowing the trumpets; but when the day was come that the walls of the city were to fall, the priests were more frequent and abundant in blowing their trumpets" (*Some Thoughts*, p. 398).

44. In his initial letter of invitation to Whitefield, even Jonathan Edwards, who would later express reservations about the Grand Itinerant's techniques, encourages an uncontainable growth of his powers: Edwards expresses the hope that Whitefield will "rise to a greater height, and extend further and further, with an irresistable Power bearing down all opposition! and may the Gates of Hell never be able to prevail against you!" (Abelove, ed., "Jonathan Edwards's Letter of Invitation to George Whitefield," p. 488). On New Light understanding of "holy violence," see Gilbert Tennent, *The Necessity of Religious Violence in Order to Obtain Durable Happiness*; the phrase "holy Violence" appears on p. 17. Tennent, interpreting Matthew 11:12,

conjectures that the phrase "*and the Violent take it by Force* . . . seems to signify, that the Kingdom of heaven is not now confin'd to one People as of old, but lies open and exposed, without any National Inclosures, that whoever will take persevering pains for it may possess it" (2–3).

45. See John Freccero, *Dante: The Poetics of Conversion*. Freccero analyzes the structural peculiarities of the conversion narrative in "Logology: Burke on St. Augustine."

46. Alexander Garden, *Six Letters to the Reverend Mr. George Whitefield*, p. 28 (letter 4).

47. Garden, *Regeneration and the Testimony of the Spirit*, p. 2. Croswell is quoted in Schmidt, "The New Light Extremism of Andrew Croswell," p. 230. According to Schmidt, Croswell's rejection of preparationism, which he understood as a "'worrying'" of the Christian "'step by step, from lower to higher degrees of horror and distress,'" suggests his anticipation of nineteenth-century sentimental Christianity: his was a "conception of Christianity as a joyful triumph over all spiritual horror and anguish" (231).

48. Garden, *Regeneration and the Testimony of the Spirit*, p. 3.

49. Franklin, *Autobiography*, p. 180.

50. The parenthetically quoted phrase appears in Gillies, *Memoirs*, p. 152.

51. Quoted in Gillies, *Memoirs*, pp. 200, 255. Clearly, Whitefield had not considered the option of silence as developed by the Quaker George Fox. Responding to the attack on the Quaker practice of silent meetings, Fox explained that "the intent of all speaking is to bring into the life . . . and to possess the same, and to live in and enjoy it, and to feel God's presence, and that is in the silence." For this reason, "words declared" promote "fellowship in the spirit of God, in the power of God, which is the gospel, in which is the fellowship, when there are no words spoken." All legitimate speech proceeds from and is directed toward the perfect restoration of silence. Quoted in Bauman, *Let Your Words Be Few*, p. 125. Cf. pp. 128–36 on the practical difficulties for Quaker ministers of negotiating the conflicting imperatives of testifying and remaining silent.

52. From a letter to the Reverend Mr. Hervey written on 28 April 1750, cited in Gillies, *Memoirs*, p. 180. Information concerning the cause of his malady is provided neither by Gillies nor by Whitefield in the remainder of the letter, published in Whitefield, *Works*, 1: 345–46.

53. See Rudolph M. Bell, *Holy Anorexia*.

54. An eyewitness account of Whitefield's death, given by one Richard Smith who accompanied the Grand Itinerant on his last American tour, is contained in Gillies, *Memoirs*, pp. 270–75, quotation from p. 273. For Ezra Stiles's Franklinesque challenge to Jonathan Parsons's account of the numbers of mourners attending the funeral, based on a calculation of the square footage of Parsons's church, see *The Literary Diary of Ezra Stiles*, 1: 79–80. On the decades-long obsession with viewing and handling Whitefield's remains, see Butler, *Awash in a Sea of Faith*, p. 188.

55. The quoted phrase is taken from the scene of Rev. Dimmesdale's death in the pulpit in Nathaniel Hawthorne, *The Scarlet Letter*, p. 279.

56. Quoted in Gillies, *Memoirs*, p. 65 n.

57. Chauncy, *Letter to Wishart*, pp. 8, 6.

58. Cole's narrative, published as "The Spiritual Travels of Nathan Cole," was recently edited by Michael J. Crawford. Further page references to this printing will appear parenthetically in the text.

59. As Daniel B. Shea Jr. noted, Cole's prose "is ignorant of the luxury of relaxation" (*Spiritual Autobiography in Early America*, p. 213).

60. Cf. Shea, *Spiritual Autobiography*, p. 221.

61. For a review of the civil, educational, and social penalties in place in Connecticut for separatist activity, see Bonomi, *Under the Cope of Heaven*, pp. 162–66.

62. Cole's exuberance in this closing passage — about his rising up from the ashes to generate and then to transfer the power of spirit through an entire community — recalls that expressed by Hawthorne's character Oberon, the frustrated amateur author. In the 1835 sketch "The Devil in Manuscript," Oberon describes his unsuccessful struggle to escape the drudgery of practicing law by becoming a famous author. When an ember from the autobiographical manuscript he had tossed despairingly into the fire one night flew up the chimney to ignite the sleeping town, Oberon recognizes his moment of triumph: "Huzza! My brain has set the town on fire!" (337). Compare Garden's reproach to Whitefield: "You boast indeed, in your *Journals*, that you have kindled a *Fire* which all the *Devils* in Hell shall not be able to extinguish! Alas (Sir) the *Fire* you have kindled is that of Slander and Defamation. A *Fire!* which no *Devil* in Hell, no nor *Jesuit* nor *Deist* on Earth, will ever go about to extinguish; but fagot and foment it with all their Might, as too effectually serving their Interests or Turn" (*Six Letters*, p. 21, letter 3).

63. See Edwards, *Some Thoughts*, p. 355.

64. The following report is contained in "A remarkable Account of a Reformation among some Gentlemen." Page numbers will hereafter be cited in the text. William Seward, Whitefield's devotee and the one whom Lambert describes as his "press agent," related a suspiciously similar incident in Philadelphia in his journal: "Heard of a Drinking Club (whereof a Clergyman was a Member) that had a *Negroe* Boy attending them, who used to mimick People for their Diversion. The Gentlemen bid him mimick our Brother *Whitefield*; which he was very unwilling to do; but they insisting upon it, he stood up and said — *I speak the Truth in Christ, I lie not, unless you repent, you'll all be damned.* — This unexpected Speech broke up the Club, which has not met since." See Seward, *Journal of a Voyage from Savannah to Philadelphia, and from Philadelphia to England*, pp. 7–8.

65. Gaustad, *The Great Awakening in New England*, quotes an advertisement issued in Boston in 1742 for a runaway slave who could " 'mimick some of the strangers that have of late been preaching among us' " (128).

66. Chauncy, *Letter to Wishart*, p. 12.

67. On Whitefield's contradictory pronouncements on the subject of slavery due to his overriding fear of blacks, see Stein, "George Whitefield on Slavery: Some New Evidence." Cf. Stout, *Divine Dramatist*. Stout's account of Whitefield's attitude to-

ward blacks is more moderate than Stein's insofar as he affirms the successful transfer of the power of authoritative speech to them, claiming that the Grand Itinerant supplied black Christians "with an evangelical vocabulary they later adapted to their own purposes" (197). Cf. Jackson, "Hugh Bryan and the Evangelical Movement in Colonial South Carolina."

68. Reprinted in Gillies, *Memoirs*, pp. 165–67. Page numbers will hereafter be cited in the text.

69. Whitefield's idiosyncratic use of Matthew 10:16 is underscored by Jonathan Edwards's more conventional invocation of the passage to caution friends of the New Light movement to act prudently so as not to provide detractors with grounds for complaint. See Edwards, *Distinguishing Marks*, p. 277.

70. It is significant that immediately after his visit to the Bermudas, while he was en route to England, Whitefield undertook to edit his journals so that he might "have a new edition before I see *America*," and bemoaned, in a letter to a supporter, his habit of verbal impetuosity which only stirred up "needless opposition": "I frequently wrote and spoke in my own spirit, when I thought I was writing and speaking by the assistance of the spirit of GOD. I have likewise too much made inward impressions my rule of acting, and too soon and too explicitly published what had been better kept in longer, or told after my death." See "Letter DCXI," 24 June 1748, in *Works*, 2: 143–45, quotations from p. 144; also cited in Gillies, *Memoirs*, pp. 172–73.

71. Reprinted in Whitefield, *Works*, 4: 473–75, quotation on p. 474. Although no date is provided, the prayer is consonant in tone with the anonymous letter of 1743 entitled "A Letter to the Negroes Lately Converted to Christ in America," attributed to Whitefield by Stein in "George Whitefield on Slavery."

72. Lydia Ginzburg offers another way of understanding the end of Whitefieldian uncontainability that has to do with a limitation inherent in what she describes as "romantic personality": the essence of such a personality, she claims, "lay in its separateness from the 'crowd.' The hero and the man of the 'crowd' could not share one and the same psychological structure or the same principles of behavior, although the 'crowd' could follow the hero, and the hero could show compassion for the 'crowd' and sacrifice himself for its sake." In sum, to the degree that conversion may be regarded as a romantic ideal, it "was not a behavioral norm, but a spiritual limit posited only for an elect." See *On Psychological Prose*, p. 22. Ginzburg's analysis of the early messianism of the anarchist Mikhail Bakunin in *On Psychological Prose*, entitled "Bakunin, Stankevich, and the Crisis of Romanticism," suggests a compelling comparison with the personality of Whitefield.

CHAPTER THREE

1. Willard's anti–spectral evidence tract, *Some Miscellany Observations*, for example, would be published in Philadelphia in 1692.

2. Willard's "A briefe account of a strange & unusuall Providence of God befallen

to Elizabeth Knap of Groton" was originally written in the form of a letter to Cotton Mather; quoted material on p. 7. Henceforth page numbers for cited material (spelling in some instances modernized) will appear parenthetically in the text. Knapp was referred to as a *"ventriloqua"* by the historian Thomas Hutchinson (*History of Massachusetts-Bay*, 2: 13).

3. "Satan," or the voice Willard understands as being Satan's, denies his satanic identity and responds to Willard's enraged charge that he is "a lyar" by replying that he is "a pretty blacke boy" and Knapp is his "pretty girle" (18).

4. Edwards's definition of conscience is offered in *Distinguishing Marks*, p. 251.

5. The phrase *"electing Love"* appears in Samuel Blair, "Revival of Religion at New-Londonderry," p. 256.

6. Timothy Walker, *The Way to Try All Pretended Apostles*, p. 5.

7. Walker, *Way to Try*, pp. 28, 15.

8. Gilbert Tennent, *The Necessity of Religious Violence*, p. 7.

9. Isaac Stiles, *A Looking-glass for Chang[e]lings*, pp. 311, 313, 318.

10. John Wilson, *A Regular Zeal in Matters of Religion justified*, p. 228.

11. Moses Bartlett, *False and Seducing Teachers*. Bartlett noted that one of the "Stratagems" employed by "counterfeit Apostles" to undermine the true was "to represent them as mercenary men" (17). The burden of his treatise is to identify the "discriminating Marks and Characters of those seducing Teachers, by which we may, if we duly attend to the Word of GOD, discern, shun, and avoid them" (28).

12. Wilson, *Regular Zeal*, p. 224.

13. Cf. de Certeau, *The Practice of Everyday Life*, chapter 10 ("The Scriptural Economy"), esp. p. 138: "The turning point that inaugurates the modern age is marked first . . . by the devaluation of the statement and a concentration on the act enunciating it. When the speaker's identity was certain ('God speaks in the world'), attention was directed toward the deciphering of his statements, the 'mysteries' of the world. But when this certitude is disturbed along with the political and religious institutions that guaranteed it, the questioning is directed toward the possibility of finding substitutes for the unique speaker: who is going to speak? and to whom? The disappearance of the First Speaker creates the problem of communication, that is, of a language that has to be *made* and not just *heard and understood*."

14. John Hancock, *The Dangers of an Unqualified Ministry*, p. 22.

15. Chauncy, *Enthusiasm described and caution'd against*, p. 23.

16. Edwards, *Distinguishing Marks*, p. 226. Cf. Bartlett, *False and Seducing Teachers*, p. 28, quoted in note 11.

17. Walker, *Way to Try*, pp. 14, 11, 9, 6, 9.

18. All quotations in this paragraph were taken from p. 366. Page numbers will henceforth be cited in the text. Extracts of Smith's sermon that do not appear in *The Christian History* may be found in Heimert and Miller, eds., *The Great Awakening*, pp. 62–69.

19. As early as 1724 Solomon Stoddard, Jonathan Edwards's grandfather and

Increase Mather's great opponent in the debate over the Halfway Covenant, was urging his readers "to try the matter of Preaching and to Determine what is Sound" insofar as "Learning is no security against Erronious Principles." Although Stoddard provides guidelines for detecting whether or not a minister is speaking "experimentally" about conversion, he does not single out individual ministers for criticism in this regard as happened during the revival. See Stoddard, *The Defects of Preachers Reproved*; quoted material from pp. i (from Salmon Treat's preface "To the Reader"), 7, 9.

20. The controversial New Light itinerant Gilbert Tennent thus complained that Old Lights had endeavored "to blacken the Characters of several *Ministers* whom GOD has been pleas'd of his pure Goodness to honour with success," and that as soon as his own preaching became effective, he too "found *many Adversaries*, and my Character was cover'd with unjust Reproaches" ("A Letter from the Rev. Mr. Gilbert Tennent," pp. 286–87, 293). Similarly, Charles Chauncy complained that those bold enough to warn against the dangers of enthusiasm "run the hazard of being call'd *enemies* to the *holy* SPIRIT, and may expect to be ill-spoken of by many, and loaded with names of reproach: But they are notwithstanding the best friends to religion" (*Enthusiasm described*, p. 26). One final aspect of the character wars touched upon by Chauncy is made explicit by Timothy Cutler in a letter to the Bishop of London on 5 December 1740. Cutler noted how Whitefield "was the subject of all our Talk, and to speak against him was neither credible nor scarce safe" (see Perry, *Historical Collections*, 3: 347). Samuel Finley called Old Light opposition "the unpardonable Sin" and added that *"the Sin against the Holy Ghost shall never be forgiven"* (*Christ Triumphing*, pp. 164, 166).

21. As the historian Patricia Bonomi writes, "once decorous [Old Light] ministers impugned the intelligence and integrity of their rivals in public sermons and essays" (*Under the Cope of Heaven*, p. 151).

22. Prince, ed., *Christian History 1743* presents Whitefield's arrival as a watershed moment in the history of American spirituality; it divided discussion of seasonal revivals into those that occurred before his arrival and those that had occurred since. See p. 113.

23. *The Testimony of . . . Harvard College, against George Whitefield*, pp. 349, 346, 345, 342.

24. Wilson, *Regular Zeal*, pp. 231, 229.

25. Bartlett, *False and Seducing Teachers*, p. 36. I also quote from Blair, "Revival of Religion at New-Londonderry," p. 251. The phrase "the sneaking Self-seeker" appears in William Tennent's "Account of the Revival of Religion at Freehold," p. 307.

26. On the transcendent power of Whitefield's voice, see James Ogilvie, who speculates in *The Christian History* whether Whitefield's "may be the Lord's last Voice to us" ("An Account of the Rev. Mr. Whitefield . . . at Aberdeen," p. 280). Benjamin Colman wrote to Whitefield along similar lines: "This is the plain, fair, and impartial Idea I have of your Mission from God . . . it is not you that have chosen him, but he

you" (quoted in Kenney, "George Whitefield, Dissenter Priest of the Great Awakening," p. 89 n. 41 [ellipsis Kenney's]).

27. Smith, *Sermon*, pp. 366, 369, 371. An initially somewhat skeptical witness of a Whitefield sermon noted, in this regard, that he *"prayed most excellently*, in the same Manner (I guess) that the first Ministers of the *Christian Church* prayed, before they were shackled with Forms" ("Account of Whitefield's New York visit," p. 360). On the Harvard faculty's critique of extemporaneous preaching as repetitious, "cursory," "perverted," and "little Instructive to the Mind, and still less cogent to the reasonable Powers," see *Testimony of Harvard College*, pp. 350–51.

28. Smith, *Sermon*, p. 371; Bordley quoted in Richard J. Cox, "Stephen Bordley," p. 305. Bordley noted that in all his discourses Whitefield "very strongly hints, nay sometimes plainly says, that he is divinely Inspired, that he is sent by God on purpose to remove the World from its abominable state of Wickedness. & particularly Where he is railing at the Clergy for preaching (as he says) ag[ains]t the Spirit, he says Yet a little while, & will come the great day of Judgment, And I shall be to Confront You (the Clergy) & to declare what Doctrines You have preached" (306).

29. Smith, *Sermon*, p. 66. Cf. Chauncy, *Enthusiasm described*, p. 16.

30. Smith, *Sermon*, p. 68. The description of Whitefield had apparently become conventional almost immediately: Rev. Colman opened his sermon in the Brattle Street Church on 21 October 1740, after Whitefield's departure from Boston and guest appearance at the church, by telling how he had been received there "as an *Angel of* GOD for JESUS sake; as the Apostle St. *Paul* was received by the Churches in *Galatia*" ("Souls flying to Jesus Christ," pp. 382–83). Later in the sermon, Colman likens Whitefield to *"David* going against *Goliah"* (for his extreme youth) and challenges his listeners to attend his own sermons as they attended Whitefield's: "You have seen, as it were, a young *Elias*, or the *Baptist* risen again, a *burning and a shining Light*, and you were *willing for the Season to rejoyce in his Light and Heat*" (384).

31. In a time of fierce denominational conflict, many statements from supporters testify to Whitefield's refusal to endorse any particular religious denomination. See, for example, "Account of Whitefield's New York visit," esp. p. 363; cf. Smith's appraisal in *Sermon*, p. 373.

32. This definition of the new birth is in Prince, ed., *Christian History 1744*, p. 362.

33. J. Willison, "Letter . . . respecting Mr. Whitefield's Character," p. 282. On Whitefield's astonishing equanimity and ministerial perseverance in the face of personal crisis, from the death of his only child to imminent shipwreck, see Prince, ed., *Christian History 1744*, pp. 288 n, 296 n.

34. William Hobby, *An Inquiry into the Itinerancy, and the Conduct of the Rev. George Whitefield, an Itinerant Preacher*, p. 23.

35. Blair, "Revival of Religion at New-Londonderry," p. 253. Also see pp. 255–56, where Blair provides an example of one of his parishioners, a thoughtful young woman, freed from the seemingly unresolvable antithesis between the typological

and the individual into a certainty of saving grace. The young woman had "heard that Sinners in closing with CHRIST by Faith received him for their Saviour, which she tho't included in it a Perswasion that he was their's in particular, and she could not clearly say that this had ever been her Case." Yet she was partially reassured by hearing of "some *Mark* of Grace, some Evidence of a real Christian laid down" in a sermon and feeling that it applied to herself. Eventually she resolves the tension between her expectation of a direct and individual relation with Christ and the typology of salvation: "she believ'd that he had suffered for her Sins; that she was the very Person who by her Sins had occasioned his Sufferings, and brought Agony and Pain upon him," enabling her to feel a visceral sense of her loathsomeness, an enjoyment that delivers her into the calm waters of salvation as inclusion in the individual promise of Christ's sacrifice for humankind. The phrase "the unerring Word of Truth" appears in Wilson, *Regular Zeal*, p. 228. Cf. Jonathan Edwards, *Faithful Narrative*, p. 181, regarding a pious old woman who one day read about Christ's sufferings in the New Testament and had a powerful realization of what she had read as "a thing that was real and very wonderful, but quite new to her"; for the first time she perceives her relation to the suffering Christ as personal and immediate. On the concept of the human document, see Ginzburg, *On Psychological Prose*.

36. Chauncy, *Enthusiasm described*, p. 25.

37. *Testimony of Harvard College*, p. 346. The complaint recalls Robert Calef's critique of spectral evidence theorists (and Cotton Mather in particular) whose enthusiasm was expressed as an undue literalism and subsequent abandonment of metaphor in public statements about the social and theological crime of witchcraft. See Calef, *More Wonders*, p. 298.

38. Willison, "Letter," p. 283.

39. Smith, *Sermon*, pp. 66, 371.

40. Quoted in Barish, *Antitheatrical Prejudice*, p. 92. Cf. Chauncy's view of Whitefield: "unsteady and variable as a *Weather-Cock*, and is yet Enthusiast enough to boast of his Inspirations, and frequent Intercourse with that Almighty Being, who *is the same yesterday and to day and for ever: His Councils immutable, and in whom is no Variableness nor shadow of turning*" ("A Second Letter," p. 7).

41. Tennent, *Necessity of Religious Violence*, p. 40.

42. *Testimony of Harvard College*, pp. 351–52. The imagery is representative of the Old Light tendency to characterize the revivalist as feminized: irrational, victimized, hysterical, and so on.

43. Smith, *Sermon*, p. 372. William Tennent characterized the Old Light ministry as the barren body of a woman in "Account of the Revival of Religion at Freehold," p. 299. Timothy Walker refers with contempt to the New Light characterization of Old Light clergy as spiritually impotent in *Way to Try*, p. 17.

44. Whitman, "Prefatory Letter to Emerson, 1856," p. 732.

45. Joseph Park, "An Account of the late Propagation of Religion at Westerly and Charlestown," p. 202. To an astonishing degree, Whitman's public persona made

available in his poetry successfully recuperated the Whitefieldian tropes not just of the religious ravisher but of the transcripted life and monumentality, as his contemporary reviews (collected in Milton Hindus, ed., *Walt Whitman: The Critical Heritage*) attest. Moncure Conway, after meeting Whitman, declared in a letter to Emerson that Whitman "is clearly his Book"; his evident popularity with "the common folks" also prompted Conway to observe "that there is much in all this of what you might call 'playing Providence a little with the baser sort'" (30, 29). A scathing anonymous review in the London *Critic* stated that "The man is the true impersonation of his book — rough, uncouth, vulgar," an impression augmented by the self-portrait which served as the book's frontispiece and title page, an image that for the reviewer "expresses all the features of the hard democrat, and none of the flexile delicacy of the civilised poet" (56). An anonymous reviewer for the *Brooklyn Daily Eagle* interpreted the relationship of book to person more positively: "the book is a reproduction of the author," the reviewer maintained, insofar as "[t]he contents of the book form a daguerrotype of his inner being, and the title page bears a representation of its physical tabernacle" (84–85).

46. Park, "Account," p. 205.

47. Cox, "Stephen Bordley," pp. 305, 304; "Account of Whitefield's New York visit," p. 361. Page numbers to both accounts will henceforth appear in the text. Bordley also noticed the negative effect that Whitefield's appearance had on the beauty of his voice: "He is very Young, has a well turned person, a fine sett of teeth, which is a great ornament in a Speaker & a Sweet and Agreeable turn of Countenance, but the beauty of this is somewhat lessened by a prodigious Squint w[i]th his left Eye" (304).

48. Prince, "Some Account," p. 381. Page numbers for Prince's anatomization of ministerial voice will henceforth appear in the text.

49. Cox, "Stephen Bordley," pp. 306, 307.

50. For the significance of the publication in the press of the Garden-Whitefield polemic, see Lambert, "*Pedlar in Divinity*," pp. 169, 175–76.

51. Garden, *Six Letters to the Reverend Mr. George Whitefield*, p. 14 (letter 3).

52. Garden, *Six Letters*, p. 13 (letter 3).

53. Garden, *Six Letters*, pp. 47, 13, 40 (letters 6, 3, 5).

54. Chauncy, *Enthusiasm described*, pp. 19, 21.

55. Garden, *Regeneration*, p. i. Perhaps the most striking account of the overwhelming effect on his listeners of the aesthetic qualities of Whitefield's voice as opposed to the content of the words he uttered is provided by the German Lutheran Henry Melchior Muhlenberg. In his *Journals*, he tells of the influence of one of Whitefield's field-sermons upon a non–English speaking German woman who afterward proclaimed the "quickening, awakening, and edifying experience" she had received solely on the strength of "his gestures, expressions, looks, and voice"; quoted in Lambert, "*Pedlar in Divinity*," p. 154.

56. Garden, *Regeneration*, p. 25. An Anglican minister from Delaware, George Ross, in a letter of 3 June 1742 to the Secretary of the Society for the Propagation of

the Gospel, made a similar point: he noted that Whitefield's sermons were far less influential when they appeared in print because their publication gave "their opponents a handle to expose their madness; and many who were carried away with their raging novelty, are come to their sober senses" (Perry, *Historical Collections*, 5: 85).

57. Garden, *Regeneration*, p. ii. Cf. the prayer the Connecticut minister Daniel Wadsworth offered on behalf of his people: "Save them from error, prevent their being Led astray by such as creep into houses to Lead captive the Silly" (*The Diary of the Reverend Daniel Wadsworth*, p. 88). Of Whitefield's diary, Wadsworth had this to say: "Met with the famous Mr. Whitefields life and read it. but what is it" (58).

58. Whitefield was often accused by his foes of Catholic tendencies, i.e., his pretense to infallibility, his discouraging alternative viewpoints, his acolytes' disregard for their own powers of judgment, etc. A point-by-point comparison forms the basis for *A short reply to Mr. Whitefield's letter Which he wrote in answer to the Querists*. In *Six Letters*, Garden taunted Whitefield with claiming the same infallibility as the Pope and the Mufti: "A motley Triumvirate of *Infallibles!*" (p. 37, letter 5).

59. David McGregore, *The Spirits of the Present Day Tried*, p. 221.

60. Gilbert Tennent, *The Danger of an Unconverted Ministry*. Page numbers will henceforth be cited parenthetically in the text. Heimert's assessment of the sermon's significance appears on pp. 71–72, quotation from p. 72.

61. Jonathan Edwards, *Distinguishing Marks*, p. 248.

62. Cf. Jonathan Edwards in *Some Thoughts* as he declaims at length against "ungodly ministers" who are "put to it continually to play the hypocrite, and force the airs of a saint in preaching" considering that so many parishioners were already awakened: "Oh, how miserably must such a person feel! What a wretched bondage and slavery is this! What pains, and how much art must such a minister use to conceal himself!" (507, 506).

63. I am grateful to Jeff Knapp for discussing with me the difference between these two terms. The Reverend Samuel Stone's remarks concerning a speaking aristocracy and a silent democracy are quoted in Perry Miller, *Seventeenth Century*, p. 452.

64. Chauncy, *Seasonable Thoughts*, p. 51.

65. Chauncy, *Enthusiasm described*, p. 9. Wilson, *Regular Zeal*, pp. 225, 224.

66. Bushman, *From Puritan to Yankee*, p. 220.

67. Park, "Account," pp. 202, 205. Page numbers will appear henceforth in the text.

68. This reversal of "the conventional flow of speech in public assemblies" is described at length from contemporary reports of Davenport's prayer meetings in Stout and Onuf, "James Davenport," pp. 568–70 (quotation from p. 570). Such descriptions are striking for the way in which they demonstrate how Whitefield's spectacular conversions were inverted by those separatist preachers most indebted to him for their preaching styles. Thus, although Stout and Onuf maintain that "Davenport's preaching was an extension of the techniques he had learned from Whitefield," the character of Whitefield's sermons — the powerful preacher whose voice could be

heard a mile away when he was surrounded by a silent audience—was inverted: Davenport led his hearers to destroy the difference between himself as preacher and them as audience, and the resultant cacophony of voices from Davenport's many "speaking companions" could be "'heard a mile from the place,'" according to a contemporary report (566, 570).

69. William Shurtleff, *A Letter to those . . . who refuse to admit the Rev. Mr. Whitefield into their Pulpits*, p. 357.

70. Shurtleff, *Letter*, p. 360. The metaphor of thirst was a conventional one: Samuel Finley used it to explain the "unusual Numbers" attending New Light sermons in *Christ Triumphing*, p. 158. For a typical radical New Light assessment of how religion had "dwindled into an empty Form" before the revival, see p. 155. Finley also pointed out that since New Light preachers were by and large unlearned, and thus possessed "less Rhetorick & Oratory" than their established colleagues, the work they wrought upon the populace must be not a work of mere man but of God; see p. 157.

71. Blair, "Revival," pp. 247, 246. Stout and Onuf noted how Davenport considered his first task as a revivalist preacher to be "to silence the voice of established authority" or, as he styled them, "'dead preachers'" ("James Davenport," p. 566).

72. Timothy Cutler, letter of 24 September 1743 to the Secretary of the Society for the Propagation of the Gospel (SPG), excerpted in Perry, *Historical Collections*, 3: 675–76, quotation from p. 676; Gilbert Tennent, "Letter," p. 297.

73. Jonathan Dickinson, "Account of the Revival of Religion at Newark & Elizabeth-Town," p. 255.

74. Quoted in Heimert, *Religion and the American Mind*, p. 222. Lambert, in "*Pedlar in Divinity*," seconds the historian T. H. Breen's call (in "Retrieving Common Sense") for a reconceptualization of the public sphere as it developed in the American context as primarily an arena for religious discussion, and one whose actors are "literate" and "reasoning" (171). Although such a refinement of Habermas's account of the rise of the public sphere to fit American circumstances would certainly be welcome, this characterization of its participants seems to me to ignore firsthand descriptions offered by supporters and detractors.

75. Joshua Hempstead as quoted in Stout and Onuf, "James Davenport," p. 561.

76. As early as 1724, Solomon Stoddard had associated formal observance with spiritual degeneracy; see *Defects of Preachers Reproved*, p. 23. Not surprisingly, there is a political analogue for the space that lay beyond formal observance that was itself, arguably, the result of the types of popular religious activity here discussed. Gordon S. Wood writes of how the philosophical statesmen of the revolutionary era, gentlemen all, came to regard "the people out of doors"—that "larger political society existing outside of the legislative chambers" whose "hovering presence" increasingly oppressed those within—as an unfortunate but inevitable development which, thanks to the "popular and egalitarian ideology of the Revolution," they were forced not just to acknowledge but to conciliate. See "The Democratization of Mind in the American Revolution," pp. 73–75.

NOTES TO PAGES 151–54

77. The phrase is quoted disapprovingly by John Wilson in *Regular Zeal*, p. 226.

78. Chauncy, *Enthusiasm described*, p. 3.

79. Chauncy, *Seasonable Thoughts*, pp. 324, 327–28, 324.

80. Chauncy, *Enthusiasm described*, p. 17.

81. James Davenport, "The Confession and Retraction of the Rev. Mr. Davenport," p. 238; Chauncy, "Letter to Davenport," p. v.

82. Chauncy, *Seasonable Thoughts*, pp. 373, 326; Weller, *Trial of Mr. Whitefield's Spirit*, p. 34. Those who fulminated against enthusiasm two decades later would have considered Chauncy's prophecy fulfilled in their time as "political enthusiasm," a term employed by Rev. Ebenezer Thompson of Scituate, Massachusetts, in a letter of 25 April 1769 to the Secretary of the SPG. The observations of William McGilchrist, Anglican preacher at Salem, concurred: in a letter of 7 December 1770 to the Secretary of the SPG, he noted with what would prove a short-lived relief, "The ferment by which the minds of the people here have been wrought up into as high a degree of Enthusiasm by the word liberty, as could have been expected had Religion been the cause, begins now to subside." Political enthusiasm, according to Joshua Wingate Weeks in his letter to the SPG of 20 June 1769, had generated "differences in opinion with regard to political matters" that recalled the religious separations of the 1740s and, according to Thompson, had placed upon those who objected to political enthusiasm as powerful a censorship as the antirevivalists complained of three decades earlier. See Perry, *Historical Collections*, 3: 546, 555, 546. On complaints of censorship from Old Lights during the revival see, for example, Chauncy, *Enthusiasm described*, p. 26; and Timothy Cutler's 14 January 1741 letter to the Bishop of London, in Perry, *Historical Collections*, 3: 350–52. On political enthusiasm, see David Lovejoy, " 'Desperate Enthusiasm': Early Signs of American Radicalism."

83. Bartlett, *False and Seducing Teachers*. The preface to *Seasonable Thoughts* explicitly links the revival not to the witchcraft crisis but to the earlier Antinomian crisis.

84. Chauncy, *Enthusiasm described*, p. 3. Page numbers will appear hereafter in the text.

85. Quoted in Chauncy, preface to *Seasonable Thoughts*, pp. xvi–xvii; cf. 359.

86. Bartlett, *False and Seducing Teachers*, p. 39; Banage, quoted in Chauncy, "Letter to Davenport," p. vii. That these professionals were also prone to self-delusion and did not operate with complete cynicism was maintained by Samuel Weller: he claimed that George Whitefield was not "really that sort of Person, which perhaps he verily believes himself to be" (*Trial*, p. 7; cf. p. 28).

87. Chauncy, preface to *Seasonable Thoughts*, pp. viii–ix.

88. Timothy Walker, *Way to Try*, p. 18. The New Lights were equally anxious to claim Scripture as their touchstone: the *Christian History*, for example, is replete with claims that New Light doctrine and the audience behaviors it elicited conform with scriptural guidelines. Even radicals like James Davenport invoked the analogy of Scripture.

89. Walker, *Way to Try*, p. 19. Chauncy devotes the entire introduction to *Season-*

450 NOTES TO PAGES 154–55

able Thoughts to a delineation of the characterological evidences for a work of God upon the individual's soul; see pp. 1–34.

90. Walker, *Way to Try*, pp. 23, 25. Note Walker's persistent feminization of the enthusiast's victim.

91. Bartlett, *False and Seducing Teachers*, p. 41.

92. Bartlett's vision of endless separations was historically fulfilled in what Stephen A. Marini calls the "new New England," the hill country of northern New England and Canada. Noting the pattern of cultural crisis that accompanied settlement in these regions during and after the Revolution, Marini analyzes the religious itinerancy characteristic of the region, and also notes that the other major form of sectarian evangelism "was systematic expansion by intrachurch schism." See Marini, *Radical Sects of Revolutionary New England*, pp. 38–39, 82–86; quoted phrases on pp. 39, 86. See also Ruth H. Bloch's excellent *Visionary Republic: Millennial Themes in American Thought*.

93. Bartlett, *False and Seducing Teachers*, p. 42; Wilson, *Regular Zeal*, p. 233. Wilson pointed out in refutation of this concept that if one wants to seduce the mob, one endeavors to cater to its proclivities, which are by definition decidedly against the stringencies of religious observation.

94. Isaac Stiles, *Looking-glass*, p. 315; Weller, *Trial*, p. 31. Weller is here referring to the *"Women-Societies"* that flourished in the wake of Whitefield's itinerancy (31), but numerous similar descriptions exist of mixed assemblies. Stout and Onuf, in "James Davenport," report that antirevivalist newspapers characterized New Light assemblies as composed of " 'idle or ignorant persons, and those of the lowest Rank' " (561). Stout and Onuf dispute this characterization on pp. 562–63; cf. Bonomi and others. It is significant that Old Light assessments of their opponents resemble an account provided by one wholly outside the debate, the physician Alexander Hamilton of Maryland. In his account of his travels through the northern colonies, Hamilton relates his experience at an inn on the Connecticut River: "After dinner there came in a rabble of clowns who fell to disputing upon points of divinity as learnedly as if they had been professed theologues. 'Tis strange to see how this humour prevails, even among the lower class of the people here. They will talk so pointedly about justification, sanctification, adoption, regeneration, repentance, free grace, reprobation, original sin, and a thousand other such pritty, chimerical knick knacks as if they had done nothing but studied divinity all their life time and perused all the lumber of the scholastic divines, and yet the fellows look as much, or rather more, like clowns than the very riff-raff of our Maryland planters" (*Gentleman's Progress*, p. 163).

95. Wilson, *Regular Zeal*, p. 230. Page numbers will appear henceforth in the text (many of the pages are misnumbered in *The Christian History*; I have corrected the numbering throughout). Cf. Jonathan Edwards, *Some Thoughts*, pp. 296–300, esp. p. 297: it is "false divinity," Edwards maintained, "to suppose that religious affections don't appertain to the substance and essence of Christianity: on the contrary, it seems to me that the very life and soul of all true religion consists in them."

96. Weller, for example, claimed that "the Word METHODEIA, or Methodism" (for all intents and purposes, a synonym for enthusiasm) appears twice in the New Testament where it "is translated *lying in wait,* or watching to take an advantage of any one: And in the other it is rendered by the Word *Wiles* or Stratagems: And in both Places denotes that *cunning Craftiness,* whereby evil Men, or evil Spirits, *lye in wait to deceive*" (*Trial,* p. 6). Such statements clearly link the realm of individual religious experience so threatening to the mid-eighteenth century to the spectral realm which threatened the late seventeenth. New Lights, of course, were not averse to etymological researches to support their reforms: in defense of affectionate preaching, Jonathan Edwards asserted that "the word commonly used in the New Testament, that we translate 'preach,' properly signifies to proclaim aloud like a crier"; Christ himself will "cry like a travailing woman." See *Some Thoughts,* p. 389.

97. Blair, "Revival," p. 261. Blair cautions: "I must not speak wickedly, even for GOD; nor talk deceitfully for HIM." The conservative notion of the naked truth (quoted in parentheses in the text) is from Chauncy, *Enthusiasm described,* p. 17. An excellent example of Wilson's sense of ontological context and the meanings of words is provided in Jonathan Edwards's *Faithful Narrative*; see the concluding cases Phebe Bartlet and Abigail Hutchinson on pp. 191-205, esp. pp. 194-95, where Edwards discusses the latter's recall and repetition of the word "truth" and of the phrases "Worthy is the Lamb that was slain" and "meek and lowly in heart."

98. Cf. melancholy, in Jonathan Edwards's view, as effecting a false revaluation of all values; he defines it in *Some Thoughts* as a "strange disposition . . . to take things wrong. So that that which as it is spoken, is truth, as it is heard and received, and applied by them, is falsehood" (392). The symbolic act associated with melancholy is thus not natural death but suicide (393).

99. Blair, "Revival," pp. 248, 247.

100. Chauncy, *Letter to Wishart,* p. 16.

101. John Cotton, "History of the Revival of Religion . . . at Hallifax," p. 268. Cf. Thomas Hooker, preface to *Survey of the Summe of Church Discipline*: "*The Sum is, we doubt not what we practise, but its beyond all doubt, that* all men are liars, *and we are in the number of those poor feeble men, either we do, or may err, though we do not know it, what we have learned, we do professe, and yet professe still to live, that we may learn.*" For the benefit of "less intelligent Readers" who might be ignorant of the fact "that *Outcries* and *bodily Distresses* attending a Work of the divine Spirit, are no new Things," *The Christian History 1743* published extracts from seventeenth-century writers who testify to their existence (pp. 215 ff.). Chauncy, not surprisingly, considered this assumption "'the most dangerous and hurtful'" aspect of such scenes: "'that very much Stress was laid on these *Extraordinaries,* as tho' they were *sure Marks,* or, at least, *sufficient Evidences* of a just Conviction of Sin on the one Hand; or, on the other, of that Joy which there is in believing, and so of an Interest in the Favour of God'" (a witness to a New Light service, quoted in *Letter to Wishart,* p. 17).

102. William Tennent, "Account," p. 309. Jonathan Edwards famously asserted

in *Some Thoughts* the probability that God will begin the project "to renew the whole habitable earth . . . in this utmost, meanest, youngest and weakest part of it, where the church of God has been planted last of all" (356; see pp. 353–58 for Edwards's reasons for believing that the millennium would probably dawn in America). Chauncy's indignation at what he considered to be Edwards's arrogance in imagining that America — and specifically Edwards's own Northampton parish — would lead the way to the millennium was registered in his answer to *Some Thoughts*, the lengthy volume entitled *Seasonable Thoughts*. There he quotes Increase Mather as saying, " 'I know there is a blessed Day to the visible Church not far off: But it is the Judgment of very learned Men, that, in the glorious Times promised to the Church on Earth, AMERICA will be HELL' " (*Seasonable Thoughts*, p. 372 n).

103. Jonathan Edwards, quoted in Prince, ed., *Christian History 1743*, p. 112.

104. Edwards, *Faithful Narrative*, pp. 160, 166.

105. This sequence of assumptions is exceptionally clear in Jonathan Edwards, *Faithful Narrative*, which includes this description of the emergence of selflessness and redeemed collectivity: he noticed that "[p]ersons after their own conversion have commonly expressed an exceeding desire for the conversion of others: some have thought that they should be willing to die for the conversion of any soul, though of one of the meanest of their fellow creatures, or of their worst enemies; and many have indeed been in great distress with desires and longings for it" (256). The 6 November 1736 version of the *Narrative* (written as a letter giving an account of the Northampton revival of 1734–36 to Rev. Benjamin Colman of Boston) was excerpted in *Christian History 1743*, beginning with the 11 June 1743 number, pp. 115–28.

106. Quoted in Bushman, *From Puritan to Yankee*, p. 198.

107. Thus Samuel Blair, faced with constant public outbursts during his sermons, asked his parishioners to "endeavour to moderate and bound their Passions, *but not so as to resist or stifle their Convictions*" ("Revival," p. 246).

108. As Jonathan Edwards put it in *Faithful Narrative*, "the difference between what is spiritual and what is merely imaginary" (189).

109. Blair, "Revival," p. 247.

110. Cotton, "History," pp. 261, 263.

111. Jonathan Edwards, "Continuation of the State of Religion at Northampton," p. 372. Edwards's observation is elsewhere supported. The Reverend Nathanael Leonard, describing for *The Christian History* the effects of the visit of the radical New Light Andrew Croswell to his Plymouth congregation, noted that "*Conversions* were so open and publick that we seemed to see Souls dead in Trespasses and Sins, revive and stand up Monuments of divine Grace" ("A brief Account of the late Revival of Religion in Plymouth," p. 313).

112. Wilson, *Regular Zeal*, p. 220; Blair, "Revival," p. 256.

113. Cotton, "History," p. 270. See also Cotton Mather, *Manuductio ad Ministerium: Directions for a Candidate of the Ministry*, pp. 2–3.

114. Blair, "Revival," p. 251.

115. Blair, "Revival," p. 247.

116. The phrase "meer *natural* or *mechanical Influence*" is Prince's, who expressed in "Some Account" his reservations about the ease with which natural fear may be confused with religious feeling (386).

117. Gilbert Tennent, "Letter," p. 297.

118. Jonathan Edwards, *Some Thoughts*, p. 315. Page numbers will henceforth appear parenthetically in the text.

119. Edwards, *Distinguishing Marks*, p. 244.

120. Edwards, *Distinguishing Marks*, p. 245.

121. Edwards, *Distinguishing Marks*, p. 268. Cf. Jonathan Parsons, *A Needful Caution*, p. 30.

122. Edwards, *Distinguishing Marks*, p. 274.

123. Edwards, *Distinguishing Marks*, p. 265.

124. Edwards, *Faithful Narrative*, p. 174. For an interesting inversion of this problem, see the complaint registered by the Anglican H. A. Brockwell of Salem, Massachusetts, in a letter of 15 June 1741 to the Secretary of the SPG: "the very Children are affected by their Parents' [spiritual] uneasiness and talk nothing less than they of renovation, regeneration, conviction and conversion, tho' neither Children nor Parents understand the meaning of the terms they continually cant about" (Perry, *Historical Collections*, 3: 357).

125. See Edwards, *Distinguishing Marks*, p. 265. Such a circumstance, Edwards argues, requires a style of preaching that resembles an interrogation as the preacher endeavors to supply his auditors with an affective language for their experience that they can signal their recognition of through nonverbal or inarticulate means: behaviors and outcries.

126. Edwards, *Distinguishing Marks*, p. 265.

127. Hobby, *Inquiry*, pp. 11, 25.

128. Chauncy, *Enthusiasm described*, p. 21.

129. Chauncy, *Letter to Wishart*, pp. 12–13.

130. Late twentieth-century analyses of the problem of authenticity and replication have been enormously influenced by the work of Walter Benjamin, especially "The Work of Art in the Age of Mechanical Reproduction." Particularly suggestive for the scenario depicted here is the essay's second section, in which he points out that reproduction "enables the original to meet the beholder halfway," in so doing "reactivat[ing]" the reproduced object and therefore "shattering" the historical tradition that determined the authenticity of the original: both processes, Benjamin claimed, "are intimately connected with the contemporary mass movements [i.e., fascism]" (220–21).

131. Edwards, *Faithful Narrative*, p. 160. He immediately qualifies this statement about the vast variety of ways of converting by claiming that "in many things there is a great analogy in all" — a typical recovery by which Edwards lauds the individuality of awakening manifestations but recuperates them for uniformity in the end. He dis-

cusses the various ways of coming to conviction after this quotation on p. 160. Cf. p. 185, where Edwards asserts that despite the extraordinary variety of means, "it seems evidently to be the same work, the same thing done, the same habitual change wrought in the heart; it all tends the same way, and to the same end; and 'tis plainly the same spirit that breathes and acts in various persons." Variety merely shows that God will not confine himself to "a particular method." Edwards's desire to resolve variety and individuality into uniformity will be discussed later in this chapter.

132. Edwards, "Continuation," p. 369.

133. Other popular accounts of the transmission of evangelical feeling were calculated to stimulate fears that such strong expressions of emotion must be linked to sexual promiscuity. Timothy Cutler, for example, in a letter to the Secretary of the SPG of 24 September 1743 remarked concerning the revivalists' use of the press that "[o]ur presses are for ever teeming with books, and our women with bastards, though regeneration and conversion is the whole cry" (Perry, *Historical Collections*, 3: 675). Chauncy, in *Enthusiasm described*, claimed that enthusiasm "has made strong attempts to destroy all property, to make all things common, *wives* as well as *goods*" (15). And Alexander Hamilton facetiously remarked concerning his hostess at a Boston dinner party that she was "a strenuous Whitefieldian. The word carnal was much used in our table talk, which seems to be a favorite word of the fair sex of that perswasion" (*Gentleman's Progress*, p. 112). Many Old Light ministers expressed a fear of Moses Bartlett's in his tract against "false and seducing teachers," that they were particularly able to *"lead captive silly Women"* (29). Some critics evinced a more subtle sense of the carnal: Samuel Weller accused George Whitefield of betraying an "Excess of a refined Carnality, in the Pleasure this Gentleman takes in describing" the numbers of persons in his audiences (*Trial*, p. 11).

134. Edwards, *Distinguishing Marks*, p. 235. Cf. *Some Thoughts*, p. 400. This did not mean that Edwards tolerated itinerancy, ministerial or lay. The reservation was widespread, even among New Light ministers extremely sympathetic to the revival and who had suffered professionally for their fidelity. See, for example, Parsons, *Needful Caution*, pp. 49–50 n.

135. William Cooper, preface to Edwards, *Distinguishing Marks*, p. 221; Edwards, *Some Thoughts*, pp. 400–401.

136. John Howe quoted in Cooper, preface to Edwards, *Distinguishing Marks*, p. 218 (brackets Cooper's).

137. Edwards protested his delicacy in this regard in *Faithful Narrative*, pp. 175–76.

138. Edwards's protest is directed toward criticisms like those delivered from the Hartford North Association (a ministerial association) from a proclamation of 11 August 1741 which decreed that "there is no Weight to be Laid upon those Visions or visional Discoveries by some of late pretended to, of Heaven or Hell, or the body or blood of Christ, *viz* as represented to the eyes of the body." Quoted in George Leon Walker, *Some Aspects of the Religious Life of New England*, p. 99 (spelling modernized).

139. Edwards, *Faithful Narrative*, pp. 189, 163; Parsons, *Needful Caution*, p. 66. As holy sepulcher, the human heart produced a fantastically self-aggrandizing mystical courting of death during the revival, exemplified not so much by Abigail Hutchinson, one of the heroines of *Faithful Narrative* who serenely endures a horrific death by starvation, as by Edwards's wife, Sarah, who wished to demonstrate her unqualified love of God by taking upon herself the greatest ill she could imagine, personal immortality. See Julie Ellison, "The Sociology of 'Holy Indifference': Sarah Edwards's Narrative." Hutchinson's story appears on pp. 191–99 in *Faithful Narrative*.

140. Gerald F. Moran, in "Conditions of Religious Conversion in the First Society of Norwich, Connecticut, 1718–1744," provides a telling example of the contentiousness Edwards bemoaned in young Nathaniel Lathrop Jr.'s public statement, recorded in the church minutes, that "it would be pleasentis sight that ever my eyes saw if Christ would come in the cloud and take vengeance on all the workers of iniquity this night and to hear Christ give a commission to the devils to drag your soul down to heel, my dear sister Anne" (quoted on p. 342 n. 27).

141. The definitive study of Edwards's moral thought, including his notion of the conscience, is Norman Fiering, *Jonathan Edwards's Moral Thought and Its British Context*. Extremely useful for the history of the notion of conscience in colonial New England is Fiering's *Moral Philosophy at Seventeenth-Century Harvard*.

142. See pp. 426–27 in *Some Thoughts* for Edwards's caveats on bold speech and the bold speech of women. Edwards is deeply ambivalent about the propriety of women speaking. On the one hand, he defended the impassioned speech of ministers by reminding his readers that the Scriptures portray Christ preaching "like a travailing woman" (389). On the other hand, women had to remember that although " 'tis beautiful in private Christians, though they are women and children, to be bold in professing the faith of Christ, and in the practice of all religion, and in owning God's hand in the work of his power and grace, without any fear of men," yet "for private Christians, women and others, to instruct, rebuke, and exhort, with a like sort of boldness as becomes a minister when preaching, is not beautiful" (427).

143. William Cooper, in the preface to *Distinguishing Marks*, also noted that "all qualities and conditions" had resolved themselves into a single work of pleasing uniformity (219, cf. 220–21). However, Cooper also observed that the work was attended by some "particular appearances"; although "conversion is the same work, in the main strokes of it, wherever it is wrought; yet it seems reasonable to suppose that at an extraordinary season wherein God is pleased to carry on a work of his grace in a more observable and glorious manner," particular appearances should be expected as "reasonable" (221). Cf. Parsons, *Needful Caution*, pp. 34–36. Parsons urges his readers that if "all their Principles and Practices [are] conformed to the Gospel of Christ," it would amount to "standing Evidence before the Eyes of Opposers, that those Operations of the Spirit which are visible in their Effects, have *indeed* a transforming Influence" (35). The aim is "to shut up the mouth of Contradiction" (35).

144. Emerson, "The Poet," p. 226.

PART II

1. The bibliography on this subject is quite extensive. See especially Bushman, *From Puritan to Yankee*, for permutations within the relationships of Old and New Lights and their political entanglements, and Marini, *Radical Sects of Revolutionary New England*, who examines Separatism in the frontier regions. For a discussion of the dynamics of separation in contemporary religious and political groups, see Gerlach and Hine, *People, Power, Change*, esp. chapter 3.

2. On this subject see Crawford, *Seasons of Grace*, chapter 10, pp. 197–222. On the history of the Quakers' paradigmatic shift in emphasis from aggressive evangelism to "the spiritual maintenance of Friends" through an increased focus upon meetings for worship — and thus a new insistence upon the value of silence and decorum (as exemplifying "innocence" and "simplicity of heart" [121]) over speech — see Bauman, *Let Your Words Be Few*, chapters 8 and 9. Historians have tied the institutionalization of Quaker practice, summarized by Bauman as "the routinization of prophecy, the process whereby a form of speaking by an individual originally responsible only to God is brought under corporate control" (138), to their increased persecution following the Restoration of 1660. Bauman's aim in chapter 9 is to examine this process not from the perspective of external pressures but rather as it occurred within the ministry itself, including the growing role of elders in the development and imposition of an organizational discipline, an increasing rationalization of formalism in religious practice, an increased sensitivity to public perceptions of internal factionalism and thus an increased intolerance of internal dissent or radical public behaviors, the gradual replacement of an incantatory with a catechetical preaching style that discouraged audience participation, and the gradual co-optation of charismatic by corporate signs of ministerial legitimacy.

3. Rhys Isaac, "Evangelical Revolt," p. 356.

4. See Goen, *Revivalism and Separatism*, pp. 228–29 (the quotations about Ledoyt in the following paragraph are from these pages).

5. Timothy Walker, *Way to Try*, p. 20.

6. The Killingly Convention of Separate churches convened in 1781, for example, conceived of the "trial of their gifts," by which individuals "convinced their fellow church members that God had indeed called them to preach," as a way to reinstitutionalize a ministry that had separated itself from traditional institutional constraints like education and ordination. According to a statement generated by that Convention, " 'all those Brethren in a Church, that have Gifts given them, that are for the Edification of the Church, ought to be improved in the Church, in their proper Place; and to be subject to the Government and Direction of the Church.' " See Goen, *Revivalism and Separatism*, pp. 174–75.

7. An example of such brief references in the historical documentation appears in a letter of 29 October 1766 from the Maryland Anglican Henry Addison to the Bishop of London. Addison complains of an itinerant, an ordained Anglican named

Colgrave or Colgreve who went by the name of Congreve. He lived "a vagrant life, strolling from place to place thro' most of the Colonies," Addison reported, and in that period had had several shady adventures. He had run a pub near Philadelphia, joined the army, acted as a schoolmaster in Maryland, married (his wife left him a week later for abuse), run into debt, disappeared, emerged in England "in holy orders," perpetrated some scandal, returned to Maryland, was deserted by his congregation, convinced his wife to return to him, and was at the time of Addison's letter head of a new parish in North Carolina. Addison asserted that such characters were "not unfrequent with respect to America" — a claim on which he bases his argument that America stood in urgent need of an episcopacy. See Perry, *Historical Collections*, 4: 332–34.

8. Such fears of the verbal excesses of democratic personality were expressed in a prevalent anxiety concerning " '*demagogues,*' 'with the *vox populi vox Dei* in their mouths,' men who were 'at the bottom, *whether of yesterday or the day before*, who under plausible pretences, . . . for dark, ambitious, or (not unlikely) speculative purposes, which they dare not own,' were 'disturbing the peace of the public, and causing the government to be bullied.' " This amalgam of quotations appears in Wood, *Creation of the American Republic*, p. 369.

9. Isaac Stiles in Alan Heimert and Perry Miller, eds., *The Great Awakening*, p. 309.

10. Cf. Warner, chapter 5 of *Letters of the Republic*. In a reading of Fisher Ames's essay "American Literature," Warner suggests that America's literary delinquency may be attributed to the republican ideology of literature which dominated the culture through the early national period: "The same republican rhetoric that had brought the nation-state of the United States into being now blocked the development of a national imaginary by its rigorous construction of citizenship in the public sphere" (149). Unlike a later, liberal generation, Ames did not worry that American literary genius would fail to materialize, but that its materialization would signal the corruption of republican virtue in a new association of print with "distinction and private appreciation" (148). My understanding of novelistic production in the republican period does not contradict Warner's reading of Ames's views as exemplifying republican literary ideology. But it does preclude my viewing this ideology as so monolithic that it may be regarded as a kind of master narrative to which all individual textual productions, whether novel or newspaper article, unambiguously refer. (I consider Warner's reading of Charles Brockden Brown's *Arthur Mervyn*, the focus of his sixth chapter, to be overdetermined in this regard.) What I am calling an incipient ethic of democratic literary creation is discernable in the rhetoric of inclusion at the heart of the republican ideology of literature as Warner so ably describes it, as well as in the uneasy recognition that the rhetoric belied the underlying practice of attempting to supervise inclusion: it belies, that is, "a recalcitrant social difference," an "implicit center-periphery metaphorics [which] registers the centralization of literacy that the thematic content of the discourse disavows" (129). An ethics of democratic

literary creation is even more discernable, however, in the represented forces in the novel which work against the republican ideal as exemplified by Brown's narrator Clara Wieland and Crèvecoeur's narrator Farmer James.

11. "Through me many long dumb voices" and "kosmos" appear in section 24 of Whitman's "Song of Myself."

CHAPTER FOUR

1. Jonathan Edwards, *Some Thoughts*, p. 423. The phrase "gentle Violence" comes from Gilbert Tennent, quoted in Heimert, *Religion and the American Mind*, p. 233; the phrase "insinuated word" comes from Rev. Calvin Colton, *History and Character of American Revivals of Religion*.

2. Bartlett, *False and Seducing Teachers*, p. 30.

3. "State of Religion in New England since the Reverend Mr. George White-field's Arrival there" (Glasgow: 1742), quoted in George Leon Walker, *Some Aspects*, pp. 96–97. C. C. Goen maintains that itinerant evangelizing was "quite without precedent" before Whitefield's arrival and that it represented "a radical innovation"; see *Revivalism and Separatism*, p. 9.

4. That the problem of itinerancy was formidable is evident from the legal measures undertaken by several colonies to limit or restrict it (Connecticut, for example, made religious itinerancy illegal in 1742, and the law was not repealed until 1750). See Bushman, *From Puritan to Yankee*, pp. 186–87, 229. The problem of lay itinerancy and its behavioral consequences among auditors in the Great Awakening was not unprecedented. Denigrations of seventeenth-century Quaker practice in England are descriptively identical to eighteenth-century American accounts. One observer in 1655 wrote: "They pretend raptures, ecstasies, swoonings, swellings, groanings, tumblings, and prostrations, shreekings, murmurings, trances, sensible feelings, and manifestations of God's Spirit coming into them; and in this politic frenzy, they pretend to have him, he is now within them, and so must speak, and must only be heard, as sent by God to give commands, directions, and advisos to the great ones of the earth" (quoted in Bauman, *Let Your Words Be Few*, p. 82).

5. Chauncy, *Enthusiasm described*, p. 12; and *Letter to Wishart*, p. 14.

6. Brockwell, Letter to the Secretary of the SPG of 18 February 1741, in Perry, *Historical Collections*, 3: 353.

7. Chauncy, *Enthusiasm described*, pp. 13, 12.

8. Bowen, "Extracts," pp. 169, 165. See my discussion of Bowen at the start of Chapter 1.

9. Timothy Cutler, Letter to the Bishop of London of 14 January 1741, in Perry, *Historical Collections*, 3: 351.

10. Thomas Dawson to the Bishop of London of 23 July 1753 in Perry, *Historical Collections*, 1: 407; Hugh Jones and Henry Addison to Lord Bishop of London on

27 August 1753 in Perry, *Historical Collections*, 4: 331; Edward Bass to the Secretary of the SPG of 25 March 1764 in Perry, *Historical Collections*, 3: 512–13; and J. W. Weeks to the Secretary of the SPG of 10 November 1770 in Perry, *Historical Collections*, 3: 551, 553–54.

11. Chauncy, *Seasonable Thoughts*, pp. 368–69.

12. Chauncy, *Enthusiasm described*, p. 11.

13. Hancock, *Dangers*, p. 22; Cutler, letter of 24 September 1743, in Perry, *Historical Collections*, 3: 676; newspapers quoted in Stout and Onuf, "James Davenport," p. 561. Stout and Onuf refute this blanket categorization on pp. 562–63, although they concede that Separatists "were poorer than established church members and held no important offices in town government" (563). On this topic, see also Bonomi, *Under the Cope of Heaven*, pp. 147, 260 n. Richard Hofstadter in *America at 1750* claims that the revival "cut across class lines"; although it appealed to "people of lower station, it took much of its driving force from its ability to reach the solid middle classes of the villages and even some of the well-to-do in the seaboard towns" (274). Gerald F. Moran in "Conditions of Religious Conversion in the First Society of Norwich, Connecticut, 1718–1744" and J. M. Bumsted in "Religion, Finance, and Democracy in Massachusetts: The Town of Norton as a Case Study" both support the perception that the revival was particularly attractive to the disenfranchised, especially young, unmarried individuals without property.

14. The phrase "very mean" is quoted in Tolles, "Quietism versus Enthusiasm," p. 37.

15. Finley, *Christ Triumphing*, pp. 157, 161.

16. The phrase "political enthusiasm" was used by Ebenezer Thompson to the Secretary of the SPG of 25 April 1769 in Perry, *Historical Collections*, 3: 546 (cf. note 82 in Chapter 3); William McGilchrist to the Secretary of the SPG of 7 December 1770 in Perry, *Historical Collections*, 3: 555. See also T. H. Breen, "Retrieving Common Sense," on the religious component of political discourse in this era.

17. Samuel Tingley to the Secretary for the SPG of 5 March 1782 in Perry, *Historical Collections*, 5: 139.

18. Weller, *Trial*, p. 34.

19. Quoted in Goen, *Revivalism and Separatism*, p. 284. Goen comments that Worcester's anxieties represent "only another instance of the contempt felt by the aristocratic conservative as he watched his congregation forsake his correct niceties to seek more spiritual food from the lips of some New Light exhorter," a "pattern that persisted well into the nineteenth century" (284). The nineteenth-century continuation and amplification of such patterns is fully and subtly analyzed by Hatch, *The Democratization of American Christianity*.

20. Parsons, *Needful Caution*, pp. 38, 41. Cf. Prince, "Some Account," p. 405.

21. For an account of this animosity, see Schmidt, "New Light Extremism." Stout, in *New England Soul*, credited Whitefield with inspiring an indigenous itinerant ministry, for which Gilbert Tennent's sermon *The Danger of an Unconverted Minis-*

try functioned as the "primer and party platform" (199). The growth of radical itinerancy led to the establishment of colleges such as Tennent's own Log College and the Shepherd's Tent. Stout points out that Tennent's ministry inspired "a wave of itinerant speakers," many of whom were recent Harvard and Yale graduates not yet established in a parish and sympathetic to the revival. Their training involved accompanying a more experienced itinerant on the road and then endeavoring, "in small group settings," to imitate extemporaneous speech; that is, they practiced trying to "speak . . . as if they had no formal training at all" (200). Goen notes in *Revivalism and Separatism* that the point of preaching extempore was to prevent "unscrupulous men [from] impos[ing] on their congregations by reading high-sounding works of other divines" (176). Extemporaneous preaching not only precluded the debased ventriloquism associated with false (mediated) speech but was a sign of the preacher's faith that God would supply him with words.

22. Prince, "Some Account," p. 385. Page numbers will appear henceforward in the text.

23. On Davenport's career, see Stout and Onuf, "James Davenport," and Nash, *Urban Crucible*, pp. 204–21. Stout and Onuf write that Davenport's "first task" upon arriving in a parish would be to demand an audience with the standing minister to insist on an account of his conversion. "Invariably dissatisfied" with it, he would then lead public prayers for the minister's conversion and in the process convert numbers of the minister's parishioners to an alliance with him. Taken together, his tactics amounted to the exploitation of "anticlericalism" among the people "for evangelical purposes, thereby tapping popular religious impulses that had never been adequately expressed" (566). Schmidt has recently made a compelling case for the more flamboyant and enduring itinerant ministry of Andrew Croswell in "New Light Extremism."

24. The incident is recounted in Stout and Onuf, "Davenport"; the quotation appears on p. 569. See also Hamilton, *Gentleman's Progress*, p. 161.

25. Quoted in Stout and Onuf, "Davenport," p. 569. Stout and Onuf point out that in Davenport's meetings, "the traditional distinctions between preacher and parishioner, pulpit and pew" were wholly obliterated (569). This description is consonant with that offered by Chauncy of such assemblies in *Letter to Wishart*, pp. 12–14.

26. James Davenport, "Confession and Retraction," p. 238.

27. Parsons, *Needful Caution*, pp. 49 n, 52 n, 48, 48 n. Page numbers will appear hereafter in the text.

28. Brockwell letter of 18 February 1741 in Perry, *Historical Collections*, 3: 354; Brockwell letter of 28 July 1744 in Perry, *Historical Collections*, 3: 387.

29. Weller, *Trial*, p. 9. On Jonathan Edwards's belief in these as the marks of regeneration, see *Distinguishing Marks*, pp. 257–58. Edwards speaks against lay itinerancy in *Some Thoughts* on pp. 424–28 and esp. pp. 484–89.

30. Hancock, *Dangers*, pp. 22, 23; Benjamin Colman, letter to Solomon Williams (1744), quoted in Goen, *Revivalism and Separatism*, p. 31. The phrase *"breeding up exhorters"* and Josiah Cotton's remarks are quoted in Schmidt, "New Light Extremism," pp. 219, 220.

31. Colman, letter to Williams, quoted in Goen, *Revivalism and Separatism*, p. 31; "*Whitefield's* Doctrine" is said to "discover itself in Multitudes" in Chauncy, *Letter to Wishart*, p. 12.

32. Walker, *Way to Try*, p. 19.

33. Edwards offered his biography of the itinerant evangelical David Brainerd, *An Account of the Life of the late Reverend Mr. David Brainerd*, as a model of the sanctified life. The subject of America's "first popular biography" was not an individual but a "representative figure," according to Norman Pettit, and the book was intended to contribute to "a larger effort to answer a basic theological question: 'What are distinguishing signs of truly gracious and holy affections?' " ("Prelude to Mission: Brainerd's Expulsion from Yale," pp. 28, 49).

34. Chauncy, *Enthusiasm described*, pp. 15, 16, 20; Bartlett, *False and Seducing Teachers*, pp. 29, 33.

35. Quoted in Schmidt, "New Light Extremism," p. 234, ellipsis in Schmidt.

36. Bartlett, *False and Seducing Teachers*, pp. 40, 38–39. Page numbers will henceforth appear in the text.

37. Chauncy, *Enthusiasm described*, p. 27.

38. Isaac Stiles, *Looking-glass*, p. 307. Page numbers will hereafter appear in the text.

39. The quoted phrase appears in a 1751 Address to the Burgesses from the Anglican Rev. Thomas Dawson in Perry, *Historical Collections*, 1: 381.

40. Brockwell, letters of 18 February 1741 and 28 July 1744 to the Secretary of the SPG, in Perry, *Historical Collections*, 3: 353, 387.

41. Chauncy, *Letter to Wishart*, p. 24.

42. Samuel Chandler's diary, quoted in Goen, *Revivalism and Separatism*, p. 181.

43. O. E. Winslow, *Meetinghouse Hill* (1952), p. 232, quoted in Hofstadter, *America at 1750*, p. 283.

44. Chandler's diary, quoted in Goen, *Revivalism and Separatism*, pp. 181–82.

45. Jonathan Edwards, *Faithful Narrative*, p. 189.

46. See Tolles, "Quietism versus Enthusiasm," pp. 38 and 40. Tolles draws another parallel, that both movements "recruited their members . . . largely from the lower classes" so that "[i]n the popular mind both groups were associated with the idea of social revolution" (43). Given that revivalism was "a movement which was in such large measure a republication of their own religion of spiritual illumination," Tolles attributes the Quakers' aversion to the evangelicals to the fact that the latter's emphasis upon instantaneous conversion ("inspirational automatism") recalled the enthusiasm, repudiated by the mid–eighteenth century, of the early Quakers (44, 45).

47. My pairing of charisma with centrifugal movement (to describe the effects of Calvinist, but not Quaker, itinerancy) is discussed by Max Weber in *Economy and Society*. Analyzing the ways in which rational discipline works to diminish charismatic power, Weber observes, "It is the fate of charisma to recede before the powers of tradition or of rational association after it has entered the permanent structures of social action. This waning of charisma generally indicates the diminishing impor-

tance of individual action" (1148–49). For the applicability of Weber's observation to the seventeenth-century transformation of charismatic into corporate Quakerism, see Richard Bauman, *Let Your Words Be Few*, chapter 9. Bauman observes of that transformation that "the structures and mechanisms of corporate control and the formal and stylistic conventions for ministerial discourse that emerged in the process of routinization came into play to channel, constrain, and guide the originally unfettered *speaking* of the prophetic ministry" (151). See also Elias Canetti, *Crowds and Power*, pp. 24–25.

48. John Woolman, *The Journal of John Woolman*, p. 23. Page numbers will appear hereafter in the text.

49. The account of seventeenth-century Quaker John Crook illustrates this disarticulation: "Out of the mouth of [the] seed of eternal life, would words proceed within me as I sat in the meetings with God's people, and at other times, which I was moved to utter with my tongue often times in the cross to my own will, as seeming to my earthly wisdom to be void of wisdom, and most contemptible to my natural understanding, not knowing the end why I should keep such words: yet I was charged with disobedience, and deeply afflicted and troubled in my spirit, when I neglected to speak them forth; and sometimes some others have spoken the same words, while I was doubting in the reasoning about them; and then I was much exercised, that it should be taken from me, and given to another that was faithful." Quoted in Bauman, *Let Your Words Be Few*, p. 133.

50. Cf. the explanation supplied by Tolles, "Quietism versus Enthusiasm."

51. Jonathan Edwards, "Unpublished Letter [to Rev. Benjamin Colman]," p. 99.

52. Thomas Prince described Edwards as a "Preacher of a low and moderate Voice, a natural Way of Delivery; and without any Agitation of Body, or any Thing else in the Manner to excite Attention; except his habitual and great *Solemnity*, looking and speaking as in the Presence of GOD, and with a weighty Sense of the Matter delivered" ("Some Account," pp. 390–91).

53. Edwards, *Faithful Narrative*, p. 206; "Unpublished Letter," p. 109. Page references to *Faithful Narrative* will hereafter appear in the text. Edwards calls melancholy "a distemper that the family are very prone to"; it is important to note that Hawley was Edwards's uncle by marriage. On Hawley's suicide and its aftermath in the form of Hawley Jr.'s enmity against Edwards, whose sermons apparently fed Hawley Sr.'s melancholy tendencies, see Perry Miller, *Jonathan Edwards*, pp. 103–4.

54. On the numbers of children reported by New Light preachers to be experiencing conversion, the Quakers, significantly, responded with skepticism. The Quaker John Smith accounted such reports among the revivalists' greatest "delusions." "I have seen a boy younger [than six] imitate a preacher very nicely," he wrote a friend, "use unexceptionable words, and deliver himself as if he was affected with what he said—but I count it as no miracle. Who does not know that children of that age, by example and tuition, are capable of imitating almost anything?" He concluded his commentary on such reports by observing that "[e]ven a parrot may be taught to

speak some few words, but he cannot give any rational account of the cause of those words. Why? Because he is destitute of the power of reflection and so incapable of understanding the difference between causes and their effects" (quoted in Tolles, "Quietism versus Enthusiasm," p. 35).

55. Edwards, "Unpublished Letter," p. 110.

56. Edwards's *Some Thoughts* indicates that this continued to be a problem: Edwards admonishes his adherents against praying for obviously unconverted people to die forthwith and be sent to hell before they can do any more harm. Edwards asks, "And why don't ministers direct sinners to pray for themselves, that God would either convert them or kill them, and send them to hell now before their guilt is greater? In this way we should lead persons in the next place to self-murder, for many probably would soon begin to think that that which they may pray for, they may seek, and use the means of" (482). The definition of conscience appears in *Distinguishing Marks*, p. 251. On revivalism and suicide, see also the letter of 3 June 1742 from the Anglican George Ross to the Secretary of the SPG in Perry, *Historical Collections*, 5: 85.

57. Chauncy, "Letter to Davenport," p. v.

58. Charles Brockden Brown, *Wieland and Memoirs of Carwin the Biloquist*, p. 1. Page numbers will hereafter appear in the text. Fliegelman's introduction to this edition of *Wieland* provides an excellent overview of the novel's major issues. Also relevant are Fliegelman's *Prodigals and Pilgrims* and especially *Declaring Independence*.

59. On domestic political violence in the 1790s, see Howe, "Republican Thought"; John L. Brooke, "To the Quiet of the People: Revolutionary Settlement and Civil Unrest in Western Massachusetts, 1774–1789"; Thomas P. Slaughter, *The Whiskey Rebellion: Frontier Epilogue to the American Revolution*; and the collection of primary and secondary texts in Steven R. Boyd, ed., *The Whiskey Rebellion: Past and Present Perspectives*. On radical unrest in Philadelphia, see Steven Rosswurm, " 'As a Lyen out of His Den': Philadelphia's Popular Movement, 1776–80"; cf. Henry F. May, *The Enlightenment in America*, pp. 243–45.

60. On the positive side of this discovery urged by midcentury rhetoricians whose writings spurred the "elocutionary revolution" of the last quarter of the eighteenth century, see Fliegelman, *Declaring Independence*, pp. 28–35. For this group of rhetoricians, including Thomas Sheridan, James Burgh, and Hugh Blair, meaning was inherent in the affective manner of utterance and not the words of which the utterance was constituted. Far from amounting to a radical separation of matter and manner, then, manner (or style) could not be separated out from matter; "natural" or "naked language," as Fliegelman points out, "embodies rather than represents thought [and thus] turns language into something that is simultaneously body and dress" (35). It is interesting with respect to Brown's *Wieland* that Fliegelman interprets the elocutionary revolution as, in part, opposed to the Ciceronian assumption that rhetoric should limit itself to ceremonial occasions, "drawn from set topics or commonplaces" rather than "the facts of the case under debate" (29).

61. Emily Dickinson, Poem 822 in *The Complete Poems of Emily Dickinson*, p. 399.

62. Bernard Bailyn identifies precisely this period with the greatest political tensions in *The Ideological Origins of the American Revolution*, p. 22.

63. This passage is interesting in the context of what Fliegelman calls "natural theatricality." See *Declaring Independence*, pp. 79–89, esp. p. 80.

64. Michel Chion, "The Impossible Embodiment," pp. 206 n. 1, 197. Chion's *La Voix au Cinéma* offers a fuller discussion of acousmatics as it functions in film; see esp. pp. 25–33.

65. On the ubiquity of this question in the novel, see Walter Hesford, "'Do You Know the Author?': The Question of Authorship in *Wieland*." Hesford's thesis is that the novel "deconstruct[s] the idea of single authorship, and, with it, belief in a single, authoritative source of meaning and action" (239).

66. The concept of artistic space is elaborated by Iurii M. Lotman in "Problema khudozhestvennogo prostranstva v proze Gogolia" (The problem of artistic space in the prose of Gogol). Interestingly, Lotman's analysis of Gogol's representation of the estate, or "the inside world," in his story "The Old-fashioned Landowners" recalls Brown's representation of Mettingen: "The inside world is achronic. On all sides, it is isolated; it has no direction; and nothing occurs within it. Actions refer neither to the past nor to the present, but represent multiple repetitions of one and the same thing. . . . Unchangingness is a property of . . . inside space, and change is possible only as the catastrophic destruction of this space" (428, 429, my translation). Lotman's analysis is also relevant for his focus upon "the path" versus "the road," an opposition whose moral valence approaches Brown's "mazy path" versus the "blissful" or "forth-right path." For an analysis of doubling and its relation to coincidence, see Norman S. Grabo, *The Coincidental Art of Charles Brockden Brown*. See also Roland Hagenbüchle, "American Literature and the Nineteenth-Century Crisis in Epistemology," pp. 138–51, and William J. Scheick, "The Problem of Origination in Brown's *Ormond*."

67. On the "third ontological domain," see Lorraine Daston, "Marvelous Facts," p. 99.

68. Bartlett, *False and Seducing Teachers*, p. 42.

69. Bartlett, *False and Seducing Teachers*, p. 29; cf. pp. 38–40, and the related text earlier in this chapter.

70. The scene is reminiscent of that in which the narrator of Hawthorne's *Scarlet Letter* exhumes the literally disembodied letter once attached by gold thread to Hester Prynne's bosom. For a suggestion that this scene resembles the opening of Georges Poulet's "Phenomenology of Reading," see Hesford, "Authorship in *Wieland*," p. 240.

71. See, for example, Brown's preface, "To the Public," to his novel *Edgar Huntley*, p. 3.

72. On Zinzendorf and the German pietists of provincial Pennsylvania, see Delbanco, *Puritan Ordeal*, pp. 246–47.

73. For a contemporary account of how Cicero provides young men with a model for ideal republican citizenry, see Joseph Stevens Buckminster, "The Dangers and

NOTES TO PAGE 222

Duties of Men of Letters," pp. 99–100. The classicist Jennifer Roberts makes the point that in his speeches, Cicero portrayed Athenian democracy as mob rule; see "The Creation of a Legacy: A Manufactured Crisis in Eighteenth-Century Thought," esp. p. 85.

74. Brown gave several indications that his choice of Cicero for Wieland's obsession was ironic. For one thing, as Brown portrays him in 1789, Cicero himself had suffered from Wieland's disease. "There never was a genius," Brown maintained in "The Rhapsodist," "that rested satisfied with its own exertions, for it is the lot of genius only to form an idea of perfection, which, though all its ambition be directed to that single object, it shall never be able to realize. Thus it was, that Cicero conceived a character of perfect eloquence, adorned with every accomplishment that mind or body is capable of possessing. He described an impossible assemblage of virtues, and surveyed with fondness a picture, to which there was no original or resemblance among mortals" (9). In "Remarks on Style," Brown named Cicero as, with Johnson, an "eminent literary manneris[t]" who "considered [his] eloquence as a deceptive art." More "censurable" than Johnson, Cicero, Brown claims, "in the most solemn acts of life, and before the tribunal of justice, . . . confesses to have protected and saved the life of many a criminal by the power of his eloquence," a statement that reflects ironically upon Wieland's obsession with restoring purity to the Ciceronian text (102, 103).

75. On the appeal of the classical writers of the Roman Enlightenment for the revolutionary generation, see Gordon S. Wood, *Creation of the American Republic*, pp. 48–53. In his rehearsals of Ciceronian orations, Wieland was apparently in good company: Bailyn reports that educated colonists "found their ideal selves, and to some extent their voices" in the classical authors, especially Cicero, and that the "enraptured" John Adams, as a young man, "declaimed aloud, alone at night in his room" Cicero's Catilinarian orations (*Ideological Origins*, p. 26). Cf. Meyer Reinhold, *Classica Americana: The Greek and Roman Heritage in the United States*, pp. 150 and 155, which point to Cicero's usefulness as a model of private and public virtue. The detail is interesting in the context provided by Wood in the penultimate chapter of *Creation of the American Republic*, "The Relevance and Irrelevance of John Adams," pp. 567–92. See also Fliegelman's observations on the anti-Ciceronian bent of "the elocutionary revolution" of the period, a rejection of Cicero's "ornamental" rhetorical style for "one of heartfelt persuasion [that] stemmed from a culture at once republican and evangelical," in *Declaring Independence*, p. 38. The fact that Wieland devotes himself to Cicero within the vacuum of Mettingen casts his obsession as a particularly vivid instance of aristocratic decadence, the gentleman's remove from real political fire, that came under popular attack during the 1790s, the age Wood associates with the "democratization of the American mind" (see Wood, "The Democratization of Mind in the American Revolution").

76. For an account of the ambiguousness of this war, see Edwin Sill Fussell, "*Wieland*: A Literary and Historical Reading," p. 186 n. 9.

77. As Christopher Looby observes, the way of life established by Wieland Sr. represents "the limit case of the displacement of a decaying public sphere by private familial life" (*Voicing America*, p. 152). Alternatively, one might characterize life at Mettingen before Carwin's arrival as an agoraphobic's paradise — one might see the happily incarcerated Wielands as anticipating nineteenth-century domestic ideology as an alternative to the excessive vitality of the public sphere. See Gillian Brown, *Domestic Individualism: Imagining Self in Nineteenth-Century America*.

78. In *Democratic Vistas*, Whitman would confess himself haunted by a vision of America composed of "conflicting and irreconcilable interiors" (368).

79. See de Certeau, *Practice of Everyday Life*, chapter 10 ("The Scriptural Economy"), esp. p. 138, for an insight into the genesis of a figure like Carwin and what drives him "to make himself the master of a space and to set himself up as a producer of writing."

80. On the thematic significance of this particular oration as featuring Cicero "at his most brilliantly specious," see Looby, *Voicing America*, pp. 161, 163.

81. For a discussion of Brown's relation to the postrevolutionary myth of an originating Saxon democracy predating and undermining the authority of Britain, see Looby, *Voicing America*, pp. 154–58.

82. Cf. Brown's own swoon into antinomianism as the enabling condition of authorship, as he represents it in "The Rhapsodist": calling himself "a hearty convert" to the belief in apparitions, he denies that he is superstitious or melancholy as a result. Instead, "[a]n interview with one of those preternatural forms is conceived in idea without disquiet or uneasiness, and is actually enjoyed without trepidation or dismay. He [i.e., Brown's persona himself] is void of terror at this tremendous moment, because he is sensible that their intents are charitable, and that they approach, accompanied by airs from heaven. Wrapt in silent ecstasy at some transporting moment, he is carried 'beyond the visible diurnal sphere:' the barrier between him and the world of spirits, has for a moment yielded to the force of heart-thrilling meditation: the film is removed from his eyes, and he beholds his attending genius, or guardian angel, arrayed in ambrosial weeds, and smiling with gracious benignity upon the bold attempts of the adventurous pupil" (7–8).

83. Ziff makes the crucial point that Lockean optimism, which he refers to as "scientific enthusiasm," in this novel is linked to sentimentalism, and that the novel, in undermining the premises of the one, undermines the premises of the other. See "A Reading of *Wieland*," esp. p. 54.

84. See Michael Warner, *Letters of the Republic*, chapter 5, esp. pp. 126, 129, 122.

85. In "Remarks on Style," Brown will assert that "style" and "thinking" are commonly disjunct: "some argue," he writes, "in favour of a natural style, and reiterate the opinion of many great critics, that proper ideas will be accompanied by proper words. But this observation, though supported by the first authorities, is not perhaps sufficiently clear. Writers may think justly and write offensively; and a pleasing style may accompany a vacuity of thought. Does not this evident fact prove that style and

thinking have not that inseparable connection which many great writers have pronounced?" (102).

86. In his article "The Symbolism of Literary Alienation in the Revolutionary Age," Lewis P. Simpson suggests a related way of reading the meaning of Carwin's face as inverted cone. Discussing Brown's characterization of the contemporary author in his inaugural essay "The Rhapsodist" (1789), Simpson notes that although (like Carwin) the Rhapsodist "has come to Philadelphia from some remote western spot [where] he has cultivated the life of the man of letters in solitary independence," yet he represents himself upon his arrival as deferring entirely to his master, the reading public, and assuming the role of vassal eager above all to demonstrate his sincerity. "Displaying an inverted pride — his gross flattery of his readers hiding his resentment, and perhaps his disdain, of them — the Rhapsodist bows to the author's dependence on the public in the age of printing and democracy" (96). The *ressentiment* of Carwin may thus be seen as related to Clara's and Brown's repeated bids for vindication from their readers.

87. For a discussion of the significance in the American Gothic of the woman's home as asylum, see Cathy N. Davidson, *Revolution and the Word*, p. 222.

88. Carwin confesses his attractions to *"the temple"* on p. 227 and to Clara's summerhouse on pp. 231–32, where he describes for her how he felt uneasy at the thought that he "should be deprived of my retreat; or, at least, interrupted in the possession of it" by her unexpected use of the space, an interruption which interrupts his possession of her maid, Judith, with whom Carwin conducts "midnight interviews" there (232). Judith is the "common" woman in the kitchen who facilitates her lover's encroachments on Clara's privacy.

89. On sincerity, see Fliegelman, *Declaring Independence*, and Trilling's classic discussion in *Sincerity and Authenticity*.

90. Even the insignificant detail of the unrehearsed play bears witness to the degree of specular doubling in the novel.

91. On disorderly walkers, cf. Bartlett, *False and Seducing Teachers*, p. 42.

92. Cf. Hagenbüchle, "Crisis in Epistemology," who also finds that Clara's self is "radically destroyed . . . at the very moment Pleyel lost faith in her [when he] began to assume the possibility that there were two Claras" (133).

93. Ziff views the trial scene as providing evidence that one of Brown's key achievements in this novel is his critique of the sentimental tradition in which *Wieland* seems superficially to participate. The trial scene demonstrates "an ex-sentimentalist's [Clara's] failure to communicate with the lover still bound by that tradition [Pleyel]" ("A Reading of *Wieland*," p. 53).

94. As Fussell notes, Clara resembles nothing so much here as she does the Constitution and the institutions to which it gave rise: "like them, Clara was worth writing down; Pleyel sounds like an infatuated version of *The Federalist Papers*" ("*Wieland*," p. 179).

95. Leslie Fiedler first observed that Charles Brockden Brown was "the inventor

of the American writer, for he not only lived that role but turned it into a myth." See his classic study, "Charles Brockden Brown and the Invention of the American Gothic," esp. p. 145.

96. Cotton Mather, *Diary*, 1: 23.

97. Cf. Fussell, *"Wieland,"* who sees Brown as having written "a diatribe against writing" for, if nothing else, writing may be seen as having instigated the American Revolution which then placed upon Brown the imperative to write the new nation. However, "within that context he split the indictment in order to show an irresponsible writer wreaking havoc and wretchedness on a hapless populace while quite another kind of writer—his kind—was quietly restoring a semblance of reason and peace to such of those people as chanced to survive. *Wieland* is a furious contest between villainous confused Carwin and our doughty daughter of the American Revolution, Clara Wieland, Brown's narrator. Clara wins, but the price of her victory is exile. Having finished her novel, she removes to Europe, never more to confront the monstrosity of these States" (172–73).

98. I use the adjective "disarticulating" to convey Clara's description of the impact the disembodied voice has upon her body: "It appeared to cut asunder the fibres of my brain, and rack every joint with agony" (97).

99. Nathaniel Hawthorne, *The Scarlet Letter*, pp. 40, 39, 40, 50, 39.

100. As Wieland insists that God authored his acts, Clara will insist that "the author of evil" authored, or at least provoked, hers. Paul De Man's "Excuses" analyzes "the deviousness of the excuse pattern" by showing how it "occurs within an epistemological twilight zone between knowing and not-knowing" (287, 286). It thus provides a provocative gloss upon this point, as well as upon the very similar excuses for spying on Clara copiously produced by both Pleyel and Carwin.

101. Carwin's admission that his culpability must be limited to his uncontrolled curiosity makes him the victim—of the false and seducing teacher, as so many Old Lights had warned would occur if curiosity was indulged. Curiosity, in their view, ended in conviction. Another consideration to add: Carwin admits to Clara as part of his confession that after she had seen his face in the act of utterance on her staircase, he had fled Mettingen, like Adam discovered in his transgression, "covered with the shame of this detection" (244). Clara's vision of Carwin in the ventriloquistic act, then, is the equivalent of Carwin's illicit scrutiny of Clara's diary, the materialization of her "inmost soul" whose "possession" gives Carwin the benefit of a knowledge of Clara "more accurate" than "conjugal intimacies" (235, 234).

102. Carwin's description of himself here fulfills the recipe for vulgarity to which conservatives from Old Lights to Federalists subscribed. His account of his powers here differs from his more confident description of the ventriloquist's art that he provides the Mettingen congregation upon first learning from them of the strange voices (86–87). In an article from 1806 entitled "What Is Literary Genius?" Brown, in refuting the idea that geniuses are born and not made, insists that "Man *creates* by *imitation*" (253). Moreover, he claims that genius is the product of chance events:

"When men of letters reflect on the manner of their own attainments, and on the literary history of others, they discover that the faculties of the mind are not *gifts* of nature, but effects of human causes, or *acquisitions* of art." "Every man of common organization," then, "has the power of becoming a man of genius, if to this he add a solitary devotion to his art, and a vehement passion for glory" as well as "the capacity of long attention"; "nature is more impartial than some of her children allow" (249). In this respect, Carwin exemplifies Brown's democratic idea of the genius.

103. Clara more forthrightly expresses her will to survive her brother, as when (on p. 260) she marvels that with all her tribulations, "still I consent to live!" while she finds (on p. 263) that, given her brother's comparable woes, she cannot wish for the "continuance of [his] being."

104. One might say that Clara has appropriated for herself a strategy she had initially attributed to Carwin, that he "had constructed his plot in a manner suited to the characters of those whom he had selected for his victims" (153). And this, of course, echoes Moses Bartlett, *False and Seducing Teachers*, pp. 22–26 (where he argues that the carnally minded are especially susceptible) and pp. 38–44 (where he notes the resemblance between false teachers and their followers).

105. See Grabo, *The Coincidental Art of Charles Brockden Brown*, pp. 23–29.

CHAPTER FIVE

1. In the introduction to *The Democratization of American Christianity*, Nathan O. Hatch elaborates three reasons why "the popular religious movements of the early republic articulated a profoundly democratic spirit" (9). First, they refused to defer to the educated clergy, associated virtue with the common people, and privileged the vernacular in speaking to or about God. Second, they encouraged "increased supernatural involvement in everyday life" in the form of dreams and visions as well as their public revelation (to the chagrin of conservatives who warned against " 'publish[ing] such visions] to the world' " [10]). Third, Hatch notes the general perception of the uncontainability of such movements which, in their zeal to challenge established ecclesiastical authority, "had little sense of their limitations" (10). As I have shown in the first four chapters of this study, these features distinguish colonial demonstrations of religious enthusiasm as well, suggesting that the "democratic spirit" significantly predated the Revolution. Like Hatch, Robert H. Wiebe identifies the Revolution, in conjunction with the Second Great Awakening, as initiating American democracy, claiming that eighteenth-century radicalism (including the First Great Awakening) was unable to sustain its antiauthoritarian force. But, like Hatch's, his description of the Second Great Awakening's exceptional revolutionary power applies substantially to what occurred in the forty years preceding the Revolution. See *Self-Rule*, pp. 17–19.

2. See Warner, *Letters of the Republic*, p. 129. Warner claims that "the problem of

the self-erasing center," in which "the same rhetoric that claims to base government on 'the wills of the people' is the rhetoric that conceives itself as mechanically fitting those wills together," only *appears* to be "the hegemonic problem of theory in a democratic movement" (129). In my view, the resemblance is far more than superficial: it bears witness to the uneasy relationship of the democratic to the republican which will continue through the transformation of republican into liberal ideology. In *Revolution and the Word*, Cathy Davidson amply documents the same center-periphery metaphorics in critical discussions of the rise of the novel, most obviously those which associated the genre with the lower classes. The novel's emergence, she claims, was itself the expression of a broad-based challenge to authority.

3. The historiography on each of these issues is enormous, and I can indicate here only the texts that have been particularly helpful to me in refining my understanding of them. On the democratizing effects of the Revolution, see Gordon Wood, esp. "The Democratization of Mind in the American Revolution" and *The Radicalism of the American Revolution*. Also useful is the collection of articles edited by Jack P. Greene, *The Reinterpretation of the American Revolution, 1763–1789*, esp. Jackson Turner Main's "Government by the People: The American Revolution and the Democratization of the Legislatures" (323–38) and R. R. Palmer's "The American Revolution: The People as Constituent Power" (338–61). On the American adaptation of European Enlightenment thought, see Bernard Bailyn, *The Ideological Origins of the American Revolution*; Henry F. May, *The Enlightenment in America*; J. G. A. Pocock, *The Machiavellian Moment*; and Lance Banning, *The Jeffersonian Persuasion*. For a corrective to our historical understanding of the agrarian myth, see Joyce Appleby, "The 'Agrarian Myth' in the Early Republic," in *Liberalism and Republicanism in the Historical Imagination*. On the elocutionary revolution, see Jay Fliegelman, *Declaring Independence: Jefferson, Natural Language, and the Culture of Performance*. The slogan *vox populi, vox Dei* was first recorded in a letter the English scholar and theologian Alcuin wrote to Charlemagne in 800 in which he denies the truth of the popular saying: "And those people should not be listened to who keep saying the voice of the people is the voice of God, since the riotousness of the crowd is always very close to madness" (*Nec audiendi qui solent dicere, Vox populi, vox Dei, quum tumultuositas vulgi semper insaniae proxima sit*); see the third edition of the *Oxford Dictionary of Quotations* (1980), p. 3. Charles Brockden Brown entitled his early political tract on the subject of women's rights *Alcuin*.

4. On the internalization of strife, cf. also Norman O. Brown, "Liberty," in *Love's Body*, pp. 3–31.

5. See Steven Rosswurm, " 'As a Lyen out of His Den': Philadelphia's Popular Movement, 1776–80," for an account of the political self-empowerment of "the radical 'lower sort' " during and after the Revolution. Also pertinent is Thomas P. Slaughter, *The Whiskey Rebellion: Frontier Epilogue to the American Revolution*, and Steven R. Boyd, ed., *The Whiskey Rebellion: Past and Present Perspectives*.

6. Gordon S. Wood names "fears of democracy" as "the fixation of the Federalist

party in the 1790's" ("Democratization of Mind," p. 77). On civil unrest, see Howe, "Republican Thought"; John L. Brooke, "To the Quiet of the People: Revolutionary Settlement and Civil Unrest in Western Massachusetts, 1774–1789"; Slaughter, *The Whiskey Rebellion*; and Boyd, ed., *The Whiskey Rebellion*.

7. Regarding the agentless popular voice, Gordon S. Wood quotes an anonymous writer for the Baltimore *Maryland Journal* for 3 August 1787 as asking in exasperation, what do "those who are continually declaiming about *the people, the people* . . . mean by the people?" "No part of the government, even their representatives, seemed capable of embodying them" (*Creation of the American Republic*, p. 398). The most thorough and subtle account of the political context for *Wieland* is Jay Fliegelman's "Introduction." Cf. Jane Tompkins, *Sensational Designs*, pp. 40–61, who finds that Brown's aim in writing the novel was to warn Americans of the "horrifying consequences" of revolution; and Warner Berthoff, "Brockden Brown: The Politics of the Man of Letters," who attributes to Brown a "suprapolitical" liberal Federalism mixed (the legacy of his Quaker upbringing) with "a preference for a truly communal democracy" (6, 9). Charles C. Cole Jr. claims that although in 1797, when he published the politically radical women's rights tract *Alcuin*, Brown was affiliated with Jeffersonian democracy, by the following year he had converted to Federalist politics; see "Brockden Brown and the Jefferson Administration." Christopher Looby has recently suggested how Brown's aborted career in the law, undertaken between 1787 and 1793 (between the writing of the American Constitution and the acceleration of revolutionary violence in France), and his exposure during those years to legal theories such as James Wilson's Philadelphia lectures concerning the so-called "revolution principle" and his philosophy of evidence, may explain his conservative ("counter-revolutionary") anxieties about the power of voice so prominent in *Wieland*; see *Voicing America*, pp. 188–92, 202. In particular, Looby persuasively claims, the novel reads "like a critical commentary" on Wilson's thirteenth lecture for the College of Philadelphia, "Of the Nature and Philosophy of Evidence," in which he argues for the primacy and reliability of information transmitted by the senses (190). The designation of democracy as an "uncontrolled" and "unrestricted" political force appears in Fisher Ames's 1801 essay "Equality," p. 212. On the political ambivalence of the Friendly Society of New York to which Brown belonged until it disbanded in 1798, see May, *The Enlightenment in America*, pp. 233–35.

8. Brown himself characterized authorship as ventriloquy in his first published piece, "The Rhapsodist." There he defined "*an author*" as one "who speaks, as it were from behind a curtain. And while he reveals himself to our view only in the most engaging attitudes, may, by the help of his disguise, render the unfavourable parts of his character perfectly secure from the searching eye of curiosity" (16–17).

9. Cf. Emerson, "The American Scholar" (1837): "The state of society," the atomized remains of an original wholeness, "is one in which the members have suffered amputation from the trunk, and strut about so many walking monsters, — a good finger, a neck, a stomach, an elbow, but never a man" (64).

10. The historians J. G. A. Pocock and Gordon S. Wood make precisely this point with reference to representational politics as it was adapted to the American context in the era in which Brown wrote. See Pocock, *Machiavellian Moment*, pp. 513–26, esp. pp. 516, 517; and Wood, *Creation of the American Republic*, pp. 363–89, 409–13, 596–600. See also Wood, "Democratization of Mind," pp. 75–77.

11. Herman Melville, *Billy Budd, Sailor*, p. 43.

12. For a discussion of how readerships, which, like authorships, had expanded in the late eighteenth century beyond the purview of a cultural elite, could place pressure upon an author by demanding "useful knowledge and rewarding amusement" from their reading as well as "presuming to judge whether they were worthwhile and thus wresting interpretation from the authors," see Ziff, *Writing in the New Nation*, pp. 31–33, esp. p. 33. On Brown's guilt, see Hagenbüchle, "Crisis in Epistemology," esp. p. 138; Maurice Bennett, "Charles Brockden Brown's Ambivalence Toward Art and Imagination," esp. p. 61; and Fussell, "*Wieland*."

13. "An Account of a Murder Committed by Mr. J——— Y———, Upon His Family, in December, A.D. 1781" was printed in the *New York Weekly Magazine* in 1796. There are indeed several parallels: Yates effaces his wife to ensure that she won't recover; he fails in his attempt to kill his sister, who manages to restrain him; he escapes several times from imprisonment; and he also disdains any suggestion that he should confess himself in error or repent. Shirley Samuels offers another possible historical source, the *Narrative of the Life of William Beadle* (1796); Beadle killed his wife and four children and then committed suicide because of financial failure. See Samuels, "Wieland: Alien and Infidel," pp. 58–60.

14. The narrator of "Account of a Murder" suggests that the event "is beyond the conception of human beings." He raises and rejects the possibility of insanity, and concludes "that [Yates] was under a strong delusion of Satan": "But what avail our conjectures, perhaps it is best that some things are concealed from us, and the only use we can now make of our knowledge of this affair, is to be humble under a scene of human frailty to renew our petition, 'Lead us not into temptation' " (28).

15. For an excellent treatment of the epistemological crisis in *Wieland* and its relation both to the European Gothic and realistic novels as well as the antebellum canon, see Hagenbüchle, "Crisis in Epistemology." On the democratic nature of this crisis and its direct association with a crisis of authorship, see Simpson, "The Symbolism of Literary Alienation in the Revolutionary Age." Simpson discusses the problematic identification of the republican "man of letters" with "the protean image of public mind or public opinion" (91). Its " 'secret influence' " (in the words of Federalist Joseph Buckminster), issuing from "the breasts of thousands," and its inability to discriminate public intention from private motive, posed a direct threat to the Republic of Letters with which the republican author wished unambiguously to associate himself (86). The result, Simpson shows, is the depletion of literary authority as the role of the man of letters in republican culture becomes increasingly ambiguous. In *The Idea of Authorship in America*, Kenneth Dauber also traces a depletion of literary authority, particularly in the years between Benjamin Franklin's authorship and

Charles Brockden Brown's. Dauber reads Brown's "Advertisement" as evidence for the disintegration of the writer-audience bond Franklin enjoyed and which authorized his writing, compelling Brown "to establish authorship not as prior, but as democratic" — that is, as struggling perpetually to negotiate the gap "between eccentricity and representativity" (53, 54). See also pp. 54–65.

16. For a thorough account of American anxieties regarding the rise of fiction, particularly as they referred to the involvement of women in the production and reception of the novel in the late eighteenth through the mid–nineteenth centuries, see Davidson's extensive study of early American fiction, *Revolution and the Word*, esp. chapters 3 and 4. See also pp. 236–39, as well as the analysis of *Arthur Mervyn* on pp. 239–53, for a discussion of the ideological, and specifically the class, significance of Brown's decision to write Gothic novels at the close of the Federalist era. Davidson's intriguing point in her study's eighth chapter is that for its creators, and Brown in particular, the American "Gothic might be rooted in the very essentials of American democracy" (237). Also useful is William Charvat, *The Origins of American Critical Thought*, esp. chapters 2 and 7. On republican anxieties about the truth-value of aesthetic writing in the early national period, see David Simpson, *The Politics of American English, 1776–1850*, pp. 138–39. See also Catherine Gallagher's account of the fear of fiction in *Nobody's Story*, esp. chapter 6.

17. This circumstance was discussed by William H. Prescott in his biography of Brown in the context of the question of whether or not Brown should have attempted to explain his *"supernaturalities"* in his "Advertisement." Wouldn't it be better, Prescott asked, "to trust to the willing superstition and credulity of the reader . . . , than to attempt a solution on purely natural or mechanical principles"? Both the ancients and the old English dramatists were willing to place their "ghosts and witches . . . in the much more perilous predicament of being subjected to the scrutiny of the spectator, whose senses are not near so likely to be duped, as the sensitive and excited imagination of the reader in his solitary chamber." But Brown's explanations of ventriloquism as the cause of events in the novel, intended to calm the reader's imagination in advance of reading, does not at all speak to the "sublimity and general effect of the narrative" but casts an ironic shadow upon everything that transpires. See Prescott, "Life of Charles Brockden Brown" (1834), pp. 142, 143, 146.

18. Thus despite the claims of the "Advertisement," Prescott found Carwin to be "contradictory, unnatural, and devilish"; quoted by Rufus Wilmot Griswold, "Charles Brockden Brown," p. 108. Interestingly, although Griswold admits that "no critic has hitherto taken a different view" on the subject, he himself is more inclined to entertain Brown's explanations for Carwin's peculiar power as well as his own claim to being an "anatomist of the mind" (109).

19. Prescott, "Life of Brown," p. 162. On Brown's ventriloquistic authorship, particularly with reference to the anti-Jeffersonian political tracts he published (in some cases anonymously) after his series of novels, see Looby, *Voicing America*, pp. 193–202.

20. William Ellery Channing, "Remarks on National Literature," pp. 346, 347,

348. Charles Jared Ingersoll would conflate print with oratory in his 1823 claim that Americans, "through the vivid medium of a free press, constitute, as it were, an auditory greatly superior to that of any other nation." Elsewhere he insisted that "crowds of listeners are continually collected in all parts of this country to hear eloquent speeches and sermons," occasions on which always "the orator is inspired, the auditor is absorbed." See "Discourse Concerning the Influence of America on the Mind," pp. 258, 260. Washington Irving would complain in 1839 that "the mystic operation of anonymous writing" had elevated the critic to an unmerited position of authority: "his crude decisions, fulminated through the press, become circulated far and wide, control the opinions of the world, and give or destroy reputation." See "Desultory Thoughts on Criticism," p. 176.

21. Charles Brockden Brown, "The Rhapsodist," p. 1. In this essay, Brown also inhabits the position of the possessed, except that he rejects the notion of an evil specter for the same reason Increase Mather did: "He [the rhapsodist] believes it derogatory to the majesty of the supreme being; nay, he holds it to be a thing utterly impossible that an evil spirit should be suffered to escape from his dungeon, or that God's own messengers should be dispatched upon errands hurtful or pernicious to the sons of men." He has no objection, however, to holding conference with "preter-natural forms" because he understands that they are sent by God and "accompanied by airs from heaven." His antinomian faith is rewarded: he sees that "the barrier between him and the world of spirits, has for a moment yielded to the force of heart-thrilling meditation: the film is removed from his eyes, and he beholds his attending genius, or guardian angel, arrayed in ambrosial weeds, and smiling with gracious benignity upon the bold attempts of the adventurous pupil" (7–8, 8).

22. Brown, "The Rhapsodist," pp. 5, 1. Wordsworth's claim, "a Poet . . . is a man speaking to men," is in "Preface to *Lyrical Ballads* (1802)," p. 603.

23. Lewis P. Simpson, "The Symbolism of Literary Alienation in the Revolutionary Age," esp. pp. 94–97.

24. Brown, "The Rhapsodist," p. 16. The entire essay represents the author's attempt to escape into character, an effort impeded by the fact that he can't quite characterize the character into whom he wishes to escape. Simpson maintains that Brown betrays a concern to represent the author as innocent through the eponymous character who is either "a representation of the American storyteller and man of letters as an 'innocent' [or] a pretender to innocence" ("Symbolism of Literary Alienation," pp. 98–99).

25. Stephen Burroughs, *The Memoirs of Stephen Burroughs*. Page references for this work will henceforth be given in the text. For the publication history, see p. ix. of Gura's introduction in which he claims that the text is "arguably one of the more popular personal narratives between the Revolution and the Civil War" (x). See also Ziff, *Writing in the New Nation*, pp. 59–71. Ziff provides an interesting parallel between Burroughs and both Godwin's Caleb Williams and Benjamin Franklin on pp. 67–71.

26. As Davidson has shown, the "reluctance to be identified as an author" was somewhat of a convention in the period, with the majority of authors remaining anonymous. Davidson proposes several motives for the "ambivalence of early authorship," which was especially acute for women authors, on pp. 31–32 of *Revolution and the Word.*

27. See Ziff, *Writing in the New Nation*, p. 66. Ziff argues that the advent of print and the decline of oral culture in the revolutionary and postrevolutionary eras, signaled by the increasing popularity of the novel beginning with Benjamin Franklin's publication of Richardson's *Pamela* in 1740, both determined and bore witness to the substitution of "immanence," wherein all created reality including the self is divinely given, with "representation," wherein reality is created from moment to moment and individual to individual (14–17). Within this context, a character like Burroughs, although "he represented himself as other than what he really was . . . in each of these representations he successfully became what he represented himself to be" (60). This tension is explicit in an argument between Burroughs and a "sober-faced clergyman": the clergyman chastises him for his "vile hypocrisy" in "assuming that character" of a clergyman which, "of all others, . . . ought to be held most sacred." Burroughs reminds the clergyman that, as "the ambassador and representative of him, who has commanded us, 'in lowliness of mind to esteem others better than ourselves,' " he was at least as guilty as Burroughs of betraying the true character of a clergyman (134–35).

28. The most hilarious instance of this failure to recognize occurs on p. 224.

29. It is significant in this regard that Burroughs refuses his parents' request that he, with a "child-like temper," recognize that his "object in life must be pursuing the labors of the field" (184). The life of the virtuous republican farmer (which Carwin allegedly adopts at the conclusion of *Wieland*, or so Clara would have us believe) is not for Burroughs, the unrepentant itinerant who has no investment in the vision of redeemed community that inspired both Edwards and Jefferson.

30. See J. Hector St. John de Crèvecoeur, *Letters from an American Farmer and Sketches of Eighteenth-Century America*, p. 37. All references to this edition will appear henceforth in the text. The text was first published in England in 1782, and in France in 1784. For the standard biographical study of Crèvecoeur, see Gay Wilson Allen and Roger Asselineau, *St. John de Crèvecoeur: The Life of an American Farmer.* For a speculative account of Crèvecoeur's arrangement of the chapters of the *Letters*, see Norman S. Grabo, "Crèvecoeur's American: Beginning the World Anew," esp. p. 166. Also interesting in this regard are A. W. Plumstead, "Hector St. John de Crèvecoeur," and Bernard Chevignard, "St. John de Crèvecoeur in the Looking Glass."

31. The philosophical and authorial problem here is reminiscent of Emerson's dilemma in positing the authorial self as a "transparent eyeball" intended to fuse "epistemological detachment" with "ontological participation." See Carolyn Porter's analysis of Emerson's metaphysics of vision in *Seeing and Being*, esp. pp. 36–40, 91–118.

32. William Tennent, "Account," p. 309.

33. Ames, "The Dangers of American Liberty," p. 377.

34. There is, of course, an irony here: as Albert E. Stone has pointed out in his introduction to the Penguin edition of *Letters*, this "new man, the American writer . . . is, first of all, a man of aliases and disguises" (9). This opinion was shared by Crève-coeur's contemporaries: in "St. John de Crèvecoeur in the Looking Glass," Chevignard quotes one troubled Loyalist who, seeking to settle the question of his fidelity to the Crown, noted that "Many Occurences in Which he has been Consulted, have proved him to be a Man of Penetration, Art and Stratagem" (175). For a reading of the ethical coherence of Crèvecoeur's pro-American but antirevolutionary politics, see Myra Jehlen, "J. Hector St. John Crèvecoeur: A Monarcho-Anarchist in Revolutionary America."

35. In "St. John de Crèvecoeur in the Looking Glass," Chevignard suggests that the immigrant Crèvecoeur more than fulfilled this pattern of becoming in the New World what he had only potentially been in the Old. Through his agonizing experience during the Revolution, Crèvecoeur metamorphosed from a "scribbling farmer," an amateur diarist, into a "man of letters," whose subsequent fame, especially in France where his account of America mirrored France's dream vision of a New World republican utopia, "metamorphosed Hector St. John into the ideal farmer he had most likely never really been" (186).

36. In his paean to Andrew the Hebridean, Crèvecoeur does not mention the significant number of Irish, Scotch, and German immigrants who came to the colonies as indentured servants for a period of from seven to fourteen years, and sometimes for life. Gordon S. Wood has estimated that from one-half to two-thirds of such immigrants arriving in the colonies between 1718 and 1775 came as indentured servants, many of whom met with a brutal treatment that was unusual in Europe. Wood quotes one British observer who claimed that they "groan beneath a worse than Egyptian bondage." See Wood, *Radicalism of the American Revolution*, pp. 51–54; quotation from p. 53. Cf. Wiebe's account of white servitude and its amelioration during and immediately following this period, in *Self-Rule*, pp. 24–27.

37. The minister proposes, that is, an explicitly Lockean authorship as the natural American one where a mind receiving impressions is like a field receiving the mark of the plough: "your mind is what we called at Yale college a *tabula rasa*," the minister assures James, and as such may be considered free from any corrupting, prior inscriptions (46).

38. Brown, *Wieland*, p. 258; discussed at the end of the second section of Chapter 4.

39. And if this metaphorical account of growth and pruning is not enough, after recounting this conversation, James reminds the Englishman who elicits his correspondence that James writes only because they are in "covenant": "Remember, you are to give me my subjects and on no other shall I write," he admonishes "Mr. F.B." "Remember that you have laid the foundation of this correspondence" (49). Like

Brown in his "Advertisement," James understands that writing is trial and expresses an anxiety to be vindicated: by allowing Mr. F.B. to "plainly see the motives which have induced me to begin [to write]," the Englishman will be unable to "reproach" the farmer "with any degree of presumption." Having clarified his motives, fears, and principles, James says, "I have now nothing to do but to prosecute my task" (49).

40. As D. H. Lawrence noted about these wasps, it was his Amiable Spouse, and not Farmer James, who had to make the jam. See *Studies in Classic American Literature*, p. 27.

41. As Warner says in *Letters of the Republic*, "As a publication, the early American novel strives for the performative virtue of republican textuality" (169).

42. Thomas Philbrick, in his biographical study *St. John de Crèvecoeur*, proposes that "the very artistry and surrealistic force of the scene argue against its basis in literal fact. The abruptness with which it is introduced, its strange transmutation of the animal imagery that appears in previous letters, the richness of its thematic implications, all suggest that it is a major instance of the shaping and creating power of Crèvecoeur's imagination, not the product of his experience" (47–48). This appears to be the consensus of opinion among Crèvecoeur scholars: Alfred E. Stone, after Marius Bewley in *Eccentric Design*, describes the scene as "a protomythic imagination at work," and argues that its artistry betrays its roots in imagination rather than experience ("Introduction," pp. 21–22). His biographers Allen and Asselineau do not comment on the origin of the scene.

43. Cf. Davidson, *Revolution and the Word*, p. 258.

44. Whitman, *Democratic Vistas*, p. 368.

45. On the influence of "blackness" (the "Africanist presence") on the American literary imagination, see Toni Morrison, *Playing in the Dark: Whiteness and the Literary Imagination*.

46. Farmer James's encounter with the slave in the cage suggests Pocock's second definition of the "Machiavellian moment" in his classic study of that name: "the moment in conceptualized time in which the republic was seen as confronting its own temporal finitude, as attempting to remain morally and politically stable in a stream of irrational events conceived as essentially destructive of all systems of secular stability" (viii). A confrontation of "virtue" with "corruption," the Machiavellian moment as Crèvecoeur stages it specifically targets the farmer's faith that the republicanism he promotes is the best—indeed, the only—system of secular stability. No longer paired with virtue, republican prosperity is from this moment associated with an unmistakable act of corruption, the white invasion of peaceable African neighborhoods, which the farmer unwittingly and grotesquely reenacts in this scene. In *The Jeffersonian Persuasion*, Banning explains the apocalyptic force of such a moment: the discovery of corruption, in the "mental universe" of the revolutionary generation, brought to mind not the need for vigorous reform but only the inevitable continuation of corruption until purity was reestablished by future revolutionary violence (113). See also Hanson, *The Democratic Imagination in America*, chapter 3.

47. The seventh chapter of Crèvecoeur's *Sketches of Eighteenth-Century America*, "The Man of Sorrows," deplores the Revolution as an annulment of his vision of an America freed from the taint of human history: "Could I have ever thought that a people of cultivators, who knew nothing but their ploughs and the management of their rural economies, should be found to possess, like the more ancient nations of Europe, the embryos of these propensities which now stain our society?" (342).

48. Joseph Fichtelberg persuasively writes that Crèvecoeur's response to the revolutionary crisis, "only a series of hypothetical half-measures perilously exposed to corruption," represents the writer's conscientious investigation (after Diderot and the Montesquieu of *The Persian Letters*) of the limits of republican ideology as they are revealed during a time of revolutionary crisis. See "Utopic Distresses: Crèvecoeur's *Letters* and Revolution," p. 88.

49. Cf. the notion of "sentimental power" to which feminist scholars attribute the antebellum vogue of the sentimental novel. See in particular Jane Tompkins's key essays, "Sentimental Power: *Uncle Tom's Cabin* and the Politics of Literary History" and "The Other American Renaissance," in *Sensational Designs*, pp. 122–85. For a powerful critique of this concept of sentimental power, see Ann Douglas's brilliant *The Feminization of American Culture*.

50. For an alternative account of competing visions of the representative American experience in Crèvecoeur, see John Hales, "The Landscape of Tragedy: Crèvecoeur's 'Susquehanna.' "

51. Charles Brockden Brown, "Remarks on Style," p. 102. The representation of the American Revolution as a conservative event, especially in the wake of the French Revolution, has been amply treated by Gordon Wood. This ideological legacy to the nineteenth century is apparent, for example, in Charles Jared Ingersoll's claim (in "Discourse Concerning the Influence of America on the Mind") that the American republic has been "always as it were in a state of temperate revolution" (282). Almost twenty years later, William Alfred Jones of Young America wrote in the *Democratic Review* that American literature should be modeled on the American Revolution, "commenced in a deliberate, though earnest spirit, after mature reflection, and with a special design. Advocated by cool heads and brave hearts, it was conducted in a spirit of intelligent zeal, and yet a wise moderation, and finally consummated with sagacity. . . . No bloody conspiracies, no Bartholomew massacre, no Sicilian Vespers, marked its course, but wise counsels and eloquent oratory, and fields fairly fought and won" (200). On the eighteenth-century obsession with sincerity and authenticity, see Trilling, *Sincerity and Authenticity*. Further historical background, with a specific reference to Renaissance and Augustan England, is provided by Jean-Christophe Agnew, *Worlds Apart: The Market and the Theater in Anglo-American Thought, 1550–1750*. Fliegelman examines the topic with reference to revolutionary America in *Declaring Independence*.

52. Theodore Dehon, "A Discourse upon the Importance of Literature to Our Country," p. 472.

53. William Charvat links democratization and commercialization in a discussion of the early American poet Joel Barlow, whom he claimed contributed to "the growth of a genuinely democratic psychology of authorship" (*The Profession of Authorship in America*, pp. 9, 10; see also chapter 5, "Cooper as Professional Author," esp. p. 77).

CHAPTER SIX

1. This epigraph is quoted in Gordon S. Wood, *Creation of the American Republic*, p. 423. Wood identifies "Candidus" as in all likelihood the pen name of Benjamin Austin, a radical Massachusetts politician.

2. Historiographical scholarship on the intersections of democratic, republican, and liberal ideologies in the period is vast and, because of the shifting meanings and complex interrelationships of the key terms, often confusing. Daniel T. Rodgers, in his article "Republicanism: The Career of a Concept," offers an excellent overview of recent scholarship on the definitional problem and marks the evolution in meaning (as contemporary historians have construed it) of keywords. Also clarifying in this regard is Robert E. Shalhope, "Republicanism and Early American Historiography." See also historians' assessments of Wood's *Creation of the American Republic, 1776–1787*, as well as Wood's response, collected in *William and Mary Quarterly*, 3d ser., 44 (July 1987): 549–640. Historians who have been especially helpful to me in understanding the transition from republicanism to liberalism as it occurred on the socio-cultural and political-theoretical levels are Joyce Appleby, Nathan Hatch, Russell Hanson, Rhys Isaac, Gary Nash, J. G. A. Pocock, Robert Wiebe, and Gordon Wood. This chapter is also indebted to Cathy Davidson's, Jay Fliegelman's, and Christopher Looby's accounts of the intersection in this period of political rhetoric and rhetorical practices (including literature). In this chapter, as throughout the study, the term "democracy" refers not to what Wood (in "Interests and Disinterestedness in the Making of the Constitution") calls the "patrician-led classical democracy" dear to democratic republicanism (83) or the pragmatic individualism of liberal democracy or "democratic humanism," as celebrated by scholars such as Harold Kaplan in his study of classic American literature as the basis of our own democratic mythology. It refers instead to the largely untheorized performance of popular empowerment through humble self-enlargement, productive of a disruptive public voice claiming its revelations to be the truest representations of invisible realities. The present chapter will examine the confrontation of democracy so defined with the rehabilitative democratic ideologies which informed both republican and liberal sociopolitical thought as imagined within literature as well as literary-critical theories of Americanness in literature.

3. I have chosen to use the gender-specific term "common man" throughout this chapter because no gender-neutral term exists to convey what we understand by it and because "common woman" has sexualized connotations irrelevant to this study. The

term "commoner" possesses connotations inappropriate to an American context and was in any case not used by those writers with whom I am concerned. Moreover, I will use the masculine pronoun to refer to the representative American author to reflect the fact that the critics with whom I am dealing here do not consider the possibility that this figure might be a woman. As is now well known, thanks to the extensive studies of antebellum sentimental literature of the past two decades, the success of women writers in the period did not materially influence that assumption.

4. See Christopher Looby, *Voicing America*, chapter 4. The quoted phrase appears on p. 246. See also Cathy Davidson, *Revolution and the Word*, chapter 7; and Lewis P. Simpson, "The Symbolism of Literary Alienation in the Revolutionary Age." Simpson observes that Brackenridge's novelistic alter ego, Captain Farrago, cannot control the ludicrous ambitions of his servant, Teague O'Regan. Whereas Teague owes nothing to Farrago, but rather, as "the symbol of public opinion, subjects the master to the servant," Farrago "is bound by the ties of his democratic idealism . . . to redeem Teague" (95). Simpson concludes that "if Captain Farrago cannot control Teague O'Regan, neither can his creator," suggesting that Teague embodies the ludicrous qualities of a terrifying character like Carwin and that his textual power or uncontainability is the effect not of his diabolism but of his banality (95). Cf. Fussell, "*Wieland*," p. 175: as embodied in Carwin, "Brown's view of literature [is] distinctly a product of postrevolutionary backlash. . . . The concept of the author is raised to almost infinite powers but with no commensurate responsibility or benevolence. He is, in a word, the devil."

5. On the Puritan plain style, see Perry Miller, *The New England Mind: The Seventeenth Century*, chapter 12. Explication of the republican emphasis on neoclassical simplicity and the agrarian ideal associated with Jefferson may be found in the works of Joyce Appleby, J. G. A. Pocock, and Gordon Wood. On the "elocutionary revolution," see Jay Fliegelman, *Declaring Independence*. Benjamin T. Spencer (*The Quest for Nationality*), Leon Chai (*The Romantic Foundations of the American Renaissance*), and Robert Weisbuch (*Atlantic Double-Cross*) discuss American adaptations of European concepts of and approaches to the "folk." The social effects of Jacksonian democracy may be gleaned from Wiebe, *Self-Rule*, esp. part I, and Sean Wilentz, *Chants Democratic*. For an overview of the era, see Arthur M. Schlesinger Jr., *The Age of Jackson*, and Robert V. Remini, *The Legacy of Andrew Jackson*, chapter 1. On American frontier literature, see Richard Slotkin, *Regeneration Through Violence* and *The Fatal Environment*.

6. Benjamin T. Spencer, *The Quest for Nationality*, p. 80. On p. 74, Spencer provides an account of why the national literature campaign intensified in the years between the War of 1812 and the mid-1840s. The stimulations he lists include the founding of new critical magazines, the example of Walter Scott, the need to respond to hostile British commentary on the national culture and its literary output, Continental theories concerning the priority of local tradition over universal reason, the growth of the popular press, and the influence of Transcendentalism.

7. Opposition to the critical prescription of silence and solitude for authentic

American authorship thus came from outside the liberal milieu. See the radical democrat Orestes A. Brownson's review of Emerson's Dartmouth address in the *Boston Quarterly Review* (January 1839): 2: 1–26. The review is excerpted in Perry Miller, ed., *The Transcendentalists*, pp. 431–34.

8. Walt Whitman, "A Backward Glance O'er Travel'd Roads," p. 723.

9. Walt Whitman, "Note at End of *Complete Poems and Prose*," p. 733. Ellipsis appears in the original text.

10. Spencer, *Quest for Nationality*, p. 159. See also pp. 111–21, 175–89.

11. Walt Whitman, "Preface to 1855 Edition of *Leaves of Grass*," pp. 710, 713. This work will be cited hereafter as 1855P.

12. Whitman, "Song of Myself," p. 52. The most important presentations of the "labile" presence of Whitman in his poetry are Tenney Nathanson's *Whitman's Presence: Body, Voice, and Writing in "Leaves of Grass,"* and Allen Grossman's impossibly concise and thrilling, "Whitman's 'Whoever You Are Holding Me Now in Hand': Remarks on the Endlessly Repeated Rediscovery of the Incommensurability of the Person."

13. George Steiner, *Tolstoy or Dostoevsky*, p. 18.

14. With this insistence that the genuine American literatus would be known by his silence or inarticulateness, the most eloquent of the nation's literary-cultural elite paired eloquence with corruption, all the while confessing, not so much in their writings as by the fact that they wrote, their own alienation from the sublime and wordless simplicity they celebrated. Whitman himself would lament at the end of his life that he had had "no way of reaching" the people: "I needed to reach the people: . . . but it's too late now." Quoted in David S. Reynolds, *Walt Whitman's America: A Cultural Biography*, p. 6. The phrase "literary delinquency" is taken from Walter Channing's 1815 essay "Reflections on the Literary Delinquency of America."

15. Henry Wadsworth Longfellow, "Review of Sydney," p. 252.

16. Whitman, 1855P, p. 717.

17. Whitman, "Song of Myself," sections 24 and 30.

18. Kenneth Dauber will identify this perceptual choice, for which the author is constrained to "making truth" no matter how he chooses, with "the ethical consequence of democratic writing"; see *The Idea of Authorship in America: Democratic Poetics from Franklin to Melville*, p. 101.

19. William Ellery Channing, "Remarks on National Literature," pp. 357, 364. In his definitive study of this issue, *Atlantic Double-Cross*, Robert Weisbuch writes that "British literary imperialism is the chief issue in American critical thought through the Civil War" (4). See esp. chapters 1 and 3. Also informative is Spencer, *Quest for Nationality*. Perry Miller's famously lively account of the internecine battles between antebellum America's pro– and anti–national literature forces, *The Raven and the Whale*, provides a detailed picture of the role of British influence in critical debates and literary production from the 1830s through the 1850s. The collections of critical writings from the late eighteenth to the mid–nineteenth centuries offered by Richard

Ruland, *The Native Muse*, and Robert E. Spiller, *The American Literary Revolution: 1783–1837*, document the longevity and urgency of the problem of British influence. For a reading of American Renaissance literature as "postcolonial," see Lawrence Buell, "American Literary Emergence as a Postcolonial Phenomenon."

20. Parkman, "The Works of James Fenimore Cooper." Page numbers will appear parenthetically in the text.

21. Walter Channing, "Essay on American Language and Literature," p. 117.

22. Parkman, "The Works of James Fenimore Cooper," p. 376; Edward Tyrell Channing, review of *The Life of Charles Brockden Brown*, by William Dunlap, p. 119.

23. Wood, "Democratization of Mind," p. 76. On the nation's "democratic destiny" as "a defeat of the exalted republican vision of the founders," see William L. Hedges, "The Myth of the Republic and the Theory of American Literature," p. 107.

24. The phrase "perspective from absence" is taken from Fanger, *The Creation of Nikolai Gogol*, esp. chapters 1 and 2, which offers through an account of the career of Nikolai Gogol a compelling portrait of Russian culture in the first half of the nineteenth century as it struggled with the same anxiety of European influence and the same range of cultural absences that Americans imagined were hindering the production of their own national literature. As he describes it, Fanger's phrase is particularly fitting to the American scene. On the early national "effort to nationalize simplicity as the true genius of American style" and a concomitant rejection of the "vulgar and florid strains" of popular oratory, see Spencer, *Quest for Nationality*, pp. 53–60. Quoted phrases appear on pp. 53, 54; cf. pp. 113, 131.

25. Charles Brockden Brown, "What Is Literary Genius?," p. 253. On Brown's editorship of the *Monthly Magazine and American Review* (from April 1799 to December 1800), *The American Review, and Literary Journal* (from January/March 1801 to October/December 1802), and, in Philadelphia, *The Literary Magazine and American Register* (from October 1803 to December 1807), see Mott, *American Magazines*, pp. 218–22. *Carwin the Biloquist* (*Memoirs of Carwin*) ran serially through the first three volumes of *The Literary Magazine and American Register*. I am assuming Brown's authorship of the pieces quoted insofar as Mott maintains that he supplied half the contents of the eight semiannual volumes. For verification of Brown's authorship, see also Alan Axelrod, *Charles Brockden Brown: An American Tale*, p. 181 n. 1.

26. Charles Brockden Brown, "What Is Literary Genius?," p. 253.

27. Charles Brockden Brown, "Remarks on Style," p. 102.

28. Joseph Stevens Buckminster, "Address of the Editors," p. 4; Dehon, "A Discourse," p. 472. Lewis P. Simpson attributes the former to Buckminster and excerpts it in *Federalist Literary Mind*, pp. 83–84. For the history of this publication, see pp. 3–41.

29. Dehon, "A Discourse," pp. 472–73. Cf. Fisher Ames, "American Literature," pp. 439–40.

30. Dehon, "A Discourse," pp. 472, 469.

31. Fisher Ames, "The Mire of Democracy," p. 53.

32. Edward Tyrell Channing, "On Models in Literature." Page numbers from the Spiller edition will appear parenthetically in the text.

33. With this critical line, Channing anticipated a future direction for those hard-pressed to understand the paucity of American literary works. Washington Irving himself would complain twenty-five years later of an "excess of criticism" evident in "the increasing number of delinquent authors daily gibbetted for the edification of the public" ("Desultory Thoughts on Criticism," p. 175).

34. Interestingly, James D. Hart points out that the conservative Joseph Dennie was the sole "champion" of Wordsworth and Coleridge when the *Lyrical Ballads* appeared in 1802. Later, Dennie would rescind his former admiration, claiming that "Wordsworth stands among the foremost of those English bards, who have mistaken silliness for simplicity, and with a false and affected taste, filled their pages with the language of children and clowns." See Hart, *The Popular Book*, p. 71. Cf. Frank Luther Mott, *A History of American Magazines, 1741–1850*, p. 231. The term "republican simplicity" to describe Wordsworth's poetry is Henry Wadsworth Longfellow's, who yet cautions that it provides "a very unsafe model for imitation." See Longfellow's "Review of Sydney," p. 258. Weisbuch provides an extensive account of Wordsworth's influence on the thought of Emerson, Thoreau, and Whitman in *Atlantic Double-Cross*.

35. Fedor Dostoevskij, "Neskol'ko zametok o prostote i uproshchennosti," p. 143.

36. Edward Tyrell Channing, review of *The Life of Charles Brockden Brown*, by William Dunlap, p. 121. Page numbers will appear hereafter in the text.

37. In *Profession of Authorship*, chapter 3, Charvat explains that "the real class animus was not between the 'haves' and the 'have-nots.' So far as the writers and intellectuals were concerned, the struggle was between their own homogeneous patrician society and a rising materialistic middle class without education and tradition" who were challenging the patricians' control of "the national culture through the professions of law, ministry, and politics; had written their own books and edited all the critical journals; had represented the people in their legislatures and garnered all the diplomatic appointments" (64). For a fuller view of the challenge posed to the patrician classes by the "middling" class, see Kenneth Cmiel, *Democratic Eloquence: The Fight over Popular Speech in Nineteenth-Century America*. For a fuller view of the transmutation of the working classes in this era, see Sean Wilentz, *Chants Democratic: New York City and the Rise of the American Working Class, 1788–1850*.

38. See Lev. N. Tolstoy, "Are the Peasant Children to Learn to Write From Us? or, Are We to Learn from the Peasant Children?"

39. Charles Jared Ingersoll, "Discourse Concerning the Influence of America on the Mind," p. 244. Page numbers to this essay will appear parenthetically in the text.

40. William Ellery Channing, "Remarks on National Literature." Page numbers will appear parenthetically in the text.

41. Joseph S. Buckminster, "Dangers and Duties of Men of Letters," p. 96.

42. Emerson, "The Poet," p. 238; Whitman, *Democratic Vistas*, p. 388.

43. Buckminster, "Dangers and Duties of Men of Letters," p. 96.

44. Emerson, "Literary Ethics," pp. 107, 110, 105. Page numbers for this essay will henceforth appear in the text.

45. Orestes A. Brownson, "American Literature," *Boston Quarterly Review* 2 (1839): 22, 21. Page numbers to Brownson's essay will appear parenthetically in the text.

46. Emerson's letter to Carlyle is quoted in Weisbuch, *Atlantic Double-Cross*, p. 211. See also Channing, review of *The Life of Charles Brockden Brown*, p. 120.

47. Evert Duyckinck, "Nathaniel Hawthorne," p. 330.

48. Quoted in Wood, "Democratization of Mind," p. 76.

49. Joel Barlow, *The Works of Joel Barlow*, 2: 376.

50. On the history of this figure in early American literature, whose literary life extended from 1776 through 1850 (sandwiched between Yankee Doodle and Uncle Sam), see Winifred Morgan, *An American Icon: Brother Jonathan and American Identity*. On Park Benjamin's and Rufus Griswold's New York magazine, *Brother Jonathan*, launched in 1839 and eventually acquired by John Neal, see Mott, *American Magazines*, pp. 359–61; Spencer, *Quest for Nationality*, pp. 76, 114, who characterized the magazine as an "attempt to democratize literature by eliminating the specialized literary class" (114); and Reynolds, *Walt Whitman's America*, pp. 41, 83. Morgan rightly observes that as a representation of the ordinary American, Brother Jonathan "was constructed by people who did not consider themselves 'ordinary,'" so that "the figure may tell us more about the producers of and myths about the ordinary American than about the ordinary American himself" (preface, n.p.). David Simpson, in *Politics of American English*, observes that "the discourse of class confrontation" that had been the subject of heated debate in the first decade of the nineteenth century was, by the 1830s, increasingly absorbed into largely comic representations, even though the actual "sense of crisis" over an influential "rhetoric of populism" was much more pronounced as the century progressed. Conservative representations of the common man were intended, Simpson claims, "to increase the appearance of popular affiliation while maintaining the fact of continued social control" (145, 146).

51. Washington Irving suggested, in an article on the deceased poet Robert Treat Paine, that there might have been no real alternative in the period to a comic portrayal of "the author": "Unfitted for business in a nation where every one is busy; devoted to literature, where literary leisure is confounded with idleness; the man of letters is almost an insulated being, with a few to understand, less to value, and scarcely any to encourage his pursuits. . . . In fact, the great demand for rough talent, as for common manual labour, in this country, prevents the appropriation of either mental or physical forces to elegant employments. The delicate mechanician may toil in penury, unless he devote himself to common manufactures, suitable to the ordinary consumption of the country; and the fine writer, if he depend upon his pen for a subsistence, will soon discover that he may starve on the very summit of Parnassus, while he sees hords of newspaper editors battening on the rank marshes of its borders." See "Original Review: The Works . . . of the late Robert Treat Paine," p. 211.

52. On the genesis of Robert Slender, see Emory Elliott, *Revolutionary Writers: Literature and Authority in the New Republic, 1725–1810*, pp. 146–49. On Freneau's relationship with Thomas Jefferson and his establishment of the *National Gazette* in Philadelphia as an alternative to John Fenno's Hamiltonian paper, see p. 133; see also Hanson, *Democratic Imagination*, pp. 77–83.

53. Philip Freneau, "Letters on Various Interesting and Important Subjects, by Robert Slender, o.s.m.," pp. iv, v.

54. Freneau, "Advice to Authors, by the Late Mr. Robert Slender," pp. 9, 10, 9.

55. Brown, "What Is Literary Genius?," p. 253.

56. Irving, "Account of the Author" (pp. 373–76) and "To the Public" (pp. 377–81), in *A History of New York*; see esp. p. 379.

57. Walter Channing, "Essay on American Language and Literature" (see esp. pp. 117, 121) and "Reflections on the Literary Delinquency of America." Page numbers to this pair of articles will appear henceforth in the text.

58. References to *The Pioneers* and *The Last of the Mohicans* will be cited in the text by page number followed by *P* and *LM* respectively. The history of Cooper's critical reception may be gleaned from the contemporary reviews of his novels collected by George Dekker and John P. McWilliams, eds., *Fenimore Cooper: The Critical Heritage*.

59. See W. H. Gardiner, review of *The Spy*, by James Fenimore Cooper, pp. 192, 193; Richard Henry Dana Sr., review of *The Sketch Book of Geoffrey Crayon, Gent.*, by Washington Irving, esp. p. 222. Richard Slotkin notes that the Indian was positively depicted "as a representative of the kind of heroism that natural, uncultivated, American man is capable of" in the mid–eighteenth century, although he was seen as racially inferior and, ultimately, as the Anglo-American's "foil, the opponent against whom he exercises and develops his heroic powers as a representative of civilization." See *Regeneration Through Violence*, pp. 189, 205.

60. In his introduction to the 1986 Penguin edition of *The Last of the Mohicans*, Richard Slotkin notes that the critical history of that novel and *The Pioneers* reveals strong doubts on the parts of Cooper's contemporaries about the "intrinsic interest of the Indian as a fictional subject," and that these doubts were linked to racial prejudice against Native Americans (xii). Far from romanticizing the disappearing Indians, Cooper "departs," Slotkin states, "from the reconciliationist model of history" offered by Walter Scott, such that his "conflicts end with the elimination (actual or potential) of one race or party" (xiii). Cooper's introduction to the 1831 edition of *Last of the Mohicans* is reprinted in the 1986 Penguin edition and cited in the text accordingly.

61. Simpson, *Politics of American English*, chapter 6, esp. pp. 196–97; cf. pp. 183, 205. Simpson notes that the "Native American quality of silence and invisibility is one that Cooper wishes to reclaim or preserve as essential to the true American character," and that for Cooper "the language of democracy" was "a language composed of silence and poetry" (197, 205). One of Cooper's critics objected to the moral valence attached to Natty's laugh as follows: "We can find nothing to quarrel with Hawk-eye about, unless it be the too frequent repetition of his 'silent and heartfelt laugh'. Not

but that he had a right to perform this noiseless agitation of his diaphragm, as often as he found it natural or refreshing; but the reader does not require to be perpetually reminded of this accomplishment of the woodsman, or 'gift,' as he would have styled it." See the anonymous review of *The Last of the Mohicans* in *New-York Review and Atheneum*, p. 94.

62. It is a well-established fact of literary-historical scholarship that in the first decades of the nineteenth century, American literature learned to accommodate explicitly as exemplarily democratic the "savages" — Indians and backwoodsmen — of an earlier era. Larzer Ziff, for example, has recently noted that by the close of the 1820s, when the fear of anarchy characteristic of the early national period had largely subsided, "the notion that American democracy relied upon a degree of wildness for its preservation gained popular acceptance," resulting in the celebration of the "crude precursors of those who actually established civil society" as "the founders and guardians of American society." See Ziff, "Wild Usages," in *Writing in the New Nation*, p. 182. My point, however, is that savagery was both celebrated and rhetorically contained in the process of transferring (domesticated) democratic personality to white liberal America.

63. On the significance of this scene, see Slotkin, *Regeneration Through Violence*, pp. 487–88.

64. Anonymous review of *The Pioneers*, p. 70.

65. Although he generally admired Cooper, the French novelist Honoré de Balzac noted his "profound and radical impotence for the comic," particularly insofar as he construed it as requiring a portrait of local (common) character: "I feel, in reading Cooper, a singular sensation, as if while listening to beautiful music there was near me some horrible village fiddler scraping his violin and harrowing me by playing the same air. To produce what he thinks to be comic he puts into the mouth of one of his personages a silly joke, invented *a priori*, some notion, a mental vice, a deformity of mind, which is shown in the first chapters and reappears, page after page, to the last. This joke and this personage form the village fiddler I speak of." See Honoré de Balzac, review of Cooper, esp. p. 198.

66. Anonymous review of *The Last of the Mohicans* in *New-York Review and Atheneum*, p. 94.

67. On Cooper's role in contributing to the genre of historical romance as it evolved from its eighteenth-century European beginnings, see George Dekker, *The American Historical Romance*, esp. chapters 1–4. Dekker comments on Cooper's use of Shakespeare on p. 52. The comparison between Scott and Cooper was universal; it plays, for example, a major role in the Russian critic Vissarion Belinsky's article on "The Division of Poetry into Kinds and Genres." It was not always a favorable comparison: the American critic John Neal observed that the "difference between the author of *Waverley* and his American follower [is] that the former, in his descriptive flourishes, shows himself an amateur of nature, whilst the latter proves himself only an amateur of the author of *Waverley*" ("The Last American Novel," p. 85).

NOTES TO PAGES 319–31 **487**

68. Reminiscent of Carwin, David Gamut is described as physically disproportionate, exhibiting a marked "contrariety in his members" such that his body constituted a "false superstructure of blended human orders," "profanely reared." Likewise his clothing is "ill-assorted and injudicious" (16 *LM*). But his voice is "as remarkable for the softness and sweetness of its tones, as was his person for its rare proportions," and his first soliloquy, an inquiry concerning the breed of someone's horse, is as excessively flowery as Carwin's request for a glass of buttermilk (17 *LM*).

69. Critical condemnation of this character as "the *bore* of the romance" is ubiquitous. See, for example, the anonymous reviews of *The Last of the Mohicans* from *New-York Review and Atheneum* (esp. p. 94) and *The United States Literary Gazette*, Gardiner's review, and William Gilmore Simms's review, "The Writings of Cooper."

70. Balzac review, p. 196. Interestingly, the great Russian critic Vissarion Belinsky, who played Evert Duyckinck to Dostoevsky's Melville, noticed that Cooper (whom he greatly admired) "seems not even to suspect the existence of the *inner* man," and attributed that feature to "the decisive preponderance of the epic moment" that required "the absence of the inner, subjective principle" ("Division of Poetry," pp. 194, 193).

71. Francis Parkman attests to the success of Cooper's strategy of making Natty Bumppo the truest representation of the tragedy of Native America. In his 1852 review of Cooper's works, Parkman notes how civilization must be held accountable for "exterminating the buffalo and the Indian" as well as the "extinction" of that "class of men" who acted as civilization's own "precursors and pioneers." "Of these men," Parkman writes, "Leatherstocking is the representative," leaving ambiguous the question of whether the Indian is to be classed with the buffalo or the human precursors of civilization. See "The Works of James Fenimore Cooper," p. 364.

72. Neal, "Last American Novel," p. 87.

73. Emerson's most famous argument against the book occurs in "The American Scholar" (1837). In a similar way, Natty Bumppo's condemnation of owning property makes a jarring comparison with Cooper's own acquisitiveness in this regard: see the incident reported in Lewis Leary, "Introduction" to Cooper's *Home as Found*, p. xiii, wherein the residents of Cooperstown, New York, protest (by, among other things, removing copies of his books from the public library) against his making inaccessible to bathing and picnicking a spit of land he owned on Lake Otswego that villagers had been accustomed to use during his seven-year stay in Europe.

74. Cf. Dauber, *Idea of Authorship in America*, chapter 3, on the self-alienation inscribed within Natty's representativity (as well as Cooper's). Just as "it is not nature that civilization opposes but itself, which it divides into civilization proper, as what is allowed by law, and nature, which is rather civilization acting outside its law," so Natty's "representativity, also, is instrumental, born out of society's confrontation with its divisions" (95).

75. Slotkin understands this paradox as played out in terms of the marriage metaphor that governs the action of the last of the Leatherstocking tales, *The Deerslayer*.

488 NOTES TO PAGES 333-35

He understands domestication, that is, to mean the restraint placed upon the masculine and "Indian sinfulness of his profession of hunter" by "the moral bounds set by the feminine symbols of civilized culture." These "conflicting demands . . . neutralize Leatherstocking and render him impotent" — unable to marry and reproduce. He is thus profoundly anomalous, unable to play "his proper role in either the Indian or the Christian frame of reference." This internalized contradiction means that Natty's "innocence is doomed to ultimate impotence." See *Regeneration Through Violence*, pp. 502–3, 506.

76. On the trajectory of Cooper's career, and the placement between the Leatherstocking bookends of his political writings, see Charvat, *Profession of Authorship*, pp. 68–83. On Cooper's decision to return to the Leatherstocking novels, see Stephen Railton, *Fenimore Cooper: A Study of His Life and Imagination*, pp. 194–96; and James D. Wallace, *Early Cooper and His Audience*, pp. 172–73.

77. Quoted in Leary, "Introduction," pp. xii and vi.

78. As Perry Miller has shown, Cooper (perhaps despite himself) served as a model for aspiring national authors of the 1840s eager to replicate the innocence of his literary creations: "Cooper and Irving had created their mighty beings in an innocent day; they hardly knew what they were doing. The point about [Cornelius Mathews, a leading figure in the literary nationalist Young America movement of the 1840s] is that he knew, he had to know, that he was willfully enacting the program of Young America. After the proclamation of nativism must come the attempt to live up to it, which means that a story can hardly be told for the story itself; it must inescapably contain what Melville would eventually call a 'part-&-parcel allegoricalness of the whole'" (*Raven and the Whale*, 143).

79. Parkman, "The Works of James Fenimore Cooper," p. 360.

80. The cultural context, and specifically the literary politics, surrounding Melville's authorial debut is provided by Miller, *Raven and the Whale*. For a collection of primary texts related to the history of Melville's reception, see Watson G. Branch, ed., *Melville: The Critical Heritage*.

81. On the reception of Cooper's political works and its effect upon the evolution of Cooper's politics in the last two decades of his life, see George Dekker and Larry Johnston, "Introduction" to James Fenimore Cooper, *The American Democrat*. See also Arthur M. Schlesinger Jr., *The Age of Jackson*, pp. 375–80, who notes Cooper's growing fear in the 1840s of the demagogue who had destroyed the general belief "in the superior innocence and virtue of a rural population" (380). Clark is quoted in Miller, *Raven and the Whale*, p. 26. Throughout his landmark study, Miller comments on the decline in Cooper's popularity, particularly for its effect upon the early career of Herman Melville, and speculates on the significance of Melville's early exposure to the "blighting majesty" of Cooper (26).

82. Gardiner, review of *Last of the Mohicans*, 112, 113; anonymous review, *United States Literary Gazette*, p. 101.

83. Neal, "Last American Novel," p. 85.

84. Grenville Mellen, review of *The Red Rover*. Page numbers (from the excerpts of the review in Dekker and McWilliams, eds., *Fenimore Cooper: The Critical Heritage*) will henceforth be cited in the text.

85. Mellen found the same fault with the white hero of Cooper's *The Red Rover*: "[t]here is too much poetry about him," he observed, "too much of the genteel villain, and too little of the Ishmaelite, in his composition" (147).

86. In Mellen's view, the problem was remedied by acknowledging that "[i]t is the author, not his theatre or his matter, that nationalizes his work." Washington Irving's *Sketches of Old England* is, in this regard, "as essentially American as it is possible for any book to be" because it exemplifies good taste according to "the English school of civilization" to which America unarguably belongs (145).

87. James Russell Lowell, *A Fable for Critics*, p. 238. On the history of this character in American literature and the extraordinary breadth of its appearances in a range of literary genres, see Slotkin's monumental *Regeneration Through Violence*.

88. Sampson Reed, "Observations on the Growth of the Mind," p. 57.

89. This view of the common man as a candidate for future authorship was in reality doubly proleptic. Not only was the common author who ate his meal from a firkin a hypothetical creature of the future whom Emerson hoped would emerge from out of the undifferentiated mass, but the type itself had been superseded by an industrialized working class. Emerson's common man represents a nostalgic throwback to agrarian America, a type of "distressed genre" in Susan Stewart's formulation in *Crimes of Writing*. According to Charvat, in the third chapter of *Profession of Authorship*, Emerson shared this nostalgic view with other prominent Unitarians and Congregationalists as revealed by their responses to the great depression of 1837. On Whitman's similar nostalgia, see Reynolds, *Walt Whitman's America*.

90. Gardiner, review of *The Spy*, p. 188. Emerson's conviction that the discovery of the American genius would require writers to abandon their voluntary enslavement to European literary conventions and themes was itself, of course, largely derived from European romantic nationalism. On the influence of German and British romantic nationalist thought in the United States, see especially Henry A. Pochmann, *German Culture in America*; Leon Chai, *The Romantic Foundations of the American Renaissance*; Weisbuch, *Atlantic Double-Cross*; and Miller, *Raven and the Whale*.

91. Gardiner, review of *The Spy*, p. 188.

92. Prescott, "Life of Brown," pp. 174, 175.

93. Henry David Thoreau, *Walden and Civil Disobedience*, p. 65; Parkman, *Essays from the North American Review*, p. 376 (quoted in Spencer, *Quest for Nationality*, p. 112).

94. Quoted in Spencer, *Quest for Nationality*, p. 113. On the ubiquity of such populist sentiments in the literary criticism of this period, see "The Impact of Democracy," pp. 111–21. On the appropriation of populist language by all political parties in the post-Jacksonian era, see Simpson, *Politics of American English*, pp. 145–48. Simpson notes how "an explicit recognition of class distinctions and differences of

interest, in Federalist discourse, is replaced by a disingenuous rhetoric of equality in which there are no workers and no employers, and in which all have the same interests and the same opportunity for profit and progress. Thus was born that enduringly vague entity and smokescreen for a multitude of political priorities, the American people." Given this strategy, the "task of the conservative was then clear: to increase the appearance of popular affiliation while maintaining the fact of continued social control" (145, 146). I generally agree, but would note that the aesthetic of innocence expressed a far more subtly conceived and ambivalently executed form of social control in its prescriptions for authorial innocence; moreover, the aestheticians of innocence occupied a wide range of political and social positions, as the polarity of Emerson and Whitman, its two greatest practitioners, demonstrates. The most complete account of the cultural generation, evaluation, and appropriation of the democratic idiom in this period is Cmiel, *Democratic Eloquence*; especially pertinent for the present study are chapter 2, "The Democratic Idiom," and chapter 3, "Saxon Eloquence: The *Sermo Humilis*." Cmiel states what was at stake in the political and cultural debates over the value and authenticity of "rustic language" that these chapters chronicle: "The nineteenth-century debate over language was a fight over what kind of personality was needed to sustain a healthy democracy" (14).

95. Margaret Fuller and Ralph Waldo Emerson, "The Editors to the Reader," p. 2. Page references will henceforth appear in the text.

96. [Emerson and Fuller, eds.], "New Poetry," p. 220.

97. Cmiel, *Democratic Eloquence*, notes the fears of the "middling" class, for whose timid conventionality Emerson and Fuller had only contempt, that as a result of a popular control of letters, "*ethos* would sink into *persona*," identity (or, in Cmiel's usage, character) would give way to vulgar theater (67).

98. Spencer, *Quest for Nationality*, p. 117.

99. Cf. Weisbuch's discussion of "actualism" in *Atlantic Double-Cross*, chapter 9, esp. pp. 217–218. The requirement of inarticulateness is Emerson's crowning contribution to the aesthetics of innocence. One finds the other requirements — poverty, solitude, exile — in numbers of other statements about the hypothetical democratic poet; see, for example, William Alfred Jones's "Democracy and Literature," which insists on the democratic poet's isolation from "the confusion and hurry of business" and other "short-lived and inconstant" pursuits (197). This observation supports, I think, Christopher Newfield's regarding what he describes — in a reading of the "Language" section of Emerson's essay *Nature* (1836) — as Emerson's "authoritarian individualism." "Liberalism," Newfield points out, "envisions the fulfillment of freedom in obedience yet insists that obedience reflect free consent. *This consent, in 'Language,' is precisely what Emerson rejects*: obedience is 'spontaneous' and unwilled, not willful and voluntary." This quality of obedience can only mean "the elimination of the term 'mind' that ordinarily forms the bridge between nature and spirit." In *Nature*, Emerson therefore "summons the most intimate, private form of freedom — individual voice, literary creation, utopian imaginings, poetic self-expression — and subordinates

it to preexisting law in *both* of the departments of being." Newfield raises the iconic example of the "liberal" Emerson in order to suggest an ongoing "difficulty in discussing the authoritarian elements of US democracy." See Newfield, "Controlling the Voice: Emerson's Early Theory of Language," pp. 20–22, and his extension of these ideas with respect to the development of what he calls American "corporate individualism" in *The Emerson Effect*.

100. John McVickar, *Tribute to the Memory of Sir Walter Scott*, pp. 36, 37.

101. Emerson, "The Poet," p. 238. Page numbers to this edition will appear henceforth in the text. Robert D. Richardson Jr. downplays this lament in *Emerson: The Mind on Fire*, p. 374.

102. Ziff suggests something akin to this dilemma in his allusion to "the paradox of representing immanence" as the particular challenge faced by Emerson, Melville, and Whitman as writers interested in arresting the slide into literacy — that is, for-eign — conventions. See Ziff, *Writing in the New Nation*, p. 188. Ziff, however, un-necessarily abridges his inquiry into this paradox by assigning "immanence" to oral culture and "representation" to print culture, and then imagining them to be succes-sive so that, for example, although the Great Awakening arguably prepared Jonathan Edwards's parishioners to assume political authority in the revolutionary era, both "the revolution and the republic that succeeded it were . . . preeminently creatures of print culture while Edwards's outlook [and thus that of his adherents] is shaped by the assumptions of oral culture" (Edwards's many publications, apparently, notwithstand-ing); Ziff, *Writing in the New Nation*, pp. 15, 17, 14.

103. The phrase is Kenneth Burke's (*Rhetoric of Religion*, p. 32).

104. The description of Whitman is taken from Tenney Nathanson's brilliant *Whitman's Presence: Body, Voice, and Writing in "Leaves of Grass,"* p. 9. The term "richest fluency" is from Whitman, 1855P, p. 715.

CHAPTER SEVEN

1. Whitman, *Democratic Vistas*, p. 474. Page numbers to this edition will be cited in the text and designated *DV*.

2. See Whitman, "Preface 1855," in Harold W. Blodgett and Sculley Bradley, eds., *Leaves of Grass: Comprehensive Reader's Edition*, p. 715. Page numbers to this edition will be cited henceforth in the text and designated 1855P.

3. In his recent biography of Whitman, *Walt Whitman's America*, David S. Rey-nolds writes that the poet's two denials of Emerson's influence force us "to realize that Emerson was at most a catalyst for [Whitman's] poetic imagination," and that "Emer-son himself expressed curiosity about what he termed the 'long foreground' of *Leaves of Grass*" (82). The reason, Reynolds suggests, that Whitman did not produce *Leaves of Grass* a decade earlier, upon the publication of Emerson's "The Poet," is because of his determination to immerse himself in popular culture, "absorbing a million

people . . . with an intimacy, an eagerness, an abandon, probably never equalled" (Whitman quoted on p. 83).

4. Ralph Waldo Emerson, "The Poet." The phrase "without impediment" appears on p. 224, the two extensive quotations on p. 240. For a record of Melville's annotations of Emerson, see Wilson Walker Cowen, *Melville's Marginalia*, 1: 524–27. Melville marked these passages with a vertical line, but did not comment on them. Although the annotation on the flyleaf of Melville's copy of Emerson's *Essays: Second Series* is dated 22 March 1861, Cowen notes that the date is erroneous since Melville was in Washington, D.C. on that day. See also William Braswell, "Melville as a Critic of Emerson." For an analysis of Melville's relationship to Emerson, see Merton M. Sealts Jr., *Pursuing Melville: 1940–1980*, pp. 250–77. Because "The Poet" is the most heavily annotated essay in Melville's edition of Emerson's *Essays: Second Series*, Sealts conjectures that this is "where his mixed feelings about the man came to their sharpest focus"; he does note, however, that no evidence exists for Melville's having read Emerson after the 1870s (274, 275). For an alternative account of Emerson's presence in *Billy Budd*, see Philip D. Beidler, "*Billy Budd*: Melville's Valedictory to Emerson."

5. Herman Melville, *Billy Budd, Sailor: An Inside Narrative*, pp. 9, 124. All further references to this text, a reediting of the 1962 Hayford-Sealts edition, will be cited parenthetically in the essay. For the text's growth and history, as well as a thorough analysis of Melville's manuscript of the novel, discovered in 1924, see Harrison Hayford and Merton M. Sealts Jr., eds., *Billy Budd: The Genetic Text*, pp. 1–24; and Hershel Parker's extension of their inquiry in *Reading Billy Budd*.

6. For evidence that Melville, during the time he was writing *Billy Budd*, had Whitman very much on his mind, see Sealts, *Melville's Reading: A Check-List of Books Owned and Borrowed*, p. 133.

7. Emerson, "The American Scholar," p. 64.

8. Melville began to write *Billy Budd* in 1886, leaving it apparently incomplete at his death in 1891. Since the discovery of the manuscript in 1924, scholars have consistently emphasized the value of the work, whatever its artistic merits or demerits, as, in John Middleton Murry's well-known phrase, Melville's "last will and testament"; see Murry, "Herman Melville's Silence." According to the chronology of his major biographers (excluding Hershel Parker, the second volume of whose Melville biography is forthcoming), *Billy Budd* represents the unanticipated flower of Melville's Dark Ages, a thirty-year period of silence and resignation commencing in 1857 with the stunning critical failure of *The Confidence-Man*. Their romantic portrait of the later Melville is conspicuous for its faithfulness to the image of the cloister, suggested perhaps by that young admirer who, having set off to Pittsfield in 1859 on a "literary pilgrimage" to the "renowned author of Typee, &c," found the writer a combination "Ishmael" and "cloistered thinker" (as quoted by Jay Leyda, *The Melville Log*, 2: 605–6). Lewis Mumford writes that "the shearing of his head, the donning of sackcloth, the last ironic act of renunciation"—that is, his acceptance of a deputy inspectorship at the New York customhouse—occurred in 1866, and the remainder

of his life passed in an appropriately "cloistral quiet" (*Herman Melville*, pp. 282, 333). Leon Howard portrays Melville as considering with La Bruyère the "advantages of renouncing the world," in despair of finding "a kindred spirit who could speak his own secret language" (*Herman Melville, A Biography*, pp. 272, 323–24). On Melville's "Hermit's Reputation" in the last decades of his life, see Sealts, "Alien to His Contemporaries: Melville's Last Years," in *Pursuing Melville*, pp. 193–220. For an account of Melville's last decades as devoted to an intense inquiry into art and the creative process, see William Dillingham, *Melville and His Circle*.

9. In *Subversive Genealogy: The Politics and Art of Herman Melville*, Michael Paul Rogin reads *Billy Budd* as Melville's elegy to his grandsires, revolutionary heroes, and to the values of the "lost revolutionary world" they had inhabited, a reconciliation with family made possible by his mature acceptance of the modern democratic state (290). Accordingly, Rogin claims that as Melville reworked the novel, "Vere gained in complexity and dominated the action" (295); through him, the sacrifice of the innocent Billy articulates Melville's revisionist account of the scandalous *Somers* mutiny of 1842 in which his cousin, First Lieutenant Guert Gansevoort, had been instrumental in the conviction and execution of the alleged conspirators.

10. For an alternative reading of *Billy Budd* as Melville's assessment of his century, see Richard A. Hocks's intriguing essay, "Melville and 'The Rise of Realism': The Dilemma of History in *Billy Budd*." Hocks sees the novel as in part a response to Melville's realization that the triumph in his century of Lockean utilitarianism, a triumph which had secured the ideology and institutions of liberal democracy, posed a threat to a particular conception of art, necessitating a new mode of artistic creation marked by indirection. See also Hocks's comments on Billy as an embodiment of the Emersonian ideal (67–69).

11. For a compilation of nineteenth-century reviews of Melville's work, see Branch, ed., *Melville: The Critical Heritage*. The issue of Melville's lack of "veracity" is especially prominent in reviews of his first two novels, *Typee* (1846) and *Omoo* (1847). On this problem, see Miller, *Raven and the Whale*, pp. 157–67, 203–8, 216–19, 247–51. The critical desire to "freeze [Melville] into silence" was expressed by George Washington Peck in his review (reprinted in *Critical Heritage*, p. 316) of Melville's novel of the trials of American authorship, *Pierre* (1852). For an assessment of the extent to which Melville courted his readership's disapproval, see Wai-chee Dimock, *Empire for Liberty: Melville and the Poetics of Individualism*; and Charvat, "Melville and the Common Reader," in *Profession of Authorship*, pp. 262–82. For Charvat's assessment of the readership's (as opposed to the critical establishment's) impact upon a writer's professional success in the mid–nineteenth century, see pp. 290–92. For an alternative reading of the novel that posits Billy's silence as directly relevant to Melville himself, see Brook Thomas, "*Billy Budd* and the Judgment of Silence."

12. Although the *Bellipotent* fights France for Britain, its spiritual champion, "the flower of [its] flock," Billy Budd, born in 1776, hung in 1797 as a mutineer, unambiguously identifies it as a setting for the dramatization of nineteenth-century Ameri-

can preoccupations: the genesis and meaning of revolution, the contradiction between liberty and authority and between individual and community, the status of innocence, and alternatively, the tensions of a contrived innocence. Fliegelman has called *Billy Budd* "a meditation on the meaning of [the French] revolutionary era," and, noting Billy's birthdate, associates him with "the idealism of the American Revolution" (*Prodigals and Pilgrims*, p. 259).

13. For the narrator's discussion in the novel of the Nore and Spithead mutinies, see pp. 21–24 and 31–32. For a critical discussion of the relationship of the *Somers* mutiny to Melville and to the composition of *Billy Budd*, see Rogin, "The *Somers* Mutiny and *Billy Budd*: Melville in the Penal Colony," in *Subversive Genealogy*, pp. 288–316. For an account of Vere as based on Lord Thomas Fairfax, Puritan warrior and patron of the poet Andrew Marvell (whose ambivalent assessment of Fairfax's moral integrity informs "Upon Appleton House"), see Charles Larson, "Melville's Marvell and Vere's Fairfax." Larson's focus on Marvell's ambivalence toward Fairfax challenges earlier accounts of the meaning of Vere's ancestry offered by Joseph L. Schneider, "Melville's Use of the Vere-Fairfax Lineage in *Billy Budd*"; and Michael Millgate, "Melville and Marvell: A Note on *Billy Budd*."

14. For an analysis of stuttering among American slaves as reported by their masters and explained by advertisers for slaves to be sold, see Gerald W. Mullin, *Flight and Rebellion: Slave Resistance in Eighteenth-Century Virginia*, pp. 98–103. "Masters generally agreed with one another when they tried to explain their slaves' problems of speech," Mullin writes, "slaves stuttered when replying to their owners' 'sharp questioning'" (98–99). Often tics accompanied the stuttering, as with one Jem who, "'when challenged with a fault, or surprised [made] an extraordinary motion with his hands, which he could not avoid'" (quoted on p. 99). Mullin's analysis of the situation and character of slave stutterers (including the preponderance of slave sailors who were stutterers) is suggestive in relation to Billy Budd.

15. Thoreau, *Walden*, p. 101.

16. Melville, *Moby-Dick*, p. 170.

17. See Barth, "The End of Religion," p. 256.

18. See "Gomorrahs of the Deep; or, Melville, Foucault, and the Question of Heterotopia," in which Cesare Casarino provocatively identifies the Melvillean ship with Foucault's notion of the "heterotopia" as a place within culture, at once real and unreal, "'in which the real sites, all the other real sites that can be found within the culture, are simultaneously represented, contested, and inverted'" (Foucault quoted on p. 2). Casarino reads the Melvillean vessel as the exemplary nineteenth-century heterotopia, and notes how Melville's (and other nineteenth-century) sea narratives "marked the very space of the ship, and all of its intricate, internal circuitries of power, as the central narrative telos" (2).

19. Stanton Garner has identified the source of the phrase "the deadly space between" as Thomas Campbell's "Battle of the Baltic," a poem written to commemorate Nelson's victory at Copenhagen. The phrase appears in stanza 3, which describes

NOTES TO PAGES 353-70

the beginning of hostilities: "But the might of England flush'd / To anticipate the scene; / And her van the fleeter rush'd / O'er the deadly space between." Hayford and Sealts had not been able to locate the source of the quotation, and more recent scholarship, to my knowledge, has not availed itself of Garner's discovery. See Garner, "Melville and Thomas Campbell: The 'Deadly Space Between,'" pp. 289–90. Garner's scholarship constitutes a gold mine for those of Melville's readers who are plagued by the "unusual number of factual errors" in *Billy Budd*; see his "Fraud as Fact in Herman Melville's *Billy Budd*." In this delightful article, Garner suggests that Melville revised passages in order to make them untrue to historical fact, and thus "did not write history, but anti-history in the guise of documentary narrative, a conscious disavowal of the literalists who dedicate themselves to 'actual men and events'" (83, 93).

20. This definition of tautology was borrowed from Eric J. Sundquist, "Suspense and Tautology in *Benito Cereno*," p. 112. On tautology as a strategy for containment, see Dimock, *Empire for Liberty*.

21. See Burke, *A Grammar of Motives*, esp. pp. xv–xxiii and 3–58.

22. As Barbara Johnson puts it, "In thus occupying the point at which murder and language meet, Captain Vere positions himself astride the 'deadly space between'" ("Melville's Fist," p. 102).

23. For instances of the tacit rule against pronouncing the word "mutiny," and the general "confining all knowledge" as to what had transpired, see *Billy Budd*, pp. 86, 99, 102, 115.

24. Whitman's channel thus offers itself as a secularized version of the Quaker understanding of the Inward Light which functioned as a pure channel for the communication of truth from one person to the next: "Because the Inward Light was everywhere unitary and identical, true communication and persuasion were effected by the reaching of the Light in another person. Truth was felt in the resonant chord struck within one's conscience by another's message." See Bauman, *Let Your Words Be Few*, p. 39. Melville's "vocal current electric" represents a profane inversion of both the sacred model and its reconceptualization as the basis for a national poetics.

25. The narrator, piling pun upon pun, refers to Billy in the introduction to his character, presumably because of his orphaned state, as a "by-blow" (16).

26. Whitman, "Prefatory Letter to Ralph Waldo Emerson, Leaves of Grass 1856," p. 737. Hereafter cited as 1856P. For a brilliant reading of the structural significance of homoeroticism in *Billy Budd*, see Eve Kosofsky Sedgwick, "Some Binarisms (I): *Billy Budd*: After the Homosexual."

27. The phrase is from Martin Price, "The Logic of Intensity: More on Character," p. 374.

28. Thus, Claggart elicits from Vere the pun on "to lie" which Christopher Ricks characterized as "striking" for the "pressure" it brings to bear on the language. During the trial, after the jury's question concerning the motive for Claggart's lie, Vere replies that no one can rightly answer, "'unless indeed it be he who lies within

there,' designating the compartment where lay the corpse" (103). Of such an unconscious reversion to the pun, Ricks remarks that it often goes "insinuatingly and insidiously unremarked: no conscious vigilance will secure a speaker against those subliminal associations which proffer themselves . . . as mere naturalnesses of a language, innocent and neutral rather than . . . potencies." The narrator may be indicating Vere's lack of "vigilance" in a "truth-testing situatio[n]" by characterizing as "soothing" the hand Vere paternally lays on Billy's shoulder, and which provokes an intensification of his anxiety to articulate, which leads immediately to the fatal blow. Ricks notes the "instructive" deflection of the verb "sooth/soothe": "from 'to prove to be true' (*OED* instances from 950 to 1588); through 'to declare to be true; to uphold as the truth' (1553–1616); into 'to put forward a lie or untruth as being true' (1591–1616); and so into the current 'to smoothe, gloss over, flatter, or render calm' (1697 on)." Ricks concludes: "So that *soothe*, far from meaning 'tell you the truth,' has come to mean 'make you feel better, probably by off-white lies.'" As for Claggart, Ricks judiciously notes of lying that it "has the special potency of immediately paradoxical possibilities, since it strikes at the roots of language and may strike, self-incriminatingly, at itself." See Christopher Ricks, "Lies," esp. pp. 122, 124, 125.

29. Melville, *Moby-Dick*, p. 144.

30. The enduring "acceptance" and "resistance" schools of *Billy Budd* criticism were initiated by E. L. Grant Watson's "Melville's Testament of Acceptance" and Philip Withim's "*Billy Budd*: Testament of Resistance." For a cogent critique of this either/or approach to the text, see Johnson, "Melville's Fist." Eve Sedgwick, in "Some Binarisms (I)," also points out that the novel is "about the placement and re-placement of the barest of thresholds" and thus "continues to mobilize desires that could go either way" (94). For a recent "acceptance" reading, see Andrew Delbanco, "Melville's Sacramental Style." See also Geraldine Murphy, "The Politics of Reading *Billy Budd*," who analyzes the resistance/acceptance dichotomy with reference to the intersections of leftist politics with American literary critical schools in the decades after the manuscript's discovery in 1924 through the Cold War period.

31. Cf. Brook Thomas, "The Legal Fictions of Herman Melville and Lemuel Shaw," pp. 43–44. Thomas regards the implicit questioning of Vere's sanity as "impugn[ing] the institutional foundation of [Judge Lemuel] Shaw's Boston." Thomas argues that Vere represents the mentality, exemplified by Melville's father-in-law Shaw, that would uphold the institution of the law over the individuals whose rights it is supposed to protect. Interestingly, Vere and Shaw voice fears of the people; Shaw regarded his judicial function as intended to contain the "encroachments of a wild and licentious democracy" and the "irregular action of mere popular will" (quoted on p. 45).

32. Whitman, "Preface, 1876, to the two-volume Centennial Edition of *Leaves of Grass* and "'Two Rivulets,'" p. 465.

33. Friedrich Nietzsche, *The Use and Abuse of History*, p. 5.

34. Terry Eagleton, *Literary Theory: An Introduction*, p. 146; and Hawthorne, "The Devil in Manuscript."

CONCLUSION

1. C. B. Macpherson, *The Real World of Democracy*, p. 1.

2. Joyce Appleby, *Liberalism and Republicanism in the Historical Imagination*, p. 92. Page numbers will henceforth appear in the text.

3. See Michael Oakeshott, *Rationalism in Politics and Other Essays*, pp. 111–36, esp. pp. 124–27.

4. Robert H. Wiebe, *Self-Rule*, pp. 6, 2. Page numbers will appear henceforth in the text.

5. Calef, *More Wonders*, pp. 298, 299.

6. Chauncy, *Enthusiasm described*, p. 25.

7. *Testimony of Harvard College*, p. 346.

8. Quoted from Hawthorne's journal for 12 November 1856 in Jay Leyda, *The Melville Log*, p. 529.

9. See Allen Grossman, "Whitman's 'Whoever You Are Holding Me Now in Hand': Remarks on the Endlessly Repeated Rediscovery of the Incommensurability of the Person," p. 116. Page numbers will appear henceforth in the text.

10. See Michael Taussig, *Mimesis and Alterity: A Particular History of the Senses*, pp. xv, xiii.

Bibliography

Abelove, Henry, ed. "Jonathan Edwards's Letter of Invitation to George White-
field." *William and Mary Quarterly*, 3d ser., 29 (1972): 487–89.
"An Account of a Murder Committed by Mr. J——— Y———, Upon His Family, in
December, A.D. 1781." *New York Weekly Magazine* 2, no. 55 (20 July 1796): 20;
no. 56 (27 July 1796): 28.
"Account of Whitefield's New York visit." Excerpted in Prince, ed., *Christian History*
1744, 358–63. Originally in *New-England Journal*, no. 659.
Agnew, Jean-Christophe. *Worlds Apart: The Market and the Theater in Anglo-American
Thought, 1550–1750.* New York: Cambridge University Press, 1986.
Ahlstrom, Sydney E. *A Religious History of the American People.* New Haven: Yale
University Press, 1972.
Allen, Gay Wilson, and Roger Asselineau. *St. John de Crèvecoeur: The Life of an Amer-
ican Farmer.* New York: Viking Press, 1987.
Ames, Fisher. "American Literature." In *Works of Fisher Ames*, ed. Seth Ames, 2 vols.,
2: 428–42. Boston: Little, Brown and Company, 1854.
———. "The Dangers of American Liberty." In *Works of Fisher Ames*, ed. Seth Ames,
2 vols., 2: 344–99. Boston: Little, Brown and Company, 1854.
———. "Equality." In *Works of Fisher Ames*, ed. Seth Ames, 2 vols., 2: 207–28.
Boston: Little, Brown and Company, 1854.
———. "The Mire of Democracy." In Lewis P. Simpson, ed., *Federalist Literary Mind*,
51–55. Originally in *Monthly Anthology and Boston Review* 2 (1805): 563–66.
Anderson, Benedict. *Imagined Communities: Reflections on the Origin and Spread of
Nationalism.* London: Verso, 1983.
Anglo, Sydney. "Evident Authority and Authoritative Evidence: The *Malleus Male-
ficarum*." In *The Damned Art: Essays in the Literature of Witchcraft*, ed. Sydney An-
glo, 1–31. London: Routledge & Kegan Paul, 1977.
Appleby, Joyce. *Liberalism and Republicanism in the Historical Imagination.* Cambridge:
Harvard University Press, 1992.
Arblaster, Anthony. *Democracy.* 2d ed. Minneapolis: University of Minnesota Press,
1994.

Arendt, Hannah. *On Revolution.* New York: Viking Press, 1963.

Armstrong, Nancy, and Leonard Tennenhouse. *The Imaginary Puritan: Literature, Intellectual Labor, and the Origins of Personal Life.* Berkeley: University of California Press, 1992.

Axelrod, Alan. *Charles Brockden Brown: An American Tale.* Austin: University of Texas Press, 1983.

Bacon, Leonard. *Thirteen Historical Discourses.* New Haven: 1839.

Bailyn, Bernard. *The Ideological Origins of the American Revolution.* Cambridge: Harvard University Press, 1967.

Bakhtin, Mikhail. "Discourse in the Novel." In *The Dialogic Imagination: Four Essays,* ed. Michael Holquist, trans. Caryl Emerson and Michael Holquist, 259–422. Austin: University of Texas Press, 1981.

———. "Forms of Time and of the Chronotope in the Novel." In *The Dialogic Imagination: Four Essays,* ed. Michael Holquist, trans. Caryl Emerson and Michael Holquist, 84–258. Austin: University of Texas Press, 1981.

———. *Problems of Dostoevsky's Poetics.* Ed. and trans. Caryl Emerson. Minneapolis: University of Minnesota Press, 1984.

Balzac, Honoré de. Review of James Fenimore Cooper. Trans. K. P. Wormeley. In Dekker and McWilliams, eds., *Fenimore Cooper,* 196–200. Originally in *Paris Review,* 25 July 1840.

Bancroft, George. *History of the United States of America.* 6 vols. New York: D. Appleton and Co., 1890–91.

Barish, Jonas. *The Antitheatrical Prejudice.* Berkeley and Los Angeles: University of California Press, 1981.

Barlow, Joel. *The Works of Joel Barlow.* 2 vols. Ed. William K. Bottorff and Arthur L. Ford. New York: Scholars' Facsimiles & Reprints, 1970.

Barth, Karl. "The End of Religion." In *The Writings of St. Paul,* ed. Wayne A. Meeks, 250–57. New York: W. W. Norton, 1972.

Bartlett, Moses. *False and Seducing Teachers.* New London: 1757.

Baudrillard, Jean. *In the Shadow of the Silent Majorities; Or, The End of the Social, and Other Essays.* Trans. Paul Foss, John Johnston, and Paul Patton. New York: Semiotext(e), 1983.

Bauman, Richard. *Let Your Words Be Few: Symbolism of Speaking and Silence among Seventeenth-Century Quakers.* Cambridge: Cambridge University Press, 1983.

Beard, Charles A. *The Republic: Conversations on Fundamentals.* New York: Viking Press, 1946.

Beidler, Philip D. "*Billy Budd*: Melville's Valedictory to Emerson." *ESQ: A Journal of the American Renaissance* 24 (1978): 215–28.

Belden, Albert D. *George Whitefield, the Awakener: A Modern Study of the Evangelical Revival.* New York: Macmillan, 1953.

Belinsky, Vissarion. "The Division of Poetry into Kinds and Genres." Trans. M. A. Nicholson. Excerpted in Dekker and McWilliams, eds., *Fenimore Cooper,* 193–96.

Original available as "Razdelenie poezii na rody i vidy," in *Izbrannye esteticheskie raboty v 2-kh tomakh*, ed. N. K. Geia (Moscow: Iskusstvo, 1986), 1: 215–83.

Bell, Michael Davitt. *Hawthorne and the Historical Romance of New England*. Princeton: Princeton University Press, 1971.

Bell, Rudolph M. *Holy Anorexia*. Chicago: University of Chicago Press, 1985.

Bendix, Reinhold. "The Lower Classes and the 'Democratic Revolution.'" *Industrial Relations: A Journal of Economy and Society* 1 (1961): 91–116.

Benjamin, Walter. "The Work of Art in the Age of Mechanical Reproduction." In *Illuminations*, ed. Hannah Arendt, trans. Harry Zohn, 217–51. New York: Schocken Books, 1978.

Bennett, Maurice. "Charles Brockden Brown's Ambivalence Toward Art and Imagination." *Essays in Literature* 10 (Spring 1983): 55–69.

Bercovitch, Sacvan. *The American Jeremiad*. Madison: University of Wisconsin Press, 1978.

———. *The Puritan Origins of the American Self*. New Haven: Yale University Press, 1975.

———. *The Rites of Assent: Transformations in the Symbolic Construction of America*. New York: Routledge, 1993.

Berthoff, Warner. "Brockden Brown: The Politics of the Man of Letters." *Serif* 3 (1966): 3–11.

Blaikie, Alexander. *A History of Presbyterianism in New England*. Boston: Alexander Moore, 1882.

Blair, Samuel. "Revival of Religion at New-Londonderry in the Province of Pennsylvania . . ." In Prince, ed., *Christian History 1744*, 242–61.

Bloch, Ruth H. *Visionary Republic: Millennial Themes in American Thought, 1756–1800*. New York: Cambridge University Press, 1985.

Bobbio, Norberto. *Democracy and Dictatorship: The Nature and Limits of State Power*. Trans. Peter Kennealy. Minneapolis: University of Minnesota Press, 1989.

———. *The Future of Democracy: A Defence of the Rules of the Game*. Trans. Roger Griffin. Ed. Richard Bellamy. Minneapolis: University of Minnesota Press, 1987.

Bonomi, Patricia. *Under the Cope of Heaven: Religion, Society, and Politics in Colonial America*. New York: Oxford University Press, 1986.

Bourdieu, Pierre. *Language and Symbolic Power*. Ed. and intro. John B. Thompson. Trans. Gino Raymond and Matthew Adamson. Cambridge: Harvard University Press, 1991.

Bowen, Nathan. "Extracts from Interleaved Almanacs of Nathan Bowen, Marblehead, 1742–1799." *Essex Institute Historical Collections* 91 (1955): 163–90.

Boyd, Steven R., ed. *The Whiskey Rebellion: Past and Present Perspectives*. Contributions in American History, no. 109. Westport, Conn.: Greenwood Press, 1985.

Boyer, Paul, and Stephen Nissenbaum. *Salem Possessed: The Social Origins of Witchcraft*. Cambridge: Harvard University Press, 1974.

———, eds. *Salem Witchcraft Papers: Verbatim Transcripts of the Legal Documents of the Salem Witchcraft Outbreak of 1692.* 3 vols. New York: Da Capo Press, 1977.

———, eds. *Salem-Village Witchcraft: A Documentary Record of Local Conflict in Colonial New England.* Belmont, Calif.: Wadsworth Publishing Co., 1972.

Branch, Watson G., ed. *Melville: The Critical Heritage.* London: Routledge & Kegan Paul, 1985.

Braswell, William. "Melville as a Critic of Emerson." *American Literature* 9 (1937): 317–34.

Brattle, Thomas. "Letter of 8 October 1692." In Burr, ed., *Narratives of the Witchcraft Cases*, 165–90.

Breen, T. H. "Retrieving Common Sense: Rights, Liberties, and the Religious Public Sphere in Late Eighteenth Century America." In Josephine F. Pacheco, ed., *To Secure the Blessings of Liberty: Rights in American History*, 55–65.

Breitweiser, Mitchell R. *Cotton Mather and Benjamin Franklin: The Price of Representative Personality.* Cambridge: Cambridge University Press, 1984.

———. "Cotton Mather's Crazed Wife." *Glyph* 5 (1979): 88–113.

Briggs, Charles Augustus. *American Presbyterianism, Its Origins and Early History.* New York: Charles Scribner's Sons, 1885.

Brooke, John L. "To the Quiet of the People: Revolutionary Settlement and Civil Unrest in Western Massachusetts, 1774–1789." *William and Mary Quarterly*, 3d ser., 46 (1989): 425–62.

Brown, Charles Brockden. "Dialogues of the Living: Dialogue II." *Monthly Magazine and American Review* 2 (1800): 96–99.

———. *Edgar Huntley; or, Memoirs of a Sleep-Walker.* Kent, Ohio: Kent State University Press, 1984.

———. "On American Literature." *Monthly Magazine and American Review* 1 (1799): 338–42.

———. "Remarks on Style." *Literary Magazine and American Register* (1806): 100–105.

———. "The Rhapsodist." In *The Rhapsodist and Other Uncollected Writings*, ed. Harry R. Warfel, 1–24. New York: Scholars' Facsimiles & Reprints, 1943. Originally in *Universal Asylum and Columbian Magazine* 3 (1789): 464–67, 537–41, 587–601, 661–65.

———. "The Use of Anecdotes." *Literary Magazine and American Register* (1806): 53–57.

———. "What Is Literary Genius?" *Literary Magazine and American Register* (1806): 247–54.

———. *Wieland and Memoirs of Carwin the Biloquist.* Ed. and intro. Jay Fliegelman. New York: Penguin Books, 1991.

Brown, Gillian. *Domestic Individualism: Imagining Self in Nineteenth-Century America.* Berkeley: University of California Press, 1990.

Brown, Norman O. *Love's Body.* Berkeley and Los Angeles: University of California Press, 1966.

Brownson, Orestes A. "American Literature." *Boston Quarterly Review* 2 (1839): 1–26.

Buckminster, Joseph Stevens. "Address of the Editors." *Monthly Anthology and Boston Review* 6 (1809): 4–5. Excerpted as "Gentle Knights and the Paynim Host" in Lewis P. Simpson, ed., *Federalist Literary Mind*, 83–84.

———. "The Dangers and Duties of Men of Letters." In Lewis P. Simpson, ed., *Federalist Literary Mind*, 95–102. Originally in *Monthly Anthology and Boston Review* 7 (1809): 146–53.

Buell, Lawrence. "American Literary Emergence as a Postcolonial Phenomenon." *American Literary History* 4 (1992): 411–42.

Bumsted, J. M. "Religion, Finance, and Democracy in Massachusetts: The Town of Norton as a Case Study." *Journal of American History* 57 (1971): 817–31.

Burke, Kenneth. *A Grammar of Motives.* Berkeley and Los Angeles: University of California Press, 1969.

———. *Language as Symbolic Action: Essays on Life, Literature, and Method.* Berkeley and Los Angeles: University of California Press, 1966.

———. *The Rhetoric of Religion: Studies in Logology.* Berkeley and Los Angeles: University of California Press, 1961.

Burr, George Lincoln. "The Literature of Witchcraft." *Papers of the American Historical Association* 4 (1890): 237–66.

———, ed. *Narratives of the Witchcraft Cases, 1648–1706.* New York: Charles Scribner's Sons, 1914.

Burroughs, Steven. *The Memoirs of Stephen Burroughs.* Intro. Philip F. Gura. Boston: Northeastern University Press, 1988.

Bushman, Richard L. *From Puritan to Yankee: Character and the Social Order in Connecticut, 1690–1765.* Cambridge: Harvard University Press, 1967.

———, ed. *The Great Awakening: Documents on the Revival of Religion, 1740–1745.* Chapel Hill: University of North Carolina Press, 1989.

Butler, Jon. *Awash in a Sea of Faith: Christianizing the American People.* Cambridge: Harvard University Press, 1990.

———. "Enthusiasm Described and Decried: The Great Awakening as Interpretive Fiction." *Journal of American History* 69 (1982): 314–22.

Butler, Judith. *Bodies That Matter: On the Discursive Limits of "Sex."* New York: Routledge, 1993.

———. *Gender Trouble: Feminism and the Subversion of Identity.* New York: Routledge, Chapman & Hall, 1990.

———. *The Psychic Life of Power: Theories in Subjection.* Stanford: Stanford University Press, 1997.

Butler, Judith and Joan W. Scott, eds. *Feminists Theorize the Political.* New York: Routledge, 1992.

Caldwell, Patricia. *The Puritan Conversion Narrative: The Beginnings of American Expression.* New York: Cambridge University Press, 1983.

Calef, Robert. *More Wonders of the Invisible World.* Excerpted in Burr, ed., *Narratives of the Witchcraft Cases*, 289–393.

Canetti, Elias. *Crowds and Power.* Trans. Carol Stewart. New York: Farrar Straus Giroux, 1988.

Casarino, Cesare. "Gomorrahs of the Deep; or, Melville, Foucault, and the Question of Heterotopia." *Arizona Quarterly* 51 (1995): 1–25.

Chai. Leon. *The Romantic Foundations of the American Renaissance.* Ithaca: Cornell University Press, 1987.

Channing, Edward Tyrell. "On Models in Literature." In Spiller, ed., *American Literary Revolution*, 154–62. Originally in *North American Review* 3 (1816): 202–9.

———. Review of *The Life of Charles Brockden Brown*, by William Dunlap. Excerpted in Ruland, ed., *Native Muse*, 118–30. Originally in *North American Review* 9 (1819): 58–77.

Channing, Walter. "Essay on American Language and Literature." In Spiller, ed., *American Literary Revolution*, 112–20. Originally in *North American Review* 1 (1815): 307–14.

———. "Reflections on the Literary Delinquency of America." In Spiller, ed., *American Literary Revolution*, 121–31. Originally in *North American Review* 2 (1815): 33–43.

Channing, William Ellery. "Remarks on National Literature." In Spiller, ed., *American Literary Revolution*, 342–72. Originally in *Christian Examiner* 36 (1830): 269–94.

Charvat, William. *The Origins of American Critical Thought, 1819–1835.* Philadelphia: University of Pennsylvania Press, 1936.

———. *The Profession of Authorship in America, 1800–1870.* Ed. Matthew J. Bruccoli. New York: Columbia University Press, 1992.

Chauncy, Charles. *Enthusiasm described and caution'd against.* Boston: 1742.

———. *A Letter from a Gentleman in Boston, to Mr. George Wishart, One of the Ministers of Edinburgh, Concerning the State of Religion in New-England.* Edinburgh: 1742.

———. "Letter to Davenport." In *Enthusiasm described*, i–viii.

———. *A Letter to the Reverend Mr. Whitefield, Vindicating certain Passages he has excepted against, in a late Book entitled, "Seasonable Thoughts on the State of Religion in New-England."* Boston: 1745.

———. *Seasonable Thoughts on the State of Religion in New-England.* Boston: 1742.

———. "A Second Letter to the Reverend Mr. Whitefield . . . by Canonicus." Boston: 1745.

Chevignard, Bernard. "St. John de Crèvecoeur in the Looking Glass: *Letters from an American Farmer* and the Making of a Man of Letters." *Early American Literature* 19 (1984): 173–90.

Chion, Michel. "The Impossible Embodiment." In *Everything You Always Wanted to Know about Lacan . . . but Were Afraid to Ask Hitchcock*, ed. Slavoj Žižek, 195–207. London: Verso, 1992.

——. *La Voix au Cinéma*. Paris: Editions de l'étoile, 1982.

Clark, Michael. " 'Like Images Made Black with the Lightning': Discourse and the Body in Colonial Witchcraft." *Eighteenth Century* 34 (1993): 199–220.

Clark, Stuart. "The Scientific Status of Demonology." In *Occult and Scientific Mentalities in the Renaissance*, ed. Brian Vickers, 351–74. New York: Cambridge University Press, 1984.

Clark, T. J. *The Absolute Bourgeois: Artists and Politics in France, 1848–1851*. Princeton: Princeton University Press, 1973.

Cmiel, Kenneth. *Democratic Eloquence: The Fight over Popular Speech in Nineteenth-Century America*. Berkeley and Los Angeles: University of California Press, 1990.

Colacurcio, Michael J. *The Province of Piety: Moral History in Hawthorne's Early Tales*. Cambridge: Harvard University Press, 1984.

Cole, Charles C., Jr. "Brockden Brown and the Jefferson Administration." *Pennsylvania Magazine of History and Biography* 72 (1948): 253–63.

Cole, Nathan. "The Spiritual Travels of Nathan Cole." In Michael Crawford, ed., "The Spiritual Travels of Nathan Cole." *William and Mary Quarterly*, 3d ser., 33 (1976): 92–126.

Colman, Benjamin. "Souls flying to Jesus Christ pleasant and admirable to behold." Included in Prince, "Some Account," in Prince, ed., *Christian History 1744*, 382–84.

Colton, Calvin. *History and Character of American Revivals of Religion*. 1832. Reprint, New York: AMS Press, 1973.

Cook, George Allan. *John Wise, Early American Democrat*. New York: Octagon Books, 1966.

Cooper, James Fenimore. *The Last of the Mohicans*. Intro. Richard Slotkin. New York: Penguin Classics, 1986.

——. *The Pioneers*. New York: Penguin Classics, 1988.

Cotton, John. "History of the Revival of Religion . . . at Hallifax . . ." In Prince, ed., *Christian History 1743*, 259–70.

Cowen, Wilson Walker. *Melville's Marginalia*. 2 vols. New York: Garland Publishing, 1987.

Cowing, Cedric B. "Sex and Preaching in the Great Awakening." *American Quarterly* 20 (1968): 624–44.

Cox, Richard J. "Stephen Bordley, George Whitefield, and the Great Awakening in Maryland." *Historical Magazine of the Protestant Episcopal Church* 46 (1977): 297–307.

Crawford, Michael J. *Seasons of Grace: Colonial New England's Revival Tradition in Its British Context*. New York: Oxford University Press, 1991.

——, ed. "The Spiritual Travels of Nathan Cole." *William and Mary Quarterly*, 3d ser., 33 (1976): 92–126.

Crèvecoeur, J. Hector St. John de. *Letters from an American Farmer and Sketches of Eighteenth-Century America*. Ed. and intro. Albert E. Stone. New York: Penguin Books, 1986.

Dana, Richard Henry, Sr. Review of *The Sketch Book of Geoffrey Crayon, Gent.*, by Washington Irving. In Spiller, ed., *American Literary Revolution*, 211–34. Originally in *North American Review* 9 (1819): 322–56.

Daston, Lorraine. "Marvelous Facts and Miraculous Evidence in Early Modern Europe." *Critical Inquiry* 18 (1991): 93–124.

Dauber, Kenneth. *The Idea of Authorship in America: Democratic Poetics from Franklin to Melville*. Madison: University of Wisconsin Press, 1990.

Davenport, James. "The Confession and Retraction of the Rev. Mr. Davenport . . ." In Prince, ed., *Christian History 1744*, 236–41.

Davidson, Cathy N. *Revolution and the Word: The Rise of the Novel in America*. New York: Oxford University Press, 1986.

de Bolla, Peter. *The Discourse of the Sublime: Readings in History, Aesthetics, and the Subject*. Oxford: Basil Blackwell, 1989.

de Certeau, Michel. *The Practice of Everyday Life*. Trans. Steven Rendall. Berkeley and Los Angeles: University of California Press, 1984.

De Man, Paul. "Excuses." In *Allegories of Reading: Figural Language in Rousseau, Nietzsche, Rilke, and Proust*, 278–301. New Haven: Yale University Press, 1979.

Dehon, Theodore. "A Discourse upon the Importance of Literature to Our Country." *Monthly Anthology* 4 (1807): 465–74. Excerpted as "With Literature as with Government," in Lewis P. Simpson, ed., *Federalist Literary Mind*, 185–88.

Dekker, George. *The American Historical Romance*. Cambridge: Cambridge University Press, 1987.

Dekker, George, and Larry Johnston. "Introduction" to *The American Democrat*, by James Fenimore Cooper. New York: Penguin Books, 1969.

Dekker, George, and John P. McWilliams, eds. *Fenimore Cooper: The Critical Heritage*. London: Routledge & Kegan Paul, 1973.

Delbanco, Andrew. "Melville's Sacramental Style." *Raritan* 12 (1993): 69–91.

———. *The Puritan Ordeal*. Cambridge: Harvard University Press, 1989.

Demos, John. *Entertaining Satan: Witchcraft and the Culture of Early New England*. New York: Oxford University Press, 1982.

Dexter, Franklin B., ed. *Documentary History of Yale University under the Original Charter of the Collegiate School of Connecticut, 1701–1745*. New Haven: Yale University Press, 1916.

Dickinson, Emily. *The Complete Poems of Emily Dickinson*. Ed. Thomas H. Johnson. Boston: Little, Brown and Company, 1960.

Dickinson, Jonathan. "Account of the Revival of Religion at Newark & Elizabeth-Town . . ." In Prince, ed., *Christian History 1743*, 252–58.

Dillingham, William B. *Melville and His Circle: The Last Years*. Athens: University of Georgia Press, 1996.

Dillon, Elizabeth Maddock. "Representing the Subject of Freedom: Liberalism, Hysteria, and Dispossessive Individualism." Ph.D. dissertation, Department of Comparative Literature, University of California, Berkeley, 1995.

Dimock, Wai-chee. *Empire for Liberty: Melville and the Poetics of Individualism.* Princeton: Princeton University Press, 1989.

Dostoevskij, Fedor. "Neskol'ko zametok o prostote i uproshchennosti" (Some remarks on simplicity and simplification). *Polnoe sobranie sochinenii v tridtsati tomakh,* 23: 141–44. Leningrad: Nauka, 1981.

Douglas, Ann. *The Feminization of American Culture.* New York: Avon Books, 1977.

Dudley, Joseph. "Letter to the Dutch and French clergymen of New York, 5 October 1692." *Collections of the Massachusetts Historical Society,* 2d ser., 1 (1884): 353. Latin original on 348–49.

Duyckinck, Evert. "Nathaniel Hawthorne." *Arcturus* 1 (1841): 330–36.

Eagleton, Terry. *Literary Theory: An Introduction.* Minneapolis: University of Minnesota Press, 1983.

Edwards, Jonathan. *An Account of the Life of the late Reverend Mr. David Brainerd . . .* Boston: 1749.

——. "Continuation of the State of Religion at Northampton . . ." In Prince, ed., *Christian History 1743,* 367–81.

——. *The Distinguishing Marks of a Work of the Spirit of God.* In *The Works of Jonathan Edwards,* ed. John E. Smith. *Vol. 4: The Great Awakening,* ed. C. C. Goen, 213–88. New Haven: Yale University Press, 1972.

——. *A Faithful Narrative of the Surprising Work of God in the Conversion of Many Hundred Souls in Northampton . . .* In *The Works of Jonathan Edwards,* ed. John E. Smith. *Vol. 4: The Great Awakening,* ed. C. C. Goen, 144–211. New Haven: Yale University Press, 1972.

——. "Letter of Invitation to George Whitefield." See Abelove, ed., "Jonathan Edwards's Letter of Invitation to George Whitefield."

——. *Some Thoughts Concerning the present Revival of Religion in New-England . . .* In *The Works of Jonathan Edwards,* ed. John E. Smith. *Vol. 4: The Great Awakening,* ed. C. C. Goen, 289–530. New Haven: Yale University Press, 1972.

——. "Unpublished Letter [to Rev. Benjamin Colman] of May 30, 1735." In *The Works of Jonathan Edwards,* ed. John E. Smith. *Vol. 4: The Great Awakening,* ed. C. C. Goen, 99–110. New Haven: Yale University Press, 1972.

Edwards, Sarah. "Narrative." In Jonathan Edwards, *Works of President Edwards: With a Memoir of His Life,* ed. Sereno E. Dwight, 10 vols., 1: 171–86. New York: G. & C. & H. Carvill, 1830.

Elliott, Emory. *Revolutionary Writers: Literature and Authority in the New Republic, 1725–1810.* New York: Oxford University Press, 1982.

Ellison, Julie. "The Sociology of 'Holy Indifference': Sarah Edwards's Narrative." *American Literature* 56 (1984): 479–95.

Emerson, Everett, ed. *American Literature, 1764–1789: The Revolutionary Years.* Madison: University of Wisconsin Press, 1977.

Emerson, Ralph Waldo. "The American Scholar." In *Selections from Ralph Waldo Emerson,* ed. Stephen E. Whicher, 63–80. Boston: Houghton Mifflin Co., 1957.

——. *The Journals and Miscellaneous Notebooks of Ralph Waldo Emerson.* 16 vols. Ed. William H. Gilman et al. Cambridge: Harvard University Press, 1960–82.

——. "Literary Ethics." In *Collected Works of Ralph Waldo Emerson, Vol. 1: Nature, Addresses, and Lectures.* Intro. and notes Robert E. Spiller. Cambridge: Harvard University Press, 1971.

——. "The Poet." In *Selections from Ralph Waldo Emerson,* ed. Stephen E. Whicher, 222–41. Boston: Houghton Mifflin Co., 1957.

[Emerson, Ralph Waldo, and Margaret Fuller, eds.]. "New Poetry." *The Dial* 1 (1840): 220–33.

Erkkila, Betsy, and Jay Grossman, eds. *Breaking Bounds: Whitman and American Cultural Studies.* New York: Oxford University Press, 1996.

"The Examination of Mrs. Anne Hutchinson at the Court at Newtown." In *The Antinomian Controversy, 1636–1638: A Documentary History,* 2d ed., ed. David D. Hall, 311–48. Durham: Duke University Press, 1990.

Fanger, Donald. *The Creation of Nikolai Gogol.* Cambridge: Harvard University Press, 1979.

Fichtelberg, Joseph. "Utopic Distresses: Crèvecoeur's *Letters* and Revolution." *Studies in the Literary Imagination* 22 (1994): 85–101.

Fielder, Leslie. "Charles Brockden Brown and the Invention of the American Gothic." In *Love and Death in the American Novel,* rev. ed., 126–61. New York: Stein and Day, 1966.

Fiering, Norman. *Jonathan Edwards's Moral Thought and Its British Context.* Chapel Hill: University of North Carolina Press, 1981.

——. *Moral Philosophy at Seventeenth-Century Harvard: A Discipline in Transition.* Chapel Hill: University of North Carolina Press, 1981.

Finley, Samuel. *Christ Triumphing, and Satan Raging.* In Heimert and Miller, eds., *The Great Awakening,* 152–67.

Fliegelman, Jay. *Declaring Independence: Jefferson, Natural Language, and the Culture of Performance.* Stanford: Stanford University Press, 1993.

——. "Introduction" to *Wieland and Memoirs of Carwin the Biloquist,* by Charles Brockden Brown. New York: Penguin Books, 1991.

——. *Prodigals and Pilgrims: The American Revolution against Patriarchal Authority, 1750–1800.* New York: Cambridge University Press, 1982.

Foner, Philip S. *The Democratic-Republican Societies, 1790–1800: A Documentary Sourcebook of Constitutions, Declarations, Addresses, Resolutions, and Toasts.* Westport, Conn.: Greenwood Press, 1976.

Franklin, Benjamin. *The Autobiography of Benjamin Franklin.* Ed. Leonard W. Labaree et al. New Haven: Yale University Press, 1964.

Freccero, John. *Dante: The Poetics of Conversion.* Ed. Rachel Jacoff. Cambridge: Harvard University Press, 1986.

——. "Logology: Burke on St. Augustine." In *Representing Kenneth Burke,* ed. Hayden White and Margaret Brose, 52–67. Baltimore: Johns Hopkins University Press, 1982.

Freneau, Philip. "Advice to Authors, by the Late Mr. Robert Slender." Excerpted in Spiller, ed., *American Literary Revolution*, 5–12. Originally in *Miscellaneous Works of Mr. Philip Freneau, containing his Essays and Additional Poems*, Philadelphia: 1788.

———. "Letters on Various Interesting and Important Subjects, by Robert Slender, O.S.M." Philadelphia: 1799.

Fuller, Margaret, and Ralph Waldo Emerson. "The Editors to the Reader." *The Dial* 1 (1840): 1–4.

Fussell, Edwin Sill. "*Wieland*: A Literary and Historical Reading." *Early American Literature* 18 (1983): 171–86.

Gallagher, Catherine: *Nobody's Story: The Vanishing Acts of Women Writers in the Marketplace, 1670–1820*. Berkeley: University of California Press, 1994.

Garden, Alexander. *Regeneration and the Testimony of the Spirit*. Charleston, S.C.: 1741. Excerpted in Heimert and Miller, eds., *The Great Awakening*, 46–61.

———. *Six Letters to the Reverend Mr. George Whitefield*. 2d ed. Boston: T. Fleet, 1740.

Gardiner, W. H. Review of *The Last of the Mohicans*, by James Fenimore Cooper. Excerpted in Dekker and McWilliams, eds., *Fenimore Cooper*, 104–18. Originally in *North American Review* 23 (1826): 150–97.

———. Review of *The Spy*, by James Fenimore Cooper. In Ruland, ed., *Native Muse*, 186–94. Originally in *North American Review* 15 (1822): 250–82.

Garner, Stanton. "Fraud as Fact in Herman Melville's *Billy Budd*." *San Jose Studies* 4 (1978): 83–105.

———. "Melville and Thomas Campbell: The 'Deadly Space Between.' " *English Language Notes* 14 (1977): 289–90.

Gaustad, Edwin S. *The Great Awakening in New England*. New York: Harper & Brothers, 1957.

Gellner, Ernest. *Nations and Nationalism*. Ithaca: Cornell University Press, 1983.

Gerlach, Luther P., and Virginia H. Hine. *People, Power, Change: Movements of Social Transformation*. Indianapolis and New York: Bobbs-Merrill, 1970.

Gillies, John. *Memoirs of the Life of Reverend George Whitefield, M.A.* London, 1772; New Haven, 1834.

Ginzburg, Lydia. *On Psychological Prose*. Trans. and ed. Judson Rosengrant. Princeton: Princeton University Press, 1991.

Glanvill, Joseph. *Saducismus Triumphatus; or, Full and Plain Evidence concerning Witches and Apparitions*. London: 1681.

Godbeer, Richard. *The Devil's Dominion: Magic and Religion in Early New England*. New York: Cambridge University Press, 1992.

Goen, C. C. *Revivalism and Separatism in New England, 1740–1800: Strict Congregationalists and Separate Baptists in the Great Awakening*. New Haven: Yale University Press, 1962; 1969.

Gould, Philip. "New England Witch-Hunting and the Politics of Reason in the Early Republic." *New England Quarterly* 68 (1995): 58–92.

Grabo, Norman S. *The Coincidental Art of Charles Brockden Brown*. Chapel Hill: University of North Carolina Press, 1981.

———. "Crèvecoeur's American: Beginning the World Anew." *William and Mary Quarterly*, 3d ser., 48 (1991): 159–72.

Greenblatt, Stephen. "The Circulation of Social Energy." In *Shakespearean Negotiations: The Circulation of Social Energy in Renaissance England*, 1–20. Berkeley and Los Angeles: University of California Press, 1988.

———. *Renaissance Self-Fashioning, from More to Shakespeare*. Chicago: University of Chicago Press, 1980.

———. "Towards a Poetics of Culture." In *Learning to Curse: Essays in Modern Culture*, 146–60. New York: Routledge, 1990.

Greene, Jack P., ed. *The Reinterpretation of the American Revolution, 1763–1789*. New York: Harper & Row, 1968.

Griswold, Rufus Wilmot. "Charles Brockden Brown." In *The Prose Writers of America*, 2d ed., rev., 107–11. Philadelphia: Carey & Hart, 1847.

Grossman, Allen. "Whitman's 'Whoever You Are Holding Me Now in Hand': Remarks on the Endlessly Repeated Rediscovery of the Incommensurability of the Person." In Betsy Erkkila and Jay Grossman, eds., *Breaking Bounds: Whitman and Cultural Studies*, 112–22.

Habermas, Jürgen. "Sovereignty and the Führerdemokratie." *Times Literary Supplement* (26 September 1986): 1053–54.

———. *The Structural Transformation of the Public Sphere: An Inquiry into a Category of Bourgeois Society*. Trans. Thomas Burger. Cambridge: MIT Press, 1994.

Hagenbüchle, Roland. "American Literature and the Nineteenth-Century Crisis in Epistemology: The Example of Charles Brockden Brown." *Early American Literature* 23 (1988): 121–51.

Hales, John. "The Landscape of Tragedy: Crèvecoeur's 'Susquehanna.'" *Early American Literature* 20 (1985): 39–63.

———. *A Modest Inquiry into the Nature of Witchcraft*. In Burr, ed., *Narratives of the Witchcraft Cases*, 397–432.

Hall, David D. "Witchcraft and the Limits of Interpretation." *New England Quarterly* 58 (1985): 253–81.

———. *Witch-Hunting in Seventeenth-Century New England: A Documentary History, 1636–1692*. Boston: Northeastern University Press, 1991.

———. *Worlds of Wonder, Days of Judgment: Popular Religious Belief in Early New England*. New York: Alfred A. Knopf, 1989.

Hamilton, Alexander. *Gentleman's Progress: The Itinerarium of Dr. Alexander Hamilton, 1744*. Ed. Carl Bridenbaugh. Chapel Hill: University of North Carolina Press, 1948.

Hammond-Tooke, W. D. "The Witch Familiar as a Mediatory Construct." In *Witchcraft and Sorcery*, ed. Max Marwick, 365–75. New York: Penguin, 1970.

Hancock, John. *The Dangers of an Unqualified Ministry*. Boston: 1743.

Hanson, Russell L. *The Democratic Imagination in America: Conversations with Our Past*. Princeton: Princeton University Press, 1985.

Hart, James D. *The Popular Book: A History of America's Literary Taste*. Berkeley: University of California Press, 1950.

Hatch, Nathan O. *The Democratization of American Christianity*. New Haven: Yale University Press, 1989.

Hawthorne, Nathaniel. "The Devil in Manuscript." In *Tales and Sketches*, ed. Roy Harvey Pearce, 330–37. New York: Library of America, 1982.

——. *The Scarlet Letter and Selected Writings*. Ed. Stephen Nissenbaum. New York: Modern Library, 1984.

Hayford, Harrison, and Merton M. Sealts Jr., eds. *Billy Budd: The Genetic Text*. Chicago: University of Chicago Press, 1962.

Hazlitt, William. "American Literature — Dr. Channing." Excerpted in Dekker and McWilliams, eds., *Fenimore Cooper*, 155–61. Originally in *Edinburgh Review* (October 1829): 125–31.

Hedges, William L. "The Myth of the Republic and the Theory of American Literature." *Prospects* IV, ed. Jack Salzman, 101–20. New York: Burt Franklin & Co., 1979.

Heimert, Alan. *Religion and the American Mind, from the Great Awakening to the Revolution*. Cambridge: Harvard University Press, 1966.

Heimert, Alan, and Perry Miller, eds. *The Great Awakening: Documents Illustrating the Crisis and Its Consequences*. Indianapolis: Bobbs-Merrill Educational Publishing, 1967.

Held, David. *Models of Democracy*. Stanford: Stanford University Press, 1987.

Henry, Stuart C. *George Whitefield: Wayfaring Witness*. New York: Abingdon Press, 1957.

Hesford, Walter. " 'Do You Know the Author?': The Question of Authorship in *Wieland*." *Early American Literature* 17 (1982/83): 239–48.

Heyrman, Christine Leigh. *Commerce and Culture: The Maritime Communities of Colonial Massachusetts, 1690–1750*. New York: W. W. Norton, 1984.

Hindus, Milton, ed. *Walt Whitman: The Critical Heritage*. London: Routledge & Kegan Paul, 1971.

Hobby, William. *An Inquiry into the Itinerancy, and the Conduct of the Rev. George Whitefield, an Itinerant Preacher . . .* Boston: 1745.

Hobsbawm, E. J. *Primitive Rebels: Studies in Archaic Forms of Social Movement in the Nineteenth and Twentieth Centuries*. New York: W. W. Norton, 1959.

Hocks, Richard A. "Melville and 'The Rise of Realism': The Dilemma of History in *Billy Budd*." *American Literary Realism* 26 (1994): 60–81.

Hofstadter, Richard. *America at 1750: A Social Portrait*. New York: Vintage Books, 1973.

Honig, B. "Toward an Agonistic Feminism: Hannah Arendt and the Politics of Identity." In *Feminists Theorize the Political*, 215–35. Ed. Judith Butler and Joan W. Scott. New York: Routledge, 1992.

Hooker, Thomas. *Survey of the Summe of Church Discipline*. London: 1648.

Howard, Leon. *Herman Melville, a Biography*. Berkeley and Los Angeles: University of California Press, 1951.

Howe, John R., Jr. "Republican Thought and the Political Violence of the 1790s." *American Quarterly* 19 (1967): 147–65.

Hunter, William B., Jr. "The Seventeenth Century Doctrine of Plastic Nature." *Harvard Theological Review* 43 (1950): 197–213.

Hutchinson, Thomas. *The History of the Colony and Province of Massachusetts-Bay*. 3 vols. Ed. Lawrence Shaw Mayo. Cambridge: Harvard University Press, 1936.

Ingersoll, Charles Jared. "Discourse Concerning the Influence of America on the Mind." 1823. In Spiller, ed., *American Literary Revolution*, 239–83.

Irving, Washington. "Desultory Thoughts on Criticism." *Knickerbocker* (1839): 175–78.

———. *A History of New York, by Diedrich Knickerbocker*. In *History, Tales, and Sketches*, ed. James W. Tuttleton, 363–729. New York: Library of America, 1983.

———. "Original Review: The Works . . . of the late Robert Treat Paine." *Analectic Magazine* 1 (1813): 208–26.

Isaac, Rhys. "Evangelical Revolt: The Nature of the Baptists' Challenge to the Traditional Order in Virginia, 1765 to 1775." *William and Mary Quarterly*, 3d ser., 31 (1974): 345–68.

———. *The Transformation of Virginia, 1740–1790*. Chapel Hill: University of North Carolina Press, 1982.

Jackson, Harvey H. "Hugh Bryan and the Evangelical Movement in Colonial South Carolina." *William and Mary Quarterly*, 3d ser., 43 (1986): 594–614.

Jacob, Margaret, and James Jacob, eds. *Origins of Anglo-American Radicalism*. London: George Allen & Unwin, 1984.

Jehlen, Myra. "J. Hector St. John Crèvecoeur: A Monarcho-Anarchist in Revolutionary America." *American Quarterly* 31 (1979): 204–22.

Johnson, Barbara. "Melville's Fist: The Execution of *Billy Budd*." In *The Critical Difference: Essays in the Contemporary Rhetoric of Reading*, 79–109. Baltimore: Johns Hopkins University Press, 1980.

Jones, William Alfred. "Democracy and Literature." *Democratic Review* 11 (1842): 196–200.

Jordan, Cynthia S. "On Rereading *Wieland*: 'The Folly of Precipitate Conclusions.'" *Early American Literature* 16 (1981): 154–74. Reprinted as chapter 3 in *Second Stories: The Politics of Language, Form, and Gender in Early American Fictions*. Chapel Hill: University of North Carolina Press, 1989.

Joyce, Patrick. *Democratic Subjects: The Self and the Social in Nineteenth-Century England*. Cambridge: Cambridge University Press, 1994.

Juster, Susan. *Disorderly Women: Sexual Politics and Evangelicalism in Revolutionary New England*. Ithaca: Cornell University Press, 1994.

Kammen, Michael. *People of Paradox: An Inquiry Concerning the Origins of American Civilization*. Ithaca: Cornell University Press, 1980.

Kaplan, Harold. *Democratic Humanism and American Literature*. Chicago: University of Chicago Press, 1972.

Karlsen, Carol F. *The Devil in the Shape of a Woman: Witchcraft in Colonial New England*. New York: Vintage Books, 1989.

Kenney, William H., III. "George Whitefield, Dissenter Priest of the Great Awakening, 1739–1741." *William and Mary Quarterly*, 3d ser., 26 (1969): 75–93.

Kibbey, Ann. "Mutations of the Supernatural: Witchcraft, Remarkable Providences, and the Power of Puritan Men." *American Quarterly* 34 (1982): 125–48.

Kittredge, George Lyman. *Witchcraft in Old and New England*. Cambridge: Harvard University Press, 1929.

Knight, Janice. *Orthodoxies in Massachusetts: Rereading American Puritanism*. Cambridge: Harvard University Press, 1994.

Konig, David Thomas. *Law and Society in Puritan Massachusetts, Essex County, 1629–1692*. Chapel Hill: University of North Carolina Press, 1979.

Laclau, Ernesto, and Chantal Mouffe. *Hegemony and Socialist Strategy: Towards a Radical Democratic Politics*. London: Verso, 1985.

Lambert, Frank. *"Pedlar in Divinity": George Whitefield and the Transatlantic Revivals, 1737–1770*. Princeton: Princeton University Press, 1994.

Lang, Amy Schrager. *Prophetic Woman: Anne Hutchinson and the Problem of Dissent in the Literature of New England*. Berkeley and Los Angeles: University of California Press, 1987.

Larson, Charles. "Melville's Marvell and Vere's Fairfax." *ESQ: A Journal of the American Renaissance* 38 (1992): 59–70.

Law, William. *The Absolute Unlawfulness of the Stage-Entertainment Fully Demonstrated*. 1726. New York: Garland Publishing Inc., 1973.

Lawrence, D. H. *Studies in Classic American Literature*. New York: Viking Press, 1964.

Lawson, Deodat. *A Brief and True Narrative Of some Remarkable Passages Relating to sundry Persons Afflicted by Witchcraft, at Salem Village* . . . 1692. In Burr, ed., *Narratives of the Witchcraft Cases*, 145–64.

———. *A Brief and True Narrative* . . . 1704. In Upham, *Salem Witchcraft*, 2: 525–37.

———. *Christ's Fidelity the only Shield against Satan's Malignity*. Excerpted in Upham, *Salem Witchcraft*, 2: 78–87, and Boyer and Nissenbaum, eds., *Salem-Village Witchcraft*, 124–28.

Leary, Lewis. "Introduction" to *Home as Found*, by James Fenimore Cooper. New York: Capricorn Books, 1961.

Lefort, Claude. *Democracy and Political Theory*. New York: Oxford University Press, 1988.

———. *The Political Forms of Modern Society: Bureaucracy, Democracy, Totalitarianism*. Ed. John B. Thompson. Cambridge: Polity Press, 1986.

Leonard, Nathanael. "A brief Account of the late Revival of Religion in Plymouth." In Prince, ed., *Christian History 1744*, 313–17.

"Letter from R.P. to Jonathan Corwin of 9 August 1692." In Upham, *Salem Witch-craft*, 2:538–44.

Levin, David. *Cotton Mather: The Young Life of the Lord's Remembrancer*. Cambridge: Harvard University Press, 1978.

——. "Shadows of Doubt: Specter Evidence in Hawthorne's Young Goodman Brown." *American Literature* 34 (1962): 344–52.

——. "When Did Cotton Mather See the Angel?" *Early American Literature* 15 (1980/81): 271–75.

Leyda, Jay. *The Melville Log: A Documentary Life of Herman Melville, 1819–1891*. 2 vols. New York: Harcourt, Brace & Co., 1951.

Longfellow, Henry Wadsworth. "Review of Sydney." 1832. In Ruland, ed., *Native Muse*, 240–60.

Looby, Christopher. *Voicing America: Language, Literary Form, and the Origins of the United States*. Chicago: University of Chicago Press, 1996.

Lotman, Iurii M. "Concerning Khlestakov." In *The Semiotics of Russian Cultural History*, eds. Alexander D. Nakhimovsky and Alice Stone Nakhimovsky, 150–87. Ithaca: Cornell University Press, 1985.

——. "Problema khudozhestvennogo prostranstva v proze Gogolia." (The problem of artistic space in the prose of Gogol.) *Izbrannye stat'i v trekh tomakh, t. I, Stat'i po semiotike i tipologii kul'tury*, 413–47. Tallin, Estonia: Aleksandra, 1992.

Lovejoy, David. " 'Desperate Enthusiasm': Early Signs of American Radicalism." In *Origins of Anglo-American Radicalism*, ed. Margaret Jacob and James Jacob, 231–42. London: George Allen & Unwin, 1984.

——. *Religious Enthusiasm in the New World: Heresy to Revolution*. Cambridge: Harvard University Press, 1985.

Lovelace, Richard F. *The American Pietism of Cotton Mather: Origins of American Evangelicism*. Grand Rapids, Mich.: Christian University Press, 1979.

Lowell, James Russell. *A Fable for Critics*. Excerpted in Dekker and McWilliams, eds., *Fenimore Cooper*, 238–40. Originally Boston: Ticknor and Fields, 1856.

Lukes, Steven. *Individualism*. Oxford: Basil Blackwell, 1973.

Macpherson, C. B. *Democratic Theory: Essays in Retrieval*. Oxford: Clarendon Press, 1973.

——. *The Life and Times of Liberal Democracy*. Oxford: Oxford University Press, 1977.

——. *The Political Theory of Possessive Individualism: Hobbes to Locke*. New York: Oxford University Press, 1962.

——. *The Real World of Democracy*. Toronto: Canadian Broadcasting Corporation, 1965.

Main, Jackson Turner. "Government by the People: The American Revolution and the Democratization of the Legislatures." In Jack P. Greene, ed., *Reinterpretation of the American Revolution*, 322–38.

Marini, Stephen A. *Radical Sects of Revolutionary New England*. Cambridge: Harvard University Press, 1982.

Marrant, John. "A Narrative of the Lord's wonderful Dealings with John Marrant, a Black, (Now gone to Preach the Gospel in Nova-Scotia) Born in New-York, in North-America, Taken down from his own Relation, arranged, corrected and published, By the Rev. Mr. Aldridge." In *Held Captive by Indians: Selected Narratives, 1642–1836*, ed. Richard VanDerBeets, 177–201. Knoxville: University of Tennessee Press, 1973.

Mather, Cotton. *Another Brand Pluckt Out of the Burning, or, More Wonders of the Invisible World.* Included in Calef, *More Wonders of the Invisible World.* In Burr, ed., *Narratives of the Witchcraft Cases*, 308–23.

———. *A Brand Pluck'd Out of the Burning.* In Burr, ed., *Narratives of the Witchcraft Cases*, 253–87.

———. *Diary of Cotton Mather.* 2 vols. New York: Frederick Ungar Publishing Co., n.d.

———. "A Discourse on Witchcraft." In *What Happened in Salem?*, 2d ed., ed. David Levin, 96–106. Documents Pertaining to the Seventeenth-Century Witchcraft Trials series. New York: Harcourt, Brace & World, 1960.

———. *Magnalia Christi Americana.* 2 vols. Hartford: Silas Andrus and Son, 1853.

———. *Manuductio ad Ministerium: Directions for a Candidate of the Ministry.* 1726. Reprint, New York: Columbia University Press Facsimile Text Society, 1938.

———. *Memorable Providences, Relating to Witchcrafts and Possessions.* In Burr, ed., *Narratives of the Witchcraft Cases*, 89–143.

———. *Selected Letters of Cotton Mather.* Comp. Kenneth Silverman. Baton Rouge: Louisiana State University Press, 1971.

———. *Wonders of the Invisible World.* In Burr, ed., *Narratives of the Witchcraft Cases*, 203–51.

Mather, Increase. *Angelographia, or, a Discourse Concerning the Nature and Power of the Holy Angels . . .* Boston: 1696.

———. *The Autobiography of Increase Mather.* Ed. M. G. Hall. Worcester, Mass.: American Antiquarian Society, 1962.

———. *Cases of Conscience Concerning Evil Spirits Personating Men.* In Cotton Mather, *Wonders of the Invisible World . . . To Which is added, A farther account of the tryals of the New-England Witches by Increase Mather*, 221–91. London: J. R. Smith, 1862.

———. *A Disquisition Concerning Angelical Apparitions.* Appended to *Angelographia.*

———. *An Essay for the Recording of Illustrious Providences.* London: 1684.

May, Henry F. *The Enlightenment in America.* New York: Oxford University Press, 1976.

McGregore, David. *The Spirits of the Present Day Tried.* In Heimert and Miller, eds., *The Great Awakening*, 214–27.

McLoughlin, William G. *New England Dissent, 1630–1833. Vol. 1: The Baptists and the Separation of Church and State.* Cambridge: Harvard University Press, 1971.

McVickar, John. *Tribute to the Memory of Sir Walter Scott.* New York: 1833.

Mellen, Grenville. Review of *The Red Rover*, by James Fenimore Cooper. Excerpted in Dekker and McWilliams, ed., *Fenimore Cooper*, 141–47. Originally in *North American Review* 27 (1828): 139–54.

Melville, Herman. *Billy Budd, Sailor: An Inside Narrative*. Ed. Milton R. Stern. Indianapolis: Bobbs-Merrill Educational Publishing, 1975.

———. *Moby-Dick*. Ed. Harrison Hayford and Hershel Parker. New York: W. W. Norton, 1967.

Middlekauff, Robert. *The Mathers: Three Generations of Puritan Intellectuals, 1596–1728*. New York: Oxford University Press, 1971.

Miller, Joshua. *The Rise and Fall of Democracy in Early America, 1630–1789*. University Park: Pennsylvania State University Press, 1991.

Miller, Perry. "Errand into the Wilderness." In *Errand into the Wilderness*, 1–15. Cambridge: Harvard University Press, 1956.

———. *Jonathan Edwards*. Amherst: University of Massachusetts Press, 1981.

———. "The Marrow of Puritan Divinity." In *Errand into the Wilderness*, 48–98. Cambridge: Harvard University Press, 1956.

———. *The New England Mind: From Colony to Province*. Cambridge: Harvard University Press, 1953.

———. *The New England Mind: The Seventeenth Century*. Cambridge: Harvard University Press, 1939.

———. *The Raven and the Whale: The War of Words and Wits in the Era of Poe and Melville*. New York: Harcourt, Brace & World, 1956.

———, ed. *The Transcendentalists: An Anthology*. Cambridge: Harvard University Press, 1950.

Millgate, Michael. "Melville and Marvell: A Note on *Billy Budd*." *English Studies* 49 (1968): 47–50.

Moran, Gerald F. "Conditions of Religious Conversion in the First Society of Norwich, Connecticut, 1718–1744." *Journal of Social History* 5 (1972): 331–43.

Morgan, Edmund S. *Inventing the People: The Rise of Popular Sovereignty in England and America*. New York: W. W. Norton, 1988.

———. *The Puritan Dilemma: The Story of John Winthrop*. Boston: Little, Brown, and Company, 1958.

———. *Visible Saints: The History of a Puritan Idea*. Ithaca: Cornell University Press, 1963.

Morgan, Winifred. *An American Icon: Brother Jonathan and American Identity*. Newark: University of Delaware Press, 1988.

Morone, James A. *The Democratic Wish: Popular Participation and the Limits of American Government*. N.p.: Basic Books, 1990.

Morrison, Toni. *Playing in the Dark: Whiteness and the Literary Imagination*. Cambridge: Harvard University Press, 1992.

Mott, Frank Luther. *A History of American Magazines, 1741–1850*. New York: D. Appleton and Co., 1930.

Mouffe, Chantal. *The Return of the Political*. London: Verso, 1993.

Mullin, Gerald W. *Flight and Rebellion: Slave Resistance in Eighteenth-Century Virginia.* New York: Oxford University Press, 1972.

Mumford, Lewis. *Herman Melville.* New York: Harcourt, Brace & Co., 1929.

Murphy, Geraldine. "The Politics of Reading *Billy Budd.*" *American Literary History* 1 (1989): 361–82.

Murry, John Middleton. "Herman Melville's Silence." *Times Literary Supplement* (10 July 1924): 433.

Naess, Arne, et al., eds. *Democracy, Ideolgy, and Objectivity: Studies in the Semantics and Cognitive Analysis of Ideological Controversy.* Oxford: Basil Blackwell, 1956.

Nash, Gary. *The Urban Crucible: Social Change, Political Consciousness, and the Origins of the American Revolution.* Cambridge: Harvard University Press, 1979.

Nathanson, Tenney. *Whitman's Presence: Body, Voice, and Writing in "Leaves of Grass."* New York: New York University Press, 1992.

Neal, John. "The Last American Novel." Excerpted in Dekker and McWilliams, eds., *Fenimore Cooper,* 83–88. Originally in *London Magazine* 16 (May 1826): 27–31.

Newfield, Christopher. "Controlling the Voice: Emerson's Early Theory of Language." *ESQ: A Journal of the American Renaissance* 38 (1992): 1–29.

———. *The Emerson Effect: Individualism and Submission in America.* Chicago: University of Chicago Press, 1996.

Niebuhr, H. Richard. *The Kingdom of God in America.* New York: Harper and Brothers, 1937; 1959.

Nietzsche, Friedrich. *The Use and Abuse of History.* Trans. Adrian Collins. Indianapolis: Liberal Arts Press, Inc., 1949.

Nissenbaum, Stephen, ed. *The Great Awakening at Yale College.* Belmont, Calif.: Wadsworth Publishing Co., 1972.

Nuttall, Geoffrey F. *The Holy Spirit in Puritan Faith and Experience.* Oxford: Basil Blackwell, 1947.

———. "Howel Harris and 'The Grand Table': A Note on Religion and Politics, 1744–50." *Journal of Ecclesiastical History* 39 (1988): 531–44.

———. *Visible Saints and the Congregational Way, 1640–1660.* Oxford: Basil Blackwell, 1957.

Oakeshott, Michael. *Rationalism in Politics and Other Essays.* New York: Basic Books, 1962.

Ogilvie, James. "An Account of the Rev. Mr. Whitefield and his Reception, Ministrations and Success at Aberdeen . . ." In Prince, ed., *Christian History 1743,* 279–81.

Ong, Walter J. *The Presence of the Word: Some Prolegomena for Cultural and Religious History.* Minneapolis: University of Minnesota Press, 1981.

Owen, Dennis E. "Spectral Evidence: The Witchcraft Cosmology of Salem Village in 1692." In *Essays in the Sociology of Perception,* ed. Mary Douglas, 275–301. London: Routledge & Kegan Paul, 1982.

Pacheco, Josephine F. *To Secure the Blessings of Liberty: Rights in American History.* Fairfax, Va.: George Mason University Press, 1993.

Palmer, R. R. *The Age of Democratic Revolution.* 2 vols. Princeton: Princeton University Press, 1959.

———. "The American Revolution: The People as Constituent Power." In Jack P. Greene, ed., *Reinterpretation of the American Revolution,* 338–61.

———. "Notes on the Use of the Word 'Democracy,' 1789–1799." *Political Science Quarterly* 68 (1953): 203–26.

Park, Joseph. "An Account of the late Propagation of Religion at Westerly and Charlestown . . ." In Prince, ed., *Christian History 1743,* 201–10.

Parker, Hershel. *Reading Billy Budd.* Evanston: Northwestern University Press, 1990.

Parkman, Francis. "The Works of James Fenimore Cooper." In *Essays from the North American Review,* 358–76. Ed. A. T. Rice. New York: 1879.

Parrington, Vernon Louis. *Main Currents in American Thought: An Interpretation of American Literature from the Beginnings to 1920.* 3 vols. New York: Harcourt, Brace and Co., 1927.

Parris, Samuel. *Christ Knows How Many Devils There Are.* In Boyer and Nissenbaum, eds., *Salem-Village Witchcraft,* 129–31.

———. *These Shall Make War with the Lamb.* In Boyer and Nissenbaum, eds., *Salem-Village Witchcraft,* 132–36.

Parsons, Jonathan. *A Needful Caution.* New London: 1742.

Perry, William Stevens, ed. *Historical Collections Relating to the American Colonial Church.* 5 vols. Hartford, Conn.: The Church Press, 1870–78.

Pettit, Norman. "Prelude to Mission: Brainerd's Expulsion from Yale." *New England Quarterly* 59 (1986): 28–50.

Philbrick, Thomas. *St. John de Crèvecoeur.* New York: Twayne, 1970.

Phips, William. "Letter to the Earl of Nottingham of 21 February 1693." *Collections of the Massachusetts Historical Society,* 2d ser., 1 (1884): 340–42.

Plumstead, A. W. "Hector St. John de Crèvecoeur." In *American Literature, 1764–1789: The Revolutionary Years,* Everett Emerson, ed., 213–31.

Pochmann, Henry A. *German Culture in America: Philosophical and Literary Influences, 1600–1900.* Madison: University of Wisconsin Press, 1957.

Pocock, J. G. A. *The Machiavellian Moment: Florentine Political Thought and the Atlantic Republican Tradition.* Princeton: Princeton University Press, 1975.

———. *Politics, Language, and Time: Essays on Political Thought and History.* New York: Atheneum Press, 1971.

———. *Virtue, Commerce, and History: Essays on Political Thought and History, Chiefly in the Eighteenth Century.* Cambridge: Cambridge University Press, 1985.

Pole, J. R. "Historians and the Problem of Early American Democracy." *American Historical Review* 67 (1962): 626–46.

Pope, Robert G. *The Half-Way Covenant: Church Membership in Puritan New England.* Princeton: Princeton University Press, 1969.

Portelli, Alessandro. *The Text and the Voice: Writing, Speaking, and Democracy in American Literature*. New York: Columbia University Press, 1994.

Porter, Carolyn. *Seeing and Being: The Plight of the Participant Observer in Emerson, James, Adams, and Faulkner*. Middletown, Conn.: Wesleyan University Press, 1981.

Poulet, Georges. "Phenomenology of Reading." *New Literary History* 1 (1969): 53–68.

Prescott, William H. "Life of Charles Brockden Brown." 1834. In *The Library of American Biography, Vol. 1*, ed. Jared Sparks, 117–89. New York: Harper Brothers, 1848.

Price, Martin. "The Logic of Intensity: More on Character." *Critical Inquiry* 2 (Winter 1975): 369–79.

Prince, Thomas. "Some Account of the late Revival of Religion in Boston." In Prince, ed., *Christian History 1744*, 374–415.

———, ed. *The Christian History Containing Accounts of the Revival and Propagation of Religion in Great-Britain, America &c. For the Year 1743*. Boston: 1744.

———, ed. *The Christian History Containing Accounts of the Revival and Propagation of Religion in Great-Britain, America &c. For the Year 1744*. Boston: 1745.

Railton, Stephen. *Fenimore Cooper: A Study of His Life and Imagination*. Princeton: Princeton University Press, 1978.

Reed, Sampson. "Observations on the Growth of the Mind." 1826. Excerpted in *The Transcendentalists: An Anthology*, ed. Perry Miller, 53–59. Cambridge: Harvard University Press, 1979.

Reinhold, Meyer. *Classica Americana: The Greek and Roman Heritage in the United States*. Detroit: Wayne State University Press, 1984.

"A remarkable Account of a Reformation among some Gentlemen, at *Boston* in *New-England* . . ." *Weekly History*, no. 28 (17 October 1741): 3–4.

Remini, Robert V. *The Legacy of Andrew Jackson: Essays on Democracy, Indian Removal, and Slavery*. Baton Rouge: Louisiana State University Press, 1988.

"Return of the Dutch and French clergymen of New York of 5 October 1692." *Proceedings of the Massachusetts Historical Society*, 2d ser., 1 (1884): 353–58.

Review of *The Last of the Mohicans*, by James Fenimore Cooper. In Dekker and McWilliams, eds., *Fenimore Cooper*, 89–96. Originally in *New-York Review and Athenaeum* 2 (1826): 285–92.

Review of *The Last of the Mohicans*, by James Fenimore Cooper. Excerpted in Dekker and McWilliams, eds., *Fenimore Cooper*, 97–104. Originally in *United States Literary Gazette* 4 (1826): 87–94.

Review of *The Pioneers*, by James Fenimore Cooper. In Dekker and McWilliams, eds., *Fenimore Cooper*, 69–72. Originally in *Port Folio* 15 (March 1823): 230–48.

Reynolds, David S. *Walt Whitman's America: A Cultural Biography*. New York: Alfred A. Knopf, 1995.

Richardson, Robert D., Jr. *Emerson: The Mind on Fire*. Berkeley: University of California Press, 1995.

Ricks, Christopher. "Lies." *Critical Inquiry* 2 (Autumn 1975): 121–42.

Roberts, Jennifer. "The Creation of a Legacy: A Manufactured Crisis in Eighteenth-Century Thought." In *Athenian Political Thought and the Reconstruction of American Democracy*, ed. J. Peter Euben, John R. Wallach, and Josiah Ober, 81–102. Ithaca: Cornell University Press, 1994. .

Rogin, Michael Paul. *Subversive Genealogy: The Politics and Art of Herman Melville.* New York: Alfred A. Knopf, 1983.

Ross, Kristin. *The Emergence of Social Space: Rimbaud and the Paris Commune.* Foreword Terry Eagleton. Vol. 60, Theory and History of Literature. Minneapolis: University of Minnesota Press, 1988.

Rosswurm, Steven. " 'As a Lyen out of His Den': Philadelphia's Popular Movement, 1776–80." In Margaret Jacob and James Jacob, eds., *Origins of Anglo-American Radicalism*, 300–323.

Ruland, Richard, ed. *The Native Muse: Theories of American Literature, Vol. 1.* New York: E. P. Dutton & Co., 1972.

Rutman, Darrett B. "Local Freedom and Puritan Control." In *Puritanism in Seventeenth-Century Massachusetts*, ed. David D. Hall, 108–18. New York: Holt Rinehart and Winston, 1968.

Samuels, Shirley. "Wieland: Alien and Infidel." *Early American Literature* 25 (1990): 46–66.

Scheick, William J. "The Problem of Origination in Brown's *Ormond*." In *Critical Essays on Charles Brockden Brown*, ed. Bernard Rosenthal, 126–41. Boston: G. K. Hall, 1981.

Schlesinger, Arthur M., Jr. *The Age of Jackson.* Boston: Little, Brown and Company, 1953.

Schmidt, Leigh Eric. " 'A Second and Glorious Reformation': The New Light Extremism of Andrew Croswell." *William and Mary Quarterly*, 3d ser., 43 (1986): 214–44.

Schmitt, Carl. *The Crisis of Parliamentary Democracy.* Trans. Ellen Kennedy. Cambridge: MIT Press, 1985.

Schneider, Joseph L. "Melville's Use of the Vere-Fairfax Lineage in *Billy Budd*." *Names* 26 (1978): 129–38.

Scott, Joan W. " 'Experience.' " In *Feminists Theorize the Political*, ed. Judith Butler and Joan W. Scott, 22–40. New York: Routledge, 1992.

Sealts, Merton M., Jr. *Melville's Reading: A Check-List of Books Owned and Borrowed.* Rev. ed. Charleston: University of South Carolina Press, 1988.

——. *Pursuing Melville: 1940–1980.* Madison: University of Wisconsin Press, 1982.

Sedgwick, Eve Kosofsky. "Some Binarisms (I): *Billy Budd*: After the Homosexual." In *Epistemology of the Closet*, 91–130. Berkeley: University of California Press, 1990.

Selijns, Henry, et al. "Reply to Dudley, 11 October 1692." *Collections of the Massachusetts Historical Society*, 2d ser., 1 (1884): 354–58. Latin original on 349–53.

Seward, William. *Journal of a Voyage from Savannah to Philadelphia, and from Phila-delphia to England.* London: 1740.

Shea, Daniel B., Jr. *Spiritual Autobiography in Early America.* Princeton: Princeton University Press, 1968.

Shoemaker, Robert W. " 'Democracy' and 'Republic' as Understood in Late Eigh-teenth Century America." *American Speech* 41 (May 1966): 83–95.

A short reply to Mr. Whitefield's letter Which he wrote in answer to the Querists . . . 1741. In Heimert and Miller, eds., *The Great Awakening*, 134–46.

Shurtleff, William. *A Letter to those . . . who refuse to admit the Rev. Mr. Whitefield into their Pulpits.* 1745. Excerpted in Heimert and Miller, eds., *The Great Awakening*, 354–63.

Silverman, Kenneth. *The Life and Times of Cotton Mather.* New York: Columbia Uni-versity Press, 1985.

———. "A Note on the Date of Cotton Mather's Visitation by an Angel." *Early American Literature* 15 (1980): 82–86.

Simms, William Gilmore. "The Writings of Cooper." Excerpted in Dekker and Mc-Williams, eds., *Fenimore Cooper*, 218–27. Originally in *Magnolia* 1 (1842): 129–39.

Simpson, David. *The Politics of American English, 1776–1850.* New York: Oxford University Press, 1986.

Simpson, Lewis P., ed. *The Federalist Literary Mind: Selections from the "Monthly An-thology and Boston Review," 1803–1811, Including Documents Relating to the Boston Athenaeum.* Baton Rouge: Louisiana State University Press, 1962.

———. "The Symbolism of Literary Alienation in the Revolutionary Age." *Journal of Politics* 38, no. 3 (1976): 79–100.

Slaughter, Thomas P. *The Whiskey Rebellion: Frontier Epilogue to the American Revolu-tion.* New York: Oxford University Press, 1986.

Slotkin, Richard. *The Fatal Environment: The Myth of the Frontier in the Age of Indus-trialization, 1800–1890.* New York: Atheneum, 1985.

———. *Regeneration Through Violence: The Mythology of the American Frontier, 1600–1860.* Middletown, Conn.: Wesleyan University Press, 1973.

Smith, Josiah. *A Sermon, on the Character, Preaching, &c. of the Rev. Mr. Whitefield.* Ex-cerpted in Heimert and Miller, eds., *The Great Awakening*, 62–69, and Prince, ed., *Christian History 1744*, 366–74.

Spencer, Benjamin. *The Quest for Nationality: An American Literary Campaign.* Syracuse: Syracuse University Press, 1957.

Spiller, Robert E., ed. *The American Literary Revolution: 1783–1837.* Documents in American Civilization Series. New York: Anchor Books, 1967.

Starkey, Marion L. *The Devil in Massachusetts: A Modern Inquiry into the Salem Witch Trials.* New York: Anchor Books, 1969.

Stein, Stephen J. "George Whitefield on Slavery: Some New Evidence." *Church His-tory* 42 (1973): 243–57.

———. "A Note on Anne Dutton." *Church History* 44 (1975): 485–91.

Steiner, George. *Tolstoy or Dostoevsky, an Essay in the Old Criticism*. New York: E. P. Dutton & Co., 1971.

Stewart, Susan. *Crimes of Writing: Problems of the Containment of Representation*. Durham, N.C.: Duke University Press, 1994.

Stiles, Ezra. *The Literary Diary of Ezra Stiles. Vol. 1: January 1, 1769–March 13, 1776.* Ed. Franklin Bowditch Dexter. New York: Charles Scribner's Sons, 1901.

Stiles, Isaac. *A Looking-glass for Chang[e]lings . . .* 1743. Excerpted in Heimert and Miller, eds., *The Great Awakening*, 305–22.

Stoddard, Solomon. *The Defects of Preachers Reproved . . .* New London, Conn.: 1724.

Stout, Harry S. *The Divine Dramatist: George Whitefield and the Rise of Modern Evangelicalism*. Grand Rapids, Mich.: William B. Eerdmans Publishing Co., 1991.

——— . *The New England Soul: Preaching and Religious Culture in Colonial New England*. New York: Oxford University Press, 1986.

——— . "Religion, Communications, and the Ideological Origins of the American Revolution." *William and Mary Quarterly*, 3d ser., 34 (1977): 519–41.

Stout, Harry S., and Peter Onuf. "James Davenport and the Great Awakening in New London." *Journal of American History* 70 (1983): 556–78.

Sundquist, Eric J. "Suspense and Tautology in *Benito Cereno*." *Glyph* 8 (1981): 103–26.

Talmon, J. L. *Political Messianism: The Romantic Phase*. History of Totalitarian Democracy, vol. 2. London: Secker and Warburg, 1962.

——— . *The Rise of Totalitarian Democracy*. London: Secker and Warburg, 1952.

Taussig, Michael. *Mimesis and Alterity: A Particular History of the Senses*. New York: Routledge, 1993.

Taylor, Charles. *Sources of the Self: The Making of the Modern Identity*. Cambridge: Harvard University Press, 1989.

Tennent, Gilbert. *The Danger of an Unconverted Ministry*. 1741. In Heimert and Miller, eds., *The Great Awakening*, 71–99.

——— . "A Letter from the Rev. Mr. Gilbert Tennent . . ." In Prince, ed., *Christian History 1744*, 285–98.

——— . *The Necessity of Religious Violence in Order to Obtain Durable Happiness*. New York: 1735.

Tennent, William. "An Account of the Revival of Religion at Freehold . . ." In Prince, ed., *Christian History 1744*, 298–310.

The Testimony of . . . Harvard College, against George Whitefield. 1744. In Heimert and Miller, eds., *The Great Awakening*, 340–53.

Thayer, James B. "Trial by Jury of Things Supernatural." *Atlantic Monthly* 65 (1890): 465–81.

Thomas, Brook. "*Billy Budd* and the Judgment of Silence." In *Literature and Ideology*, ed. Harry R. Garvin, 51–78. Lewisburg: Bucknell University Press, 1982.

——— . "The Legal Fictions of Herman Melville and Lemuel Shaw." *Critical Inquiry* 11 (1984): 24–51.

Thomas, Keith. *Religion and the Decline of Magic*. New York: Scribner, 1971.

Thoreau, Henry David. *Walden and Civil Disobedience*. Ed. Owen Thomas. New York: W. W. Norton, 1966.

Tocqueville, Alexis de. *Democracy in America*. Trans. George Lawrence. Ed. J. P. Mayer. New York: Anchor Books, 1969.

Tolles, Frederick B. "Quietism versus Enthusiasm." *Pennsylvania Magazine of History and Biography* 69 (1945): 26–49.

Tolstoy, Lev N. "Are the Peasant Children to Learn to Write from Us? or, Are We to Learn from the Peasant Children?" In *The Works of Count Lev. N. Tolstoy, Vol. 4: Pedagogical Articles*, ed. and trans. Leo Wiener, 191–224. Boston: Dana Estes & Co., 1904.

Tompkins, Jane. *Sensational Designs: The Cultural Work of American Fiction, 1790–1860*. New York: Oxford University Press, 1985.

Totalitarian Democracy and After: International Colloquium in Memory of Jacob L. Talmon, Jerusalem, 21–24 June 1982. Jerusalem: Magnes Press, Hebrew University, 1984.

Tracy, Joseph. *The Great Awakening: A History of the Revival of Religion in the Time of Edwards and Whitefield*. Boston: 1842.

Trilling, Lionel. *Sincerity and Authenticity*. Cambridge: Harvard University Press, 1971.

Trinterud, Leonard. *The Forming of an American Tradition: A Re-examination of Colonial Presbyterianism*. Philadelphia: Westminster Press, 1949.

Tyerman, Luke. *The Life of the Rev. George Whitefield in Two Volumes*. 2d ed. London: 1890.

Upham, Charles W. *Salem Witchcraft*. 2 vols. 1867. Reprint, Williamstown, Mass.: Corner House Publishers, 1971.

Van Doren, Carl. *Benjamin Franklin*. New York: Penguin Books, 1991.

Wadsworth, Daniel. *The Diary of the Reverend Daniel Wadsworth, 1737–1747*. Ed. George Leon Walker. Hartford, Conn.: Case, Lockwood & Brainard Co., 1894.

Walker, George Leon. *Some Aspects of the Religious Life of New England with Special Reference to Congregationalists*. New York: Silver, Burdett and Company, 1897.

Walker, Timothy. *The Way to Try All Pretended Apostles*. Boston: 1743.

Wallace, James D. *Early Cooper and His Audience*. New York: Columbia University Press, 1986.

Walsh, John. "Methodism and the Mob in the Eighteenth Century." In *Popular Belief and Practice*, ed. G. J. Cuming and Derek Baker, 213–27. Cambridge: Cambridge University Press, 1972.

Walzer, Michael. *The Revolution of the Saints: A Study in Radical Politics*. Cambridge: Harvard University Press, 1965.

Warner, Michael. *The Letters of the Republic: Publication and the Public Sphere in Eighteenth-Century America*. Cambridge: Harvard University Press, 1990.

Watson, E. L. Grant. "Melville's Testament of Acceptance." *New England Quarterly* 6 (1933): 319–27.

Watters, David H. "The Spectral Identity of Sir William Phips." *Early American Literature* 18 (1983/84): 219–32.

Weber, Donald. *Rhetoric and History in Revolutionary New England*. New York: Oxford University Press, 1988.

Weber, Max. *Economy and Society: An Outline of Interpretive Sociology*. 2 vols. Ed. Guenther Roth and Claus Wittich. Berkeley: University of California Press, 1978.

Weisbuch, Robert. *Atlantic Double-Cross: American Literature and British Influence in the Age of Emerson*. Chicago: University of Chicago Press, 1986.

Weisman, Richard. *Witchcraft, Magic, and Religion in Seventeenth-Century Massachusetts*. Amherst: University of Massachusetts Press, 1984.

Weller, Samuel. *The Trial of Mr. Whitefield's Spirit*. Boston: 1741.

Welles, Benjamin. "Political Methodism." In Lewis P. Simpson, ed., *Federalist Literary Mind*, 55–56.

Wesling, Donald, and Tadeusz Sławek. *Literary Voice: The Calling of Jonah*. Albany: State University of New York Press, 1995.

Whitefield, George. *George Whitefield's Journals (1737–1741), To Which is Prefixed His "Short Account" (1746) and "Further Account" (1747)*. Ed. William Wale. Gainesville: Scholars' Facsimiles & Reprints, 1905; 1969.

——. *The Works of the Reverend George Whitefield*. 6 vols. London: 1771–72.

Whitman, Walt. "A Backward Glance O'er Travel'd Roads." In Floyd Stovall, ed., *Prose Works 1892*, 711–32.

——. *Leaves of Grass: Comprehensive Reader's Edition*. Ed. Harold W. Blodgett and Sculley Bradley. New York: New York University Press, 1965.

——. "Note at End of *Complete Poems and Prose*." In Floyd Stovall, ed., *Prose Works 1892*, 733–34.

——. "Preface 1855 — Leaves of Grass, *First Edition*." In Harold W. Blodgett and Sculley Bradley, eds., *Leaves of Grass: Comprehensive Reader's Edition*, 709–29.

——. "Preface, 1876, to the two-volume Centennial Edition of *Leaves of Grass* and 'Two Rivulets.'" In Floyd Stovall, ed., *Prose Works 1892*, 464–74.

——. "Prefatory Letter to Ralph Waldo Emerson, Leaves of Grass 1856. *Emerson to Whitman*, 1855. *Whitman to Emerson*, 1856." In Harold W. Blodgett and Sculley Bradley, eds., *Leaves of Grass: Comprehensive Reader's Edition*, 729–39.

——. *Prose Works 1892. Vol. 2: Collect and Other Prose*. Ed. Floyd Stovall. New York: New York University Press, 1964.

——. "Song of Myself." In Harold W. Blodgett and Sculley Bradley, eds., *Leaves of Grass: Comprehensive Reader's Edition*, 28–89.

Wiebe, Robert H. *Self-Rule: A Cultural History of American Democracy*. Chicago: University of Chicago Press, 1995.

Wigglesworth, Edward. *A Letter to the Reverend Mr. George Whitefield By Way of Reply To his Answer to the College Testimony against him and his Conduct*. Boston: T. Fleet, 1745.

Wilentz, Sean. *Chants Democratic: New York City and the Rise of the American Working Class, 1788–1850*. New York: Oxford University Press, 1984.

Willard, Samuel. "A briefe account of a strange & unusuall Providence of God befallen to Elizabeth Knap of Groton." In *Groton in the Witchcraft Times*, ed. Samuel Abbott Green, 7–21. Groton, Mass.: 1883.

———. *Some Miscellany Observations On our present Debates respecting Witchcrafts, in a Dialogue Between S. & B.* 1692. Reprint, Boston: 1869.

Williams, Daniel E. " 'Behold a Tragic Scene Strangely Changed into a Theater of Mercy': The Structure and Significance of Criminal Conversion Narratives in Early New England." *American Quarterly* 38 (1986): 825–47.

Williams, John R. "The Strange Case of Dr. Franklin and Mr. Whitefield." *Pennsylvania Magazine of History and Biography* 102 (1978): 399–421.

Williams, Raymond. *Keywords: A Vocabulary of Culture and Society*. Rev. ed. New York: Oxford University Press, 1985.

Willison, J. "Letter . . . respecting Mr. Whitefield's Character." In Prince, ed., *Christian History 1743*, 282–84.

Wills, Garry. "The Phallic Pulpit." *New York Review of Books* (21 December 1989): 20–26.

Wilson, John. *A Regular Zeal in Matters of Religion justified, and vindicated from the Charge of Enthusiasm, Madness, Dissimulation, etc.* Excerpted in Prince, ed., *Christian History 1744*, 220–34.

Withim, Philip. "*Billy Budd*: Testament of Resistance." *Modern Language Quarterly* 20 (1959): 115–27.

Wolin, Sheldon S. "Norm and Form: The Constitutionalizing of Democracy." In *Athenian Political Thought and the Reconstruction of American Democracy*, ed. J. Peter Euben, John R. Wallach, and Josiah Ober, 29–58. Ithaca: Cornell University Press, 1994.

Wood, Ellen Meiksins. "Democracy: An Idea of Ambiguous Ancestry." In *Athenian Political Thought and the Reconstruction of American Democracy*, ed. J. Peter Euben, John R. Wallach, and Josiah Ober, 59–80. Ithaca: Cornell University Press, 1994.

Wood, Gordon S. *The Creation of the American Republic, 1776–1787*. New York: W. W. Norton, 1969.

———. "The Democratization of Mind in the American Revolution." In *Leadership in the American Revolution*, 62–89. Library of Congress Symposia on the American Revolution. Washington: Library of Congress, 1974.

———. *The Radicalism of the American Revolution*. New York: Random House, 1991.

Woolman, John. *The Journal of John Woolman*. Ed. Janet Whitney. Chicago: Henry Regnery Co., 1950.

Wordsworth, William. "Preface to *Lyrical Ballads* (1802)." In *William Wordsworth*, ed. Stephen Gill, 595–615. Oxford: Oxford University Press, 1984.

Young, Alfred F. "English Plebeian Culture and Eighteenth-Century American Radicalism." In Margaret Jacob and James Jacob, eds., *Origins of Anglo-American Radicalism*, 185–211. London: George Allen & Unwin, 1984.

Ziff, Larzer. *Puritanism in America: New Culture in a New World*. New York: Viking Press, 1973.

———. "A Reading of *Wieland*." *PMLA* 77 (1962): 51–57.

———. *Writing in the New Nation: Prose, Print, and Politics in the Early United States.* New Haven: Yale University Press, 1991.

Žižek, Slavoj. "Formal Democracy and Its Discontents: Violations of the Fantasy-Space." *American Imago* 48 (1991): 181–98.

Index

In this index an "f" after a number indicates a separate reference on the next page, and an "ff" indicates separate references on the next two pages. A continuous discussion over two or more pages is indicated by a span of page numbers, e.g., "57–59." *Passim* is used for a cluster of references in close but not consecutive sequence. Fictional characters discussed in this book appear as individual name entries.

Adams, John, 465n75
Addison, Henry, 456n7
"Advice to Authors" (Freneau), 310–11
Aesthetic of innocence, 188–89, 309, 314, 361; development of, 291–94; and gap between being and representation, 293–95, 333, 337, 340f, 349; and absence of national literature, 296–97, 333, 337; and Cooper, 333f, 448n78; and Emerson, 333–35, 340–43, 490n99; and Whitman, 333, 341–46 *passim. See also* Inarticulateness; Innocence
Afflicted, 4, 57–58, 424n97; wounds of, 52–53, 60–61, 422n84, 423n88, 425nn107, 110, 113, 426n114; connection of specter to, 57–69; beliefs about, 59–60, 425n106; C. Mather on, 62, 63–66, 425nn107, 113; revelations of, 67–69; authority of, 75–76; identity of, 77–81
African Americans: as religious exhorters, 31, 113–14, 192, 199, 438n39; as invisible American character, 283–84. *See also* Slaves
Agora, 16, 401n44
Ahlstrom, Sydney, 406n6
Alden, John, 47, 424n97
Alden, Noah, 183
Allen, Timothy, 85

American literature. *See* National literature
American Revolution, 260, 478n51; and evangelism, 84f, 433n3, 434n8; and Great Awakening, 84, 433n3, 434n8; Crèvecoeur on, 284, 476nn47, 48; as origin of democracy, 381ff
"American Scholar, The" (Emerson), 333, 338, 340–41
Ames, Fisher, 276, 290, 300, 457n10
Anderson, Benedict, 4, 433n3
Andros, Edmund, 41
Anglo, Sydney, 429n148
Antinomian crisis, 36, 39, 73–74, 153, 394n8, 410n19
Antinomianism, 321, 341, 384, 410n19, 431nn159, 60; literary, 249–50, 258, 263
Appleby, Joyce, 6, 379–80
Arendt, Hannah, 397n26
Austin, Benjamin, 479n1
Authorship: as ventriloquism, 189, 191, 255–56, 267–68, 473nn17, 19; transformation in, in *Wieland*, 217–18, 242–58, 263–65; Hawthorne on, 248–49; as secularized antinomianism, 249–50, 258, 263; linked with democratic personality, 259f, 270, 288–89, 291–92, 329–34, 337, 469n2; American, and C. B. Brown, 267–69, 467n95, 468n97,

471n8, 473n17, 474nn21, 24; reluctance to be identified with, 270–71, 475n26; S. Burroughs on, 270–71; Crèvecoeur on, 274–82 *passim*, 288–89, 476n39; and gap between being and representation, 293–95; and inarticulate common man, 296, 481n14; comic portrayal of, 310–11, 484n51; Native American as model for, 312–14. *See also* Poet, American

Bailyn, Bernard, 6, 464n62, 465n75
Bakhtin, Mikhail, 8–9, 17, 101, 363, 396n18, 436n22
Balzac, Honoré de, 325, 486n65
Bancroft, George, 393n5, 403n3
Baptists, 182–84
Barlow, Joel, 309, 479n53
Bartlet, Phebe, 208
Bartlett, Moses, 152, 154–55, 201, 227, 442n11, 454n133, 469n104
Baudrillard, Jean, 395n15
Bauman, Richard, 456n2, 462n47
Baxter, Richard, 411n25
Beadle, William, 472n13
Beard, Charles A., 398n31
Being and representation, gap between, 8, 312, 328; and democratic personality, 10, 186, 289; and poet, 189, 337, 377; and aesthetic of innocence, 293–95, 333, 337, 340f, 349
Belcher, Jonathan, 99
Belinsky, Vissarion, 487n70
Bendix, Reinhold, 393n6
Benjamin, Walter, 453n130
Bentham, Jeremy, 399n35
Bercovitch, Sacvan, 38, 399n36, 412n36
Billy Budd (Melville), 12–13, 189, 347–75, 377–78, 385–88; "deadly space between" in, 13, 352–62 *passim*, 378, 385f, 494nn18, 19, 495n22; interpretations of, 348, 492n8, 493nn9–11, 496n30; "vocal current electric" in, 348, 352, 356, 361f, 378, 495n24; historical context of, 349, 493n12, 494n13; plot of, 349–50, 493n12; death sentence in, 350–61; narrator role in, 361–75. *See also individual fictional characters*
Bishop, Bridget, 45ff, 61, 425n110
Blacks, as limit to uncontainability, 116–19, 284. *See also* Slaves

Blair, Samuel, 131, 160, 162–63
Bobbio, Norberto, 12, 16, 401n44
Bonomi, Patricia, 443n21
Bordley, Stephen, 129–30, 134–36, 137, 446n47
Bourdieu, Pierre, 401n42, 402n45
Bowen, Nathan, 31–32, 192, 404n2
Boyer, Paul, 46, 405n5; on spectral evidence, 407n9, 409n17, 417n60
Brackenridge, Hugh Henry, 291, 480n4
Bradbury, Mary, 47, 418n65
Bradbury, Thomas, 47
Brainerd, David, 159, 461n33
Brattle, Thomas, 45–46, 52–58 *passim*, 407n9, 422nn84, 87
Breen, T. H., 394n15
Breitweiser, Mitchell, 7, 395n15, 411n30
Bright, John, 397n25
Brockwell, Charles, 32f, 192, 203, 405n5
Brockwell, H. A., 453n124
Brother Jonathan, 309, 484n50
Brown, Charles Brockden, 31, 185ff, 210, 266–67, 291, 465n74, 466n82; politics of, 262, 471n7; and authorship, 267–69, 467n95, 468n97, 471n8, 473n17, 474nn21, 24; as literary critic, 299–300. *See also individual fictional characters*
Browne, Mary, 45
Brownson, Orestes, 74, 307–8, 339
Buckminster, Joseph S., 306
Budd, Billy (*Billy Budd*), 350–68 *passim*, 372, 375; as innocent poet, 347–48, 361–62, 377; as symbol of American Revolution, 493n12
Bumppo, Natty (Leatherstocking tales), 314–20 *passim*, 324; whiteness of, 324–28; as innocent author, 329–34 *passim*
Burke, Kenneth, 15, 91, 353–54
Burr, George Lincoln, 406n6, 410n17, 414n48, 423n91
Burroughs, George, 66–67, 75f, 78, 291, 418n68, 419n75
Burroughs, Stephen, 187; *Memoirs*, 270–74; on character, 272, 273–74, 475nn27, 29
Bushman, Richard L., 147, 403n3
Butler, Judith, 397n26

Caldwell, Patricia, 411n27
Calef, Robert, 69, 75, 383–84, 419nn70, 75; on C. Mather, 55–56, 412n30,

425n103, 428n121, 445n37; on afflicted, 72, 424n97; on spectral evidence, 407n9, 409n16, 410n17

Calvinism, 28–29, 173, 197, 386

Candidus, 290, 479n1

Captain Vere (*Billy Budd*), 349–60 *passim*, 367f, 385, 470–73, 494n13, 495n28, 496n31

Carrier, Martha, 61

Carwin, Frank (*Wieland*), 185–87, 211–12, 255–62 *passim*, 267–68, 468nn101, 102, 473n18; voice of, 212, 214–17, 226; and Clara, 225–42 *passim*, 260–66

Cary, Elizabeth and Nathaniel, 34

Casarino, Cesare, 494n18

Channing, Edward Tyrell, 301–4, 308, 338, 483n33

Channing, Walter, 311–13, 314

Channing, William Ellery, 268, 298f, 305

Character: as variant of spectral space, 145; as threat to redeemed community, 175–76; American, 182, 276, 277–78, 283–84, 289, 293, 297, 298–99, 476n34; ontology of, in early American novels, 186–87, 260–70 *passim*, 275; ethical priority of, 187–88, 288–89, 290–92; uncontainability of, 265–66, 286–89; as without essential identity, 270–74, 475n27; S. Burroughs on, 272, 273–74, 475nn27, 29. *See also* Common man; Visible character

Character references, in Salem witchcraft trials, 47–48, 81, 418nn65, 67

Charity, 181, 226; Puritan concept of, 21f, 48; and beliefs about afflicted and witches, 58–59, 60; and individuality, 124, 142; renewal of, in Edwards, 180–81

Charvat, William, 479n53, 483n37

Chauncy, Charles, 131, 138, 209, 406n8, 410n19; on Whitefield, 92, 93–95, 106, 384, 445n40; on character of ministers, 126, 131, 146–47, 443n20; on enthusiasm, 151–53, 154, 158, 449nn82, 89, 454n133; on lay exhorters, 192f, 201–4 *passim*

Cheever, Ezekiel, 45, 50

Chevignard, Bernard, 476nn34, 35

Chion, Michel, 216

Churchill, Sarah, 78

Cicero, 213, 221–22, 224, 253, 464n73, 465nn74, 75

Claggart, John (*Billy Budd*), 347–78 *passim*, 385, 495n28

Clark, Lewis Gaylord, 335

Clark, Michael, 415n52

Clark, Stuart, 430n148

Clark, T. J., 15

Clarke, Mary, 61

Class. *See* Social classes

Cloyce, Sarah, 81, 417n61

Cmiel, Kenneth, 402n47

Colacurcio, Michael J., 418n63

Cole, Charles C., Jr., 471n7

Cole, Nathan, 107–13, 183, 215, 252, 440n62

Cole, Sarah, 45

Colman, Benjamin, 99, 127, 199, 443n26, 444n30

Colton, Calvin, 458n1

Common man, 291f, 479n3; national literature from, 292–95, 301–9, 338–42, 489nn89, 94; as inarticulate, 293, 296, 480n7, 481n14; national character from, 300–304, 483n37. *See also* Simplicity

Confidence-Man, The (Melville), 348, 492n8

Consent to representation, 22, 44–50 *passim*, 57–59, 70, 414n48, 415n49, 50, 416nn54, 55, 59

Conway, Moncure, 446n45

Cooper, James Fenimore, 191, 292, 298, 313, 488n81; *The Last of the Mohicans*, 294, 313–19 *passim*, 326, 335; *The Pioneers*, 294, 313–19 *passim*, 328, 331–33; and aesthetic of innocence, 314, 333f, 488n78; on Native Americans, 314–27, 335–36, 485nn60, 61; *The Deerslayer*, 333, 337; *The Pathfinder*, 333; criticism of, 335–37, 486n65, 487nn70, 71, 73–75, 489n85. *See also* individual fictional characters

Cooper, William, 127, 171–72, 455n143

Corey, Giles, 425n110

Corey, Martha, 50, 56, 425n110

Cory, Hannah, 204f

Cotta, John, 430n148

Cotton, John, 158, 160, 162

Cotton, Josiah, 199

Crèvecoeur, J. Hector St. John de, 187, 291; *Letters from an American Farmer*, 270, 274–89, 477n46; on authorship,

274–82 *passim*, 289, 476n39; on American character, 276, 277–78, 476n34; biography of, 276–77, 476n35; on visible character, 277–78, 282; on American Revolution, 284, 476nn47, 48. *See also* Farmer James
Crook, John, 462n49
Croswell, Andrew, 102, 199f
"Custom-House, The" (Hawthorne), 245, 248–49
Cutler, Timothy, 149, 152, 192–93, 443n20, 454n133

Dana, Richard Henry, Sr., 314
Dane, Francis, 82
Dansker, the (*Billy Budd*), 364–65, 369
Daston, Lorraine, 36, 417n60, 431n157
Daston, Sarah, 407n9
Dauber, Kenneth, 481n18
Davenport, James, 147–48, 151–52, 197–98, 199, 405n5, 447n68, 448n71, 460nn23, 25
Davidson, Cathy, 470n2
De Certeau, Michel, 1, 394n9
Deerslayer, The (Cooper), 333, 337
Dekker, George, 486n67
Delbanco, Andrew, 496n30
De Man, Paul, 468n100
Democracy, 1–2, 10, 403n3, 479n2; and liberalism, 2, 11–16, 391n1, 397n28, 399nn35, 37; origin of American, 2, 11–15, 379–83, 399n37; as negative term, 15, 26, 398n31, 399n32, 404n9; reconceptualizing, 15–16, 401n42; Federalists' fear of, 262, 470n6; radical, 262, 391n1; Jacksonian, 292, 480n5
Democratic literary production, ethics of, 187–88, 260, 269–70, 290–92
Democratic personality, 3f, 15–16, 388; origin and history of, 3–6, 393n7; in Salem witchcraft crisis, 4–5, 20, 22–24, 75, 383–84, 403n3; as variant of constructed subjectivity, 9, 10–11; emergence of, 20, 22–27; and Great Awakening, 20, 24–27, 85, 118–19, 259, 469n1; linked with authorship, 259f, 270, 288–89, 291–92, 469n2. *See also* Domestication of democratic personality
Democratic subjectivity, 10–11, 15–16, 397n25

Democratic Vistas (Whitman), 189, 295, 344–45, 347, 376f
"Democratic wish," 394n13
Demos, John, 418n62
Dennie, Joseph, 483n34
DeRich, John, 61
Devil: I. Mather on, 70, 416n58, 430n148; Puritanism on God and, 70–71, 429n148; Knapp's possession by, 120–24; as voice to nation, 122–23; C. Mather on, 427n117, 430n149
Dickinson, Emily, 211
Dickinson, Jonathan, 149–50
Domestication of democratic personality, 3, 186, 193, 290–95; through common man, 291, 293; in Cooper's novels, 292, 294, 314–33; in Whitman's *Leaves of Grass*, 293–97 *passim*; allied with author, 294–95; in literary criticism, 295, 298, 335–43; through Native Americans, 312–14, 486n62
Dostoevsky, Fyodor, 302
Dudley, Joseph, 407n9, 420n78
Dunlap, William, 303

Eames, Rebecca, 79
Easty, Mary, 24, 69f, 81, 243, 257, 403n5, 417n61, 424n97
Edwards, Jonathan, 83, 122, 205, 313, 405n5, 441n69, 461n33; on truest representation, 28–29, 168–71, 210, 384; on spectacular conversion, 113, 161–62; on voice and visible character, 126–27, 163–77, 191, 450n95, 453nn125, 131, 454nn134, 138, 455nn139, 140, 142; on character and voice of ministers, 136, 143, 145, 447n62; on America as leading into millennium, 159, 451n102, 452n105; theory of redeemed representation of, 180–82, 384; on Hawley suicide, 208–11, 462n53; on Whitefield, 438nn43, 44
Edwards, Oliver. *See* Effingham, Oliver
Effingham, Oliver (Leatherstocking tales), 328–31
Elocutionary revolution, 260, 463n60
Emerson, Ralph Waldo, 293, 339–40, 471n9, 475n31, 487n73; quoted, 83, 177, 259; "The Poet," 296, 306, 333, 346; on American poet, 306–8, 333, 338–46 *passim*; on literary isolationism, 306–7, 308; and aesthetic of innocence,

333–35, 340–43, 490n99; "The American Scholar," 333, 338, 340–41; on national literature, 338–39, 489n90; on inarticulateness, 340–43, 346–47, 490n99; as influence on Whitman, 346, 491n3; and Melville, 347f, 492n4

English, Mary, 425n110

Enthusiasm: Chauncy on, 151–53, 154, 158, 449nn82, 89, 454n133; and evangelism, 154–55, 450nn92–94; political, 194–95, 449n82

European witchcraft trials, spectral evidence in, 409n17

Evangelism: and American revolutionary thought, 84f, 433n3, 434n8; as tautology, 97, 437n38; and religious enthusiasm, 154–55, 450nn92–94; and suicide, 208–11, 463n56. *See also* Great Awakening; Itinerants

Exhorters, lay, 192–95; Chauncy on, 192f, 201–4 *passim*; social class of, 193–94, 459n13; and New Light ministers, 195–99. *See also* Itinerants

Faith, and identity, 81–82

Fanger, Donald, 482n24

Farmer James (*Letters from an American Farmer*), 187, 275, 277–89, 476n39, 477nn39, 46

Faulkner, Abigail, Sr., 426n115

Federalists, democracy feared by, 262, 470n6

Fichtelberg, Joseph, 478n48

Fielder, Leslie, 467n95

Field-sermons, 85, 91–92, 96, 101, 105–6

Finley, Samuel, 194, 448n70

Fliegelman, Jay, 402n47, 463nn58, 60, 464n63, 494n12

Foucault, Michel, 397n26, 494n18

Fox, George, 439n51

Franchise, democratic, 13–14, 399nn34, 35, 401n43

Franklin, Benjamin, 7, 472n15, 475n27; on Whitefield, 102, 226, 434nn4, 8

Freccero, John, 101

Freneau, Philip, 309–10

Frontier mythology, 292, 331

Fuller, Margaret, 339–40

Gamut, David (Leatherstocking tales), 318, 319–20, 487n68

Garden, Alexander, 102, 137–46, 147, 437n26

Gardiner, W. H., 313–14, 339

Garner, Stanton, 494n19

Gerrish, Joseph, 69

Gillies, John, 437n37

Ginzburg, Lydia, 17; on personality, 8, 9–10, 396n20; on epochal personality, 91f; on romantic personality, 441n72

Godbeer, Richard, 421n82

Goen, C. G., 183, 458n3, 459n19, 460n21

Goodwin, John, 71, 430n150

Goodwin, Martha, 63–64, 65, 76

Goodwin children, 61

Gould, Philip, 406n5

Grabo, Norman, 258

Grand Itinerant. *See* Whitefield, George

Great Awakening, 20, 83–84, 182; democratic personality in, 20, 24–27, 118–19, 259, 469n1; and representation, 26–28; criticism of, 31–33, 404n2, 405n3; as similar to witchcraft crisis, 31–33, 36–37, 405n5; and American Revolution, 84, 433n3, 434n8; Second, 259, 382–83, 469n1. *See also* Evangelism; Itinerants

Greenblatt, Stephen, 436n23

Griswold, Rufus Wilmot, 473n18

Grossman, Allen, 387

Hale, John, 57, 61, 68–72 *passim*, 410n17, 429n140

Halfway Covenant, 40, 412nn34, 36

Hall, David D., 421n82

Hamilton, Alexander (Dr.), 197, 435n12, 450n94, 454n133

Hancock, John, 193

Hanson, Russell L., 391n1

Hart, James D., 483n34

Hartz, Louis, 391n1

Hatch, Nathan O., 269n1

Hathorne, John, 49, 419n74

Hawley, Joseph, Sr., 208–11, 257, 462n53

Hawthorne, Nathaniel, 344, 378, 385, 418n63, 464n70; "The Custom-House," 245, 248–49

Heckewelder, J. G., 335

Heimert, Alan, 17, 142, 433n3

Herbert, George, 157

Herrick, Mary, 69–70, 429n145

Heyrman, Christine Leigh, 392n5, 405n2

Higginson, Joseph, 410n17
History of New York (Irving), 311
Hobbs, Abigail, 416n55
Hobbs, Deliverance, 77–78, 415n53
Hobby, William, 169
Hobsbawm, E. J., 4, 393n6
Hocks, Richard A., 493n10
Honig, B., 397n26
Hooker, Thomas, 158
How, Elizabeth, 423n96
Howard, Leon, 493n8
Howe, John, 172
Huckins, Hannah, 205
Humble self-enlargement, 5, 20f, 181, 403n2, 435n10; and Whitefield, 83ff, 96, 118–19, 201–2; and N. Cole, 111ff; and voice of convert in Great Awakening, 115–16, 159–61; and black Christians, 117–18; and rise of individual, 159–61; as authorial strategy, 186, 233, 275f, 279f; and democratic literary ethics, 187–88, 269–70; and domesticated democratic personality, 329
Hutchinson, Abigail, 208
Hutchinson, Thomas, 65

Inarticulateness: of democratic voice, 6–8; of American poet, 188–89; of common man, 293, 296, 480n7, 481n14; of Native Americans, 316–19; Emerson on, 340–47 *passim*, 490n99; Whitman on, 344–46; Melville on, 347–50; of slaves, 494n14
Indentured servants, 476n36
Indians. *See* Native Americans
Individualism, 5, 24, 394n10; possessive, 23, 403n4; emergence of, 26, 380–81; and charity, 124, 142; of religious vocalizations, 159–60, 176–77; contained by community, 183–84
Ingersoll, Charles Jared, 290, 304–5, 474n20, 478n51
Ingersoll, Sarah, 78
Inner voice, 204–9; of conscience, 174–75; and Quakers, 205–7; and suicide, 207–9. *See also* Voice
Innocence: in Puritanism, 69, 429n141; of Whitefield, 97; of author, 269, 474n24. *See also* Aesthetic of innocence
Irving, Washington, 311, 474n20, 483n33, 484n51, 489n86

Isaac, Rhys, 182, 395n15
Itinerants, 85, 153, 382–83, 458nn3, 4; charismatic, 184, 456n7; New Light's animosity toward, 195–99; objections to lay, 195, 199–205; Whitefield's inspiration of, 196f, 459n21; scriptural critique of, 200–203; effect of, 203–5; Quaker, 205–7, 458n4, 461n46. *See also* Carwin, Frank; Exhorters, lay

Jacksonian democracy, 292, 480n5
Jacobs, George, Sr., 81
Jacobs, Margaret, 61, 81
Johnson, Barbara, 496n30
Jones, William Alfred, 259, 478n51
Joyce, Patrick, 7, 395n15, 397n25

Karlsen, Carol F., 408n10
Kibbey, Ann, 410n20
Kittredge, George Lyman, 409n17, 414n48
Knapp, Elizabeth, 59–60, 120–24, 169
Knickerbocker, Diedrich (*History of New York*), 311
Knight, Janice, 412n31
Konig, David Thomas, 410n19, 416n56

Lambert, Frank, 17, 106
Last of the Mohicans, The (Cooper), 294, 313–19 *passim*, 326, 335
Law, William, 96
Lawson, Deodat, 34, 56, 67–68, 431n157; on consent to spectral representation, 44, 49–50, 57, 415n49, 416n59
Leatherstocking tales (Cooper), 189, 292. *See also individual fictional characters and specific novels*
Leaves of Grass (Whitman), 189, 293–97 *passim*, 333, 376–77, 491n3
LeDoyt, Biel, 183, 215
Lee, Jarena, 259
Lefort, Claude, 16, 401n42
"Letters" (Freneau), 310
Letters from an American Farmer (Crève-coeur), 187, 270, 274–89, 477n46. *See also* Farmer James
Levin, David, 413n40
Lewis, Mercy, 67
Liberalism, and democracy, 2, 6, 11–16, 391n1, 397n28, 399nn35, 37
Liberal republicanism, 262

Literary criticism, 309; domestication of democratic personality in, 295, 298, 335–43; on absence of national literature, 296–309, 481nn14, 19, 483n33; British influence on, 298, 481n19

Literary delinquency, 296, 299, 481n14. *See also* National literature, absence of

Longfellow, Henry Wadsworth, 297, 483n34

Looby, Christopher, 291, 402n47, 466n77, 471n7, 480n4

Lotman, Iurii M., 464n66

Lowell, James Russell, 336–37

Ludloe (*Wieland*), 211–12, 213–14, 239–40

Lukes, Steven, 403n4

McGilchrist, William, 449n82

Macpherson, C. B., 6, 379, 394n12, 400n39; on individualism, 5, 394n10, 396n20; on liberalism as origin of democracy, 13–15, 399nn35, 37

McVickar, John, 341

Maleficium, 34, 46, 52, 408n10

Marini, Stephen A., 402n47, 450n92

Marrant, John, 438n39

Martin, Susannah, 48, 418n68

Massachusetts Bay Colony, 38, 40–41, 383

Mather, Cotton, 57, 162, 392n5, 411n30, 429n140, 437n37, 445n37; quoted, 31, 191; on spectral evidence, 34–35, 51–52, 408n14, 419n70, 421n81, 429n144; on invisible world, 41–43, 53–54, 63, 413n40; on spectral representation, 44, 59, 70, 415n50, 424n103; on visible character, 48, 50, 420n75; on afflicted, 62, 63–66, 72, 76, 425nn107, 113, 428n124; on devil, 427n117, 430n149

Mather, Increase, 406n7, 411n23, 482n102; on spectral evidence, 35, 48, 71f, 406n9, 409n15, 414n48; on challenges to Puritan beliefs, 40f; on devil, 70, 416n58, 430n148; on visible/invisible world, 426n115

Mellen, Grenville, 335–36, 489nn85, 86

Melville, Herman, 344; *Billy Budd*, 12–13, 189, 347–61, 385–88, 492n8, 493nn9–11; and Emerson, 347f, 492n4; on inarticulateness, 347–50; and Whitman, 347, 361–63, 366, 492n6, 495n24; *The*

Confidence-Man, 348, 492n8; and democratic personality, 385–88; biography of, 492n8. *See also individual fictional characters*

Memoirs (S. Burroughs), 270–74

Memorable Providences, Relating to Witchcrafts and Possessions (C. Mather), 42–43, 44

Methodists, 87f

Middlekauff, Robert, 40f

Miller, Arthur, 394n9

Miller, Joshua, 391n1

Miller, Perry, 33, 37, 393n5, 410n20, 411n29, 414n48, 420n75, 481n19, 488n78

Mimesis, 387–88

Ministers: character and voice of, 125–46, 442nn13, 19; change in function of, 148–49, 448n71. *See also* New Light ministers; Old Light ministers

Morgan, Edmund S., 411n25, 426n115

Morone, James A., 394n13, 399n36

Mouffe, Chantal, 401n42

Muhlenberg, Henry Melchoir, 446n55

Mullin, Gerald W., 494n14

Mumford, Lewis, 492n8

Murphy, Geraldine, 496n30

Murry, John Middleton, 492n8

Naess, Arne, 398n31

Nash, Gary, 395n15

Nathanson, Tenney, 17

Nationalism, 11, 397n27

National literature: invention of, 289–93 *passim*; and common man, 292–95, 301–9, 338–42, 489nn89, 94; absence of, 296–309, 333, 337, 481nn14, 19, 483n33; and aesthetic of innocence, 296–97, 333, 337; Whitman on, 376–77

Native Americans, 320–21, 486n62; romanticization of speech of, 312–14, 316–20, 485n61; Cooper on, 314–27, 335–36, 485nn60, 61; as exemplary democrats, 320–24; representation among, 321–24

Naturalization, 278, 281

Neal, John, 327, 335, 486n67

Newfield, Christopher, 490n99

New Light ministers, 84, 101–2, 195–99, 448n70; vs. Old Light, 25, 26–27, 128f,

132–33, 443nn20, 21, 445nn42, 43; on individual Christians' vocalizations, 155–64, 173, 181, 449n88

Nietzsche, Friedrich Wilhelm, 378

Nissenbaum, Stephen, 46, 405n5, 407n9, 409n17, 417n60

Novel, early American, 260, 291–92, 469n2, 473n16

Noyes, Nicholas, 56–57

Nurse, Rebecca, 49, 77, 419n74

Oakes, Urian, 31

Oakeshott, Michael, 380, 393n7

Ogilvie, James, 443n26

Old Light ministers, 202–3; vs. New Light, 25, 26–27, 128f, 132–33, 443nn20, 21, 445nn42, 43; on individual Christians' vocalizations, 151–55, 163–73 passim, 180, 449n82, 450n94

Onuf, Peter, 460nn23, 25

Opposition: Whitefield's concept of, 84, 86–90, 435n12, 437n26; internalization of, in early American novel, 187–88, 261–62, 265, 270, 291–92

Osgood, Mary, 80

Paine, Robert Treat, 484n51

Park, Joseph, 147–48

Parkman, Francis, 298, 487n71

Parrington, Vernon Louis, 398n31

Parris, Samuel, 56, 58, 71, 420n76

Parsons, Jonathan, 174, 196, 198–99

Pathfinder, The (Cooper), 333

Personality: representative, 7, 395n15; development of term, 8–10, 396n20; secularization of, 17–18, 402n50. *See also* Democratic personality

Pettit, Norman, 461n33

Philbrick, Thomas, 477n42

Phips, William, 35, 69

Pioneers, The (Cooper), 294, 313–19 passim, 328, 331–33

Pleyel (*Wieland*), 213, 222–30 passim; and Clara, 231–42 passim

Pocock, J. G. A., 6, 400n37, 472n10, 477n46; on secularization of personality, 17–18, 402n50; on individualism, 394n10, 396n20

Poet, American: inarticulateness of, 188–89, 344–48; Whitman on, 295–96, 297, 343–47 passim, 386; Emerson on, 306–

8, 333, 338–46 passim; Billy Budd as, 347–48, 361–62, 377. *See also* Authorship

"Poet, The" (Emerson), 296, 306, 333, 346

Popular voice, 17, 182, 386; as transition to democratic popular speech, 21, 25–26, 404n7; in *Wieland*, 262, 471n7

Prescott, William H., 268, 339, 473nn17, 18

Preston, John, 39

Prince, Thomas, 120, 136–37, 196–97, 462n52

Proctor, Elizabeth, 78

Proctor, John, 78, 81, 407n9, 422n87

Proctour, G., 45–46

Protestantism, 411n21

Prynne, William, 132–33

Public speech, 203–4; during Great Awakening, 25–26, 31–32, 103–6; as Puritan prerequisite, 38, 411nn25, 27; by individual Christians, 147–51 passim, 155–63 passim, 175–76, 447n68

Public sphere, 3, 150, 392n2, 395n15, 401n44, 448n74

Pudeator, Ann, 81

Puritanism, 18, 36–37, 84, 392n5, 403n3; congregationalism of, 2, 391n1; concept of visible sainthood of, 21, 37–41; end of era of, 33, 72, 81–82, 431n159; on visible/invisible world, 36, 38–40, 410n20, 421n79; public speech in, 38, 411nn25, 27; on devil/God relationship, 70–71, 429n148; plain speech of, 292, 480n5

Putnam, Ann, 61

Putnam, Ann, Jr., 66–67

Putnam, Edward, 50

Quakers, 433n3, 439n51; itinerancy among, 194, 205–7, 458n4, 461n46; shift from evangelism to community by, 207, 456n2, 462n49; on conversion of children, 462n54

Readers, 266–67, 472n12

Reinhold, Meyer, 465n75

Representation: and Great Awakening, 26–28; Edwards on, 28–29, 168–71, 180–82, 384; truest, 28–29, 168–71, 384; theory of redeemed, 180–82, 384;

in *Wieland*, 210–11, 264; Ziff on, 272, 475n27; among Native Americans, 321–24; Whitman on, 386f; and democracy, 400n39. *See also* Being and representation; Spectral representation
Representative personalities, 7, 395n15
Revivalism. *See* Evangelism; Great Awakening
Revolution, elocutionary, 463n60. *See also* American Revolution
Reynolds, David S., 491n3
Richards, John, 412n34
Ricks, Christopher, 495n28
Rogin, Michael Paul, 493n9
Ross, George, 446n56
Ross, Kristin, 401n42
Ruland, Richard, 481n19
Rule, Margaret, 66, 422n84, 424n103

Sainte-Beuve, Charles-Augustin, 120
Salem witchcraft crisis, 32–82, 393n8, 413n43; emergence of democratic personality in, 4–5, 20, 22–24, 75, 383–84, 403n3; tactics vs. strategies in, 5, 394n9; as similar to Great Awakening, 31–33, 36–37, 405n5; significance of, 33, 405n5, 406n6; spectral evidence in, 34–35, 43–44, 406n9, 414n46; crimes alleged in, 46, 52–54, 408n10, 418n62, 421nn82, 83; character references in, 47–48, 418nn65, 67; and visible/invisible world, 51–57
Saltonstall, Nathaniel, 419n71
Samuels, Shirley, 472n13
Scott, Joan W., 394n12
Scott, Walter, 341
Secularization of personality, 17–18, 402n50
Sedgwick, Eve, 496
Self-representation, 4–5, 85, 91–92
Separatism, 38, 84–85, 182–83
Sewall, Joseph, 99
Seward, William, 440n64
Shaw, Lemuel, 496n31
Sheldon, Susannah, 425n110
Short, Mercy, 61, 65f, 76, 422n84, 424n96, 428n136, 429nn140, 145
Shurtleff, William, 149
Silverman, Kenneth, 42, 413nn40, 41
Simplicity, 290, 300, 312, 337, 482n24; republican, 301, 483n34; comic portrayal of, 309–11, 484nn50, 51. *See also* Common man
Simpson, David, 314, 484n50, 489n94
Simpson, Lewis P., 269–70, 474n24
Slaves, 494n14; and Whitefield, 114, 116–18, 440n67; in *Letters from an American Farmer*, 187, 282–85, 287–89, 477n46
Sławek, Tadeusz, 17
Slender, Robert ("Advice to Authors," "Letters"), 309–11
Slotkin, Richard, 330–31, 485nn59, 60, 487n75
Smith, John, 462n54
Smith, Josiah, 127–30 *passim*
Social classes: and identity, 11, 397n27; of lay exhorters, 193–94, 459n13; antagonism between, 262, 303–5, 483n37; lower, 298–304 *passim*, 393n6, 395n15. *See also* Common man
Social disorder, 31–33
Spectacular conversion, 3, 20, 24, 85, 261f; Whitefield's configuring of, 87–89; voice in, 105–7, 115–16, 118–19
Specters, 5, 44, 71, 394n9, 425n110; relationship of, to afflicted, 57–69; and visible/invisible world, 63, 426n115
Spectral evidence: C. Mather on, 34–35, 51–52, 408n14, 421n81, 429n144; in Salem witchcraft trials, 34–35, 406n9; I. Mather on, 35, 71f, 406n9, 409n15, 414n48; as presumption of guilt, 46–47, 416n56; and visible character, 47, 48–51; debate on, 60, 69–72, 425n106, 429n144, 145, 431n157; in European witchcraft trials, 409n17
Spectral evidence theory, 22–28 *passim*, 124, 181, 423n93; as groundwork for democratic personality, 35–37, 74–75; in Salem witchcraft trials, 43–44, 414n46; circular logic of, 46, 417n60; on visible/invisible world, 218–19
Spectral exhibitions, 57–67 *passim*
Spectral eyes, 32–33
Spectrality, of inarticulate, 6–7
Spectral possession, 3, 4–5, 19
Spectral representation: consent to, 22, 44–50 *passim*, 57–59, 70, 414n48; 415nn49, 50, 416nn54, 55, 59; C. Mather on, 44, 59, 70, 415n50, 424n103
Spectral space: character as, 145; as space

beyond formal observance, 151, 179; human heart as, 173–74; Mettingen (*Wieland*) as, 185, 218–23, 261; slavery as, 187, 282–87; and novelistic-democratic space, 218, 261–62, 291–92; and textuality, 268; in Cooper, 329

Spencer, Benjamin T., 292, 340, 480n6

Starkey, Marion, 48, 406n6, 407n9

Steiner, George, 296

Stiles, Isaac, 202–3

Stoddard, Solomon, 40, 442n19

Stone, Albert E., 476n34, 477n42

Stone, Samuel, 38

Stoughton, William, 414n48, 416n56

Stout, Harry S., 402n47, 433n3, 460nn23, 25

Subjectivity, 8, 397n26; democratic, 10–11, 397n25

Subject's experience, 6, 394n12

Suffrage. *See* Franchise

Suicide, 208–11, 257, 405n5, 462n53, 463n56

Swan, Timothy, 61

Taussig, Michael, 387

Taylor, Edward, 104

Tennent, Gilbert, 136, 142–46, 149, 164, 196, 443n20, 445n43, 458n1, 459n21

Thayer, James B., 410n17

Thomas, Brook, 496n31

Thomas, Keith, 52

Thoreau, Henry David, 280, 339, 349

Tocqueville, Alexis de, 2, 15f, 29, 393n5, 403n3

Tolles, Frederick, 205, 461n46

Tolstoy, Leo, 304

Toothaker, Allen, 61

Truth, Sojourner, 259

Tyler, Martha, 79–80

Uncontainability: of Whitefield, 98–99, 100; limits to, 117–19, 284; of democratic personality, 185–86, 187–88, 291–92; of character, 265–66, 286–89; Crèvecoeur on, 286ff

Upham, Charles W., 408n9, 414n48, 416n56

Ventriloquism, 189, 191; authorship as, 255–56, 267–68, 473nn17, 19

Visible character, 21f, 420n78; and spec-tral evidence, 47, 48–51; destabilization of, 76–79, 81; of ministers, 125–27, 131, 146–47, 442n13, 443n20; and voice, 126–27, 131, 134, 138, 163–77, 191, 450n95, 453n125, 455nn139, 140, 142; Burroughs on, 272, 475n27; Crèvecoeur on, 277–78, 282

Visible/invisible world: Puritanism on, 36, 38–40, 410n20, 421n79; and C. Mather, 41–43, 413n40; and witchcraft, 51–57; and wounds of afflicted, 61, 62, 426n114; and specters, 63, 426n115; Antinomians on, 73–74; and slavery, 187, 282–87; and Carwin (*Wieland*), 214, 216–17; and spectral evidence the-ory, 218–19; and American national lit-erature, 337–39; Protestantism on, 411n21

Visible sainthood, 21, 37–41, 411n23; and Halfway Covenant, 40, 412nn34, 36; and Massachusetts Bay Colony charter, 40–41

Voice: popular, 17, 21, 25–26, 182, 262, 386, 404n7, 471n7; in spectacular con-version, 105–7, 115–16, 118–19; devil's possession of Knapp's, 120–24; of con-science, 122, 133–34, 144ff, 175, 205, 209; and visible character, 126–27, 131, 134, 138, 163–77, 191, 450n95, 453n125, 455nn139, 140, 142; minis-terial, 128, 137, 144–46; of Whitefield, 134–40 *passim*, 147, 446nn47, 55; inner, 174–75, 204–9; in *Wieland*, 212, 214–17, 224–29 *passim*, 236–37, 244–45, 247, 466n82, 468n98; and democratic personality, 215–16

Vox populi, vox Dei, 260, 470n3. *See also* Popular voice

Wadsworth, Daniel, 447n57

Walker, Timothy, 124–25, 127, 154, 184, 445n43

Warner, Michael, 225, 260, 392n2, 402n47, 469n2

Warren, Mary, 45, 78, 422n87

Watson, E. L. Grant, 496n30

Waugh, Edwin, 7, 397n25

Webb, John, 99

Weber, Donald, 402n47

Weber, Max, 461n47

Weeks, Joshua Wingate, 449n82

Weisbuch, Robert, 481n19, 483n34
Weisman, Richard, 52, 406n9, 408n10, 421n82
Weller, Samuel, 152, 194–95, 437n35, 449n86
Welles, Benjamin, 404n7
Wesley, Charles, 87f
Wesling, Donald, 17
Whitefield, George, 4, 5, 83–119, 193, 215f, 384, 402n47; popularity of, 20, 84, 106, 402n1, 434n5, 439n54; conversion by, 24–25, 87–89, 107–14, 435n15, 440n62; individuality modeled by, 24–25, 84f, 118–19; and humble self-enlargement, 83ff, 96, 118–19, 201–2; concept of opposition of, 84, 86–90, 435n12, 437n26; on drama, 89–90, 436n16; self-representation of, 91–92, 101–2; Chauncy on, 92, 93–95, 106, 384, 445n40; impersonation of God by, 92–101, 131–32, 141, 437nn28, 35, 37, 447n58; Franklin on, 102, 226, 434nn4, 8; health of, 102–5; voice and speech of, 103–6, 134–40 *passim*, 147, 443n26, 444nn27, 28, 446nn47, 55, 56; and slaves, 114, 116–18, 440n67; Josiah Smith on, 127–28, 129f; ministerial character of, 128–42, 145, 443nn20, 22; nondenominationalism of, 130, 444n31; Garden on, 137–46; as origin of itinerancy, 196f, 459n21; Edwards on, 438nn43, 44
Whitman, Walt, 10, 16, 134, 283, 376–77, 401n40, 445n45, 481n14; quoted, 1, 259, 290, 344; *Democratic Vistas*, 189, 295, 344–45, 347, 376f; *Leaves of Grass*, 189, 293–97 *passim*, 333, 376–77, 491n3; on American poet, 295–96, 297, 343–47 *passim*, 386; and aesthetic of innocence, 333, 341–46 *passim*; on inarticulateness, 344–46; Emerson's influence on, 346, 491n3; and Melville, 347, 361–63, 366, 492n6, 495n24; on representation, 386f
Wiebe, Robert H., 4, 381–83, 391n1, 469n1
Wieland; or, The Transformation: An American Tale (Brown), 185–87, 210–58, 468n97, 472n15; representation in, 210–11, 264; voice in, 212, 214–17, 224–29 *passim*, 236–37, 244–45, 247, 466n82,

468n98; Cicero in, 213, 221–22, 224, 253, 465nn74, 75; Clara's transformation into author in, 217–18, 242–58, 263–65; artistic space in, 218–20, 223, 464n66; power struggle in, 260–65; political context of, 262, 471n7; historical parallels in, 266–68, 472nn13, 14. *See also individual fictional characters*
Wieland, Catharine (*Wieland*), 213, 222, 224
Wieland, Clara (*Wieland*), 186–87, 213, 217–25 *passim*, 231, 259, 384, 469nn103, 104; transformation of, into author, 217–18, 242–58, 263–65; and Carwin, 225–42 *passim*, 260–66; and Pleyel, 231–42 *passim*
Wieland, Theodore (*Wieland*), 212–13, 252–53, 256–57; and Cicero, 213, 221–22, 224, 465nn74, 75
Willard, Samuel, 54, 58, 59–60, 124, 416n54, 422n86; and Knapp incident, 120–24, 169
Williams, Abigail, 49
Williams, Daniel E., 435n14
Williams, Raymond, 8f, 404n9
Wills, Garry, 438n38
Wilson, John, 147, 155–57, 163–64, 169, 313
Wise, John, 4, 392n5
Wishart, George, 170
Witch wounds, 52–53, 60–61, 422n84, 423n88, 425nn107, 110, 113, 426n114
Women, 399n34, 455n142
Wood, Gordon S., 6–7, 299, 448n76, 465n75, 470n6, 471n7, 472n10, 476n36, 478n51
Woolman, John, 205ff
Worcester, Noah, 195, 459n19
Wordsworth, William, 280, 301–2, 483n34

Yates, John, 266, 472nn13, 14
"Young Goodman Brown" (Hawthorne), 418n63

Ziff, Larzer, 392n5, 393n7, 491n102; on representation in fiction, 272, 475n27; on witchcraft crisis, 405n5, 410n20, 413n43; on Brown's *Wieland*, 466n83, 467n93
Žižek, Slavoj, 400n38

Library of Congress Cataloging-in-Publication Data
Ruttenburg, Nancy.
Democratic personality : popular voice and the trial of American
authorship / Nancy Ruttenburg.
p.   cm.
Includes bibliographical references (p.   ) and index.
ISBN 0-8047-3096-2 (cl.)
ISBN 0-8047-3097-0 (pbk.)
1. American literature — 19th century — History and criticism.
2. St. John de Crèvecoeur, J. Hector, 1735–1813. Letters from an
American Farmer. 3. Popular literature — United States — History
and criticism. 4. National characteristics, American, in literature.
5. Authorship — Political aspects — United States. 6. Politics and
literature — United States. 7. Innocence (Psychology) in literature.
8. Democracy in literature. 9. Aesthetics, American. 10. Self in
literature. I. Title.
PS201.R85   1998
810.9′358 — DC21   97-42315
CIP
REV.

⊛ This book is printed on acid-free recycled paper.

Original printing 1998
Last figure below indicates year of this printing:
07 06 05 04 03 02 01 00 99 98

DATE DUE